Being and Motion

BEING AND MOTION

Thomas Nail

OXFORD
UNIVERSITY PRESS

Oxford University Press is a department of the University of Oxford. It furthers
the University's objective of excellence in research, scholarship, and education
by publishing worldwide. Oxford is a registered trade mark of Oxford University
Press in the UK and certain other countries.

Published in the United States of America by Oxford University Press
198 Madison Avenue, New York, NY 10016, United States of America.

© Oxford University Press 2019

All rights reserved. No part of this publication may be reproduced, stored in
a retrieval system, or transmitted, in any form or by any means, without the
prior permission in writing of Oxford University Press, or as expressly permitted
by law, by license, or under terms agreed with the appropriate reproduction
rights organization. Inquiries concerning reproduction outside the scope of the
above should be sent to the Rights Department, Oxford University Press, at the
address above.

You must not circulate this work in any other form
and you must impose this same condition on any acquirer.

Library of Congress Cataloging-in-Publication Data
Names: Nail, Thomas, author.
Title: Being and motion / Thomas Nail.
Description: New York, NY, United States of America : Oxford University Press, [2019] |
Includes bibliographical references and index.
Identifiers: LCCN 2018013561 (print) | LCCN 2018028422 (ebook) |
ISBN 9780190908928 (Updf) | ISBN 9780190908935 (Epub) |
ISBN 9780190908904 (hardcover : acid-free paper) | ISBN 9780190908911 (pbk. : acid-free paper)
Subjects: LCSH: Human beings—Migrations—History. | Emigration and
immigration—Political aspects. | Migration, Internal—Political aspects. |
Political science—Philosophy.
Classification: LCC GN370 (ebook) | LCC GN370.N35 2019 (print) |
DDC 304.809—dc23
LC record available at https://lccn.loc.gov/20180

CONTENTS

Acknowledgments   ix

Introduction I: The Age of Motion   1

BOOK I: The Ontology of Motion

Part I: Ontology and History
1. Historical Ontology   13
2. Ontological History   21
3. Philosophy of Motion   36
4. Realism and Materialism   52

Part II: The Theory of Motion
I. Flow
5. Continuum   67
6. Multiplicity   77
7. Confluence   86

II. Fold
8. Junction   99
9. Sensation   106
10. Conjunction   118

III. Field
11. Circulation   129
12. Knot   145

Introduction II: Kinos, Logos, Graphos   159

BOOK II: The Motion of Ontology

Part I: Being and Space
I. Kinos
13. Centripetal Motion   175

II. Logos
14. Prehistoric Mythology: Venus, Egg, Spiral   187

III. Graphos
15. Speech: The Body   207

Part II: Being and Eternity
I. Kinos
16. Centrifugal Motion   227

II. Logos
17. Ancient Cosmology I: The Holy Mountain   239
18. Ancient Cosmology II: Theomachy   252
19. Ancient Cosmology III: Ex Nihilo   262
20. Ancient Cosmology IV: Plato and Aristotle   276

III. Graphos
21. Writing I: Tokens   285
22. Writing II: Alphabet   300

Part III: Being and Force
I. Kinos
23. Tensional Motion   317

II. Logos
24. Medieval Theology I: Aether   331
25. Medieval Theology II: Impetus   343
26. Medieval Theology III: Conatus   358
27. Medieval Theology IV: The Trinity   373

III. Graphos
28. The Book I: Manuscript   389
29. The Book II: Printing Press   406

Part IV: Being and Time
I. Kinos
30. Elastic Motion   427

II. Logos
31. Modern Phenomenology I: Series   443
32. Modern Phenomenology II: Circulation   456
33. Modern Phenomenology III: Multiplication   472
34. Modern Phenomenology IV: Process and Interval   479

III. Graphos

35. The Keyboard I: Typewriter   *493*
36. The Keyboard II: Computer   *509*

Conclusion   *517*

Notes   *525*
Index   *589*

Being and Motion

Being and Motion

INTRODUCTION I

The Age of Motion

We live in an age of movement. More than at any other time in history, people and things move longer distances, more frequently, and faster than ever before. All that was solid melted into air long ago and is now in full circulation around the world, like dandelion seeds adrift on turbulent winds. We find ourselves, in the early twenty-first century, in a world where every major domain of human activity has become increasingly defined by motion.[1]

Socially, life is becoming increasingly migratory.[2] At the turn of this century, there were more regional and international migrants than ever before in recorded history.[3] Today, there are more than one billion migrants.[4] With each new decade the percentage of migrants as a share of the total population continues to rise, and in the next twenty-five years the rate of migration is predicted to be higher than in the past twenty-five years.[5] More than ever, it has become a necessity for people to migrate due to environmental, economic, and political instability. Climate change, in particular, may even double international migration over the next forty years.[6] By 2050 more than two billion more people are expected to migrate to urban centers around the world.[7] While many may not cross a regional or international border, people do tend to change jobs more often, commute longer and farther to work,[8] change their residence repeatedly, and travel internationally more than ever before.[9] This general increase in human mobility and expulsion affects us all in one way or another, and it is now widely recognized as a defining feature of our epoch.[10]

This global movement has also given birth to an explosion of bordering techniques for managing and circulating human movement. Since the mid-1990s, but particularly since 9/11, hundreds of new borders have emerged around the world—miles of new razor-wire fences, tons of new concrete security walls, numerous offshore detention centers, biometric passport databases, and security checkpoints of all kinds in schools, airports, and along various roadways across the world—all attesting to the increased social anxiety about controlling social motion.

Contemporary politics can no longer be adequately understood through the paradigm of static states, immobile borders, and stationary citizens. This theoretical framework no longer fits the reality of global mobility, fluctuating borders, and constant migration. An increasing number of scholars across a range of disciplines are coming to recognize the primacy of social mobility and movement.[11] The expectation that the world of mobile bodies will conform to a static model of states, borders, and political behavior is causing millions of people around the world to undergo immense suffering. If we want to understand contemporary social reality, and thus respond to it appropriately, we need a new set of conceptual tools based on the primacy of motion.[12]

Scientific knowledge in the twenty-first century also reveals that we live in a world of continuous motion. At the macroscopic level, cosmologists just before the turn of the twenty-first century discovered that the universe is not only expanding in every direction but also that the speed at which it is doing so is rapidly increasing.[13] We live in what physicists call an "accelerating universe." What Einstein thought was an immobile and finite universe is actually defined by increasing movement in all directions.[14] The very fabric of space-time is now defined by the primacy of a continuously expansive movement.

At the mezzoscopic level, the development of nonlinear dynamics toward the end of the twentieth century showed decisively that even the predictable particles of classical physics are subject to irreversible thermodynamic and kinetic flows of energy. Chaos theory, the often touted "third" scientific revolution of the twentieth century, has shown that the flux, turbulence, and movement of energy are more primary than the relative or metastable fixity of classical bodies.[15]

At the microscopic level, it is also increasingly clear that space-time and gravity are not preexisting, fundamental aspects of reality but actually products of more primary quantum motions. What we used to think of as solid bodies, elementary particles, and background parameters are actually products of nonlocal vibrating quantum fields. Unifying the macroscopic theory of gravitational space-time (general relativity), and the microscopic fit the twenty-first-century reality of interactive electrical circulations and continually modulated images.[23]

ONTOLOGY

Ontological practice, the primary subject of this book, has also become increasingly mobile. This is in part due to the increasingly mobile nature of the social, scientific, and aesthetic events of our time (described above), whose being ontology attempts to describe. As the world has become increasingly mobile, our ontological descriptions of it have struggled to reflect this. Furthermore, ontology is in turn actively and practically shaped by the contemporary political, scientific, and aesthetic conditions it describes. Those who write ontological descriptions, for example, travel longer distances and more often than ever before—and thus participate to some degree in a vast global-migration regime.[24] Their digital and printed texts now circulate faster, in more media forms, and more broadly than before. Even the technical conditions of written images and their distribution are now faster and more dynamic due to the equations of quantum field theory that structure the computers that philosophers write with. In short, ontology today is more mobile than ever before because it is *practically entangled* with all the increasingly mobile events of our time.

Ontology has traditionally been defined as the universal description of being as it is in itself (i.e., being qua being). This definition can no longer be upheld today.[25] This is not because we have discovered that there is no reality independent of our sensation of it but because it has become almost impossible to ignore the now manifold and expressly mobile material conditions that shape and are shaped by ontological description itself, as a performative practice.[26] The way we describe the world is shaped by the apparatus of description we use—and the world is in turn really and materially shaped in some way by our description of it.[27] Ontologies matter. Ontologies are real acts or processes of materialization with their own sets of tools and networks of mobility. They are not neutral representations. This is what makes them historical, practical, and entangled with the contemporary conditions they describe. They are aspects of the same historical process. The vast proliferation, mixture, and global circulation of old and new media technologies today has thus increasingly forced us to confront how incredibly mediatized, and thus material and historical, our ontological practices have become (and have been).

Theorists today increasingly acknowledge this situation.[28] According to Friedrich Kittler, "Ontology has been hostile from its very beginnings to media, whether physical or technical. More than any other theorists, philosophers forgot to ask which media support their very practice."[29] The aim of this book is therefore twofold: first, to provide a new ontology of motion for our present that responds more appropriately to the increasingly mobile conditions of our time, as described above; and second, and more specifically, to apply this new ontological framework to the material history of ontological practice itself—thus also revealing the kinetic conditions of contemporary ontological practice itself, including this book.

Being and Motion thus makes at least three novel and intertwined interventions: it provides (1) an original and systematic ontology of motion alongside (2) the first history of the philosophy of motion in the Western tradition, in relation to (3) the history of its material and practical conditions of inscription.

THE TWENTY-FIRST CENTURY

The major historical events described above are part of a larger shift taking place in the early twenty-first century, a shift toward the increasing importance of motion. The exceptions to the rules of the previous static paradigms have now themselves become the rules in a whole new kinetic paradigm.[30] Global migration, climate change, and border politics are no longer marginal issues but have increasingly come to destabilize the nation-state system itself.[31] In the West, mobile devices and their mobile images are no longer luxury items for the privileged few but have transformed every aspect of daily life, including the human brain itself.[32] Quantum field theory is no longer an obscure area of scientific speculation about microscopic exceptions to the rules of classical physics—nonlocality, entanglement, and tunneling—but has become what physicists now call "the standard model,"[33] which now underpins almost every new contemporary technology, from global-positioning systems to computer processing techniques.

The difference between the end of the twentieth century and the beginning of the twenty-first, however, is not a difference *in kind*, but rather a difference *of degree*—from solid to liquid. The transition has been dramatic, but it has nonetheless also been continuous and incremental. Only in the twenty-first century, however, have the events described above ceased to be aberrations or emerging trends, as they have now become foundational events of our time. They are the beginning of a new paradigm defined by motion.[34]

The political, scientific, and aesthetic consequences of this new kinetic paradigm are enormous and thus beyond the range of this book. They are, however, important contemporary conditions that situate and motivate the ontology of motion put forward in this book. Twenty-first-century transformations in each of these domains (politics, science, art, and ontology) should be considered together, even if each requires its own full-length treatment. They are interrelated parts of a single project inaugurated by this author's books *The Figure of the Migrant* and *Theory of the Border*, and now continued in *Being and Motion*. Although motivated and co-conditioned by these other domains, the focus of the present book is on the strictly ontological aspects of this new kinetic paradigm—the details of which will be introduced in the next few chapters.

The point of this introduction is this: I believe we have entered a new historical era, defined in large part by the primacy of movement and mobility, and are now in need of a new ontology appropriate to our time. The observation that the end of the twentieth century and the beginning of the twenty-first was a period marked by an increasingly "liquid" and "mobile" modernity is now something widely recognized in the scholarly literature.[35] Almost twenty years into the twenty-first century, we now find ourselves situated on the *other side* of this heralded transition. Our situation today is therefore importantly different from the transition to postmodernity, beginning in the 1970s. The question that confronts us today is thus a new one: how to fold all that has melted back up into something new. Answering this question requires a new and different set of theoretical tools.

The challenge for theory today is to look afresh at the perspectives, problems, and possibilities that are opened up to us by our new historical conjuncture. In other words, what do the major events of our time reveal about the nature of being as it is for us today? At no point in history have beings ever been anywhere near as mobile as they are today, so what does this say about the nature of reality such that it is capable of this degree of mobility? If being is defined by the historical primacy of motion today but existing ontologies are not, then we need a new historical ontology of the present.[36] This is what *Being and Motion* provides.

BOOK I
The Ontology of Motion

PART I
Ontology and History

CHAPTER 1
Historical Ontology

More than ever before, the fact that everything is up in the air and on the move requires us to seriously rethink not only global migration, the problem of knowledge in quantum field theory, and the nature of affect and image in an age of digital mobility but also the conceptual and ontological frameworks we use to describe the *being* of these kinds of events. This task is the special focus and unique contribution of *Being and Motion*: to provide an ontological and historical framework for describing the being of motion and the motion of beings.

The central contribution and importance of this book is therefore twofold. On the one hand, it aims to produce a new conceptual and ontological framework for describing the being of motion. The purpose of such a framework is to provide a new and more fitting lens by which to interpret a wide range of kinetic phenomena across scientific, aesthetic, and social fields. This is the framework deployed systematically in the companion volumes to *Being and Motion* mentioned in the Introduction.

This framework applies both to the contemporary events of our time and more widely to the historical ways in which movement has been distributed and organized into various patterns or regimes. In other words, being is not just in motion because of a few big events at the turn of the twenty-first century. Such events, with their dramatic and epoch-defining mobility, are simply the historical occasions that force us to see the importance of something that has been there all along, though previously hidden or explained by something else. What is at stake in this book, therefore, is the invention of a conceptual framework that would allow us to describe and identify a whole new dimension or aspect of present and previous beings from the perspective of movement. This methodological perspective is not just a matter of novelty, although its novelty is also important. It is also a matter of becoming equal to the historical events of our time that increasingly force us to think about things in ways we never did before. What is at stake, therefore, is not simply a more appropriate ontological description of current events but also a unique insight into a certain hidden or occluded dimension of Western ontology.

On the other hand, the second important contribution of this book is to turn this kinetic perspective back on the practice of ontology itself. If being is in motion, then the act of doing ontology itself is also a motion and must be included in the analysis. What are the material-kinetic conditions or regimes of motion under which a specific ontological inscription itself has been performed, and how does it relate to the kinds of descriptions of being it generates? Even in the rare cases where philosophers have taken movement seriously, or where mobilities scholars have taken ontology seriously, no one has done a kinetic analysis of ontological practice itself. In fact, no one to my knowledge has even attempted to write a history of the philosophy of movement. Books abound that contain philosophical histories of time, space, eternity, and even force—but not of motion. Motion, for the most part, has been treated as a nonphilosophical category best left to physics.

Those who have attempted to treat motion as a more philosophical or ontological category have paradoxically not treated their own ontological practice as *in movement,* or as part of any larger historical pattern of motion.[1] Any ontology of motion that follows such traditional methods of inquiry into the nature of "being qua being" risks falling back into the same ahistorical, fixed, and immobile methods of older static ontologies. Even if the universal nature of being is paradoxically said to be "in motion" forever and all time, such a claim, by its very structure, pretends to be outside the movement of its own historical description, and therefore not in the motion it describes.

This is not what *Being and Motion* does. The production, distribution, and consumption of this book itself is the performance of the historical and material conditions described in this book. Ontology is entangled with, and emerges from, its material conditions. All the old historical techniques of inscription described in Book II—speech, writing, books, and keyboards—merge and mix together in the hybrid performance of contemporary ontological practice. For example, the ontological practice of this book has taken many kinetic forms. It was spoken about with colleagues and drawn on classroom walls. It was inscribed in written language. It was written by hand in a series of seven manuscript notebooks. It was typed out on a keyboard and put into digital form. It was printed out by a printing press. It was then circulated verbally, digitally, and in print among peers and editors, who then made their own verbal, written, and digital marks. It was put into circulation around the world and into the hands and computers of readers who will perhaps talk about it, make marks in the margins, copy and paste it, and so on. All this material-kinetic activity is part of its historical ontological practice, but it remains typically occluded in most philosophical ontologies. The practical activity of doing ontology is typically considered to be nonphilosophical because it is too material, too kinetic, too historical, or too technical to have any bearing on the purely abstract description of being qua being.

Therefore, the second novel contribution of *Being and Motion* is to show that the act of doing ontology itself is a historical, material, and kinetic one. Ontological description is not a passive representation—it is real material coproduction. Furthermore, different patterns of motion, and different tools of inscription, are linked to very different historical descriptions of the nature of being, as we will see in Book II.

These are the twin theses of this book. The first thesis is particularly difficult because it refers to the philosophy of movement in its most general conceptual formulation. This is challenging because, although examples are given from the domains of politics, science, and art, in order to show the concepts in action, the full scope and application of the framework to these exemplified domains requires book-length treatments for each domain. Since this is an ontology, the reader should expect to find in these chapters of Book I a relatively original, internally consistent set of self-referring concepts, vocabulary, and diagrams that offer a new way of thinking through the primary questions of ontology: quality, quantity, relation, modality, identity, unity, causality, subject, and so on.

So, aside from the occasional examples taken from the companion volumes on politics, art, and science, and used to clarify various points, Book I will not be drawing on the ever-growing range of empirical studies of movement and mobility from other disciplines and domains because I have already done this in the companion volumes.[2] Developing a systematic conceptual framework that responds to all the demands of ontology is no small task. There is thus no way for this book to both develop such a framework *and* apply it across all the empirical areas it could possibly be applied to *and* still be able to prove the second major thesis about the material historicity of ontological practice. Thus, the primary focus of *Being and Motion* will be on ontology and the history of Western ontology. If the reader is curious to see how the main concepts of this book are applied and developed to domains outside ontology, please see the companion volumes.[3]

Furthermore, if the reader is curious to read more about the other limits that define this project, he or she can peek ahead at the Conclusion of this book for a list of its four major limitations and future projects.

HISTORICAL METHOD

The primacy of motion is a unique ontological perspective in Western philosophy. Throughout history, being has been understood in many ways, but rarely has it been said to be, primarily and above all, *in motion*.[4] However, defined as it is by constant movement and mobility across every major area of social, scientific, and aesthetic life, the present age is, if not the first, then certainly the loudest to proclaim *"omnia moveri!"*

The central question of this book, therefore, is, "What do these events reveal about the nature of reality such that it is capable of producing this present?" Now that such a present has emerged, it has become possible in a way it was not previously to inquire into the conditions of its emergence. In other words, the present reveals something new about the historical nature of being so far: what it must *at least* be like to be defined by the primacy of motion and mobility. At no point in history have beings ever been anywhere near as mobile as they are today, so what does this say about the nature of our reality? If being is defined by the historical primacy of motion today, yet existing ontologies are not, then we need a new ontology. *Being and Motion* aims to produce such a conceptual framework based on the historical primacy of motion.[5]

The Present

The present, however, is not a homogenous, closed set of things and dates. The present is not a presence but an open process. So by "our present" I simply mean "the flux of things and dates in the twenty-first-century so far." We live in an age increasingly defined by movement and mobility, but not exhaustively or reductively so. The present cannot be fully grasped or totalized by any single epochal concept. Motion is not the essential core of the present. It is simply one aspect of the present—albeit an increasingly prevailing and powerful "anchoring point" worthy of our critical attention.[6]

At least two consequences for this project follow from this definition. First, since the present is contested and multiple, what seem like important events at the time (global migration, quantum field theory, and digital media) can turn out retroactively to have not been important. But even further along they may become, retroactively, important again. It is not the object of this book to proclaim anything about what future generations may or may not think of the events of our time—but rather to show what they reveal to us *now*. This project, and this book in particular, is thus not a view from nowhere but a specific view from the early-twenty-first-century under the conditions described above.

If there is a philosophical deduction of motion in this book, it is not an epistemological one like Kant's nor an existential one like Heidegger's but rather a kinetic one. The concepts of flow, fold, and field deduced in Book I are the minimal features needed to describe the historical being of motion. They are the features that must be the case for being to be in motion today. Therefore, the motivation for this book and the others connected to it is tied, by necessity, to contemporary events that most people, including me, currently believe are and will be defining events for the twenty-first century. The importance of these events is thus not fundamental but historical: Relative to what we currently know, these things seem important enough to challenge previous social, scientific, and aesthetic paradigms— and to expose a new kinetic one.

The Past

Similarly, the past is not an objective set of fixed events. Depending on the conditions of the present, different aspects or dimensions of the past will appear and disappear. New lines of development between the past and the present can be put forward on the basis of new social, scientific, and aesthetic discoveries or events that emerge in the present. For example, once Newton discovered the inverse square law of gravity, this appeared to be true not only for his present, but also for the entire past as he and others knew it. Newton and others then told a retroactive evolutionary story about the development of this truth, just as Hegel told a similar social story about the development of human sociality into its highest present form: the nation-state. In both cases, however, their error was the attribution of necessity, causality, and finality to these developments. From the perspective of the present, the entire past appeared as one or more long lines of retroactive precursors.

As the present changes, however, so do the lines of the past that lead to it. This does not mean that history is illusory and false but rather that it is composed of multiple real coexisting and divergent historical series. There is no other starting point outside of the present from which to begin. Luckily, the present is divergent enough to accommodate many lines. This book is not exempt from the limits of the present—even if it does not rely on necessity, causality, and finality for its explanation. As a historical ontology, *Being and Motion* simply adds one new and previously hidden historical trajectory to the others: the line of motion. Once we discover motion at the core of some of the most important social, scientific, and aesthetic events of our time, we can see that it was there all along.

The Future

The future is that which is not yet. As such, it bears no necessary resemblance to the present nor the past. This has two consequences for *Being and Motion*. First, it means that there can be no ontology of the future—unless we mean by this some paradoxical ontology that simply exposes the impossibility of fundamental ontology. This book remains entirely agnostic about the being of the future and about any description of being that would hold true forever. The ontology of motion developed here pertains only to a few major dimensions of the present, and to what these reveal about the historical practice of ontology.

Second, *Being and Motion* remains open to the possibility that new events in the future will reveal yet another hidden dimension of the past that could in turn re-describe everything that appeared to be in motion from the perspective of the early twenty-first century. However, it is also possible that this might not happen. We will see.

In either case, no historical ontology, and certainly not this one, could ever foreclose in advance the possibility of another in the future, no matter how apparently seamless the historical line. It is also true that every voice speaks by the omission of others. Even as the present work of historical ontology gives voice to a previously occluded region of being (motion), it also leaves out other regions and other histories. This is not a reason not to do a new historical ontology, but it is a reason to multiply such histories—of which this is only one.

The primary inquiry of this book is therefore ontological but not foundational. It is historical. In other words, it does not aim to identify the absolute and immutable structure of being forever and all time (being qua being). It rather seeks to identify, given a particular historical emergence, the real conditions of that emergence—*really* constitutive of ontological practice itself. Being is surely much more than motion, but no matter what else it is it must *at least* be in motion in a way that makes a present like ours possible.

The contribution of *Being and Motion* is to locate a new historical ontology of motion—a minimal condition that, from the perspective of the present, appears to have always been a hidden dimension of the past. The aim is therefore to take one of the most important (not the only or essential) features of contemporary reality (motion) and use it reinterpret the dominant notions of ontology, such as space, time, force, quality, quantity, relation, and so on. From the vantage point of the present, the past can now be reinterpreted anew, without foreclosing the future.[7]

Accordingly, the method deployed by this book cannot be a naive realism in which the discovery of the contemporary primacy of motion gives pure access to being in itself. Rather, it is a kind of historical realism of the *minimal ontological conditions* of the emergence of the present itself. It is therefore also a *critical* or *minimal* realism in the sense in which being is interpreted only with respect to that aspect of previous being that must at least be the case for our present "to have been possible" (i.e., actual). Therefore, the method deployed throughout this book is neither realist nor relativist in their traditional senses, but rather *minimally, critically, or historically* realist.

The question is not what the conditions of the human mind must be for the present to be what it is but rather what *previous reality itself* must *at least* be like such that the present and its ontological inquiry have come to be defined by the primacy of motion. The question is not what the conditions of language, the unconscious, economics, power, and so on must be like for the present to be *possible* but rather what previous being must at least be like so as to render actual these anthropic structures in the first place.[8] Without a doubt, contemporary reality is shaped by multiple human structures, but these structures are in turn conditioned by other real, nonanthropic material structures that precede and constitute them. The two then work on each other in turn, *really co-constituting each other*. The aim of this work is to locate the real conditions necessary for the emergence of contemporary being in motion.[9]

To be absolutely clear, *Being and Motion* is not seeking the minimal *fundamental* conditions of all reality (past, present, and future) such that motion appears as primary today but rather only the minimal *historical* conditions (of the past) for the present. As Marx writes, "All the mysteries which lead theory to mysticism find their rational solution in human practice and in the comprehension of this practice."[10] But human practice is never reducible strictly to anthropocentric structures. *Being and Motion* is a strictly historical and regional ontology of ontological practice itself, limited only to the present and the past—without any ontological claim on the being of the future. Following Marx's retrograde reading of history, we can say that it was precisely the contingent appearance of increased mobility in the present that makes possible a new (and no less real) history from the viewpoint of that event: a historical ontology of motion.

CHAPTER 2

Ontological History

If the critical events of our age are defined by the primacy of their motion, then we need a new set of concepts appropriate to this motion. However, if being is in motion, then so is ontological practice itself. The observations, descriptions, and inscriptions of ontological practice are themselves *transformative* and *kinetic* actions. They are in motion. There is no neutral activity of representation, contemplation, or communication that does not already introduce motion into the process of ontological description. Thus, any ontology of motion that does not have a theory and history of the structure of its own kinetic practice remains yet another universal claim about being qua being as problematic and metaphysical as any other immobile ontology. The mysteries of ontology can therefore only be solved by the practice of ontology itself.

For example, when philosophers describe something, they always do so through some material process of inscription—language, writing, books, typography—that has a material-kinetic structure that changes something about reality through its usage. The invention of language, writing, and the printing press, for example, all introduced real kinetic changes that are not independent from the ontological descriptions inscribed on them. All kinds of social, sensory, and quantitative factors contribute to the material conditions within which an ontologist describes reality. Ontological description, therefore, does not stand isolated apart from the whole network of material, social, and technical motions within which the description is inscribed. How ontological practices describe and inscribe the world is bound up with the way people and things move in it, and vice versa. The consequence of this important kinetic insight is that the ontological apparatus of description and inscription is itself an aspect or dimension of being's motion.

This poses a real problem for traditional ontology, which tends to bracket its own material and historical agency and conditions in favor of pure concepts. However, if ontological practice is part of reality and introduces changes into the reality that it describes, then its descriptions cease to be representations and become *kinetic aspects or dimensions of reality*. Ontological practice is not a view from nowhere; it is situated in the moving present along with everything else. Therefore, the ontology of motion requires not only a new conceptual framework for describing the motion of beings but also a kinetic reinterpretation of ontological practice itself and of its historical kinetic conditions of emergence. If ontological practice itself is a kinetic activity, how does it move? How do its ontological descriptions and inscriptions circulate within various patterns of motion? *Being and Motion* provides a historical and kinetic answer to this question.

This second major thesis, that ontological practice is itself a historical and kinetic activity, therefore makes an important intervention into the study of ontology more broadly. What is at stake, therefore, in the development of an ontology of motion is a solution to two major problems in ontology: stasis and reductionism.

ONTOLOGICAL STASIS

The first problem is that ontology has been understood as the saying or thinking of the unchanging and static properties of being *in itself*. In this way, ontology has been relegated to serving a secondary or representational function. The structure of being remains unchanging and fixed according to an immutable formal structure that we mobile, changing humans glimpse through epistemological, linguistic, structural, or mathematical formalisms. In other words, the introduction of an ontological division between things as they are *for us* and things as they are *in themselves* is at the heart of the problem of a static being and a representational saying of it. Once the division is introduced, there is no way to get the "for itself" and the "in itself" back together again.

Subjectivism and metaphysics are two sides of this same intractable problem. On the one hand, subjectivist philosophies argue that as humans we have access only to our sensations of nature through various anthropic, linguistic, economic, unconscious, and historical structures—as it is *for us*. We have no access to what being is *in itself*. Any descriptions of being in itself are by nature completely speculative, and we must remain agnostic toward them. Although subjectivism claims to have no ontological access to being in itself because of the finite anthropic structures of thought, society, language, and so on, it must also accept as the precondition of such structures at least one minimal ontological condition: that being in itself must be structured in such a way that it can produce the self-affection of the anthropic subject, since this is the condition for human sensation, experience, and philosophical practice as such.[1] Without ontological self-affection or differentiation, there can be no anthropic experience. In this way, subjectivism falls into an uncritical metaphysics.[2]

On the other hand, metaphysical positions argue that humans have direct, unmediated access to mind-independent reality as it is in itself. In this definition, ontology is a speaking of being qua being that represents it and gets it right. In this case of naive and uncritical metaphysics, we have the inverse problem of subjectivism. In the first case, the "for itself" is cut off from the "in itself" and ends up assuming a metaphysical position. In the second case, the "for itself" can, through proper mediation, come to know the "in itself" but ends up assuming the existence of something called "mind-independent reality," which by definition exists independently of the mind and must therefore remain in some sense distinct from the mind, qua independent. If the "in itself" ever made itself fully known to the mind, it would no longer be independent from the mind. Naive metaphysics thus falls back into subjectivism and idealism.

HISTORICAL ONTOLOGY OF ONTOLOGY

In response to the problem of a static and representational view of ontology, I argue that if we want to understand what ontological practice is, there is no need to introduce a metaphysical division between being and our description of it. Since we ourselves are also beings, as are ontological descriptions, we can examine ontological practice from the perspective of what being *does* in the act of description and inscription. Thus, ontology should no longer be understood as a static, neutral, or total description of being in itself, but must be understood *kinetically* as an action or material practice that *really does something*.

In other words, this book does not adopt an absolute ontological position from which to dismiss certain ontologically "incorrect" subjective and metaphysical claims about being for or in itself. It is neither a critique of anthropic constructivism nor a deconstruction of metaphysics. This is because its domain of inquiry is not the nature of being in itself, but rather the historical practice of ontological description itself. Thus, the core philosophical presupposition of the ontology of motion is strictly historical (the primacy of motion in the present) and neither metaphysical nor implicitly subjective.

Being and Motion does not waffle between metaphysics (i.e., fundamental ontology, or being-qua-being) and subjectivism (i.e., correlationism, or being-qua-thought) but tries to develop a third way. Since the ontology of motion does not claim anything positive or negative about the future, it cannot be, by definition, fundamental ontology. However, since its claims about the being of motion extend well before the advent of human life and posit motion as a minimal feature of previous beings, it also cannot be, by definition, correlationist—since correlationism has no access to anything beyond present human thought, or at most all previous human thought. *Being and Motion* is strictly and by definition a regional ontology of motion, though it includes the largest possible region of being, excluding only the future.[3] Therefore, when "ontology" or "being" are mentioned here, please read: "the strictly historical study of being up to but not including future being."

Rather than putting forward a theory of being qua being or even an epistemological theory of being qua thought, this book offers a description of the minimal ontological commitments entailed *by the very kinetic practice of ontological description itself*. Given that the act of ontological description is a *real action* that changes reality in some way, and that the act of inscription relies on the material-kinetic activity of a historical media of inscription, a realist theory of motion is presupposed by both.

What is at stake in *Being and Motion* is therefore an immanent critique of ontological practice and the discovery of its minimal or regional, but no less ontologically real, material conditions. The theory of ontological practice presented in this book is thus a kind of historical ontology of ontology, but not, strictly speaking, a metaontology.[4] Metaontology presupposes a theory of being qua being from which to order and evaluate other ontologies. In contrast, *Being and Motion* puts forward a strictly historical ontology of the present by which previous ontological practices can be interpreted but without making any claims about the absolute nature of being in itself.

Admittedly, this may seem like an unusual project, and one hardly worthy of the grand title *Being and Motion*, since the crux of its argument is quite different from what is typically considered to be ontology or even history. In the end, however, this book remains "ontological" insofar as it offers nothing less than a wholesale redefinition of all the major categories of traditional ontological inquiry—space, eternity, force, time, quality, quantity, relation, and so on—as well as ontological practice itself, from the perspective of motion.

ONTOLOGICAL REDUCTIONISM

The second problem this book aims to overcome is that of ontological reductionism. In particular, there are two kinds of ontological reductionism that are of concern here. The first, and more common, is an idealist reductionism which claims that the contents of ontological descriptions are accurate mental representations of being in itself, regardless of the material-kinetic media of inscription. For the idealist, ontological practice is entirely reducible to the *thinking* of being. The material and historical conditions by which such thoughts are inscribed as content on a surface are completely irrelevant to what can be thought about the nature of being. In other words, the contents of ontological description and inscription are stripped of their materiality and reduced to the pure thought of being.

At least one major problem with this move to universally identify thought and being, in addition to the antinomy of naive metaphysics described above, is that the thought of the ontologist engaged in such an activity is not directly expressible to anyone else without some medium of inscription or communication. The history of ontology cannot be studied by looking at the *thoughts* of dead philosophers, scientists, and theologians but instead requires a material study of the *graphic inscriptions* they have produced. Thought is not something that can be studied independently of the material and graphic conditions of that thought.

The second kind of reductionism with which this book is concerned is a technological, material, or media reductionism, which claims that any ontological description of being, including thought or any other sensation, is a simple product of the technological or media conditions through which ontology expresses itself. In its most extreme formulation,[5] everything becomes media, and all human culture, including ontological practice, is determined by the form of the medium of inscription. In this case, ontological practice says or thinks what it does about being simply because of the formal structure of the media used to inscribe it. Contrary to anthropic idealism, media materialism argues that humans are not the creators of technology, but that technology develops autonomously, *using* humans as *its medium*. This kind of reductionism goes too far in the other direction from the first. Instead of the ontological content or description explaining away or neutralizing the form of expression or inscription, the media form ends up completely explaining away or neutralizing the content of description.

ONTOLOGICAL GRAPHISM

The problem with both these kinds of reductionism is that they operate under a metaphysical presupposition of a division between humans and nature. The relationship between description (idealism) and inscription (materialism) is poorly understood as one of unidirectional causality: Does the human description of reality cause us to make new technologies of inscription (instrumentalism), or do new technologies of inscription determine in advance that very description in the first place (determinism)?

Reductionism thus relies on the very division it tries to resolve. If nature is the movement and organization of matter, and if technology is the strictly human organization of matter, then the problem becomes clear. If nature creates humans, then humans themselves become the technologies of nature. The human body becomes a technical machine created by nature for increasing entropy. Humans in turn create their own kinds of technical objects, such as clothing and tools. However, if we grant that the technologies created by nature, namely humans, and the technologies created by humans both in turn have some transformative effects on their creators (nature and humanity), then nature and humanity equally become the technologies of technologies. In other words, if we admit a recursive determination between nature and humanity via technology, the distinction collapses entirely.[6] An ontological difference between nature, humanity, and technology cannot be sustained. The whole reductionistic debate between instrumentalism and determinism starts from faulty assumptions.

Therefore, in *Being and Motion* there are only kinetic regimes of collective transformation, coordination, or synchronization, not causalities (linear or otherwise). Descriptive content and inscribed form are simply two collectively coordinated aspects of the same kinetic regime mutating through history. These regimes are neither strictly natural, human, or technological, but *kinetic*.

Accordingly, if ontological practice is part of this mutual kinetic transformation, then it is in motion and should thus be redefined kinetically. The word "ontology" comes from the Greek word ὄντος, *ontos*, "to be," plus the Greek word -λογία, *-logia*, "study, logic, or saying," and it has been traditionally interpreted as the study or speaking of being qua being. Alternately, however, the Greek word *logos* also comes from the root word λέγω, *légō*, meaning "to pick up, gather together, to choose, to arrange."[7] Thus, contained in the roots of the traditional definition is also the key to a more kinetic definition of ontology—one that highlights the *material activity* of picking up, selecting, gathering, drawing together, and arranging of being. The word *légō* explicitly emphasizes the kinetic activity of the hand, and thus of gesture, that picks up and puts together: graphism.

Following this alternate definition, we can offer a reinterpretation of ontological practice as a kinetic activity comprising two distinct but interrelated gestural or "kinographic" actions: description and inscription. Ontology is "de-scriptive" in the sense in which it is a picking out and picking up that re-moves (de-) something from a previous graphic or material arrangement, but also "in-scriptive" insofar as it produces a new gathering together (in-) of the graphic. By this definition, an ontological description can no longer be understood as a representation or reflection of being in itself in thought. Description is active and creative. It selects something from the world and removes it from where it was already inscribed or gathered. Once it has been removed from one region, it can appear as the "content" of a new form gathered on a surface: the inscription. A bit of charcoal, for example, can be removed from a campfire and used as a writing implement, leaving a trace of itself on a new surface of inscription—a wall. In this sense the Greek word *logos* should be understood as a dimension of the more primary graphic and kinetic act of the hand that gathers and marks. Ontology is thus fundamentally kinographic.

Description

A "description" is a system of marks and signs arranged on an inscription surface. Different signs do not represent or have any resemblance to being in itself, but are arbitrary marks gathered from elsewhere and placed in a relation on an inscription surface that are kinetically coordinated with certain material actions or gestures in nature.[8] Although descriptive signs today seem obviously and necessarily connected to sensory and material beings, all those connections and coordinations had to be historically created (as will be shown in Book II). They were not already there.

In other words, the understanding of ontological description as a representation of being is a historical artifact, not an essential feature of ontological practice. Because it is a historical artifact, we can give a historical and kinetic analysis of the emergence of the practice of ontology "as representational." This is what Book II does.

Inscription

"Inscription" is the process of gathering descriptive marks and signs onto a recording surface. As such, it is impossible to separate description from inscription. To speak of one or the other is to speak of two sides of the same thing, not two different things or parts of a whole. Surfaces of inscription are rarely understood to be representing anything about the nature of being, but are more often reduced to utilitarian instruments for communicating information. However, just as description is nonrepresentational, inscription is noninstrumental. Inscription surfaces—bodies, tablets, books, and so on—all have their own material-kinetic structure that really introduces new motions into the world. Technologies of inscription do not represent or facilitate human needs but are an articulation of the larger kinetic regime in which those needs emerge *at the same time*. There is no discoverable system of simple causality between human utility and technical innovation—there is only historical coemergence and constant conjunction or coordination, which appear afterward as causally connected. Insofar as inscription is tied to material technologies, it is both kinetic and historical and in no way offers a view from nowhere.

What distinguishes ontology from other kinds of graphism is that it privileges or focuses on the immanent relation between the descriptive signs and the inscriptive surfaces themselves. One is not the cause of the other. They are two aspects of the same kinographic process. Together, ontological description and inscription produce a written document whose kinetic coordinations follow the same dominant pattern of motion as the other major graphic events of its time—not by mimesis but by resonance or synchrony.

Social motions, for example, are described by flows of bodies and inscribed by borders, aesthetic motions are described by affects and inscribed in images, and scientific motions are described by quantities and inscribed in objects—but ontological motions are described by graphic signs and inscribed on recording surfaces.[9] During each major historical period, the same dominant pattern of motion is produced in each domain, according to its own graphic elements.

Historical Mixture

Each domain has its own kind of descriptive content and inscription, but they all mix together in history. Each also has dimensions of the other. Literature, for example, makes graphic inscriptions on recording surfaces such as books, but the main aim of aesthetic practice is to produce certain kinetic patterns of sensation through images. By contrast, the privileged function of ontology is not to produce sensations on our bodies, although it also does this, but rather to produce a kinetic pattern of marks on a surface.

Table 2.1 KINOGRAPHY

Domain	Description	Inscription
Politics (kinopolitics)	Bodies	Borders
Art (kinesthetics)	Affects	Images
Science (kinometrics)	Quantities	Objects
Ontology (kinographics)	Signs	Surfaces

Since each graphism includes aspects of the others, a metaphysical or absolute division between politics, art, science, and ontology is untenable (see Table 2.1). Everything can be examined according to each of these four dimensions at once.[10] However, this should not prohibit us from methodologically separating out the different kinds of graphisms that define each dimension of reality, even if they are always mixed in practice and history. Only when they have been separated out is it possible to see them *as a mixture* of distinct aspects or dimensions of being. This analytic task is the contribution of philosophy.

Ontology, therefore considered on its own, is philosophically different from the other domains simply because it tends to privilege or focus its study on the internal and immanent relations of kinographic signs gathered on a recording surface, and not on the affects, social movements, or quantities that are related to them. This does not make ontology any more "pure" of a domain than the others. Just because ontology privileges the graphic over the affective, social, or quantitative does give it any special primacy. It is simply a different domain of inquiry.

Ontology is the graphic movement of signs and surfaces that create a regime of motion. This is not a representation but a real material creation. It is a real practice and performance. The descriptive content creates an internally consistent material sign system of kinetic relations, while the surface of inscription creates a kinetic structure for recording these signs. Both resonate with or follow the same dominant regime of historical motion of their age, alongside the other domains of social, aesthetic, and scientific practice. Through this process, ontology gives a descriptive name to the inscriptive pattern of being's motion as it appears within the dominant regime of motion. The great names of being are thus each connected to a different regime of historical motion, which their ontologies describe.

These regimes are neither strictly chronological nor merely a priori universal "types." The real movements of history contingently produce certain nonuniversal types or patterns of motion. Once each of these patterns emerges, it can be reproduced, altered, mixed, or destroyed through history.

PLAN OF THE BOOK

The plan of *Being and Motion* is as simple as it is ambitious: to develop an ontology of motion. This has two different but complementary objectives following its two core theses: (1) the development of a transdisciplinary conceptual framework, or ontology, useful for describing the motion of beings; and (2) a historical ontology of the motion of ontological practice itself. These two tasks cannot be separated. The second relies on the conceptual framework of the first, just as the first relies on the historical conditions and movement of the second. Separating these two kinds of inquiry from each other results in either ahistorical idealism (the first without the second) or historical constructivism (the second without the first). *Being and Motion* is therefore divided into two books: one focusing on the ontology of motion, which we will call "kinology," and one focusing on the descriptive and inscriptive motions of ontological practice itself, or what we will call "kinography."[11]

Kinology

The primacy of motion and mobility across several major domains at the turn of the twenty-first century has forced us to take motion seriously—not only for understanding those events, but also for understanding a previously subordinated dimension of all previous events that has now become visible. For example, the advent of the modern clock and the rise of industrial capitalism had similar historical effects on ontologies of the nineteenth and twentieth centuries with respect to the primacy of time. The question today, however, has shifted from time to motion—that is, given the novel emergence of the primacy of motion, what then must be the real minimal ontological features of being such that it is *capable of being in motion*? This is the fundamental question of Book I. In brief, the answer to this question is a deceptively simple one, but from it numerous consequences follow. The historical condition for the primacy of motion in the present age is that being must flow. From this initial thesis, an ontology of movement is possible.

Theory of Motion. The ontology presented in Book I is thus organized around three major concepts, which together form the theoretical framework for describing the motion of beings. The first concept, from which the others are derived, is that being is composed of *flows*, or continuous movements. As beings flow, they intersect with one another, forming confluences, and bend back over one another, forming folds. The second concept, therefore, is the *fold*. The outcome of these continuous intersections and folds is a relative kinetic stability. Once these folds occur, they can be entrained together into a circulatory system or field that orders and maintains a set of internal kinetic synchronies between them. The third concept therefore is the *field* of circulation. Flows, folds, and fields are the *historically* necessary conditions for being in motion.

A full description of each of these three concepts, their relations, and their consequences for important issues in ontological inquiry are developed in Book I. Together, they form the minimal theoretical framework entailed by the contemporary revelation of the primacy of motion, and provide the conceptual tools for reinterpreting the motion of beings both past and present more broadly.[12]

Kinography

While Book I deals strictly with the kinological conditions of moving being, Book II deals with the way in which these conditions have been distributed into specific kinographic regimes of description and inscription. While Book I is more conceptual because it describes the historically ontological commitments of moving being generally, Book II is more concrete, material, and historical, since it examines the specific graphic arrangements or regimes of motion that structure ontological practice itself.

In other words, although Book I comes first logically and conceptually, Book II comes first historically as the material and graphic conditions for the production of the logical concepts of Book I. As Marx says,

> Of course the method of presentation must differ in form from that of inquiry. The latter has to appropriate the material in detail, to analyze its different forms of development and to track down their inner connection. Only after this work has been done can the real movement be appropriately presented. If this is done successfully, if the life of the subject-matter is now reflected back in the ideas, then it may appear as if we have before us an *a priori* construction.[13]

But we do not have an a priori construction, only a material and historical one. Only because we stand today at the relative end of this long historical process are we now able to invent concepts appropriate to the process itself. Since this is a work of philosophy, and the owl of Minerva flies at dusk, we begin with concepts to help explain the things that have made us what we are today. In short, the question of Book II is this: What are the kinetic conditions under which ontological practice itself describes and inscribes reality?

The history of ontology has always taken specific forms. Being has been given several major historical names: space, eternity, force, and time. Each of these names has been used historically to provide a description of the fundamental nature of being qua being. At some point each has also been used to explain all the others, and has thereby justified its own claim of ontological primacy. At certain points or ages in history, these names take on a more widely accepted status resonant with the other relevant inventions and discoveries in the domains of politics, art, and science. Then, at other times, the same names wane with the emergence of a new descriptive name that comes to explain the previous names. This does not mean that there is some developmental logic of ideas at work here that precedes the historical battle and politics of truth. It only indicates a shifting and mobile battleground as these names are redistributed, revalorized, or retheorized and mixed together in new relations or descriptive primacies alongside various other historical patterns of motion. New combinations and hybridizations occur among the regimes until we arrive at the present, the most hybrid and complex so far, not de jure but de facto.[14]

The thesis of *Being and Motion* is that the events of the twenty-first century have introduced yet another prevailing, but not exclusive, historical name for being: motion. Just like the others, this name is capable of describing all the others, and thereby justifying its own claim to historical ontological primacy. Or at least this is what I would like to argue. In fact, only by showing precisely such an explanatory power over all the previous ontologies can motion be said to have proven its historical equality with these other names—which have all done precisely this. To claim that being is in motion is therefore to claim that space, eternity, force, and time are all ontologically describable by motion. It is an ambitious claim, and it is the core thesis argued in Book II.

In one sense, *Being and Motion* is not quite playing the same game as other ontologies, since its ultimate claim is not that all previous names for being are wrong and it alone is right and primary forever and all time. Unlike the other great names in the history of ontology, motion is not another name for being qua being. Since it makes no claim to the future, it does not do battle on the same grounds. It is ultimately a historical and regional ontology, rooted in the present, and thus can at most lay claim to a single dimension or historical trajectory in being leading up to a certain region of the present. Such a "regional realist ontology" is one possible answer to the question of what can be done at the "end of metaphysics" without returning to metaphysics (speculative realism), or simply destructing it (deconstruction), or abandoning it altogether (constructivism).

In another sense, though, *Being and Motion* is on the same ontological battleground, insofar as every other great historical name for being has only ever been just that: a historical and regional ontology for its time. And ultimately, as I want to argue, the ontology of our time is an ontology of motion. This is a big claim, and to succeed it has to be demonstrated with an appropriate historical depth and breadth that occupies all of Book II. More specifically, the thesis of Book II is composed of three interlocking theses.

First Thesis. The history of ontology can be grouped according to at least four major historical periods (prehistoric, ancient, medieval, and modern) in which a single name (space, eternity, force, time, respectively) comes to predominate the ontological descriptions of the age, even if it is not the only one in use.

Second Thesis. During these same historical periods, a certain technology of inscription (speech, writing, books, typography), used to write the ontological descriptions, also rises to dominance.

Third Thesis. Description and inscription are not derived from one another. Rather, during each historical period, the dominant ontological description and the dominant technology of inscription have the same kinetic pattern or regime of motion, which allows us to put forward an original *kinetic ontology* of space, eternity, force, and time.

HISTORICAL RATIONALE

Put succinctly and concretely, the grand labor of Book II is therefore to connect the *ontological names* of space, eternity, force, and time to their *historical descriptions* in prehistoric mythology, ancient cosmology, medieval theology, and modern phenomenology; to their *graphic inscriptions* in speech, writing, books, and typography; and to their respective *kinetic patterns* of centripetal, centrifugal, tensional, and elastic motion (see Table 2.2).

Together, these three theses support the core thesis of Book II: that ontological practice itself is historical and kinetic. This thesis has three consequences, which are the *rationale and motivation for the historical labor of Book II*:

Table 2.2 HISTORICAL ONTOLOGY

Ontology	Space	Eternity	Force	Time
Kinos (type of motion)	Centripetal	Centrifugal	Tensional	Elastic
Logos (type of description)	Mythology	Cosmology	Theology	Phenomenology
Graphos (type of inscription)	Speech	Writing	Book	Keyboard

1. It shows that all the great names for being rise and fall historically and are therefore on the same historical footing with a regional ontology of motion. In other words, all the previous names of being are tied to their historical techniques of inscription and thus to certain kinetic patterns of motion and mobility. Therefore, the history of ontology is also a history of motion.
2. This allows us to analyze the contemporary mixture of their kinetic structures, insofar as they continue to circulate and persist in the present under the same names of space, eternity, force, and time in contemporary ontology.
3. Most importantly, the historical analysis of these four major periods and their dominant names in Book II allows us to develop original kinetic theories of space, eternity, force, and time that form the second set of major concepts in the ontology of motion.

It is only through the historical labor of Book II, therefore, that the second half of the core concepts of the ontology of motion can be developed: a kinetic theory of space defined by centripetal motion, a kinetic theory of eternity defined by centrifugal motion, a kinetic theory of force defined by tensional motion, and a kinetic theory of time defined by elastic motion. In this sense, the rationale for Book II is to produce an immanent critique of the history of ontology that reveals, at the same time, original kinetic descriptions of space, eternity, force, and time. These form part of *the conceptual core of the ontology of motion itself.*

In short, Book II is not just a history in the same way that Book I is not just an ontology. Book I is a historical ontology—which is limited to the conditions of the present—and Book II is an ontological history—which derives its ontological concepts from the historical conditions of its own ontological practice. They are two inseparable sides of the same ontological project.

However, before the finer details of the theory of motion can be put forward, we first need to lay out the methodology of its formulation and application. Therefore, we now move on to the philosophical, realist, and materialist orientations of the ontology of motion.

CHAPTER 3

Philosophy of Motion

Being is in motion, and so is ontological practice itself. This twin formulation at the heart of *Being and Motion* raises several methodological issues about how to go about doing an ontology of motion, if ontology is already in motion. Thus, before moving on to the theory of motion in Part II, there are three more interrelated methodological issues to tackle regarding 1) the definition of the philosophy motion and its difference from the ontology of becoming, 2) the meaning of philosophical realism, and 3) the nature of historical materialism.

THE PHILOSOPHY OF MOTION

The philosophy of motion is the analysis of phenomena across social, aesthetic, scientific, and ontological domains from the perspective of motion. As such, the ontology of motion is only one part of the philosophy of motion. Most importantly, and quite simply, the philosophy of motion is defined by the methodological primacy of motion with respect to the domain of study. Therefore, the difference between simply describing the motion of things—which almost every philosopher and even every lay person has done—and the philosophy of movement is the degree to which movement plays an analytically primary role in the description. For example, if we describe a body moving through a space (x,y,z) over a time (t), we are describing motion, but we are also assuming a more primary nonkinetic and immobile space-time within which this motion occurs. From the perspective of motion, however, space and time are not immobile at all but only relatively immobile patterns of some matter in motion upon which another pattern or trajectory is traced by something else. Everything is in motion, but all motions are relative to others. This is a basic tenet of contemporary physics.[1] Giving analytical primacy to motion, however, does not mean that we cannot speak of space or time. It just means that motion is a unique dimension of reality not reducible to space or time.

Given this simple and quite general definition of the philosophy of motion, we can already see it at work across several contemporary domains of inquiry, to varying degrees.

The Study of Motion

At the most basic level, there are a number of domains and subdomains where the *movement* of bodies defines the study of the domain itself, such as fluid and nonlinear dynamics,[2] interactive and generative art,[3] or migration and transportation studies,[4] to name only a few. If everything is in motion at one level or another, then quite literally everything deals with motion. The difference, however, is how the study deals with this motion. Does it treat its domain of inquiry like static nodes in a network, like abstract numbers, or like preserved works of art? Or does it focus almost exclusively on the vectors, oscillations, and circulatory patterns of mobility itself within which people, things, states, particles, proteins, and so on are all metastable aspects of a more primary kinetic process?

In most major domains the study of motion is not a dominant one. The study of motion is often defined solely by the very fact that its domain of inquiry itself deals exclusively with the study of bodies as *movements*. In this sense, studies of motion adhere to a kind of regional de facto primacy of motion. Their work is a relevant and important contribution to the philosophy of motion, even if such studies take no broader position on the primacy of motion in any other domain. The limitation of such studies, however, is that they are often, although not always, limited to a single domain, subdomain, historical period, or methodology.

The Mobilities Paradigm

In 2006 Mimi Sheller and John Urry announced the emergence of a "mobilities paradigm" or "mobility turn" in the social sciences.[5] Their edited journal issue on this topic showed quite dramatically what many scholars studying movement across several different disciplines had already felt was going on for some time—that despite their different domains and topics of study they were in fact studying the same thing, motion, but from different perspectives. The recognition of a common something that was being studied, despite the empirical differences in the areas of study, was an important event and has led to further expansions of the paradigm into the humanities over the ensuing years.[6]

This has had at least two consequences for the development of a philosophy of motion. First, it took the study of motion one step further by explicitly expanding the de facto methodological starting point of the primacy of motion to multiple areas and topics of study in the humanities and social sciences, including anthropology, cultural studies, geography, science and technology studies, tourism and transportation studies, and sociology, to name only a few.

Second, and even more importantly, this expansion introduced the possibility of a theoretical or methodological unity to the study of motion, as well as the possible limits for such a method. Does this method apply only to studies where things are obviously, dramatically, and empirically moving around, such as tourism, migration, the spread of viral epidemics, portable computers, airports, automobiles, and so on?[7] Or should we still adopt the methodological primacy of motion in cases where things seem more immobile, such as borders, states, prisons, desktop computers, roads, and so on? Or for these should we go back to the spatial turn of the 1980s for a different method and set of concepts? Should we still begin our method with the primacy of motion if the events are older than the contemporary event of our "liquid" and "mobile" modernity, as Zygmunt Bauman, Marc Augé, Manuel Castells, Paul Virilio, and others all heralded at the turn of the century?[8] Or for older events, when the world was more static, should we just rely on the traditional static methods of our discipline? There are as many answers to these questions as there are mobilities scholars, but it is easy to see where this is going. The mobility paradigm extends only as far scholars are willing to take it. At the moment, mobility studies is largely, although not exclusively, focused on more obviously mobile bodies (cars, dance, diaspora, airports, and so on), and mostly in the social sciences, sometimes in the humanities, and rarely in the natural sciences.[9]

In their description of this mobilities paradigm, Sheller and Urry make clear that they "do not insist on a new 'grand narrative' of mobility, fluidity, or liquidity. The new mobilities paradigm suggests a set of questions, theories, and methodologies rather than a totalising or reductive description of the contemporary world."[10] The mobilities paradigm is, according to the authors, not a metaphysics that describes everything forever and for all time. Nonetheless, it also seems arbitrarily limited in its scope and content. At times this limitation threatens to undermine the methodological primacy of motion all together, such as when a binary division is introduced between space-time immobilities, fixities, or moorings, on the one hand, and mobilities, on the other. This is particularly limiting when immobility itself is understood to be the condition of mobility. This can be seen in Urry and Sheller's claim that "the multiple fixities or moorings . . . enable the fluidities of liquid modernity," or that mobilities "presume overlapping and varied time-space immobilities."[11] Surely there are relative relations of motion and rest, but, physically speaking, nothing is absolutely immobile. Why then limit the paradigm of movement in this way?[12]

Despite the rather banal empirical fact accepted by every contemporary physical scientist that everything is in motion, some mobilities scholars have really dug their heels in on this point, arguing that "if everything is mobile, then the concept has little purchase."[13] Imagine saying that "since everything is in space or time, the concept has little purchase"! This critique is preposterous.[14] No wonder so few natural scientists seem interested in the mobilities paradigm. I agree that it is at least analytically useless, and at most politically pernicious, to *merely* say "everything is in motion" or "motion is a good,"[15] but that is true of anything. On the contrary, the methodical goal of the philosophy of motion is to give us another robust perspective on reality—with the same rigor across every domain of inquiry that space and time have.

Surely there is a third way between a metaphysics of motion and only studying some contemporary things that move a lot. Surely it is possible for paradigms and theoretical frameworks to offer a description of everything that has been without being the only coherent or reductive description of those things. There can be and certainly are multiple coexisting descriptions of the same things from different perspectives. Why, then, can't the mobilities paradigm offer us a new perspective on or dimension to everything in the same way that we quite easily talk about spatial and temporal dimensions to all things? Movement is just as real of an irreducible dimension of being as space or time. There is nothing that is not or has not been in motion. To believe otherwise is precisely to reduce motion to space and time.

A regional ontology of motion can therefore be stretched a long way without impinging on the future or becoming "total," "absolute," or "reductive." In other words, a theory can have a large region and still be regional. Certainly such a theory can be pushed beyond the last fifty or one hundred years. Everything moves. So why restrict a movement-oriented theoretical perspective to a couple of domains, or historical periods, or anything else outside the nonexistent future itself? If something moves, why can't a movement-oriented perspective be used to understand it?

So while the mobilities paradigm has made and continues to make excellent contributions to the philosophy of motion to some degree, it also seems to have some arbitrary de facto limitations to its domains, historical scope, and content that leave plenty of room for the emergence of a more robust nonmetaphysical and nonreductionist philosophy and ontology of motion.

THE ONTOLOGY OF MOTION

The ontology of movement presented here has several important precursors in the history of philosophy, as well as several related contenders in contemporary philosophy. To help clarify the continuity and genuine novelty of *Being and Motion* with respect to this tradition, it is worth considering carefully where it is similar and where it diverges from its precursors and contemporaries.

Historical Precursors

Here I will give only an abbreviated history of the main ideas and contributions of three major philosophers of motion, since elsewhere I have given each of them a much more careful and book-length treatment.[16] Also, I will not provide in this brief history the exact reasons why other philosophers are *not* on this list, because most of those arguments are included throughout Book II.

Lucretius. The first historical precursor in the ontology of motion is the Roman poet and philosopher Lucretius (c. 99 BCE–c. 55 BCE). Lucretius comes after a long line of Greek atomist philosophers from around the fifth century BCE, including Leucippus, Democritus, and Epicurus. According to Aristotle, one of the primary ontological tenets of atomism for Democritus and Leucippus is "that there is always motion." With the exception of Parmenides, in fact, most of the pre-Socratic philosophers accepted the thesis of continuous motion. However, not all of them accepted that this motion was ontologically primary. Leucippus, Democritus, and Epicurus alone affirmed the ontological primacy of movement without a static, eternal, or first origin. "The atoms," Epicurus writes, "move continuously for all time."[17] Their movement has no origin and no end, no God and no immortal soul. There is only matter in motion. There are no static phenomena to appear to a stable observer, but only *kinomena*, or bodies in motion. All of being is produced by a curvature in the flows of this motion that subsequently generates a series of spiral vortexes that appear as solid discrete material. Stability and stasis are therefore products of a more primary vortical movement.

However, the difference between Lucretius and the earlier, Greek atomists is precisely that—the atom. For Leucippus, Democritus, and Epicurus, atoms are always in motion, but the atom itself remains fundamentally unchanged, indivisible, and thus internally static. Instead of positing discrete atoms as ontologically primary, as both ancient Greek and later modern theories do, Lucretius instead posited *the movement or flow of matter as primary*. Lucretius could have used the Latin word *atomus* (smallest particle) in his poem, but he intentionally did not use it, nor did he use the Latin word *particula* (particle) to describe matter. The English translations of "atom," "particle," and others have all been added to the text based on a certain Greek and modern bias. The idea that Lucretius subscribed to a world of discrete particles called atoms is therefore both a projection of Epicureanism, which used the Greek word *atomos*, and a retroaction of modern scientific mechanist theories onto *De Rerum Natura*. Instead, Lucretius uses the word *materies* (matters) to describe the continuous and turbulent flow (*flux*) of movement without rest and without space or time (*exiguum clinamen principiorum nec regione loci certa nec tempore certo*).[18] No one before Lucretius had ever given such a direct and clear ontological primacy to motion. He is therefore the prince of motion. Based on this ontological position, he provides a number of shockingly contemporary-sounding theories on physics, epistemology, aesthetics, history, and meteorology. Unfortunately, the one short book we have left from him hardly constitutes a full-fledged ontology.

Marx. The second historical precursor in the ontology of motion is the German philosopher Karl Marx (1818–1883). As a young philosopher, Marx had read Epicurus and Lucretius before he ever read a single word of Hegel. He was of course deeply influenced by Hegelian philosophy, but he was also deeply critical of its idealist and historically determinist character. His first attempt to overcome Hegel and create his own philosophical and materialist philosophy began with his doctoral thesis on *The Difference Between the Democritean and Epicurean Philosophy of Nature*. By looking at his notebooks, we can see this was written alongside his thinking about the nature of matter in Feuerbach and in Hegel's *Philosophy of Nature*.

By engaging with Greek atomism, Marx was able to work out the philosophical and ontological foundations of his own philosophy on different terrain. The key discovery of his thesis was that for Epicurus and Lucretius, in contrast to Democritus, matter itself was creative and free in its movement or swerve. This meant that being was not idea but matter, not logically determined but materially free. History was open to a revolutionary communist horizon beyond the Hegelian state. In his reading, Marx was also the second philosopher after Lucretius to reject the existence of a solid and static atom in atomism, seeing instead its movement as more ontologically primary than its solidity:

> The consequence of this [the primacy of the flow of matter] for the monads as well as for the atoms would therefore be—since they are in constant motion—that *neither monads nor atoms exist*, but rather disappear in the straight line: for the solidity of the atom does not even enter into the picture, insofar as it is only considered as something falling in a straight line.[19]

Based on this early methodological conviction about the primacy of motion, Marx's work takes on a decidedly historical and material-kinetic character—focusing on the mobility of labor and the circulation of capital. He treats labor (and thus society) not as a static thing but as a material "flow" or "motion,"[20] which becomes "congealed"[21] or "crystalized"[22] into commodities, which in turn flow, circulate, and congeal into larger and larger social metabolic structures. Marx does not provide a metaphysics or a pure ontology of motion or of anything else and should not be conflated with the more metaphysical remarks of Engels in the *Dialectics of Nature*. Therefore, one is only able to discern a historical ontology of motion in Marx's work by seeing it, appropriately, in practice here and there as it is put to use.

Bergson. The third historical precursor in the ontology of motion is the French philosopher Henri Bergson (1859–1941). Bergson continued Lucretius's legacy by publishing his first book as an annotated commentary on *De Rerum Natura* in 1884. The influence of Lucretius on Bergson is readily apparent in Bergson's rejection of atomistic and mechanistic materialism, as well as the affirmation of the ontological primacy of motion. Instead of fixed states, Bergson describes "fluid masses" in "a moving zone." "States," he says, "thus defined cannot be regarded as distinct elements. They continue each other in an endless flow."[23] Nature is "one single immense wave flowing over matter."[24]

Despite his numerous comments about a continuum of matter and motion, Bergson is often read as a "vitalist" philosopher, or a philosopher of time and duration (*duré*)—and not of movement per se. In other words, all the passages about motion are often read as being derived from something else more primary: a *vital force* or unquantifiable energy inside all of life that causes it to move or explains its motion.

In fairness, Bergson often lends himself to this kind of reading in most of this writing by not always clarifying the ontological status of exactly what this "vital impetus" or "force" is. Still other passages, from *Matter and Memory*, make it sound like it is time or "pure duration" that is ontologically primary and is doing the flowing and moving.[25] In all this it is easy to mistake Bergson's ontology for one of vital force or time.

However, what is less well known is that Bergson finally cleared all this up in his final and most definitive work, *La Pensée et le mouvant* (*Thought and Mobility*, 1934)—for some strange reason translated into English as *The Creative Mind: An Introduction to Metaphysics*. With respect to "vital force," he argued that it "is known and estimated only by the movements which it is supposed to produce in space . . . [but it is] one with these movements."[26] Vital force, therefore, is not some kind of mystical or ethereal substance or vague energy. It is nothing other than *movement itself*. On the issue of time/duration, Bergson writes very clearly in this final work that "time is mobility."[27] "Mobility," he argues, "or what comes to the same thing, duration,"[28] is becoming, but becoming is not "becoming in general" as an "immobile medium"[29] through which things pass. Becoming is the continual mobility of reality itself.[30] "Reality is mobility itself." In this final work Bergson could hardly be any more unequivocal and clarifying when he writes that "[i]f movement is not everything, it is nothing."[31] Whatever apparent primacy he had given to so-called vital force/impetus or time/duration should now be understood to be *nothing other than the primacy of motion itself*.

This wonderful book gives us a way to return to and rethink many of Bergson's previous works on time, mind, and vital force with respect to the absolute primacy of mobility. It is only unfortunate that it was so late in his life before he was able to clearly and systematically identify duration and the *élan vital* with movement itself.

Limitations. All of these historical precursors have their limitations: We have only one short book from Lucretius, Marx did not write a historical ontology, and Bergson came late to the explicit ontological primacy of motion. In some sense, Marx is the most limited, since he does not explicitly put forward anything like a systematic historical ontology. In another sense, however, Lucretius and Bergson are even more limited, since their ontologies are not nearly historical enough. Unlike Marx's more historical methodology, which takes place explicitly under the regional and historical conditions of nineteenth-century industrial capitalism, Lucretius and Bergson offer largely universalist sounding accounts.

Being and Motion, however, is a quite different project that seeks to overcome both the ontological and historical limitations of these precursors by presenting a historical ontology and an ontological history of motion. This is something none of these precursors did. *Being and Motion* thus owes a great debt to these figures, but it also moves beyond them in its own way.

Process Ontology and Becoming

These historical precursors of the ontology of motion have also had a major influence on a number of contemporary process ontologies, or ontologies of becoming. Process ontology, like the ontology of movement, emphasizes flux and becoming but is not identical to the ontology of motion. There can be all kinds of fluxes: fluxes of time, fluxes of space, fluxes of force, and so on. The ontology of motion is strictly the flux of matter. Time, space, and force do not transcend matter in motion. Space and time are dimensions of reality, but they are irreducibly material-kinetic dimensions in the ontology of motion.[32] It is easy to see how the two are connected but also important to see where they diverge.

Whitehead. One of the first major systematic process philosophers was Alfred North Whitehead (1861–1947), although a whole other set of historical precursors could be drawn up, which would likely include Heraclitus, Duns Scotus, Spinoza, Nietzsche, Leibniz, and others. For Whitehead, process is real, but change and motion are not. For example, according to Whitehead, change is only "the difference between actual occasions comprised in some determined event," and thus it is "impossible to attribute 'change' to any actual entity."[33] "Thus an actual entity never moves: It is where it is and what it is."[34] Change and motion thus relate to a succession of actual entities and are constituted only by the *differences* among them. Every entity is simply "what it is," and it "becomes" as the whole of reality enters a succession of different states, but no entity ever technically changes or moves.

At least one scholar has aptly observed that this is a purely logical kind of change, or what has come to be known as a "Cambridge change," after the school of logicians Whitehead worked with, and not a kinetic one. Whitehead's transition, the same scholar observes, "is not a real transition, not a flow or flux, and change so understood is merely a fact consequent upon the successive existence of a series of different unchangeable and static actual entities. *The very notion of change has been made incurably static.*"[35] If there was still any doubt on this matter, Whitehead quite clearly writes in *The Concept of Nature* that "Motion presupposes rest. A theory of motion and a theory of rest are the same thing viewed from different aspects with altered emphasis."[36] There is "no continuity of becoming," Whitehead says, but only "a becoming of continuity."[37] This is the direct inverse of Bergson's claim that immobility presupposes mobility and that everything is in motion. Here we see that process ontology can be quite different from an ontology of motion, and can even eliminate motion entirely and still be considered a process ontology of becoming.[38]

Deleuze. Gilles Deleuze (1925–1995) was the philosopher of process and becoming par excellence. Influenced both by the ontologists of motion (Lucretius, Marx, Bergson) and the great philosophers of becoming more broadly (Duns Scotus, Spinoza, Nietzsche, Leibniz, Whitehead, and others), Deleuze was the first to unify these two traditions into a vast synthetic and systematic philosophy of becoming.

Instead of developing a single ontology limited to a single name for being (space, eternity, force, time, motion, etc.), Deleuze developed an inclusive and pluralistic ontology in which all the great names of being are said equally and univocally of the same being—but only, however, on the strict condition that this single being be understood as the being of pure becoming or differential process. The ontology of becoming, therefore, is not a naive and contradictory affirmation of all other ontologies, but rather a complete reinterpretation of all ontology itself as process, as becoming. As such, Deleuze develops and applies process theories of space, thought, force, time, motion, and others across numerous domains.

This incredible coup de grâce at the end of the twentieth century has given birth to a number of inspired efforts extending the application of becoming to new areas. Of particular interest are those Deleuzeans such as Michael Hardt, Antonio Negri, Manuel DeLanda, Brian Massumi, Erin Manning, Jane Bennett, William Connolly, Rosi Braidotti, and others who have made a concerted effort to apply this ontology to questions of materiality.[39] Even object-oriented ontologists and speculative realists such as Levi Bryant,[40] Steven Shaviro,[41] and Didier Debaise,[42] have explicitly drawn on Whitehead and Deleuze to theorize a process philosophy of objects and things. In short, the ontology of becoming has become an extremely fecund starting point for numerous new ontologies at the end of metaphysics.

Deleuze's great contribution to the philosophy of movement was therefore to have shown the ontological primacy of becoming over being as well as the coherence of this minor historical tradition stretching from Lucretius to Whitehead. But becoming means continual flux, matter, and motion for Deleuze just as equally as it means difference, thought, and stasis. There is a becoming of both—hence the division and ambiguity between what are now called "new materialism" and "speculative realism," both drawing on different strands in Deleuze's work. This split, however, attests to the difficulty and perhaps impossibility of affirming both becomings equally without falling back into one or the other, or introducing, as Deleuze ends up doing, a third "pure becoming" that traverses them all: force.

For Deleuze, there is a "force of thought"[43] just as there is a "force of matter."[44] Everything becomes because everything is a force of becoming. He is quite explicit about the ontological primacy of force against Marx's and Lucretius's kinetic materialism in his book on Nietzsche. "Atomism," Deleuze writes, "would be a mask for an incipient dynamism."[45] Deleuze's position has at least three important limitations, which by way of contrast, will help highlight the novel contribution of *Being and Motion*.

Motion. The first limitation is his *theory of motion*. If the flux of matter, like every other flux, is ontologically equal to every other flux, then we should expect to find in Deleuze's pluralist ontology of becoming a continuous becoming of motion, without stasis, immobility, cut, or break. But in almost every one of his major works we find the opposite.[46] He always ends up reintroducing stasis or immobility into his definition of motion.

For example, in *Difference and Repetition* he explicitly subordinates movement to time: "The [third] synthesis is necessarily static, since time is no longer subordinated to movement; time is the most radical form of change, but the form of change does not change."[47] In *Logic of Sense*, the subordination of movement and matter to time is explicit in his theory of "an empty form of time, independent of all matter."[48] Accordingly, the whole of Chapter 16 is dedicated to what he calls, "Static Ontological Genesis," and Chapter 17 to "Static Logical Genesis." In *Anti-Oedipus*, he and Guattari frequently describe society as an "immobile motor,"[49] and they even define the concept of "flow," taken from Marx, as continually "broken up," "interrupted," or "cut." "Every 'object'," they say, "presupposes the continuity of a flow; every flow, the fragmentation of the object."[50] In *A Thousand Plateaus* they even write, "It is thus necessary to make a distinction between *speed* and *movement*: a movement may be very fast, but that does not give it speed; a speed may be very slow, or even immobile, yet it is still speed."[51] Hence the nomad's "motionless voyage."[52]

These quotes are not rare aberrations in his texts, nor by citing them am I trying to introduce some clever interpretation. Deleuze explicitly and consistently describes motion in terms of stasis—reminiscent of Whitehead. Speed, time, stasis, and difference are each explicitly given ontological primacy over motion. Therefore, in Deleuze's pluralist ontology of becoming, motion all too often resides unequally alongside the other kinds of flux. This does not mean Deleuze clearly privileges immobility over motion in every case, just that, despite all he says about continuous motion and the "movement" of becoming, he nevertheless consistently includes in it stasis, breaks, and immobilities whose existence is ultimately incompatible with the ontology of motion. On the plane of motion, everything moves continuously. Stasis cannot be introduced without dividing continuous movement. Thus, at the least, Deleuze's theory of motion is extremely uneven and fractured, and at the worst (from the vantage of an ontology of motion), it is explicitly subordinated to stasis, time, immobile speed, vital force, and other such attributes. A similar issue occurs in the secondary literature, especially those following in the same Spinozist tradition.[53]

Matter. The second limitation of Deleuze's ontology of becoming is his *theory of matter*. If motion is the flux of matter, then Deleuze's pluralism must also be able to show at least an ontological coprimacy or immanence of matter to the other fluxes. Again, this is not what he does. In *What Is Philosophy?* Deleuze and Guattari define philosophy not as the movement of matter, but as an "infinite movement of thought" that lays out a philosophical "plane of immanence" and populates that plane with concepts through a "finite movement of thought."[54] These various movements of thought lay out philosophical planes defined not by material beings and things but by an "extraction of events from things and beings," and by giving an ontological description of being as "space, time, matter, thought, and the possible."[55] In short, philosophy has always given a name to being and thus "handed over immanence to Something = x"—and thus mimicked the discovery of something transcendent.[56]

However, according to Deleuze, the ontology of becoming is "THE plane of immanence, [which] is, at the same time, that which must be thought and that which cannot be thought. It is the nonthought within thought. It is the base of all planes, immanent to every thinkable plane that does not succeed in thinking it."[57] THE plane of immanence cannot be thought, since it is the *infinite movement of thought itself* which thinks all the other planes. According to Deleuze and Guattari, this plane was first discovered by Spinoza, "the Christ of philosophers." Substance, for Spinoza, is one, but it has an infinity of parallel and ontologically coprimary attributes, including thought and matter. However, Spinoza is also quite explicit that thought is the only attribute that can think its own plane and all the other planes: "By attribute I understand *what the intellect perceives of a substance,* as constituting its essence [*quod intellectus de substantiâ percipit*]."[58]

Therefore, even though Spinoza's attempt to make thought and matter ontologically equal and thus not reducible to each other is radical, there still remains a fundamental inequality between them if only one of those attributes can reproduce all the others. This is a well-known issue in Spinoza scholarship.[59] In his book on Spinoza, however, Deleuze passes over this fraught issue all too quickly, saying that "[t]he intellect only *reproduces* objectively the nature of the forms it apprehends."[60] Deleuze thus makes clear, against other commentators, that thought does not create matter and the other attributes—it just objectively reproduces them all in a way that they cannot do themselves. Thus, one inequality (subjective idealism) is thrown off only to reveal another (speculative idealism).

From his first book to his last, Deleuze grants a similar ontological primacy to what he calls "the image of thought."[61] Thought, for Deleuze, following Spinoza, is just one plane of becoming among many, but more importantly, it is also the only plane capable of thinking its own plane and THE plane which is "the base of all planes" (matter, space, time, possibility, etc.).[62] Again, this is not an interpretive discovery of a hidden meaning in the text. Deleuze and Guattari are explicit about this: "Spinoza *thought* the 'best' plane of immanence—that is, the purest."[63]

Strangely then, Deleuze and Guattari's description of the "infinite movement of thought" that defines philosophical practice must be understood as a kind of pure motion without matter—an oddly abstract, ideal, and "purely formal motion," as Marx might say.[64] If ontological practice had even the smallest bit of materiality to it, it could not be an infinite and objective survey or reproduction of THE plane of immanence that thinks all the planes as their unthought presupposition.[65] Rather, it would have to be productive, positional, and kinographic.[66]

History. The third limitation of Deleuze's ontology of becoming is his *theory of history*. Deleuze's thesis that being is becoming is an explicitly metaphysical claim, even if it is a paradoxical-sounding one. The claim that THE plane of immanence is the base of all the other planes is not just a regional or historical claim about all previously invented planes but about *all planes*, past, present, and future. Just like Spinoza, thought, for Deleuze, stretches out and surveys infinitely across itself and all the other planes without limit. This is possible because thought is freed of any materiality that would connect it to practices of inscription and thus history. However, ontological practice, or "thought," for Deleuze is not outside of history but immanent with all of history—past, present, and future:

> But if it is true that the plane of immanence is always single, being itself pure variation, then it is all the more necessary to explain why there are varied and distinct planes of immanence that, depending upon which infinite movements are retained and selected, succeed and contest each other in history.[67]

In other words, there is only one pure plane of becoming forever and for all time, which only thought can reproduce, but which is *thought of* differently depending on the historical and geographical circumstances. "History," for Deleuze and Guattari, is thus simply the "set of conditions from which one turns away in order to become, that is to say, in order to create something new."[68] "Philosophy is becoming, not history, it is the coexistence of planes, not the succession of systems."[69]

Deleuze and Guattari are right to reject a simple succession, dialectic development, or deterministic evolution of historical ontologies, but this does not necessarily mean that all ontological descriptions coexist for all time. How could they coexist, for example, before they were historically invented by humans? There was no Platonic description of eternity 400 million years ago. Ontological practices are created in history, not discovered on a speculative plane of becoming. Only after they are created in history can they coexist and mix with other ontological descriptions, as they do today.

In practice, postulating the coexistence of future planes adds nothing to philosophical analysis. Furthermore, why say that thought (becoming) is an escape from matter (history) and not that matter is an escape from thought or from itself? Deleuze and Guattari are right that history is not deterministic. But then why does becoming require thought to become other than history? If there is truly an ontological equality of fluxes, then history and matter are fully capable of becoming other than themselves through their *own flux*: motion. Humans are, after all, matter with the capacity for creating new ontological descriptions and inscriptions. A glimmer of this point is most apparent in *Anti-Oedipus*, their most Marxist book, where Deleuze and Guattari describe the historical and material conditions of inscription. However, in *Anti-Oedipus* these are understood only as the social conditions of *desire*, to be "turned away from" with the thought of becoming—as is later made plain in *What Is Philosophy?* The plane of matter and its movement through history is thus just another plane to be traversed by infinite thought.

Limitations. The historical precursors of the ontology of becoming thus have several limitations: Whitehead's ontology is completely static and ahistorical, while Deleuze's is more nuanced but ultimately limited by its theories of stasis, thought, and becoming. Both philosophers provide robust theories of becoming, but *neither provides an ontology of motion*. Deleuze says that all fluxes are ontologically equal, but motion is continually cut up and mixed with stasis.[70] Unlike the planes of space, force, and time, which do not seem to pose a contradiction when combined, the planes of stasis and motion pose an explicit contradiction at the heart of Deleuze's philosophy. He says that philosophy is a "movement" of thought but then abolishes this same movement by purifying it of all matter with the Spinozist thought of THE pure plane of becoming. He says that thought is not outside history but then claims that all planes past, present, and future coexist and become only by turning away from history. Contemporary vitalist new materialisms have favored this same ahistorical approach.[71]

Thus, despite the ontological nature of their claims, Whitehead's and Deleuze's philosophies fit very much with the Einsteinian paradigm of the twentieth century, which prevailed publicly well after Hubble disproved it: that the universe is absolutely static but internally and spatiotemporally dynamic; that it is immobile but creative and becoming; that it is an ontologically "motionless voyage." Today, new discoveries in cosmology, quantum gravity, and other fields render visible the dated and historical nature of such claims, but they also set up new conditions that force philosophy to create a new historical ontology for the twenty-first century.

In this light, *Being and Motion* should be viewed as a complete inversion of the ontology of becoming. But, like Marx's inversion of Hegel or Lucretius's inversion of Plato, the inversion is also a transformation. *Being and Motion* is not a simple *ontological* inversion that merely positions the continuous becoming of motion and matter as more primary than the becoming of difference, stasis, and thought. Nor does the primacy of motion reject the existence of relative stasis and thought. The ontology of motion turns process philosophy right-side-up with its mobile feet on the ground and renders all becoming fully material. Stasis becomes an eddy or vortex of flows. Thought becomes a coordinated rhythm of self-affective matters: bodies, brains, tools, and all kinds of prosthetics. Ontology becomes historical ontology, grounded in the material and kinetic conditions of its time.

Just as Marx extracted a "rational kernel" of the dialectic from the "mystical shell" of Hegel's speculative philosophy, which resulted in a new historical materialist dialectic, so the ontology of motion extracts from the speculative ontology of becoming the "rational kernel" of flux, resulting in a new historical materialist ontology of motion.[72] The methodological primacy of motion, therefore, is not a strictly ontological claim about being qua being, or even being qua becoming but rather a historical ontological claim about becoming qua history. What we know now is that everything is in motion. Einstein, Whitehead, and Deleuze were wrong in certain ways not because they made ahistorical claims about the nature of becoming (which they also did) but precisely because their claims were *historically limited* in certain ways they could not see beyond and are only now apparent to us. The same will likely be true of *Being and Motion* at some point. That is what makes it a properly *historical and regional ontology*.

All the other great names for being, past, present, and future, do not coexist in a pure becoming, but only those that have been historically invented so far coexist and mix together, and only with respect to the material-kinetic conditions of the present conjuncture. Furthermore, all previous claims to transcendence are not "illusions," as Deleuze says, contrasted with the true plane of becoming, but are all real dimensions of their kinetic present.

Before moving on to the theory of motion that forms the basis of this ontological history, two final methodological issues raised in this chapter must now be dealt with in the next: realism and materialism.

CHAPTER 4
Realism and Materialism

TRANSCENDENTAL REALISM

The main methodological move that needs further elaboration at this point is the most general and overarching of *Being and Motion*: transcendental realism, which is the study of the real minimal ontological conditions for the actual emergence of the historical present. The purpose of this method is to give a description of what previous being must *at least* be like given that it appears as it does today: in motion.[1]

In previous chapters, I described this method as a kind of *minimal realism*. From the vantage point of the regional transcendental structure of our time—motion—historical being must at least have some minimal kinetic attributes such that this motion *is*: flow, fold, and field. If being does not have any kinetic attributes, we risk positing a miraculous ex nihilo origin of motion. Thus, the transcendental is a minimally real ontological structure of historical being—but not the *only* one. There are multiple coexisting real transcendentals; motion has simply emerged today as a relatively dominant and undertheorized one, thereby making possible a new ontological description of the present from this perspective.

In addition to the minimal ontological commitments entailed by the dominance of this new transcendental structure of motion, there are certain historical consequences as well. If the present has truly revealed something minimally real about the nature of historical reality, then it is not just real for us here and now. In other words, *Being and Motion* is not simply a historical or anthropological constructivism. Being is not just in motion now, for us. If it is truly a minimally real aspect of being now, then being must have always been capable of motion and thus in motion (since motion does not come from stasis without positing its ex nihilo creation) for all of history—just circulating under different names and in a subterranean fashion.

The conclusion that ontological practice is not only in motion for us now but has always been in motion is no small claim. This means that the entire history of ontological practice, which has systematically marginalized, repressed, and explained motion by some other more foundational category, has not only failed to properly define what motion is but has more importantly failed to define the very mobility of being and its own immanent ontological practice.

In short, the transcendental conditions of ontological practice itself, as a kinetic practice, have yet to be understood—because they were continually subordinated to other aspects of being in previous ages. This is true of past practices as well as present ones. The historical emergence of dominant ontological descriptors such as space, eternity, force, and time have not gone away; they are mobilized throughout contemporary ontology. For example, Peter Sloterdijk describes his spheres project as *Being and Space*.[2] Since Alain Badiou defines events as "eternal truths,"[3] his book *Being and Event* could just as easily be named *Being and Eternity*. Insofar as Deleuze argues that the question of becoming is always a "question of forces,"[4] his ontology could aptly be called *Being and Force*, and of course Heidegger's *Being and Time* is quite explicit about the ontological primacy of time.[5] Historical descriptions and inscriptions of being are thus still part of present ontological practice.[6] To understand the hybrid nature of ontological practice today, then, we must understand its material and historical conditions *in motion*.

Understanding contemporary ontological practice thus requires a kinetic reinterpretation of the historical transcendental structures of the past that persist in the present. Through this effort, *Being and Motion* aims to show that the previously dominant names for being have had a hidden *kinetic* dimension and structure.[7] If ontological practice requires descriptive and inscriptive graphism, then it necessarily requires motion. If it requires motion, then there must be a particular distribution of motion for each practice. This might not be an intuitive claim, but Book II of this volume attempts to prove it at length. The method of transcendental realism, therefore, is what makes possible and orients these aims.

But here is where a methodological note is required to tie the two books together. The transcendental structure of the present appears to us as nothing other than the mixture of historical-kinetic transcendentals of the past. This is the case precisely because the transcendental structure of the present always appears *as an ontological structure* from the vantage point of the present. This is the meaning of historical ontology. From the vantage point or region of being of the present, one can explain all the various transcendental structures of the past, but one's own structure simply appears as the apparent universal structure within which all the others are ordered—that is, until the future.

However, the only way to get through the present to the future is through the practice of ontology *in the present*.[8] In order for there to be a transcendental structure for the future to look back on, one must have been created previously. Therefore, only in trying to understand the ontology of the present will it be possible to move beyond the region of our present and toward any future ontology—which will then be capable of describing the transcendental structure of what is now the present.

The present and the past, therefore, are like two sides of the same transcendental Möbius strip: One side of the strip is *transcendentally historical*, insofar as it is ordered by several previous fields of circulation, while the other side is *transcendentally real*, insofar as all the previous fields of circulation become dimensions or aspects of the ontological framework of the present—in this case motion. In other words, when transcendental realism is applied to the present, we tend to call it ontology, but when it is applied to the past, we tend to call it history. Transcendental realism thus earns the contradictory-sounding titles of "historical ontology," "ontological history," or "history of the present." The important point here is that both dimensions are part of the same methodology.

The alternative to transcendental realism is either metaphysics or constructivism. On the one hand, metaphysics aims to reduce all of being to a single ahistorical and nontranscendental description qua being. In this case, being will never move or change such that its fundamental conditions will need redescription. On the other hand, constructivism aims to reduce all of being to anthropocentric transcendental structures such as language, mind, society, the unconscious, and so on. In this case, these transcendental descriptions are either said to have nothing to do with any *real* aspect of being (antirealism) or all of being is said to be reducible to them (reductionism). No real movement of being has any bearing on the status of these anthropic structures. In the first case (metaphysics), there are no transcendental structures; in the second case, there are only anthropic transcendental structures of the Kantian, phenomenological, structuralist, or post-structuralist variety. In both cases, however, being is static, either as unchanging essence or inaccessible outside of such anthropic structures.

For a kinetic transcendental realism, however, there are a multiplicity of mutating transcendentals (both anthropic and nonanthropic), each describing *a real dimension or aspect of being*. The method of transcendental realism thus makes possible, among other things, a pluralistic theory of ontological practice based on the analysis of the historical transcendentals that compose it. This analysis is developed in Book II. The movement of ontology is the movement of kinographism that describes and inscribes being.

The Transcendental

Transcendental realism puts forward a new definition of the transcendental, roughly identical to the concept of the kinetic "field" developed in Part II. Since the entirety of Book II traces a historical typology of kinographic fields at length, it is worth noting here how this method differs from the original Kantian theory of the transcendental developed in *The Critique of Pure Reason* (1781). There, Kant succeeds in overcoming the problems of both metaphysics and empiricism by introducing a theory of the transcendental. On the one hand, "[m]etaphysics is a speculative cognition by reason that is wholly isolated and rises entirely above being instructed by experience."[9] In other words, the knowledge of what the world is like *in itself* cannot have any foundation in our experience, and thus no application and no verification. On the other hand, empiricism assumes that "all our cognition must conform to objects. On that presupposition however, all our attempts to establish something about them a priori, by means of concepts through which our cognition would be expanded, have come to nothing."[10] In other words, the empirical sciences bombard us with specific information but tell us absolutely nothing about more general (a priori) conditions of knowledge under which that information appears to us as such. Thus, Kant's solution to this problem is to invert it, just as Copernicus did in astronomy. Let us assume instead, Kant says, "that objects must conform to our cognition" in the same way that "the spectator revolve[s] and the stars remain at rest" for Copernicus.[11] In other words, Kant proposes to instead identify the rules "that I must presuppose within me even before objects are given to me, and hence must presuppose a priori; and that rule is expressed in a priori concepts. Hence all objects of experience must necessarily conform to these concepts and agree with them."[12] Kant names this philosophical inquiry into the conditions of possible experience "transcendental idealism" or "critique."

Kant should be credited for his critiques of metaphysics and empiricism, but he was wrong to arbitrarily limit the transcendental to consciousness alone and cut it off from access to the reality of being, matter, and movement. By way of contrast, transcendental realism puts forward the following six theses on the status of the transcendental.

One. The transcendental is *not a condition of possibility*. There is no such thing as a condition of something that is merely possible if there are not already actual things that define the immanent relations of the field to begin with. Transcendental relations are therefore extrinsic and not intrinsic. Before there are folds distributed according to their degrees of flux in a field, there is *no preexisting field* to order them. A field without folds or things is just an unordered flow. Conditions of possible motion presuppose an independence or transcendence of the conditions beyond the folds or things that are conditioned. In short, possible conditions are an idealist abstraction.

Two. The transcendental is *not an empirical condition*, either. The conditions of empirical things cannot be other empirical things. If they were, there would be no transcendental difference between the conditions and conditioned. Everything would simply be empirical all the way down, without any relations or field of circulation to order them. Logically, moreover, if the conditions for the empirical were also empirical, then we would have failed to explain the *conditions of the empirical*. We would have tautologically presupposed precisely what we set out to explain: the empirical itself.

Three. The transcendental is *not a universal condition*. If the transcendental field is kinetic and actual, then it is necessarily historical, and if it is historical, then it cannot be universal, since all of history has not happened yet. The future is yet to come. Moreover, if there have already been transcendental fields in the past, and the present is not among them, then it is possible for new ones to emerge in the future following new fields of the present.

Four. The transcendental is *not an idealist or subjective condition*. For Kant, there is only one kind of transcendental: consciousness. However, such an anthropocentric proposition fails to explain the historical and material *conditions of the emergence of that transcendental structure itself*. There was a time, Kant must admit, when there were no humans and thus no transcendental structure, and later on there was. Kant offers no account of the properly historical and material modulation that must have occurred in order to produce the transcendental structure of consciousness. Kant thus falls into an ahistorical and ex nihilo creation myth of the anthropocentric transcendental ego by failing to properly historicize its material and nonhuman emergence. Structuralism and post-structuralism fall into the same trap when they fail to account for the material and historical conditions of the production of new transcendental fields.

Five. The transcendental is *a real condition*. If there is no ontological division between being in itself and being for itself, then each transcendental is a real slice, dimension, or local region of being itself. Since there are a multiplicity of transcendentals, there can be no single or total transcendental of all the others that could wrap them all up. Transcendentals are not separate or individual structures, nor parts in a whole, but are mutable and entangled dimensions of the same kinetic process of materialization.

Six. The transcendental is *kinetic.* As Kant says, a transcendental condition describes the "rules" or ordering relations between empirical things. Relations or order are therefore not things. However, a relation, contra Kant, is not a merely ideal or mental faculty, "the unity of apperception"; relations are strictly kinetic relations because movement is neither ideal nor empirical. It is not a thing; it is the *kinetic process* by which things themselves are distributed. Thus, the movement of things is immanent to the things themselves but not reducible to them or to our perception of them.

A transcendental is thus not strictly human or even biological. Nor is it simply mutable or even merely lacking absolutely fixed boundaries. It is, like a kinetic field (see chapters 11 and 12), a local region of order that is globally entangled with other ordered and ordering regions, not as separate individuals but as a single continuously changing manifold surface. Kinetic transcendentals, therefore, do not exist a priori but are emergent material structures, patterns of circulation, immanent to the kinetic processes that produce them.

PROCESS MATERIALISM

The next methodological move that needs further elaboration is *Being and Motion*'s materialism. Transcendental realism describes the structure and process of motion—but *what,* one may ask, is in motion? Matter is the historical name of what is in motion, but what matter *is* is *in process* and thus must remain ontologically indeterminate for transcendental realism, because motion is by definition a kinetic process of materialization.

In other words, the ontological primacy of motion entails that the being of matter must also be a kinetic *process*, and thus not reducible to strict empirical or metaphysical substance. The terms "motion" and "matter" used throughout this book should thus always be read as "matter-in-motion." Matter is not the passive object of ontological representation, but something mutually produced and producing or enacted through motion—including, and not limited to, the motion of ontological practice itself.

Again, the mysteries of theory find their rational solution in the process materialism of practice itself.[13]

Empiricism

Process materialism is, first of all, in contrast to the empiricist definition of matter as some discrete, deterministic, or probabilistic substance. It is precisely *because* being is in motion that the substantial being of matter—as atoms, particles, fields, and so on—must remain a historically open and interactive process. Physics, for example, routinely assembles new matters and even actively changes how matter is treated, as with the introduction of Einstein's theorem of matter energy conversion, or $E = mc^2$. Energy and momentum currently define all "matter" for contemporary physics. The ontology of motion, however, is not conceptually limited to this specific determination, because matter could be distributed differently, even if historically we do not yet know what that will look like.[14] The point is that matter may be distributed in many ways and given many names, but that in every case the distributions and descriptions are all *real* and immanent aspects of its materialization, not merely names or ideas *about* matter. Matter is really shaped in the *process* of knowing or describing it.

Being and Motion thus makes no metaphysical claims about the nature of matter as a continuous or discrete *substance*. This is because matter is not a substance at all but rather an indeterminate kinetic process. Matter, along with space and time, occurs in and through constant movement. There is not a static thing, stuff, or substance, we can ontologically designate as "matter" any longer. As the Italian physicist Carlo Rovelli writes, "The impossibility of anything being entirely and continuously still in a place is at the heart of quantum mechanics."[15]

This is quite different from other contemporary theories defined by an ironic or post-structuralist "failed materialism" in which matter is only that which appears in our failed attempts to describe or construct it anthropically.[16] Process materialism is an attempt to move beyond a post-structuralism that remains yoked to the analysis of human structures and ontologically cut off from the real.[17] Process materialism is also quite different than a "negative materialism" or "materialism without matter" in which the reality of matter is what infinitely withdraws from our descriptions of it.[18] Against these two kinds of contemporary materialisms, *Being and Motion* adopts a realist historical materialism in which our descriptions are not failed or negative representations but real practical and performative constructions of matter in process.[19] Right now, we know historically and performatively that matter is *at least* quantum fields in continuous motion.[20] This is the historical name given to the continuous process of materialization. Matter, like a fluctuating and folded topological surface, is never lacking or withdrawn but is simply redistributed in different regions where the kinetic process of folding and unfolding occur.

The ontology of motion is therefore not incompatible with contemporary physical theories, but neither is it reducible to them or any theory of fundamental particles or substances. Process materialism is not a classical, "mechanistic" or "substance-based" materialism. Matter is an indeterminate and relational process. Process materialism is not just a revitalization of seventeenth-century mechanistic theories of bodies-in-motion, or what Marx rightly calls "crude materialism."[21] Bodies are processes. There is no discrete, static atomic body which is itself not internally in flux and motion. Process materialism is thus different from classical, mechanistic, or crude materialism in at least three ways:

1. Matter, like quantum fields, is not reducible to static, discrete, or passive stuff that gets moved around like billiard balls, following universal natural or divine laws. Matter is creative, unstable, and in constant motion all the way down without fundamental substance.
2. Matter, unlike classical materialism, is not completely observable, measurable, or predictable.[22] Matter therefore is not strictly empirical or "actual" in the classical sense.
3. Matter, is also not causal or deterministic but rather pedetic and stochastic. It moves in unpredictable but emergent patterns of constant conjunction.

All these features of matter are *historical features* consistent with but *not reducible to* the descriptions of contemporary quantum science. They clearly distinguish process materialism from classical or mechanistic materialisms.[23]

Metaphysics

Second, matter is not simply a concept or logical category of all material things, as it was for Aristotle. Matter is not an idealist and immaterial abstraction that exists independently from or that transcends various historical processes of materialization, including ontological practices. This conceptual or idealist version of materialism is what Marx calls "contemplative materialism."²⁴ "The chief defect of all hitherto existing materialism (that of Feuerbach included) is that the thing, reality, sensuousness, is conceived only in the form of the *object or of contemplation.*"²⁵

Matter is the name for what reality is *and* for that portion of reality enacted in what we are doing, thinking, and performing through description, and nothing more until that something more emerges historically through motion. Our ontological descriptions are not separate from matter but are themselves material enactments. Matter, like motion, is historical. All so-called universal descriptions (ideas) of matter are themselves material and historical kinetic processes. Although every description introduces its own kind of exclusions, the exclusions are creative and not lacking. They recirculate, redistribute, and bifurcate without logical negation.

Thus, there cannot be a single and absolute idea or definition of matter, just as there is no single and final empirical description of matter for the same reason: Matter is an open *process of motion*. Matter performs its own description through practice, including, but not limited to, the human sensuous practice of ontological description. The material techniques of inscription themselves participate in the performance as well. Human practice is just one aspect or mediation among other mutually mediating processes.

Process materialism is also distinct from a "vital materialism" in which the motion and activity of matter is explained by recourse to something else: either external forces (as with Newton) or internal immanent forces (as with Spinoza, Deleuze, and other neo-vitalist new materialists).²⁶ The ontological recourse to vital forces to explain matter's generativity and motion is an old move in the history of metaphysics and merely another way to rob matter of its own autonomous movement.²⁷ Vital materialism treats matter-in-motion as synonymous with mechanistic materialism and therefore sees the injection of force as the only pathway to a "new" kind of materialism. In fact, as we will see in detail in Part III of Book II, the idea of "vital forces" (both external and immanent) is not new at all.

The description of a so-called immanent "life" or "vitality" of inorganic matters is also symptomatic of a more general biopolitical and ideological bias in contemporary politics.²⁸ Instead of starting with the primacy of matter, vital materialism starts with the primacy of biological life (another historical move common in the nineteenth century, with the invention of the biological sciences) and retroactively attributes such living vitality to inorganic matter—when the historical ontological situation is precisely the opposite.²⁹ Organic matter emerges from inorganic matter, not the other way around. The vital materialist attempt to theorize a post-humanist new materialism succeeds only by introducing a new biocentrism and by resubordinating matter and motion to something else.[30]

Therefore, the empirico-scientific determinations of matter and the metaphysico-conceptual determinations of matter are both fundamentally limited and limiting because they both attempt to foreclose, fix, or render static the kinetic flux of matter. They attempt to explain matter by something else. Matter, however, *is* the real kinetic *process* of materialization itself—and nothing else. Thus, if matter is not fixed or static, then it can receive neither a fixed empirical/constructivist nor a fixed metaphysical/conceptual definition. The best way to describe what it is is by what it does, or how it moves.

Historical Materialism

The ontology of motion therefore adopts the name of "matter" not in an empirical or metaphysical way but in a strictly *historical* way, from the perspective or *kairos* of our present, in which motion in the West has been ontologically connected to the motion *of matter*.

From Aristotle to Hegel, motion has always been the motion *of matter*.[31] Together, the two have suffered the same fate in Western ontology: They have been subordinated to some other ontological category. In the ancient world, matter and motion were subordinated to eternal forms and unmoved movers. In the medieval world, they were subordinated to the vital forces or via inertia that directed their motions and formed their matters. In the modern world, they have been subordinated to mechanism, rationalism, and natural laws. Book II traces the Western history of this twin subordination.

However, just as the historical subordination of one almost always entailed the subordination of the other, so the historical liberation of one also entails the liberation of the other. If motion is ontologically primary, creative, and pedetic, then so is the matter that moves. In *Being and Motion* matter is thus de-substantialized through motion, and motion is immanently incarnated through materialization. If matter is liberated, then so is the motion by which it is moved. Without matter the concept of movement remains a "formal" or idealist category.[32] Without pedetic movement, however, matter remains static, discontinuous, law-bound, substantial, and merely passive.

Being and Motion therefore puts forward both a new kinetic materialism and a material kinetics, neither "crude," "contemplative," "failed," "negative," nor "vital." If historical being is in motion and all of motion is pedetic, and matter is what is in motion, then matter can no longer be defined by mechanism or metaphysics; neither substance nor subject. Process materialism is therefore neither a Copernican revolution in which it is we who move around the fixed stars nor a Ptolemaic counterrevolution in which we are at rest while the stars move around us but a Hubblean revolution where *everything is in motion*.

The big metaphysical names of being, according to this revolution, now appear to us as real descriptions of certain tendencies or aspects of matter in motion and have no representational being independent from the kinetic processes they describe. Matter is really constructed and shaped in part by ontological acts of description. The history of metaphysics is thus a history of conceptual fetishes—products masquerading as productive powers (atoms, ideas, structures, life, and so on). Transcendental realism, therefore, describes the material processes that function as the historical conditions of these names.

With these methodological definitions in place, we can now move on to develop our theory of motion in Part II.

PART II
The Theory of Motion

I
Flow

CHAPTER 5
Continuum

Being flows. This is the first and central thesis from which the entire theory of motion follows. Part II of Book I is dedicated to a theory of motion and in particular to the three core concepts that define it: flow, fold, and field. These concepts were not chosen arbitrarily. The argument of Part II is that they are the most minimal and internally consistent features of being such that it is capable of being in motion.[1]

If the movement of being seems to be so central for us today, it is from this precise historical vantage point that we now pose the question of its minimal conditions. What must the basic features of being be such that this motion is actually happening? The thesis of Part II is that being must flow, it must fold, and it must circulate through fields. Although I have presented these concepts here as logically building on one another for the sake of analytical clarity, ontologically speaking, the three are coprimary and inseparable from one another. There is never really one without the other. The following chapters of Part II thus aim to show that in order for there to be motion, being must flow, fold, and circulate. If it does not, then being does not move. Flows, folds, and fields are the *historically* necessary conditions for movement.

The chapters in Part II are also the most abstract chapters of *Being and Motion*, not because they are a priori concepts but because they have been selected from the historical conditions described in Book II and isolated in order to show the hidden presuppositions at work in the history and practice of ontological description. Furthermore, in the service of making these concepts more concrete and of showing their dynamic range of applicability, Part II also provides a series of different examples from the domains of politics, art, and science, as well as some diagrams to illustrate them. These examples are not meant to stand in for the more robust treatment these topics received in the companion volumes to *Being and Motion*. They are presented simply to help clarify the concepts more concretely and provide the reader with a glimpse into the wider range of conceptual analyses that can be done with them—as well as the wider non-ontological conditions of ontological practice itself.[2]

Without further ado, we begin our theory of motion with the first and most basic condition for being in motion: flow. Flows have three main features: continuity, multiplicity, and confluence. This chapter and the next two describe each of these features in turn.

CONTINUOUS MOVEMENT

A flow is a continuous movement. Being flows *if and only if* the twin conditions of *continuity* and *motion* are satisfied. If being were *only continuous* (i.e. a continuous substance) it would be a homogeneous totality. Being would be One—a finite or infinite unity—without the possibility of change or motion outside of itself, since there would be no outside to it. In this case, all movement, as Zeno and Parmenides once argued, would be an illusion. Furthermore, if being was One total being that contained all of being, the being that contained all of being would have to be different from the being that was contained by it. Being would thus be separate from itself, or nontotal. We thus reach the paradox of the One that Gödel and others discovered long ago: that the One cannot be included in that which it contains.[3] Ontological continuum without motion thus results in a paradoxical conception of totality that cannot include itself in its own totality. In cosmology, the fantasy of a static and total universe initially held by Einstein was destroyed by Hubble's kinetic discovery of the expanding universe in 1925.

However, if being were *only movement* without continuity, there could paradoxically be no motion at all. Strictly speaking, a discontinuous movement is not a movement. For example, without the continuous movement of translation between point A and point B the movement cannot be said to be the *same* movement. Without continuity, point A and point B would remain completely different points divided by an infinity of intermediate points, themselves divided by an infinity of intermediate points, and so on ad infinitum. We can say there is a "change" that occurs, since an entity is now at point A, now at point B—it "changes" from point A to B. However, if there is no continuity between A and B, then these points are not different aspects of the same movement, but radically different points without any movement between them at all. Movement without continuity is thus not movement at all but merely discontinuous, formal, occasionalism, or logical *change:* strobe being.[4]

According to the Greek philosopher Zeno, the problem with "discontinuous movement" is that if space is infinitely discontinuous or divisible, we would have to traverse an infinite distance of intervals in order to arrive anywhere else. Movement would therefore be impossible. The same result occurs, according to Zeno, when we understand movement as a series of temporal now-points or instants. If every unit of time is infinitely divisible, it will take an infinity of time to move from one point to any other. In both cases the problem remains the same: movement cannot be divided without destroying it. By thinking that we can divide movement into fixed, immobile stages, we spatialize, temporize, and thus immobilize it. "Discontinuous movement" is simply the *difference* between divisible points of space-time and has nothing to do with movement at all.

Alternatively, if movement were only the movement of discrete units through space (atomism) then the units themselves would be internally static, as would be the background space-time through which they moved. Again, there would be no real fundamental movement. Therefore, if we want to say that being actually moves, then such movement cannot emerge from mere discontinuous change but must emerge from the twin conditions of continuity and motion: flow.

CONTINUITY AND DISCONTINUITY

Real motion cannot be derived from stasis, and continuity cannot be derived from discontinuity, but the reverse is not true. Relative stasis and discontinuity can be derived from movement and continuity.[5] If being is fundamentally flow (continuous movement), then discreteness would simply be a relative or regional stability of that flow. For example, point A and point B would not be fundamentally separate from each other, divided by an infinite series of midway points, but would rather be regional stabilizations, folds, or cycles *of* the continuous line AB itself. In the same way that point A and point B presuppose the continuity of the line AB on which they are points, discrete and static being presupposes the flow of being of which it is a regional fold, like the foam of an ocean wave.[6]

Here is the crux of the ontological problem of movement: Either we begin with it, or we never get it. This is a fundamental question for ontology. Either we begin with discrete and static being and have to say that real motion is an illusion, or we begin with flow and are able to explain stasis as relative or folded forms of movement. All the discrete objects in the world will never give birth to a single motion. They are nothing more than the "dead and artificial reorganization of movement by the mind," as Bergson writes.[7] Their bodies fill a graveyard by the sea. As Valéry writes,

> Zeno, Zeno, cruel philosopher Zeno,
> Have you then pierced me with your feathered arrow
> That hums and flies, yet does not fly! The sounding
> Shaft gives me life, the arrow kills. Oh, sun! —
> Oh, what a tortoise shadow to outrun
> My soul, Achilles' giant stride left standing!
>
> No, no! Arise! The future years unfold.
> Shatter, O body, meditation's mould!
> And, O my breast, drink in the wind's reviving!
> A freshness, exhalation of the sea,
> Restores my soul . . . Salt-breathing potency!
> Let's run at the waves and be hurled back to living![8]

Only the flows of moving being can save us from Zeno's graveyard of dead objects by the sea.

INTENSIVE AND EXTENSIVE MOVEMENT

Movement and stasis, continuity and discreteness are not opposed. Each is one way of describing the same process or flow. It is thus more appropriate to distinguish between two dimensions or axes of the same movement: extensive and intensive. Along the first axis, extensive movement is made up of units of space-time *pace* Zeno. It is quantitative, measurable. Extensive movement is movement as change of place, locomotion, or translation. It moves from one discrete point to another by changing places. It is nothing other than the difference or change between points.

Along the second axis, movement is intensive and qualitative. It is a change in the whole, a transformation. In the example of the line AB, it is "already motion that has drawn the line"[9] to which A and B have been added afterward as its endpoints. A and B presuppose the continuous motion of the line on which they are points. The division into A and B is always a division or freeze frame *of a kinetic process*, an attempt to impose arbitrary divisions into a continuous movement. Intensive movement is already primary, but we imagine it is not in order to explain it later as derived from something else. According to Bergson, however, "It is movement which is anterior to immobility."[10] Thus, extensive movement is simply a regional or relative movement within a larger intensive movement. When an extensive movement occurs from A to B, the whole line AB undergoes a qualitative or intensive transformation, like a wave.[11] An extensive point is nothing other than a stabilization or fold in an intensive flow.

For example, the difference between extensive and intensive motion can be seen, among other places,[12] in the theory of quantum complementarity—that all matter can be described in terms of both extensive particles and intensive fields. Visible discrete particles appear to move from point A to point B under an electron microscope. However, these discrete particles are also nothing other than the continuous vibrations of quantum fields. What appears to be an isolated self-identical particle moving from A to B in "empty space" is actually the modulation of the same quantum field in a series of successively observed patterns transforming itself continuously at one point and then another. The extensive motion of a particle is thus only one limited aspect of the intensive wave motion that transports it.

At the level of visible particles, there appears to be "space" between A and B, and even spaces within the particle itself between its components, but as we look closer and closer the space is increasingly filled with a continuously vibrating quantum field.[13] Particles and waves are therefore two aspects of the same continuous flow of matter. This is why quantum entanglement—the simultaneous change in electron spins at a distance—only appears to be "spooky" in the world of extensive particle physics. Intensively speaking, we are simply looking at two different dimensions or local regions of the same globally entangled field.[14] There is no action at a distance because there is no distance between discrete particles and no external action in the first place. There is simply a simultaneous and intensive change of the whole field.

All movement is therefore both extensive and intensive at the same time. The two occur as dimensions of the same continuous process that produces both the qualities and quantities of things. Particles are aspects or dimensions of moving fields, but fields are not the product of static particles.[15] However, since particles are not ontologically static, their extensive or quantitative translation is also part of a simultaneous and intensive transformation of the whole flow of which it is a regional point. The two are always present together, like the latitude and longitude of a kinetic cartography.

PEDESIS

So far we have said that being flows in continuous motion and that flows have an extensive and intensive aspect or dimension. However, for these flows to be capable of intersection and composite creation, they must also be capable of *curvature*. This is only possible through pedesis. Pedesis (from the proto-Indo-European root **ped-*, meaning "foot") is the motion of semi-autonomous self-transport: the motion of the foot to walk, to run, to leap, to dance unpredictably. Nature has no straight lines because it moves.

The concept of pedesis is derived from two of the most important kinetic discoveries of twentieth-century physics: Einstein's kinetic theory of matter (1915) and Heisenberg's quantum uncertainty principle (1927). In the first, Einstein argued that all matter is a product of the stochastic or pedetic motion of innumerable smaller materials—molecules, atoms, and so on. For example, the atoms of gases move faster and farther, those of fluids less so, and those of solids even less. All matter, Einstein showed, was not only in motion but in pedetic or Brownian motion. Each movement is continuous with its previous position, but where it will go after that is indeterminate. The macroscopic conclusion is that the form of matter is fundamentally kinetic or kinomorphic but also fundamentally and irreducibly pedetic.

However, by showing that all matter was in turbulent or pedetic motion, Einstein introduced a fundamental kinetic uncertainty and unpredictability into the heart of being, initially suggested by Ludwig Boltzmann. Since this discovery, science has been completely unable to produce a successful deterministic theory of turbulent motion beyond minimally probabilistic models. The description of kinetic turbulence goes all the way back to the Roman poet Lucretius, and its precise kinetic structure remains one of the last, and greatest, unsolved problems of classical physics.[16] The unsolved problem of classical turbulence, combined with Einstein's kinetic theory of matter, has an enormous ontological consequence: that all matter is in motion and that all motion is fundamentally nondeterministic. This, and the related theory of entropy, has given rise to an entire field of chaos theory and nonlinear dynamics.[17] Heisenberg was said to have once remarked that he wanted to ask God two questions: "Why is general relativity so weird?" and "How do you explain turbulence?" He then said that he was certain God would know the answer to the first question.[18]

In the second kinetic theory, Heisenberg showed that there is a fundamental limit to the precision with which the position and momentum of a particle can be known at the same time. The more precise the position of a quantum field, the more it looks like a stable particle, and the less we know about its momentum. The less precise the position of a field, the more it looks like a wave, and the more we know about its momentum through its diffraction pattern or waveform. In other words, Heisenberg teaches us that motion cannot be reduced to position without destroying its motion, and the trajectory of a position cannot be predicted without the fundamental uncertainty of motion.

This fundamental uncertainty about the motion of matter is not just an epistemological effect of observation.[19] It has been experimentally shown that this unpredictable or pedetic effect is inherent in the motion of the matter waves of all quantum objects.[20] The uncertainty principle and indeterminacy are fundamental properties of all quantum systems. Indeterminacy, however, is not random or even probabilistic, because position only occurs in continuous relation to momentum. Heisenberg thus showed that even at the quantum level, matter in motion is both relational and uncertain, or pedetic.

Pedesis may be irregular and unpredictable, but it is *not random*. What is interesting about movement is not simply that it is pedetic, but that it is through pedesis and turbulence that metastable formations and emergent orders are possible. By contrast, the ontology of randomness is quite bleak. In a purely random ontology, all of matter would be moving randomly, and thus nonrelationally, at all times. Since random fluctuations from disorder to order are physically rare, the likelihood that anything like the sun or even our galaxy would just suddenly pop into existence would be unimaginably rare, and would likely fall apart immediately due to further random motion. It would even be statistically possible for a human brain to pop into existence just long enough to think a thought and then disperse.[21] The very idea of a purely random motion presupposes that it was not affected by or related to anything else previously, which presupposes that it was the first thing and before it was nothing, which is a version of the internally contradictory hypothesis of ex nihilo creation: something from nothing. The ontology of random motion claims that from pure disorder of discrete nonrelational particles comes high-level composite order. Given the high level of order and complexity in our present age, randomness is demonstrably not the case.

Pedetic motion, on the other hand, is not random at all, but instead emerges from and is influenced by other motions, just not in a completely determined way. Unlike randomness, pedetic motion is not unpredictable because it is *not influenced* by any other motions; rather, motion is pedetic *precisely because* it occurs in relation to other motions. It is the interrelation and mutual influence of matter with itself that gives it its unpredictable character. Over a long period of time, the pedetic motion of matter combines and stabilizes into certain patterns, synchronies, and relations, giving the appearance of stability and solidity, only to become turbulent again and enter into new conjoined relations.

A correlate of this attribute is that if being is currently in motion, it must have always been in motion. If not, there would have been a time when there was no motion, so that motion emerged out of something immobile, which is an ex nihilo contradiction. If being was always in motion and all motion is fundamentally pedetic, then it also follows that the motion of being has always been pedetic.

Unlike randomness, pedesis is not defined strictly by disorder. Turbulence is a disordered motion, but it is a disordered motion that is capable of producing order because it responds to itself and others. Nonrandom disordered motion—alternately called pedesis, Brownian, or stochastic motion—is capable of producing emergent metastable states precisely because it is responsive to and continuous with what came immediately before it, but *not determined* by it or its longer history. In other words, pedesis is neither random, determinate, nor probabilistic but strictly indeterminate and relational.

This relational indeterminacy produces ordered metastable patterns, much like the pedetic air currents in a room produce invisible spiral patterns on which visible motes of dust float in the sunshine, as Lucretius described so beautifully.[22] The emergence of spacetime itself from patterns of "quantum foam," the turbulent and spiraled and ring patterns of cigarette smoke, and the spiraled storm systems that emerge from the turbulence of global air currents, are all metastable states originating in pedesis.[23] Endless examples of this "order from pedesis" can be cited.[24]

WAVES

If flows are completely continuous and undivided but also pedetic, their motions are also interconnected motions of a whole, or *waves*. Flows are continuous but only insofar as they are themselves already simplexes whose topological distribution and micro-curvature is capable of stretching, bending, and modulating itself infinitely without breaking. A flow is thus composed of different curvatures and topological regions, or waves.

Waves are simplex, or one-folds. They bend, curve, and undulate, but they do not yet loop over themselves in a duplex. Because all motion is pedetic, flows are not straight or static lines, but bent, curved, or wavy. What appears to be a straight line at one level is made of innumerable undulations and curves at lower levels, like a fractal coastline or Mandelbrot set. From a continuous sequence of curved or bent lines (waves), a one-dimensional simplex is capable of producing an n-dimensional manifold.

For example, in mathematical topology, a simplex is a purely continuous, one-dimensional, single-sided flow that is capable, by bending and morphing, of producing multiple higher dimensional simplexes, or what topologists call "simplicial complexes" (see Figure 5.1). In other words, all higher dimensionality is *simply* the product of the folding and morphing of a single n-dimensional simplex, as in string theory. On the other hand, a 0-simplex or nonsimplex is a point, meaning an unfolded and unfoldable discrete particle. A 1-simplex is a line segment; a 2-simplex is a triangle; a 3-simplex is a tetrahedron, and so on into higher-dimensional topological figures.

The difference between the mathematical definition and the kinetic definition of the simplex proposed here, however, is that there is no such thing as a "line segment" in the theory of motion. It is a mathematical abstraction. The "line segment" problematically presupposes that it is dealing with discontinuous, discrete quantities, when in fact no such things can exist independently of flows. All the images in Figure 5.1 should therefore be corrected by extending all of their lines to infinity. Furthermore, each line would also be composed of an infinity of curves and waves, each giving an infinite dimensionality to each n-dimension.

In other words, the simplex is also a flow. Nothing is kinetically discrete or static; all of nature flows. The simplex flow or wave is simply the most basic topological dimension from which all higher dimensions are composed. Each simplex flow or wave also has its own kinotopological regions: in some places the flow is more curved, in others less, and some waves are closer to other waves by virtue of their morphology (what topologists call "neighborhoods").[25] These topological morphisms in the simplex are the waves, bends, and curves capable of producing the vertices of n-dimensional waveforms.

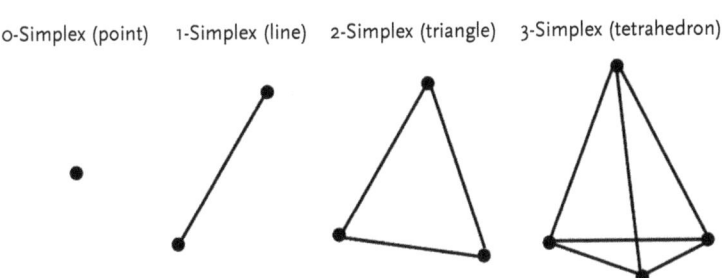

Figure 5.1 Simplicial Complexes

However, these waves are not parts of a whole, since parts need to be discrete from one another with respect to the whole. Waves will never have the power to separate themselves from the flow in this way. They are nothing other, beyond, or above the flow itself. The waves are the kinotopological modulations or morphisms in the flow, and thus constitute the primary features of the flow itself.

Just as waves of water are not separate from the ocean, so the curvatures are not separate from the flows. We can describe the different dimensions of a wave (crest and trough) without introducing a discontinuity in the movement of the ocean. The crest cannot be separated from the trough without destroying the whole wave. Wave transport is thus intensive, since it moves by the transformation of the whole. The topological modulation of the waves is the internal self-differentiation of the flow with itself. A flow is thus different from itself not by discontinuity, but by curvature. The waves of a flow are not parts that were brought together at some point to create a whole flow, but the topokinetic modulation of the flow itself that gives it its dimensionality and self-relation—and nothing else.

The continuity of flows, however, are not only continuous simplexes, but also continuous multiplicities. This is what we will see in the next chapter.

CHAPTER 6

Multiplicity

Being flows, but is there one flow or many? If there is only one flow, then being would be a totality—a pure substantial continuum, without movement—which is impossible. If there are many flows, then each would be ontologically discrete, which destroys movement by introducing a static difference between moving flows. There is a third way, however: flows are neither one nor many, but multiple. This is precisely why it is difficult to measure "a" flow. Every flow both composes and is composed by at least one other flow, ad infinitum. As a nested kinetic continuum of entangled and folded flows, there is never only one flow or any simple totality of flows but a rather continuous process, an open multiplicity of flows. As such, a flow is by definition a nonunity and nontotality.

INFINITY

As continuous movements, flows are by definition infinite; that is, they have no discrete beginning point and no discrete endpoint, since these points would render their continuity discontinuous, at a point. Since nothing comes from nothing, being has no kinetic first or final cause. Flows are therefore neither created nor destroyed, only rearranged. If flows are infinite in motion, and being is composed of flows, then the movement of being must be infinite. If being had an end after which it was destroyed, we would have already reached it. If there was nothing before it began, it could not begin from nothing. Therefore, being has no beginning and no end—just like its flows.

Contemporary cosmologists call this lack of beginning and end the "Big Bounce" theory. According to everything we currently know about the universe, it will ultimately unfold itself faster and faster in all directions until every atom is unraveled back into the constitutive vibrating quantum fields that composed it all in the first place, often referred to as "vacuum energy" or the "cosmological constant."

> Astronomers estimate that the last dim star will wink out around 1 quadrillion (10^{15}) years from now. By then the other galaxies will have moved far away, and our local group of galaxies will be populated by planets, dead stars, and black holes. One by one, those planets and stars will fall into the black holes, which in turn will join into one supermassive black hole. Ultimately, as Stephen Hawking taught us, even those black holes will evaporate. After about 1 googol (10^{100}) years, all of the black holes in our observable universe will have evaporated into a thin mist of particles, which will grow more and more dilute as space continues to expand. The end result of this, our most likely scenario for the future of our universe, is nothing but cold, empty space, which will last literally forever.[1]

However, cosmologists also estimate that after roughly $10^{10^{10^{56}}}$ years, another universe could be created by pedetic quantum fluctuations or quantum tunneling.[2] According to the Poincaré recurrence theorem, thermal fluctuations, and the fluctuation theorem,[3] over an infinite amount of time there would be a spontaneous entropy decrease. At the point of universal heat death it would only take a little bit of gravity to gather all the quantum flows back together in a spontaneous inflation.

Big bounce cosmologists argue that our universe was not the first but rather the effect of a previous contracting universe that had condensed to a very small but not singular region and then exploded back outward. This process may have been repeated infinitely. Nature has neither a beginning singularity where there was no movement nor an end where movement would stop—only an infinite multiplicity of flows continuously expanding in every direction and then bouncing back again.[4]

Being never stops flowing. In physics, fluctuating fields are the immanent producers of material motion. It is precisely their unstoppable kinetic energy that is responsible for the Big Bang, heat death, the big crunch, and their endless cycle of composition and recomposition. The fact that there is a universe now is thus already a demonstration that there must be some nonimmobilizable flows from which all other things are composite.

One important consequence of this discovery is that there is no essential ontological hierarchy (verticality) or ontological democracy of things (horizontality).[5] Flat ontology, as Adriana Cavarero argues, merely "reinstalls the verticality of paternal authority in the horizontal plane of fraternal equality."[6] They are two sides of the same modernist political schema. Instead, being is twisted, curved, inclined, woven, and folded. Regions of verticality (authority) and horizontality (equality) are emergent regional properties or products of a more primary and constitutive kinetic inclination or curvature of being.

If being is in constant and continuous motion, then flows do not and cannot form a finite totality or even an infinite totality but rather an infinite and continually expanding sum or series—an open or expanding and manifold whole.[7] If being is in motion, therefore, it cannot be a monism or pluralism but must be an infinite multiplicity.

DELIMITATION

Being may be infinite, but kinetic infinity does not mean "unlimited."[8] In fact, being is a concrete infinite sum precisely because it is actively *delimited* by its flows. Delimitation is the process by which flows continuously mark a limit at a certain point but in the very act of doing so also go beyond that limit. Thus, delimitation is both the marking of a limit and the removal of that same limit in one and the same continuous kinetic act. This occurs because every limit presupposes a division on either side of itself. On one side of the limit, things are included; on the other, they are excluded. Each limitation therefore presupposes both that which *is limited* and that which *it is limited by*. If things were only limited but not *limited by* anything else, they would not be limited. Therefore, all limitation presupposes that which does the limiting: the flows.

However, that which does the limiting is itself not contained in the limits that it produces. If it were, it would be no different from that which is limited, and thus there would be no limit. Therefore, since every limit presupposes that which is limited and that which it is limited by, nature cannot by definition of limitation be a totality, a unity, or "one." Just because there is no absolute or final limit, it does not follow that there is not an infinite multiplicity of limitations continuously alternating in turn.

If being flows and flows are infinite, then they are not infinite in only one direction but in all directions. If being flows in all directions, then it is delimited in all directions. Being is therefore becoming infinitely large and infinitely small at the same time. It is becoming larger as it continuously surpasses its previous limit, but it is also becoming smaller at the same time with respect to its future limits—which it is increasingly infinitely smaller than. The same logic applied to the infinitely large is also applied to the infinitely small. Thus, the universe is not only expanding and surpassing its own limits outward but also inward at the same time. In other words, because matter is nothing but flows in motion that make larger and smaller limitations and these limitations are fundamentally delimited in all directions, there can be no absolute limit in any direction.

There is nothing smaller than the purely continuous motion of the *flows themselves*, but these flows also have kinotopological ripples and waves in them that are not divisible or made of anything smaller. Thus, there are larger and smaller infinities, each defined by a delimitation of one folded flow by another, but there is no smallest infinity. This is possible because the infinity here is a kinetic infinity and not a substantial one. The flow of movement is infinitely continuous and at no level divided or static. Accordingly, folds are capable of an infinity of smaller internal limitations. Every wave can be composed of smaller waves, like a continuous fractal fold in motion. The *process* of delimitation, therefore, has no absolute limit, because the movement of flows is absolutely continuous. There is no point at which the flows can no longer move or fold, or else they would no longer be continuous at that *point* but in fact discrete and static—which would destroy their motion.[9]

COMPOSITION

If flows are infinitely delimited, then it follows that they are also infinitely composite. That is, we will never find a "single" or "pure" flow that is not already a composite multiplicity of smaller flows or waves. A flow is always already a flow of flows, a curve composed of curves, a labyrinth of labyrinths. Therefore, because being is a multiplicity of flows, the ontology of motion cannot be a theory of fundamental particles. *Being and Motion* makes no claims as to what the smallest building blocks of matter are. Whatever matter is it flows, and all flows can be composed of other flows. As Marx writes of the motion of Epicurean atoms, "Since they are in constant motion . . . the solidity of the atom does not even enter into the picture."[10] Everything is caught in the flow of things and is therefore caught in the process of composition.

Being, therefore, is not just infinite—it is an infinity of larger and smaller continuous and composite infinities.[11] This is the case because composition itself, like delimitation, is infinite. Every time a flow delimits an interior and exterior, it produces a composite of interior folds, but every interior and exterior composite is itself capable of holding together an infinity of subfolds within it.

Composition is therefore not just infinitely large but also infinitely small insofar as it has no inner or outer limit to how many flows it can compose. Every given composite makes possible an infinity of smaller composites within it. As noted previously, this infinity is possible because of the infinite continuity of the flow itself but also because this infinite continuity, through composition, opens up an infinity of delimited larger and smaller composites. Each delimited composition is therefore its own *actual infinity* insofar as it contains an infinity of smaller composites. Each composite is actually and not just potentially infinite. Infinity is not a substance but the creative flow or process of materialization itself.

VISIBILITY

If flows are infinite composites, then no flow can be rendered completely empirical or fully present. The empirical itself flows. A flow is the movement of matter that renders the empirical sensible in motion. In other words, the fundamental kinetic conditions of visibility are themselves not fully visible substances but *processes of visibility*. If they were simply visible they would no longer be the conditions of the visible but would fall back into identity with visible things, and we would have gleaned nothing of the real conditions of things at all.

Empiricism denies the reality of anything that cannot be directly sensed. As such, a strict empiricist must reject, for example, the current scientific consensus regarding the existence and reality of quantum fields, since they cannot be observed directly or independently of the particles they produce.[12] Quantum fields have energy and momentum that can only be indirectly observed by their macroscopic visible effects, like the recently discovered Higgs field.[13] Although the popular press fetishized the "God particle," the most important discovery for physicists was actually the nonempirical discovery of the Higgs *field*, not the empirical particle. The visible particle only proved the reality of the more important and more fundamentally constitutive invisible kinetic field.[14]

Flows are an active and creative process that one can never see in a pure or uncomposite state, since they are not a state at all but a *process*. A flow is something that can only be known immanently as the ontological condition of the things that flow. The visible will always have as its condition a relatively or not fully isolatable kinetic substratum that distributes it for observation. Things never appear on their own or fully present but in relation and in motion. In other words, in contrast to naive empiricism or naive materialism, *Being and Motion* adopts a transcendental empiricism or transcendental materialism that aims to discover the real conditions for the emergence of the empirical and material *in relational motion* (see Chapter 4).

Since motion is not a thing but a process, kinetic relations are not strictly empirical, because one cannot directly sense a process "as such," but only the fragmentary sense perceptions within that relational process.[15] But kinetic relations are not metaphysical either, since they are material processes, not substances. The conditions of the empirical cannot be anything empirical in themselves, but this does not mean that the kinetic conditions are not thoroughly real. It only means that flows in themselves are not necessarily and fully empirically present or sensible discrete "things."

Let's take another example from quantum field theory. First, quantum fields are in a state of indeterminacy. The act of measurement interacts with the field itself and gives determination to the indeterminate fields. Prior to this interaction or measurement there is no objective discrete state or states, only a continuous and indeterminate flux. Humans, however, are not the only ones that interact or "observe"—fields interact with themselves at every level. Fields are the real construction of themselves. Thus, empirical observation can only take place as a series of entangled and creative observations, not as a total observation of a passive state or substance.[16] There is thus no single objective "flow" that is "the flow" independent of anything else. There is only an indeterminate fluctuation that comes to be determined through its interaction with other flows. The quantum indeterminacy of matter is therefore kinetically real without being entirely empirically actual or sensible.[17]

TIME AND SPACE

If being is in motion and motion is infinite, then the origins of motion cannot come from anything other than motion. In other words, flows are neither reducibly temporal nor spatial. Flows do not occur in a fixed background of time or space—"*motus nec tempore certo nec regione loci certa*," as Lucretius sings.[18] Rather, time and space emerge through flows. If there were a time before flows, then the flows would no longer be continuous and infinite but would begin at a moment in time. If there were a space prior to the flows, then the flows would similarly be limited and made discontinuous by this space where there were not yet flows.

Thus, the ontological priority or fundamentality of time and space as independent of movement and flows is incompatible with the theory of flows and of quantum gravity.[19] It is impossible to explain the emergence of flows from time or space. But again, the inverse is not true. Current scientific work points to the idea that space-time emerged in and through the *motion* of at least one cosmic explosion of quantum fields in which space and time were unfolded into the known universe: the Big Bang.[20] All the quantum fields we currently know of emerged from a single continuous field whose symmetry has bifurcated in different ways, producing the particles that compose the known universe. This is what physicists refer to as "spontaneous symmetry breaking."[21]

The "arrow of time," for example, is a historical product of the contingent fact that the initial conditions of our early universe happened to be relatively lower entropy ones: a superdense quantum state. What we call "time" is nothing other than the thermodynamic process of increasing entropy, as the physicist Sean Carroll puts it.[22] Because we experience macro-level entropy, the arrow of time does not seem to go backward; we do not remember the future. However, in a heat-death universe with extremely high entropy, the process would be reversed in order, with low entropy eventually emerging from high entropy.[23] The arrow of time is an effect of entropy, but the second law of thermodynamics does not *guarantee* entropy in every case. Entropy is not a universal law, only a high likelihood at our level of our observation. For example, at the level of quantum gravity (the Planck scale) time continually fluctuates back and forth.[24] Thus, time is not ontologically fundamental; like space, it is the emergent product of a thermokinetic process. Lucretius was right.

The flows of matter do not flow through a static background space, but space is produced by flows. Space does not preexist matter in motion; it is created by matter in motion at the same time as it flows. This is echoed at the macro and micro levels of contemporary physics: cosmology and quantum gravity. In contemporary cosmology, for example, not only does the theory of a Big Bang show there to be a relative origin of space and time produced through an inflationary process of superdense quantum matter, but even recent discoveries about the early nature of the universe reveal that in the beginning of the cosmos, space-time was not a perfectly smooth, preformed background fabric. Rather, it had an extremely turbulent unfolding *when it was produced and unfolded by matter in motion*, which only gradually settled down into what we now perceive as the relatively smooth background space-time of reality.[25] In short, kinetic turbulence is at the heart of the cosmic origins of space-time itself.

At the micro level of quantum field theory, the fundamentality of space is now increasingly questioned by recent models in theoretical physics. According to physicists Carlo Rovelli and Lee Smolin, space is itself a product of quantum fields flowing and looping below the level of empirical observation (i.e. at the Planck level).²⁶ Loop quantum gravity theory demonstrates that it is mathematically possible (and experimentally verifiable, although not yet verified) for space itself to be a product of the more primary process of the folding and bubbling of quantum fields.

This theory is called the "spin foam" theory of space because the flows of quantum fields fold up into tiny bubbles that compose larger foam structures; these provide the seemingly smooth but actually quite folded and bubbly topology of space.²⁷ Movement occurs first in the quantum kinetic theory of gravity.²⁸

BIFURCATION

Flows are continuous movements, but this does not mean that they cannot be divided. The idea of dividing a flow remains a contradiction by definition only if we think of division as introducing a radical discontinuity, lack, or break into the flow. However, as I hope to show in this brief section, this need not be the case. Division is not subtractive but additive—it multiplies by division—through *bifurcation*.

Multiplication by Division

In order to make the above point, it is important to distinguish between two kinds of division following the two types of motion distinguished previously: extensive and intensive. The first kind of division, the extensive, introduces an absolute break—producing two quantitatively separate and *discontinuous* entities. The second kind of division, the intensive, adds a new path to the existing one, like a fork or bifurcation, producing a qualitative change in the whole *continuous* flow. The bifurcation diverges from itself while still following the "same" continuous movement.

Although division is typically understood according to the extensive definition, this is only relative to or a side effect of the intensive kind of division. Division occurs when a continuous process reaches a bifurcation point. By definition, a flow does not start or stop; instead, it bifurcates and is redirected. Thus, every bifurcation is a bifurcation of a bifurcation and so on, ad infinitum, without any unbifurcated taproot or final accumulation of all the bifurcated flows. It is an open-ended process—a multiplicity of coexisting levels of bifurcation. After the bifurcation point in a flow, a qualitative divergence occurs and two distinct pathways can be identified.

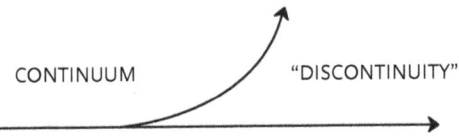

Figure 6.1 Bifurcation

The result of this bifurcation is that the division is experienced both as a continuity and as a discontinuity, depending on where one is in the flow.

In both cases, however, what remains *primary* is the continuous flow that allows one flow to continue on ahead and another to be redirected elsewhere. In other words, division is an active process of bifurcation that does not simply divide once and for all, but continuously redirects flows across or away from itself (see Figure 6.1). The division only appears as lack or discontinuity from the binary perspective of the divided region. From the perspective of the continuum, the division appears conceptually as a secondary or derivative phenomenon.

But the problem with the extensive definition of division is that it presupposes precisely what it proposes to explain. If we begin with divided discrete objects, we fail to explain how these objects came to be delimited or divided in the first place. In contrast to Zeno's infinitely divided solid medium, we propose instead an infinitely bifurcated fluid medium. While the former results in immobility, the latter results in movement. This movement is not mechanistic but stochastic, thus making possible the confluence and intersection of flows with one another.[29]

This in turn raises the subsequent question of how such multiple and bifurcated flows interact with one another. This is what we call the "confluence" of flows and is the subject of the next chapter.

CHAPTER 7
Confluence

If the flows of being are pedetic and capable of bifurcation, then it is also possible for them to flow together in a confluence, which is an intersection or connection of two or more flows that intersect one or more times. In this type of connection, multiple flows move together and intersect with one another without directly folding back over themselves.

Confluence does not, therefore, divide flows but instead brings them together and distributes them without division. This type of collective connection is possible because flows do not necessarily move along straight, mechanical paths that would eliminate the possibility of intersection between heterogeneous flows. Being connects because it moves together following a multiplicity of pedetic trajectories. The collective effect of this pedesis makes it impossible to assign a single original causal motion to the stochastic trajectory of any given flow.

Stochasticism (from the Greek word στόχος, *stókhos*, meaning to "take aim" or "guess"; from the Greek word στείχω, *steíkhō*, "to walk, march, go or come"; from the proto-Indo-European root **steyg-*, "to walk") is the experimental aim of the wandering foot, or pedesis. The French poet Paul Valéry describes beautifully the way in which the pure stochastic toil of the sea produces the manifold confluences of its elusive foam:

> What grace of light, what pure toil goes to form
> The manifold diamond of the elusive foam![1]

This is why the "problem" of turbulence remains unsolvable. There is no first or final cause, only an infinite multiplicity of nonlinear variables-in-motion. Any classical series traced back far enough exposes this stochastic uncertainty. Since the variables that would determine the trajectory of being include all of being itself, a single causal source remains unassignable. All of being is self-caused. Given the kinetic possibility of confluence, several consequences follow.

EVENT

The first consequence is the *event*. Once the motions of two or more flows intersect or connect with one another, they create an event, which is a singular point at which two or more flows cross (see Figure 7.1).

An event is still not a thing or an object but rather a kinetic hinge or terminal through which intersecting flows pass. The intersection between flows is not identical to the flows that intersect, but it is not anything separate from them either. Something new is produced by their composition. An event is thus a singular point shared by two or more intersecting flows that changes their possible trajectories: It opens up a new world of motion.

As a singular intersection, the event is also fleeting, like Valéry's "elusive foam." A new future or trajectory of motion is opened up at this intersection. However, as an intersection the flows also continue on, leaving the event to dissolve immediately after its creation. The event then retroactively appears only as a trace or flash of something that might have once occurred. However, the event is also that which makes possible a potentially infinite new practical trajectory for movement. There is thus a double nature to the kinetic event. On the one hand, it is a common occurrence, happening all the time and dissolving immediately, such as when one passes exits on a highway. On the other hand, it is a rare occurrence, when any given intersection becomes a new trajectory, such as when one chooses an exit.

Novelty occurs when a flow crosses another flow. In this way the event is fundamentally collective, as it always requires more than one. It occurs through an unpredictable encounter with an other or an outside. However, the consequences of this encounter are only realized by additional motions, by following out the new vector opened up by this intersection. For an

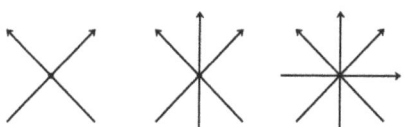

Figure 7.1 Event

event to be anything more than a fleeting spark,[2] its new region of kinetic possibility has to be further developed by folding. Without folding, the event remains an affect without object.[3]

The event does not cause or preexist the flows, nor does it have any characteristics independent of the flows that intersect and constitute the event. However, once the flows intersect, following their pedetic motions, the event appears retroactively as the destination of the preceding flow. An event thus makes possible a kind of kinetic "perspective," a singular point from which a new world is distributed. It is a kinetic or vectorial orientation, or "the fundamental condition of all life," as Nietzsche writes.[4] Kinetic perspective is not merely opinion or visibility; it is more general. It is a vector point along a trajectory of matter in motion that opens up a new world of visibility. It is the kinetic condition of intersection that makes perspective possible. A perspective is always from somewhere, but a somewhere or localization is only possible on the minimal condition that two flows briefly intersect to form a point of view between more than one trajectory. From this point at least two infinite trajectories stretch out. Kinetically, an event is a *pivot, joint,* or *relay* along a trajectory that makes possible a relatively stable position from which the intersecting flows can be interpreted and traversed. The event is thus a product of the flows—the first bit of stability that makes possible a new world.

Since everything is in motion, there are all kinds of kinetic events. Over the course of Part II, I use various political, aesthetic, and scientific examples to help demonstrate the concepts of flow, fold, and field. In the service of showing the most expansive range of examples possible in such a short space, I have chosen two running examples from two domains otherwise not exemplified elsewhere in Part II: one nonhuman example (the plant) and one human political example (Zapatismo). I could have used others, and indeed have used many others elsewhere. If the reader is looking for closer kinetic analyses of other natural and political kinomena, please see the companion volumes to this one. However, since the focus of this book is ontological, I treat these domains here only as examples to illustrate an underlying kinetic concept and not to reproduce the more robust theories of motion already developed in other books.[5]

EXAMPLE 1: THE PLANT

The historical emergence of the first plant is a kinetic *event*. A plant is an intersection of heterogeneous material flows that converge on a single point or event and then follow out of this new perspective. The life or event of a plant was initially constituted by the intersection of two heterogeneous flows: algae flows and bacterial flows. About 700 million years ago, a single blue-green algae (glaucophyte) swallowed a single cyanobacterium (*Cyanophora paradoxa*) and began extracting energy from its photosynthetic process. This event was singular and occurred only once, as evidenced by the fact that following this event, but not before, all subsequent plants shared a genetic structure.[6] All plants owe their existence to this singular algae-bacteria event.

There was no necessity of such an intersection, only the pedetic contingency of their confluence in a fluid medium. As flows of prey decreased and flows of light increased, this new form of life was capable of developing itself and becoming more powerful by following the new trajectory opened up by the algae's initial intersection with the cyanobacterium. Although the event itself occurred only once, this unique life form was able to genetically internalize and self-generate, or to reproduce within itself a new cellular component: the chloroplast. This change made possible a new movement, trajectory, or "perspective" of the algae toward the sun.

The perspective of plant life is thus defined by the new intersections that compose its vectorial being: water, air, sun, and nutrients. Without a continuous supply of any of these four flows, most plants will die. Given a continuous intersection of these flows, different plants develop and evolve along the different trajectories that follow these flows. Some plants move more toward water (seaweed), others toward the sun (trees), others under the earth (tubers), and others toward the air (epiphytes). Plants literally moved underground or up to the sky or into the ocean to follow one of their confluent vectors more than the others.

Like the capture of cyanobacteria, events make possible new perspectives or trajectories that a life can follow. A kinetic life-world comprises the vectorial intersections in which a life is lived.[7] The more confluent flows that intersect and can be sustained, the more complex the form of life.[8] From the simple to the most complex, all beings are potentially subject to the transformative power of events.

The event is a "point" of intersection, but this does not mean that it is immobile; indeed, far from it. The event is like a terminal through which the flows pass ceaselessly and change as they pass. The motions of the flows produce fluctuations in the event, but the event persists in the connection or intersection between the flows if it is sustained. An event is a dynamic nonequilibrium state or homeorhesis between at least two confluent flows. It does not necessarily block or redirect flows, but it makes possible their bifurcation at certain intersections. The event lasts only as long as its flows do. Thus, the event is an effect of the flows and not the other way around.

As soon as the flows change direction and no longer intersect, the event dissipates. Events are thus ephemeral by nature and exist only in the new trajectories they produce or the folds that preserve them.

Since flows are in continuous motion, and thus different at each moment, their intersections are singular. Events occur only once, but the consequences can be sustained indefinitely. Millions of years ago, one algae swallowed one bacterium that could photosynthesize. After that, a genetic modulation produced plants that could make their own chloroplasts for millions of years. The emergence of plant life is singular in the algae-bacteria event, but the confluence of water, air, sun, and nutrients must be continually replenished for the plant to reproduce itself. When one or more of its confluent flows dries up from lack of sun, nutrients, air, or water the plant dies. The plant's perspective can no longer be maintained. This does not mean that the molecular flows of the plant stop; they are simply redirected elsewhere. At the atomic level, flows of atoms continue on in another form, since energy is neither created nor destroyed but only rearranged.[9]

Plants are only one example. There are just as many kinds of events as there are kinds of flows that can intersect—animal events, political events, artistic events, and so on. As more flows enter into a confluence at a singular point, an event gains new perspectives or new conditions for development. A life becomes more complex and powerful. As the number of flows that intersect an event diminish, the event becomes less complex and less powerful. For example, once the algae intersects with the cyanobacteria, it becomes more complex. If it loses its ability to photosynthesize, it becomes less complex. Each new intersecting or connecting flow adds another point of entrance and exit to the event. In other words, each new confluent flow produces a transformation of the whole event, and of the flows it could potentially harness and repeat. An event changes in nature each time a flow is added because it gains another unique trajectory for development—opening up a new possibility for all the previously connected flows.

A kinetic event is like a transportation terminal, telecommunication terminal, or axon terminal in the brain. It allows new flows to enter and then be redirected or connected to other flows through this new point. The more flows intersect it, the greater the degree of kinetic freedom in destinations and the greater the collective transformation of the flows arriving there. In this sense, kinetic events have no essence. If the event is nothing other than the product of the intersection of any flow that crosses it and changes each time a new flow is added, then it can have no unchanging essence or fundamental qualities. Its qualities are only those that intersect it at any given point in the flow. When an event dissipates, the same flows continue on but are simply directed elsewhere. Unlike essences, events do not preexist or persist after the confluence of flows.

Finally, events do not happen in time, but time happens through events. Events occur first as the intersection of flows; only afterward can the flows begin to bifurcate from their trajectory and curve back around to the event in order to sustain and support it with affective folds. These folds in turn make possible a sensation of temporality as the succession of folds, but the event itself is not temporal; instead, it produces temporality.[10]

CONSTELLATION

The second consequence of kinetic confluence is the emergence of a constellation of events. Since the flows of being are multiple, there is not only one event but a multiplicity. When two or more flows intersect at two or more events, they form a constellation—a site, region, or surface produced by the intersection of flows (see Figure 7.2). Constellations have five characteristics.

First, a constellation has no essence. Since the constellation is composed solely of events, which are composed only of flows, the constellation has no preexistent or persisting essence, quality, or existence independent of the flows that compose it. Like an event, a constellation of flows does not block or capture the movement of flows but simply defines and gives a consistency to a region where the flows intersect with one another. Once the flows are redirected elsewhere, the constellation, like the event, ceases to persist in that form. The constellation is an assembly of affects without a fixed thing or object to which they refer. It is composed of "streaks" and "arrows of sensation," as Virginia Woolf calls them, without unification or substance.[11]

Second, a constellation is a kinetic surface. Once the constellation appears at the intersection of several events, something like a metastable domain of motions can be discerned. This gives rise to the possibility of multiplying new events ad infinitum within the parameters of the constellation. Each

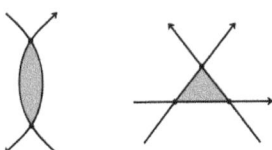

Figure 7.2 Constellation

new event along the outline of the constellation gives further definition to the constellation as a whole. Just as events become more complex and powerful the more flows intersect them, constellations also become more defined the more flows pass through the events that define the contours of the constellation. Furthermore, just as events can be the intersection of an infinite number of flows, so constellations can be outlined by an unlimited number of events without ever completely totalizing it. Since the flows that outline the constellation are continuous, they can intersect an infinite number of finite points. As continuities, there will always be room for another event between two others.

Third, a constellation is abstract but not in the sense that it is an illusion, a fantasy, or a purely mental entity. A kinetic constellation, just like an astronomical constellation, is *really there*, but only as the composition or confluence of heterogeneous stars. The diagram of Ursa Major, for example, does not literally appear as lines between stars in the sky but rather as relatively "abstract" relations of space-time from a certain kinetic perspective. The constellation is abstract, but the flows that populate and define its outline and motion are concrete. The constellation thus has no transcendence. An astronomical constellation is made visible by its stars, but a kinetic constellation is made visible by its events. As the concrete flows that compose it change, so the abstract constellation changes its configurations and relations.

Fourth, the constellation is multiperspectival. Each event in the constellation is a perspective, terminal, or relay point along the kinetic vector of a flow. As a confluence of flows and events, the constellation arranges a kinetic domain that contains a multiplicity of heterogeneous perspectives without unifying them into a single perspective or totality. Movement in the constellation is distributed across singular events, each with its own perspective and set of connecting flows. The constellation is not a totality of these flows but rather a fragmentary and open whole across which movement arrives and departs. Each time a new flow or event is added, the constellation changes and increases its conditions for development. The more flows and events populate the constellation, the stronger it becomes.

Fifth, the constellation is additive. That is, since the constellation is defined by nothing other than the collective set of movements that compose its concrete body, each new flow that is added changes the structure of the constellation. There is no static being of the constellation, only an additive and compositional becoming defined by motion. There is no discontinuity between one articulation of the constellation and another, only bifurcation.

EXAMPLE 2: ZAPATISMO

This time let's consider a political example: a constellation of political events. The Zapatista rebellion in Chiapas, Mexico, can be defined by the constellation of at least two heterogeneous flows: the flow of Marxist vanguard revolutionaries led by Subcomandante Marcos out of the cities and into the mountains, and the flow of indigenous peasants expelled from their land and forced into those same mountains. After ten years of quite literally pedetic wandering and uncoordinated efforts of resistance, the implementation of NAFTA brought the two flows to a decisive intersection: the revolutionary event of 1994. Armed men and women from the indigenous communities, co-organized by Marxist revolutionaries, took seven towns and more than five hundred privately owned ranches by force in the state of Chiapas. The intersection of these two groups with very different political trajectories (reformist versus revolutionary) intersected to produce a political event defined by the creation of a new political body—the Ejército Zapatista de Liberación Nacional (Zapatista Army of National Liberation, or EZLN)—a revolutionary military structure prepared to engage in warfare with the Mexican state in Chiapas.

This brief event in 1994 made possible a whole new world and set of trajectories by showing that what was previously impossible was now possible through a mutual transformation of confluent motion. Disjoined flows of indigenous refugees and disjoined flows of vanguardist revolutionaries were mutually transformed by their revolutionary encounter or event, which now made possible a self-organized autonomous conjoining of political power (the EZLN) capable of expropriating the expropriators.

The event of Zapatismo (see Figure 7.3) made possible at least two new major trajectories or *stókhos*: (1) achieving regional autonomy by force, and (2) mobilizing the Mexican people in revolutionary action against the state. Again, this movement is not metaphorical; the vanguardists actually wanted to march into Mexico City, and the indigenous groups actually wanted to move freely through the land that had been stolen from them. Neither of these movements seemed possible before the event; now they were.

After the event, however, neither of these trajectories could be sustained for very long. Most of the Mexican people supported the Zapatistas, but they did not support the armed overthrow of the government. The city of San Cristobal was captured, but soon military and paramilitary forces took it back. A single event could not sustain the revolution.

After almost ten more years of struggle, the new trajectories curved toward one another again and intersected in 2003 in the creation of the

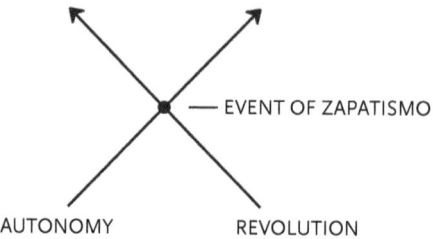

Figure 7.3 Event of Zapatismo

Juntas de Buen Gobierno (Councils of Good Government). This second event marked a huge shift in the vectors of Zapatismo: from direct confrontation with the Mexican government and paramilitary forces to the regional attainment of autonomy and self-government. During this time the Zapatistas openly criticized the military structure of the EZLN, the unequal status of women, the destruction of the environment, and the uneven development of the five *caracoles* (regions of the Zapatistas' territory, literally "snail shells"). The *Juntas* were the result of a decision not to wait for the revolution to fix these things, but to make the revolution happen where they were—by building their own schools, managing their own economic cooperatives, developing their own political egalitarian decision-making process, empowering women, protecting their environment, and so on.

In this second event the flows of indigenous people—disappointed with the original failure to achieve regional autonomy again, having intersected with the flows of Marxists, and disappointed with the failures of vanguardism and class struggle to produce a new revolutionary system—intersected again to create autonomous self-government: the *juntas*.

Zapatismo demonstrates each of the five characteristics of the constellation (see Figure 7.4). First, it has no essence, but instead has two events: the uprising and the Juntas. These events did not block or capture political motion but were connected together at two major intersections that retroactively reveal a consistency in their heterogeneous political actions occurring between 1994 and 2003. If the flows were ever to disperse, the movement would dissolve. The events have no destiny or essential features beyond their singular intersection. Not all revolutionary action everywhere in the world is supposed to or will look like it did in Chiapas, nor do the Zapatistas intend for it to.

Second, the two events created a kinopolitical surface that eventually became connected to a multiplicity of new events that occurred during and after the formation of the constellation: the alter-globalization movement, the Occupy movement, the global encounters against neoliberalism,

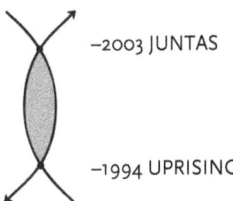

Figure 7.4 Constellation of Zapatismo

and numerous solidarity movements around the world. "Anyone can be a Zapatista," as they say. Any flow whatsoever can connect up to this constellation, with no limit on the number of points of connection. Since there is no essence, then anything can potentially connect up in global solidarity.

Third, Zapatismo is abstract. Like an astronomical constellation, Zapatismo is not a thing or an object; it is a kinetic relation between flows, a pattern or process of motion. One either sees the Zapatista constellation and can connect to it, or one sees a host of disconnected stars and spontaneous actions without consequence—"just a bunch of angry peasants." Zapatismo also has no transcendence or being independent of the eventual connections that shape its contour.

Fourth, Zapatismo is multiperspectival. Connected to it are numerous different progressive groups, from environmental activists to revolutionary anarchists. Zapatismo is not a doctrine, program, or state; it is a constellation or series of terminals that people move into and out of without creating a single total perspective. Each terminal or connection adds a new perspective, alliance, or way that Zapatismo can move—in solidarity with the Palestinians, with the Kurdish rebels, with fair trade organizations, and so on. Anyone can be a Zapatista.

Fifth, Zapatismo is additive. Each of its new perspectives or trajectories that connect up to the kinetic constellation it produced between 1994 and 2003 contributes to the mutation of the constellation. Zapatismo mutates alongside its connections with the Internet and to its global solidarity projects that fund it and visit it in Chiapas. It is not static but constantly moving in multiple directions at once.

CONCLUSION

The concept of flow developed in Section I of Part II provides us with a kinetic theory of the pedetic process and thus the real possibility for confluence within the process of continuous motion. However, it does not yet provide us with a theory of how such a confluence could maintain any kind of stability after an event. Confluence shows us how novelty is possible but not how such a novelty could come to exist as a stabilized pattern of motion connected to other concrete things or objects in the world. For this we require a theory of the fold, developed in the next section.

II
Fold

CHAPTER 8
Junction

Being flows, but it also folds. All that is air condenses into solid. This is the second conceptual component of the theory of motion. Being flows, but it also folds over itself in habitual cycles and patterns of dynamic equilibrium, creating regional stabilities-in-motion. If we begin philosophy from discontinuity and stasis, the challenge is to theorize movement. However, if we begin philosophy from the primacy of movement, the challenge is to theorize stability. This section provides a kinetic theory of how folds emerge from flows through junctions and conjoin with one another to produce larger composites or conjunctions.

A fold is produced by the junction or intersection of a flow *with itself*.[1] If all of reality is made of continuous flows, folds explain the kinetic structure of the relative stasis or stability that emerges from this process. A fold is like an eddy or whirlpool in the flows of being. It is a relative stasis that is always secondary to the primacy of the flows and events that compose it. As such, a fold is nothing other than a flow. A fold does not transcend or pre-exist the flow; it is simply the redirection of a flow back onto itself in a loop or junction. It is therefore a mistake to think of the fold as a mere product of a flow, as if the two were ontologically separate. The fold that moves already presupposes a more primary constitutive flow that composes and moves through it: the creative movement of the flow itself. Flow and fold are thus co-constituted in the same immanent kinetic process.

In this way, a fold is distinct from a confluence. A confluence is an open whole of two or more intersecting and heterogeneous flows, but a fold occurs when a single flow loops back over itself. A confluence is a novel but fleeting intersection, but a fold is what occurs afterward as an attempt to

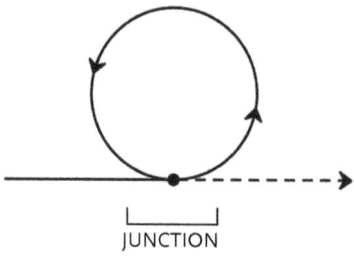

Figure 8.1 Fold and Junction

stabilize or repeat the unique moment of intersection. A fold is the repetition of a kinetic differential: a cycle. A fold remains a kinetic process, but it is a vortical one that continues to repeat in approximately the same looping pattern, creating a kind of mobile stability or homeorhesis.[2] The point at which the flow returns to itself may be an evental point whose trajectories have moved on, or it may be a fold in an evental or noneventual trajectory. In this way the junction constitutes a point of self-reference or haptic circularity in matter that yokes the flow to itself (see Figure 8.1).[3]

The fold then acts like a filter or sieve that allows some flows of matter to pass through the recurrent attractor of the cycle, and other flows to be caught in the repeating fold. The movement of the captured flow can then be connected to the movement of another captured flow and made into all manner of mobile composites, or conjunctions. However, the yoking or joining of the flows into a fold also augments them, not necessarily by moving them faster or slower but by subordinating them to a cycle that begins and ends at the same haptic point.

PERIOD

Let us call this point at which a flow intersects with itself its "period." Although the flow is continually changing and moving around the loop, this haptic point appears to remain in the same place. In this sense, the point appears to absorb and regulate all the mobility of the yoked flow while itself remaining relatively immobile—it is a relative immobility that moves by the movements of others.

The concept of the fold stands in contrast to the concept of node developed in various network theories and spatial location theories in the geography of movement. For example, John Lowe and S. Moryadas define movement as the routes between prior discrete nodes. Movement is purposive, "and each bit of movement has a specific origin and destination. . . .

Our schema," they say, "is predicated on the existence of nodes prior to the development of networks and movement. . . . Without nodes, why is there movement, and where is it consigned?"[4]

Kinology offers the inverse of this static and spatialized theory of motion.[5] In fact, one should turn Lowe and Moryadas's question on its head and ask, "Without movement, how did nodes or stable points emerge in the first place?" Placing the fixed nodes first means that movement is always already bound to an origin and destination. In this spatial definition there are no flows, and thus no confluences or junctions. As argued in the previous chapter, however, we will never understand movement by beginning with immobile nodes. Movement cannot be understood as a route between presupposed origins and destinations, and junctions are not fixed nodes given in advance of movement.[6] As the joining of flows to themselves, folds are secondary to the continuous movement of those flows.

Folds occur only in that which is continuous. This is because a fold is defined by the curving or bending of something back over itself, and *not over something else*. The intersection or junction of a flow with another flow is not a fold but an encounter or event. The structure of the fold is kinetically different. The fold is capable of producing reoccurring cycles and periods, while the event is fleeting and singular. If being were not in continuous movement, there could be no folds or even events. Folding presupposes continuous movement, and continuous movement makes possible the fold of being.

CYCLE

Being flows and folds over itself, but once it returns and connects to itself again it creates a cycle. A *cycle* is the movement between the departure of a flow from a bifurcation point and its return or arrival to that same point. This point is the periodic attractor of the cycle with itself. While the concept of identity has been historically conceptualized as a purely logical or formal concept, often relating to essences, the terms *period* and *cycle* more accurately reflect the primacy of motion (see Figure 8.2).

Identity is therefore rethought here as a product or an effect of the primary process of cyclical or habitual motion. Simply defined, the period is the point in a cycle where a flow recurrently intersects with itself in some degree of iterative frequency or density. The period of a cycle does not always create a perfect regularity, equilibrium, or classical "identity" so much as a metastable aperiodicity around an "attractor" that tends to overlap with itself again and again at irregular but frequent and infinitely differential approximate intervals.

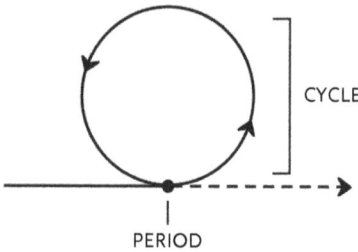

Figure 8.2 Cycle and Period

Thus, a kinetic period is simply a tendency toward a certain region of intersection around an attractor, and not always a mere repetition or regularity. The period and cycle are thus unstable and differential at the local level and stable and only approximately identical at the global level. Each cycle returns somewhere between perfect periodicity and strange or irregular periodicity.

A cycle is the whole process of self-intersection of a flow with itself, but this does not mean that the flow has been arrested or rendered completely discrete. The period is simply a slice or selection from the whole continuous cycle. When we mistake the periodic attractor for a simple static or fixed point we lose the flow entirely, so that we see only an abstract product without the motion that composed it. It is as if we looked at a Jackson Pollock painting and wondered how he was able to paint such wonderfully detailed replicas of paint splatter. In this case we have misunderstood everything about the kinesthetics of painting; we have abstracted the product from the process.

The cycle produces identity but only through motion. Since a flow is a continuous movement, the fold is not only continually receiving a constant source of new motion from outside, but it is also losing some motion that passes through its junction. Thus, a fold is only a regional capture of motion in a certain period. This is because when it intersects itself it is actually intersecting itself at a different point in the flow each time. Since a flow is also a continually moving and self-differentiating process, it is impossible that it should ever be the same, in a strict sense, as itself.

However, insofar as it is redirected into a repeating pattern of motion, the pattern of motion returns and we say it is "identical." Thus, we *can* step in the same river twice, but only on the condition that the river also turns over itself in local eddies and whirlpools.[7] The fold remains the *same*, but only on the condition that *others* flow through it. As Heraclitus writes,

Ποταμοῖς τοῖς αὐτοῖς ἐμβαίνομέν τε καὶ οὐκ ἐμβαίνομεν, εἶμέν τε καὶ οὐκ εἶμεν
(On those stepping into rivers staying the same, other and other waters flow).[8]

For Heraclitus, each eddy or fold in the river is like another river within the river. Each flow below the surface of the river is already multiple, but it is this multiplicity that composes the stream itself, as Virginia Woolf writes in *The Waves*: "Like one carried beneath the surface of a stream, is interrupted, torn, pricked and plucked at by sensations, spontaneous and irrelevant."[9]

Each period in the eddy of the river is composed of entirely different water molecules, but the cycle of the whirlpool persists. The cycle remains "the same," like Valéry's depiction of Narcissus's reflective pool:

> Admire in Narcissus the eternal return
> toward the mirror of the water which offers his image to his love,
> and to his beauty all his knowledge.
> All my fate is obedience
> to the force of my love.[10]

As the continuous flows of being slow and pool into cyclical folds, they make possible a smooth and stable surface in which sensible forms can emerge. Gide writes,

> Alas, when will Time cease its flight and allow this flow to rest? Forms, divine and perennial forms which only wait for rest in order to reappear! O when, in what night, will you crystallize again?[11]

The flow from period to period prime (P-F-P'), considered as a whole process, is thus the limit cycle of the fold. A cycle is not a static unity but a fluid or kinetic unity, like the recreation of Narcissus's pool from the flows of rain and river drainage. Since the fold is only a fold in a continual flow that constantly enters and exits it, renewing it each time, its cycle cannot be said to be the unity of an ideal identity but of a kinetic process. A cycle is the unity of a process of kinetic differentiation. Just like a whirlpool in a river, a cycle is only a unity of a differential process refreshed each time with new water—"paradise re-created in appearance," as Gide writes. The theory of motion thus replaces the concepts of identity and unity with the concepts of period and cycle.

EXISTENCE

The coemergence of periodic identity and cyclical unity constitutes the existence of the fold. Existence is the persistent but differentiated self-recurrence of something with itself. Kinetic existence is simply a homeorhetic point of habitual stability and self-affection within a world of differential flux and process. If being is pure continuous flow, something comes into concrete existence precisely when it is able to reproduce a consistent cycle of self-identity. In other words, it continually moves in such a way that its own movements are not movements other than its own.

In this sense, a flow that has not folded into some kind of persisting, stable, nonsingular structure does not "exist." Existence is therefore tied to self-sensation—not the sensation of a human observer only, but a minimal and kinetic self-sensation. If a thing has no sensation of itself, it does not exist as a thing. Unicorns, for example, do not exist not because the material that would compose them is ontologically absent from the world, but because the flows of this material have not yet folded into the proper periodic and cyclical structures that would give them self-sensation: existence.

Existence, therefore, is not static or formal, but kinetic and practical. Existence is a process or motion. Being must persist to exist. If Plato formulated the problem as "essence precedes existence," and Sartre reformulated it as "existence precedes essence," *Being and Motion* reformulates it again as "process precedes existence."

NECESSITY

Since being is in motion and motion is pedetic or stochastic, there is no ontological necessity or universal determinism. Flows have no necessity. This does not mean, however, that an apparent necessity cannot be regionally produced or constantly conjoined.[12] The structure of necessary existence, therefore, still requires a kinetic explanation. The structure of cycles is also what produces the regional effect of necessity. Once a flow is bifurcated and folded back over itself in a cycle and connected with itself at a period, its point of departure and point of arrival become the same point—even though this point must be continually reproduced. In other words, what looks to be an original vector will have already been the path that led to the being that it is/was. The fold is repetitive, even if it is a differential repetition.

Necessity is simply the kinetic effect of beginning where one ends and ending where one begins. Necessity is therefore a circular function of the identity of a unity or the period of a cycle. By definition, cyclical movement is always already movement back to where one began, and in this sense it is a kind of kinetic necessity. If beginning and end are the same, both merge together and disappear in unity, thus giving the appearance of a necessity and the idea that one was the necessary cause of the other. In fact, however, they only appear to be the cause of each other because of kinetic proximity and their cyclical motion. Kinetically speaking, necessity is the habit or compulsion of a flow to move in a cyclical and repetitive pattern such that its beginning is also its end. Opposed to an absolute necessity, flows produce a kind of regional or kinetic necessity: constant kinetic conjunction.

This habitual self-intersection of a flow with itself also produces an affect or sensation. This is the second main feature of the fold, and it is the subject of our next chapter.

CHAPTER 9

Sensation

A fold can contain one or more cycles. Each cycle departs from and returns to the same period in larger or smaller intercalated loops. As each cycle returns to the same periodic point, it reproduces the kinetic identity of the cycle with itself, as well as the unity of all the intercalated cycles with the same periodicity (see Figure 9.1). This structure also makes possible an important kinesthetic effect: sensation.

Sensation occurs at the period where a flow folds back over itself and touches itself. Sensation is the ambiguous kinetic structure of the period itself—the double or split affect of periodicity. It is a single and same period, but also an intersection of two different points in the same flow. Sensation is the *kinetic difference* between sensibility and the sensed. The two are identical in the period of sensation (the sensed) but differentiated in the continuous movement of the flow across its cycle (sensibility). Sensation is the kinetic differentiation internal to existence that makes possible self-affection or self-sensation. In short, sensation is the sense of the sensed as the kinetic identity of the kinetically different.

Sensation is what happens when a flow affects itself. It is a calm pool or an eddy in the flows that make possible the sensation and beauty found by Narcissus. As Baudelaire writes,

> There all is order and beauty,
> luxury, calm, and sensuousness.[1]

Without the difference between one point in a flow and another, there would be no sensation, only logical static identity. On the other hand, if

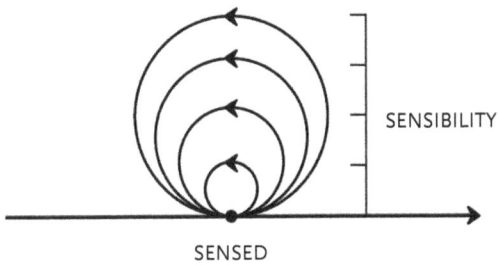

Figure 9.1 Intercalation and Sensation

sensibility and the sensed were fundamentally discontinuous entities, they could not produce the same sensation of the sensed, but only different sensibilities without sensation.

The antikinetic idea of discontinuous sensation has given rise to the philosophical division between so-called primary and secondary qualities, from at least Locke onward. Primary qualities inhere in things in themselves, since they are objectively in the *sensed*; secondary qualities appear in things only as they are subjectively sensed by human *sensibility*. Sensibility has been thus divided along the lines of the "in itself" and the "for itself."

Under these conditions, *real* sensation is impossible. Real sensation occurs only when something senses *itself* as other. "I is an Other," as Rimbaud says.[2] If the *for itself* and the *in itself* are not two aspects of the *same* being, they are incapable of sensing *themselves* as other. They are ontologically, simply, or merely other. Only when they are continuous and undivided is a proper "self-affection" possible.

Sensation must therefore be a kinetic structure of *self*-receptivity, a capacity to be affected and to affect at the same time. Simply put, a flow has the capacity of being receptive to other points in the same flow. Two different regions of the same continuous flux have the capacity to touch, intersect, and respond to each other as *different* points sensed in the *same* period. Sensation is the junction at which a flow returns to itself at a period in a continual cycle of acting and reacting back on itself. The *two* points of the flow become *one* period, but in doing so each point becomes twofold or duplex. The one folds into two, but the two also fold into one.

In other words, in sensation each point becomes *itself* as an *other* to itself. The point is still a singular point in a flow, but in joining with another singular point it is both itself and another. Every cyclical repetition of a sensation is thus a *repetition of kinetic difference* or manifold.

The sensed is the exact point of intersection where the two different points become one period in their *being sensed*. Therefore, the sensed being does not precede the process of sensation itself. Every flow contains a great many possible capacities or points of junction, but not every sensation is always expressed in action or intersected at the same periods. For example, fish have the capacity to taste, but they are not always tasting. The sensation of taste requires the flow of food to fold in the mouth on a tastebud. If the food is not folded at the right period where it intersects with the fish's tastebud, no sensation occurs. When the flow intersects, sensation occurs; when the junction unfolds, sensation does not occur. Since sensation is practical and not essential (predetermined or fixed), we never know with absolute certainty what sensation is capable of.

RECEPTIVITY AND REDIRECTION

The kinetic process of sensation thus has two distinct operations: receptivity and redirection. Sensation either allows flows to pass through or it delays them by redirection. The period adds nothing to what it receives. Sensation should thus be contrasted with representation, which is a duplication or mimesis of one discrete thing by another. It thus presupposes the existence of a distinct original that precedes the copy, as if one point in a flow were simply a copy of another and not a fold or period.

Sensation, on the other hand, is produced only at the unique point of intersection between two differentiated regions of the same flow. Sensation is the repetitive *intersection of differences* and not *a replication of a previous point*. Sensation is a crossing-over or chiasm that combines the operations of receptivity and redirection at a single period. The hand that touches is also touched back by what it touches.[3] At the chiasm of sensation, the flow that actively bends and returns back on itself is also the same flow that receives this folded flow. At the point of intersection, the flow either passes across itself, continuing elsewhere, or it is taken back up into a periodic cycle for a delayed release later on.

The operations of receptivity and redirection are crucial for the persistence of events. An event produces a new intersection of flows that can also become the site of a new cycle. On the one hand, an eventual intersection may very well remain a fleeting and strange moment with only minimal or ambiguous persistence.[4] As such, it can open up a new trajectory or perspective, but it does not necessarily sustain it.

On the other hand, one or more of the intersecting flows passing through an eventual point can return and fold over itself at that point in order to sustain it. This requires both the receptivity of the flow and the redirection of its trajectory back into a stabilizing fold. While the original event was singular, the fold is cyclical and periodic. The event lives on in the self-generating consequences of the fold.

EXAMPLE 1: THE PLANT

To continue with our example from the previous section, plants first emerged from the single rare event of bacterial capture. After this evental mutation, however, the organism began to genetically "repeat" the initial operation of photosynthesizing sunlight to use as energy. This is not an analogy; the organism really repeated the same motions again and again.

After the event, the plant cell began to both receive and redirect flows of sunlight energy to itself without having to continually absorb a new bacteria each time. The plant then had its own capacity to affect itself in a new way—in the form of a chloroplast that can photosynthesize. Instead of intersecting with a new flow of cyanobacteria every time, the cellular transport system of *Legionella* now moved cyclically entirely *within the plant cell itself*. The flow of bacteria was taken up and repeated in the cell. The photosynthetic cycle could then be completed entirely within the haptic sensory system of the plant cell. The plant creates its own periodic fuel source: receiving flows of light and redirecting them into usable energy. The affective cycle of the plant is thus *unified* in the *existence* of the cell and made retroactively *necessary* for the survival of the new organism.

It also follows from this kinetic definition that sensation does not refer only to human sensation or even to the sensations of organic life. Sensation occurs wherever there is a receptivity and redirection of flows. Even minerals have a receptive capacity to be affected and to redirect the kinetic flows of temperature and pressure. For example, according to Einstein's kinetic theory of matter, a piece of basalt is composed of innumerable atomic flows that move extremely slowly and vibrate in dense patterns. Some of these flows are redirected away from this dense compound by erosion, but most move only until they reach a certain limit and then fold back into the rest of the receptive vibrating and cycling atoms bouncing off one another within certain periodic limits. The flows of silica and oxygen atoms in basalt, for example, move in slow general cycles outward and inward, folding and refolding at certain junctions and forming ionic compounds. However, once another flow of more rapidly moving atoms or photons (heat) collides with this basalt rock, the silica and oxygen become receptive to this motion and respond by redirecting their flows elsewhere, melting into a liquid between 984 and 1260 degrees Celsius. Similar capacities for receptivity and redirection can be given from physics to biology. At a general level, all matter has some capacity for kinetic sensation.

Thus, sensation is different from kinetic perspective. Perspective is produced by events, and sensation is produced by cycles. Perspective is the intersection of two or more heterogeneous flows or vectors. Perspective opens up a new trajectory or possibility in being able to move in new ways, given a certain eventful intersection, mutation, or kinetic constellation. It is defined not by its receptivity or redirection but by its action and constellation. Sensation, on the other hand, is the intersection of the same flow with itself. It is a cyclical return of the different with itself to generate a homeorhetic identity, unity, stability, and existence. It is not an orientation that opens up new ways of acting, necessarily, but an accumulation that captures and redirects a series of cyclical repetitions into a stable form of existence. Events flow; sensation cycles. Perspective adds new vectors of action; sensation captures and repeats them. It is a cycle of *both* active and reactive motion.

QUALITY

Periodic cycles produce sensation, but from these sensations also come differing qualities of sensation. When a flow folds back and intersects with itself, it produces a sensation *of something*: the sensed. Events produce a flash or streak of sensation that disappears immediately without being connected to some particular *thing*. It is a flash of light or color without a clear source, a feeling of urgency without a plan or program of action, an ambient sound without discernible instrument, and so on. Affects sustain these sensations, but if they are not yet conjoined to any others, they are still not necessarily *things*. In *The Waves*, for example, Virginia Woolf describes the way in which motion reveals the affects that compose individual things:

> Observe how dots and dashes are beginning, as I walk, to run themselves into continuous lines, how things are losing the bald, separate identity that they had as I walked up those steps. The great red pot is now a reddish streak in a wave of yellowish green. The world is beginning to move past me like the banks of a hedge when the train starts, like the waves of the sea when a steamer moves. I am moving too, am becoming involved in the general sequence.[5]

In motion there is no pot, only a streak of red, a wave of yellow; no hedges, only a streak of green; no waves, only a streak of blue; and ultimately no subject but the general affective sequence or flow of sensation. Things lose their discrete identity and gain a kinetic identity in the persistence or flow of their affects. Outside of this affective kinetic sensibility there is no transcendent essence of the thing. Things are made of affects, not the other way around.

This affective kinetic quality produced by flows differs from traditional ideas of quality in several ways. First, a kinetic quality never exists independently of a kinetic flow; it exists only through periodic sensation. Quality, contrary to Plato, does not transcend its concrete manifestations in matter.[6] The same quality can appear in different things without there being an unchanging transcendent form of this quality, independent of the fold, because flows are capable of being moved and affected in similar *patterns* or *synchronies* in more than one place at a time.[7] Furthermore, the same junction can be shared by more than one flow at a time as they converge and cycle around the same affective point. This movement does not require any immaterial form or idea.

Second, a kinetic quality is not an attribute of a preexisting substance. Kinetic quality, contrary to Aristotle, is not a mere attribute of "one and the selfsame substance" that "while retaining its identity, is yet capable of admitting contrary qualities."[8] A kinetic quality is not attributed after the fact to a preexisting thing to which the quality is attached as something other than the thing. The quality and the thing are produced at the same time in the fold because the thing is nothing other than the conjunction of its kinetic affects.

Third, a quality is not an essence. An essential quality is a quality that a thing has independent of any observation of it, and that must remain the same for that thing to be what it is. For example, a primary or essential quality of a book is that it must have pages. If we remove all but one page of a book, a single piece of paper is by definition no longer a book. However, the color of the book is an accidental quality or property of the book. If a book is first white but then painted black, it remains a book regardless of its color.

Kinetic qualities do not follow this opposition between objective essential and subjective accidental qualities because all qualities are affective functions of the same fluent process. "Qualities belong to matter as much as to ourselves: They belong to matter, they are in matter, by virtue of the vibrations and numbers that punctuate them internally."[9] In other words, what a thing "is" changes each time one of its qualities changes. For example, the book with one page has a diminished capacity for being read but an increased capacity for portability; the black book has diminished capacity for reflecting light waves but an increased capacity for absorbing them. There are no essential or accidental qualities, only diminished and increased capacities for specific kinetic sensations.

The Waveform Theory of Quality

The self-intersection of a flow is a period of sensation, but it also defines the kinetic quality of the sensed. Periodicity is the process by which two different aspects of a flow become one in the same period. This period appears not as an abstract or logical identity (A = A), but as a kinetically *qualified identity*—as a *certain* solidity, size, speed, color, temperature, and so on. Depending on the way the flows are folded over one another, they produce different qualities.

For example, kinetic theories in physics have elaborated fairly robust accounts of qualities based on the thesis that all particles constantly move and vibrate in continuous frequencies or cycles and waveforms. In physics all sensible matter (i.e. matter above the Planck scale) can be understood according to its kinotopological waveform. Subatomic particles, atoms, and molecules all move and thus have a frequency of some kind. If all matter moves, all matter also has a frequency or waveform of movement that defines its qualities at different levels of emergence—atomic, molecular, cellular, organic, social, planetary, and so on.

For example, the kinetic *density* of folds determines the solid, liquid, or gas quality of the thing, while the kinetic *frequency* determines the visible, audible, gustatory, olfactory, and temperature of the thing. The wavelength across the electromagnetic and pressure spectrums produces the qualities of color and sound, the different vibratory frequency of atoms and molecules determine the taste and smell of matter, while the kinetic speed of the folds determines the quality of their temperature. In short, the waveform theory of matter is that the qualities of matter are defined purely by the waveform of their motion.[10]

Qualities are therefore the result of kinetic affections—flows whose density, shape, speed, and frequency are receptive and directive. A fold has a waveform and frequency because it has a period in which it goes out and returns to itself more or less quickly, in larger and smaller cycles. Insofar as matter exists, the movement of its component parts—atoms, molecules, cells, and so on—move outward and back in at periods or limits that define its form and quality.

Degrees of Quality. Kinetic quality also admits degrees—more or less solid, more or less large, more or less hot, more or less dark, and so on.

This is because there can be larger and smaller intercalated cycles that all return to the same period of sensation. A degree of a quality (more or less) is thus always relative to its period or point of sensation through which all the intercalated cycles pass. One cycle is "more" than another the more smaller cycles it envelops with respect to their shared period of intersection: sensation. The period of sensation is the point of arrival (reception) and departure (redirection) for all the intercalated flows.

Just as it is possible to distinguish between larger and smaller infinities in mathematics without knowing the exact numerical difference between these infinities, so is it possible to distinguish between more or less of a quality without considering the exact quantitative difference between them.[11] Something can feel more or less hot in relation to a point of sensation without considering the exact magnitude of the difference between two qualities. As Nietzsche writes, "We cannot help feeling that mere quantitative differences are something fundamentally distinct from quantity, namely that they are qualities which can no longer be reduced to one another."[12] The difference between any two cycles of sensation is thus not a quantitative difference but a qualitative difference.

Without this periodic structure of repetition, a quality like solidity, for example, would quickly dissipate if the flows did not return to one another in a certain density. If, for example, flows of magma disjoined all the silica flows in a basalt rock and mixed them elsewhere with other metamorphic flows, the rock would lose its qualitative degree of solidity. Its flows would not return in the same cycle or qualitative degree. In this case the rock would be destroyed (a qualitative transformation) and would no longer exist, since the identity function of periodicity is required for the existence of qualities.

QUANTITY

However, qualitative folds are also quantitative insofar as their continuous cycles are treated as numerically discrete unities. There is therefore no fundamental or ontological division between quality and quantity; there are only flows and folds. The kinetic theory of folds thus allows us to go beyond the simple opposition between heterogeneous quality and homogenous quantity. Quality and quantity are simply two dimensions of the same continuous movement of the fold.[13] While quality describes the period or point of sensation of the fold, quantity describes its periodicity as a whole, identical, and unified complete cycle (see Figure 9.2). Greater or lesser quantities are determined by counting the smaller subcycles they contain.

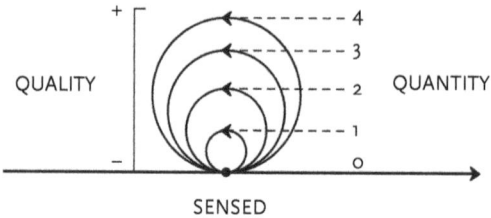

Figure 9.2 Quality and Quantity

For example, ten degrees of temperature is hotter than at least nine other measurable qualitative subcycles or degrees. In this way, a cycle can be counted as a quantitative multiplicity without presupposing an ontological division between the period and cycle of a fold. Contemporary physics, for example, accepts the qualitative continuity of matter's movement as quantum fields, but also the quantifications of those fields at different emergent levels: particles, atoms, molecules, cells, animals, plants, galaxies, and so on.[14] This is possible only because quantity is nothing more than the cycle of a qualitative fold of motion, considered as a unity or "one." Quantity is a movement of expansion or identification of the kinetic period to the whole unity of the cycle, while quality is a movement of contraction of the unity of the cycle back to the single point of its self-sensation or affection. Quantity and quality are therefore two dimensions of the same kinetic process.[15]

PORES

The process of folding not only produces a period and a cycle related to the quality and quantity of the fold, it also produces a pore, or opening, that occupies the middle of the fold.

Folded Pores

By definition, every fold requires such a pore or opening, or else the fold would be completely solid and undifferentiated and therefore not a fold at all. The pore of the fold is what differentiates the fold from itself, making it not a single solid point but rather a junction of two distinct points on the same flow. The two points of the same flow are both differentiated and united by the fact that the flow must move in a cycle, around the pore, from one to the other in order to return to the same period (P-F-P'). If the fold lacked a pore, it would be completely homogenous, self-identical, and static, because it would *already be* identical to that which it was without requiring any motion at all (P). A fold only remains a fold when it retains a difference between itself and itself; the pore is that difference. Without this difference, no kinetic quality or quantity would be possible at all.

Periodic Pores

The same must be said for the intercalated cycles of the fold that define its qualitative and quantitative degrees. Between one degree or cycle and another, there must be a pore or difference that keeps them apart and distinct. Without such a difference, the cycles would, like the loop of the fold, collapse into a simple static identity with each other.

With respect to qualities, pores create a difference inside the fold that forces a flow to go around the cycle, thus introducing the sensory difference between P and P' and defining the qualitative waveform of motion. With respect to quantities, pores create the difference between one cycle and another. If all the cycles of a fold were completely filled in, there would be no basis for numeration because numbers require a minimal difference between counting and what is counted for the numbers to be kinetically coordinated. By forcing a flow to move around the fold in a cycle, the pore introduces a difference between the kinetic act of counting, which requires its own cycle, and the other cycles being counted by it.[16]

Every fold is thus pockmarked with the pores and openings of sensation that occur between its cycles. These pores are like so many eyes, ears, mouths, noses, and other orifices that draw a flow into a pool through their openings and make possible a sensation of the same through kinetic difference. Pores are like wounds or knotholes embedded in the body of a thing that expose its inside to its outside and its outside to its inside, making possible differences in both quality and quantity.

Multiple Pores

The pore should in no way be thought of as a negative or empty space in the middle of the fold. The pore is more like the core or *chora* of the fold.[17] The pore is nothing other than the positive and creative process of the flow itself, making or opening up a space through its own motion. The pore does not preexist the fold but is made by the fold, as the result of its junction. Flows are literally wrapped around the pores, but it is the very wrapping or encircling that produces the pore in the first place. The pore therefore emerges through the fold, but it is nothing other than the fold itself. Flow and pore are two sides of the same *duplex* motion.

Since every flow is composed of an infinite multiplicity of other flows, every fold is also composed of an infinite multiplicity of other folds. The difference between a fold and itself is the pore, but between this pore and this fold is yet another fold and therefore yet another pore that distinguishes this fold from itself, and so on. In this way there is an infinite multiplicity of infinite multiplicities. The multiplicity of folds alternates with the multiplicity of the pores that they opened up. In this way being is kinetically self-differentiated and infinitely self-affective.

What appears to be a discontinuity at one level is a kinetic continuity at another. However, what appears as an identity in one fold also appears as the difference of another. Just as skin appears flat and smooth to the naked eye but highly porous under a microscope, so folds appear as simple unities on one level, even though they are filled with highly porous subfolds on another level. At one level, folds appear smooth, at the next level rough, but just like skin there is a kinetic continuity between all the layers. This kinetic process unites the inside with the outside through an infinite multiplicity

Figure 9.3 Menger Cube
Source: Niabot/Wikimedia Commons.

of pores, like a Menger sponge, a topological shape with an infinite surface area and almost zero volume (see Figure 9.3).

Flows are related and connected together through confluence, but how are folds connected together? This brings us to the final defining feature of the fold: conjunction. This is the subject of the next chapter.

CHAPTER 10

Conjunction
The Theory of Motion

Folds are connected together through one or more conjunctions. A *conjunction* is the connection between two or more junctions or intersections. As such, it is also the connection between different qualities and quantities, each with its own affect and number.

The conjunction of folds is a "thing." However, since every fold is both qualitative and quantitative, so is every thing. Therefore, with respect to the connection of the periods of folds, sensate qualities, or affects, let us call the conjoined thing an "image." With respect to the connection of cycles or numerical quantities, let us call the conjoined thing an "object." Quality and quantity, image and object are two kinetically distinct but inseparable dimensions of a thing (see Figure 10.1).

For example, a chair is a conjunction of kinetic waveform qualities of a certain solidity, temperature, texture, color, and so on that define its sensory image. However, it is also a conjunction of certain determinate quantities—four legs, one seat, two arm rests, all of a certain length, width, and height—that define its numerical objectivity. Together, the combination and arrangement of these qualities and quantities produces a relatively cohesive grouping that defines the thing called "chair."

Things are conjunctions of folds but also disjunctions of others, thus giving them the appearance of discreteness relative to their environment. A pore is the difference between flows, but a thing is the difference between what is conjoined in it and what is not. These are the two sides of the thing that define its existence. Just like the folds that make them up, things alternate to infinity in a series of mutual self-limitations where the

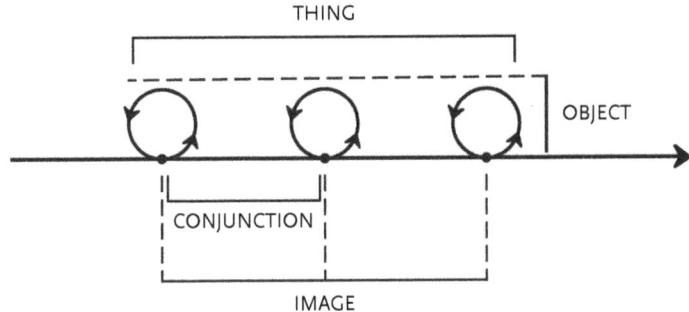

Figure 10.1 Conjunction, Thing, Object, and Image

things are only the exact kinetic outline of a relative difference between their conjunctions and disjunctions, even though flows also recede and exceed these determinations as multiplicities.

For example, the "thingness" of the chair is the difference between all its conjoined qualities and quantities and all of the qualities and quantities it does not have, that are disjoined from it. This is not an absolute or discontinuous difference but rather a regional one, like the folded neighborhood of a topological surface. A wooden chair might have the conjoined quality of solidity but not the quality of burning-hot temperature, or the quantity of nine legs, and so on. The list of disjoined qualities and quantities is obviously much larger than those of a singular chair.

The more qualities a thing has, the more pores it has. The more pores it has, the more it can be divided or penetrated by other flows and folds, transforming it from within and from without.[1] However, once a thing has only one or less of its qualities, it ceases to be a thing. This is because for a quality to appear as a quality *of a thing*, it must appear as a quality *of* at least one other quality. The kinetic structure of this "of-ness" is made possible by the process of conjunction that links one fold to another. If a quality is just a quality and not a quality of something else, it is not a thing—it has no conjunction.

Every conjunction of folds is also supported solely by flows that move through the whole series. For example, living organisms are only relatively stable pools or folds in a continuous flow of expenditure and transformation of energy moving from the sun, conjoined by the organism, reproduced in its offspring, and disjoined in death. The folds of life are only eddies in the kinetic stream.

Even the inorganic bodies of minerals are nothing more than relatively stable combinations of folds in the continuous transformation of kinetic energy. Igneous, sedimentary, and metamorphic rocks are simply three relative stages of a continuous mutation and conjunction of the earth's liquid body—the rock cycle. Solid, liquid, and gas, or ice, water, and air—these are simply the three relative stages of a continuous conjunction in the earth's fluid body—the water cycle.

At the microscopic level, all organic and inorganic bodies are conjunctions of smaller bodies, and those of even smaller bodies, and so on, all of which are in constant motion at every level. Flows of molecules, particles, and subatomic particles are continually moving and conjoining with one another. Quantum fields ebb, flow, conjoin, disjoin, diffract, and collapse into particles on the luminous shores of the vast "Dirac sea."[2] As the Italian physicist Carlo Rovelli writes, "The world is a swarm of elementary events, immersed in the sea of a vast dynamic space that sways like the water of an ocean."[3] Even at the macroscopic level, all these bodies do not produce a final stability. Everything is moving through an accelerating universe at incredible speeds. Since all things are products of kinetic conjunction, they are metastable. Things are always supported by flows at a smaller level.[4]

"Essential" qualities and quantities, such as an extension, volume, shape, and so on, are nothing more than the products of the process of continuous and constant conjunction. It is only after a series of qualities and quantities have been added together in a conjoined structure of periodic cycles that things emerge. Thus, it is only retroactively that they appear to have these qualities and quantities by necessity or essence. Necessity and essence are again only kinetic effects produced by pedesis. They are based on kinetic limit cycles.

Without conjunction there are no things, only fragmented sensations—a degree of heat, a flash of color, a pop of sound. Flows keep moving, folds keep cycling, but without conjunction nothing holds together. Nothing seems to be attached to or part of anything else. Everything flows, but motion is not a thing, it is a process. Flows are vectors and tensors in things and not reducible to them. For example, at a given time a body of water may not be frozen. At that moment there is no *thing* called ice. However, as the kinetic waveform of water changes, slows down, cools, folds, and congeals, ice comes into existence as a thing. Once hydrogen and oxygen slow down enough to conjoin together at slower speeds, there is ice. Things emerge through kinetic processes, but the processes are not separate or independent from the things. Flows are the processes by which things come into and go out of existence. They are the wharfs, woofs, and vectors by which existence is woven, folded, and unfolded.

The conjunctive process is additive, "one by one," not something attributed once and for all. This is the case because there is no single substance to which the conjunctive process is attributed. Matter is not a substance but a process of materialization. Since flows are multiplicities and being is nontotal, conjunctions can only be regional. The conjunctions that compose kinetic things are, like the flows themselves, in constant motion and can always undergo a change or recomposition. The determination of the qualities of a thing is thus never total, complete, or final because the flows that compose them always leak or connect to something else outside them. As a process of flows, the kinetic thing is thus not reducible to any fixed set of qualities or quantities conjoined at a given moment.

However, it is also important to distinguish between three kinds of conjunctions: injunctions, circuits, and disjunctions.

INJUNCTION

The first type of conjunction is injunction (see Figure 10.2), which is the inclusive joining of two or more junctions such that the cycle of one is equal to the cycle of the other. In other words, injunction occurs when two or more folds share exactly the same cycle and periodicity. Injunction is thus the inclusive identity or unity of two or more folds. Injunction also entails that two or more folds have exactly the same affective capacities, expressed as identical qualities and quantities.

EXAMPLE 2: ZAPATISMO

Let us continue our political example of Zapatismo. On May 2, 2014, members of the paramilitary organization Central Independiente de Obreros Agrícolas y Campesinas Histórica, funded and organized by the regional and national government, attacked the Zapatista autonomous community of La Realidad. They destroyed the autonomous school and clinic and injured fifteen Zapatistas; one of them, José Luis Solís López (nicknamed Galeano), a teacher at the Escuelita Zapatista, was brutally murdered. On May 25, 2014, Subcomandante Marcos, the spokesperson for the Zapatista

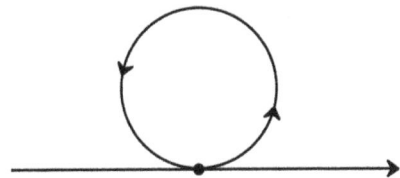

Figure 10.2 Injunction

uprising, changed his previous nom de guerre from "Marcos," after a previously fallen comrade named Mario Marcos, to "Subcomandante Galeano."

The injunction "Subcomandante Galeano" is composed of all the same affects as Subcomandante Marcos: black mask, tobacco pipe, riding his horse through crowded streets, wearing his headset microphone, and so on. In this way the original Galeano, who shared none of these affective junctions, lives on, but only through the kinetic injunction of Subcomandante Galeano, who shares every single one of Subcomandante Marcos's affects and is in fact kinetically identical to him. The two are conjoined in one. "We think that one of us must die so that Galeano can live, so death does not take a life but a name," as Marcos/Galeano says.

CIRCUIT

The second type of conjunction is the circuit (see Figure 10.3). A circuit is the conjunction of one or more folds in a third larger fold. The third fold functions as a common background for the others and brings them together. In this way, a flow conjoins multiple folds together by using another. Thus, all the flows in the circuit cycle through at least one shared period. The subjunctions that compose the larger circuit may have no shared qualities or capacities with one another, but they are all limited in their cycles by a third cycle that constrains or underlies their comotion. A kinetic circuit works in much the same way as an electrical circuit board: It provides a pathway or material foundation for electrical current to pass through via multiple components—capacitor, transistor, diode, and so on.

Each component fold has its own capacities, but the circuit ties them together and binds them to another component, without which the others would be disjoined. Together, the folds in a circuit are different qualities of a single quantity because they are part of the thing. Since conjunctions are nothing but flows, a circuit has no support independent of the folds that compose it. Every larger circuit depends on the support of all the smaller

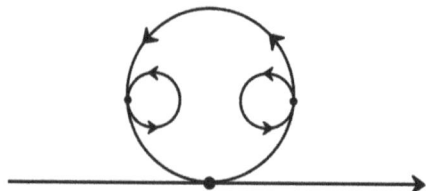

Figure 10.3 Circuit

subcircuits and junctions that compose it, all the way down and all the way up.

Causality

This relation of dependence also produces the effect of causality or, kinetically speaking, constant conjunction.[5] Kinetically, we can say that smaller subjunctions "cause" larger circuits. When we use the term "causality" we seem to be offering an explanation, but we are not. The concept of causation simply functions as a shortcut for a much more lengthy description of the kinetic components of the situation.

For example, when we say that heat *causes* a solid to become a liquid, what we are really saying is that the molecules inside the solid are moving relatively quickly. When we say that the pile of books on my desk is the *cause* of my messy desk, what we are really doing is describing the fact that there are books on my desk. What seems to be an explanation is actually just a description at another level.[6]

Furthermore, since a circuit is just a fold that contains other folds, whether a flow is a fold or circuit simply depends on the level of kinetic analysis. At one level silica and oxygen are ionic folds within the circuit of the basalt rock; on another level the basalt rock is itself a fold in the mountain slope circuit, and so on.

Continuing with our political example, the military front of the Zapatistas (EZLN) functions as a common circuit through which the affective folds of masculinity and femininity cycle within a relative equality. In 1994 the EZLN voted by consensus to enact the Women's Revolutionary Law, giving women the right to receive a just salary, be educated, plan their families, choose their romantic partners, and hold leadership positions in the EZLN—all of which were denied to women outside the EZLN. Thus, the EZLN, although far from achieving a perfect equality between men and women, began to increasingly function as a common circuit in which everyone's movement could count and flow through the larger fold of the military organization.

As a circuit, the EZLN allowed its subjunctions to move together as one cohesive kinetic body, as one *thing*. Despite the differences between masculine and feminine subbodies, everyone shares cooking and cleaning tasks. Each fold has its own capacities, but the circuit holds the differences together in a common background through which they are received and redirected and without which they would be disjoined. Together, the soldiers in the EZLN are different qualities of the same numerically unified military body. The EZLN, as a circuit or thing, also depends on the comotion of the solider folds that constitute it.

DISJUNCTION

The third type of conjunction is disjunction (see Figure 10.4). Disjunction is the kinetic process by which one or more flows leaves its fold, periodic orbit, or conjunction. Disjunction is the entropy of flows. Every junction and conjunction leaks. That is, every seemingly stable object or image, being kinetic, is also subject to decay and degeneration. Folds have to be made and remade continually in order to keep them from sinking like a leaking ship. The arrangement and order of folds does not have an eternal form or essence that preexists its concrete conjunction. Things must be built, and they must be constantly conjoined.

Entropy

Every kinetic conjunction thus has a degree of disjunction or entropy. The more disjunctions there are in the folds and the faster the flows flee the folds, the less stable the junctions and their conjunctions are. The less disjunctions there are, the more stable, predictable, and ordered the folds or conjunctions. For example, a refrigerated pear is a relatively stable conjunction of flows compared to a pear left in the hot sun. As the sun heats up the pear, the conjoined folds of the pear become increasingly disjoined through oxidation, cell rupture, bacteria, and hungry insects. Eventually the pear will decompose and its flows will be completely disjoined. The new folds—carbohydrate molecules, fiber, and so on—will no longer share any common qualities with the pear (juicy, sweet, green). However, these disjoined folds can then be reconjoined into other conjunctions (soil,

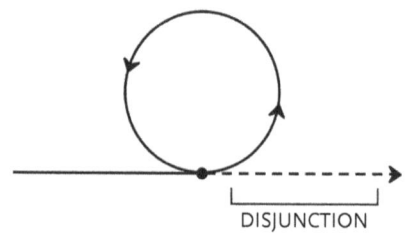

Figure 10.4 Disjunction

bacteria, insects, grass, and so on) that absorb the kinetic energy of its carbon, fiber, and water.

The sun is the largest mass of conjoined folds in the solar system, but it also produces the most disjoined folds in the form of heat—photons. Ultimately, according to the laws of thermodynamics, flows of energy tend toward increasing disjunction as the universe expands toward complete disjunction. Heat is ordered and disordered *through motion*. Without motion there is no thermodynamics and no entropy. Heat and energy are simply names that describe the motion of matter and have no existence independent of it.[7] Thermodynamics is thus derived from kinetic theory and not the other way around, as Einstein discovered in 1905.[8]

The energy of the sun grows plants on the earth, which in turn release energy in the form of oxygen, which is in turn used as energy for animals to breathe, which is excreted as waste, and so on. By continually fleeing itself, nature is increasing the total entropy in the universe. However, the second law of thermodynamics only says that motion tends to increase in disorder but not that it necessarily will in every case. Since motion is stochastic, it is also possible that order or negentropy can also emerge, although it is less likely. Regional entropy in open systems, like the earth, is certainly capable of producing order and conjunction, but only at the cost of the sun's destruction.[9]

We conclude this chapter with a demonstration of kinetic disjunction in the case of Zapatismo. The Zapatistas in Chiapas have been and continue to be under constant threat of violence from paramilitary forces and the Mexican state. The regional economic crisis in Chiapas, in part the result of NAFTA, has resulted in the mass expulsion of hundreds of thousands of indigenous people from their land to make way for hydroelectric dams, cattle ranches, and foreign mining companies. The entire region, along with the Zapatistas, is in a state of constant kinopolitical disjunction. As migrants flee, as mining companies and dams destroy the environment and capture the flows of water that sustain Zapatista communities, the folds and their conjunctions lose the shared affective points that bound them to the region and the people of the region. Migrants who may have been directly connected to a large number of conjoined affects of Zapatismo may now connect to only a few, or perhaps none, because they no longer live there. They no longer experience many of the same singular struggles. Those that no longer share any of the same affects are completely disjoined from Zapatismo. The Zapatistas call it the "nightmare of global migration." "If Mexicans could find in their own land what now is denied them," they say, "they would not be forced to look for work in other countries."[10] In kinopolitical terms, if the Mexican people were able to create sufficient conjunctions to one another and to the land in Mexico, they would not be disjoined from their local circuits of Zapatismo by migration.

The concept of the fold developed in this section provides us with a kinetic theory of the processes by which confluent flows are capable of taking on a regional homeorhetic stability in cycles and combining with one another in conjunctions to produce larger metastable composites or things.

However, the theory of flows and folds developed so far still does not allow us to determine how such composites would be *ordered or distributed* in the process of conjunction. The theory of folding shows us how stability is possible for a flow but not how such heterogeneous stabilities could be arranged and related to one another in larger kinetically ordered systems. For this we require a kinetic theory of the circulatory field, which is developed in the next section.

III
Field

CHAPTER 11
Circulation

Being flows and folds, but it is also distributed by a field. Flows join into stable folds, and folds are conjoined into things, but things are also arranged or ordered together through a field of circulation. This is the third concept in the theory of motion. If flows intersect and folds periodically cycle, fields organize them all in a continuous feedback loop. This chapter provides a kinetic theory of how conjoined flows become organized according to distinct regimes or fields of motion.

THE FIELD OF CIRCULATION

A field is a single continuous flow that has a kinetic vector for each period on its surface. It is a continuous flow that provides a path of circulation that binds together and orders a regional distribution of folds. This is different from conjunction. A conjunction adds folds together into larger and smaller composites of qualities and quantities. Conjuctions are composed entirely of larger and smaller folds. A field, however, binds together conjoined groups of folds but is itself not another fold. A field is a binding and ordering flow that moves through all the folds and subfolds and then repeats the process. Folds allow flows to persist, but fields allow conjunctions to be distributed.

The field of circulation is the kinetic condition for the ordered distribution of motion. It is a flow that moves through all the different conjunctions, but at a certain limit junction it folds back over itself and returns to at least one other junction, beginning the process again. The movement of circulation across the field thus secures the conditions in which a relation or order

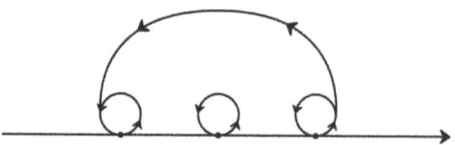

Figure 11.1 Field of Circulation

between two or more folds can persist through repetition. Without a field, conjoined folds only exist as disordered partial objects—a grin without a cat, or a walking hand without a body. Only through circulation are folds kinetically ordered and put into relation.

This in no way means that the field of circulation is anything other than flows. Just like folds, fields have no transcendent reality independent of the flows that constitute them. An ordering of flows does not preexist the flows themselves. Ordering is produced by flows. The circulation of a field is therefore also immanent and continuous with the folds that constitute it. In other words, the kinetic condition is immanent to what it conditions. This is precisely because there is a complete continuity between the flow that connects one fold to another and the flow that connects the other back to the first. This circulatory field is what gives folds a consistent and repeatable relation to one another, such that the grin does not float away from the cat (see Figure 11.1). Without the differential repeatability of this relation, folds have no persistent arrangement or structure. They exist as folds, but they do not move together.

Example 1: The Plant

Continuing the biological example from the previous chapters, it was noted that the intersection of two heterogeneous flows, glaucophytes (algae) and a cyanobacterium, was an event. By marking a new common point between two flows, this evental intersection made possible a whole new regime of circulation that ordered a specific set of additional relations between algae and other bacteria as well. The evental intersection between a glaucophyte and a cyanobacterium is not sufficient on its own to stabilize and reproduce a plant cell. This initial relation had to be genetically internalized and repeated through reproduction, or through folding. However, it is also not enough for the algae to merely reproduce the cyanobacterium; it has to be reproduced *as a chloroplast, or as an organ within a new order of the algae*.

In other words, the reproduction of the chloroplast introduces a new order into the cellular field of circulation. In addition to its previous circulation of flows, from feeding channel to food vacuole to nucleus to waste, it now adds a chloroplast that introduces a transformation of the whole order, from photons to chloroplast, to nucleus, to waste as oxygen. A different order of the same folded components of the organism does not work. The chloroplast cannot be used as a vacuole to store food or waste, and all the components need to be inside the cell walls, or they will fall apart. The field of kinetic circulation for early plants must therefore be ordered according to a particular kinetic pattern in order to make use of a reproduced chloroplast.

Incapacity

A field is not a thing, and it thus has no sensible qualities independent from the sensible folds that compose it. Since a field itself is not a fold, it has no affective capacity, no qualities, and cannot be a thing or even part of a thing, *relative to its folds*. Instead, the field of circulation is the continual flow that traverses things, binds them together, orders them, relates them, and conditions their comotion and relation to one another. It is the way things move together relative to one another. The field is nothing but a folded flow that connects with itself only indirectly through two or more related folds. The path of circulation is thus not an a priori order waiting to be filled with folds, nor is it an a posteriori fiction that only seems to order the folds. The field of circulation is the real and immanent relational constitution of order by the flows that traverse the folds.

In turn, the folds are nothing other than the constitutive flows that join themselves into these folds. The whole process—flow, fold, field—is one continual motion. This is the *incapacity* of the field. Since the field is nothing other than flows and folds, it has only the capacities and affects created by the cycles and periods of those folds. Circulation is therefore an incapacity in a dual sense—it has no affective capacities or qualities of its own, *and* has only its capacities in or through its constitutive folds.

However, just because a field is not a thing does not mean that it is an absence or negativity. The field is a positive and immanent ordering that is entirely continuous with what it orders. It is not a negativity because it is not the opposite of the folds but rather their support or structured coordination. Since the field of circulation has no positive, or negative being independent of the folds, it cannot be their opposite. It is the kinetic relations between things, that order things, but is itself not a thing. This language sounds tricky, but what it describes is quite simple and intuitive: motion is not a thing, but it is the process through which or way that things are related. The field is therefore the collective capacities of things that is itself neither a capacity or a thing: it is an incapacity or no-thing.

The specific distribution of a field, the existence of its folds, and the conjunction of its circuits are not universal or necessary relations. There is nothing essential about them. Instead, any given series of folds only exists with respect to the ordering relations of a given field of circulation. Without an ordering circulatory flow, things remain disjoined, fragmented, and incoherent. In other words, there are no grins without cats or hands that walk on their fingers without bodies. All folds that are outside a given circulation are not regionally ordered under its constituting relations. Ontologically, however, each local entanglement or ordering is continuous with a larger global entanglement with which it is connected. A more complete treatment of this issue is developed in the next chapter, on knots.

In the context of our plant example, the incapacity of the field is the *kinetic process* of genetic mutation that orders the things within the cell: various captured bacteria and cellular components. Such ordering and reproduction is only possible on the condition of the primary process of genetic extraction and reproduction, which qua process is itself not a thing but also not the opposite of the cellular components. The plant cell has no capacities other than those expressed by the specific bacteria, cell walls, and mitochondria that perform its operations and allow it to generate energy, defend itself, transport RNA, and so on. The process of ordered reproduction itself is therefore a kinetic pattern of things and not a thing.

Theory of Fluxions

Everything moves, not as a totality but as an infinite sum.[1] Therefore, there is no single immobile point from outside by which to measure the objective and absolute motion of any flow. If there were, there would also be another point further along from which to measure that one, and so on, in an expansive kinetic infinity. It therefore follows that there is only an infinity of points from which to measure the strictly *relative* but no less *real* motion of being. The theory of fluxions provides a logic for understanding the relative or ontologically regional ordering of motion.

Folds move differently in their field of circulation. A fluxion is a degree of motion relative to the motion of the field it is on, and to its neighboring motions. Depending on its degree of flux, a fold moves more or less with respect to its other neighboring folds, and all of those move with respect to the field of motion that measures or orders them all.

Relative to one body, another appears to be moving; relative to another the same body appears to be still. In his *Principles of Philosophy*, Descartes gives the example of the motion of a ship. Relative to the shoreline, a passenger on a ship appears to be *moving* down the river. Relative to the ship, the same passenger is *not moving* with respect to the neighboring bodies aboard the ship. However, if the ship was being pulled by the wind upriver at the same speed that the current was pulling it down-river, the ship would *not be moving* relative to the shore, but it *would be moving* relative to the changing wind and water surrounding the ship.[2] The point is this: Everything is moving but only relative to other motions. A fluxion is the relative kinetic difference between folds. The field is the background flow or continuous function, as in calculus, within which the fluxions are related or derived.[3]

Each fold has its own periodic motion but is also related to other folds in the same kinetic field. Every field of motion is therefore composite. For example, Descartes continues, if you are walking along the deck of a ship with a pocketwatch, the wheels of the watch have their own motion. However, added to this motion is the motion of your body along the deck, and added to your body's motion is the motion of the ship tossed about on the waves, and added to that motion is the motion of the ocean as whole, and added to this is the motion of the whole rotating earth, and so on.[4] All of these motions are part of the same field of motion. But each also moves more or less relative to the others. Relative to the watch, your walking body is less mobile; relative to your walking body, the ship is less mobile as you walk across it; but relative to the ship, the waves are less mobile as it sails across their surface—and so on in relatively *decreasing* degrees of mobility or fluxion. From the inverse perspective, the waves move across the surface of the ocean, the ship moves across the surface of the waves, and so on in relatively *increasing* degrees of mobility or fluxion.

The great contribution of Einstein's theory of special relativity to kinetic theory was to show that space and time themselves are relative to each other *with respect to motion*. Motion is what relativizes space and time. As the degrees of fluxion increase, time slows down or "dilates," and space "contracts," relative to the moving body or fold. Every degree of flux, therefore, also determines a degree of space-time, not the other way around.

Following special relativity, the theory of fluxions thus offers a description of space-time grounded in motion. A fluxion is simply a difference in degree of motion relative to a given kinetic field (see Figure 11.2). A kinetic field, on the other hand, is the relatively immobile background or surface from which the different fluxions are measured. A field is that which has zero motion relative to the rest of the degrees of motion on it.

CIRCULATION

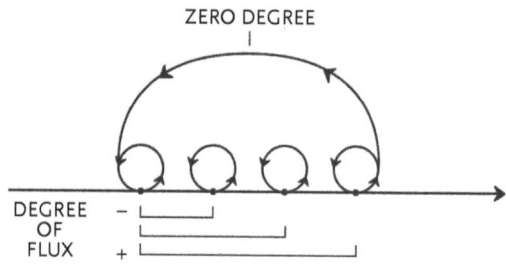

Figure 11.2 Fluxions

Three correlates follow from these definitions. First, a field of circulation requires at least two folds and a relation between them such that the flow of one is kinetically relative to the flow of the other. If this is the case, it is possible to directly compare the cycle of one fold with the cycle of another. This makes possible a measure of their fluxion, or kinetic degree of "more or less" motion, on the basis or support of a single continuous flow that binds them together and apart: the field.

In other words, folds differ with respect to one another only through and relative to a relatively immobile background or zero degree of motion that flows among them. Thus, the flux of one fold is relative to another fold only on the basis of the other's relation to the first *and* to their shared and triangulated relation to the field. Folds thus appear as different from one another or the same as one another to varying degrees of flux only relative to their shared field of circulation. The theory of the field presupposes at least two related folds and at least one fluxion or kinetic difference between them. Every kinetic ground presupposes its figures, and every figure presupposes its kinetic ground; the two are relationally defined.

A field with no folds is simply a flow. A field with just one fold is simply a fold—a quality without fluxion or relation. A flow with just one fold can only have larger and smaller intercalated folds intersecting at the same period, as described in the previous chapters. However, for multiple different folds to be related together *as different*, as fluxions, in some ordered way, they require a field of circulation that binds them together but also holds them apart.

The second correlate of these definitions is that for something to have its own distinct motion it must have a higher degree of flux than all its lower degrees. For example, relative to the shore, the motion of the sitting passenger is identical to that of the ship. Only if the passenger moves while on the ship does she appear to have her own motion. However, if she moves in the opposite direction of the ship's motions at the exact speed of the ship, from the shore she will not appear to be moving. Her degree of flux in this case would be identical with that of the shore. Only when her degree of flux is greater than all the other relative degrees in the field does she appear to have her own positive motion in the field.

The third correlate is that if two folds have the same degree of fluxion relative to the zero fluxion of a given field, then they appear more or less identical or injoined relative to the other degrees in that field. If two folds have the same fluxion, they will coappear in motion as injoined. If their fluxion is different only with respect to a third fold, they are part of a third fold or circuit. If a fold has no degree of flux it will not appear; it will be disjoined—it will be part of the relatively immobile background.

Example 1: The Plant

Let us continue with our example from biology. The different components of a plant cell (organelles) move more or less according to a degree of flux through the field of the cell. Once a cyanobacterium is fully domesticated and genetically reproduced by a cell, it is called a chloroplast. A chloroplast is one of the earliest and most strongly defining features of a plant cell. Without it there would be no plant cell. Its use of chlorophyll, a green-colored pigment that absorbs sunlight, not only allows the plant to make its own food through photosynthesis but also determines the macro appearance of many plants as green because of its abundance in the cell.

The cell is the field of circulation through which nutrients enter from outside and out of which waste is excreted. Within this kinetic field the cytoplasm of the cell has a relatively small degree of flux because it provides the relatively immobile fluid medium through which the motion of all the organelles, nucleus, and chloroplasts move. Its subfolds are also relatively conjoined into circuits, since its motion is relatively undifferentiated and homogeneous. Relative to the cell, however, the nucleus is more differentiated and has a higher degree of flux. With respect to the circulatory process of genetic reproduction, the fluxion of the nucleus has a greater degree of flux than the cytoplasm because its motion of genetic reproduction occurs in the cytoplasm and introduces new differentiated motions back through it. Chloroplasts have an even higher degree of flux in the cell because their motions are in turn based on the relatively stable and predictable motions of the nucleus. The chloroplasts are highly mobile and active folds in the cell, constantly converting photons into energy, using it, and directing it to storage. As the most recent addition to the cell, the motion of the chloroplast both relied on the background mobility of previous fluxions and also surpassed them in mobility.

The Waves

For clarity and scope of the theory, let's add an example from literature. In Virginia Woolf's *The Waves*, six characters meet in a restaurant on the occasion of saying farewell to their old schoolmate Percival, who is going away to India. Let's consider the aesthetic field of circulation of "Percival's farewell dinner." First of all, in contrast to the other characters, who all speak in the first person in the novel, Percival has no voice. Additionally, no representational narrative is given of Percival, or the restaurant, or anything else in the background by the author. We read only what each character says in turn about the kinetic and affective background *from their degree of flux in the field*. The aesthetic field is not a thing that can be objectively sensed or described by an omniscient author but only lived in the affective folds of the six characters who meet with Percival. It is the zero degree of motion on which the relative affective movements of the characters play out.

Neville arrives at the restaurant before anyone else. Since no one sees him arrive, his movement appears with the least degree of flux possible relative to the restaurant itself. All the other characters find him already there, sitting and unmoving like a piece of furniture, relatively unaffected by their arrival. As the first and only fold in the field, his sensation of the restaurant is one of complete indifference and anticipation. "Things quiver as if not yet in being," he says. "The blankness of the white table-cloth glares. The hostility, the indifference of other people dining here is oppressive." The field of Percival's farewell dinner has transformed the restaurant, but as Neville observes, without the others "things have lost their normal uses—this knife-blade is only a flash of light, not a thing to cut with. The normal is abolished." There are only affective flashes or events without things or order to hold them together.

Louis arrives next, but he does not come to the table immediately. His motion is first one of hesitation and self-reflection as he fixes his hair in a mirror. He is the next degree of fluxion—more than Neville who is unmoving and unaffected, but less than the others whose movements will have still greater affect. He arrives; he moves unremarkably through the restaurant. His motion is oblique and has no effect on anyone or anything. Now Louis describes the next arrival, Susan, who enters like "a creature dazed by the light of a lamp. Now she moves. She has the stealthy yet assured movements (even among tables and chairs) of a wild beast." Susan comes in immediately after Louis and has a similar but not identical degree of affective fluxion, since she moves while Neville and Louis sit, but she moves in a dazed manner, by instinct, toward the table, "touching no one." "Rhoda comes now, but from nowhere, having slipped in while we were not looking," says Louis. Although entering later, Rhoda appears as if she had never moved and already been at the table next to Neville, unaffected. The kinetic pair of Neville and Rhoda thus also have similar but not identical degrees of flux in relation to the affective field.

Susan then describes the entry of Jinny. "There is Jinny. She stands in the door. Everything seems stayed. The waiter stops. The diners at the table by the door look.... She brings things to a point, to order.... Now she sees us, and moves, and all the rays ripple and flow and waver over us, bringing in new tides of sensation. We change." Jinny is the maximum degree of fluxion for the field. Her movement is so affective that it radiates out, making everything else look like a relatively immobile background upon which she moves. Everyone is affected by her. Her final degree of fluxion shows, by triangulation, the relative degrees of fluxion for all the others. The sequence or chain of fluxions is complete. The maximum, minimum, and middle can now be measured and ordered across the affective field.

Finally, Bernard comes in without pushing a door. He does not look in the mirror. "He has no perception that we differ, or that this table is his goal," Neville says. Bernard does not feel as if he is coming into a room of strangers. He has a very high but not maximal degree of flux. He talks to everyone as he moves, both affecting them and being affected by them. "He half knows everybody; he knows nobody." With respect to his relatively maximal affection, no one appears to have any more or less significant degree of difference or degree of flux at the table.

"Now is our festival; now we are together. But without Percival there is no solidity. We are silhouettes, hollow phantoms moving mistily without a background.... Nothing can settle," Neville says. Once Percival arrives, "the reign of chaos is over. He has imposed order. Knives cut again." "He is like a stone fallen into a pond . . . like minnows . . . we undulate," Rhoda observes. Now there is "a chain whirling round, round, in a steel-blue circle beneath," as Louis puts it. Susan says, "That is the furious coal-black stream that makes us dizzy if we look down into it." "Yet these roaring waters," Neville states, "upon which we build our crazy platforms are more stable than the wild, weak and inconsequent cries that we utter when, trying to speak . . . 'I am this; I am that!'" Percival is the poetically insensible field that brings the friends together and allows their "common emotion" (love) to circulate, and is therefore not reducible to Percival the person but becomes the kinetic occasion of comotion. "No, that is too small, too particular a name," says Bernard, "We cannot attach the width and spread of our feelings to so small a mark."[5]

The poetic figures each enter and flow like waves on the ocean across the restaurant in different affective motions, all distributed on the background field of Percival's unaffective, undescribed arrival.

KINOMENA

If every fold and circuit in a field has a degree of flux, then the appearance of one fold is also related to and entails the simultaneous coappearance of the others in the same field. Kinomena are the coappearance of folds in an ordered field of circulation.[6] They are immanent, collective relations between two or more fluxions. Kinomena are thus different than phenomena. Phenomena are what appear to *consciousness* and are related to one another strictly through consciousness. Since phenomena are the appearance of movement *only through consciousness*, which for Kant is not itself in motion, they remain static representations of motion: frozen, fixed, and arrayed by the intentionality of the human subject. As long as motion remains something *for* consciousness and not a feature *of* a material consciousness itself, phenomenology will always be a graveyard of immobile forms.[7]

Kinomena are defined by their relations, but their relations are always constitutive. In other words, folds that are related through a continuous field are themselves nothing but folds *in this field*. There are no relational flows between folds until there are folds to be related, and vice versa. The two emerge at the same time. Kinetic relations are something that must be made through the primary process of folding and do not precede it. Kinetic relations are thus neither strictly extrinsic or intrinsic. External and internal relations are two sides of the same continuous process of folding.

The folds, therefore, are not exhausted by their relations, because the flows themselves that connect and compose the folds are two aspects of the same kinetic process. Folds and relations co-appear in motion. Matter can always redistribute its relations differently because flows and folds are continuous with one another and not ontologically discrete entities.

The theory of kinetic relation is thus in contrast to the theory of intrinsic or essential relations that precede the things they relate. Intrinsic relations are fixed relations or properties that define a concrete thing before anything appears as that thing. For example, the intrinsic relations of a chair bind together four legs, a seat, and a back, and so on. The intrinsic relation between these affects defines them as a chair, whether or not such a thing actually exists or appears as a thing. If a thing fails to fulfill these relations, it is not a chair.

In contrast to this, kinomenal relations are constituted immanently, one by one, through the affects produced by folding. A fold creates an affective capacity, but it also makes possible a new relation with other folds based on what it can do. For example, the kinomenal appearance of the chair depends on what it can do within the immanent relations in its field. A rock could be a chair at an outdoor picnic, a small table could be used as a chair, anything elevated off the ground that can be sat on has at least one affect in common with a chair can function *as a chair*. However, the rock at a picnic is not "like" a chair, and the chair is not "like" a rock. Their affects are not representational or analogical; they are real. The rock really can be sat on, as can a chair. A chair can also "do" more than its dictionary definition. It can be used for all kinds of things other than just sitting; it can be part of a street barricade, or with a blanket over the top it can become a child's fortress. All these things, and more, constitute the external relations a chair is capable of entering into. It is not stuck or fixed by one set of formal features. What a chair is (internal) and what a chair does (external) are two dimensions of the same continuous kinetic process. Ultimately, we cannot know all the affects a chair is capable of. It can always do one more thing. Because flows are continuous and infinite, fields are always capable of adding one more fold to their flow. Circulation is thus the process or flow capable of holding together an infinity of affective points or folds in the same field of kinomenal relation.

Things are the product of conjunction. For example, a chair is composed of a conjunction of a quality of brown, a region of flatness, a certain height or elevation. However, only when these folds and conjunctions are co-ordered in their kinetic function are they able to take on the collective appearance of "something to be sat in." A chair is thus not simply a series of qualities, but a particular order and actual coappearing of these qualities in such a way that they work or function together to form the chair as something to be sat in, or used as a barricade, or whatever: a kinomena.

Triangulation. Kinomena are thus defined not only by their relation to the field of circulation in which they appear as fluxions, but also by all the other kinomena in the field. In other words, the kinetic capacity to act depends on the comotion of the other folds that support it. Since there are at least two folds in a field, every fold is supported by a flow from at least one other. The second fold secures the relation through the direct support of the first. Given the security of this first relation, it is then possible for this first relation to support a third fold that is related directly to the other two, producing a triangulation. A fourth fold can then also connect to the first two, producing yet another relation different from the third, and so on in higher levels of relation. At each higher level of triangulated relations between kinomena, a new parallax relation is possible that modulates and supports the capacities of the others.

For example, plant cell circulation developed a whole new set of internal relations between early kinomena that had to be developed in *media res*. To the first evental relation between glaucophyte and cyanobacterium, a second relation was added with a third kinomena: a bacterial parasite called *Legionella*, from which genetic material was extracted in order to transport food from the cyanobacterium to the host cell. This relation was then augmented by a fourth kinomena, another bacterial parasite that differed in function from the others and whose genetic material was horizontally transferred to the cell in order to perform other cell functions augmenting and facilitating the third: the creation of mitochondria to generate energy (ATP). This fourth kinomenal organelle was then augmented by a fifth, the development of a *rigid* cell wall, and so on. This process of genetic transformation or relational triangulation was ongoing for thousands of years, continually adding one more kinomena to the rest, creating a new parallax affect that modulated the immanent field of the others with respect to the new addition.

LIMIT JUNCTIONS

Within a field of circulation there are two types of junctions: limit junctions and nonlimit junctions (see Figure 11.3). Limit junctions are the final junctions in the field, after which flows are disjoined from the field and/or enter into another field of circulation. The limit junction is thus a kind of filter or redirector of flows. Once a flow moves through a series of conjunctions and reaches a limit junction or bifurcation point, it is either expelled or recirculated back across the previous conjunctions.

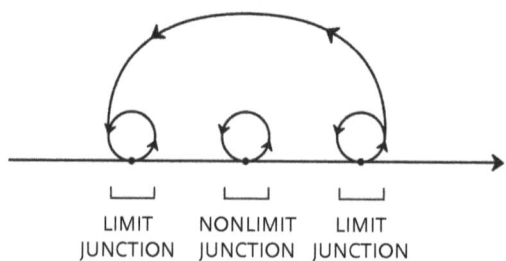

Figure 11.3 Limit and Nonlimit Junctions

There are two kinds of limit junctions: exit junctions and entrance junctions. The task of the exit junction is to actively expel, destroy, or unbind flows. It removes flows from circulation; it detaches or disjoins them. However, limit junctions also redirect circulation back to previous folds and circuits. Entrance junctions are filters that allow some flows to enter into circulation and others to be blocked or redirected. Limit junctions are thus responsible for the flows that define circulation in the first place; they are the kinetic conditions for ordered interiority and relatively disordered exteriority. However, limit junctions or folds are not determined in advance as limiting junctions. Their role as points of bifurcation or limits is only relative to their operation in the field and to other relative degrees of flux. Any junction or period in a flow can thus take on a limiting function insofar as it disjoins, conjoins, and recirculates a field. It is therefore possible for any field to both shrink and grow according to the expansions and expulsions of its limit junctions.

A nonlimit junction is simply a fold in the field of circulation. At the end of each circuit or fold, a flow can either start over or move on to another circuit until it reaches the limit junction of its field. Nonlimit junctions thus do not filter what comes in or out of a circulatory system but simply sustain and constitute the affective capacities of the field itself.[8]

Expansion by Expulsion. Every limit junction or border is composed of three operations: an outward expansion, an inward fortification, and a recirculation (see Figure 11.4). The first motion pushes outward, expanding the limits and reach of the field, while also possibly expelling or disjoining a flow. The second motion follows the second, securing, supporting, and retracing this first motion through an expansion of the circulation. The

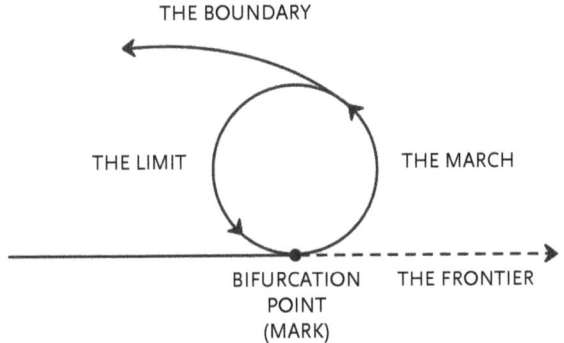

Figure 11.4 The Border

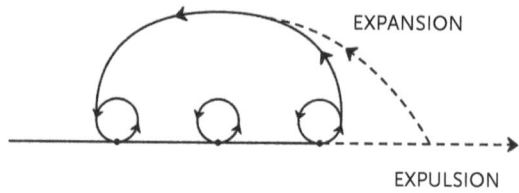

Figure 11.5 Expansion by Expulsion

third motion transports and recirculates newly incorporated flows back through the field.[9]

The field, just like the flows, is not well understood by the concepts of exclusion and inclusion. The conceptual basis of circulation is that something goes out and then comes back in, again and again. In this sense, circulation is both inside and outside at once. It is a manifold or complicated process, creating a folded system of relative insides and outsides without absolute inclusions and exclusions. The insides and outsides are all folds of the same continuous process or circulating flow. Each time circulation captures a fold or pleat, both a new inclusion and a new exclusion are created.

The circulating field feeds off disjunction. Each newly disjoined flow can be captured, redirected, and looped back around to the beginning of the series. Circulation is an attempt to recycle and redistribute waste back into a relatively stable field of order. This does not stop kinetic entropy, but simply rearranges things, more or less (see Figure 11.5).

For example, ecological systems can be more or less kinetically efficient. Some plants inhibit the growth of others by releasing certain chemicals or blocking their sunlight. However, different plants in turn may feed off these same chemicals and thrive in the shade. An ecological, economic, or social system is a circulation of flows across multiple folds that maintains a certain homeorhetic network: a dynamic stability or collective trajectory.[10] Instead of a mere series of conjoined folds, circulation is like an overfold that connects the conjoined series of folds back to itself in a particular order.

This not only gives rise to the possibility of the persistence of a kinetic order of fluxions but it also allows the order itself to expand and contract. The folds remain distinct, but the field adds or subtracts them from circulation. By the action of the limit junctions, the more folds act together the stronger and more complex the field becomes, whereas the more folds separate through disjunction the weaker and less complex the field becomes. Circulation, through limitation, sets some folds loose and merges others together in an expanding network. As the circulatory or metabolic field increases its folds, it increases its qualitative and quantitative dimensions.

It becomes more complicated and more powerful. Circulation is thus more complex than unordered movement or even harnessed movement (the fold); it is the controlled reproduction and redirection of collective movement across a certain limited field.

However, the expansion of a field always comes at the cost of some kind of expulsion. Either the field expels some folds of its own field in order to take in relatively more from elsewhere, or it expels folds from other fields or flows in order to enlarge itself. Just as there is no ontologically "free" energy in thermodynamics, so there is no expansion of a given field without the expulsion from some other kinetic process. Flows are neither created nor destroyed but only redistributed according to the various expansions and expulsions of fields of circulation.

Example 1: The Plant

The rigid cell wall of the plant cell, for example, is a limit junction that facilitates the expansion of cell circulation. It is the final junction after which a flow is no longer conjoined in the field of a cell. Plant-cell walls are porous and allow certain nutrients and water to flow inward, with specific size restrictions, and also allow certain waste products to be expelled from the cell.

There are thus three layers of the cell wall corresponding to the three kinetic operations of the limit or border (see Figure 11.6). The first layer is called the *middle lamella* and is the outer layer of the cell through which cells directly touch other cells and entities outside of them. This is the final layer through which flows are expelled before leaving the cell. The second layer is called the *inner lamella* and is the inner layer of the cell that forms and hardens once the cell is fully grown. It secures and supports the expanded state of the cell. The third layer is called the *primary cell wall* and is a thin flexible membrane that develops as the cell grows, allowing it to pass all the nutrients and water that will be the circulatory fluid of the cell body. The cell thus expands both by expelling waste from inside and by expelling nutrients from the environment and circulating them through itself in internal systems of storage and capture.

The key to understanding the thermodynamics of the living system is not so much energy flow (stressed by many commentators, such as Prigogine, Morowitz, and Ulanowicz) as energy capture and storage under energy flow. Energy flow is of no consequence unless the energy is trapped and stored within the system, where it is mobilized to give a self-maintaining,

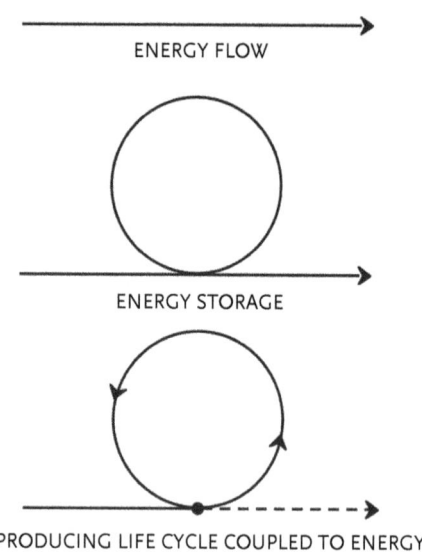

Figure 11.6 Plant Cell
Source: Mae-Wan Ho, "Circular Thermodynamics of Organisms and Sustainable Systems," *Systems Review* 1.3 (2013): 30–49, http://www.mdpi.com/2079-8954/1/3/30/htm.

self-reproducing life cycle coupled to the energy flow. (By energy, I include material flow, which enables the energy to be stored and mobilized.).[11]

This theory of circulation, however, also raises another issue: how such fields of circulation interact and relate to one another. This is the subject of our next chapter.

CHAPTER 12
Knot

Fields circulate and order folds as degrees of flux, as we have seen, but fields can also combine themselves into larger and smaller knotworks based on their shared circulations and folds. A knot is thus the intersection of two or more fields at two or more of the same folds or junctions (see Figure 12.1).

Knotting is what makes possible the continuous intersecting of *composite* fields of circulation. In a kinetic knot, each field remains distinct but also becomes connected at specific junctions to other fields, making possible a series of shared or collective qualities and quantities. Folds are what tie the knots together. One circulation kinetically becomes or flows into another not by mimesis, analogy, or representation, but by actually sharing and continuously reproducing the same affective capacities or folds as another field. Two fields are knotted together by their shared affects, but these shared affects can also produce their own field in turn: a knot.

Knots are different both from the constellation of flows and from the conjunction of folds. Constellations do not require folds, since they are simply the intersection of flows. However, the intersections or events in a constellation can become the site of two or more folds or conjunctions if folding occurs at the points of intersection. Fields, however, can then connect these two folds together in an ordered pattern similar to that of the original eventual encounter.

In other words, an event can become stabilized by repeating its *trajectory* and *intersections*. A constellation can become a field, but a constellation is different from a field because a constellation has no folds, whereas fields require them. Accordingly, constellations cannot have knots, since knots have to be bound together by folds.[1]

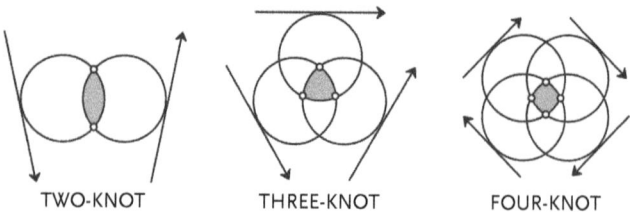

Figure 12.1 Knots

NESTS

Knots are also different from nests. A pore is the inside of a fold. A pore is the difference between larger and smaller folds, which are not discontinuous but simply appear porous, depending on their regional order. However, just as there are larger and smaller folds, each containing the previous one but without a final one above or below, so there are larger and smaller nested fields of circulation.

The difference between these nested fields is similarly porous. Within any given field only the kinomena appear; the field itself does not. However, at the next larger level or nest a subfield will appear *as a thing* and *not another field* relative to the larger field that contains it. In other words, with respect to, or from the perspective of, the larger field, the smaller nested field is treated as a particular conjunction of folds, and not as a field. Each field is therefore a real synthesis of all its components at each level. There is no largest or smallest field, however, only a multiplicity of knotted and nested fields. The difference between a nest and a knot, therefore, is that a knot is created by a *nontotalizing overlap* of one field with another that entails the sharing of at least two folds, and *not a nested relation* of one field completely inside another.

KNOTTING

Knotting entails the emergence of a third field or knot between the two overlapping fields. This shared circulation between the two fields makes possible a third condition for ordered relations—a third distribution of folds shared by two differing fields, but distinct from them. A knot is thus the product of overlapping but distinct fields. If all the shared affects should dissolve or be redirected, the knot is destroyed. Its circulation exists only on the condition of the other fields that support it. It has nothing to do with essential or accidental properties. Knots are simply the practical affects produced by kinetic overlap. If a fold is unfolded, the knot is loosened; if a new fold is added, it is strengthened. When the kinetic qualities that create the knot are gone, the knot is gone. Thus, knots can appear and disappear as flows fold and unfold.

The fundamental question of kinomenology is not linguistic, conceptual, or indexical, such as "What is x?" This kind of question tries to determine the intrinsic relations of the thing before the thing has folded these relations. The question should instead be material, practical, and kinetic: What can it *do*? How can it *move*? Being is nothing but movements—flowing, folding, and the knotting together of different fields across shared folds. To describe a thing is simply to identify its kinetic capacities and the field of circulation that orders it. The more folds it shares with other circulations, the greater the degree of connection or entanglement between them.

Fields of circulation are knotted together, but they also produce a knot or new field that occurs only as the intra-action between the fields.[2] A knot is like a dance in which two fields directly coordinate their motions around a few shared capacities. The knot is not an interaction between two separate individual fields, but rather their mutual transformation: the entangled dance of their motion. Both fields thus undergo a mutual transformation by coordinating their motions. Instead of two or more fields, the knot becomes a single field with two or more *dimensions*, or pathways.

Knots also make it possible for fields of circulation to morph or change their patterns of motion without changing the number of shared junctions or crossings. As long as the morphisms or movements in the circulations do not disjoin from the shared junctions, the two fields remain knotted. However, as circulatory fields change and move, their flows and folds may move either closer to or farther away from one another, forming different kinotopological "neighborhoods" or proximities. Kinotopological neighborhoods may change, but the number of shared folds will remain the same in the knot. In other words, knots are what allow composite sensations and things to persist in their composition without dissipating, even when they are moved around or morphed. The organs of a body, for example, are tightly knotted fields of circulation insofar as they share many of the same kinetic capacities of DNA, electrochemical connection through the nervous system, blood flow, oxygen, and so on, but they also remain distinct in important ways. They can also be moved around and changed to some degree without becoming unknotted from the body.

Shared junctions in the knotted circulations are shared sensations as well as points of bifurcation where a flow from one circulatory system can pass over into another circulatory system. This makes it possible for one circulatory system to drain all the flows from another. Fields of circulation are thus capable of consuming and being consumed by others. Consumption

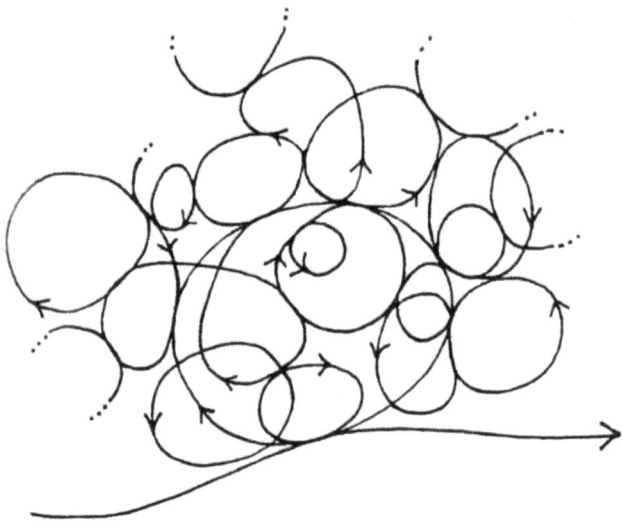

Figure 12.2 Knotwork
Source: Mae-Wan Ho, "Circular Thermodynamics of Organisms and Sustainable Systems," *Systems Review* 1.3 (2013): 30–49, http://www.mdpi.com/2079-8954/1/3/30/htm.

occurs when all the flows, folds, and eventually knots between the fields are undone. When two or more knotted fields remain stable, there is a kinetic equality of circulation. When one expands at another's expense, there is an inequality in production and consumption.

Ecologies, for example, are also tightly knotted woven knotworks (see Figure 12.2). In every ecology there is a general economy of motion—a movement of consumption, production, and equality. There are predators, prey, and equals. An invasive species can consume large parts of an ecosystem by overpopulating it, but overpopulation can also cause an imbalance and even the self-destruction of the overpopulating species. In this way there is a political ecology of nonlinear expansion and expulsion, of knotting and unknotting.[3] Knotworks can thus be quite complex.

EXAMPLE 2: ZAPATISMO

The more shared capacities two or more circulations have, the more ways in which it is possible for them to interact and function together—the stronger their knot, in other words. Continuing the political example from the previous chapters, Zapatismo has created a kinopolitical knot in the form of a global and mutual solidarity movement. In Chiapas, the Zapatistas have created their own regional field of political circulation called "Zapatismo," defined by the various folds and conjunctions described in the previous chapters. In addition to the regional circulation of this field, however, the Zapatistas have also knotted it together with a number of other political fields through global gatherings like the Intercontinental *Encuentros* for Humanity and against Neoliberalism.

The aim of the first *Encuentro* (Encounter) was to gather the "minorities of the world: the indigenous, youth, women, homosexuals, lesbians, people of color, immigrants, workers, peasants, etc.,"[4] and create a space in which they could share their struggles and create bridges or shared junctions of mutual global solidarity. Here some of the first knots were created, such as the Committees in Solidarity with the Zapatista Rebellion, and charged with the further organization of more *Encuentros* on the five continents—Europe, Asia, America, Africa, and Oceania—in the coming years. The closing remarks of this first *Encuentro* (Second Declaration of La Realidad) defined two central aims of this new knotwork. The first was to make a collective network of all singular struggles and resistances:

> This intercontinental network of resistance, recognizing differences and acknowledging similarities, will search to find itself with other resistances around the world. This intercontinental network of resistance will be the medium in which distinct resistances may support one another. This intercontinental network of resistance is not an organizing structure; it doesn't have a central head or decision maker; it has no central command or hierarchies. We are the network, all of us who resist.[5]

The second aim was to create an intercontinental network of alternative communication among all struggles and resistances that would "search to weave the channels (*tejer los canales*) so that words may travel all the roads (*camine todos los caminos*) that resist . . . [and] will be the medium by which distinct resistances communicate with one another."[6]

In 1997 the Second *Encuentro* was held in southern Spain, drawing more than three thousand activists from more than fifty countries. It was here that the plans originated for the creation of an offshoot group, the Peoples' Global Action (PGA), in order to "move beyond debate and exchange and propose action campaigns against neoliberalism, worldwide."[7] Beginning in 1998, the PGA organized a series of direct actions and interventions in various global elite summits (G7, WTO, and so on) that are now identified as the alter-globalization movement. Over the years the many similar forums on global resistance—the World Social Forum (2001–present), regional social forums, and so on—have all emphasized the core proposals made at the First *Encuentro*: horizontal (nonhierarchical) organization and global alternative communications without centralization.

Kinopolitically, the *Encuentros* were gathering sites where different fields of political struggle could determine which of their folds were actually the same folds and which were different, and to coordinate their movements through communication. This intercontinental knotwork was not itself an "organizing structure," as they say, because it was not a *nested relation* of hierarchical fields but rather an *overlapping relation* of horizontal knots. This is the kinetic meaning of "recognizing differences and acknowledging similarities."

One of these important political similarities was the use of consensus decision-making as a deliberative process. Because all the groups at the *Encuentros* used consensus, they then began using this same method in their own fields of circulation. Similar practices were also knotted together, such as the use of spokescouncils; the wearing of ski masks; nonviolent resistance; direct democracy; and the equality of ecological, feminist, queer, racial, and economic concerns in revolutionary practice. The social affects of dignity, justice, exploitation, and oppression were also shared to varying degrees. All the social practices and affects that the different global justice groups shared or began to share at the *Encuentros* are the common folds between them that make the knots.

The resulting kinopolitical structure of shared affects or knots with the Zapatistas is called Zapatismo. This is why the Zapatistas say that "anyone can become a Zapatista." Any field of political circulation can attend these global gatherings and share some kinetic practices or knots with the groups there. The resulting new field of circulation or knot that grew out of the shared folds of numerous global justice groups was eventually called the alter-globalization movement.

Knotting is simply the coordinated operation of the same fold of motion in a distinct but entangled field. The original organizers of the PGA, such as David Graeber, for example, had worked with the Zapatistas directly and introduced the same consensus process into the different field of the Occupy movement. There is thus a direct and kinetically coordinated historical connection. Quakers also use consensus, but there is no shared junction in the knotted struggle against capitalism because there is no direct kinetic connection or coordination.

Since all folds are singular and defined practically, shared junctions must serve the same kinetic function in both fields, in this case as a coordinated way to deliberate in the struggle against political oppression and global capitalism. For example, the alter-globalization movement is only a kinetic knot insofar as the groups within it *act* as if their interlocking oppressions are *actually the same* shared oppressions, such that a common battle can be *waged* against capital. In other words, knotting is not a nominalist or merely formal similarity, but a kinetic and practical one. The alter-globalization movement emerged because people were actually oppressed by the same structures and aimed at emancipation through some of the same acts.

As the Zapatistas describe it, knotting is a horizontal activity made possible only by those who act on and reproduce the knots. When the Zapatistas say that they "will search to weave the channels (*tejer los canales*) so that words may travel all the roads (*camine todos los caminos*) that resist," they are describing the weaving of knots into the flows of circulation. These are real roads. Political movements require actual movement. A knotwork of communication must be set up in which the fields of struggle can coordinate the shared folds of their actions or motions and thereby move or travel along the same kinetic paths (practices and affects). The kinetic knots of solidarity are not unilateral, like soviet or colonial solidarity, but multilateral, because multiple fields circulate, traveling the same road back and forth and coordinating their actions. When the Zapatistas say they are trying to create "a world in which many worlds fit," they are not referring to a single revolutionary program, but to a knotted global network of coordinated solidarity: a horizontality of knots. The more knots are formed, the stronger the movement. These are practical kinetic knots based on the repeated use of shared collective events or actions of the *Encuentros*, as well as subsequent global gatherings where knots could be directly coordinated and plans made for their collective struggle.

THE SCIENCE OF KNOTS

The concept of kinetic knotting, however, cannot be strictly identified with the mathematical concept of knots developed in topology. While there are some similarities, there are also some important differences. First, both concepts aim to account for the creation of order and morphisms in continuous systems, but the main difference is that mathematical knots are defined as conceptually "closed loops."

Each closed loop is defined by a series of crossings under or over itself. When the loop can be continuously morphed without changing its number of crossings, it is a knot. A mathematical knot is thus a closed, abstract, and immobile concept. This is quite different from the theory of kinetic knots described above. A kinetic knot is an open loop occurring in the middle of a

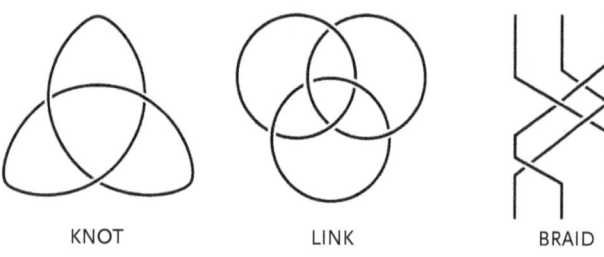

Figure 12.3 Knot, Link, and Braid

flow extending without beginning or end. It has at least one entrance and one exit through which flows conjoin or disjoin. Mathematical knots, however, are abstractions. Unlike kinetic knots, mathematical knots have no entropy or dissipation. Kinetic knots are closer to, but again not identical to, mathematical "links," interlocking circles, or open-ended "braids" (see Figure 12.3).

Second, kinetic knots are not defined by their crossings over or under, but by their points of intersection and bifurcation. Mathematical knots have no intersection—this is what defines them *as knots*. This makes it quite difficult to establish anything more than a mere surface similarity between actual flows in dynamic systems defined by superposition and diffraction and purely abstract, closed-loop, nonintersecting mathematical knots. This does not mean that knots in a physical flow cannot cross over and under one another, and therefore be categorized similarly to many mathematical knot diagrams. However, without the ability to theorize intersection, bifurcation, and movement, mathematical knots remain unhelpful for theorizing real fluid systems that can intersect, conjoin, bifurcate, and diffract.[8]

Third, kinetic knot theory is distinct from the nineteenth-century physicist William Thomson's (Lord Kelvin's) vortex theory of knotted atoms. Kelvin, the inventor of knot theory, argued that atoms emerged from swirling ether knotted into immutable structures. *Being and Motion* does not claim that being qua being is pure ether or any other substance, only that "being flows." Furthermore, Kelvin treated these knotted flows as classically stable fluids, which we now know to be fundamentally unstable at the quantum level. This makes his atomic models of unchanging knot patterns untenable. Kelvin wanted his atomic circulations to be eternal, but since flows are open-ended and always subject to disjunction and pedesis, his model fails.[9]

UNKNOTS

An *unknot* occurs when the knot between two fields is undone. Unknotting is thus the process of co-circulatory transformation. However, not all unknotting produces the same kind of transformation in kinetic circulation. There are four kinds of unknotting.

Destructive Unknotting

The first kind of unknotting is destructive. Unknotting is destructive when it unfolds all the junctions that sustained the knot. In this case the capacities that sustained a kinetic becoming are no longer actively expressed. Furthermore, an unknot can also be destructive if a flow becomes disjoined from circulation but does not intersect with any other flows or produce any new confluence or fold.

Expansive Unknotting

The second kind of unknotting is expansive. In this case the knot between two or more circulations is simply unfolded and quickly refolded at a different point in the circulation in order to expand or add a new circulation. The knot changes but only in order to expand its regimes of circulation. It may even disjoin certain flows or folds entirely in order to incorporate them further along in a process of expansion by expulsion.

Evental Unknotting

The third kind of unknotting is evental. In this case not only are all the folds that sustained the knot unfolded, but one or more flows disjoin from the co-circulation entirely and intersect or create a confluence elsewhere between two or more flows. In this case a new event is produced from the unknotting process, opening up the possibility of an entirely new order of motion. However, a new event or even a constellation is not sufficient on its own for sustaining a new regime of motion.

Constructive Unknotting

The fourth kind of unknotting is constructive. Unknotting is constructive when it has not only unfolded the junctions that sustain a knot and created a confluence of disjoined flows, but also when this confluence becomes the basis of a new distribution of motion and its affects are stabilized by a new series of folds and circulation. Constructive unknotting occurs when a flow that previously did not move together with the other folds between two more knotted circulations disjoins from the circulations and now moves with a maximum degree of fluxion as the condition or field of a new distribution of motion.

EXAMPLE 2: ZAPATISMO

The kinetic operation of unknotting can be elucidated in four trajectories of Zapatismo. Just as there are knots of solidarity, so are there knots of oppression. The Zapatistas confronted a knot of kinopolitical oppression in Chiapas. This knot was the product of the intersection of at least two circulations: the Mexican government and paramilitary forces in Chiapas. These two fields are knotted together by at least two shared folds: the active capacity of putting down indigenous resistance in Chiapas, and the defense of the so-called private property of the ranchers who occupy indigenous land there. The unknotting of this knot of oppression was achieved in several ways.

First, the knot of kinopolitical oppression in Chiapas was *destroyed*. The initial aim of the Zapatista uprising in 1994 was to destroy or unfold two major capacities of kinopower that bound the Mexican government and local paramilitary forces. The Zapatistas took back the land that belonged to them and expelled those who put down their revolt. They succeeded, though only briefly. Additionally, the first communique of the Zapatistas announced that the group would disjoin itself from the political knot completely through the military capture of the Mexican state. Unfortunately, the Mexican people did not support this. Had the Zapatistas pursued this revolutionary course anyway, they may have succeeded in destroying the regional knot of oppression in Chiapas, but they would also have destroyed themselves if they attacked the state capital without popular support.

Second, the 1994 uprising in Chiapas may have unknotted the circulations of Mexican and paramilitary power in Chiapas temporarily, but they also inadvertently created the opportunity for an *expansion* of state and paramilitary kinopower to reknot themselves together at new junctions. For instance, indigenous groups directly or indirectly in support of Zapatismo became the targets of coordinated attacks by paramilitary groups directly or indirectly supported by the Mexican government. The most dramatic example is the Acteal massacre, the December 22, 1997, killing by the paramilitary group Mascara Roja (Red Mask) of an indigenous pacifist group, Las Abejas (The Bees). Forty-five supporters of the

Zapatistas died, including women and children. Mexican soldiers knowingly allowed the massacre to occur, and even tried to hide the evidence by washing the blood off the church walls. By unknotting oppression in one place it was intensified and reknotted in another—the intensified expansion of (para)military control in the region.

Third, the confluence of disjoined Marxist vanguardists and indigenous peasants also created a new *event*: the EZLN 1994 uprising. This eventual intersection not only unfolded the knots that held together local governance in Chiapas; it also created a new intersection of kinopower: Zapatismo. This new event was produced from the unknotting process and opened up the possibility of a new order of motion. However, on its own this new eventual unknotting was not sufficient for sustaining a new regime of motion in the region. In fact, the initial gains of the uprising in 1994 and the San Andrés Accords were slowly taken back by the government. Without further construction, Zapatismo could not be sustained as a regional power on the basis of this single event alone.

Fourth, after years of struggle the Zapatistas were able to build from the 1994 event a new field of circulation that connected this first event to a second: the creation of the *Juntas de Buen Gobierno* in 2003. Thus, the constellation of events in 1994 and 2003 not only unfolded the regional folds of knotted kinopower, but they also disjoined from them to produce a new constellation that could be sustained through a new field of revolutionary affects. The constructive unknotting of Zapatismo took the previously invisible flows of the situation in Chiapas, the indigenous peoples and vanguardists, and disjoined them from the knotted field of oppression in order to create a new revolutionary field of affects.

HISTORICAL TYPOLOGY OF FIELDS

Not all fields of circulation follow the same kinotopological pattern of motion. To date, there have been at least four major kinotopological types of fields that have risen to dominance at different periods in history: centripetal, centrifugal, tensional, and elastic.[10] Each of these types of fields describes the kinotopology of motion across social, aesthetic, scientific, and ontological domains of the period.[11] The historical exposition of this typology across social, aesthetic, and scientific domains is reserved for other works, since this book will focus strictly on the historical practice of ontology. In hopes of signposting for the reader the main types of kinetic fields dealt with in this book (and others), a general description of each is provided below.

Centripetal Fields

The first type of field is defined by centripetal motion. Centripetal fields are defined by a motion moving from their periphery more or less toward their center, without necessarily creating a center (see Figure 12.4). Centripetal circulation is produced when a flow is folded over itself in two or more junctions that remain largely at the periphery of the field that circulates between them. By moving a series of junctions and circuits at the periphery of a field, centripetal circulation creates one big field in which all the folds are included and increasingly concentrated. In this way the chaos of pedetic flows can be captured and ordered into a single and undifferentiated interior surface. This surface is made possible by a curvilinear motion that is captured from the periphery and turned inward toward a centripetal basin of attraction.

Centrifugal Fields

The second type of field is defined by centrifugal motion. Centrifugal fields move predominantly from the center of the field to the periphery (see Figure 12.5). Centrifugal circulation is produced when a single megajunction emerges at the center of the field and begins to redirect all motion through this center fold. The megajunction becomes a radial point through which all flows move and through which all flows must pass; the megajunction becomes a radial fold that regulates and directs all the internal motions of the field. Movement is then redirected from the center outward to the

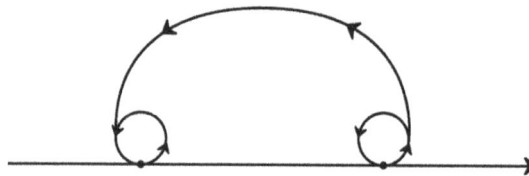

Figure 12.4 Centripetal Field

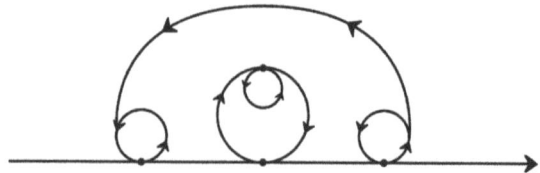

Figure 12.5 Centrifugal Field

periphery. As flows are redirected from the center to the periphery, this periphery makes possible a conjoined movement of rotation around the center.

Tensional Fields

The third type of field is defined by tensional motion. Tensional fields conjoin their folds and circuits together through a system of rigid links (see Figure 12.6). These rigid conjunctions keep the folds together and apart from one another. In this way rigid conjunctions decenter the motion of centrifugal circulations while also strengthening their connection. Kinetically, fields are relatively autonomous orders, with their own distributions of motion, but since their movements are held together by the tension of a rigid conjunction, the motion of one fold becomes restricted by the motion of the other. Tensional motion occurs when there are two or more folds or circulations whose movement is inelastically relativized by the others, like the movement of the human arm. The human arm is composed of several radial joints connected by several bone linkages. Each ball joint rotates in its own orbit with its own degrees of freedom, while the rigid linkage between them both decenters and strengthens their movement. This motion makes possible a *linked rotation* between multiple folds in the same field or multiple fields themselves.

Elastic Fields

The fourth type of field is one of elastic motion. Elastic circulation conjoins the folds and circuits of a field together through a system of elastic links (see Figure 12.7). These elastic conjunctions allow its folds to move together but also to return to their previous position or degree of flux after a contraction

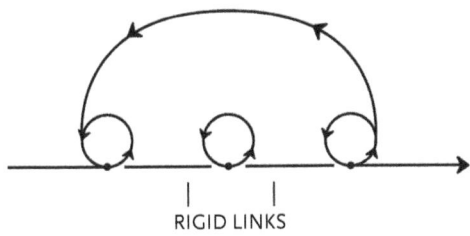

Figure 12.6 Tensional Field

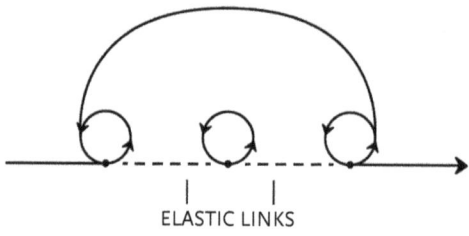

Figure 12.7 Elastic Field

or expansion of their motion. In contrast to the rigid conjunctions that constrain the motion of tensional fields, elastic conjunctions are flexible and allow the field to oscillate back and forth, expanding and contracting, without becoming disjoined.

CONCLUSION

This chapter concludes the kinetic exposition of the minimal necessary features for being in motion. If being can truly be said to be in motion today more than ever before, it must at least be capable of flowing, folding, and circulating across a field. The theory of motion gives the ontology of motion its own proper concepts. Without them, motion appears to be only a derivative or even illusory construction of more fundamental, spatial, eternal, dynamic, or temporal processes. The theory of motion thus also provides an original conceptual framework in order to understand the historical ontological primacy of motion across social, aesthetic, and scientific domains—dealt with in the companion volumes.

However, the theory of motion put forward in Part II of Book I remains ontologically insufficient in an important way—it remains entirely *conceptual*. I have so far presented the kinetic *concepts* of flow, fold, and field largely abstracted from their detailed historical and material emergence. For this reason, what can be said of kinetic operations at this level is extremely minimal and general. The theory of motion tells us nothing about how these concepts are actually deployed in the movement of ontological practice itself. Being is motion, but it does not always appear as such in ontological description. Thus, it remains to be explained what role kinography itself plays in the historical distribution of the motion of being. This is the aim of Book II.

INTRODUCTION II
Kinos, Logos, Graphos

Book II is divided into four parts corresponding to the four dominant historical regimes of motion that define ontological practice. Each historical regime marks the emergence and rise to dominance of a certain descriptive name for being in Western ontological practice. In the prehistoric period, being is predominantly characterized by space, in the ancient period by eternity, in the medieval period by force, and in the modern period by time. These are not the only names for being during these periods, nor are they progressive practices in the descriptive development of being as such. They are simply the prevailing descriptive names of being *for their time*. Moreover, they continue to be major names of being today, just as their inscriptive techniques remain the major forms of contemporary ontological practice.

The purpose of this historical periodization, to remind the reader, is twofold. The first aim is to kinetically and materially demystify Western ontology—to show that all the great names of being are not absolute ones, but rather historical ones directly coordinated with the dominant kinetic patterns of their own material practices of inscription. Accordingly, these four historical periods have been chosen not because they are the only periods for which such descriptions have ever been given but because these are the periods during which each name is most widely described and inscribed as the most ontologically fundamental structure of being.

The second aim is to extract from each period a properly kinetic theory of its dominant name for being. This allows us to demonstrate a clear historical ontological primacy of motion capable of describing all the previous names of being. It allows us to reinterpret the dominant history of Western ontology using one of the most systematically subordinated concepts of this tradition: motion. As such, it allows us to reinterpret the history of Western ontology as more than a series of great names, such as space, eternity, force, and time but as a mixture of material-kinetic patterns, which persist in various degrees up to the present.

In other words, the conditions for contemporary ontological practice, in which this book is itself engaged, are to be located in the admixture of descriptive names and inscriptive techniques found throughout the history of ontology. If we want to provide an ontology of our present, or an immanent critique of our own ontological practice, this history is absolutely crucial. Without it, ontology remains mystified and mystifying.

Most importantly, though, the following historical analysis of these four major periods and their dominant names allows us to develop original kinetic theories of space, eternity, force, and time for use in the broader philosophy of motion. In other words, Book II is not *just* a history—although it is a history, and perhaps the only one, or at least the most systematic one, of the philosophy of movement to date. More fundamentally, however, it is an ontological and kinetic reinterpretation of four of the most dominant categories in Western ontology: space, eternity, force, and time. While traditional ontologies provide largely formal and ahistorical definitions of space, eternity, force, and time, *Being and Motion* adopts instead a robustly historical materialist approach grounded in the uniquely kinetic study of ontological practice itself. It thus offers new definitions of space, eternity, force, and time. Without such a historical method, ontology remains purely formal, sterile, and idealist. A truly material-kinetic ontology must, therefore, emerge not from the contemplative mind that thinks of being as becoming or process *as such*, but from the concrete material practices that co-condition contemporary ontological practice itself. Since these conditions are resolutely historical ones, ontology must also be historical ontology.

The central argument of Book II is that each of these historical periods, along with its dominant description and inscription of being, follows a precise kinetic pattern that allows us to put forward an original kinetic ontology of space, eternity, force, and time. The structure of Book II is ordered accordingly. Each major ontological practice during its historical period has its own part, which is further divided into three sections, each corresponding to a kinetic dimension of its ontological practice: kinos, logos, and graphos.

KINOS

The first section of each part of Book II draws on the conceptual framework developed in Book I in order to provide a purely *kinomenological definition* of each historical name of being. In other words, each section offers an interpretation of each historical name of being from the ontological vantage point of motion. Instead of interpreting each name as a metaphysical entity, it treats it rather as an ordered coappearance of motion or kinomena. Kinomenology is the analysis of the transcendental kinetic conditions under which the being of motion comes to appear. While the kinology or theory of motion in Book I provides us with the general conceptual framework necessary to understand the minimal historico-logical operations that must be the case in order for being to be in motion, the kinomenology of Book II provides us with the historical typology of fields necessary to understand the specific regimes of circulation that order and distribute the coappearance of ontological practice.

Being flows, folds, and circulates in fields, but it has not always appeared as such. Being has been described in many ways. However, if being is in motion and motion is not derived from some more primary determination (space, eternity, force, or time), then it is first necessary to understand why being has consistently appeared as primarily something *other than motion*. Furthermore, if being is motion, it is then necessary to understand how it is that motion—its flows, folds, and fields—could have moved in such a way as to produce the appearance of at least four different dominant ontological determinations of being in Western history: spatial, eternal, dynamic, and temporal.

The first section of each part of Book II is dedicated to a purely kinomenological answer to this question. Although these sections occur first in each part, they are actually derived from the subsequent historical chapters as a purely conceptual synthesis of the concrete history of ontology. They are strategically placed prior to the historical chapters, however, to help the reader identify the existence of a simple kinetic pattern among the more complex historical details of their description and inscription. Therefore, these patterns of motion are not a priori forms applied to history but rather derived from it.

Kinomenology is the analysis of the different fields of motion that condition and order the coappearance of motion *as something other than motion*. Being has always been in motion, but only now has it become possible to understand how this became the case. Such a thesis cannot simply be asserted as a conceptually coherent fact—or this book would have been much shorter—it must be demonstrated by a history of our present. Such a history not only reveals the composite fields of motion that persist in the present from the past, but also retroactively discovers the kinomenological regimes that obscured the historical motion of being.

This does not mean that the history of Western ontology has been a history of "illusion" or the "forgetting of being."[1] Plato was not "wrong" in his de/inscription of eternity as ontologically primary. Rather, his philosophical practice itself participated in the active co-constitution of a real field of circulation, a certain kinomenological order or pattern of motion that really appeared as "eternity." This is not a nominalism. The name "eternity" is really and materially part of a real pattern of graphic circulation bound up with other political, scientific, and aesthetic practices of the time. Even nominalism is itself a performative kinetic action and thus part of a regime of real ontological practice.

Just like the concept of motion, the concept of eternity should not be interpreted as a strictly ontological thesis about the nature of being qua being. Eternity should instead be interpreted as a kinomenological thesis regarding the emergence of a certain historically dominant field or regime of motion that came to appear as eternal motion in the ancient world: circular and centrifugal motion. In this way kinomenology is not a history of the conceptual representations of being or how being has been thought or forgotten but rather a history of how being has really circulated in certain historical patterns of motion.

In this sense, Book II is not a historical constructivism but a *historical realism*. The rise to dominance of each new name for being is not just another field of circulation for humans, or simply a way that humans think or talk about being. Reality actually moved differently in each period. In the "long Anthropocene" the human transformation of reality is inseparable from the transformation of nature itself. Changes in the movements of human culture really changed the movements of nature.

This is not, however, because ontological practice simply causes the rest of reality to move differently, or vice versa. Rather, one of the most interesting theses of kinetic philosophy is that the fields of circulation across multiple domains of social, aesthetic, scientific, and ontological motion in the West *all begin to follow the same pattern or regime of motion* around the same periods of history. Kinetic philosophy, therefore, does not put forward a metaphysical argument about why this happened, nor does it posit a reductionistic argument about how one field caused the others to move differently. It simply presents a historical ontology that describes these *real kinetic resonances* or *synchronies* without attributing any particular set of reductionist or metaphysical causalities between them. Thus, in each historical period of Western ontological practice, there is *really* a different kind of pattern of motion at work.

Based on the underlying kinomenological structure of each historical field of ontological practice laid out in the first section of each part, the second and third sections then move on to interpret the kinographic structure of this historical field—its descriptions and inscriptions. The second section focuses on the history of ontological *description*—the logos of being, while the third focuses on the history of ontological *inscription*—the graphos of being. Together the logos and graphos of being define the historical practice of ontology. As a practice, ontology is kinetic and constitutes the flip side of the ontology of movement (kinology): the movement of ontology (kinography). The "movement of ontology" is the kinetic act of description and inscription that defines ontological practice.

LOGOS

The second section of each part theorizes the historico-ontological descriptions or logos of being and deals primarily with the textual canon of mythological, cosmological, theological, and phenomenological writings. However, it does so in an original way. Instead of studying the history of ontological descriptions as representations of being qua being, each second section seeks to identify the *implicit and explicit kinetic structure* deployed by the dominant logos or description of being during each historical period.

Instead of studying the history of ontological practice as a series of texts that represents the *thought* of a thinker, which in turn represents the nature of *being qua being*, each second section treats the historical descriptions of being as immanent sign systems whose internal relations, both explicit and implicit, describe or presuppose a certain pattern of motion of an ontological practice. In other words, ontological texts are not treated in Book II as representing anything outside the texts themselves, but as enacting or performing an internally consistent set of textual and semiotic patterns that rely on implicit and explicit kinetic regimes.

For example, in ontological description, certain words or signs are said to be necessarily related to others by motion. In ancient cosmology, the "sphere" of being is said to be necessarily related to the perfection of its circular motion. The question of Book II is not whether being is actually spherical but what pattern of motion is explicitly described and implicitly presupposed in the ontological description itself (in this case centrifugal motion), and what historical resonance or synchrony it has with the technology of inscription shown in the subsequent section.

Kinetic philosophy is therefore not interested in the symbolic or representational aspects of these descriptions or what they mean either to the people who invented them or to people today. Nor is it concerned with the metaphysical, psychological, or evolutionary theories that attempt to explain the causal origin of these descriptions or what they tell us about human consciousness, our imagination, and so on.

Kinetic philosophy is simply interested in how these ontologies describe different patterns of motion hitherto unnoticed. Ontological description is not studied here as a psychic or anthropological structure that represents reality, as mythologists such as Joseph Campbell argue.[2] For *Being and Motion*, such structures are only possible under the conditions of real historical and material movements. In other words, the sections on the logos of ontology perform an immanent critique of the kinetic structure implicitly described by ontology and not an *interpretation* of the structure as it refers to or symbolizes something else, like human minds, psychoanalytic structures, evolutionary biology, and so on. The question is not empirical— "Were there actually eternal gods then or not, what were they like, and why did humans invent them?"—but rather kinetic— "How must things have moved such that being could appear to ontological practice as eternal gods?"

The thesis put forward more generally in Book II is that the kinomenological, descriptive, and inscriptive structures of each major historical period follow the same pattern of motion. In this way, ontological description can be studied not as an arbitrary sign system but as a historical sign system of specific kinetic signs in resonance or sync with their material technology of inscription. Kinography is the study and classification of the immanent relations used to tie kinetic signs together in a particular order on an inscribed surface of circulation. In other words, kinography gives systematicity to the hidden kinetic structures used in the history of ontological practice.

Unfortunately, ontological description has tended to explain away its use of kinetic vocabulary as mere metaphor. The reduction of motion to the status of so-called descriptive "metaphor" in ontological practice has been used as a weapon against taking matter and motion seriously. Ontology describes patterns of motion, but at the same time it cautions us not to take these descriptions too literally. For example, Hegel systematically uses the word "movement" (*bewegung*) to describe the logical movement of the dialectic. The formal logic of dialectics, however, has no materiality, and it thus makes no sense to say that it can be *in motion*, as Marx rightly comments.[3]

Ontologists have tended to borrow kinetic and material descriptors and apply them to immobile and immaterial concepts as a way to make it *seem* as if the metaphysical notions of space, eternity, force, and time are real moving things while at the same time holding on to them as immobile ideas and causal explanations of motion. Through the use of metaphor, kinetic descriptions have been used in ontological descriptions to define the semiotic relations of beings, but at the same time they have been used to disavow or repress motion as "merely metaphorical" in order to maintain the pure, idealist, formal, logical, or immaterial character of being qua being—untainted by some particular kinetic or material relations.[4] Ontologists have thus used metaphor in the way vampires drink the blood of their victims. Their own immortal living death is sustained only by secretly draining movement in the middle of the night from the circulating blood of living bodies. They treat metaphor as Aristotle does, as a process of "giving the thing a name that belongs to something else."

However, the dualism between metaphor and literality that ontologists desire cannot be sustained, in part because metaphor *is itself a motion*. In fact, the word "metaphor" comes from the Greek word μεταφορά, *metaphorá*, meaning "to transfer or carry over." Based on this definition, metaphor is necessarily in literal motion, and literal motion is, qua motion, also metaphorical. Therefore, one cannot say that the movement of immaterial concepts is somehow metaphorical without implying a literal relation of motion required to produce the metaphor in the first place. The very act of using the metaphor presupposes the mobility of the person who performs the connection. Kinetic metaphor is therefore not a rhetorical structure of ontological description to be ignored in favor of the "real" descriptive content of the text as a representation of being qua being. The kinetic metaphors used by ontologists are bound up with the literal content of the description (logos) itself. Thus, the whole process of ontological description is shot through by a repressed kinetic structure that this book hopes to reveal.[5]

GRAPHOS

The third section of each part of Book II interprets the prevailing historical name of being according to the material techniques used to *inscribe* ontological descriptions. In these sections, each dominant name for being is examined from the perspective of the kinetics of four dominant graphic regimes that are coordinated with the ontological descriptions of the previous sections. In historical order, these major graphic regimes are the speaking of being (phonography), the writing of being (scriptography), the codexing of being (bibliography), and the typing of being (typography).

The aim and method of these sections is twofold. The first is to provide a description of the kinetic structure of the dominant recording surfaces of ontological inscription. If being is nothing but matter in motion, then all ontology must have a material-kinetic structure of inscription that can be studied. This is accomplished through a detailed historical and material analysis of the kinetic relations of each technology of inscription during its period of emergence and dominance: its component parts, how they function, what they are made of, how they combine with the mobility of the human body, and so on. This is possible because the body of the ontologist is not discontinuous with or outside of the kinetic process of ontological inscription. There is no such thing as a thinking of being qua being without the kinetic process of inscription. Human thought does not transcend all the material-kinetic flows that constitute it—it is embedded in them.

The surfaces of inscription are not limited to the biological body that supports the brain—they also include the technical objects that conjoin kinetically with the body. For example, the human body's upright posture and oral musculature are technical objects of linguistic thought, just as systems of visual markings on durable surfaces are technical objects of written thought. Thinking is thus not simply "supported" by an external material-kinetic object as if thought were something independent from the object that supported it, nor are technical objects mere "extensions" of a preexisting mind.[6] The brain, the body, and its inorganic tools are all part of *the same kinetic process*.[7] The study of ontological inscription provided in Book II is the study of the whole kinographic process of recording required by ontological practice.

The second aim and method of these sections is to show the historical synchrony of the technologies of ontological inscription with the ontological descriptions of the same period. The thesis here is that although the kinetic sign system of markings (description) and the recording surface (inscription) bear no formal resemblance to each other, they both follow the same kinetic patterns during the same historical periods. This is not due to any direct causality or even mutual causality between independent parts but to a concurrent kinetic change in the whole field of historical reality.[8] These regimes of motion are therefore neither strictly general or particular, human or inhuman, but rather hybrid regimes in which the historical inscriptions of individual human ontologists are entangled and inseparable from their media. Inscriber and inscription are media for each other. They are two sides of the same kinetic process.

The method of the third section then is not to show how the technologies of inscription caused, determined, or shaped a way of thinking about or describing being, nor is it to show how the human desire for progressively new technologies made possible new technological invention. The question of whether the invention of written language, for example, gave birth to the concept of eternity, or whether the description of eternity was created by social hierarchy, or whether it was organized armies that gave birth to writing, which in turn gave birth to the cosmologies of eternal father sky-gods, is poorly posed. The search for a direct and linear causality in history is a metaphysical one.[9]

Thus, the method pursued by Book II is simply to describe the kinetic structure of ontological description and ontological inscription, and then demonstrate by comparison how both follow the same pattern of motion conceptually synthesized for the reader in the first section of each part. The existence of this kinetic pattern then gives us a historical foundation for a kinetic ontology of space, eternity, force, and time.

PLAN OF BOOK II

Book II provides a kinomenological and kinographic analysis of four dominant regimes of motion to which ontological practice has given the historical names of space, eternity, force, and time. However, these four regimes and their corresponding concepts are not necessarily the only regimes, nor are they even the exclusive regimes of motion at any given time. None of these concepts is more advanced or developed than the others; there is no chronology, development, or teleology. Together, the history of these three intersecting practices not only defines the material conditions of contemporary ontology but also provides the descriptive foundations for a kinetic ontology of space, eternity, force, and time.

The remainder of this book is organized into four parts, each analyzing the dominant patterns or fields of ordered motion in ontological practice during four major historical periods, and through them it develops its own original ontological concepts. Part I begins in the Neolithic period (10,000 BCE–5,000 BCE) by analyzing the rise to dominance of a certain centripetal, inwardly directed regime of motion that appears ontologically as space and graphically in the material invention of speech. Part II continues in the ancient period (5000 BCE–500 CE) by analyzing the rise to dominance of a certain centrifugal, outwardly directed regime of motion that appears ontologically as eternity and graphically in the material invention of writing. Part III demonstrates the rise to dominance during the long medieval and early-modern periods (500 CE–1700 CE) of a certain tensional, rigidly linked, rotational regime of motion that appears ontologically as force and graphically in the material invention of the codex or book. Part IV concludes with the modern period (1800 CE–2000 CE) by analyzing the rise to dominance of a certain elastic or oscillating regime of motion that appears ontologically as time and graphically in the material invention of typography.

Each of these parts is subdivided into three sections: kinomenology (kinos), ontology (logos), and kinography (graphos). Although I have separated them analytically to highlight their different dimensions, the three are inseparably part of the same process from which the ontology of motion derives its theories of space, eternity, force, and time. This is possible because the material-kinetic conditions of the invention of these ideas tells us something about the structure of these ontological descriptors themselves—even if ontologists are unaware of this pattern. For example, even though it is possible to distinguish between the kinetics of a descriptive structure insofar as it appears under the name "eternity" and the kinetics of its graphic structure insofar as it appears as clay jars, tokens, tablets, and scrolls in the invention of written language, both also share the same field of motion conceptually described in kinomenological terms as centrifugal motion.

Together, the transcendental and materialist-historical study of the kinos, logos, and graphos of ontological practice comprise perhaps one of the strangest investigations in the history of philosophy: a history of ontology in which the *thought* of being is no longer central. This is not the case because human thought is not part of the kinographic process or because it is immaterial but because kinetic ontology is the study of practices of description and inscription, and not ideas about being.[10] The two are materially and historically inseparable, of course, but if we accept that there is no direct or simple causality between logos and graphos, then it becomes possible to analytically separate them as different dimensions of the same continuous kinomenological process, as we will see in the following chapters.

BOOK II
The Motion of Ontology

PART I
Being and Space

I
Kinos

CHAPTER 13
Centripetal Motion

Being is in motion, but motion appears first and foremost historically as space. During the period of time roughly defined as the Neolithic (10,000 BCE–5,000 BCE), movement begins to take on a certain dominant mode of distribution or circulation, defined by an inward trajectory from the periphery toward a center. This centripetal motion is the condition for the dominant description of being's motion as fundamentally spatial. This is not the only type of movement or regime of circulation during this time, only the most dominant one that defines and orders the others.[1] Furthermore, this is not the first appearance of this type of motion in the history of the earth, only the period of time in which this type of motion begins to take on an increasingly dominant function on earth during the early Anthropocene.[2]

The aim of this chapter is to put forward a kinetic theory of space as centripetal motion. However, kinomenological analysis is not anthropological analysis. The *concept* or *experience* of space is a purely anthropological determination of the appearance of motion *for humans*. However, the material-kinetic regime or field of centripetal motion that directs and organizes the flows of matter into the field described as "space" is the real material condition under which Neolithic humans and their technical appendages come to appear together as part of the same historically dominant distribution of motion. The centripetal motion of being is the condition for the ontological description of being as space and its inscription through speech. Centripetal motion is an entirely real and kinetic condition, not a metaphysical concept. Space and speech are simply two material and kinetic expressions of the same regime of centripetal motion.[3]

Part I, "Being and Space," is divided into three sections: the first offers a strictly *kinomenological* theory of space as centripetal motion; the second offers a kinetic analysis of the historically *descriptive* features of space provided by the dominant mythologies of the time; and the third offers a kinetic analysis of the historical technology of *inscription* (speech) within which these descriptions were inscribed.

KINOMENOLOGY OF SPACE

Kinomenologically, being emerges as spatial through a constitutive regime of centripetal motion. Provided below is a materialist and kinetic description of space, but without resorting to the metaphysical postulation of some independent background entity or idea of space.

Centripetal Motion

Being flows, but since it is pedetic, it can also change its trajectory to produce loops or folds in its flow, as we saw in Book I. Centripetal circulation is created when flows begin to curve and fold, increasingly gathering multiple flows together toward a central area. As the flows gather and move increasingly inward from the periphery toward the center, they begin to form a spiral pattern. From this spiral pattern it becomes possible for the continuous flows to bifurcate and intersect themselves between the arms of the spiral. Through additional folds, these intersections can create junctions that bind the loop within the spiral pattern to itself. Once at least two junctions are formed, a basic field of circulation has been established. Now the circulation can support not only the increasing centripetal accumulation of flows that enter it from elsewhere but also the increasing centripetal gathering of subjunctions and conjunctions that populate its center.

For a loop or circulatory accumulation to occur, something must be pulled back toward itself, forming two limit junctions—one at the point of bifurcation where it breaks away from itself, and one at the point of intersection where it returns to itself. Centripetal motion gathers flows from the periphery toward a center and then circulates them there. Without at least some centripetal motion, there can be no field of circulation in general. All the other regimes of circulation include and modulate this basic movement of the accumulation and repetition of flows. By its kinetic definition, a field requires this return to itself: a turn from a continual outgoing

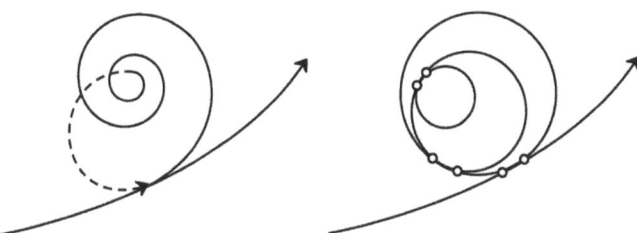

Figure 13.1 Spiral Space

to a generally returning centrality. Once this occurs, it makes possible an infinite number of larger and smaller circulations, all connected together through the continuous spiral arm. This makes possible stable sites of gathering and accumulation. In other words, centripetal motion is the process of spatialization. Motion does not occur in or on a preexisting space, but rather space emerges from a more primary kinetic material pattern of centripetal motion (see Figure 13.1).[4]

Internalization

Centripetal motion produces one of the defining features of space: internalization. The process of internalization is not the same as having an absolute interior or exterior. Space is not a thing that comes already made like a fully completed and enclosed circle with an inside and outside. Such a concept of a pure and complete a priori spatiality is either metaphysically or transcendentally idealist.

Neither of these theories tells us how space is created; they simply posit it as an absolute and necessary concept without history or materiality. This is the case either as an ahistorical pure intuition of human reason, as in Kant, or as a nonhistorical natural determination of being, as in Hegel. In both cases a spatial division within being is presupposed without an explanation of its production. This is why Jean Hyppolite calls space the "first myth of outside and inside."[5] It is the geometrical core at the heart of the most profound metaphysics.[6] The division between being and nonbeing, between mind and body, between being and being-there all rely on and modify this first spatial division—this "implicit geometry which, whether we will or no, confers spatiality upon thought."[7]

However, kinomenology allows us to go one step further in the theorization of space by considering it as a product of a more primary process of material-kinetic folding.[8] Space is a product of matter in motion. Being in motion has no ontological interior and no exterior because the flows that compose it are multiplicities without the totality of an outer shell or finality of an inner core. There are only flows of flows, folds of folds, and fields of fields, all the way down. The *process of internalization* thus occurs only when these flows begin to curve and fold back around themselves to create a division between an interior and exterior of a given loop.[9] This closed-loop circle created by flows is thus a product of curved flows and not a preexisting form. "The very permanence of its form is only the outline of a movement," as Bergson writes.[10] Form is a product of motion: a kinomorphism.[11]

The division in being between inside and outside is therefore not an illusion. Space is not a fiction. Being really is capable of folding and looping over itself into circles, each with its own relative inside and outside, even if being in motion itself remains fundamentally undivided and continuous. This is possible precisely because of the centripetal motion of the flows that gather and fold inward in the pattern of a spiral. The kinomorphic figure of the spiral has no center, only an infinite process of internalization as each fold returns to itself deeper and deeper toward a center without ever reaching it. Centripetal motion is thus centric without having a center. The spiral also has no absolute periphery, only an infinite gathering inward. The inside of the spiral is its outside—they are two sides of the same movement of internalization or folding. Space, as a product of spiral motion, is thus without an absolute center, periphery, inside, outside, top, or bottom.[12]

However, this does not mean that space is without the possibility of local or regional insides and outsides formed by the closing off of loops within the spiral, like a nautilus. In other words, space is both continuous and discrete.[13] Space is smooth insofar as it is the product of a continuous and undivided centripetal movement of accumulation, gathering together various flows, but it is also striated insofar as it brings these flows into regional folds and fields that subordinate the flows to a relative satiability, basin of attraction, and repetition.[14] This is not an absolute binary, opposition, or normative distinction; it is simply a description of two aspects or regions of the same motion. In one movement, a continuous centripetal motion accumulates flows toward a center without dividing itself; in another movement these flows are folded over themselves and bound into a field of circulation capable of stabilizing, renewing, and extending them. Each movement builds off the other without totalizing or synthesizing it. Continuous flows are captured, stabilized, and circulated, but circulations are also disjoined and unknotted only to be circulated elsewhere. There is no negation here because these two types of motion are part of the same process of internalization. One does not necessarily lead to the other, synthesize the other, or negate the other. Movements simply change their trajectory.

Place

A place is a regional circulation of flows. Places are made by the continuous centripetal accumulation and folding of flows. They are like local eddies in the great spiral flows of space. The concept of place can be contrasted with the concept of "abstract space," which is defined by discrete positions in a homogenous continuum. Discrete position and homogeneity, however, already presuppose a centripetal accumulation of flows and a stabilized field of circulation in which they would appear as folds or objects. All abstract coordinate conceptions of space are thus derived from or modifications of kinomenological space. Place, on the other hand, is precisely the regional stability or condition through which such discrete positions appear in the first place on the kinetic field of space.

Merleau-Ponty calls this the place of the lived body. He contrasts what he calls "external space," "objective space," and "intelligible space" with "bodily space," "orientated space," and "lived space."[15] For Merleau-Ponty, lived space is not a container, ether, or Cartesian coordinate system of x, y, and z axes where things are laid out,

> since space is anterior to its supposed parts, which are always cut out of it . . . [it is] the means by which the position of things becomes possible. That is, rather than imagining space as a sort of ether in which all things are immersed, or conceiving it abstractly as a characteristic they would all share, we must think of space as the universal power of their connections.[16]

For Merleau-Ponty, the place of the primordial living body is beneath the abstract, Cartesian, or objective space. The body, he writes, "eventually finds its *place*, a primordial spatiality of which objective space is but the envelope and which merges with the very being of the body. As we have seen, to be a body is to be tied to a certain world, and our body is not primarily in space, but is rather of space."[17] The place of the lived body is not a coordinate on a homogenous plane; it is a regional orientation of the human body's being-*in*-the-world. As such, its place and consciousness is fundamentally structured according to the body's material and kinetic affective conditions for motion, its "motor intentionality," or "motricity."[18]

Place is thus the fundamentally kinetic and affective and circulatory condition for orientability (in, out, up, down, left, right). However, the human body is not the first body or even the only body of kinomenological analysis. Nor is its type of circulation extractable from the technical prostheses that compose its affective capacities and motoricity. The human body is simply one field among others distributed and ordered by larger centripetal motions of space itself, as we will see later in this chapter. Space folds itself up centripetally into the body, which then orients itself to other folds.

Space has no absolute inside or outside, but places have regional insides and outsides with respect to others. Since places are simply regional circulations within the centripetal spiral of space, they too have no absolute inside or outside. However, this does not mean that their regional circulations are not able to produce relative insides as part of the process of internalization. Place is therefore not something things are "in," like a container, but something *through which* flows circulate.[19] As Tim Ingold writes, "There could be no places were it not for the comings and goings of human beings and other organisms to and from them, from and to places elsewhere. Places, then, do not so much exist as occur—they are topics rather than objects, stations along ways of life."[20] Since it is the fold in the flows that constitutes space, a place cannot be something separate from the flows and conjunctions that constitute it. In this sense, places or localized spaces of circulation can be relatively nested but only on the condition that these nests are part of the same centripetal spiral motion. Places are not in space as if in a container because space has no absolute inside or outside in which they could be contained. Places are completely continuous with space; they are the regional circulations or centripetal motions of matter.

Gathering

Spatiality is the process of centripetal motion that gathers together flows and folds them into conjunctions or things. While place is the regional circulation of flows that creates a relative ordering or orientation of inside and outside, gathering is the regional folding of conjunctions or things within the place of circulation. Things are nothing but folded flows, motions gathered together and ordered through fields and places.

However, things are not reducible to their extension in space. There is not first an abstract space that becomes populated by three-dimensional objects in that space. Things are not first extensions in space (length, breadth, depth), but rather space is first a centripetal motion of material gathering folded into relative insides and outsides within a path of oriented circulation that can be divided up into extended dimensions *only after its regional internalization in a place*. In other words, movement precedes extension.

Things are not crystallizations but folds in a continuously moving trajectory. They are flows, but they are also folds capable of producing the effect of extension. Space is thus a centripetal gathering of flows, but it is also capable of producing the effect of interiority. The extended thing is thus a product of centripetal gathering and does not precede it. Things are conjunctions of affects within the place or site of circulation.

Heidegger defines the thing in a similar fashion, as a gathering and folding. The word "thing," Heidegger reminds us, comes from the ancient Germanic word *thingam*, meaning gathering or assembly. Before the word "thing" ever had extension or properties, it was originally a gathering-together. "In the course of Western thought," Heidegger writes, "the thing is represented as an unknown X to which perceptible properties are attached. From this point of view, everything *that already belongs to the gathering essence of this thing* does, of course, appear as something that is afterward read into it."[21]

Historically, the thing has been treated as a set of primary and secondary properties, but these properties are only intelligible once a centripetal gathering of heterogeneous flows of light, sound, air, and other matters have already accumulated into a thing such that the so-called perceptible properties of this thing can be determined and attributed in the first place. After the determination of the properties of the thing, we retroactively attribute them to the essence of thing as if they had been there all along, emanating from it. We have thus treated the thing only as a preestablished and already completed end rather than as a constitutive process of the centripetal motion of flows gathering into the thing.

In doing so, Heidegger writes, we also overlook the process by which the thing is a continuous process of gathering and folding of the flows of earth, sky, mortals, and divinities into space. For Heidegger, space is not given in advance of this gathering. Space is what is produced by the more primary process of gathering and folding. The thing is gathered together into a region of circulation that Heidegger calls a locale. The locale is both the regional gathering of flows into a series of folds and their continuous conjunction and circulation through a place. The circulation of things through their place or locale is both regionally limited and spatially delimited, as it connects up to the larger centripetal motion that constitutes space as gathering. Heidegger calls this the boundary of the thing. "A boundary is not that at which something stops but, as the Greeks recognized, the boundary is that from which something begins its essential unfolding."[22] At the boundary of a regional circulation of things, their movement does not stop but simply unfolds or disjoins from its conjunctions.

The centripetal motion of space literally opens up a pathway or circulation through which Dasein (being-*there*) moves. Being-there is precisely a centripetal gathering of being into a local being-*there*. The circulation of being-there through space is what Heidegger calls "dwelling":

> Spaces open up by the fact that they are let into the dwelling of man. To say that mortals are is to say that in dwelling they persist through spaces by virtue of their stay among things and locales. And only because mortals pervade, persist through, spaces by their very essence are they able to go through spaces. But in going through spaces we do not give up our standing in them. Rather, we always go through spaces in such a way that we already sustain them by staying constantly with near and remote locales and things.[23]

Kinomenologically speaking, dwelling is the persistence of being-there in its movement and circulation through space. As flows, the movement of being-there through spaces is not disjoined but rather *sustained* precisely through its regional circulation and conjunction with other near and remote folds. The conjunction of motion through which the space of circulation is sustained is what Heidegger calls "building." "Building," he writes, "accomplishes its essential process in the raising of locales by the joining of their spaces. *Only if we are capable of dwelling, only then can we build.*"[24]

Kinetically, we can say that only if there is continuous flow and movement can there be conjunction and circulation through space. Building is thus the process of "making room" that "shelters" and "houses" the kinomenal dwelling or circulation of being-there through its locales. The house is such a building, the first building insofar as it gathers together the flows of the earth, (rock, dirt, and wood) under the flows of the sky (wind, water, and light) and conjoins them into a locale of circulation through which being-there kinetically dwells. It is the site to which being-there returns along its paths and trajectories. The house is a folded space of circulation, as we will see more historically and technically in the following two sections.

In addition to the theory of space developed here, it is also important to see the connection to the prehistoric and material conditions of the mobile body and the house itself.[25] It is also important to see that in both descriptions it is not only the primacy of matter but, more importantly, the primacy of movement than makes spatialization possible in the first place—something the ontology of motion explicitly adds to the contemporary descriptions of space offered by Merleau-Ponty and Heidegger.

In this chapter I have offered only a theory of the centripetal motion of space. However, it remains to be seen how the concept of space emerges historically as the dominant name for being, and in what sense the concept itself *describes* a centripetal motion. Therefore, we turn now to an exposition of the historical description of space, not as it appears only to humans but also as it distributes the motion of matter through which humans move and through which their description and inscription of being as space is produced.

11
Logos

CHAPTER 14

Prehistoric Mythology

Venus, Egg, Spiral

MYTHOLOGY

The dominant description of being as space coincides roughly with the historical period called the Neolithic, although traces of it certainly began earlier, in the Paleolithic, and remain later in certain areas of the Mediterranean.[1] This ontological description was articulated not in written language or an alphabet, which would not be invented for several thousand more years, but through another language altogether—one of images.

Toward the end of the Upper Paleolithic period, humans began to produce an incredible amount of graphic signs coinciding roughly with the advent of agriculture.[2] These signs are not pictorial representations or copies of being,[3] but mythological images that themselves perform and create a region of being.[4] They are not merely pictorial descriptions, more or less abstract or real from a referent in the world but have an immanent religious or mythological significance in the act of material creation that can be studied.

They are what the paleoanthropologist André Leroi-Gourhan calls "mythograms."[5] Mythograms are graphic images that have ontological, mythological, or religious importance. They are graphic signs directly connected to an internally consistent mythic description.[6] They tell a visual story alongside and entangled with the oral account to which they are connected.[7] Mythology, from the ancient Greek word μῦθος, *mûthos*, meaning "mouth," is an oral or verbal description of reality. Together, mythology and mythograms form the dominant kinography of ontological practice during the Neolithic period and provide the material and historical basis for the kinetic theory of space as centripetal motion. We find in the most dominant and prevailing prehistoric descriptions of being as space a description of centripetal motion.

Just as there is a syntax and grammar in written language, so there is a syntax and grammar in mythograms.[8] Therefore, just as we would look at written texts as more than mere descriptions of reality and as having an internal descriptive relation to one another, we can also look at prehistoric mythograms in a similar way. This is because these graphic signs "represent the grammar and syntax of a kind of metalanguage by which an entire constellation of meanings is transmitted," as the archaeomythologist Marija Gimbutas writes.[9]

Since there are no existing linguistic records of the mythologies and creation stories of Neolithic peoples, this chapter relies on the nonlinguistic but nonetheless structured descriptions given by the mythographic signs of these peoples. However, prehistoric peoples produced a manifold of different graphic signs. Only some of these signs are mythologically primary insofar as they reveal how all other beings came into being. If we want to understand not only how being moves in such a way as to produce space but also how such a motion could come to be described as spatial, we must look to the most primary of these mythological signs: those that describe or explain the primary process of the creation and structure of being.[10]

There are three interrelated sign groups with this ontogenetic status that rise to dominance across almost all European Neolithic groups during this period: the Venus, the egg, and the spiral. These graphic signs are not like the others—dogs, goats, combs, tools, lunar images, and so on—but have a privileged status not just in the sheer number of their creation and geographical ubiquity across Neolithic Europe during this time, but in the primacy of their ontogenetic function to explain how being comes to be what it is.

THE VENUS

Venus is the name retroactively given to the thousands of female figurines found during the Upper Paleolithic and Neolithic periods. The Venus is not only the single most common figurative graphism for tens of thousands of years; it is also the very first human figure ever produced.[11] The oldest is the Venus of Hohle Fels, which dates to around 35,000 BCE.[12] Whatever the precise mythological system of prehistoric peoples, "the frequency and longevity of this symbol in the archaeological record (over thirty thousand years) speaks for its essential role" in it.[13]

The Venus can thus tell us something about the prehistoric mythological description of being—how it came to be or appear. The question here is not what the Venus represents (fertility and so on) or what people thought about it but rather how its kinetic structure describes or materially depicts the nature of being in prehistoric mythology. The Venus is not just an abstract symbol; it has an embodied kinetic structure that expresses a specific field of motion resonant with Neolithic goddess worship and the mythology of the Great Mother.

The Neolithic description of mythological femininity, however, is also quite problematic insofar as it remains naively essentialist and naturalist at its core. It circumscribes femininity into a spatial ontology that treats femininity as a primary container or vessel from which all beings flow. The flows of matter then are not treated as primary but as secondary effects coming from the womb of the Great Mother. In other words, feminine spatiality in these prehistoric descriptions is not something materially and historically constituted, but rather mythologically a priori, or natural and essential. The Neolithic description of the female container, however, is not described as a negativity, passivity, or lack. The description of the feminine as a lack is something that emerges only with the later rise of ancient patriarchal religions, as we will see in Part II. Instead, the problem with the prehistoric description of being as female/spatial, from a material-kinetic and feminist perspective, is that the product (the sexuated body) is placed before the process that creates it in the first place (material practices and performances of sexuation).

What I try to show in this section, therefore, is precisely this: that such prehistoric descriptions of the a priori nature of feminine spatial being already presuppose the productive performance of material-kinetic flows that produce the spatial and female body itself. Sexuated bodies are emergent phenomena from more primary kinetic *processes of sexuation*. The processes of sexual differentiation are, as Judith Butler writes, material and performative, and not a priori, or essential.[14]

The Venus mythogram gives us the first major graphic image of prehistoric ontogenesis (see Figure 14.1). In prehistoric mythologies, as Marija Gimbutas has shown, the Venus is first and foremost a description of how being comes to be what it is: through the internalization and externalization of birth. The Venus is therefore a historical description of how matter in motion is internalized, organized, and generated into *space*. More specifically, the prehistoric mythology of the Venus describes a *centripetal motion*

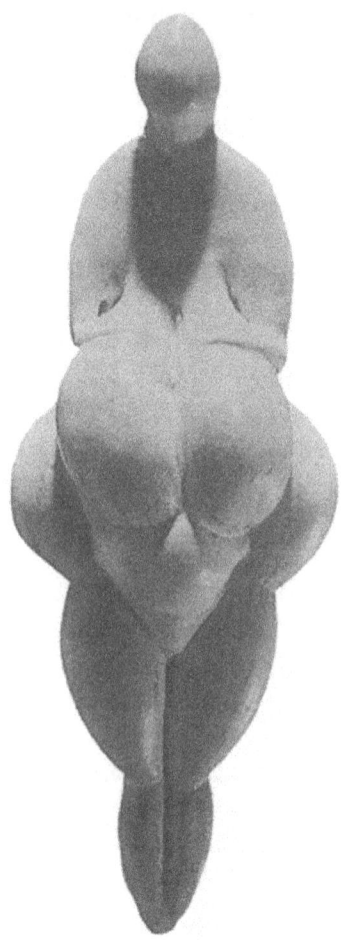

Figure 14.1 Venus of Lespugue, c. 23,000 BCE
Source: This image was taken from Plate 5 of Marija Gimbutas, *The Language of the Goddess* (San Francisco: Harper Collins, 1991).

that orders the appearance of being *as space*. This is attested to historically in two major ways: first in the material kinetics of the Venus mythogram itself, and second in its resonance with the mythological significance of perceptual, social, and natural motions of the Neolithic period.

The material kinetics of the Venus figurines are almost universally composed of a series of rounded or curved ovoids: the head, the breasts, the belly, the thighs, vulva, and buttocks. These ovoids are curves, folds, or pleats in the flows of matter that curve back around and intersect with themselves in a continual circulation. These kinetic relations are connected by a series of places or chambers where flows (milk, amniotic fluid, blood) are stored in the female body—the places or regions of Venus-space.

The rounded figurine of the Venus is similarly a product of an accumulation of terrestrial flows of dirt, clay, stone, and ivory and their centripetal contraction into a series of pools, bulbs, or sacs where they are stored. This contraction of flows is described by the frequent marking of Venus figurines with a series of parallel straight or wavy lines—"streams."[15] Sometimes the only markings on Venus figurines are a line or flow of straight lines into and out of the vulva. These streams or lines have a double kinetic function: they are both a centripetal accumulation of flows folded into rounded ovoids or bulbed spaces, and a disjunction of these same flows through the vulva, where they are released. The flow of lines across the body of the Venus is an open one that draws a continuous circulation between inside and outside. As a container of flows, the Venus is the space or series of places (bulbs) where the flow of matter folds, is internalized, persists, and circulates.

Second, the Venus mythogram describes a resonance with three other processes of spatialization. Contrary to typical archaeological interpretations, we should not think of these Venus figurines as representations of the female body or analogies for animal birth, seed germination, or lunar cycles. All these processes *actually* or *metonymically* share the same kinetic pattern of centripetal motion of gathered flows. The Venus mythogram is thus a visual contraction or resonance of all these motions into a single spatial figure that defines the whole of reality.

Perceptual, social, and natural motions all become intersecting circulations distributed by the same dominant regime of motion. The Venus figurine is simply the graphic resonance that makes explicit their kinetic similarity as spaces and describes the exact field of motion by which they are formed. Kinetically, the Venus is the figure whose sexuated bodily space is produced through the kinetic process of centripetal accumulation of material flows. Space is not a priori but rather something constituted or produced through the material distribution and connection of multiple spaces or places, like the fluid-filled vessels of her breasts, belly, buttocks, and thighs distributed on her body. These materially important processes are thus described and mythologically tied to the being of the Great Mother goddess herself—creatrix, nurturer, and destroyer. In other words, the Venus mythogram must be put alongside an oral mythology of the primary and creative power of the Great Mother goddess worshipped by Neolithic societies that also described the structure of lived reality.[16] The Venus also describes a series of perceptual, social, and natural motions.

Perceptual Motion. First, the Venus graphically describes the perceptual appearance of being as space to regional and mobile beings on the surface of the earth. The perceptual field of a mobile being on the surface of the earth is encompassed by the curved limits of the horizon. One can turn around 360 degrees and still be limited by a surrounding horizon. Terrestrial movement is thus limited on all sides and encompassed and enclosed by the perceptual "roundness" and limitedness of space. Given this basic perceptual orientation with respect to the largest possible frame of terrestrial motion (the horizon), being appears on the surface of the earth as curved and *spatially bound*—not as abstract space, of course, but as lived space: the space of orientation, perception, and action for mobile beings.

As such, all perceived things begin to look like or take on the fundamental spatialization of the curved mother. Even time itself is described as cyclical within the curvature of lived space. Some of the earliest experiences of lived time are connected to the spiraling movement of the sun across the sky in returning patterns or seasons. This spiraled movement is in turn limited by the spatial enclosure of the perceptual horizon. This spatialization of temporal being is still ontologically dominant today among several Native American peoples, such as the Lakota, Navajo, and Hopi.[17] The rounded ovoid signs of the Venus describe a curved and rounded being that is connected to perception and bodily orientation. Being thus appears as the same rounded space that the Venus describes with its rounded sign-body.

Social Motion. Second, the Venus also describes a regime of centripetal motion in resonance with the first dominant distribution of human social motion in space. At some point the trajectories of Paleolithic hunter-gatherers began to curve their wandering paths and return to the first sites of social accumulation: grave mounds. Before villages, shrines, or pottery, the grave mound was the first permanent sociotechnical enclosure. The tomb is the return to the womb of the earth, the resting space that allows for rebirth. Life is born in space (the womb) and returns to space (the tomb).

The dead, as Lewis Mumford observes, "were the first to have a permanent dwelling: a cavern, a mound marked by a cairn, a collective barrow. These were landmarks to which the living probably returned at intervals, to commune with or placate the ancestral spirits."[18] The tomb hollows out a rounded space of encapsulation and internalization, where the bodies of the ancestors are centripetally accumulated. Their family *re-turns* its pathways again and again to the same space of memorial internalization, creating a social centripetal gathering at the tomb. The tomb is therefore not an ending point or hermetically sealed inside and outside, but a life beyond death, a rebirth in the form of a memory or spirit made possible through a localization of being in space. The rounded vulva and belly of the Venus describe the same kinetic image of life and death in a single space.

The social cycle of life and death is made visual in the semiotic image of the rounded belly.

Furthermore, according to Mumford, early human societies were formed not only by the regular return to the tombs that centripetally accumulated bodies into a single space of encasement and containment but also to other areas of the earth that were particularly sacred: "The first germ of the city, then, is in the ceremonial meeting place that serves as the goal for a pilgrimage: a site to which family or clan groups are drawn back, at seasonal intervals, because it concentrates, in addition to any natural advents it may have, certain 'spiritual' or supernatural powers, powers of high potency and greater duration, of wider cosmic significance, than the ordinary processes of life."[19]

The centripetal gathering of certain natural and social powers is thus fundamentally spatial. There must be sites of potency where flows intersect and loop over one another like the gathering of fluids in the swollen breasts and belly of the Venus. Space is the swollen body of the earth; it is matter pregnant with form. Humans returned and gathered at all kinds of spaces—the natural hollows or folds in the earth like caves, and the natural accumulations of water, such as lakes, ponds, and springs. Nature gathers and pools into spaces.

Human motion follows these flows and lingers in its folds, eventually taking up residence as social space. "Thus even before the city becomes a place of fixed residence, it begins as a meeting place to which people periodically return: the *magnet comes before the container*, and this ability to attract non-residents to it for intercourse and spiritual stimulus no less than trade remains one of the essential criteria of the city, a witness to its inherent dynamism."[20] The magnet of centripetal motion and social gathering comes before its containment in houses and built social infrastructure.

Additionally, the domestication of plants and animals around 10,000 BCE also produced an increasingly dramatic accumulation of natural flows into social spaces. The process of settlement came with a "systematic gathering and planting of the seeds from certain grasses, the taming of other seed plants, like the squashes and the beans and the utilization of herd animals, the ox, the sheep, finally the ass and the horse."[21] The process of domestication centripetally gathered the wild flows of plants, water, and animals and contained them in a given space of socially directed reproduction.

The same is true of human reproduction, which became a primary activity and concern of Neolithic humans. Instead of predation, the focus of social life slowed down, settled, and focused on containing and protecting children, young animals, and seeds and sprouts in enclosed spaces. Security, receptivity, enclosure, nurturing—these are the primary functions of the early village, itself a containing space. "They give us back areas of being," Gaston Bachelard writes, poetically echoing Heidegger, "houses in which the human being's certainty of being is concentrated, and we have the impression that, by living in such images as these, in images that are as stabilizing as these are, we could start a new life, a life that would be our own, that would belong to us in our very depths."[22]

The house, the oven, the byre and bind, the cistern, the storage pit, the granary—these are all internalizations and spatializations, places for the concentration of being. "In line with this, the more primitive structures—houses, rooms, tombs—are usually round ones: like the original bowl described in Greek myth, which was modeled on Aphrodite's breast."[23] But this Greek myth is already modeled on the Neolithic one of the Great Mother described by the Venus figurines. The Venus is the mythographic description of all of these containers. Their rounded containing shape is modeled not only on her breast but also on her belly, buttocks, and thighs. Each is also modeled on the other, since they all come into being at the same time and through the experience of creation as a fundamentally spatial creation.

Venus is the mythographic historical archetype of this space, the sign of being and all reality. Her arms and legs are small and held close to her body. They are used less for movement than for enclosing, "whether it be a lover or a child; and it is in the orifices and sacs, in mouth, vulva, vagina, breast, womb, that her sexually individualized activities take place."[24] This spatialization is the very condition for social life and reproduction. To be is to be in space is to be in the Mother.

The Neolithic age is thus the age of containers. Paleolithic humans had little need to store flows; containers would only have inhibited their movement as they hunted. By staying in the same place, by creating a place, the Neolithic agricultural revolution also invented numerous kinds of containers: stone and pottery utensils, vases, jars, vats, cisterns, bins, barns, granaries, and houses, as well as the great collective containers such as irrigation ditches and villages. Agriculture brought a surplus of food, and containers made it possible to store this surplus over the winter and to remain in the same place during that time. The rounded shape of the container made possible the rounded return to the same place, and through this kinetic circulation the reproduction of the place itself. The Venus is the mythological image of the multivesseled vessel—the body vessel whose swollen parts form the regional vessels where fluid is stored and life is made and remade. The Venus is the semiotic vessel that contains, creates, and multiplies other vessels: the arche-vessel or ur-vessel.

Natural Motion. Third, the Venus describes a pattern of natural motions that come to appear as spaces. The sun, the moon, and stars are round containers or bodies of light. The earth itself appears as a similar body: a living body or living container. The description of the earth as a living body is attested to in countless mythologies.[25] However, the sun, moon, planets, and earth do not come to appear as bodies or spaces because they are modeled on the anthropological body but rather because human and nonhuman bodies are both part of the same kinetic condition of centripetal motion that gathers heterogeneous flows together into an enclosure.

Even the motions of the celestial bodies are curved. The movement of the sun, the moon, and the stars do not appear in straight lines; they appear in curved motions across the horizon. This is the case because the earth itself is already curved. They curve, rotate, and return not in a perfect circle, but in an ellipse or spiral that is different each time. This difference is correlated with the change of the seasons, which themselves return in cycles. These curves and ovoids demarcate, internalize, and enclose a spatial field, just like the rounded orbs of Venus's body enclose their own fields.

The Venus is also a descriptive mythogram of the animal and plant motions that create space. Animal and vegetable motions are not modeled on human ones but precisely the reverse. Before humans settled down, they observed the cyclical kinetic return of animals and reptiles to their rounded nests to lay their rounded eggs. They watched crustaceans build shells around themselves and fish deposit rounded eggs. They observed the way that plants bind themselves to a place through roots and store surplus energy for the winter in their fattened tubers. They noted the way in which plants reproduced themselves by enclosing their flows in seeds, from which emerged again the entire plant.

Space is not an anthropological construction; it is a real kinetic distribution produced by matter in motion—first in nature, and then in human action. Human movement, including the kinetic signs of the curved Venus, is simply part of this larger regime of motion. It is no coincidence that eggs, shellfish, tubers, and seeds became some of the most important foods for agricultural and sedentary societies, as well as descriptive images in the history of goddess mythology.

The worship of and focus on lunar cycles of the crescent or curved and rounded moon in agriculture also finds its kinetic description in the curved bulbs of the Venus. It is no coincidence that human motions are so similar to these natural ones and that their most primary mythogram concentrates all of these perceptual, social, and natural images of space into a single kinetic sign: the Venus.

Accordingly, we can see more clearly now that the mythographic description of the Venus figurine and its attendant goddess mythologies are not at all a priori feminine spatial structures but rather are themselves products of a more primary nonsexuated and nonhuman material and kinetic process of centripetal accumulation. Matter becomes sexually differentiated through patterns of motion, not the other way around. Only after the historical event of organic sexuation is it possible for the prehistoric female body to be mythologically described as the retroactive origin of all other beings—the space or womb from which all things come.

THE EGG

The egg is the second dominant ontogenetic mythogram of the Neolithic that visually describes the creative nature of being as space. The rounded ovoid shape of the egg is kinetically related to the ovoid bulbs of the Venus, but it appears historically much later—by at least 12,000 BCE.[26] Although the two are related and one comes after the other, one is not modeled on the other. Both the Venus figurine with her double-egg-shaped buttocks and breasts and the single egg shape are mythograms of the same centripetal motion of internalized creation: space.[27]

In Upper Paleolithic and Neolithic cultures, the egg mythogram is predominantly associated with birds. Early bird mythograms dating from at least 18,000 BCE provide some insight into the kinetic origin of the creation of the egg. In particular, there is a long legacy stretching back to the Upper Paleolithic of correlation between bird graphisms and the "V" symbol or chevrons that decorate these birds, as well as the exaggerated bulbous egg-shaped bodies of the birds (see Figure 14.2). Bird, V, and egg appear together as part of the same mythokinetic structure.[28]

The kinetic meaning of this mythographic trifold is the following: Just as the body of the Venus was frequently marked with straight or wavy lines to indicate the condensation of flows into her fluid-filled bulbs, so too is the bird's body marked with V's. The V image is different from the straight or wavy lines of water that fill the Venus because the V is where two flows of water are centripetally gathered or *funneled* together. The V appears not only on birds but also very often on the Venus herself as a pubic triangle or V shape. The V draws an image or sign of centripetal collection and condensation for both the bird and for the Venus. Once the flows of nature have been gathered together, the body of the bird can then swell with eggs. The condensation of flows produces a space of internalization.

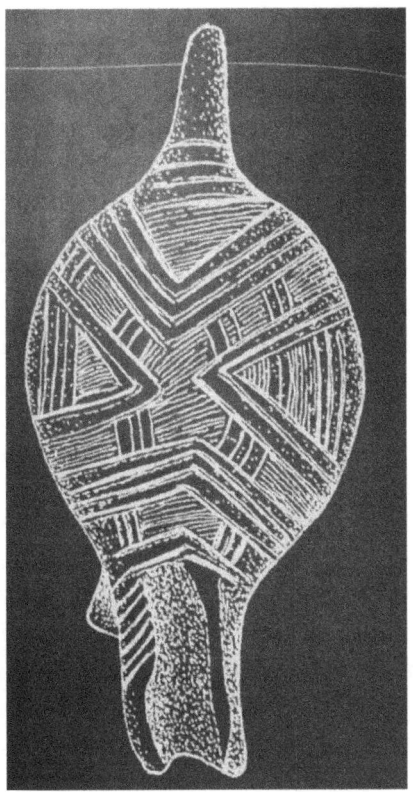

Figure 14.2 Bird with Chevrons
Source: This image was taken from Page 2 of Marija Gimbutas, *The Language of the Goddess* (San Francisco: Harper Collins, 1991).

In prehistoric mythological description, the egg is a fundamentally creative space. From the pure flows of chaos it gathers a space for organization. It takes the chaotic and dynamic processes of nature and binds them together into a consistent form: the ovoid ellipse. As the embryologist Albert Dalcq writes, "Forms are contingent upon kinematic dynamism. It is secondary whether or not an orifice forms in the germ. All that counts is the process of immigration itself."[29] Continuous flow gives birth to kinomorphic stability.

The bird, associated with air and water, gathers its flows into a V and gives birth to a dynamic egg from which being is created. The egg is a space of enclosure, of inside and outside, but also a permeable space or membrane through which selective exchanges of moisture and ventilation between inside and outside are regulated. The egg is not an absolute container but an open container or circulatory process that both produces a creative internalization and allows flows to be conjoined and disjoined through it. The egg is less a space of birth than a space of rebirth and repeated creation.

The egg is the mythogram of a dynamic cycle or process repeated again and again. It is not undifferentiated like a perfect circle but continually produces differentiation like a spiral motion that continually creates new inner and outer layers without ever ending its motion. As Deleuze and Guattari write, the "egg [is] defined by axes and vectors, gradients and thresholds, by dynamic tendencies involving energy transformation and kinematic movements involving group displacement, by migrations: all independent of accessory forms because the organs appear and function here only as pure intensities."[30] The egg creates a spatial body, but a body that has no preexisting organs or organization. Organs and organization are the products of kinetic transformations and folds that occur through the more primary circulating space of the egg itself.

During the Neolithic period the egg takes on a dominant mythographic role with respect to the ontogenetic meaning of birth and death. For example, the Lepenski Vir shrines that originated with the Upper Paleolithic circa 11,000 BCE continued to be used by later Neolithic agriculturalists following the same bird and egg mythography. Built near the banks of the Danube, these shrines were decorated with both bird images and egg-shaped sculptures with carved vulvas. As Marija Gimbutas reports,

> Besides the obvious implication that a bird or fish egg holds a new life source, the egg also signified the womb. Red ocher, connoting blood and the life essence, covered many of the sculptures. The triangular outline of the sanctuary representing the goddess' regenerative triangle, the altar depicting the birth canal, and the egg- (or womb-) shaped stones reflecting the uterus at the head of the birth canal together give a clear representation of the regenerative organs.[31]

Placing a person's body within the tomb returned him or her to the regenerative egg womb from which life was renewed. Other tombs in Italy, Malta, Sardinia, and Western Europe reveal similar bird, egg, and spiral mythography indicative of a similar description of space as primary and generative of existence.

The egg has mythological significance in numerous cultures across several time periods. "Through its magical symmetry and its quintessential form, the egg has served as the primal symbol for the cosmization of chaos since Neolithic conceptions of the world," Peter Sloterdijk writes in his own contemporary ontology of space.[32] It is part of the oldest recorded types of myths, or what David Leeming calls "primordial waters"—myths in which chaos is mythologically primary but becomes condensed into an egg, which gives birth to an ordered world or primary deity, often a bird.[33]

For example, "in the African Shangaan creation account, a bird was responsible for the origin of humans. N'wari, the bird god, laid an egg in a reed. The first human hatched from this egg."[34] In the African Fang creation account, a spider god lowered a smooth mother stone or egg into the sea. When the egg cracked, three people came out of it."[35] In a Baltic myth a cosmic egg explodes, its yolk becoming the earth, its white the waters, and its shell pieces the sky with the celestial bodies.[36]

There is also an ancient Indian myth called the Brahmanda Purana that describes the "emergence of a cosmic egg out of the cosmic waters." Another is a Polynesian myth of Samoa, "in which the creator lived in a cosmic egg and broke out, thus allowing parts of the shell to fertilize the primordial waters, causing the formation of the Samoan Islands."[37]

In Egyptian mythology the world emerges from primordial waters as a mound of dirt. Ra, the sun god, was contained within an egg laid on this mound by a celestial bird. In ancient Greek Orphic mythology the cosmos emerged from a cosmic egg that gave birth to the golden-winged hermaphroditic bird-god Phanes, who created all the other gods (see Figure 14.3). In the Kalevala, the Finnish national epic, the world is created from the fragments of an egg laid by a diving duck on the knee of Ilmatar, goddess of the air.

One of the most detailed recorded egg mythologies is the African Dogon cosmic egg myth, assembled by the French anthropologist Marcel Griaule in his book *The Pale Fox* from his conversation with the blind hunter Ogotemmeli.[38] "In the beginning, before all things, was Amma, God, and he rested upon nothing. 'Amma's egg in a ball' was closed, but made of four parts called 'clavicles,' themselves ovoid and attached, as if welded together."[39] This primordial egg created the first space for creation. "The word amma means: to hold firmly, to embrace strongly and keep in the same place. . . . To pronounce the name of Amma is to preserve all space."[40]

According to this myth, the fundamental matter of the universe was flows of water through which the design of the world was traced in space by Amma. "Amma preserved the whole, for he had traced within himself the design of the world and of its extension. For Amma had designed the universe before creating it. The material for the design was water with which he traced figures in space."[41] When the egg broke open the world emerged in a spiral (see Figure 14.4). "When Amma broke the egg of the world and came out, a whirlwind rose. The *po*, which is the smallest (thing), was made, invisible at the center; the wind is Amma himself."[42]

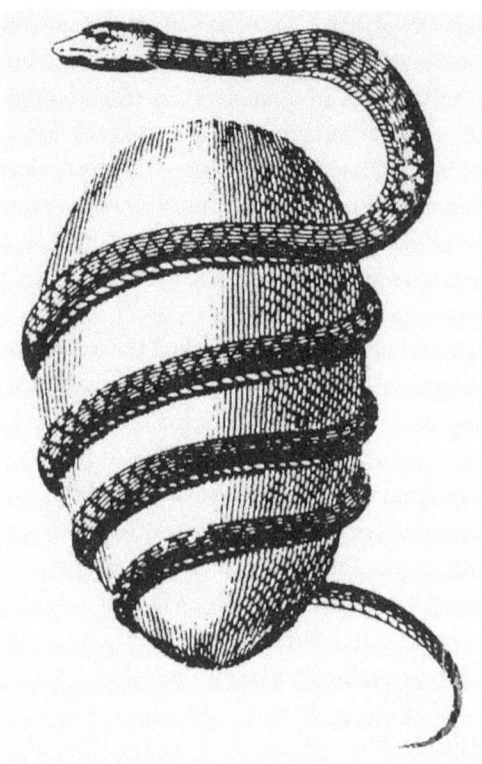

Figure 14.3 The Orphic Egg
Source: Jacob Bryant/Wikimedia Commons.

The commonality of all egg creation myths is the primacy of chaos and the necessity of the primordial spatialization of being to be able to generate the world and gods. In the end, however, it is important to note that the gods, for the Neolithics, almost always remain less powerful than the dark maternal waters of the universal space-womb from which they emerged.[43]

THE SPIRAL

The spiral is the third dominant ontological mythogram of the Neolithic that describes the nature of being as space. The spiral mythogram appears as early as 13,000 BCE in paintings and 6000 BCE on pottery.[44] Even before this time, however, humans observed and collected unique spiral objects such as gastropod-shell fossils, a testament to the "mystery of strange forms," as Leroi-Gourhan writes.[45] The spiral mythogram is also related to snakes, whose association with water, motion, and eggs connected them to

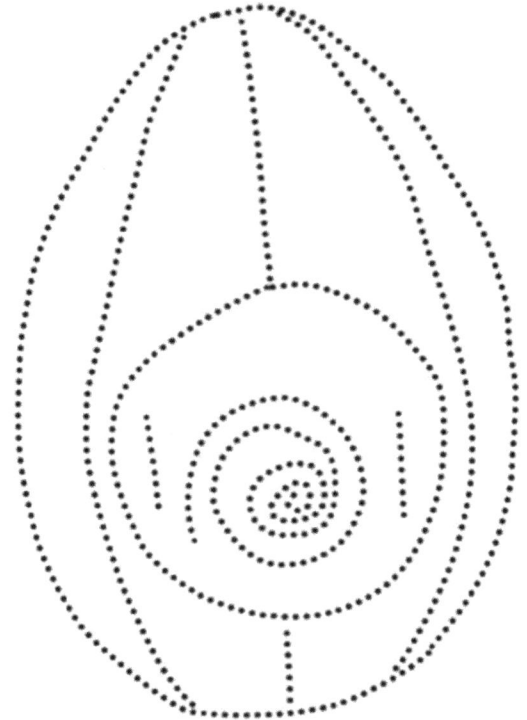

Figure 14.4 The Dogon Egg

the Venus as well. If the egg is the graphic form of being as space, the spiral snake is the graphic shape of the mythological movement that brings the space of the world into being.

Interestingly, with the rise of Indo-European civilization, the spiraled snake was increasingly replaced with the circular snake, or Ouroboros. This change in mythography is kinetically significant, as we will see in the next chapter. In addition, "spirals are often located on uniquely feminine body parts in figurines such as the breasts and uterus. The hook is a shortened version of the spiral and can be found on megalithic tombs of western Europe," as well as alongside moon and lunar cycle images.[46] The spiral is almost universal throughout Neolithic Europe and is encountered on seals, plaques, altars, dishes, elaborately decorated bases, anthropomorphic vases, and figurines.

In all its prehistorical expressions, the spiral is a graphic description of the continual and mythological cycle of folding that creates the primal space on and through which being moves. The being of space is spiral. The spiral is a mythographic description of spatialized motion by which matter folds over itself into a space of circulation. It is the mythogram of cyclical processes manifested by signs of dynamic motion: whirling and twisting spirals, winding and coiling snakes, circles, crescents, horns, sprouting seeds and shoots.[47]

It is the union of opposites. Inside and outside, light and dark, male and female are all copresent by way of their spatial differentiation and unity within the folded arm of the spiral. As one travels a spiral, the inside slowly becomes the outside and the outside the inside. The two are connected in the single continuous stream of motion. This is attested to in numerous spiral designs on Neolithic pottery and vessels. Two antithetic spirals whirl around a beautiful lidded vase from the Neolithic, simulating the generative power of the central egg.[48] Amma's egg moves in a spiral just like Venus's vulva. Spatial being is not eternal because it is centripetal. It is neither created nor destroyed but is rather *sempiternal*, because it is constantly being created *and* destroyed. It is a kind of anti-eternity, a continual process of folding and unfolding in the coils of the snake.

The triple, three-legged, or "triskelion" spiral plays an important role in Malta between 4400 and 3600 BCE, and in Irish Neolithic megaliths at Knowth, Dowth, and Newgrange, built around 3,200 BCE. The three-legged spiral and triple interlocking spirals of Neolithic Europe and the Celts also appear on numerous megalithic sites and burial areas. Interlocking spirals graphically depict the continuum and intertwining of a single motion into discrete spaces or folds. Interlocking spirals can indicate discrete forms and phases of the continuous motion of the moon or other movements tied to birth and gestation. Interlocking spirals demonstrated not only the folding of flows into spaces but also the interlocking and continuum between spaces themselves.

Ontogenetic serpent and spiral myths can still be seen today among many of the aboriginal tribes of Australia in what is known as the "Rainbow Serpent" myth. In these myths the rainbow serpent is most commonly a primeval creator mother-god who emerges from the formless, flat, bare earth (egg). One day the Rainbow Serpent emerges from its Dreamtime egg and pushes up through the surface, gives birth to all the animals, carves out the mountains, and spills water over the land, making rivers and lakes. She makes the sun, the fire, and all the colors. The Rainbow Serpent lives and moves between the important water holes and rivers of Australia, sustaining life or drowning it in floods.[49] The Rainbow Serpent creates a space for life on which all the regional paths or song lines of reality are traced. Thus, for the Walbiri, an aboriginal people of the Australian Central Desert, "The life of a person is the sum of his tracks, the total inscription of his movements, something that can be traced out along the ground."[50]

In all these concrete historical ways during the Neolithic period, being is described mythologically as spatial, using the dominant images of the Venus, egg, and spiral. However, these mythological descriptions were also inscribed simultaneously on the bodies of the speakers themselves through speech or phonography. This is the subject of the next chapter.

III
Graphos

CHAPTER 15

Speech

The Body

The spatial description of being first emerged as historically dominant in the mythology and mythograms of prehistoric and Neolithic peoples, but at the same time it was also inscribed on the body of the speaker of those same mythologies through *speech*. Therefore, the mythological description of being as space also presupposes a kinetic and historical transformation of the human body into a *speaking body*. The kinetic structure of this new surface of inscription is the subject of the present chapter. The thesis that follows is that the historical coemergence of spatial mythologies explored in the previous chapter and the new kinographic technology of speech follow the same dominantly centripetal field of motion during this time.

THE ORIGINS OF SPEECH

The origins of human speech precede its dominant kinetic distribution by tens of thousands of years. Hominids, all their precursors, and many other animals were capable of making and responding to sound waves well before these sonic flows were increasingly gathered and circulated by *Homo sapiens* into a dominant field of mythological description. At the kinetic level, therefore, there is not a difference in kind between the speech of animals and the speech of humans but rather a difference in degree or in distribution of motion.

In fact, what makes possible the human increase in sonic accumulation is nothing other than a kinetic transformation in the *animal body itself*—from quadrupedalism to bipedalism. Once the early ancestors of humans began to move on two legs instead of four, their bodies underwent a dramatic intensification of kinetic capacities. Bipedalism gave birth to two interrelated kinetic processes made possible by the liberation of the paw from being a strictly pedetic tool focused almost exclusively on locomotion to becoming a free-moving appendage capable of all kinds of new patterns of motion. The mobility of the graphic hand is thus a kinetic extension of the pedesis of the foot.

First, the liberation of the hand made possible a massive diversification of digital movement and grasping. This in turn allowed for an explosion in the diversity and function of tools that could be manipulated by the hand, including gesture or graphism—the manipulation of matter with the hand. Gesture and graphism increasingly enabled the gathering or centripetal contraction of an extremely wide diversity of rhythmic motions of the arm and hand. The freedom of the hand made possible not only an increased kinetic capacity for grasping and accumulating things toward the center of the body, including putting food into the mouth, but it also permitted a rhythmic accumulation of natural motions in the arm and hand itself.

In other words, the hand began to mimic certain natural motions—waves, wind, water, and so on—that became concretely expressed in the descriptive patterns or mythograms discussed in the previous chapter. The liberation of the hand thus gave birth to both the centripetal motion of grasping and the accumulation of natural motions concretely recorded in graphic patterns—spiral, ellipse, and so on.

Second, the disjunction of the hand also produced a simultaneous disjunction of the mouth and tongue from its almost exclusive function as a primary grasping mechanism. Instead of having to forage and manipulate food almost entirely with the mouth and lips, the freed-up hand could simply grasp and forage and deliver the food directly to the mouth.

The free movement of the hand and arm thus also made possible the free movement of the mouth, lips, and tongue, which could now develop independent kinetic functions—phonism. The evolution of the tongue was a diversification of its motions. As it evolved, it increased its degrees of freedom and motility just as the evolution of the fingers and hand increasingly diversified the kinds of tools and graphism they could make. Like graphism, phonism began to mimic and accumulate a repertoire of natural sounds made possible by the new freedom of the tongue to modulate a flow of air.[1]

The important takeaway from the historical origin of speech and gesture is that these two kinetic disjunctions of the hand and the mouth made possible by bipedalism occurred and developed together in close parallel, though one was not modeled on the other. Speech is not a representation of graphism, and graphism is not a representation of speech. One did not emerge first and then cause the other to adapt to or supplement it; the two coemerged in the same kinetic distribution. "As soon as there are prehistoric tools," Leroi-Gouhan writes, "there is a possibility of a prehistoric language, for tools and language are neurologically linked and cannot be dissociated within the social structure of humankind."[2]

Graphism and phonism are therefore dimensions of the same material-kinetic field, not essences, representations, or transcendent forms. Both are creative, both "form part of the same human aptitude, that of reflecting reality in verbal or gestural symbols or in material form as figures."[3] The two kinographic operations—the contraction of sounds into descriptions and the contraction of rhythms into graphic inscriptions—are two parts of the same centripetal process of accumulating an increasingly diverse collection of sounds and gestures *in the human body*.

INSCRIBING THE SURFACE OF THE BODY

In order to understand how mythological speech became kinetically inscribed on the surface of the human body and occurred alongside the mythograms studied in the previous chapter, we begin with the centripetal accumulation of sound waves in the body.

Just as graphic space gathers together certain privileged rhythmic motions of matter into figures like the Venus, the egg, or the spiral, which themselves follow the same kinetic patterns of the sun, moon, birds, snakes, vessels, graves, wombs, and so on, so phonetic space gathers together certain privileged flows of sound toward a central body that itself reproduces those sounds through vibration and resonance.[4] Before the body was capable of creating any kind of mythogram, it first had to undergo the kinetic transformation to bipedalism, which made possible a centripetal phonism and graphism through the kinetic disjunction of the mouth and the hand.

In other words, human speech, and thus the condition for centripetal mythology itself, is not independent of the continuous process of material motion. Mythology is only possible because of the body's kinomorphology. The ear is shaped like a whorled spiral to funnel a wide range of sound waves into a central point of accumulation, producing vibrations in the eardrum, which in turn produces vibrations in the tiny bones of the middle ear, which in turn vibrate the fluid of the inner ear, which moves the tiny hairs that send electrical flows to the brain. Sound is kinetic. It is the vibration of matter. As received by the human body, it also produces a series of kinetic movements inside the body. These are the centripetal sonic inscriptions that change and move the body.

However, the body is also capable of generating its own kinetic phonisms through speech. By pushing air across the narrow opening of the mouth and modulating it with the movement of the lips and tongue, a flow of air produces an internal vibration in the ear, in the whole body, and in the bodies of others nearby. The body centripetally gathers air into its lungs from outside and distributes it throughout the whole body in the flow of blood. This kinetic distribution produces four major rhythmic cycles: (1) the coming in and going out of air in the lungs, (2) the fluctuations of the nostrils, (3) the opening and closing of the mouth, and (4) the rise and fall of the chest. Each is a cycle kinetically coordinated with the others. Before there is speech, there is already a series of synchronized kinetic cycles of the body within which speech acts and redistributes this synchrony. This is more than a question of hand gestures. Speech itself is a fully material and gestural performance. Speech is bodily gesture—the two are kinetically inextricable.

Hearing and speaking form two aspects of the same circulation of pressure waves, but this circulation only works when it is centripetal, when it gathers diverse sounds inward toward and through a resonant and hollow body. In other words, the entire body becomes an instrument, a hollowed-out space through which vibrations gather and circulate. Although speech can also travel outward, its proximity is extremely limited and only works through the transmission of vibrations centripetally gathered in another body. In these ways, speech centripetally gathers diverse flows of peripheral sounds toward the center of the local space, where they are inscribed through vibrations on the body.

Kinetic sounds did not emerge ex nihilo from the speaking body; they were *gathered from elsewhere*. All human phonemes already existed in natural and animal sounds before the human ear ever heard them and before the human tongue ever spoke them. Human language began by humans centripetally collecting and mimicking these resonant sounds.

In the eighteenth and nineteenth centuries, several philosophers argued a version of this thesis. The eighteenth-century Italian philosopher Giambattista Vico argued that the first human words must have come from expletives spoken in response to dramatic natural sounds or from mimicking events like the crack of lightning or rumble of thunder.[5] In France, Jean-Jacques Rousseau argued that sonic expressions of feeling were the earliest forms of language. In Germany, Johann Gottfried Herder claimed that human language originated from the sounds and shapes of the natural world.[6] Mostly famously of all, however, Charles Darwin wrote, "I cannot doubt that language owes its origin to the imitation and modification, aided by signs and gestures, of various natural sounds, the voices of other animals, and man's own instinctive cries."[7] It was Darwin who drew up the first and most extensive empirical list of gestural and phonetic movements shared by humans and animals.

The intuition of these thinkers has some truth to it. The sounds of many words still have primitive connections to the natural sounds of the things. The howling of wind; the chattering of brooks; the roar of waterfalls; the thrumming of crickets; the rushing, splashing, gushing, and washing of the river—these are not metaphors.[8] Speech belongs to natural motions just as much as these natural motions belong to speech. They are expressions of the same sonic patterns.[9]

Many of these shared motions *and* their shared meanings persist, but many others do not. Natural and animals sounds do not reveal a true or total account of the connection between sounds and actions for many reasons, which are dealt with shortly. As an idealist linguistic theory, "natural mimesis" fails as a good explanation, but as a kinetic theory it provides the beginnings of a materialist linguistics. In particular, what the mimesis between natural and human sounds reveals is that human speech began as a centripetal gathering of sounds into the space or site of the body. Sound is a profoundly internal, kinetic, and vibratory phenomenon that is unique to the space in which it occurs: the singularity of a voice, an acoustic or social milieu. Space is what internalizes or folds the outside and the inside into a single site of vibration. Sound permeates the natural world but becomes folded and gathered in the hollow body of the speaker, where it resonates internally. Humans speak, but through their speech the sonorous vibratory world speaks within their resonant and inscribed bodies.

As the French philosopher Maurice Merleau-Ponty writes, "The things have us and—it is not we who have the things. . . . It is being that speaks within us and not we who speak of being."[10] Language, he writes, "is the very voice of the trees, the waves, and the forests."[11]

PHONOGRAPHISM

Speech is thus the confluence and circulation of two types of material-kinetic flows: sonic flows and gestural flows. Flows of sound (natural and animal noises) are centripetally gathered in the body through synchrony and resonance, while gestural flows of rhythmic matter and bodies are centripetally gathered and reproduced through the body's gestural and graphic expressions.

The motions constitutive of the roundness of the egg or the waviness of the water are really and metonymically synchronized in the arms and fingers of the body. This is not a representational metaphor. The graphic figure or figurine is the product of this motion, as well as a gathering of numerous motions into a single graphic action. The sun, moon, belly, and breast are all graphically contracted into a single bowl, egg, or Venus. The origins of art are fundamentally abstract and nonrepresentational because they are based precisely on the *performative* contraction or concentration of material rhythms.

If a thousand different curves and ovoids can be expressed in a single curve or mound, this is not because one curve represents the others but because each is metonymically transferred to the others *in the same kinetic pattern or field*. In this light, the human body can be interpreted as a specialized bipedal body that can collect, reproduce, and inscribe more graphic motions than any other single natural body. The human body is therefore the space or site of a centripetal gathering together of phonetic and graphic flows in a single phonographic regime.

Kinosigns

As these two kinds of flows are centripetally gathered into the same space of the body, they enter into a confluence and intersect with one another. In the moment of this intersection or utterance, the flows of sound become contemporaneous, coordinated, or synchronized with a given distribution of motion or gesture. The two flows momentarily appear as two dimensions of the same thing.

Flows of sound and flows of rhythmic gesture are distinct from one another but do not form a parallelism or a representation of one by the other—they simply flow together creating a mutual presupposition, synchrony, or kinetic coordination. What is said and what is seen or done converge in a particular fold, but this convergence does not form a static identity; it forms an intersection, event, confluence, or synchrony between heterogeneous flows. Each sound accomplishes an action, and the action is accomplished in the sound. We call this confluence or intersection a material-kinetic sign, or *kinosign*. Kinosigns are not phonemes, morphemes, or simple sounds that refer to gestures or actions—they are specific connections or links formed between a sound and a situation or act. They are sound-actions or *phonographisms*. Sound and action occur at once in the same moment or sign.

Acts or gestures do not cause or produce sounds, nor do sounds cause or produce acts; the two are heterogeneous to each other and simply become intercalated or intertwined in the advent of bipedalism. Kinosigns are not purely signifying phonological structures or "deep syntactical structures," nor are gestures merely external nonlinguistic factors that have no role in linguistic structure. Nor can the connections between the two be fully explained by the social conditions of their production. All of these options treat phonism or graphism as reducible to a structure of discrete constants when in fact the two are flows of continuous variation without totality or predetermined structure.

In other words, sounds mean nothing outside the gestures and circumstances in which they occur. For example, the phrase "Get it!" has no meaning outside particular subjects, addressees, and collective social gestures that intersect with it at a given point. For this sonic gesture to work, it must be said by someone with authority in a place where that person has authority at a certain point and where someone else could respond to the command to get "it." If there is any deviation from this kinetic context, the kinosign fails.

Sound and gesture are therefore mutual presuppositions or mutual coordinations. They do not describe each other or represent each other, but combine, order, and delimit each other. They begin as continuous and heterogeneous flows, but through a series of intersections and overlaps they form a constellation of audio-actions. Sounds are bound to situations and situations are bound to certain sounds such that when one appears it anticipates, combines, or delimits the other. One does not cause the other, but causality is only something that is attributed retroactively after their mutual intersection. A change in one kinosign is preceded by a change in another; however, this does not necessarily imply causality but rather implies only a constant conjunction and kinetic coordination.

Marriage vows, juridical verdicts, and imperatives, for example, are speech acts that reorder or transform a gestural situation in the same way a change in the situation can make possible the meaningful utterance of a phrase like "I love you," without which it would have no other practical intersection. Said on a first date, the phrase will likely fail to connect with the situation to which it is attributing love, but said after six months of dating, the phrase "I love you" may be a successful mutual attribution of love to the situation. In this case, either the situation will have changed such that a phrase can be attributed to it or the phrase, by being uttered, can create a transformation of the situation. The question of whether the phrase caused the situation to be an amorous one or the situation caused the phrase to be uttered is undecidable, because in the moment of the kinetic utterance the two flows intersect and result in a mutual presupposition or mutual coordination of order and retroactive causality.

Once the intersection between sonic and gestural flows occurs, it can, like a kinetic event or constellation, be differentially repeated by folding the flows back around into a loop or cycle. In other words, through kinetic habit a body can make the same sound and repeat the same gesture or graphism at the same time. Sound and action can be reconnected again and again, like the eddy of the river in the same whirling motion but with different spinning water.

As a material-kinetic intersection, however, the kinosign is in some sense arbitrary (but not random). What is said and what is done can be connected together differently and continuously. One is never done once and for all. For the habit of connection to persist, it must be folded again and again until the kinetic cycle appears to be natural, as if it had always been that way. However, like all kinetic folds in continuous flows, they must be made. The product is always a product of a process. The product of a discrete word with meaning is the product of a kinetic process of intersection between the two continuous flows of sound and gesture.

After a series of kinosigns have been folded, they can then be distributed or ordered together through a field of circulation. Circulation allows them to persist in a given order. It therefore presupposes a relatively large repertoire of sonic and graphic motions that can be reproduced in increasingly complex patterns or "grammars." For example, the sound "I" creates a different kinosign depending on the different bodies, voices, tones, and rhythms it is spoken in and what the gestural or practical situation is when it is uttered. Because kinosigns are composed of flows, speech functions as a continuous variation between what is said and what is done. Because each sound and situation is unique or singular, the utterance "I" is something different each time. The situation has changed each time, even if only a little. Now I speak as father, now as son, now as professor, and so on. However, the ordering or continuous circulation between sign junctions allows the kinetic operation to persist in and through all its different gestural situations. For example, the phrase "I swear!" is not a fixed statement. "It is a different statement depending on whether it is said by a child to his or her father, by a man in love to his loved one, or by a witness before the court."[12]

The utterance of sounds always occurs in the context of a larger circulation of sounds and practical gestures. Because of the continuous circulation of phonographic habits, their relations ascribe all kinds of seemingly stable mutual presuppositions and attributions (conjunction, disjunction, or dependence). In a courtroom or classroom, for example, the sounds of the judge or teacher are already distributed as authoritative sounds in relation to others before they even speak.[13] When they do speak, all their words presuppose a connection to the situation in which they are heard as authoritative. Their words confirm their authority, and their authority in the situation confirms and supports their words. If the body is the space of centripetal inscription, linguistic communities (courtrooms, classrooms, and so on) become the regional spaces of circulation where a larger order of kinosigns is contracted and outside of which certain kinosigns do nothing.

Accordingly, not all sonic and gestural flows are ordered in circulation. Just as every circulation conjoins flows, each one also continuously disjoins them. The same flows that may have folded into habitual and ordered kinosigns can also become disjoined from their confluences, folds, and fields. The incredible diversity of languages, minor languages, and the history of etymology clearly attest to the continuous variability of phonographic intersections, their audio mutation, and their geopolitical transformation.

At certain points in history there are flows of sound that no longer intersect with their habitual gestures and begin to intersect elsewhere. This is not because there are first standard language structures or circulations and then, afterward, deviations from them, but rather because so-called standard language rules, syntax, grammars, and so on are already products of continuous intersections between heterogeneous sonic and gestural flows. Because the movement of centripetal accumulation and confluence in the body or community is primary, new intersections or kinosemiotic habits are continually forming.

For example, as the American linguist William Labov has shown, Black English is not a deviant structure from the standard rules of English. First of all, Black English does not follow a fixed structure. Labov's studies show that the second consonant in Black English is absent *more often* only when the following word begins with a consonant rather than a vowel. There does not seem to be a fixed rule for this kinosign, but rather a continuous variation in the language itself over time. Second, and consequently, Black English cannot be a derived structure from English because it is does not consistently follow the same basic structure. Thus, Labov argues that "social pressures are continually operating upon language [to change it] not from some remote point in the past, but as an immanent social force acting in the living present."[14] The sonic and gestural flows of Black English disjoin from their previously ordered circulations and create new and continuously variable circulations, not as secondary deviations but as expressions of the primary kinetic process that has allowed all languages to emerge and mutate in the first place.

Kinomenological Consequences

If speech is the centripetal gathering of sonic and gestural flows into the concentrated space of the phonographically inscribed body, and into the folded circulation of these flows, then several kinomenological consequences follow.

Communication. The first consequence of the kinetic theory of speech reveals that speech is not the communication of information. This is because the first body of space to gather such a diversity of audiograms, the human body, does not preexist the sounds and gestures that are centripetally gathered in it. In other words, the speaking subject is the product of the centripetal confluences that are gathered in it and is not given as a subject in advance of the gathered flows. The product must not be confused with the process.

The subject does not preexist the kinomenological regime of motion that distributes, moves, and orders it through bipedalism, as a hollowed-out space for gathering and inscribing sounds and gestures. If communication is something that occurs between a sending subject and a receiving subject, then kinosigns cannot be communication because it is the condition of the speaking subject in the first place.

Speech is not the information that passes between and independently of the "communicating" subjects. This is because the subjects and their kinosigns are already ordered or distributed in a regime of circulation that has linked the gestural situation with certain sounds. Information is simply a redundancy of the kinosigns or habits already distributed as the kinetic conditions under which subjects are constituted and flows are bound. For example, the phrase "Guilty!" uttered by a judge in a courtroom is not informational because the social distribution of subjects and their connection with certain sounds have already been pre-prepared such that the sound "Guilty!" is immediately an action that changes the attribution of the situation to be one of guilt. Action and sound are accomplished *in the same phonographic moment* without requiring an intermediary of "information." In other words, if there are only intersections of flows between sound and gesture, their connection or link is already established and there is no third thing like information that passes between sound and action.

Reference. The second consequence of the kinetic theory of speech is that it is not referential. Sounds do not refer to gestures, just as gestures do not refer to words as something external to them. Instead, the two form a confluence or event in which they immediately intersect at the same point: the phonogram or kinosign. There is no need for reference or representation because there is no practical difference between them in what they do; they are two sides of the same thing. There is no correspondence or correlation, only a confluence, coordination, and mutual presupposition.

Linguistics. The third consequence is that there is no science or linguistics of kinosigns. This is because linguistics and the study of languages presumes a set of fixed linguistic constructions containing constant and discrete elements in a coherent totality. For Saussure, this takes the form of a logical structure of arbitrary but constant linguistic habits or phonemes that "allow an individual to understand and be understood, for which a community of speakers is necessary."[15] For Chomsky, it takes the form of a fixed syntax or rule for ordering that underlies the "mental reality" of all language and the "human essence."[16]

In both cases the science of language is assumed to be composed primarily of constant and discrete sonic-gestural products, when in fact such phonemes and rules are *secondary* to the primary process of the material-kinetic flows that produce the intersections between sounds and gestures in the first place. Labov's studies, for example, show that language cannot be separated from the continuous variation of sonic and gestural flows that constitute a whole kinomenology or social distribution through which the flows are connected in the first place. On this point our kinetic theory is in agreement with Deleuze and Guattari when they write that "[a]s long as linguistics confines itself to constants, whether syntactical, morphological, or phonological, it ties the statement to a signifier and enunciation to a subject . . . it consigns circumstances to the exterior, [and] closes language in on itself."[17]

Furthermore, linguistics tends to ignore the gestural or material flows that constitute kinosigns by interpreting language as a purely ideal realm of meaningful mental entities or purely phonetic entities: phonemes. However, since kinosigns are not ideal structures of meaning but rather material-kinetic developments that occur first and foremost in the centripetal space of the inscribed body, speaking bodies would not have considered mythology to be a representation of a transcendent realm of meaning. This kind of idea does not emerge until after the invention of writing, as seen in Part II.

By treating language as a realm of arbitrary but internally self-referential meanings, linguistics forgets the body's material-kinetic conditions of production as first and foremost a space or historical site of sonic and gestural gathering.[18] Linguistics has made the mistake of taking the metaphysical product of a certain historical kinetic distribution of being, as transcendent meaning invented in the ancient world, and projected it back onto all language itself. The science of language is therefore the "history of an error," as Nietzsche would say.[19]

As Deleuze and Guattari again rightly observe, "The constants of language do not indicate permanence as much as they function as centers, in which the search for essences is implicated, the scientific model taking language as an object of study is one with the political model by which language is homogenized, centralized, standardized, becoming a language of power, a major or dominant language."[20] This scientific model follows the same kinetic pattern as the political one developed in the ancient world, but that did not yet exist in the prehistoric and Neolithic world. Thus, by not going back in history far enough, linguistics fails to understand the original kinetic structure of language.

However, just because there is no *science* of kinosigns does not mean there can be no *study* of kinosigns. Instead of the science of universal and constant elements, a kinetic theory of signs would analyze the continual variations and heterogeneous intersections created by the conjunction, disjunction, circulation, and knotworks of flows as accumulated and inscribed in regional spaces: human bodies, animal bodies, social bodies, cosmic bodies, and so on. Such a study would be analytic but also diagnostic insofar as it would examine the points of sonic and gestural disjunction that lead to the creation of new speech habits and new circulations of mutual presupposition and attribution.

SPEECH AND MYTHOLOGY

The kinetic intersection between sound and gesture or phonographism is also coordinated with the kinetic pattern of oral mythologies themselves. For example, ancestral oral mythologies are not simply told once and for all, they are told again and again. This is because the intersection between sound and gesture does not occur only once, but must be retold in a periodic, cyclical, and differential repetition that binds and rebinds the community through the very speech act of the story.

Since being is fundamentally spatial and space is fundamentally spiral and centripetal, phonographic mythology cannot be gathered or told once and for all but must be differentially repeated in ritual enactments, initiatory ceremonies, and annual songs and dances of the hunt and the harvest. In each ritual reenactment, the community reweaves its own rhythms and audiograms back into the cosmos through a specific series of repeated speech acts that are tied to specific places.

In oral cultures space is experienced as a series of interconnected but segmented places, each with its own power and animism. A ritual mythology thus binds sounds and gestures to bodies and places not as representations of something else but as centripetal gatherings and phonographic inscriptions in the being of space itself.

In many oral cultures, mythic creation stories do not describe events that only happened once long ago but also events that occur again and again through the speech acts of those involved in the retelling. Oral mythologies do not simply speak of a past event but also bring that very event back into being through the retelling of the story.

Furthermore, the recreation or persistence of the mythological universe relies on this very retelling. Human and cosmos intersect in the folded junction of the divine phonogram. "The myths preserve and transmit the paradigms, the exemplary models, for all the responsible activities in which men engage. By virtue of these paradigmatic models revealed to men in mythical times, the Cosmos and society are periodically regenerated," as Mircea Eliade writes.[21] By performing the same sounds and gestures of the ancestral powers, one actually becomes the ancestral being and accomplishes the act of creation again for the first time, using the same sonic and gestural powers.

The spatial and repetitive structure of oral mythologies demonstrates precisely that speech does not represent being but enacts being in the ritual space of gathered speech acts. Just as the cosmos brings together sound and gesture at the highest possible level of being in space, so ritual repeats this centripetal condensation of sound and gesture at the level of the inscribed body in space. The cosmic ocean of space whirls, eddies, and settles in the tide pools of place, which are continuously replenished and interconnected by the sea. The structure of oral mythology thus attests directly to the dominant kinetic description of being as space through speech.

Much of the content of archaic oral creation mythologies attests to this point. For example, within the cosmogony of indigenous Australians, the world was created and given its forms, first the spiral rainbow serpent that burst from the formless matter of the earth (egg), but further formed and localized by "creator beings" who walked across the surface of the earth and sang its places into existence. The trails they left behind in their track are called "songlines." The songline is the audiographic flow or speech act that brings the world into being through sound, and that brings sound into being through the gestural rhythm of walking.

Sound and act are not representations of each other, but are instead two mutually attributive dimensions of the same ontogenetic process that creates the regional places within the larger folded snake spiral of space. As aboriginal peoples perform the ritual walkabout, they really perform, not represent, the footsteps of the creator beings' songlines while they reperform the same songs and gestures that brought the world into existence. They sing the world back into existence. This mythological conception of being only makes sense if sound and gesture are not representational but performative, creative, kinetic, and fundamentally spatial.

According to Ogotemmeli, an elder of the Dogon tribe of Mali, the cosmic egg that created the world was filled with spiraling "traces" "like that left by a snake or insect moving across the ground,"[22] movements, or *bummo*, that create a "transformation of continuous movement" that eventually brings being into existence. These kinetic traces are what Ogotemmeli calls "signs." A Dogon sign is not simply a sound, a gesture, or a motion; it is the kinetic intersection of all three produced by the spiral motion in the egg.[23] "Amma's signs, which he sent into the world, went, entered into things which (at that moment) became."[24] Signs, sounds, and gestures do not represent one another but intersect and create the localization of being in spiraled space. Dogon signs are the kinetic intersection of sound and gesture in spatialized being-there: they are kinosigns. "It is said: 'When life increases, it increases by spiraling,' which is a repetition of Amma's first act, because 'that indicates how Amma came out of the egg of the world.'"[25] Each creation is a spiraled repetition of the first creation; each individual phonogram brings being back into existence again as a repetition of the first divine speech act that brought the world into existence in the first place. Speech and space are united through the kinetic spiral of being.

Other archaic creation myths, like those of the Lapps, the Ostyak, the Chukchee, the Yakut, and the Tungus, refer to a "secret language of nature," which in each case is synonymous with an animal speech or song.[26] As the kinetic intersection of sound and gesture, animal speech is also creative and even more primordial than human speech. If humans have language, it is accumulated and contracted from the creative force of natural and animal speech. Many other oral archaic creation myths attest to the ontogenetic power of speech acts. For example, Hopi, Pomo, and Acoma Native American creation myths include a "song of life".[27]

The power of speech to create is also attested to in the nearly universal cultural history of incantation or magic spells. By speaking certain sounds out loud, the aim of the magic spell is not to speak about or represent the world, but to bring it into existence or transform it. The emergence of a cultural mythology of magic spells makes no sense outside the archaic practice in which sound and gesture are fundamentally intertwined not as sign and signifier but as kinetic intersection, mutual presupposition, and kinetic coordination. By using or gathering a sound or gesture, the other comes into being in the regional body or space of a particular speaking community. Thus, the word "incantation," from the Latin word *cantare*, meaning "to sing," and the Old French word "enchantment" thus connect the history of magic back to the very oldest oral creation myths based on songlines and creation songs.

This is the same legacy that connects speech, song, oral mythology, poetry, and space beyond the Neolithic period and, to some degree, into the Homeric, Hesiodic, and Orphic poems of archaic Greece (800 BCE–480 BCE).[28] Homer, Hesiod, and Orpheus were divine figures of song whose sonorous words produced and transformed reality. It is therefore no coincidence that all their oral mythologies give ontogenetic primacy to space. Being may be fundamentally chaotic, but for these bards, creation is not possible without the intermediary of a concentrated creative space.

In Homer's song it is Oceanus, the spiraling and chaotic waters that encircle the world, and Tethys, the rounded and delimited mother ocean goddess,[29] from whom all of creation and the other gods originate (γένε σιν).[30] In Hesiod, Chaos, meaning "space" in Greek, is ontologically primary, but through a centripetal ontogenetic concentration of chaotic space comes, the broad breasts of Gia (Γαῖ᾽ εὐρύστερνος), the Mother Earth, the "solid foundation" on which all other gods are birthed. The rounded, ovoid, cosmic breasts of the earth shelter and nourish creation like a womb, egg, bowl, or vessel, gathering all the flows of chaos into "broadpaths" (εὐρυόδεια) or "tracks" through which it circulates as the internalized place of ontogenesis.[31]

In the collective fragments of the Orphic songs/hymns, several fragments describe creation as coming from an egg wrapped in a spiraling snake coil;[32] others claim that it was Chaos that created the egg;[33] still others claim that it was Night (Nyx) and Ether that produced the silver egg from which the world was born.[34] Despite the differences between these fragments, Orphic cosmogony is largely described as one in which chaotic or formless motion is centripetally gathered together into a creative world-egg.[35] As the German poet Rilke writes of this in his *Sonnets to Orpheus*:

> All things were in her sleep:
> The trees I marveled at, the enchanting spell
> Of farthest distances, the meadows deep,
> And all the magic that myself befell.
> Within her slept the world.[36]

The terrestrial trees and meadows, the enchanting spell of song and speech, the depths of space and dream, the magic of phonographism, and the radical ontological interiority of the egg are all part of the kinographic structure of phonographic and mythological space.

In the prehistoric and Neolithic period, being is described predominantly as spatial and inscribed through speech. Both of these graphic performances implicitly and explicitly rely on a centripetal regime of motion. During the ancient period, however, the rise of cities, the invention of writing, and the description of being as eternal emerged according to an entirely different centrifugal regime of motion, as we see in Part II.

PART II
Being and Eternity

I
Kinos

CHAPTER 16

Centrifugal Motion

Beginning around 5,000 BCE, alongside the rise of cities and written language, a new regime of motion came to dominate ontological practice in the West: centrifugal motion. Clearly visible in the Bronze Age (3,500 BCE) and culminating in ancient Greece by 500 BCE, a newly powerful kinetic pattern of ontological practice emerged that descriptively and inscriptively relied on a centrifugal movement from the center to the periphery. This is not to say that the dominantly centripetal motions of the Neolithic period disappeared or were sublimated but rather that they were transformed and taken up by another motion.

There is no absolute succession of kinetic epochs, only a range of degrees in mixture with other motions. The ancient period is thus simply the period in which the regime of centrifugal motion first became dominant or more powerful than the others. There are no logical contradictions or negations in the ontology of motion, only vectors, constellations, and circulations. Movements do not contradict one another; they simply combine and change trajectories.

The task of Part II is to analyze how the motion of ontological practice was concretely sustained and what sorts of descriptions and inscriptions it produced. The argument of Part II is that the historically dominant ontological description of being as eternal and its inscription in written language are two expressions of the same kinetic field of centrifugal motion that rose to historical prominence in the ancient West—and that defines the kinetic concept of eternity in the ontology of motion.

More than the concept of space, the concept of eternity is described as a transcendence of motion, change, time, and space. In contrast to primitive descriptions of space linked to spiral cycles of birth, death, and rebirth, eternity never dies. However, the concept of eternity and the invention of writing rise to power historically not because they discover some metaphysical truth about the nature of being but because they produce a new kinographic description in resonance or coordination with a real change in the movement of reality at the time.

Part II is divided into three sections, just like Part I: the first offers a strictly *kinomenological* theory of eternity as centrifugal motion; the second offers a kinetic analysis of the historically *descriptive* features of eternity provided by the cosmological writings of the time; and the third offers a kinetic analysis of historical technology of *inscription* (writing), within which these descriptions were inscribed.

KINOMENOLOGY OF ETERNITY

This chapter offers a purely kinomenological theory of eternity as a pattern of centrifugal motion. The thesis of this chapter is that it is possible to give a material and kinetic description of the motions that define eternal being. The concept of eternity may be a metaphysical fiction, but the kinomena of eternity are not.

Centrifugal Motion

Centrifugal motion presupposes a centripetal motion that gathers the pedetic flows of being from the vast periphery toward a center. However, centripetal motion does not necessarily produce a center. As a spiral curvature it produces an open-ended fold or internalization, as we saw in Part I. However, once this centripetal motion has gathered and folded several flows into the internalized regional places of circulation, a new centric movement becomes possible.

Once a pattern of internalized circulation is sustained, it is possible to produce or localize a center within this circulation. Ontologically speaking, being has no center. Kinetically speaking, however, regional circulations can produce centric motions. While a centripetal spiral has no absolute center or periphery, it is also possible to demarcate both by closing off the loops of the spiral at certain points, in effect creating a regionally central and peripheral fold in being. This is the first operation of centrifugal motion.

Once a centripetal spiral motion is accumulated into a central fold it becomes possible for this central fold to then redirect flows outward, from the center to the periphery. However, centrifugal motion does not negate or abolish centripetal motion. It is not enough to simply accumulate motion once and for all; centrifugal motion relies on the constant replenishment of its concentrated central fold, or megajunction, with new folds brought in from elsewhere. Centripetal flows provide the support and sustenance for the reproduction of the center but become increasingly organized, stratified, and redirected according to a more powerful centrifugal motion that both holds them in and pushes them away according to a new regime of movement.

The regime of centrifugal motion is thus not simply defined by a one-directional outward motion but also by the constitutive motions that create the center in the first place. It is thus defined by both a convergence of influx and a redirection of outflow. What makes a regime centrifugal is that both influx and outflows are all directed toward, circulated through, and redirected outward from a central megajunction.

Centralization

Centralization is the process by which the center reproduces its conditions of persistence and redirects motion from the center back to the periphery and in again. The center is a product of a centripetal accumulation, but it is not the necessary aim of the tendency of internalization.

However, centralization is the starting point and presupposition of centrifugal radiation. Centralization does not strictly define centripetal motion, but it does define centrifugal motion. In short, centralization presupposes the uncreated and unending existence of a central fold from which and to which all things flow.

Circle. Several kinomenal forms follow from this regime of motion. The first is the circle, the geometric figure of eternity. Centripetal motion gathers toward a center, but centrifugal motion closes off the spiral at a central fold and then radiates outward from this fold toward the periphery. Another name for a closed spiral is a circle, but a circle is not only defined by its center. Closing off a center is only the first step, as Euclid notes: "A circle is a plane figure contained by a single line [which is called a circumference], (such that) all of the straight-lines *radiating towards [the circumference] from one point* amongst those lying inside the figure are equal to one another."[1] All the heterogeneous lines radiating outward become equal to one another by virtue of the limit of the circumference and the mold of a single common point: the center, from whence they originate.

In other words, the creation of the circle requires not only a center but the radiation from that center to an equidistant periphery. "To draw a circle," Euclid observes, all we need is "any center and radius."[2] According to Euclid, in order to draw a circle, we do not start with the periphery but with a single point that will become the center, as a compass draws a line around the center. This is the ideology or metaphysics of the circle.

Kinomenologically and historically speaking, however, we do begin with the periphery; we begin with space—with rounded bowls, ovoids, eclipses, eggs, breasts, wombs, and so on. Circulation is not necessarily circular but cyclical. The two are not the same. Only when the productive space of centripetal accumulation has been accomplished is it possible for a megajunction to emerge.

However, once this megajunction is created it reacts back outward, radiating and redirecting motion in all directions. In other words, centralization begins its motion from the center and radiates it in every direction, producing a new organization of the periphery as equidistant from a preexisting center. Kinetically, Euclid had it backwards, he subordinated motion to eternal geometric forms. Historically, however, he began from exactly the dominant kinetic starting point of the ancient West: the center. The description of the circle, therefore, is as the centrifugal effect *of the center*, not the centripetal effect *of the periphery*.

Rotation. If the circle with its ex nihilo center and perfectly equidistant radii is the geometric image of eternity, circular rotation is the "movement" of eternity. While the center of the circle itself remains kinomorphically unchanged, the periphery circulates or rotates around the perfect and unchanged center. Circular rotation thus allows for total motion, mobility, and circulation while itself being modeled on a relatively immobile center around which everything else rotates. The center is the sole point of reference that keeps in and holds out the periphery. The periphery appears differential while the center appears identical to itself.

Rotation is the process by which different heterogeneous folds move, cycle, and change but only with respect to a center that orients their motion. Circulation goes out, but in going out it follows the exact same arc in its return around the center. Rotational motion thus presupposes centralization. Through rotational circulation, different flows and folds are relatively homogenized with respect to the perfect arc of their circulation and with respect to their equal distance from the center. Centralization thus produces the homogeneity of motion but also a radical unification of motion as a whole in the unity of the relatively immobile center.

In other words, through circular rotation differences in time (past, present, future) and space (here and there) are reconciled through motion. Motion between different points is also reconciled in the unity of the circle. Through radiation and rotation the center becomes everywhere and nowhere. It becomes the eternal idea. As Hegel writes, "The Idea, Spirit, transcends time because it is itself the Notion of time; it is eternal, in and for itself, and it is not dragged into the time-process because it does not lose itself in one side of the process."[3] "Eternity," he continues, "will not come to be, nor was it, but it is. . . . The true Present, therefore, is eternity."[4] It is worth quoting at length Hegel's incredible insight on this point:

> This return of the line is the circle; it is the Now, Before and After that have closed together in a unity in which these dimensions are indifferent, so that Before is equally After, and vice versa. It is in circular motion that the necessary paralysis of these dimensions is first posited in space. Circular motion is the spatial or subsistent unity of the dimensions of time. The point proceeds toward a place that is its future, and leaves one that is the past; but what it has left behind is at the same time what it has still to reach: it has been already at the place that it is reaching. Its goal is the point that is its past; and this is the truth of time, that the goal is not the future but the past. The motion that relates itself to the center is itself the plane, motion as the synthetic whole in which exist its moments, the extinction of the motion in the center, the motion itself and its relation to its extinction, namely the radii of the circle. But this plane itself moves and becomes the other of itself, a complete space; or the reversion-into-self, the immobile center, becomes a universal point in which the whole is peacefully absorbed. In other words, it is motion in its essence, motion that has sublated the distinctions of Now, Before, and After, its dimensions or its Notion. In the circle, these are in a unity; the circle is the restored Notion of duration, Motion extinguished within itself. . . . Motion is the process, the transition of Time into Space and of Space into Time: Matter, on the other hand, is the relation of Space and Time as a peaceful identity.[5]

This is a dense passage, but there are three important points relevant to our kinomenological theory of eternity here.

> First, the differences in time (past, present, future) are like three different folds on the periphery of the circle of circulation. Through circular motion each of these differences is unified in the circle as a whole. Time itself is not eternal but only becomes eternal in its circular unity in relation to an immobile center around which it moves.

Second, this circular movement produces a circular and closed-off space of homogenous, peaceful, and immobilized unity.

Third, the circular, rotational, movement itself that unites the differences in space and time is itself unified in the radii of the circle and is extinguished in the immobile and eternal center. Although Hegel grants logical primacy to time and space, we can easily see from a kinomenological perspective that the concept or notion of eternity is something constituted first and foremost by circular motion.

Stasis. The concept of eternity is constituted by motion, but it is a special type of motion: a circular motion capable of producing an "immobile" center. Centralization produces a center and a circular motion of the periphery around this center. Through the rotational motion of the circle around the center, everything moves except the center that everything moves around. Undying immobility is thus achieved only through a double kinetic motion.

On the one hand, this is achieved by the more primary centripetal motion that gathers the flows toward a common region; on the other hand, the center continues to persist precisely because of the rotation of its own centrifugal radii around it. In other words, its verticality and immobility is a gyroscopic product of motion. Eternity is like a spinning top held upright by virtue of the centripetally gathered structure of the material of the top and by the rotational and centrifugal motion of the top. The center is thus a product of a double kinetic constitution capable of giving the appearance of an eternal unmoved immobility produced by a continual centrifugal motion. This kinomenological function gives rise to the appearance of a relative immobility often described as an immutable and eternal essence.

This is apparent in Hegel's analysis of circular motion insofar as motion is ultimately "extinguished" because it returns to where it started from. In a circle, origin is already destination. Before leaving, one has already arrived and therefore goes nowhere. In the closed circle, however, motion also suffocates itself and becomes a pure eternal notion in its immobile unity.

But in affirming this thesis, Hegel is forced to admit that the notion of eternity is in fact a *product* of motion itself. Eternity is only the apparent or conceptual exhaustion of motion. The materiality of centrifugal motion and the process of centralization are still required for the persistence of the center.

In other words, ideality is a product of a material-kinetic process, not its exhaustion. Hegel's thesis only gets off the ground if we grant him what Euclid already assumed—the presupposition of a center, a *Punctum*

Archimedis, or Archimedean point of fixity. If a center preexists its periphery ex nihilo, then motion is always already immobile and extinguished. However, by definition, stasis cannot give birth to motion. Motion is either primary or it is nothing.

Therefore, if the origins of centralization are themselves nothing central (i.e., if they are centripetal, spiral, kinetic, and composed of open flows), then we do not and cannot begin with a center and closed circle—and Hegel is wrong. Every circle is already open to an outside that continually supplies it with and entropically depletes it of motion. In other words, since center and circle are products of a more primary kinetic process of pedesis and centripetal motion, eternity is a conceptual effect or product of motion, not the other way around.

Through centrifugal motion, this immobile point not only appears as undying and uncaused, but it also appears as unchanged. While the periphery spins, rotates, and changes, the center remains an unchanged essence, everywhere and nowhere spread throughout its radii. Just as peripheral motion appears to be the effect of the center, so peripheral folds appear to be mere appearances emanating from an unchanging center. Centralization therefore produces the holy trinity of centrifugal motion: stasis, essence, and eternity. These are real distributions of motion with real consequences for the way in which being appears in its kinomenological distribution. Being really becomes "eternal," if by eternal we mean the ontologically descriptive name for "the kinetic effect produced by a centrifugal regime of motion."

Sphere. Centralization produces circular motion, but circular motion is not only two-dimensional, it is three-dimensional or spherical. The sphere is the kinetic product of a centralized motion radiated outward in all directions to its periphery. The sphere produces a kinetic transformation of space from being ovoid, spiraled, open, and rounded to becoming spherical, circular, closed, and perfectly round.

Kinetically, space is the centripetal condition under which a center is accumulated, but once this central point occurs, it reacts back on the open peripheral space of the spiral and closes it off such that all points in the delimited place become like homogenous radii, modeled on the center.

In other words, the sphere transforms space into a series of homogenous points in relation to a center. Each of the points has a positionality as a possible extension or direct link to the fixed, immobile point of the center. When space is given ontological primacy, it is a lived space of orientation and interconnection, like the enveloping spiral horizon of Homer's Oceanus. Time then is not a sequence but a cycle. However, when eternity is given ontological primacy, space becomes empty, void, a chasm, lack, darkness, and negativity. Time, then, is no longer cyclical but abolished in the unity of the absolute present. The future and past, the here and there are no longer heterogeneous realities but exchangeable homogenous fragments unified in the glory of the One, the Whole, the Beyond, the Eternal. The sphere is the perfect image of the immediate unity of time in its circular motion and of the homogeneous unity of space as an empty void waiting to be traversed by radii from the center. In the sphere, time and space become simultaneous in an eternal present.

Concentricity. Centralization produces circular motion, but circular motion in turn makes possible a concentric motion. The spiral of centripetal motion has numerous folds. Once a central point is secured and repeated through folding, however, it can produce radii and thus a circle. This process can also be continually reproduced on a larger and larger scale moving outward, closing off each of the spiral "rings" in turn.

As each of the spiral rings is closed off and reoriented around the center, a concentricity of larger and smaller circles is produced, each modeled on the first central circle. Centrifugal circulation is no longer the circulation of a spiraled space with regionally interconnected places but rather the closure of their interconnection in favor of a single connection of all regional folds to a single central no-place. Instead of forming a decentered collection of regional places, the circle subordinates all places to a single place or site of redirection.

The center of circular circulation is not a place "in" space, but is instead like a no-place "above and beyond" space. This is the origin of the language of verticality that appears in ontological descriptions of eternity. Insofar as the center becomes the organizing model of the periphery through its radii, it is everywhere throughout the circle, but insofar as it is everywhere throughout the circle, it is nowhere in particular. Insofar as it is nowhere in particular, it appears as a special kinetic place beyond and above the sphere where motion is always already redistributed from elsewhere—from a seemingly transcendent central megajunction.

All the larger and smaller circulations are centralized around a single megajunction producing a concentricity of circles more or less distant from the center. This kinogeometric structure also makes possible a hierarchy between concentric circles. Since all movement is directly connected and redirected through the center, it retains the highest degree of kinetic power: the power to control circulation. Those concentric circles more distant from the center transmit centrifugal motion to fewer peripheral circles than the circles closest to the center. The outer circles are all held in place and secured by the eternal foundations of the center, around which they orbit. All orbits are secured because of this center, like a geocentric universe of perfect planetary spheres, each sustained by an eternal and divine force, which itself remains unmoved and unchanged.

Concentric hierarchies have numerous historical manifestations in the ancient cosmologies, as we see in the following chapters—from concentric city planning, architectural forms, hierarchal numerals, class and social concentricities closer and farther from the center of eternal forms, or heaven.

Opposition. Centralization also makes possible a new kinetic structure of opposition. When being is dominantly distributed centripetally as space, oppositions can only take the form of regional differences, not ontological binaries. Kinetically, the material conditions for opposition cannot be achieved in spiraled and open space. In the spiral, the egg, and the ovoid, differences are held together, intertwined, or folded together. Light and dark, good and bad, inside and outside are simply two sides of the same spiraled motion that connects them together through division. If being is first and foremost spatial, there can be no ontological division inside and outside. The inside of a fold is simply an outside fold over itself, and an outside is simply an inside folded again—the spiral.

However, with the rise of centrifugal motion, the spiral arm of kinetic space is closed off and cut up into a series of concentric circles or spheres relatively divided between smaller and larger and insides and outsides. Kinetically, there are no divisions in flows, only bifurcations, which is why every circle is built on top of a spiral. However, insofar as circular and spherical motions rigidly repeat their orbits around a central megajunction, they seek to close off the bifurcation paths of the spiral. The circle is a product of motion, but insofar as its regime of motion remains bound to a central megajunction, it reproduces a distinction between the inside of the circle—where the megajunction resides, and the outside of the circle—where the subordinate microjunctions reside.

Again, this not a metaphysical opposition but rather a centrifugal and kinetic bifurcation only made possible by the process of centralization and the production of a center megajunction. The binary oppositions between male and female, heaven and earth, divine and profane, inside and outside are not metaphysical determinations but historical and kinomenological ones. The kinetic structure of eternity is thus predicated on a fundamental division or opposition between what is eternal, divine, and unmoved on the one hand and what is mortal, terrestrial, and moved, on the other.

It now remains to be seen how this kinetic regime of centrifugal motion is historically described in the cosmological writings of ancient civilizations as the eternity of being. In the next chapters we turn to the cosmologies of eternal being in which the ontological description of eternity emerges its first period of historical dominance.

11
Logos

CHAPTER 17

Ancient Cosmology I

The Holy Mountain

The previous chapter set out a kinomenological theory of eternity as a pattern of centrifugal motion. In this chapter and the next three we look at how the kinetic *description*, or logos, of eternity emerged historically as the dominant name for being. The thesis of these four chapters is to show that the dominant ancient ontological description of being implicitly and explicitly relies on a description of centrifugal motion.

COSMOLOGY

The dominant determination of being as eternity coincided roughly with the historical period of ancient cosmologies found in the writings of the Mesopotamians, Egyptians, Semitic peoples, and the Greeks, beginning around 5,000 BCE and lasting to around 500 CE, although traces of it certainly began earlier in some areas and lingered later in others. In Part I, the exposition of the concept of space as a dominant ontological description of being was tied to the rise of mythographic images made by Paleolithic and Neolithic humans. Part II, however, showed how the rise of written language made possible the invention of ontological descriptions that claim to be distinct from the being they describe. Far from being actually transcendent, this type of practice helps give rise to a new kinetic pattern of centrifugal motion.

Mythology and cosmology are in many ways distinct, but in one important way they are similar: they both provide a description of the fundamental origins of being. In other words, they both provide an ontological description. If one of the aims of this book is to offer a kinetic theory of the dominant historical descriptions of being, cosmological descriptions provide us with the primary material for analysis during the ancient period.

However, ancient cosmology, from the ancient Greek word κόσμος, *kósmos*, meaning "world or universe," is different from prehistoric mythology, in part because the material domain of their descriptive and inscriptive ontologies is quite different. While mythology is kinographically tied to the inscription of sound and action on the speaking or *mythic* body, cosmology is tied to a written inscription of a silent universal or *kosmic* logos on the surface of the mute tablet or scroll. While mythology is structured around speech and thus the resonant living body, cosmology is structured around writing and thus the silent and dead bodies of the tablet and scroll. This has important implications for the kinetics of ontological practice.

The aim of this chapter (and the next three) is therefore to examine the historical rise to dominance of a new centrifugal regime of ontological description defined by the name of eternity in ancient Western cosmology. The rise of this descriptive dominance occurs in four distinct historico-kinetic operations: (1) the division between center and periphery, (2) the immobility of the center, (3) the retroactive determination of centrifugal motion, and finally (4) the introduction of an absolute center. These four kinetic operations correspond to four major descriptions found in the cosmologies of the ancient Mesopotamians, Egyptians, Semitic peoples, and the Greeks and adopted throughout the West: (1) the separation of heaven and earth, (2) the deification of the king, (3) theomachy, and (4) ex nihilo creation (see Table 17.1). These four operations are the subjects of these four chapters on the logos (description) of eternity.[1]

Table 17.1 FOUR KINETIC OPERATIONS OF ETERNITY

Kinetic Operation	Cosmological Event	God
Division (center/periphery)	Separation (heaven/earth)	Enlil
Immobile Center	Deification of the King	Dumuzi
Retroactive Centrifuge	Theomachy	Marduk
Absolute Center	Ex Nihilo Creation	Yaweh

THE SEPARATION OF HEAVEN AND EARTH

The primary description of being as eternal began as early as the Bronze Age (3,500 BCE–2,400 BCE) with the first cosmologies of ancient Sumer. Eventually, the rise to dominance of this description reached its apex around the Iron Age (1,200 BCE–500 BCE) with the appearance of a single eternal sky god.

The rise to dominance of being as eternity therefore took place over the course of thousands of years and included four major kinetic operations of cosmological description corresponding to four major gods: (1) Enlil, (2) Dumuzi, (3) Marduk, and (4) Yaweh. The emergence of each of these gods marks a further kinetic transformation of being toward a certain description of eternity as centrifugal.

The first kinetic operation was introduced by the Sumerian god Enlil and the Egyptian god Atum; it describes the beginnings of an ontological separation of heaven from earth.

Enlil

This first descriptive cosmological operation began with the birth of the Sumerian god Enlil. However, the very oldest recorded documents of Sumerian cosmology begin with Nammu, the goddess of the sea, "the mother, who gave birth to heaven and earth."[2] Heaven and earth were thus originally united in the creative primordial sea. Through her they were birthed. Nammu herself was not born at a previous point to any other god but always existed. Within her, heaven and earth are united as the gods An (heaven) and Ki (earth). The "Cattle and Grain" myth describes this original unity of heaven and earth as a "mountain," in reference to the prehistoric goddess of space and earth.[3]

The mountain begins at the base of the earth and stretches to a peak in heaven. According to the Sumerian "Creation of the Pickax" myth, the union of An and Ki produces Enlil, meaning "air," who then separates heaven and earth from each other:

> The lord, that which is appropriate verily he caused to appear,
> The lord whose decisions are unalterable,
> Enlil, who brings up the seed of the land from the earth,
> Took care to move away heaven from earth,
> Took care to move away earth from heaven.[4]

Not only does Enlil separate heaven from earth, but this separation also creates a further separation of the exterior of the mountain from its interior, which becomes the "deep" or "underworld":

> After An had carried off heaven,
> After Enlil had carried off earth,
> After Ereshkigal had been carried off into Kur [under the mountain] as its prize.⁵

Enlil splits the earth into two: the surface (Ki) and her sister, the abyss of the deep (Ereshkigal). Since Nammu is the primordial serpent goddess of the deep, the separation of heaven and earth also produces a separation between the earth as it is exposed to the air (Ki) and the earth as it remains abyssal and hidden (Ereshkigal). In creating this trifold division of the primordial waters (Nammu) into heaven, earth, and underworld, Enlil also acquires the powers of creation and the power to bring up seed from the earth—previously the powers of the water and earth goddesses alone. In carrying away the earth goddess Ki as his bride, Enlil becomes the supreme creator and takes up residence at the top of the cosmic mountain, his temple, on top of the body of the earth.

Atum

Around the same time as the descriptive emergence of Enlil in Sumeria, Atum-Ra, the sun god, was described in Egypt and introduced a similar division between heaven and earth. There are several versions of Egyptian cosmology, depending on the time period and region, as told in the cities of Hermopolis, Heliopolis, Memphis, and Thebes. Despite their differences, however, they all share one common cosmo-kinetic operation: They all perform a separation between heaven and earth.

According to all four major versions of creation, in the beginning there were the primeval waters, or Nun, from which all life and being emerged. In the city of Heliopolis, however, the god Atum, the "Complete One," emerged out of the waters as a cosmogenetic "mound of the first time." In other versions of this same myth, the mound is an egg, surrounded by swirling waters. Atum has several different forms: as a visible divinity he is Khepri, as the divine craftsman he is Ptah, and as the sun he is Ra. Atum first creates Shu (male, air, life) and Tefnut (female, moisture, order) by masturbating or spitting them into being. His spittle or sperm mixes the breath of life into the liquid flux. Through a spatial localization (mound, egg) of chaotic waters (frothing spit/semen) came the ordered world.

The liquid unity of being as an interior of living flows is torn asunder when Shu, like Enlil, divides being into two: heaven and earth. Shu says to Atum,

> I am that space which came about in the waters
> I came into being in them, I grew in them,
> but I was not consigned to the abode of darkness.[6]

Shu and Tefnut give birth to Nut, Sky (female), and Geb, Earth (male). As Air, Shu separates Sky and Earth from one another. Shu stretches Nut upward and supports her so she can birth the stars and circulate them across her watery body. In graphic depictions of this event, Geb lays prone under Nut waiting for her life-giving waters. All creation and life is thus mediated through the air and defined by an ontological division between Sky and Earth.

In the Memphite version of this cosmogony, Atum-Ptah is an intellectual craftsman who thinks the nature of being, and by thinking creates it. This is not a physical creation but a mental one developed in Ptah's heart—the seat of human thought for ancient Egyptians. Through breath and air he draws their messages into his heart, which thinks, and then manifests creation in matter as physical tongue:

> The seeing of the eyes and the breathing of the nose bring messages to the heart . . . It is the heart which causes all decisions to be made, but it is the tongue which reports what the heart has thought out. . . . All is in accord with the command which the heart has devised and which has appeared upon the tongue. Thus is determined the peculiar nature of everything.[7]

Kinetic Analysis

These two cosmological accounts in Sumer and Egypt describe the first of the four kinetic operations of a new regime of "eternal" centrifugal motion: the division between center and periphery.

Enlil. The cosmology of Enlil, father of the gods and creator of man, begins just like the previously dominant mythologies of the Neolithic: with the primacy of a centripetal accumulation of chaotic flows into a protective and divine unity. Nammu, the goddess of flowing waters and ocean, begins to centripetally accumulate her chaotic flows into an enclosed region: a primordial holy mountain.

As the accumulation increases and piles up toward the center of the mountain, the mountain grows higher and higher into the sky, ultimately uniting it with heaven. In Nammu, heaven and earth are two sides of the same spatial gathering. The base of the earth spirals up toward heaven. The extreme centripetal accumulation of being produces a growing verticality and centrality from a relatively dispersed horizontality. While this motion is already distinct from the purely spatial and earthly gathering of the previous kinetic age, it still follows roughly the same dominantly spatial and spiral determinations of prehistoric mythologies.

However, everything changes with the birth of Enlil. The spiraled "one" (Nammu) bifurcates into two enfolded bodies (An and Ki), but the two produce a third (Enlil) that divides the two and thus destroyes the unity of the one (Nammu). Space is a dynamic folded unity, but it is also constituted by a centripetal movement of accumulation. However, Enlil introduces a cut into this infinitely narrowing accumulation, thus producing a mountain "peak." The top of the mountain no longer directly connects to heaven but only to the air at the center of a spherical cosmos. The mountaintop becomes the omphalos, or central navel that marks the point of division where Enlil has broken off from Nammu's body. Once this break occurs, motion continues to accumulate upward toward the top of the mountain, but it stops at its peak instead of connecting to heaven. Inversely, the motions of the heavens now gather and concentrate downward at the closest region where they touch the earth: the windy mountaintop.

Enlil's division of Nammu's body therefore introduces a kinetic inversion, from a centripetal to a centrifugal motion. With Enlil, the two centripetal motions of heaven and earth are now divided by the air at the mountaintop. As their mutual medium and region of intersection, the air now exerts its own powers back out in both directions from this central location or omphalos where Enlil was born. Enlil becomes the father of both gods and men, the king of heaven and earth.[8] His power now radiates centrifugally outward in both directions, up (in the creation of gods) and down (in the creation of men). Enlil becomes the eternal center from which motion now descriptively emanates upward and downward from a single skyfather. The center rises above the periphery but then becomes the center of a cosmic sphere by radiating outward in all directions in a fantastic kinetic torsion. Furthermore, with Enlil the spoken word is transformed from a centripetal accumulation of sound and gesture in a body to becoming a disembodied divine voice coming from above and beyond the earth, from the air.

Atum. A similar centralized division of being occurs with Atum. Although creation begins with the chaotic waters, and is concentrated in the egg, it then begins to accumulate vertically in the mound. The shape of the universe is no longer ovoid but circular or spherical. Ra, the visible manifestation of Atum as the sun, is depicted as a circle. The circle of the sun moves across the circle of the cosmic waters in a perfect image of eternity. The sun moves but never changes in its movement—unlike the fluctuating moon cycles. The sun persists from on high as the radiating eye that sees all. Alone in his circle, Atum creates centrifugally through ejaculation, from the central hole of his "eye" or "orifice," like the volcanic opening at the peak of his "primordial mound." As George Bataille writes in "The Solar Anus,"

> The two primary motions are rotation and sexual movement...
> In fact, the erotic movements of the ground are not fertile like those of the water, but they are far more rapid.
> The earth sometimes jerks off in a frenzy, and everything collapses on its surface.[9]

From his autoerotic creation, Atum introduces division into the world. The rotation of the centripetal waters combine with the sexual movement of ejaculate that ultimately separates sky from earth with air.

As a circle, Atum is described in the *Pyramid Texts* as the "Complete One," because his movement is unified and self-collected in the completeness of the circle. The movement that goes out is the same movement that returns. The "mound of the first time" is also the eternal "mound of all time." This is why the Egyptian symbol for eternity, *"shen,"* is depicted as a circle and comes from the word *"shenu,"* which means "to encircle." Its elongated form was also the cartouche that surrounded the king's name. The *shen* ring or symbol renders explicit the kinetic motion of eternity in the form of the circle that appears almost ubiquitously in Egyptian art: on headgear, clothing, architecture, or held over Pharaoh's head by birds with their wings outstretched in a gesture of protection (see Figure 17.1).

The most important content of the *shen*, however, is the sun disk of Atum-Ra (see Figure 17.2). The circle of Atum's eternity is held at the center, radiating its solar power out and down on the earth. This is the perfect cosmogenetic image of ancient Egypt. The circle of solar eternity is never an unsupported pure circle but only occurs at the center, like a volcanic mound, within a larger fold or loop of flux connected to the cosmic circulation of Nun's primordial waters. *Shen* is thus depicted as a fold in a rope with two ends extending indefinitely away from the circle.

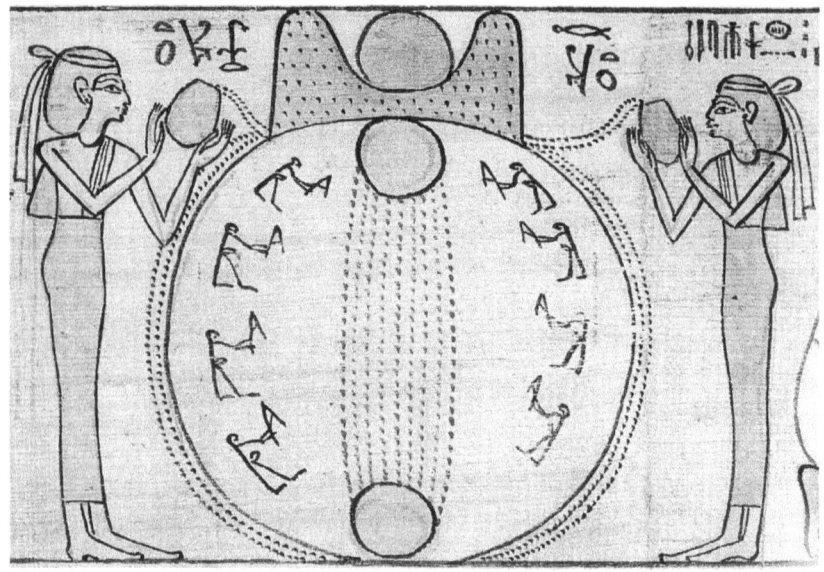

Figure 17.1 Egyptian Sphere with Waters
The sun rises over the circular mound of creation as goddesses pour out the primeval waters around it.
Source: Wikimedia Commons

Figure 17.2 Shen and Ra with Serpent Sun Disk
Source: The image of Ra was created by Jeff Dahl/Wikimedia Commons.

Just as Atum-Ra emerged from the primordial flux of Nun's waters, so his sun-disk circle appears at the center of her centripetal flows that have folded or looped into his central circle. This is nowhere more evident than in an image of Horus the falcon wearing a serpent-wrapped sun disk above his head. The cosmokinetics are striking: the spiral serpent of the goddess Nun has folded over herself to create a spatial circle whose center is occupied by the sun disk of the eternal Atum-Ra. The centripetal space of the fold creates the kinetic conditions for the centrality of eternity. The image stands at the center and above various deities such as Horus and Isis, expressing their eternity.

It is no surprise then that alongside the Egyptian image of eternity (*shen*) we also find the invention of the Ouroboros—a snake eating its own tail (see Figure 17.3).

For thousands of years preceding the Ouroboros, the mythogram of the snake expressed the spiraled and centripetal motion of space, and it continued to do so in the *shen* mythogram. However, the appearance of the Ouroboros marks a profound kinetic turn in the concept of eternity coinciding with the circle and sun disk. While the serpent *shen* is a loop or fold in a continuous flow, the Ouroboros goes one step further to separate itself from its source of cosmological motion altogether. Instead of folding it in an open circle, the Ouroboros takes this same image of the snake and connects it back with itself in a closed circle.

We should therefore distinguish between two kinds of circular motion: open and closed. An open movement shows how a circle or center is the product of a more primary centripetal flow of motion, while a closed movement shows how a circle acts as a "Complete One" on its own, in

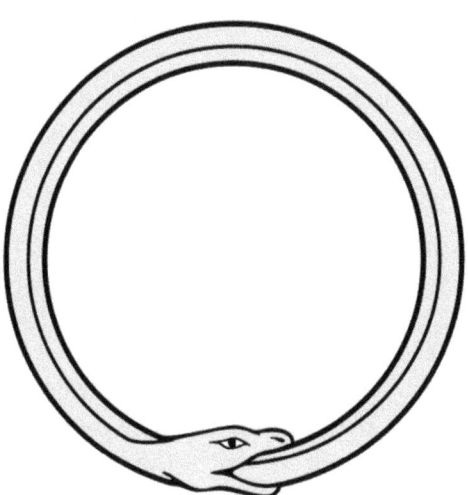

Figure 17.3 Ouroboros
Source: AnonMoos/Wikimedia Commons.

perfect equilibrium. The Ouroboros attempts to visually emancipate the circle from the flows and folds that produced it. Accordingly, after its invention in ancient Egypt, the Ouroboros cosmogram appeared in India, Greece, Rome, Ireland, and almost everywhere else one finds the metaphysical description of eternity. All stem back to the same kinetic attempt to divide being into two binary poles: eternity and mortality, center and periphery.

Although commonly interpreted by Carl Jung and others as "representing" the undifferentiated state of the pre-ego, the Ouroboros does not represent human consciousness at all; rather, it is a kinetic description of the order of things. More importantly, the kinetics of the Ouroboros are not undifferentiated, but precisely the opposite. They are absolutely differentiated between inside and outside. The Ouroboros is one image among many others during the Bronze and Iron Age of ontological binary differentiation between inside and outside, center and periphery, eternity and morality. Only an ahistorical imagination could ignore the fact that the Ouroboros was invented within an autoerotic cosmology in which Atum has *broken the unity* of Nun and ontologically divided sky from earth. The sun-disk, the circle, and the Ouroboros are all images of ontological division, not unity. The ontology of motion must restore the circle to its properly historical and kinetic definition. However, this is only the first cosmokinetic operation in the increasingly dominant description of being as eternity in the ancient West.

DEIFICATION OF THE KING

The second descriptive cosmological operation (the immobility of the center) occurred when the divine power of creation became deified in the singular body of an immortal priest-king on earth.

Dumuzi-Tummuz

In Sumerian cosmology this occurs in the description of the creation of the god-king Dumuzi, or Tammuz in Akkadian cosmology. After Enlil rapes Ninlil, the goddess of air, she gives birth to Nanna, the moon god, who in turn marries Ningal, the goddess of the moon. They have two children: Inanna, Queen of the Moon, and Utu, the sun god. As early as 3,500 BCE, Inanna, or Ishtar as she is called in Akkadia, was elevated to the status of the great goddess of Sumeria under the name of the "Virgin Queen of Heaven and Earth."[10]

As the queen of both heaven and earth, Inanna was similar to Nammu, except she was still divided from her abyssal sister Ereshkigal, banished to the deep of the inner mountain. In the "The Descent of Inanna to the Nether World," the oldest ritual dramatization of lunar myth,[11] Inanna goes to visit her sister in the deep. As she descends she is stripped of her jewelry and regalia at each of the seven gates of the underworld. When she reaches the deep, Ereshkigal fastens "the eye of death" on her and Inanna hangs like a carcass on a hook. After three days Inanna is released, but is forced to sacrifice someone else to take her place for half of the year. She chooses her husband, Dumuzi. Each year he dies and is resurrected. With this Inanna "placed Dumuzi in the hands of the eternal."[12]

In the Babylonian story the goddess Ishtar's son-lover is mortally wounded by a wild boar, and Ishtar descends into the underworld to wake him from his sleep in the dark. Ishtar also descends through seven gates (of the waning moon), and stays for three days (of the dark moon). While she is in the netherworld the fertility of the earth is stopped. When she returns with her son-lover the earth blooms again.

Dumuzi and Tummuz are both sons and husbands of Inanna and Ishtar. They are also both shepherd-gods of food and vegetation, "Lords of Life."[13] "The role of the newly risen vegetation god Dumuzi-Tammuz was enacted by the high priest or king of the city, who in the earliest times was one and the same person and may have actually replaced the previous sacrificed king."[14]

The Sumerian practice of sacrificing the priest-king is thus important not only for his eternal regeneration but also to ensure the eternal regeneration of crops and life on earth.[15] This is the first cosmology on which numerous others are based wherein an earthly king is interpreted as the son of earth and heaven and therefore becomes divine and immortal through regeneration. For example, this was the case with one of the most powerful Sumerian kings, Sargon, "Monarch of Agade." In the legend, Sargon is conceived by a temple priestess, birthed in secret, sent down the river and raised by Ishtar, and then becomes king of the land.[16] Another one of the greatest late Sumerian kings, Ur-Nammu (c. 2,100 BCE), calls himself "servant of the goddess Nammu"[17] and gains his powers from her.

Kinetic Analysis

This cosmological account describes the second of the four kinetic operations of a new regime of "eternal" motion: the immobile movement of a central point. In the first kinetic operation, a centripetal movement accumulates into a vertical mountain, but at the peak it divides heaven from earth and emanates back out its own centrifugal power. In the second cosmokinetic operation, however, heaven, earth, and underworld are reunited, but not all at once as in the primordial unity of Nammu. Instead, heaven, earth, and underworld are united only through *a continual cyclical movement between the three*; it is only by continually moving up and down that all three areas are brought together.

This is not a haphazard continual motion but one that is concentrated or focused around a single, central axis of motion: the son-lover, Dumuzi-Tummuz. Inanna-Ishtar moves from top to bottom and back, uniting heaven and earth. On her way down from heaven she marries him in the temple at the top of the mountain; on her way up she sacrifices him to the underworld. Through this continual motion she transfers to him all the divine powers of heaven, earth, and underworld in the single body of the priest-king on the mountaintop.

This produces two kinetic axes of motion in the cosmic sphere: the vertical axis of Inanna-Ishtar's cyclical and unifying movements, whose center is the mountaintop, but also the horizontal axis of the deified son-lover-king whose creative power radiates outward and downward centrifugally from the mountaintop. In the first motion the center is produced as an effect of the movement of birth-death-marriage. In the second the motion of the central point is not only consolidated in the material body of the priest-king, but from this central point of consolidation the priest-king redirects the power of motion outward and downward on earth. It is only through the cyclical motions of Inanna-Ishtar that the king becomes deified and immortal, and it is only through his sacrificial death that he lives forever. Individual people may die, but the deified king on the center mountaintop can now live forever due to Inanna-Ishtar's circular rotations. The king is dead—long live the king!

This is distinct from the motion of Enlil's separation of heaven, earth, and underworld. As air, Enlil is already immortal, since he has escaped the endless cycle of life and death and rebirth that defined the goddess Nammu's dynamic unity. This immortality, however, is regional and cannot be directly transferred to the particular human priest-king through deification, since kings remain tied to the earth. It is explicitly only through the priest-king's repeated sacrifice that he can be deified as the only human being who lives, dies, and lives again as the *same being*. All other beings are transformed and reborn as something or someone else; only through the circular movement of Inanna-Ishtar can a stable and immortal center be created on earth.

Unlike Enlil, the priest-king is not outside the cycle of life and death but actually at the center of the process itself. As such, he is defined by motion, but he appears not to move or change each time he dies. His body changes, but he remains the same lord of life on earth. Through Inanna-Ishtar the deified and sacrificial priest-king thus attains a kind of relative immobility for the first time. His immortality is not sui generis but artificially sustained by the goddess who rotates around her son-lover. He lives and dies again and again, but is reborn as the same king each time and returned to the same central mountaintop temple as Dumuzi-Tummuz. The priest-king becomes the immobile and immortal site in which an unchanging center is reproduced, but only through the moving circle of life and death woven by the movements of heaven, earth, and underworld.

Inanna-Ishtar is thus the movement of the whole returning to itself in the closed circle of life and death and no longer the open spiral unity of Nammu. The spiral was divided and centralized by Enlil and bounded by the limits of heaven and earth. This is attested to in Inanna-Ishtar's iconographic symbol: a central circle radiating outward in an eight-pointed star or rosette.

Her circular whole also produced a central part or point different from the other beings in the cycle, through which it was directly expressed as the radial and creative centrifugal power of life—Dumuzi-Tummuz as the deified priest-king on earth. While Enlil created a central region of aerial and centrifugal power, Dumuzi-Tummuz further concentrated the power of heaven and earth into a single *concrete point of power*: the deified body of a priest-king.

This immobility of the center makes possible a third kinetic operation of cosmological eternity found in the historical description of the battle of the gods (theomachy), as the next chapter will show.

CHAPTER 18

Ancient Cosmology II

Theomachy

The third cosmological description occurs when the sky father kills the mother and her son-lover and becomes the sole creator—and the origin of centrifugal motion. This occurs in historical description of theomachy.

MARDUK

The Babylonian cosmology found in the *Enuma Elish* (*From on High*) was written around the turn of the Iron Age in Mesopotamia (1,200 BCE) and adds another dimension to the previous Bronze Age cosmological descriptions. The epic of Marduk tells the story of how the gods were created from a primordial mother and father, Tiamat and Apsû:

> When the heights of heaven and the earth beneath had not been named, and when Apsû, their father [the waters that fell from heaven and the sweet river waters], and Tiamat, their mother [the saltwaters of the sea], still mingled their waters; when no field or marsh was formed and no gods had been called into being, then were the great gods created within the primal pair. The first gods were Lahmu and Lahamu, then Anshar and Kishar were created [probably the Sumerian An and Ki, Heaven and Earth], and then Anu and Ea. But these new generations of gods disturbed Apsû with their clamor, and he consulted his minister, Mummu. Together they went to Tiamat to tell her of their decision to destroy them, so that once again there could be peace and quiet. Tiamat protested

their plan: "Why destroy what we ourselves have brought into being?" she cried, but Mummu counseled Apsû to proceed, and together they plotted the downfall of the younger gods.[1]

In the beginning the chaotic waters were primary. Being flowed. From their centripetal gathering together they produced the cosmic unity of heaven (Anshar) and earth (Kishar) as well as other gods. However, once Apsû plotted to kill the gods, Ea drew a magic circle around himself for protection and killed Apsû in his sleep. Ea and his wife, Damkina, then gave birth to Marduk, a superior god-king, in order to kill Tiamat. Anu provoked Tiamat with turbulent winds to bring her to battle.

> Anu formed and gave birth to the four winds,
> He delivered them to him, "My son, let them whirl!"
> He formed dust and set a hurricane to drive it,
> He made a wave to bring consternation on Tia-mat.
> Tia-mat was confounded; day and night she was frantic.[2]

These turbulent winds disturbed Tiamat's waters, and she gathered a brood of sea creatures for battle, including Kingu, her son-lover, depicted as a winged sea creature. The younger gods made Marduk king of the whole world. He proved his power by making the night sky appear and disappear, and they armed him with weapons for battle.

> We give thee sovereignty over the whole world.
> Thy weapon shall never lose its power, it shall crush thy foe.[3]

They gave him a scepter, a throne, a ring, and the thunderbolt. Marduk "placed lightning before him, / And filled his body with tongues of flame."[4]

> The lord spread out his net to enfold her,
> The Evil Wind, which followed behind, he let loose in her face.
> When Tiamat opened her mouth to consume him,
> He drove in the Evil Wind that she close not her lips.
> As the fierce winds charged her belly,
> Her body was distended and her mouth was wide open.
> He released the arrow, it tore her belly,
> It cut through her insides, splitting the heart.
> Having thus subdued her, he extinguished her life.
> He cast down her carcass to stand upon it.[5]

> The lord trod on the legs of Tiamat,
> With his unsparing mace he crushed her skull.
> When the arteries of her blood he had severed,
> The North Wind bore it to places undisclosed.
> On seeing this, his fathers were joyful and jubilant,
> They brought gifts of homage to him.
> Then the lord paused to view her dead body,
> That he might divide the monster and do artful works.
> He split her like a shellfish into two parts:
> Half of her he set up and ceiled it as sky.[6]

This Babylonian story is important not only as one story among others but also because of its unique cosmological description of a recreated being. After Marduk killed the water-serpent queen Tiamat, he remade the cosmos out of her dead body. He created the twelve-month year and the constellations, and placed the sun and moon in the heavens.

> He heaped up a mountain over Tiamat's head,
> pierced her eyes to form the sources of the Tigris and Euphrates,
> and heaped similar mountains over her dugs,
> which he pierced to make the rivers
> from the eastern mountains that flow into the Tigris.
> Her tail he bent up into the sky to make the Milky Way,
> and her crotch he used to support the sky.[7]

Later Marduk decided to create servants for the gods "so they might be at ease," and fashioned humans from the blood and bone of Kingu, who is sacrificed for siding with Tiamat.

> They bound him [Kingu], holding him before Ea.
> They imposed on him his guilt and severed his blood vessels.
> Out of his blood they fashioned mankind.[8]

Marduk thus sacrificed the sacrificers Tiamat (Inanna-Ishtar) and her son-lover Kingu (Dumuzi-Tummuz). The father-sky-wind-sun god Marduk killed the earth and water goddesses and their priest-king sons and rebuilt the world. This has several kinetic consequences for the description of being, which we look at more closely after we consider the second major theomachic figure of Zeus.

ZEUS

Later in Archaic Greece, a similar cosmological theomachy emerged between 800 BCE and 480 BCE. Hesiod's *Theogony* gives us one of the oldest and clearest accounts of Archaic Greek cosmology and theomachy. Like many previous oral mythologies, Hesiod's cosmology begins with the ontogenetic primacy of space. Being begins in chaos but becomes stabilized and creative through the centripetal contraction of space: "Verily at the first Chaos came to be, but next wide-bosomed Earth, the ever-sure foundations of all the deathless ones who hold the peaks of snowy Olympus, and dim Tartarus in the depth of the wide-pathed Earth."[9]

The spiral of chaotic space moved centripetally inward and upward toward an increasing accumulation that resulted in a giant mountain whose center peak reached the very top of heaven. Gaia is the unity of heaven, earth, and underworld in a single primordial mountain. However, according to Hesiod, Chaos also gave birth to Erebus and black Night, who birthed Aether (air) and Day. Gaia then birthed Heaven, "equal to herself, to cover her on every side,"[10] and then with Aether birthed her son-lover Ouranos, the Air-Sky-Father with whom she conceived the first eight Titans. "After them was born Cronus the wily, youngest and most terrible of her children, and he hated his lusty sire."[11]

> So many were born of Gaia and Ouranos,
> most dreadful of children, and they hated their father
> from the beginning. As soon as one of them was born,
> Ouranos would conceal them all in a hiding place in Gaia and
> did not sent them back into the light, and he delighted in his
> evil deed. Monstrous Gaia was groaning within.[12]

By concealing all the children in Gaia they remained part of the cyclical unity of heaven (Ouranos) and earth (Gaia). In revenge, however, Gaia pleaded for one of her children to castrate Ouranos. Cronus was the only one who consented. Gaia then gave him a diamond sickle or curved sword, and Cronus castrated his father. He then assumed the throne at the vertical center of the mountain. However, Ouranos and Gaia told him that he too would be overthrown by his son. Thus Cronus devoured all his children birthed by Rhea except Zeus, whom she gave to Gaia.

> Monstrous Gaia received him
> in broad Krete to nourish and foster. There she arrived,

> carrying him through the swift black night,
> first to Lyktos. Holding him in her arms, she hid
> him in a high cave, beneath the ways of divine Gaia,
> on densely wooded Mount Aigiaon.[13]

In place of baby Zeus, Rhea gave Cronus a swaddled rock, which he devoured. Raised according to the divine ways of Gaia, Zeus became strong enough to force Cronus to vomit up all his children, including the rock, which Zeus placed in the center of the earth as the sign of a new beginning, an omphalos, and "a wonder for mortal men." Then Zeus released all the brothers of Cronus, the Gigantes, the Hecatonchires, and the Cyclopes, from Tartarus. In return they gave him "thunder and gleaming lightning and flash."

However, against Gaia's wishes and with the help of those he liberated, Zeus used his newfound powers to overthrow Gaia and her son-lovers Cronus and the other Titans, condemning them to Tartarus. According to Hesiod, "life-bearing Gaia screamed as she burned, and all the earth was boiling as well as the streams of Ouranos and the unplowed sea." Gaia burned upward and Ouranos (the heavens) fell from above onto her. With fire, Zeus reunited heaven and earth through destruction and claimed his throne at the central peak of Mount Olympus to become the father, ruler, and god of all immortals and morals.

Despite the fact that Zeus was not the original creator of cosmological motion, he fundamentally reordered it by overthrowing those who originally birthed it, declaring himself the retroactive father of all the gods, since he liberated them from his father's stomach and overthrew the Titans. As Homer writes, "Even the gods who are not his natural children address him as Father, and all the gods rise in his presence."[14] Zeus's cosmogenesis is thus an inverted one. Instead of a birth that creates by remaining one with its offspring, as Gaia did, Zeus's creation is a violent one that separates the product from the producer.

Gaia was angered by this overthrow and gave birth to Typhoeus, a hundred-headed fire-breathing serpent. Zeus's lightning bolts melted Typhoeus "like tin heated beneath the skill of craftsmen. In this way, Gaia was melting from the flame of the blazing fire."[15] Zeus threw Typhoeus into Tartarus, but still his winds blew over the sea, scattering ships and destroying sailors. According to Hesiod, Typhoeus's mate, Echidna, was half beautiful maiden and "half monstrous serpent, dreadful and huge, swift eater of raw flesh, beneath the ways of holy Gaia."[16]

KINETIC ANALYSIS

This third cosmological account describes the third kinetic operation of "eternal" motion: the retroactive determination of centrifugal motion. Let's begin with a kinetic analysis of the cosmology of the *Enuma Elish*.

Marduk. The *Enuma Elish* begins like the oldest Mesopotamian myths—with the wild pedetic flows of being. Eventually the flows of rain, river, and sea begin to curve and fold around one another in a centripetal accumulation, producing an open spatial unity: heaven and earth and the other gods. In the *Enuma Elish* this centripetal accumulation continues until so many gods are created that their motions begin to introduce a turbulence or disturbance into the enclosing and protecting spiral of space. To preserve the stability and peace of centripetal space, Apsû plots to kill the gods and restore balance. Instead, Ea draws a magic *circle* for protection and killed his father.

> He fashioned it and made it to be all-embracing [circular],
> He executed it skillfully as supreme—his pure incantation.
> He recited it and set it on the waters,[17]
>
> He bound Apsû and killed him[18]

The motion of the circle here is significant. As we saw in Part I, the mythological space of water gods is spiral. It folds over itself without beginning and without end. By drawing a magic all-embracing invincible circle and setting it on the spiraling waters of Apsû, Ea binds him and kills him—binding him kills him. Once the open spiral is closed, it becomes the all-embracing, supreme, and eternal circle: death. In closing motion in on itself, Ea aims to extinguish it.

Once Apsû the father is dead, Ea sets up a dwelling place on top of Apsû's body and names it Apsû. By drawing a circle and taking up residence in its center, Ea destroys Apsû and begins building on top of him, centrifugally from the center of his circle outward. From this new center Marduk, the king of the gods, is born.

> In Apsû was Marduk born,
> In pure Apsû was Marduk born.
> Ea his father begat him,
> Damkina his mother bore him.[19]

Marduk is born at the center of the circle, in the dead body of Apsû. That which was once birthed from a centripetal motion (Ea) has now destroyed that motion and begun a new centrifugal motion directed outward (Marduk) toward the periphery (Tiamat). However, this centrifugal motion was not yet the single and supreme cosmological motion. The center was secured and bound, but the periphery had yet to be delimited around it. Tiamat, the Queen of the Waters, still spiraled at the periphery. Ea bound the center through his magic circle, but Marduk was required to bind the periphery. To completely encircle the universe and set up an eternal central throne, she and her son-lover had to be killed.

Against her fluid, spiral, and centripetal motions around the cosmos, Anu (heaven) uses disruptive and turbulent aerial motions to undermine her movement of stabilizing interiorization. Marduk proves his sovereignty and readiness for battle by changing the night into day. In other words, Marduk becomes the sun god, moving across the sky. Unlike the moon, the sun moves without changing; it has no lunar flux. The sun is the pure and eternal unchanged mover. Through its movement it creates, but in its creation it loses nothing and is unaffected by that which it creates. It is the image of eternity: unchanging creator.

Marduk's battle with Tiamat is kinetically significant as well. Tiamat's spiral waters try to envelop and internalize him back into the megajunction from which he was born. Marduk responds by binding her movement in a net and penetrating her with an evil wind that expands her. Kinetically, he forces an inversion of her motion from a centripetal accumulation to a violent centrifugal expansion. Then he bursts her expanded belly, the womb of the cosmos, right through the center into her heart. He erects his own vertical body on her horizontal body by standing on her. He then splits her corpse into two great binary pieces, like the two halves of a shellfish.

Kinetically, for thousands of years the shellfish has been the mythographic depiction of the unity of being as space, the image of enclosed, fecund, internalized, and feminine ontogenesis. Marduk divides this ontogenetic cosmos and remakes it, but this time through craft, not birth. One half of Tiamat's body becomes the heavens above and the other half becomes the earth below.

> One half of her he set up and stretched out as the heavens.
> He stretched the skin and appointed a watch
> With the instruction not to let her waters escape.
> He crossed over the heavens, surveyed the celestial parts,
> And adjusted them to match the Apsû, Nudimmud's abode.
> He measured the shape of the Apsû
>
> He settled in their shrines Anu, Enlil, and Ea.

To complete this "death by centrifuge," Marduk cuts open her vessels and radiates her blood upward and outward into the wind to announce his victory. When he turns her body into heaven, he not only confines and blocks her fluid movements into a fixed celestial dome with newly ordered constellations, but he then measures and reshapes her body to conform precisely to the model of the new center constructed by Ea, "Apsû." Marduk thus recreates the periphery from his new residence in the center as the king of the gods in the shrines of his sky-god forefathers: Anu (heaven), Enlil (air), and Ea (craft, mind).

Marduk destroys the lived space of Tiamat, the deep, and transforms her into a pure empty and dead surface on which he stands and radiates his light from his central shrine. He even remakes the mountains of earth from Tiamat's corpse. Opposed to Tiamat's biological creation in which what she birthed remained part of her as the unity of heaven and earth, Marduk *makes* the cosmos. What he makes remains external and cut off from him; it is not a part of him. Against the material ontogenesis or kinomorphism of Tiamat, Marduk is a purely formal and intellectual cause that shapes the lifeless, formless matter of Tiamat's body. He stops up all Tiamat's centripetal flows only to redirect and recreate them outward from his centrifugal command; he punctures her eyes and breasts where he wants the water to flow. The flow of fluid is no longer free, but centrifugally commanded like vast canals and viaducts along the Tigris and Euphrates whose movement is manipulated and directed according to the demands of the central cities.

Finally, Marduk butchers Kingu, the god-priest-king who used to occupy the earthly center of power at the top of the mountain. From his guilty blood, humans were created to serve the gods. The kinetic difference here is key. In the previous kinetic operation, the priest-king was the realization of god on earth as a central product of the cyclical process of life and death. In this model, immortality was a product of a constant peripheral cycle of the unity of life and death, heaven and earth, in the goddess Inanna-Ishtar. It was an effect of a moving periphery. However, after this concrete center is produced, Marduk sacrifices it, fundamentally removing any direct earthly connection to the divine and eternal.

The divine now stands truly transcendent. The blood of the sacrificial victim (Kingu), repurposed through artifice and craft, becomes earthbound humanity. By sacrificing Kingu, Marduk ensures not only an absolute and inaccessible transcendence over the earth but also that humans will remain fundamentally artificial technical objects cut off from and distinct from divine craft, power, and knowledge. They will forever owe a debt of guilt to the gods. As the technical assemblage of blood and bones of the once immortal son-lover, humans strive to partake in his immortality through their own individualized heroism, like Gilgamesh and others, but the task is extremely difficult.

Marduk thus produces a new form of eternity through a double sacrifice. Marduk becomes eternal not only in the sense in which he will never die but also insofar as he has destroyed his original creator—there is no one from whom he was born. The movement of Marduk's eternity now appears as "neither created, nor destroyed." By sacrificing Tiamat, Marduk not only destroys the primal unity of heaven and earth from which he produced a new center and new eternity, but he also destroys the very cyclical condition under which a central point could emerge on earth that would connect it to that larger unity.

If the first kinetic movement creates a central *region* of immortality in the air (Enlil), and the second creates a central *point* of immortality on the earth (the priest king), the third sacrifices both in favor of a central transcendent point of unborn and undying eternity in heaven (An) and mind craft (Ea). Marduk's cosmology is thus the first truly artificial and truly centrifugal cosmology of eternity, even if it is only attained retroactively through the sacrifice, overthrow, and total reconstruction of the cosmos, of which he is now the center.

Zeus. Zeus accomplishes something kinetically similar in the Titanomachy. Although he was raised by Gaia, as Marduk was by Tiamat, he rises up against her and his mother's son-lovers Cronus and Ouranos. By dethroning them from the top of the central holy mountain and placing himself at the center, he retroactively claims the "fatherhood" and centrifugal cosmogenesis of all the other gods. His powers of the sky, like Enlil's, separate earth from heaven and from the underworld. From on high, his power radiates outward and downward like his lightning bolts and the "many streams flowing from its peak," as Homer writes.[20]

After Chaos, Oceanus, and Gaia centripetally accumulate the flows, Zeus captures them and inverts them centrifugally back outward. Zeus overthrows and expels the Titans out and down, from the mountain into the lower periphery. Zeus sits transcendent, above the world. Just a bit lower the Muses dwell at the base of Mount Olympus. Zeus's fires burn and melt the earth into molten material to be shaped by divine craft. Space, or Gaia, is thus reduced to a melted surface to be pounded out and stretched "like tin," as Hesiod says. After space has lost its serpentine motion and been tortured by fire, it can be remade in the image of the new centralized rulership. Just as Marduk used craft to refashion the world, Zeus gave the world or cosmos rational order through supreme rule, reforged it, and made humans from it via Hephaestus/Prometheus.

The earth, in Hesiod, thus becomes a monster that gives birth to monsters, the most powerful and aggressive of which are Typhoeus and Echidna. Their multiplicity of heads challenge Zeus's centralized unity, their spiraling coils challenge his singular centralization, and their hiddenness in the ground and sea challenge his verticality and radiating visibility. In order to secure his position as retroactive and centrifugal father of the gods, Zeus must do battle with and defeat them.

These are only the first three cosmokinetic operations that secure the dominance of eternity in the ancient West. The fourth and final movement, developed in the next chapter, is the ultimate coup de grâce in the kinetic history of eternity.

CHAPTER 19

Ancient Cosmology III

Ex Nihilo

The fourth and final cosmokinetic description of eternity occurs in the description of the figure of the ex nihilo eternal sky father, the first and only creator of all of being. In this final kinetic operation we reach the ultimate inversion of centripetal motion. Eternity appears not as the product of a theomachy or prior motion, but as the original and immobile process constitutive of all motion as such. Ex nihilo creation therefore does not refer here strictly to the creation of the world by God but more generally to the ex nihilo creation of motion from immobility.

YAHWEH

This final motion rose to dominance with the description of the emergence of the creator god Yahweh in Hebrew cosmology, around the ninth century BCE:[1]

> In the beginning God created the heaven and the earth.
> And the earth was without form, and void: and darkness was upon the face of the deep.
> And the Spirit of God moved upon the face of the waters.
> And God said, Let there be light; and there was light.
> And God saw the light, that it was good: And God divided the light from the darkness.

And God called the light Day, and the darkness he called Night. And
the evening and the morning were the first day.
And God said, Let there be a firmament in the midst of the waters,
and let it divide the waters from the waters.
And God made the firmament,
And divided the waters which were under the firmament from the
waters which were above the firmament: and it was so.
And God called the firmament Heaven. And the evening and the
morning were the second day.
And God said, Let the waters under the heaven be gathered together
unto one place, and let the dry land appear: and it was so.
And God called the dry land Earth;
And the gathering together of the waters called the Seas: and God saw
that it was good.[2]

In the beginning there was only one all-powerful and eternal God: Yahweh. His first action was to create heaven and earth, not to divide their prior unity but to create them as fundamentally divided *from him*. The earth he created was *tohu wa-bohu* (formless, chaotic), *hosekh* (dark), and the waters upon it were *tehom* (deep). These are the attributes of the primordial chaotic waters of the mother goddesses Nammu, Tiamat, and Inanna-Ishtar, who had, since the beginnings of cosmology, described being by a spatial, spiral, and centripetal interiority.

Now, for the first time in history, space, void, darkness, and chaos became descriptively secondary to eternity. This was not a temporal primacy but an ontological one that transformed space itself from spiral circular. Just as Ea did to Apsû, Yahweh traced a circle, or *chug* in Hebrew, across the face of the deep, thus dividing it from itself as heaven and earth, and placing himself in vertical and transcendent center. This is attested to in numerous places in the Hebrew Bible:

He has described a circle on the face of the waters, at the boundary between light and darkness.[3]

When he established the heavens, I was there, when he drew a circle on the face of the deep.[4]

It is he who sits above the circle of the earth, and its inhabitants are like grasshoppers; who stretches out the heavens like a curtain, and spreads them like a tent to live in.[5]

In the first book of Genesis, the death of Tehom—the equivalent of the Semitic-Babylonian Tiamat murdered by Marduk—has already been accomplished. Instead of Marduk splitting open the dead body of Tiamat, "fixing" her waters, and placing her corpse above and below, Yahweh abstractly created heaven and earth and gathered their waters in the form of a circle. From the beginning, space was already emptied out, or void. Yahweh did not stretch a corpse, but rather made a *raqiya* (circular dome or firmament) above and below. The Hebrew word *raqiya* is derived from the root *raqa*, "to beat or spread out," such as making a dish from thin metal. From a single point God stretched outward to make a continuous dome or sphere divided into above and below.

Once Marduk had sacrificed the cosmological center, its emptiness or abstract centrality became the only attribute of its transcendence. The center of the circle no longer appeared concretely anywhere, not even in the visage and form of a god. By beginning creation from a center that paradoxically preceded its periphery as Yahweh did, everything appeared to come from nowhere outside and above the sphere: ex nihilo.

Strikingly, however, this transcendent above and beyond is defined in precisely the same way that the center of the cosmic sphere was: immobile, unchanged, and eternal. Space, time, and all being appeared to emerge from an atemporal, nonspatial creator who must logically not "be," since he preceded the creation of being. If he "was" before being then he did not create being, but something must have created him. The ex nihilo creation of motion from immobility therefore relies on a kinetic sleight of hand: the creator creates outward, around, above, and below, but also is somehow not included in the creation itself, since he "sits above the circle."

Despite the apparent lack of theomachy in the Hebrew Bible, Yahweh still engaged in a number of battles against the beasts of the deep (*Tehom*). Despite Yahweh's attempt to begin creation from nothing other than himself, the deep still returned as the chaotic, watery depths that had to be traversed, divided, and lightened. The deep became the surface or space across which God moves—"And the Spirit of God moved upon the face of the waters."[6] The deep remained the condition of his mobility, if it makes any sense to speak of such mobility.

God created on and illuminated the surface, but monsters dwell in the deep. Under the sea was Leviathan, the spiraling sea snake historically associated with the goddesses Nammu, Tiamat, and others. Under the earth was Behemoth, the large-bellied bovine associated with the agricultural cow goddesses of the Neolithic and Bronze Ages. Although the decimation of *Tehom* was preaccomplished in Genesis, she continued to reappear and be redecimated throughout the Hebrew Bible. "Tohu, in the phrase *tohu wa-bohu* [formless, chaotic], becomes Tehom and Tehomot. Bohu becomes Behom and Behomot, a variation of Job's Behemoth, 'the dry-land counterpart of the sea-monster Leviathan.'"[7] Both had to be slain.

"In that day the Lord with his sore and great and strong sword shall punish Leviathan the piercing serpent, even Leviathan that crooked serpent; and he shall slay the dragon that is in the sea."[8] The danger of Leviathan is the same danger of the Babylonian mother goddess Ishtar, who threatened to "devour" the people of Judah by interiorizing them in captivity. Like the mother goddesses of space, Leviathan threatened to interiorize and envelop. "In the Book of Job, Behemoth is associated with the hippopotamus and Leviathan with the crocodile. Both these animals were sacred to Seth, the Egyptian god who personified the destructive forces of nature."[9] Leviathan threatened to swallow Judah with her mouth and bring it into her crooked spiral body. The strength of Behemoth, however, was in her loins, and her force was in the navel of her round belly. Behemoth could drink up an entire river and swallow the entire city of Jordan. God made her, and only God could destroy her at the end of time.[10] Throughout the Hebrew Bible, Yahweh and his chosen people laid waste to the old goddesses and sun worshippers, and on numerous occasions they destroyed all their "high places" or temples.[11]

Kinetic Analysis

This cosmological account describes the fourth and final kinetic operation of "eternal" motion: absolute centrifugal motion. Once a central megajunction has been fixed, it can then draw or delimit its periphery by the radiation from the center to all the infinity of points along its circumference. The retroactive determination of centrifugal motion was accomplished by Marduk through battle, but only became truly dominant when the center appeared as a preaccomplished absolute origin from which all other motion was derived. As such, the center loses its merely embodied immortality and takes on a truly disembodied eternity, neither created nor destroyed, neither in the sphere nor something simply beyond it. In other words, the center point of the circle becomes infinitely centralized and vertically unreachable at the same time that it is extended in its infinite radii along the cosmic circumference. The vertical point of transcendence above simply becomes an ontologically descriptive extension of the spherical center itself—taking on all the same characteristics (eternity, immobility, etc.), while also needing to deny any direct participation in the sphere "below." Yahweh's creation of the circle does not, in this final motion, appear as retroactive; instead, the periphery appears to emerge from a preexisting center that, in centrifugally reaching out, creates the cosmos as a circle around itself—and ultimately "below" it. The center remains unmoved and unchanged while the periphery rotates and changes around it.

The cosmological circle Yahweh draws in Genesis produces a double binary or kinetic bifurcation in being. The first division is between the inside and outside of the circle. Inside the circle is all of being, outside the circle is nonbeing. Above the circle is the dome of heaven, and below it is the dome of earth. The two domes are created through division and divided through (circular) creation. In Genesis "the Spirit of God moved [*merahepet*] upon the face of the waters," but in Job and Proverbs it becomes clear that this movement is a circular one, and that the circle is in fact produced by movement and not preaccomplished.

In other words, the periphery is the product of a centrifugal center. But this is the paradox of eternal motion: How can eternity move without changing or becoming something it is not? Yahweh's solution is that circular motion allows for the spirit of God to move without moving; hence the alternate translation of *merahepet* as "hover." Hovering is a static movement from above, but it is an "above" that is modeled purely on the center itself. By hovering above, Yahweh unifies and immobilizes himself as the center of the circle being drawn, just as Hegel's theory of circular motion unifies differences in time (past, present, future) and space (here and there) in the single motion of the circle.

In this simple kinetic motion, an entire centrifugal regime becomes visible. Movement is described as emerging from a preexisting vertical center. Kinetically, however, what we see in this description is that this center is a historical product of several preceding kinetic operations that now function as the kinetic and descriptive conditions under which a central junction (Yahweh) can react back on them and appear to have been their origin. Furthermore, this central junction now appears as a disembodied voice and unrepresentable image through the kinomena of wind, breath, and smoke.

Kinetically, the megajunction cannot actually disappear or transcend above the materiality of its kinetic conditions, but Yahweh solves this paradox by creating a megajunction so large that it appears everywhere, radiating in all directions—and thus from nowhere in particular, or from a transcendent "above and beyond." Yahweh appears as air, as wind, and as breath precisely because these kinomena also have an invisible atmospheric ubiquity to them.

In the beginning there was the center. By moving outward from the center in a centrifugal motion, Yahweh draws a circle on the surface of the deep, thus transforming kinetic space from being ovoid, spiraled, open, and rounded to becoming spherical, circular, closed, and perfectly round. Just like the deep, space is flattened out, unified, and homogenized, while at the same time being is cosmologically and not merely regionally oriented between above and below, inside and outside. Space becomes molded, flattened out (*raqiya*), surface, while the center radiates throughout the sphere, everywhere and nowhere, "hovering above."

Additionally, Yahweh unifies all of time into a single present and eternal moment of divine creation. Since God is everywhere throughout the sphere, he occupies all time and all space at once. Eternity is therefore not only a trans-temporal concept, it is also a trans-spatial concept: eternity obliterates time, space, and motion in a single unifying stroke of vertical centralization.

However, the description of the Hebrew God, like every centrifugal motion, still relies on a continual centripetal movement of support in order to function. In the Hebrew Bible this takes the form of Leviathan and Behemoth, who function as the natural spaces of accumulation on which the Creator creates. It is said that God created Leviathan and Behemoth and only he can destroy them at the end of time, but there is no end of time in eternity. Why then would he create monsters so strong that no one else could destroy them, ultimately not even himself, since there is no end of time?

In other words, although God is purported to be their creator, kinetically speaking, their movement is actually the spatial and centripetal condition of natural life on earth. Leviathan in the sea is the great spiraled, centripetal force that accumulates the waters that support all life, and Behemoth is the great ovoid womb of the earth that accumulates great waters and fields into its powerful belly, and births by its powerful loins. Although they are rendered as monsters in the Hebrew Bible, they are quite generally the creative and destructive powers of nature requisite for all material-kinetic activity on earth. Therefore, space and centripetal motion do not go away, even if they appear to have been the product of an eternal creative motion. Eternity still needs their interiorizing motions to sustain its centralizing redirection of motion from on high.

Yahweh's circular motion not only results in an ontological binary between heaven and earth, light and dark, mind and body, creation and created—it also produces an asymmetry between them. Heaven becomes the realm of eternal grace; the earth becomes the world of flesh and sin. God divides light from dark but sees the light as good and the dark as bad. The mind is pure, eternal, and unmoved, while the body is impure, mortal, and in motion. Creation is active, good, and unchanged, while what is created is passive, imperfect, and mutable.

In contrast, since the centripetal movement of the spiral has only regional divisions, it prohibits any fundamental or ontological asymmetry.

The centrifugal movement of the center of the circle has ontological divisions, but it permits absolute hierarchies and great vertical chains of being.

THE GREEK PHILOSOPHERS

We can see this same kinetic description of eternity and ex nihilo creation in the writings of almost every major ancient Greek philosopher from around 600 BCE to 300 BCE. In contrast to the archaic Greek poets Homer and Hesiod, the movement of being becomes increasingly deanthropomorphized and abstract in Greek philosophy. Being appears as centralized and centrifugal from the very beginning but without any theomachic or anthropomorphic motion. The creation of motion thus occurs ex nihilo from an immobile origin.

Although there are many important differences in the writings of the Greek philosophers from Anaximander to Aristotle, there is a single common thread that can be traced through almost all of them: the description of being as primarily determined and distributed by an eternal, unchanging, and "immobile" center. Kinetically, however, the appearance of this so-called immutable and immobile eternity is conditioned on a specifically centrifugal and spherical regime of motion. This section considers the ancient Greek kinomena of spherical motion in several of the most important Greek philosophers, which will influence and inspire Western ontology for thousands of years to come.

Centrifugal Motion

According to the Greek historian Diogenes Laertius, in Anaximander's cosmology being is ontologically boundless, unlimited, unchanging, and immaterial. "He laid down as his principle and element that which is unlimited (*to apeiron*) without defining it as air or water or anything else. He held that the parts undergo change, but the whole is unchangeable; that the earth, which is of spherical shape, lies in the midst, occupying the place of a centre."[12]

Unlimited being is immaterial and abstract, in the sense in which it is not reducible to any of the elements—air, water, fire, earth—of which material reality is composed. As a whole, being remains immutable even if the parts within it appear to undergo relative changes. However, in the beginning, Plutarch reports, Anaximander held that a single generative part of boundless being became distinct within being "at the coming to be of the world-order and from this a sort of sphere of flame grew around the air about the earth like bark around a tree. This subsequently broke off and was closed into individual circles to form the sun, moon, and stars."[13]

Thus, in the beginning, there was boundless being, but soon the creative part of this boundless being appeared at the center. Through further separations, being began to centrifugally produce a series of concentric spheres in perfect orbits.[14] This everlasting motion was creative, like the centrifugal growth of rings of bark around a tree. "Motion is everlasting, as a result of which the heavens come to be."[15] For Anaximander, boundless being creates motion by itself without the aid of anything else.

Even though being moves, it never changes. It is this eternal movement, Hippolytus says of Anaximander, that is creative of the heavens but itself is not changed by its creation, just like the divine craftsman in previous cosmologies. Additionally, Anaximander is said to have argued that "the cause of motion and coming to be [are] a single [motion]."[16] In other words, the cause of original motion and the cause of creative becoming are one and the same act of changeless, unlimited, and centrifugal creation.

Kinetically, then, for Anaximander, ontogenesis begins with a determinate and spherical center and builds outward from this center in concentric spheres, rings, and circles toward an unlimited periphery.[17] All of this occurs through an everlasting and centrifugal motion that is one with the motion of being itself—moving without changing. But how can there be movement without some kind of change? The history of ancient Greek cosmogony is the history of resolving this kinetic problem first posed by Anaximander.

For Pythagoras, ontogenesis is similarly spherical and centrifugal. Being begins with a single "monad," or unit. From this monad arises ex nihilo an undefined dyad, other, or material substratum with which it is contrasted, and that causes the rest of being to come into being. Diogenes Laertius describes his cosmology in the following way:

> The principle of all things is the monad or unit; arising from this monad the undefined dyad or two serves as material substratum to the monad, which is cause; from the monad and the undefined dyad spring numbers; from numbers, points; from points, lines; from lines, plane figures; from plane figures, solid figures; from solid figures, sensible bodies, the elements of which are four, fire, water, earth and air; these elements interchange and turn into one another completely, and combine to produce a universe animate, intelligent, spherical, with the earth at its centre, the earth itself too being spherical and inhabited round about.[18]

Kinetically, being begins from a static, uncreated, and eternal singularity. However, without matter, this monad has nothing to work on or form, so it creates an undefinable other or matter to shape. Just as Yahweh required the chaotic, undefinable void of Tehom to create the world, so Pythagoras's monad requires an "undefinable material substratum" to create his cosmos.

Instead of the center being produced centripetally by a spatial and material spiral, the center produces the "undefined" material periphery. Space is reduced to the empty, dead, and undefinable area extending outward from the center. Without any trace of anthropomorphism that might have remained in Yahweh, the monad of Pythagoras creates an intelligent (*nous*) and spherical universe with earth at its center, just as Yahweh did in Genesis.

From a single point, the monad creates outward around itself and in this way forms a sphere through centrifugal motion. This is precisely why Pythagoras "held that the most beautiful figure is the sphere among solids, and the circle among plane figures," according to Diogenes Laertius.[19] Pythagoras's cosmogony moves us closer to the kinetic reasons for privileging a cosmic sphere, but it does not yet resolve the problem of "eternal motion."

Spherology

According to Aristotle, Xenophanes, the great founder of the Eleatic school, makes explicit the anti-anthropomorphism already present in the ontologies of Anaximander and Pythagoras and further contributes in particular to the ontology of the sphere. "Homer and Hesiod," he says, "have ascribed to the gods all things that are a shame and a disgrace among mortals, stealings and adulteries and deceivings of one another."[20] According to Xenophanes, by anthropomorphizing the gods, the Greek poets infected the appearance and motion of being with their own failings, and in this way had not understood the true nature and motion of being. Furthermore, by modeling being on the human, "mortals deem that the gods are begotten as they are, and have clothes like theirs, and voice and form."[21] If horses could paint with their hands they would paint the forms of gods to resemble horses, he says.[22]

To overcome this anthropological bias, Xenophanes abstracts God from all human body and thought. "One god is greatest among gods and men, not at all like mortals in body or in thought."[23] As one god, he is the totality of being. His sensations lack nothing—"whole he sees, whole he thinks, and whole he hears."[24] There is no gap or void in his being. Without effort or physical locomotion his thinking alone moves all things—"but completely without toil he shakes all things by the thought of his mind."[25]

God's thought alone is thus sufficient for the movement of being, but thinking is not a movement—it is an unmoved and immaterial moving power. As Xenophanes continues, "[A]lways he abides in the same place, not moving at all, nor is it seemly for him to travel to different places at different times."[26] Thus God's everlasting thought moves and creates the cosmos, with which he is one but does not cause him to move. For Xenophanes, all motion is thus the product of a more primary intellectual and static process.

The sphere is the perfect ontological model of this motion. According to Diogenes Laertius, Xenophanes believed that "the substance of God is spherical, in no way resembling man. He is all eye and all ear, but does not breathe; he is the totality of mind and thought, and is eternal."[27] Aristotle reports the same thing about Xenophanes: "God is everlasting and one, all alike and spherical, neither unlimited, nor limited, neither at rest nor in motion."[28] Although it is not explicit in the extant fragments, Aristotle draws the conclusion that the kind of movement Xenophanes must be talking about is the rotation of a sphere around a center. The sphere is privileged by Xenophanes, Aristotle writes, precisely because its rotational movement allows for the center to be at rest unmoved and for the periphery to move around the center, thus neither moving nor moved. God is the whole sphere, but he abides, thinks, senses, and creates only from the point where he can remain unmoved: the center. This is perhaps the first explicit answer to the kinetic dilemma of eternal motion—the rotating sphere—even if it is retroactively posited here by Aristotle.

As the student of Xenophanes, Parmenides expands on his teacher's kinetic spherology. In his poem "On Nature," which begins with a proem or kinetic journey from night to day led by sun goddesses, he writes,

> On this way there are very many signs: that Being is ungenerated and imperishable, entire, unique, unmoved and perfect; . . . it never was nor will be, since it is now all together, one, indivisible. For what parentage of it will you look for? . . . And how could what becomes have being, how come into being, seeing that, if it came to be, it is not, nor is it, if at some time it is going to be? Thus becoming has been extinguished and perishing is unheard of. Nor is it divisible, since it is all alike and not any more in degree in some respect, which might keep it from uniting, or any inferior, but it is all full of Being. Therefore it is all united, for Being draws near to Being.[29]

Being is neither created nor destroyed; it is eternal, singular, unmoved, and perfect. It is one being without division, or becoming. As a perfect being it does not change, since change presupposes lack, void, or a state of imperfection. "It lies by itself and remains thus where it is perpetually."[30]

For Parmenides such perfection can only be kinetically achieved by the movement of a sphere. Parmenides explains the perfection of the sphere beautifully:

> Since now its limit is ultimate, Being is in a state of perfection from every viewpoint, like the volume of a *spherical ball*, and equally poised in every direction from its centre. For it must not be either at all greater or at all smaller in one regard than in another. For neither has Not-being any being which could halt the coming together of Being, nor is Being capable of being more than Being in one regard and less in another, since it is all inviolate. For it is equal with itself from every view and encounters determination all alike.[31]

If being is eternal, unmoved, and perfect, it must move equally in every direction *from its center*. In other words, the centrifugal movement from the center to the periphery as the radii is what defines the sphere and its equal limits. Without the centrifugal radiation of the center, the periphery is not definable as spherical. The center is first, eternal, and unmoved, while the periphery is derived, mutable, and moved. Parmenides makes this explicit in the image of the sun as the "origin" and source of "invisible deeds."[32] As the concentric rings of the universe become narrower, the more pure and unmixed the fire is toward the center.[33] The sphere must move by both centrifuge and rotation.

In the beginning, according to Anaxagoras, there was boundless, autonomous, pure mind (*nous*). From this single self-identical and singular mind, the universe was created ex nihilo, ordered, and set into a rotational motion by which things were brought together and separated. The concept of rotation is crucial to his cosmology. It is worth quoting the wonderful Fragment 15 at length:

> For it is the finest of all objects and the purest, and it exercises complete oversight over everything and prevails above all. And all things that have soul, both the larger and the smaller, these does mind rule. And of the whole revolution did mind take control, so that it revolved in the beginning. And first it began from a small revolution, now it is revolving more, and it will revolve still more. And things mixed together, things separated, and things segregated, all these did mind comprehend. And the kinds of things that were to be—such as were but now are not, all that now are, and such as will be—all these did mind set in

order, as well as this revolution, with which the stars, the sun, the moon, the air, and the aether which were being separated now revolve. For this revolution made things separate. And from the rare is separated the dense, from the cold the hot, from the dark the bright, and from the wet the dry. But there are many portions of many things. And nothing is completely separated nor segregated the one from the other except mind. Mind is all alike, both the larger and the smaller.[34]

For Anaxagoras, all of being is in motion but only because it is moved, ordered, and comprehended by an unchanging and self-identical mind that causes a rotational motion of the being to occur that mixes everything together except itself. Cosmokinetic motion begins small, but it moves outward centrifugally in larger and larger concentric revolutions. "Everything participates in motion being moved by mind," as Fragment 17 states. Kinetically, revolution is always a revolution around a center or single point.

For Anaxagoras, all of being rotates and by rotating mixes. However, one thing remains unmixed: *nous*. Being unmixed, it logically follows that it remains unmoved by rotation. As the revolutions of being get farther and farther from the center, they get more and more mixed and inferior to the pure self-identical and all-powerful mind at the center. Here again we see the figure of the unmoved mover-mind. Although the sphere is not mentioned explicitly in the extant fragments of Anaxagoras, Hippolytus's *testimonia* reports that, according to Anaxagoras, "things in the heaven are ordered by circular motion."[35] By deduction, the only three-dimensional figure capable of revolution and circular motion without change or mixing is the sphere.

In his poem "On Nature," Empedocles expands on Anaxagoras's theory of centrifugal mixing by adding two kinetic forces to his theory of cosmogenesis: love and strife. First, however, there is the sphere:

> There views one not the swift limbs of the Sun, Nor there the strength of shaggy Earth, nor Sea; But in the strong recess of Harmony, Established firm abides the rounded Sphere, Exultant in circular solitude. (Fragment 27, translation modified)

> Nor faction nor fight unseemly in its limbs. (Fragment 27a)

> The Sphere on every side the boundless same, Exultant in surrounding solitude. (Fragment 28)[36]

Being is spherical. Its movement is perfectly circular and self-identical. However, Fragment 35 of the poem eventually reveals that this perfect sphere was only perfect in the beginning before the creation of sun, earth, and sea. At some point strife begins to grow, and one by one the limbs of God start to move around the central joint of the sphere that binds them.

> Yet after mighty Strife had waxen great
> Within the members of the Sphere
>
> For one by one did quake the limbs of God
>
> The joint binds two.[37]

At this point the perfect harmony of the sphere is disrupted by a dynamic ontokinetic process consisting of two motions: a centripetal motion that accumulates being and a centrifugal motion that creates, orders, and mixes it. Being may be an eternal and perfect sphere, but it is also the product of a more primary centripetal process of accumulation or "love" that centralizes being into an omnipotent force of creation and order that centrifugally expands outward. Fragment 35 of "On Nature" describes this dual cosmological movement:

> But hurrying back, I now will make return
> To paths of festal song, laid down before,
> Draining each flowing thought from flowing thought.
> When down the Vortex to the last abyss
> Had foundered Hate, and Lovingness had reached
> The eddying center of the Mass, behold
> Around her into Oneness gathered all.
> Yet not a-sudden, but only as willingly
> Each from its several region joined with each;
> And from their mingling thence are poured abroad
> The multitudinous tribes of mortal things.
> Yet much unmixed among the mixed remained,
> As much as Hate still held in scales aloft.
> For not all blameless did Hate yield and stand
> Out yonder on the circle's utmost bounds.

The kinetics of the poem itself already reveal that the thinking and verse of the poem are a "flowing" and "draining" down a path. From this liquid thinking pours the idea that all of being is centripetally accumulated into a cosmic vortex. Once being becomes so contracted and accumulated at the center of the universe, it produces a unified matter or mass: love. In this spiraled, spatial, and material mass, the first beings are joined and poured abroad. However, in their birth they still remain mixed with differences that, through their own pedetic and autonomous motion, begin to separate them from the unity of love toward the periphery of hate. Once they reach the periphery, their desire for reunification brings them back together.

Empedocles's cosmokinetics can then be described as follows: The movement of love is centripetal insofar as it accumulates increasingly immobile unities, while hate is centrifugal insofar as it reintroduces movement back into the unities and separates them by ordering them outward toward the periphery. However, cosmologically, being is first and foremost eternal, boundless, self-identical, unchanging, and spherical. Only when motion begins does it become dynamic, delimited at the periphery by frenetic hate, and concentrated at the center by immobile love.

In other words, it is as if in the beginning the center of the sphere—immobile love—was everywhere, infinite, singular, lonely, and pure, and the circumference nowhere, since the sphere was boundless. In the beginning hate was not around to keep love company. There was no movement, only pure immobile center. But from this center motion began, and with it differentiation, both moving toward the periphery. In other words, the first movement of being is centrifugal. The centripetal accumulation of love is already assumed and presupposed as a boundless *solitude*. Immobile love is presupposed, but mobile bounded hate must be explained. Only after being moves to the periphery does it move back again to the center. Here the inversion of cosmological primacy of centripetal and centrifugal motions is now clear. Being is immobile, unity, love, harmony, circular, pure, isolated, self-same, and spherical. Once this unmoved being creates movement, it introduces an endless cycle of hate, difference, and chaotic mixing into the cosmos.

In this way early Greek philosophy sets the stage for the ultimate cosmospherologies of Plato and Aristotle, as will be seen in the final chapter on the ancient logos of eternity.

CHAPTER 20

Ancient Cosmology IV

Plato and Aristotle

After the preceding account of the early Greek philosophers,[1] it is now possible to appreciate the truly incredible but hardly original cosmological synthesis of centrifugal motion and spherology achieved by Plato (with the help of Socrates, who was the contemporary of many early Greek philosophers) and Aristotle.

PLATO

In Plato's work, the single clearest exposition of the kinetics of eternity occurs in his dialogue *The Timaeus*. Similar accounts are given throughout Plato's work, but since the focus of *The Timaeus* is on cosmology, it provides the most robust account. *The Timaeus* begins just after Socrates has given an account of "the city in speech" in *The Republic*, and now someone else will give an account of how such a city would look "in motion." The speaker meant to deliver the speech is missing, so Timaeus steps forward to tell the story of the material emergence of the city from its cosmokinetic beginnings.

Timaeus begins his speech with what he calls "a likely story," *eikôs logos*. In the beginning was a divine craftsman (*demiurge*) who created the universe based on an eternal model: "Well, if this universe of ours is beautiful and if its craftsman was good, it evidently follows that he was looking at an eternal model, while he was looking at a created model if the opposite is the case—though it's blasphemous even to think it. . . . it necessarily follows from these premises that this world of ours is an image of something."[2]

According to this account, being is eternal, perfect, and uncreated. The craftsman is also uncreated, since he is the one that will create the existing cosmos from this model. When the craftsman looks to the visible world he is to work on in order to create the cosmos, "he found everything visible in a state of turmoil, moving in a discordant and chaotic manner, so he led it from chaos to order, which he regarded as in all ways better."[3] The craftsman then gathers this chaotic, pedetic motion into a single totality, without remainder.[4] He then shapes the visible totality into a sphere. "And so he made it perfectly spherical, equidistant in all directions from its center to its extremes, because there is no shape more perfect and none more similar to itself—similarity being, in his opinion, incomparably superior to dissimilarity" (33b).

As we saw in the early Greek philosophers, Plato's sphere is also a perfectly self-similar form of eternal, unchanging being. The sphere is defined by the equality of the radii from the center, thus a center point is presupposed as the measure and basis of his spherology. After the craftsman creates the cosmic sphere, he puts a "soul" in its center, to be "the ruler, with the body as its subject,"[5] which paradoxically Timaeus says must have also been there all along as the origin of the sphere itself. He then sets it into motion. "Once he had set in the centre a soul, which he then stretched throughout the body and with which he also coated the outside, he set the body spinning and made it a single, unique universe."[6]

Thus the craftsman, in the following order, (1) creates a central soul; (2) stretches the central soul outward in equidistant radii, creating a smooth and spherical body; and (3) spins the sphere in a perfect circle, the natural motion of reason. "The motion he assigned to it was the one that was natural to its body and that, of all the seven kinds of motion, has the most to do with reason and intelligence. And so he gave it circular movement, by starting it spinning at a constant pace in the same place and within itself."[7] The natural and good motion of the sphere is circular rotation. Rotation is the motion that most has to do with reason (*logos*) and intelligence (*nous*) because it remains exactly itself and in the same place as it moves. It is the most immobile of mobilities. We now see the clear Platonic synthesis of the following features united in the rotating sphere: intelligence, order, the good, superiority, hierarchy, authority, eternity, totality, unity, centrality.

Kinetic Analysis

The important point to be made here is that all of these Hebrew and Greek concepts began to take on the same kinetic distribution as they rose to conceptual dominance during the ancient period. There is not a causal relationship between them, but rather a shared kinetic regime, a shared distribution of motion in which they all participate. One feature is not derived from the others, but they all coemerged under the same kinetic conditions of ontological description.

In *The Timaeus* we begin with an eternal, immobile, single point: cosmological mind craft. From this point the craftsman uses his mind to order and form the unformed, chaotic matter around him into a perfectly smooth and beautiful sphere. He orders this sphere by placing a soul in the center and centrifugally stretching it outward to the periphery. He then spins it in a perfect rotation. Since the cosmos is an image modeled on a more perfect, eternal, and unmoved model, we have to assume that the eternal model is even more perfect than this moving sphere-body. But since "no shape [is] more perfect and none more similar to itself" than the sphere, we must also assume that the eternal being is also spherical, but more perfectly so.

However, the only way it could be more perfect is if it was completely immobile and unchanging, unlike the spinning, corporeal cosmos. This is precisely why Timaeus calls the cosmos a "*moving* image of eternity":[8] because eternity does not move. "Now the nature of the ideal being was everlasting, but to bestow this attribute in its fullness upon a creature was impossible. Wherefore he resolved to have a moving image of eternity, and when he set in order the heaven, he made this image eternal but moving according to number, while eternity itself rests in unity."[9]

The only part of the sphere that does not move is the center; therefore we must conclude, and Plato must *implicitly presuppose*, that the eternal and perfect model is at the absolute, transcendent, and immobile center of all creation. Even as Plato posits the model and craftsman as above, outside, or beyond the living mobile cosmos, all the features he ascribes to them remain identical to the center of a sphere: eternal, unchanged, immobile, etc. Again, a kinetic sleight of hand is at work. Plato explicitly wants the ex nihilo creation of motion to occur before or outside the sphere, and yet his description of this "above and beyond" the sphere is implicitly identical with the center of the sphere itself!

The persona of the divine craftsman thus implicitly and kinetically becomes identical to a centrifugal movement of creation that radiates outward from the immobile center, like the hierarchical rule of the soul over the cosmic body, without being the same as the body. Spherical rotation presupposes centrifugal motion. The centrifugal motion of the cosmic sphere is thus both unified and binary. Being is one, but within its totality there is that which is immobile, creative, eternal, unchanging, good, and perfect (the vertical and transcendent center), and that which is mobile, created, mortal, mutable, inferior, and chaotic (the spherical periphery). Kinetically, therefore, the model of eternal being is an immobile centrifugal center that creates and orders a mobile sphere around it.

In the ancient concept of eternity, the apparent contradiction between eternity and mortality, between unity and duality, *can only be resolved kinetically*. Being must be a rotating sphere. In *The Republic* Plato gives the example of a spinning top: the classical image par excellence of centrifugal motion. In the dialogue Socrates refutes those who would say that a spinning top is both standing still and moving at the same time. Rather, Socrates argues, the standing still and moving refer to *two different aspects of the same top*: the part that stands still in the center and the part that spins at the periphery. "We'd claim that they have in them something straight and something surrounding it, and stand still with respect to the straight part, since they don't tilt in any direction, but move in a circle with respect to the surrounding part; and when the straight axis is leaning to the right or the left, or forward or back, at the same time it's spinning around, then it's not standing still in any way."[10] The eternity and mortality of unified being are thus possible only in the same sense in which mobility and immobility are possible in a top: circular rotation.

However, if this kinetic model is truly the basis of Plato's cosmology, we find a dramatic ontological torsion. What was initially conceived of as ontologically primary (immobile eternity) now becomes derivative of the spherical rotation, which is now revealed as its true kinetic condition. Without spherical rotation to hold the center in its place through centrifugal motion, being, just like the spinning top, collapses on its own sterility. Without spherical rotation to hold the periphery in place, the center falls off its axis, destroying its immobile perfection.

The first cosmology told by Timaeus in the dialogue the "likely story" is relatively short and quickly complicated by the later introduction of the *chora*.[11] However, the concept of eternity in the first account is by far the most historically dominant among Greek philosophers and the one reiterated by Socrates throughout the dialogues. In *The Statesman*, for example, Socrates proposes a cosmology of a divine craftsman who moves the cosmos while remaining unmoved himself.[12] In *The Axiochus* he claims that the heavens are spherical and centric.[13] In *The Phaedrus* he argues that the "self-mover is also the source and spring of motion in everything else that moves; and a source has no beginning,"¹⁴ and accordingly that the self-mover is an immortal soul that moves the body.¹⁵

ARISTOTLE

As Plato's student and a close reader of early Greek philosophy, Aristotle provides the final and most complete kinetic synthesis of the movement of eternity in the ancient world. For Aristotle every movement is caused by a mover (*kinoun*) that is itself moved, and so on from the earth to the planets to the celestial spheres until we reach that thing that moves without being moved itself: the unmoved mover (*kinoun akinêtôs*). Even though Aristotle begins with the primacy of immobility, he is careful to not reduce motion to a temporalized or spatialized object; rather, he conceives of movement as "being-potentially-something."¹⁶

He defines κίνησις/kinēsis (movement) and μεταβολή/metabloē (change) as distinct from ἐνεργέω/energeia (being-at-work). In an absolutely dense and rich passage, Aristotle says that "the being-at-work-staying-itself [*entelécheia*] of whatever is potentially [*dunamis*], just as such, is motion: of the alterable, as alterable, it is alteration."¹⁷ Motion is not what is completely active, but alteration as such. The motion of what can grow and shrink, for example, is the process of growth and shrinkage. The motion of the generable and the destructible is its process of coming-to-be and passing away. The motion of the movable in place is its changing of place. Bronze is potentially a statue, but it is not the *entelécheia* of bronze as bronze that is motion; it is the bronze in process of becoming-statue that is motion.

Motion and change are also distinguished in Aristotle. They are two poles of a single continuum between four types of change/motion: thinghood, quantity, quality, and place. Change of place is the highest degree of motion, but it involves the least change. Change in thinghood is the greatest kind of change, but it involves the least degree of motion. After defining motion in this manner, Aristotle defines the unmoved mover accordingly. While motion is the *incomplete process* of being-active-and-complete, the cause of this movement (the unmoved mover) is "already *complete* in its activity" such that it lacks, by definition, any potentiality (*dunamis*) that would allow for motion.¹⁸ The unmoved mover is thus pure *energia*. He is activity as it is always already completed. Movement and potentiality are thus secondary to immobility and potentiality.

Just as in Plato, the apparent contradiction of "eternal motion" or "unmoved mover" is resolved in Aristotle by centrifugal and spherical motion.

[280] *Being and Eternity*

The cosmos is a sphere whose center is unchanged and immobile but whose periphery moves and rotates around it.

> Any one point as much as any other is alike beginning, middle, and end, so that they are both always and never at a beginning and at an end (so that a sphere is in a way both in motion and at rest; for it continues to occupy the same place). The reason of this is that in this case all these characteristics belong to the centre: that is to say, the centre is alike beginning, middle, and end of the space traversed . . . [the locomotion of the periphery] is proceeding always about a central point and not to an extreme point; and because this [the center] remains still, the whole is in a sense always at rest as well as continuously in motion.[19]

The center of the sphere is eternal because it is beginning, middle, and end all at once, just like the unity of the first and final cause himself: the unmoved mover. Just as "there must be something at rest at the center of the revolving body," so there must be something at rest in the center of the revolving body of the heavens, which is itself not a body. The cosmos itself must be "of necessity spherical; for that is the shape most appropriate to its substance and also by nature primary."[20] "The sphere is in a certain way both moving and at rest, for it holds the same place. And the cause why all these things happen is in the center; for it is both a beginning and a middle of the magnitude, and an end as well."[21]

If, as Aristotle clearly says, the cause of motion is always at the center of a rotating sphere (the identity of the first and final cause), and that the cosmos is shaped like a sphere or concentric series of celestial spheres, then it seems that we have to conclude that the cause of the motion of the cosmic sphere comes from the center as well. In other words, the cause of cosmic mobility emanates explicitly from the center to the periphery centrifugally—from the unmoved center to the moved periphery.

From these passages one might conclude that the unmoved mover is concretely at the center of the universe. But not so. In a brilliant sleight of hand, Aristotle, like Plato, descriptively displaces this concrete center and elevates it into an abstract region above and beyond the sphere itself. "Now the action of this unmoving cause must be felt either at the center or the periphery, for these are the determining principles; and since the swiftest movements must be those of the parts closest to the moving force, and the movement of the outermost sphere is such, it is there that the motive influence is felt."[22] The strongest force of the unmoved mover is felt at the periphery because the unmoved mover is above and beyond the sphere itself.

In a shocking kinetic inversion, all the features that Aristotle explicitly used to define the center (identity of first and final cause, eternal, and unmoved) now become displaced to an abstract outer region of the sphere itself, as if they had been there all long as an unmoved eternal cause—similar to Yahweh or Plato's craftsman.[23] The identity of his explicit description of the center of the sphere and the vertical region above it where the unmoved mover resides is no coincidence. Aristotle's unmoved mover, everywhere and nowhere beyond the sphere of being, is modeled directly on the center of the sphere itself, and therefore implicitly modeled on centrifugal motion.

Kinetically, we can now make sense of Aristotle's strange definition of the unmoved mover as the being with one part that causes motion and another part that moves. "Of the thing that itself moves itself," he says, "one part causes the motion and another part is moved."[24] Just as in Plato and many other Greek philosophers, the part that remains unmoved is the center of the sphere, and the part that gets moved is the periphery. Aristotle is very clear on this: "the cause why all these things happen is in the center." Being begins with the unmoved mover, eternal and uncreated, and from this point the cosmos is set into everlasting, spherical, ordered and circular motion around the center,[25] which continually causes the perpetual motion of the world around it.

CONCLUSION

Over the course of the ancient period, the description of being as eternity emerged and rose to dominance over the previous mythologies based on the primacy of space and interiority. Through its emergence the concept of eternity went through four major descriptive kinetic transformations, analyzed above. However, alongside this change in the description of being from spatial to eternal, another transformation took place in the technical inscription of this "eternal" being: written language. Cosmology and written language are two dimensions of the same kinetic regime or field of centrifugal motion, as we will see in the next two chapters on ancient inscription.

III
Graphos

CHAPTER 21

Writing I

Tokens

In the major cosmologies of the ancient West, the movement of being is described as a centrifugal motion. This description, however, is also kinographically inscribed through the technology of written language. The two emerged during the same historical period and followed the same pattern of centrifugal motion—not because of a causality between the two, but as a topokinetic coordination or synchrony of two regions or dimensions of the same field of motion.

It is all too easy to succumb to the temptation of an explanatory causality or push-pull theory, as one finds in so the work of many historians and communication theorists who want to know "*why* writing came about," or "how writing *caused* a change in human consciousness." Many well-respected theorists have argued that the invention of writing determined the structure of ancient consciousness.[1] They are right in noting a contemporaneous change in both ontological description and inscription, but so many other domains were also involved in this change that it is impossible to say what was a cause and what was an effect. Thus, we must resist this temptation to attribute to writing alone a special causality denied to other historical elements.

At the same time, however, we should also avoid the inversion of this argument: that writing was invented as a product of an evolutionary desire or a developing human consciousness that "needed" a system of accounting, state bureaucracy, and so on.[2] In the first case we risk a kind of materialist reduction, and in the second an idealist one. Undoubtedly, the coemergence of writing and cosmologies of eternity entail some degree of entanglement, intertwining, or kinetic conjunction, but so many other non-ontological factors also coemerged alongside them that any unilateral claims to direct causality can only be speculative at best.

For this reason, these are not the kinds of questions or arguments put forward in this book. Opposed to questions of causality, origin, and development, this chapter examines the way in which the invention of writing *moves* and *resonates with* the same descriptive regime of centrifugal circulation in ancient cosmology. Every major historical period is co-constituted by a multiplicity of heterogeneous movements, all clamoring, overlapping, and battling for dominance. No single event or kind of event caused writing, and no single consequence was a consequence of writing alone. Writing coemerges and participates in the same kinographic regime as several other major events during this time that all share the same regime of motion: cosmologies of eternity, the figure of the barbarian, debt and slavery, states, the invention of walls, cardinal numbers, and aesthetic formalism. All of these factors enter into a collective, mutual transformation that should not be understood in terms of causality but in terms of kinetic *resonance, coordination,* or *synchrony*.

These domains (kinography, kinopolitics, kinesthetics, and kinemetrics) all require their own treatment, without reducing their relationship in a shared kinetic regime to one of determinate causality. This chapter treats only the kinographic dimension, but such a treatment must also be read alongside the history of politics, art, and science in the companion volumes to this book to see all the dimensions at work within the regime of centrifugal circulation.

SCRIPTOGRAPHY

Writing did not emerge out of nowhere. It took thousands of years for it to rise to its place of kinetic dominance, particularly toward the end of the ancient period. Writing emerged, like the concept of eternity, through four similar kinetic operations, resulting in a reproducible pattern of centrifugal motion. These operations were not evolutionary, developmental, or even historically sequential, since most of them coexisted alongside one another for long periods of time. Even when the dominance of the final operation occurred, this does not preclude the coexistence of the previous operations.

The following three sections of this chapter each look at one of the four major kinographic operations as it emerged during a certain time: the appearance of the first tokens of the ancient Near East, dating from around

8,500 BCE, around the time of the invention of agriculture; their storage in clay spheres around 3,700–3,500 BCE; and the first abstract inscriptions as numbers (3,400 BCE) and pictographs on tablets (3,300 BCE). The fourth major kinographic operation, the creation of written letters in alphabetic systems, around, 1,850 BCE, will be discussed in the next chapter.[3]

Each of these four kinographic operations is shown to resonate historically with the same four cosmological operations described in the preceding chapter that consolidate the kinographic dominance of centrifugal motion. However, before these four operations began in the ancient Near East, a graphic recording system of tallies and mythograms had already been in place for tens of thousands of years before the rising dominance of tokens that we are looking at now. Since I have already developed a kinetic theory of tallies elsewhere, we will begin with the emergence of tokens in the ancient world.[4]

TOKENS

The tally system began to change with the introduction of tokens. However, there were two kinds of tokens—plain tokens and complex tokens. Thus, the first major kinetic operation toward the rise of centrifugal motion was the increasing accumulation of plain tokens into bowls and finally into a centrifugal accounting system of complex tokens around 4,400 BCE. The first kinetic operation was an increasing division between the center of token accumulation and its periphery.

Plain Tokens. At the beginning of token systems, around 8,000 BCE, tokens were not pictographic images of particular objects but "small clay counters of many shapes, such as cones, spheres, disks, and cylinders, which served for accounting in prehistory."[5] The first tokens measured about one to two centimeters across, were hand-molded from clay, and sometimes baked in an oven.[6] These plain tokens originally functioned in a way similar to tallies: by one-to-one correspondence. "The tokens lacked a capacity for dissociating the numbers from the items counted: one sphere stood for 'one bushel of grain,' and three spheres stood for 'one bushel of grain, one bushel of grain, one bushel of grain.'"[7] Each token was singular and tied to one singular animal or object. Once the animal or object was dead or gone, the token was discarded.[8]

Just like the tally, the original plain tokens were kinetically centripetal accumulations of flows of clay into more mobile objects for easier computation. Just like the Neolithic invention of the bowl, whose centripetal accumulation allowed for a radical new mobility of flows, the token was a centripetal condensation of flows for increased economic mobility. Unlike tallies, however, the shape of the token itself began to express a singular quality. The repetition of each singular qualified token—sphere, cone, and so on—was its count. Thus the plain token began to slowly bring together in a centripetal gathering the coincidence of quality and quantity in singular concrete objects in a vessel.

It is not coincidental that the rise of the token system coincided with the rise of plant and animal domestication in the Neolithic, but it does not imply a causality. Both systems shared the same kinetic regime of centripetal motion. Both aimed to gather from the periphery and increasingly stored their flows in a central location.[9] The same centripetal motion of accumulating plants and animals by families and individuals was the same motion of gathering singular tokens for individual computing.[10]

Paleolithic and Neolithic peoples used plain tokens to compute or calculate quantities of accumulated time, quantities of accumulated food, and so on.[11] Kinetically, this was a centripetal form of counting, since its functions were based on the accumulation of singular tokens by noncentralized groups of people. Each individual or family used the tokens to compute what they had centripetally stored up, and not for purposes of lending or for reckoning numerical debts or credits.[12]

By 6,000 BCE these loose plain tokens began to be increasingly accumulated into bowls, bags, and jars of various kinds as certain individuals began to accumulate and exchange more plants and animals. The two accumulations occurred together (tokens and objects), each reacting to the other. The increased accumulation of tokens in jars would not have occurred had there not been an increased accumulation of grain, water, and animals by individuals, which itself would not have occurred without the usage of token systems that facilitated organized accumulation.

Complex Tokens. This centripetal counting and accumulation contrasts with the centralized and centrifugal accounting that emerged with the rise of complex tokens and political states around 4400 BCE.[13] The emergence of what Denise Schmandt-Besserat calls complex tokens marks the first major kinographic operation of centrifugal motion. In contrast to plain or simple tokens, complex tokens began to take on increasingly diverse naturalistic forms. For example, tokens that counted sheep began to be shaped like sheep or sheep heads. In addition to their complex figuration, complex tokens also increasingly became a graphic recording surface on which markings such as parallel lines, crosses, and/or punctuations or depressions punched in various patterns on the token's surface were inscribed.[14] In other words, descriptive signs began to become centralized on the surface of the token itself.

Complex tokens emerged during the same time and within the same kinopolitical regime of what Schmandt-Besserat calls the urban "redistributive economy," or the rising urban economy, in which urban merchants received agricultural products from farmers and then redistributed them according to the demands of city dwellers.[15] City dwellers could then redistribute these agricultural products to the temple bureaucracy as donations, or to another location. As a system of exchange, complex tokens, with their new diversity of types and subtypes and their markings, presupposed a specialized group of accountants to interpret, verify, and reckon the credits and debts that came in and out of the most centralized point of token accumulation: the temple.

What began as a clerical accounting practice quickly became an economic centrality as the temple became the main source of credit, debit, and redistribution management. While regional accumulations of plain tokens followed a largely centripetal, computational, and distributive motion toward the center, the centralized accumulation of complex tokens followed a largely centrifugal, accounting, and redistributive motion from the center back outward. The temple gave birth to a scribal elite who managed accounts, just as a literate scribal elite would after the development of writing. "The redistributive economy relied upon a system of record keeping and, indeed, could not have succeeded without it. This function was fulfilled in the third millennium BCE by cuneiform writing and, going back further in time, by pictographic writing and tokens."[16]

This first kinetic operation of writing presupposes not only an amplification of the previous centripetal motion but also its inversion or redistribution through taxation, monumental architecture, and a new monopoly of political force. All of these practices followed the same centrifugal motion of the complex tokens, which accumulated specialized markings on them. Taxation, or the massive accumulation of a fixed amount of goods from all individuals and guilds under penalty of sanctions from the periphery toward the central temple or palace, required a great specificity of goods and a record of debts owed by those who had not paid their taxes. Both of these were made possible only by the new diversity of multiple token shapes and the complex markings inscribed on their central surface. Taxation not only amplified the forced centripetal accumulation of goods from the agricultural periphery; it also inverted this motion in the form of a separate centrifugal redistribution of these goods toward public works, monumental architecture, canals, and roadways, as well as supporting its elite bureaucracy and its armies—all paid for by complex tokens accounted for and radiating out from the city center.

This enormous centrifugal redistribution of goods, people, and power was not a rejection of centripetal motions but rather an intensification that invented new ways of "pooling surpluses, as well as . . . new ways of administering those surpluses, including a more precise accounting method. The construction of public buildings also required a large workforce, suggesting new ways of controlling labor, such as the corvée (i.e., labor exacted from individuals at little or no pay or instead of taxes)."[17] Centripetal motion reached its height of kinetic accumulation—of people, tokens, water, stone, metals, and materials of all kinds—at the urban center of Uruk, literally amassing a pile so high it stretched toward the sky in the form of temples, towers, obelisks, and palaces. Centripetal accumulation began to amass a central verticality: A holy mountain. Once this verticality began, a centrifugal redistributive motion emerged as the center took almost total control of all reallocations of the accumulated surplus motion in the form of public works and warfare, paid for by complex tokens.[18]

The kinetics of urbanization and of writing follow the same general centrifugal motion. As Leroi-Gourhan observes, "For reasons that connect architecture with writing and with spatial integration, the city is the reference point of metrology. Land surveying plays a major role, and the farthest confines of the earth are connected by the symbolic radii of the wheel of distances. The result is a geometrical image of the world and of the city involving a whole network of corresponding spatial elements."[19] The city center that regulates the exchange and accounts of accumulated tokens becomes a cosmic center and point of radial survey across a whole world of concentric circles around it.[20]

Kinetic Analysis

The emergence of the complex token marks the first kinetic operation of centrifugal motion because it inscribes *a separation between heaven and earth*. While plain tokens were used to compute and calculate accumulated singularities, complex tokens were pooled into a growing verticality at the central site of the temple in the form of taxes, donations, debts, and so on. Complex tokens literally accumulated vertically following the movement of the holy mountain or temple. Goods were accumulated at the periphery and piled high in the center of the temple through the holy hands of the priest-bureaucrats who kept the specialized records of the complex tokens' meaning and system of equivalence.

Thus, the complex token was not merely a figurative token with some marks on it; it also kinetically introduced a radical separation between two kinds of beings or values. The token became the mediating division between the value of actual goods to be used—barley, sheep, milk, and so on—and the value granted to the goods by the heavenly hands of the priest-bureaucrats, based on the demand for their exchange. The use value of barley would remain relatively constant for the farmer, but the demand for barley in the city would fluctuate as more or less of it reached the city center for exchange. Although complex tokens were not the same as money, they did have a similar variability of exchange value since their value was regulated by priests in an urban market.

Thus, the division between token, use value, and exchange value produced a kinetic operation similar to what the god Enlil did in relation to being. At one point heaven and earth were united as the holy mountain of the earth touched heaven, but like the complex token, Enlil, the air, introduced a division between heaven and earth. The accumulations of the earth were now centripetally pooled at the central top of the mountain-temple in the hands of priests and kings, as did the heavenly powers that deified the priest-kings. From this vertical and central holy mountain, the centripetal motions were then inverted and redistributed back down the mountain in the form of debts, credits, and changing exchange values, and projected back up into heaven in the form of the cosmological narratives devised by priests and kings. The plain token became qualified by a variable value determined by centralized priest bureaucrats. Enlil may have retroactively become the creator of gods and men, but the priest-bureaucrat retroactively became the creator of Enlil though *written cosmology* itself. The world was now divided at its vertical center between a heavenly exchange value determined by priests and an earthly use value determined by an increasing agricultural and laboring class that had no control of the value of the new complex tokens.

Complex token numbers thus made possible a kind of numerical immortality: grain and sheep are eaten, and tally sticks are meaningless outside their temporal geographical context, but complex tokens and their numerical inscriptions remain and persist in quality and quantity beyond the singular objects they count. This was the first kinographic division between immortal inscriptions and mortal lives.[21]

SPHERES

The second major kinographic operation in ancient inscription occurred when plain and complex tokens became accumulated into sealed clay spheres. According to Schmandt-Besserat's discoveries, these spherical "envelopes" or "pods" "began being used in the Middle Uruk period, about 3700–3500 B.C."[22] and they persisted in some form or another until c. 1200 BCE.[23] Enclosed clay spheres were able to prevent cheating that might occur by adding or removing tokens to a set or archive. If the contents were ever in doubt, the sphere could be broken open and verified. The major drawback of this system, however, was that the spherical envelopes *concealed the tokens inside*. Furthermore, the verification of the contents could only occur once, since the process would break the clay. For this reason, tokens were also threaded together on a piece of string bound at each end. This ensured high visibility and resistance against tampering.[24] However, the string of tokens was awkward to store and manipulate and ultimately fell out of use, according to Schmandt-Besserat.[25]

By using a system of markings on the outside of the spheres that indicated not only the number of tokens inside, but also the shape of each token, administrators eventually solved the problem of spherical storage.[26] In addition to sealing the sphere "with a cylinder seal,"[27] a number of interesting graphic techniques were devised for marking the spheres, according to Schmandt-Besserat: "(1) attaching tokens to the surface; (2) stamping the tokens in the soft clay; (3) impressing signs with a stick or stylus; (4) pressing with the thumb; (5) scratching the clay when hard; and (6?) securing by a string. Most proved to be dead ends and disappeared."[28]

The technique that persisted was the stylus, as will be seen in the next section. What is important here is that the sphere introduced a graphic duplication of its contents, even if "the markings only repeated the information encoded in tokens for the convenience of accountants."[29] For example, if there were six tokens in the sphere, the token could be impressed six times on the outside of the sphere or only once with the addition of a marking indicating "six."[30] According to Schmandt-Besserat, this type of counting remained "concrete" because it remained tied directly to a specific type of commodity. However, the duplication and separation of these markings from the complex tokens themselves onto another surface of inscription, the sphere, further transformed the kinetic structure of graphism.

Kinetic Analysis

The introduction of token-containing spheres had several important kinographic consequences. The first is that it revealed that the conditions of centrifugal motion (redistribution) are first and foremost materially centripetal. Before tokens could be properly and officially distributed by a bureaucratic center, they first had to be accumulated into bowls, jars, and bags. Once they were accumulated in these open vessels, the open vessel was plugged to produce a total enclosed unity: the sphere. In particular, the clay-token spheres were actually shaped by a centrifugal method: first by making a solid ball of clay, and then by poking a hole in the ball and working a hollow in the middle *from the inside out*.[31] The plug sealed the contents and covered the tracks of the constitutive motion. In other words, the centrality of the sphere, along with its closed division between center and periphery, is a product of a centripetal vessel. The open vessel thus preceded the closed sphere. Open centripetal gathering preceded centrifugal radiation.

The second kinographic consequence of the token sphere is that it sacralizes the center of the sphere. By sealing up the clay vessel with an official cylinder seal devised, protected, and managed by an elite priest-bureaucracy, the contents of the sphere went through a kind of material deification. Two important events occurred at once in this operation: The flow of tokens became invisible through concealment in the center of the sphere, *and* the seal itself became the sole visible guarantee of its absent presence. The cylinder seal was not only the material condition that literally sealed up or closed up the open vessel; it also sacralized the contents of the sphere in the name of the god whose temple the priests managed. One trusted the seal because of who the makers and managers of the seal were. These Priests or deified priest kings were in turn trusted because of the gods that granted them power and expression on earth. In other words, the cylinder seal was the deified earthly or visible form of a heavenly promise of a valuable and invisible center: the tokens.

A similar kinetic operation occurred with Inanna's deification of Dummuz. It was Inanna's circular motion between heaven and the underworld that made possible a center of her motion. In a similar kinetic manner, it was the circle of the cylinder seal around the entire surface of the sphere that produced the closed and inscribed centrality of the sphere.[32] The cosmological resonance here is explicit in the images of the cylinder seals that were impressed around the sphere: portrayals of priests and kings slaying snakes and monsters, and even war scenes of besieged cities and prisoners with their hands tied behind their backs.[33]

As we saw in the previous chapters, the image of the priest-king slaying the snake monster is a founding kinetic cosmology of the ancient period, where the spiral and centripetal motion of the snake-mother (Tiamat, Tehom, Tethys, and others) is murdered by the hero (priest-king-god) who then takes her corpse and remakes the world with it, spreading it centrifugally outward in all directions into a cosmic *sphere* around himself, the divine center. It is therefore unsurprising, although kinetically revealing, that the construction of the clay token sphere repeats these exact same cosmological motions—sealing itself with images of the same cosmopolitical movement. One is not the model of the other, of course, but the two are part of the same centrifugal regime. Kinographically, this first material step toward invisibility is crucial. Without it the description of eternity and the inscription of writing never get off the ground, as we shall see.

The third kinographic consequence of the token sphere is that it creates a centrifugal or outward motion of the token from the center to the periphery of the sphere. Once the sphere is closed in on itself and sealed, the contents are centralized, sacralized, and made invisible, fixed, and static. Once this occurs, however, the tokens and their graphisms begin to radiate outward onto the outside surface of the sphere in a variety of forms: attaching tokens or strings to the sphere, creating impressions of the invisible tokens on the surface, or inscribing the token image with a stylus on the outside. These are real movements. Graphic signs actually changed location from one place to another, while the whole of the clay sphere was qualitatively moved from smooth to *inscribed*.

While the first kinographic operation of the token divided earthly use values from heavenly exchange values, the second operation of the sphere rendered the tokens invisible and immobile but secured their presence through divine inscription. While the first allowed for a centrifugal economic redistribution, the second created a centrifugal graphic radiation: the immobility of the center.

TABLETS

The third major kinographic operation of ancient inscription occurs when the spheres become autonomous surfaces of inscription, without tokens. The strength of the spherical storage system for tokens was that it secured the tokens from tampering; its weakness was that it concealed the tokens from view and made it difficult to confirm and modify accounts.

As we saw, this problem was solved by moving the inscriptions centrifugally from the invisible inside to the visible outside. However, once the inscriptions moved to the outside of the hollow sphere containing concealed tokens, the tokens became superfluous to the process. It was thus not long after the introduction of token spheres (c. 3,700 BCE) and their attendant graphic system that the concealed tokens inside were sacrificed entirely in favor of solid clay spheres and convex tablets (3,500 BCE). The importance of this kinographic operation in the emergence of writing cannot be overemphasized. According to Schmandt-Besserat,

> The substitution of signs for tokens was a first step toward writing. Fourth-millennium accountants soon realized that the tokens within the envelopes were made unnecessary by the presence of markings on the outer surface. As a result, tablets—solid clay balls bearing markings—replaced the hollow envelopes filled with tokens. These markings became a system of their own which developed to include not only impressed markings but more legible signs traced with a pointed stylus. Both of these types of symbols which derived from tokens were picture signs or "pictographs." They were not, however, pictographs of the kind anticipated by Warburton. The signs were not pictures of the items they represented but rather, pictures of the tokens used as counters in the previous accounting system.[34]

Since the impressions and markings on the outside of the sphere rendered the tokens inside obsolete, the clay ball no longer needed to be hollowed out. Instead, the same ball of clay was simply flattened into a rounded convex mound, producing a new inscription surface.[35]

This was not the only important kinographic transformation in this operation. With the disjunction of the tokens from the graphic system, graphism was able to create new inscriptions. "Whereas the markings on envelopes repeated only the message encoded in the tokens held within, the signs impressed on tablets were the message. The first tablets were a decisive step in the invention of writing and amounted to a revolution in communication technology."[36]

In addition to using token impressions on the surface of these convex tablet-mounds and retaining the official seal over the top, additional stylus inscriptions were added to tablets at the time of their emergence.[37] Increasingly, inscription took the place of token impressions, since the inscriptions could show finer detail, especially of complex or marked tokens, than an impression could. These inscribed images of tokens became the first pictographic images.

This is kinetically key. The brilliance of Schmandt-Besserat was to prove this thesis by fully documenting the following sequence in numerous instances:

A. A type of token found at large.
B. The same token enclosed in an unmarked envelope.
C. The corresponding marking on the surface of an envelope.
D. The matching sign impressed on a tablet.

E. The occurrence on a pictographic tablet as an impressed sign, an incised pictograph, or an impressed/incised sign.[38]

The token/impression/sign coordination clearly shows that the origin of pictographic writing did not spontaneously emerge from someone's mind as a two-dimensional image but rather emerged from a fundamentally kinographic and three-dimensional system of tokens. Pictographs introduced a radically new type of graphism that no longer referred to a singular tally or even a concrete type of object or token. Once graphism was detached from the token, it appeared as an arbitrary sign that referred not to a concrete token-object but to an abstract meaning. In other words, the pictograph for "sheep" no longer referred to any specific sheep or even any specific token of specific sheep, but to the general idea or meaning of sheep, which included all sheep and no sheep in particular at the same time.

While tokens were singular and designed for one-time use, pictographs and numerals "held information *permanently*," as Schmandt-Besserat writes, since they did not refer to any concrete object in particular.[39] Once the concrete tokens and number were disjoined from the graphic process, nothing stood in the way of creating pictographs of objects that had no tokens and no number. By about 2,900 BCE, writing had begun to record historical events and religious texts.[40]

> It was not by chance that the invention of pictography and phonetic writing coincided with that of numerals: both were the result of abstract counting. The abstraction of the concept of quantity (how many) from that of the quality of the item counted—concepts that were merged inextricably in the tokens—made possible the beginning of writing. Once dissociated from any notion of number, the pictographs could evolve in their own separate way. Symbols formerly used for keeping accounts of goods could expand to communicate any subject of human endeavor. As a result, things such as "the head of a man" or "mouth"—items which never had a token—were expressed by a picture. True pictography, wherein concepts were represented by their images, was an outcome of abstract counting.[41]

Kinetic Analysis

Several kinographic consequences followed from this historical transformation. The tablet continued the kinetics of the sphere, but in a new way, evidenced by the fact that the tablet was nothing other than the same ball of clay flattened, instead of hollowed. Since most tablets retained a convex dome-like structure, they also retained a similar kinetic structure.

The first kinographic consequence of this change was the transcendence of the center. By removing the tokens and flattening the sphere, the graphic process was no longer concretely tied to a specific object in the center of the sphere. However, this does not mean that there was no longer a sphere or center; rather, the sphere was simply enlarged such that the convex tablet was only one piece of its enormous curvature, and the center was now expanded to everywhere in general and nowhere in particular. Graphism was no longer tied to singular objects but to "general" objects, which were all types of objects but none of those objects in particular.

In other words, graphism became tied to ideas and meanings. The kinographic structure of this meaning, following the material kinetics of the token, was that the pictographic inscriptions referred to the nonconcrete center of the sphere. In a certain sense, they were inscriptions of nothing at all, or in some cases traces of something that had already disappeared. Graphism now became subject to the same dilemma as spherical cosmology: the center of the sphere is everywhere in the form of its infinite radii that extend equally to the periphery, and nowhere in particular. Just like the center of the cosmic sphere, an abstract "sheep" is static—it is not a thing—it does not move or change. It has an infinite number of concrete manifestations but is irreducible to any one of them in particular. The graphic "idea" of sheep becomes *eternal*—neither created nor destroyed, since it is not a concrete token, and neither here nor there, since it has no concrete place.

However, just because one removes the token from the sphere does not mean that the material-kinetic conditions that support the graphic act have disappeared. The material movement of graphism remains a singular act and is still connected in this immanent practice to a singular object, even if it becomes conventional to allow the same mark to be connected to other singular objects as well.

The materiality of the tablet here is crucial. The tokens in the sphere are mobile and thus disposable, but the tablet has no mobile components, so it relies on the practice of using the inscriptions more than once, even though *each time is still kinetically unique*.

The immobility of the signs on the tablet gives rise to the graphic notion of identity across singularities: abstraction. This is the second kinographic consequence of the tablet. It is no coincidence that the very first abstract inscriptions were numerical. The idea that an abstract sign can refer to multiple sheep already presupposes a unity across the differences in sheep. The archaeology of the token reveals this fact: Abstraction emerges as numerical abstraction first and foremost; only later does qualitative abstraction arise from this. All other abstractions derive from this first kinetic abstraction of the singular flow of tokens into identical and immobile pictographs.

However, being has never stopped moving; the sheep will always be singular. In fact, as archaeology now shows, the very material usage of the immobile, two-dimensional tablet inscriptions was predicated on a system of movable tokens. The stasis of the pictograph is only possible because of the mobility of the token, not the other way around. Movement is primary, and stasis is derived and abstracted from it like a slice of space-time taken from a continuum.

This point also bears directly on the rise to dominance of "oneness" in cosmology. The invention of abstract numbers made possible the invention of being or God as one. It is not a coincidence that the very possibility of such an idea would summon the very first abstract idea: oneness. Abstract oneness is not any particular one but all and none. As such, it could not have been created or destroyed by another particular one, nor could it reside in any particular place on earth. From the beginning of "one," the very notion of abstraction was eternal. This is the same idea that occurs in the history of cosmology. Over the course of several thousands of years, cosmologies slowly began to lose their multiple gods in favor of one creator god, from which all the others derived. The belief in eternity is the belief in the primacy of abstraction, even if it must retroactively cover over its true material-kinetic conditions in the mobility of tokens.

The third kinographic consequence of the tablet is the centrifugal creation of new pictographs. There is an interesting kinetic resonance here with theomachic cosmologies. Just as Marduk murdered Tiamat, took up residence in the center of Ea's magic circle, and recreated the universe centrifugally outward from the center with the dead body of Tiamat, so the concrete tokens in the sphere were removed, the center of the sphere (the origin of meaning) became transcendent, and the scribes now began to create a new world of pictographs radiating outward as divine craft. After the tokens were removed from the sphere, meaning continued to reside in the center, even if the center had become a transcendent center, or no longer the concrete center of the sphere. In Babylonian cosmology, Ea, the first centrifugal god of the center, was defined by his mind craft. When Marduk became the king of the gods, he took on Ea's divine mind craft in his recreation of the world. In a similar fashion, the priest-bureaucrats of the social-economic center sacrificed the centripetal concrete center of the sphere only to replace it with their own mind-crafted images of anything whatever: pictographs.

This had a kinographically fascinating effect. Since signs or pictographs originally referred to a more primary and preexistent concrete object, the creation of new pictographs produced a similar effect of presupposing the prior existence of the thing to which it referred. In other words, new pictographs not only began to refer to new types of objects already known, but they also began to produce new objects—gods, divine forces, heroic events, and so on—that, through their pictographic inscription, attained a retroactive existence.

The kinographic inversion here is absolutely amazing. The graphic signs were once markers of the concrete, but now the signs have become the concrete markers of the abstract. In other words, the signs refer to nothing other than themselves. They refer to what they themselves have brought into creation through their marking. It is for this reason that all written ontological description functions as a system of immanent kinosigns and not as representations or signifiers. The inverse of this is only apparently possible because of these specific historical and material conditions of inscription—a whole kinetics of written language.

This circular structure also attests to an important connection between writing and cosmologies of eternity: a transcendent god secures the realm of meaning in words, words that in turn secure the graphic inscription of the god as retroactively transcendent. All of this occurs historically and materially within the same kinetic pattern of centrifugal motion.

These three operations, however, also pave the way for the emergence of a fourth and more radical kinographic operation of inscription in which phonetic sound itself is mutually subordinated to these abstract signs in the phonetic alphabet.

CHAPTER 22

Writing II

Alphabet

The fourth major kinographic operation in the ancient world finally occurred when the graphisms created by tablets and the phonisms of speech entered into a mutual subordination to an abstract meaning or idea. In other words, once graphism was liberated from its concrete tokens, it could create abstract signs for anything, including the discrete sounds made in human speech called phonemes.

PHONETIC ALPHABET

The practice of connecting written graphisms to speech first emerged in Sumer (modern-day Iraq) around 3,500–3,390 BCE—specifically in Uruk, which is "likely the birthplace of writing in Mesopotamia"—with the use of cuneiform, a written means of representing the Sumerian language.[1] Independent of this, Egyptian hieroglyphics connected to language emerged around 3,300 BCE.[2] The earliest alphabet—the linear phonetic alphabet, Sinaitic, proto-Sinaitic, proto-Canaanite, Old Canaanite, or Canaanite—is traced to proto-Sinaitic inscriptions (c. 1850 BCE) and is a hybrid of Egyptian hieroglyphs and West Semitic word sounds[3] developed by foreign Semitic workers who had little literate knowledge of the hieroglyphic meanings.[4] All other known alphabets derived to varying degrees from this proto-Sinaitic alphabet, albeit through its full-fledged or "stabilized" form in the Phoenician alphabet (c. 1100 BCE).[5]

Once graphic signs became *signs of sounds*, they could no longer be read independently of language. This was a big historical shift. As noted in the previous chapter, sound and gesture emerged historically as heterogeneous material-kinetic processes that had been centripetally collected in the human body as speech. There was no representation or causality there, only a constant conjunction or coordinated gathering of sonic and graphic junctions. With the emergence of the phonetic alphabet, sound and gesture were radically redistributed according to a new kinographic regime of mutual subordination to abstract meaning.

The Subordination of Graphism to Phonism

There are three different aspects of this mutual subordination of phonism and graphism. The first aspect is the subordination of graphism to phonism. One of the most important conclusions of Denise Schmandt-Besserat's work is that writing and its token precursors were originally not modeled on language. Writing did not start with a pictography modeled on language, as most scholars argued. Graphism had previously been free to create its own autonomous nonlinguistic syntax of tallies, tokens, and impressions. This produced an incredible amount of pictographs, since each new type of thing required its own pictograph.

However, once graphism began to model its signs on phonetic syllables and eventually discrete phonemes, the enormous number of pictographs was reduced down to a single alphabetic sequence. Now, instead of needing a new pictograph for every type of thing, one could simply use the same graphic signs in different and infinite combinations that were coordinated to spoken sounds. As André Leroi-Gourhan writes, "At the linear graphism stage that characterizes writing, the relationship between the two fields undergoes yet another development: written language, phoneticized and linear in space, becomes completely subordinated to spoken language, which is phonetic and linear in time. The dualism between graphic and verbal disappears, and the whole of human linguistic apparatus becomes a single instrument for expressing and preserving thought—which itself is channeled increasingly toward reasoning."[6] In this great alphabetic reduction, the indefinite expansion of an autonomous graphism was subordinated to a finite combinatorial and linear phonetic alphabet. The hand became subordinated to the mouth.[7] What could be written was now reduced in form and content to what could be uttered.

The Subordination of Phonism to Graphism

The second aspect of this mutual subordination is the inverse subordination of phonism to graphism. With writing, graphism may have been reduced to the finite combinatoric of the phonetic alphabet, but in this same move phonism was also tied to or subordinated to a finite graphic syntax. The structure of spoken sounds now became tied to its graphic dimensions through reading. In the activity of reading a recorded text, one is no longer forced to remember the entire text in order to recite and transmit it orally. Through reading, one subordinates one's bodily sound to the graphic order on the recording surface. Numerous consequences follow from this.[8]

One is the homogenization of cultural memory as divergent oral traditions are standardized, preserved, and canonized by those with the power to write and preserve texts. Another is that speech takes on an increasingly passive relationship with regard to writing. This is the case not only because what is written is already there all at once and spoken reading has to move in time linearly to realize it but also because speech simply becomes a concrete duplication of what was already written. In speaking what has been written, one is forced to reproduce out loud in one's own body a series of sounds. The body becomes a cog in an imperial megajunction, a resonance chamber of a higher power, and a forced and homogenized instrument of sonic internalization. Therefore all the syntactical innovations, orderings, and political fluctuations of the where, why, and how of writing become the primary conditions under which the reading eye is able to speak what has been written.

The Subordination of Phonism and Graphism to Meaning

The third aspect of this mutual subordination is the subordination of both phonism and graphism to a third dimension: meaning. Phonism and graphism enter into a mutual subordination, but in doing so they achieve a new kind of "balance" or "coordination," as Leroi-Gourhan writes.[9] This new balance is the mutual loss of autonomy between the two and their increasingly fixed or bound relationship. Phonism and graphism become like two sides of the same Möbius strip; they are united on the strip but function as two different articulations of the same thing.

In other words, they produce the effect of a discrete homogenous identity. This is in contrast to the heterogeneous assembly of sonic and gestural motions produced by prewritten speech. This new balance between phonism and graphism is also achieved by a third subordination that coordinates and distributes the other two: the subordination to meaning, thought, or a transcendent mute voice from on high. It is worth quoting Deleuze and Guattari at length on this point:

> Primitive societies are oral not because they lack a graphic system but because, on the contrary, the graphic system in these societies is independent of the voice; it marks signs on the body that respond to the voice, react to the voice, but that are autonomous and do not align themselves on it. In return, barbarian civilizations are written, not because the voice has been lost, but because the graphic system has lost its independence and its particular dimensions, has aligned itself on the voice and has become subordinated to the voice, enabling it to extract from the voice a deterritorialized abstract flux that it retains and makes reverberate in the linear code of writing. In short, graphism in one and the same movement begins to depend on the voice, and induces a mute voice from on high or from the beyond, a voice that begins to depend on graphism. It is by subordinating itself to the voice that writing supplants it.[10]

The inversion here is amazing. Mutual subordination not only binds graphism to phonemes, and vice versa, but it also binds both to a new written or "mute" voice that occurs in one's head and body as one reads the writing. Writing triumphs precisely by subordinating itself to the voice, which it supplants at the same time by creating a mute voice that speaks the phonemes without speaking. Thus, writing realizes in an instant what speech can only realize through motion.

Phonetic writing becomes absolute eternal, silent speech—something that concrete speech and concrete graphism can only be in a single instance and never attain completely all at once. The relative immobility of the graphic code now takes on a phonetic immobility as well. Both merge together in a third dimension of what we might call "meaning." The entire apparatus of writing relies on the identity of the spoken and written words in meaning. Both must mean the same thing, or the whole system falls apart. Furthermore, writing is predicated on the belief that the meaning of a word must also remain the same, regardless of how, when, where, and who writes it: repeatability. All concrete determinations of a word should not fundamentally alter the meaning of the word. In these ways meaning becomes the coordinating power between the mutual subordination of phonism and graphism.

Kinetic Analysis

Two important kinographic consequences follow from this mutual subordination. The first is the emergence of a kinographic megajunction. Kinetically, the megajunction is a concrete material junction, but its radial extensions appear everywhere throughout circulation and thus nowhere in particular in the circulation. In the case of writing, this megajunction took on this paradoxical-sounding abstract definition, first as the concrete centralizing accumulation of tokens, then, after they were removed, as an empty center containing all types of an object but no concrete object in particular. As long as the center remained hidden, like the inner temples and sanctums of most ancient cities, anything could be inside. Abstraction is a material-kinetic effect of enclosed centralization. Wherever we find enclosed centralization we find the emergence of abstractions of one kind or another.

From a kinetic perspective, however, these abstractions have no such metaphysical status beyond their embodied practice. They are like images floating on the surface of a pool of water. If, like Narcissus, we mistake them as having an autonomous reality, we forget the beauty, mobility, and materiality of the water on which they exist. What must be explained then, from a kinetic perspective, is precisely how such images are effects of the material-kinetic regimes that condition them.

The thesis being advanced here is that the emergence of the belief in immobile and eternal abstractions was a historical event made possible by the material-kinetic condition of an active but hidden center. The dark recesses of the central temples and palaces where politics and religion emerge are historically mirrored by the dark recesses of the clay sphere that once contained concrete tokens. With the tablet, the container became an infinite hollow space as big as the world. Anything could come out of it.

All this was achieved by the tablet. The phonetic alphabet, however, presupposed it and began with it. The belief that inside a darkened sphere there are abstractions that are all things and no things in particular is also to accept the following correlates:

1. If there is such a thing as an abstraction it cannot have been created. This is because if it were created it would have to have been created by something particular, but if something particular created it, the creator would have created something particular. However, since abstractions are not reducible to their particularity, they cannot have been created as a particular by a particular.

2. It also follows that since abstractions are not particular they cannot exist in any particular place but instead exist in all places in general and no place in particular. For this same reason, it follows that abstractions are immobile, since extensive movement presupposes spatial location.
3. It further follows that an abstraction cannot change its nature without violating its identity and producing a contradiction.
4. Finally, if abstractions are not created, neither can they be destroyed. By definition they are eternal. If they are eternal while others are not, they are cosmologically primary in relation to these others. Furthermore, if they are cosmologically primary, they must be prior to and causally responsible for the creation of noneternal beings.

In order for the phonetic alphabet to work, it must presuppose the identical, repeatable, immobile, immutable, and eternal nature of an abstract meaning, since it is abstract meaning that coordinates the mutual subordination of graphism and phonism to one another. For instance, if the written word "sheep" had a different meaning than the spoken word "sheep," there would be no mutual subordination. If writing relies on this coordination, it relies on the existence of meaning; and if it relies on the existence of meaning, it relies on the belief in abstractions; and if it relies on the belief in abstractions, it assumes they are eternal, uncreated, and as such ontologically primary with regard to the particular graphemes and phonemes that are being coordinated. In short, if there is a coordinating power or meaning, it must, as abstract, be ontologically primary and thus creative of the concrete particular sounds and gestures that articulate it in any given instance.

The kinetic inversion from centripetal accumulation in the heart of the darkened sphere to the centrifugal radiation from its abstract center outward in the creation of concrete signs is now complete. The central product has now become the centrifugal producer. Abstract meaning has now recreated, reorganized, and subordinated the circulation of concrete all phonographisms in a single kinographic coup de grâce, in perfect coordination with the cotemporaneous cosmological description of eternity and God.

The second kinographic consequence of the phonetic alphabet is the centrifugal distribution of meaning. In this final move, we can finally see the kinetic synchrony, the history of ancient cosmology, the emergence of writing, and the primary determination of being as eternal. This is possible because both cosmological description and inscription encounter the same problematic opposition between the abstract and the particular. As Harold Innis states, "Writing made the mythical and historical past, the familiar and the alien creation available for appraisal. The idea of things became differentiated from things. This dualism demanded thought and reconciliation. Life was contrasted with the eternal universe, and attempts were made to reconcile the individual with the universal spirit."[11]

WRITING AND COSMOLOGY

The argument in this final section is that this so-called reconciliation between the eternal and the particular (gods and men, meaning and writing) took a fundamentally kinetic form: spherical rotation. This was already shown in the cosmologies of the previous chapters; now we see how a similar operation was introduced to reconcile the growing graphic tension between abstract meaning and concrete writing/speaking.

Greek Philosophy

Plato's *Phaedrus* remains a key demonstration of this tension and its kinetic dimensions. In this dialogue, Socrates describes writing to Phaedrus in the following way:

> You know, Phaedrus, writing shares a strange feature with painting. The offsprings of painting stand there as if they are alive, but if anyone asks them anything, they remain most *solemnly silent*. The same is true of written words. You'd think they were speaking as if they had some understanding, but if you question anything that has been said because you want to learn more, it continues to *signify just that very same thing forever. When it has once been written down, every discourse roams about everywhere,* reaching indiscriminately those with understanding no less than those who have no business with it, and it doesn't know to whom it should speak and to whom it should not. And when it is faulted and attacked unfairly, *it always needs its father's support*; alone, it can neither defend itself nor come to its own support.[12]

A number of important aspects of writing are described here. First, it is important to note the fundamentally kinetic structure of writing: It roams around everywhere, far from its original meaning. This is literal. Arguably one of the most important aspects of the emergence of writing is that it allowed an incredible mobility of communication never before seen on earth. Writing has a greater range and mobility than speech by far. Writing really addresses more audiences in more places because of its mobility.

This is precisely Socrates's problem with writing: It is too mobile! Writing allows the concrete inscriptions to kinetically wander too far from their central source of authorial meaning, historically granted in the central cities by the central priests, kings, and scribes in their darkened temples and palaces. On the other hand, the meaning of the word is completely mute and eternal. The tensions here between the eternal, silent, and immobile meaning and concrete mobile writing are extremely clear.

Furthermore, according to Socrates, writing is defenseless on its own and always requires its father. It is easy to read this passage as a representational metaphor, but it would be a mistake to ignore the historicity and cosmological context of this point. The father of writing is not just the "meaning" who created writing from his mind; in Socrates's cosmology this creation is quite literal. The male God (father without mother or wife) is the eternal craftsman at the center of a sphere who radiates centrifugally outward toward the moving periphery.

The parallel between writing and cosmology explicitly converges at this point. At the center of his rotating sphere, God creates by his mind centrifugally outward toward his rotating periphery. As we saw in the previous chapter, his eternity is reconciled with this mobile, mutable creation because the center of the sphere does not move when it rotates. There is only one single sphere, one eternal motion, but with one part that moves and one part that remains motionless. Therefore there is no paradox. This same eternal God is the one responsible for creating all the immutable eternal ideas and meanings in the world, which coordinate the mutual subordination of concrete phonemes and graphemes. Therefore God and his creations of eternal meaning reside in the center of the cosmic sphere, while the concrete written words and sounds made by humans wander errantly and indiscriminately at the periphery.

God functions at the center of his rotating sphere like a transcendent eye that radiates vision without touching or being touched by his creation that might change him or alter his eternal essence, which by definition cannot be altered or moved. Socrates's God thus creates according to an *edios*, from the PIE root **weid-*, "to see, to know," in the same way that writing accords a kinetic privilege to vision and thought in the mute voice. Vision and knowledge both occur from a distance, just as the immobile center of the sphere views and extends to all its radii without becoming absorbed by them or reduced to them. The immobile eye of God watches everything move without itself moving, like the static meaning that organizes and distributes the mobile written text without moving or changing.

In this way the model of ancient knowledge is also based on the kinomena of eternity. Knowledge is what does not change; it is the knowledge of static essences, unmoved motions, unspoken voices, and uncreated creators. However, despite its pretensions to immobility, the structure of this kind of knowledge and eternity is fundamentally kinetic because it emerges from the centrifugal motion radiating outward from the darkened sphere as tokens, impressions, and concrete signs on the exterior/periphery of the recording surface.

Furthermore, knowledge still relies on the kinetics of vision to view the mobility of the written word. Meaning may be invisible, but it still cannot be known without the concrete kinetic act of graphic inscription and vision. While speech is centripetal because it gathers and accumulates sounds and gestures in the resonating, moving body, writing is centrifugal because it presupposes the central accumulation of these senses but also radiates back outward away from the body as a single visible image on an exterior recording surface to be viewed by an invisible gaze. While the body allows for a heterogeneity between phonism and graphism in the mutual autonomy of the face and hand, the written word enforces a mutual subordination in a single *visual image*.

The visual image binds phonism and graphism, but it also produces a bifurcation of phonographic circulation between inside and outside, between viewer and viewed, between center and periphery. While the hearing-speech couple operates by centripetal resonance in both the bodies of the speaker and the audience, the vision-writing couple operates by centrifugal radiation from the eye that sees the written word outside the body without itself being seen by the written word. This produces a kinographic asymmetry between what moves and changes in the world (written texts) and the unchanging meaning that organizes the universal viewability/intelligibility of the texts.

As noted in the previous chapters, this apparent ontological division is resolved in early Greek philosophy through the rotation of a sphere. Although the explicit discussion in the remaining fragments and *testimonia* of their work deals directly with cosmological issues of eternal and mortal being, the same solution is also used for writing insofar as writing postulates an abstract and eternal realm and a concrete phonographic one. We can therefore solve Plato's problem of writing in the following synthetic formulation drawn from numerous Greek philosophers leading up to Plato's explicit solution of it in the *Phaedrus*: There is no contradiction or ontological division between motionless eternal meaning and mobile finite phonographics, because being is a rotating sphere whose periphery spins while the center remains unmoved. Just as the divine eternal God creates all of being from the center of his immobile sphere, this is also where abstract meaning resides that gives birth to writing. As the sphere rotates, the center remains motionless and unchanged while the periphery of concrete sounds and graphic inscriptions moves.

We can now produce the following series of kinetic conjunctions of cosmographic terms: If meaning is abstract, it is eternal; if it is eternal it is unmoved; if it is unmoved it is incorporeal; if it is incorporeal it is solemnly silent and invisible. If it is all of these things it has the same definition as God, the one, the sphere god, the unmoved mover. Phonetic written language thus resonates kinetically with a spherical cosmology.

Mesopotamia

All major ancient cosmologies describe a similar centrifugal account of kinographic inscription. As in many things, Plato offers an excellent and poetic synthesis of a much older phenomenon that can be traced all the way back to Mesopotamia and Semitic religion. In both of these cases we can see that writing introduces an increasingly centrifugal motion, moving outward from a transcendent or invisible center of meaning toward a mobile and immanent periphery.

In Sumer, for example, the historical emergence and superiority of the air/breath god Enlil not only plays a cosmological role, as noted in the previous chapters, but also a kinographic one, which emerged around the same time as the emergence of abstract pictographic writing: c. 3,200 BCE.[13] "With the appearance of Enlil, creation is no longer imagined as a birth from the mother, but as 'the word' that speaks all things into being."[14]

> Your word—it is plants, your word—it is grain,
> Your word is the floodwater, the life of all the lands.[15]

Enlil's word is no longer the embodied gestural word of a body but the silent disembodied voice of the air or sky that radiates out and down from the top of the holy mountain. From the beginning of Enlil's emergence in Sumerian mythology, he is known as "the father of the gods," "the king of heaven and earth," and "the king of all the lands."[16] Enlil creates from the center, not through bodily reproduction but through meaning. He is not a biological father but a kind of divine father craftsman who creates by his *words*.

However, his words must have a specific kinographic structure for him to retain his airy transcendence. His words must have a concrete graphic existence that grants them appearance as grain or water, but they must also have a concrete phonetic existence in the spoken name "grain" or "water." In addition to these two dimensions, his words must also have a third dimension: their transcendence as divine meaningful words spoken by the mute voice of the god Enlil. Not everyone's words are grain. Enlil's voice or breath, just like Enlil, transcend all concrete expressions so he can create again. His voice does not die when the plants do because his voice is a mute voice, a silent word, pure meaning.

A silent word makes no sense within previous oral cultures because words are absolutely tied to their phonographic expression. A silent word is a thought, an abstract meaning, a voice that occurs within and above the concrete: a transcendent inner breath-soul-voice. With Enlil, this mute voice from on high creates centrifugally, just as abstract meaning mutually subordinates phonetic and graphic elements. The cosmological and the kinographic motions here are part of the same centrifugal regime.

Semitic Religion

This same kinographic motion is also described by the creative voice of Yahweh in the Hebrew Bible. As an abstract and transcendent center, Yahweh does not visibly appear in the Hebrew Bible. He creates with his "voice": "And God said . . ." However, the speech of eternity no longer comes from a centripetal accumulation of sound into a gestural body; rather, eternal speech now radiates outward and downward from a disembodied center. Instead of a parity and assembly of accumulated phonisms and graphisms, there is now an eternal, unheard, and unseen expression, a voice without sound because it has no body to resonate. The material sounds and bodies that once connected with one another have now become subordinate to an eternal meaning that now becomes their retroactive origin. With the emergence of eternal and creative meaning, concrete sounds and bodies become products or signs that merely represent or signify the eternal and creative power of God.

> And, behold, the Lord passed by, and a great and strong wind rent the mountains, and broke in pieces the rocks before the Lord; but the Lord was not in the wind: and after the wind an earthquake; but the Lord was not in the earthquake:
>
> And after the earthquake a fire; but the Lord was not in the fire: and after the fire a still small voice.[17]

God has no concrete embodiment in anything else, only "a still small voice." Speech is movement, resonance in the body. Immobile speech is a paradox.

It is a speech that is not a speech, a voice that is not one. It is a "mute voice" coming from nowhere and everywhere at once, "from on high," like the center of a circle forming its periphery through centrifugal radiation. It is as if one hears the voice of God from within a sphere of speakers. Moses said to his people,

> And ye came near and stood under the mountain; and the mountain burned with fire unto the midst of heaven, with darkness, clouds, and thick darkness.
>
> And the Lord spake unto you out of the midst of the fire: ye heard the voice of the words, but saw no similitude: only ye heard a voice.[18]

"God speaks from the mountain tops, out of clouds, fire, lightning, storm, wind and thunder, much as the Semitic and Aryan gods before him: the Sumerian Enlil, the Babylonian Marduk and the Canaanite gods El and Baal."[19]

God "speaks" creation and then "sees" it is good. Just as God's speech is not spoken, his vision is not seen. His vision is not a vision "from somewhere" that would limit his perspective, it is a vision from an absolute and vertical center that sees all without itself being seen. It sees everything from everywhere.

God's eternal form also has no representable image in space-time.

> Take ye therefore good heed unto yourselves; for ye saw no manner of similitude on the day that the Lord spake unto you in Horeb out of the midst of the fire: Lest ye corrupt yourselves, and make you a graven image, the similitude of any figure, the likeness of male or female.
>
> And lest thou lift up thine eyes unto heaven and when thou seest the sun, and the moon, and the stars, even all the host of heaven, shouldest be driven to worship them, and serve them, which the Lord thy God hath divided unto all nations under the whole heaven.[20]
>
> Thou shalt have no other gods before me.
> Thou shalt not make unto thee any graven image or any likeness of any thing that is in heaven above, or that is in the earth beneath, or that is in the water under the earth.[21]

Not only does God have no representable image that can be found on earth or in the skies, but his being so far transcends any concrete image that to make an image or sound of any kind to speak his name or see his face would be blasphemy. When Moses asks him his name, Yahweh replies, "I Am That I Am . . . Thus shalt thou say unto the children of Israel, I Am hath sent me to you."[22] Once the concrete center has been sacrificed, there is nothing left but a pure being beyond all predication, an infinite center beyond any possible approximations of its location. "Typographically, the Name [Yahweh] is represented by four Hebrew consonants, but etymologically it is a modification of the verb 'to be,' which also means 'to breathe.'"[23] Breath, wind, smoke, and fire thus all become the closest physical signs of Yahweh's pure eternal being,

> who maketh the clouds his chariot: who walketh upon the wings of the wind:
> Who maketh his angels spirits; his ministers a flaming fire.[24]

Yahweh is also a divine craftsman. He does not create through birth but makes with his disembodied thought, like Ea in the *Enuma Elish*, whose name means both "mind" and "craft." The craft of the mind never dulls or ages but remains eternally creative and unchanged by what it creates. However, unlike Ea or Marduk, Yahweh does not have any anthropomorphic figuration, predication, or attribution that would leave its trace or could be affected by his creation. Yahweh requires no tools and no other gods. His disembodied voice and vision (thought/meaning) is enough to create.

CONCLUSION

This chapter concludes Part II's kinetic analysis of being as eternity and its regime of centrifugal motion. Historically, however, this regime began to wane with the fall of the Roman Empire, and a new regime of motion began to rise to ontological dominance during the period from about the fifth century to the seventeenth century CE, as discussed in Part III: Being and Force.

PART III
Being and Force

I
Kinos

CHAPTER 23

Tensional Motion

Beginning around the fifth century CE, alongside the decline of the Roman Empire and the increasing decentralization of political power in the West, a new regime of motion began to take hold: tensional force.

The task of Part III is to create a kinetic concept of force and explain the theological (descriptive) and kinographic (inscriptive) conditions of its dominant historical emergence in the West. The argument of Part III is that the theological description of being as force and the kinographic invention of the codex or book are two expressions of the same kinetic regime of tensional motion that rose to prominence during what I am calling the long "medieval period," in which being was defined primarily by its *force* or *power*. For lack of a better term, and from the perspective of the types of kinetic regimes, the designation "medieval" will henceforth refer to the long period covering the Middle Ages, Renaissance, and early-modern periods. These periods are different in many ways, but here I will focus on their seminaries as distinct from ancient and modern periods.

In addition to the ancient description of being as eternal, the medieval world added a new description that, over the course of this long historical period, became even more dominant: force. Similar to space and eternity, the description of being as force is an attempt to explain why things move. However, just like space and eternity, force, as Bergson writes, "is known and estimated only by the movements which it is supposed to produce in space . . . [but it is] one with these movements."[1] There is no secret cause or "action at a distance" behind different types of movement. "Has a force ever been demonstrated," Nietzsche asks, with the answer, "No, only effects translated into a completely foreign language."[2] Force thus remains entirely immanent to the motions that constitute it, but it gets translated into the language of metaphysics: causality, impetus, conatus, and so on. Therefore, in addition to our previous kinetic concepts of space and eternity, we now add to our growing historical ontology of motion a kinetic theory of force as tensional motion.

Part III is divided into three sections: the first offers a strictly *kinomenological* theory of force as tensional motion; the second offers a kinetic analysis of the historically *descriptive* features of force provided by the theological writings of the time; and the third offers a kinetic analysis of the historical technology of *inscription* (the book) within which these descriptions were inscribed.

KINOMENOLOGY OF FORCE

This chapter offers a purely kinomenological theory of the tensional motions that define being as force. The thesis of this chapter is that dynamic being is defined by a material and kinetic tensional motion. The kinetic concept of force has three major kinetic features: tensional motion, triangulation, and relation.

TENSIONAL MOTION

The first kinetic feature is tensional motion. Kinetically, tensional motion is the movement created by at least two folds bound together by a rigid link.[3] The rigid link keeps them both together and apart. It decenters their motion while also strengthening it. Two or more folds are relatively autonomous centers with their own form of motion, but since their movements are held together by the tension of the link, the motion of one is always restricted by the motion of the other. Tensional motion is inelastically relativized by the motion of others. This can be exemplified by the movement of the human arm.[4] The human arm is composed of several radial joints connected by several bone linkages. Each ball joint rotates in its own orbit with its own degrees of freedom, while the rigid linkage between them both decenters and strengthens their movement.

Tensional, rigid, or linked motion is defined by a rigid or inelastic connection or relation between two or more circulations. While conjunctions refer only to the relations between folds, and knots deal only with the coordinated or shared affects of fields, linked motion deals with regimes of circulation that are connected together by a third flow that links them and keeps them apart from one another at the same time.

Tensional motion presupposes a centripetal motion insofar as it relies on the connection between already established circulations that have gathered motion into distinct regimes. Furthermore, tensional motion also presupposes that this centripetal movement has produced a center large enough to redirect motion outward beyond its regional accumulation to become a connecting flow. What tensional motion adds to the previous two regimes is simply an inelastic link between fields of circulation.

Flows, by nature, are always leaking from their circulations and connecting to others. Once a flow escapes from one circulation it can connect to another, thus producing a linkage or tension between the two. This link can then be cycled back and forth between the circulations and sustained. This holds the two circulations both together and apart, granting them a degree of unity and autonomy without releasing them entirely from subordination to another. In this sense they are different both from conjunctions and knots.

As a dominant form of motion, tension resolves an important problem that confronts the cosmology of centrifugal motion. The idea that being is a single cosmic sphere where motion and order move outward from the perfect eternal center to the imperfect mortal periphery introduces the problem of impurity. In the sphere the center and the periphery are united in a single continuous being and distinguished only by degrees or gradations of difference, as concentric spheres. The problem, however, is that the center bleeds into the periphery, and vice versa, making it ultimately difficult to determine a clear kinotopic difference that is not simply a *degree* of difference. The older centrifugal model thus poses a kinetic problem for medieval theologies of creation. The difference between creator and created cannot be described as one of degree, but of kind. The pure transcendence of God does not tolerate gradation.

First Problem

The first problem of God's creation receives its kinetic resolution in the system of rigid linkages that are able to keep circulatory regimes together but also distinctly separate. For example, an eternal and centrifugal circulation can be connected to a finite centripetal one through a third flow that links the two together without reducing them to the same circulation. Their movement, however, is now a combinatory motion.

Instead of all circulations simply rotating around a single center, multiple centers, each having their own centrifugal or centripetal motion, can move with and alongside one another in a decentered but shared motion. Therefore a rigid or tensionally linked motion both keeps the center from bleeding by gradation into the periphery and keeps the center and periphery apart as distinct fields, all while still participating in the same linked motion. Tensional motion is composed of at least three distinct components.

Externalized Motion. The first component is a centrifugal and centralized flow whose externalized motion has gone out too far and escaped its circulation. This flow remains distinct from centrifugal motion insofar as it remains peripheral to it, but also remains part of it as a leaked or escaped flow.

Internalized Motion. The second component is another circulation that centripetally receives or internalizes this linking flow but also redirects it centrifugally back to the previous circulation, producing a mutual connection between two or more circulations, each requiring some degree of centripetal and centrifugal motion. However, this mutual connection does not necessarily entail a symmetry of motion. The motions of each affect the other through the link, but some circulations are larger and more powerful than others. To put this into the historico-theological language of the Middle Ages, God remains the creator of nature even if nature's movements also modify God's movements through their linkage as his extended body.

Interrelational Motion. The third component of tensional motion is the connecting or interrelational flow itself. The connecting link is the constituent force that binds the two circulations together and apart. Without the power or force of a linking flow, a given kinetic field is unable to link itself to another circulation and is thus incapable of sustaining a kinetic relation, whether symmetrical, asymmetrical, or elliptical, with other fields.

In other words, it remains cut off from its power of creative motion. A tensional flow makes creative and coordinated motion between circulations possible. Additionally, the linkage goes both ways. A linking connection between the mover and the moved allows for the moved to interpret, internalize, and redirect that motion elsewhere as a mover itself. This not only makes possible the "great chain" of being linked downward in a relation of hierarchal authority; it also makes it possible for those in the chain to coordinate and reproduce their motion horizontally within this chain and interpret or contemplate the "force of law," whether natural or divine, that orders their being.[5]

Second Problem

This third component of linked motion solves another problem: prime movement. Without an initial or first force or power to rotate the sphere, the asymmetrical kinetic relation between the static center and mobile periphery is impossible. Without a first motion, the periphery would not move and thus would not be mobile with respect to the center. Furthermore, without a first motion, the center itself would not be able to transmit a force from itself outward to the periphery. The center and periphery are connected together by a continuous force.

Ancient philosophers simply asserted that the divine mover moved the cosmos, but medieval philosophers argued that this initial motion was possible only through the introduction of a forced or linked motion. "Force" is the name for what allows the linked transfer of motion from the center to the periphery and elsewhere. The tensional flow between fields is what allows the transfer of motion between them. Without it there is no motion, and with no motion there is no spinning sphere. Without any way for God to transmit his kinetic impetus outside himself in creation, he remains theologically impotent and nothing would exist outside him. In short, a God without force or tension could not be a true *creator* God. The problem of God's creative power is thus central to the medieval theology of force.

TRIANGULATION

The second kinomenological feature of force is triangulation, which is the process by which the three components of tensional motion reproduce the linkage that holds them together, keeps them apart, and relativizes their shared motion. Triangulation is distinct from the previous two kinetic processes that define being as space and eternity. In the description of being as space, the flows of motion curve inward toward an indefinite spiral process of internalization. In the description of being as eternity, the curved flows are radiated outward toward an endless externalized periphery.

In the ontological description of force, the linkage between processes of internalization and externalization is emphasized and thus produces a tripartite structure. This does not mean that being is shaped like a triangle. Triangulation simply means that being cannot be reduced to a single or even multiple centers; the centers are connected through and move through *linking flows of force or tension*. The triangle is the simplest polygon in the polygonal world of linked fields. Just as the flows that produce space are not discrete curves but form a continuous spiral, and the flows that produce eternity are not discrete circles but continuously rotating spheres, so triangulation is not a triangle but a continuous triple fold or trefoil that links together three distinct elements through a single continuous process of polygonalism.

Each major historical description of being is based on a real, material-kinetic pattern that the abstract descriptions of space, eternity, and force describe. Therefore each idealist historical description is conditioned by a topokinetic figure of continuous, polymorphic, and folded motion (see Figure 23.1).

Triangulation is continuous because force is immanent to its motions. Once the connecting linkage between circulations is forged, it appears as the primary determination or condition for the circulations it connects. It becomes the relatively inflexible flow that binds, separates, and regulates the kinetic reproduction of the circulations.

Once the linkage is forged, the circulations appear to be continuations of the linkage itself. Its flows become the constitutive power that moves through them and makes possible all their attributes. In the case of God, force becomes immanent to God's creative and motive act; in the case of nature, force becomes the immanent physical laws that govern its behavior. Force becomes the constitutive flow that traverses God, nature, and all of being. Without the force to act and persist, there is no motion and no existence. Thus, not only do force, power, vitality, become synonymous with relation in general, but relation becomes constitutive of the things being related, as folds in unifying relation. However, the new unity produced by force is also a *folded unity* of triangulation that also keeps the related circulations distinctly and separately folded.

Third Problem. Triangulation therefore solves another problem posed by the centrifugal motion of being: multiple centers. The analysis of

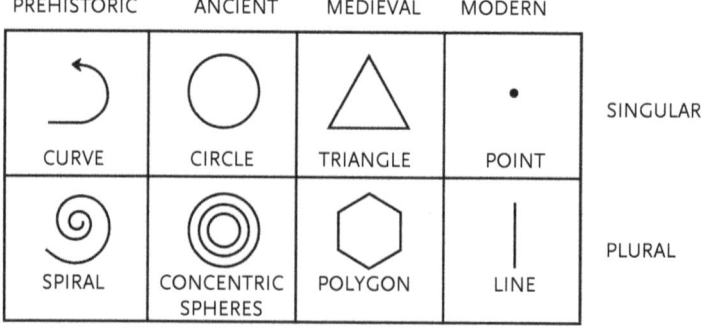

Figure 23.1 Singular and Plural Patterns of Historical Motion

centripetal and centrifugal motion alone cannot explain the relation between multiple coexisting centers because the relation between multiple centers is not defined by either centripetal or centrifugal motion—but by their connection. If there is more than one nonconcentric sphere, the cosmic image of the sphere as purely centrifugal begins to break down.

Tensional motion thus emerges most dominantly during the medieval and early-modern periods with the rise of nongeocentric (nonspherical and nonconcentric) astronomical models, beginning around the fifth century with Martianus Capella and his ninth-century commentators, leading up to Copernicus's postulating of multiple planetary centers and moons, and Kepler's discovery of elliptical orbits. The tensional force between rotating planets, held together and apart, increasingly becomes the defining motion of being.

In Christian theology a similar move begins to occur with respect to the ontological problem introduced by God's embodiment on earth in the form of his son Jesus. A third term is required to connect the two without conflating them: the Holy Spirit. With the introduction of the son and the Holy Spirit, the spherical nature of being is slowly complicated by a triangular tension between two terms linked together by a relation of theological force, as we see in the coming chapters of Part III.

RELATION

The third kinomenological feature of force is relation. Tensional motion and triangulation both rely on a linkage or constitutive relation between relata. The idea of relation in some form is very old, arguably present in the very first prehistoric mythologies up through Aristotle's theory of relation in the *Categories* based on the logical predication of accidents to substances. None of these theories, however, makes relation itself an ontologically primary substance, as occurred for the first time in the medieval and early modern ages. However, in the current chapter it is important to first show in a strictly kinomenological way the constitutive movements of this ontological description.

The ontological primacy of force presupposes the ontological primacy of relation, but the primacy of relation also presupposes a conjunction of movement. There are at least three kinds of relations: relations in space (proximity or contiguity), relations in time (priority, or sequence), and relations of repetition in circumstance (constant conjunction). Relations of causality, association, resemblance, and dependence are all derived from these three kinds of relations. The thesis of this chapter is that all these kinds of relation are further derived from a single and more primary kind of relation: *kinetic conjunction*.

As Book I has shown with the concept of conjunction, relation is fundamentally kinetic. The quality and quantity of folds and things are not defined by fixed or predetermined essences but by limit cycles in the continuous flows of motion. The discreteness of things is only a kinetic effect of their folding. Solid, liquid, and gas are three types of folds in the continuous cycles of kinetic matter, such as water cycles, rock cycles, and so on.

Contiguity in space, as Part I has shown, is already a product of a centripetal motion of flows gathering and folding over one another into spiraled regions of proximity. When flows fold over themselves they produce the kinomena of contiguous relations of space and place. The discreteness of a thing in space is due to the cyclical periodicity or self-relation created by folds.

As will be argued in Part IV, priority in time is also a product of kinetic conjunction insofar as the kinomenon of sequence or seriality relies on the continuity of motion between at least three types of decentered but conjoined and ordered junctions—past, present, and future—required by the moving "arrow of time."

Finally, constant conjunction, or the repetition of similar things in similar circumstances, was shown in Book I to be a function of kinetic cycles. Unity, necessity, resemblance, and identity were shown to be products of the continual process of folding. As a flow folds back over itself again and again, although differently each time, it continues to intersect with itself at the same relative point or period in a relatively stable cycle of kinetic "identity." Constant conjunction is nothing other than the kinetic process of continually bringing together or joining flows in a relatively similar periodicity. Flows are joined into folds, which produce a cycle, period, and affective resemblance to themselves. A thing's resemblance to itself is thus its tendency or habit to continually fold its flows in the same manner again and again.

Once these relatively discrete folds are produced they can retroactively identify their constitutive flows as relations (of contiguity, priority, and conjunction) between themselves and other folds. In other words, the kinomena of relation already presupposes junction, and junctions already presuppose a flow. The strictly kinetic determination of relation is therefore a tertiary one, but this does not mean that being is incapable of reorganizing its dominant form of motion according to a tensional and triangulated regime described by force relations. As we will see, this is precisely what occurs during the medieval and early-modern periods. Movement produces relations, but during the medieval and early-modern periods, relations are described as preexisting their relata. This consequence of this inversion is that being appears as the force or power of relationality as such.

Hume. The metaphysical ideas of force, power, connection, and relation are therefore all derived from the kinetic relation of conjunction. The eighteenth-century empiricist David Hume was one of the first to realize this:

> There are no ideas, which occur in metaphysics, more obscure and uncertain, than those of *power, force, energy,* or *necessary connexion*, of which it is every moment necessary for us to treat in all our disquisitions. We shall, therefore, endeavour, in this section, to fix, if possible, the precise meaning of these terms, and thereby remove some part of that obscurity, which is so much complained of in this species of philosophy.[6]

This is precisely what Part III of this book aims to do in a specifically kinetic and historical way. The metaphysical idea that there is something that is called power, force, energy, or relation that is knowable independently and a priori of our sensory impressions of the world is the most obscure because it appears nowhere to our senses and yet is used everywhere by philosophers, historians, physicists, and others to explain all forms of relation, as Hume complains.[7]

The universe is continually moving—one motion follows another in uninterrupted succession—but as Hume writes, "the power or force, which actuates the whole machine, is entirely concealed from us, and never discovers itself in any of the sensible qualities of body. . . . It is impossible, therefore, that the idea of power can be derived from the contemplation of bodies, in single instances of their operation; because no bodies ever discover any power, which can be the original of this idea."[8] This is the case because matter and motion are "complete in themselves and never point out any other event which may result from them."[9] Matter is distributed in regimes of motion, and we can have sensory impressions of this, but the idea that there is an unobservable secret power of relation or causality hidden in them (either as immanently internal or transcendently external) is a purely speculative and metaphysical notion.

According to Hume, all relation is fundamentally kinetic and can thereby be exemplified by the simple and universal model of two billiard balls colliding. "Here is a billiard-ball lying on the table, and another ball moving towards it with rapidity. They strike; and the ball, which was formerly at rest, now acquires a motion. This is as perfect an instance of the relation of cause and effect as any which we know, either by sensation or reflection. Let us therefore examine it."[10] When the first ball hits the second there is a spatial contiguity, since there is nothing between the two balls that acts as an intermediary; and there is a temporal priority, since one ball moves first before the other ball is affected. Furthermore, we know from similar instances "resembling" this one (other balls in the same kind of situation) that the same motion occurs: constant conjunction. "Beyond these three circumstances of contiguity, priority, and constant conjunction, I can discover nothing in this cause," Hume writes.[11]

Although an infinite number of other motions are logically possible, only one effect is predicted and only one cause is determined. Our predictions and descriptions of relations are derived purely from our sense impressions and experiences, which are finite and empirical and therefore cannot support infinite or universal claims to absolutely necessary relations. Hume therefore concludes that the belief that there is a *necessary connection* between two separate events is simply a matter of custom or habit. "Tis not, therefore, reason, which is the guide of life, but custom. That alone determines the mind, in all instances, to suppose the future conformable to the past. However easy this step may seem, reason would never, to all eternity, be able to make it."[12]

For Hume, necessary connection and causality are habits of the mind, but this does not mean that the mind is somehow a separate transcendent substance from the body. Rather, the mind, as brain, is also composed of material elements which are kinetically habituated following a similarly kinetic model. Mind and body are two sides of the same regime of conjoined or habituated motion. This is precisely why we are just as ignorant of the "manner or force by which a mind, even the supreme mind, operates either on itself or on body," as Hume says. "We have no idea of the Supreme Being but what we learn from reflection on our own faculties. Were our ignorance, therefore, a good reason for rejecting anything, we should be led into that principle of denying all energy in the Supreme Being as much as in the grossest matter."[13]

Not only do we have no coherent idea of the necessary relation between objects, but for the same reasons we have no idea of the necessary relations between the mind and the body, the mind and itself, and even the force of God in the universe. From top to bottom, the same kinetic model holds true: there is no necessary relation, only kinetic conjunction.

Kinetic Conjunction. Hume's rejection of necessary connection, causality, force, power, energy, and other metaphysical notions of relations is radical. His material-kinetic explanation goes far, *but not far enough.* The so-called discrete billiard balls analyzed by Hume as "separate events" are themselves already products of a habitual motion of smaller particle flows that constantly conjoin in a specific field of folds as "balls." Discrete matter, even particles, is itself already a habit of periodic motion of flows conjoined with themselves and to others. Therefore we cannot speak, as Hume does, of separate balls or a separation between cause and effect, but rather of a continuous periodic feedback loop or circulation of cause and effect in which two or more folds are continually conjoined by the continuous flow within which they are simply folds. The causal object (ball A) and the effected object (ball B) are two folds continuously conjoined by a flow (C) that folds them up, binds them together, and holds them apart: the tensional or relational flow. What is called "force," therefore, is nothing other than a material-kinetic relation of habit or fold.

Furthermore, if necessary relation and causality are habits of the mind, the mind is itself already a habit of matter impressed by material-kinetic flows of sensation. Flows are folded and constitute the affective structure of the brain, which in turn forms habits of thinking of matter as necessarily connected. Matter and mind are again two sides of the same regime of kinetic conjunction. Finally, if God himself is simply a habit of the mind, as Hume says, and the mind in turn a habit of matter, which is in turn a habit of motion, God is nothing other than a kinetic habituation of conjoined matter. Here we have the basis of a whole kinotheology, which will be explored further in Chapter 27.

It now remains to be seen, however, how this kinomenological regime of tensional motion is historically described in medieval physics and theology by the concept of force. In the next four chapters, therefore, we turn to a kinetic analysis of these historical descriptions.

11
Logos

CHAPTER 24

Medieval Theology I

Aether

The descriptive regime of tensional motion rises to historical dominance during the period from around the fifth century CE to around the end of the seventeenth century—roughly the long medieval and early-modern periods. The rise of this new regime occurs alongside the rising predominance of a new theological description of being as force.

THEOLOGY

The theological description of force took two historical forms during this period: the physics of force and the doctrine of the Trinity. Each expressed two aspects of the same descriptive regime of motion, and each emerged within the same ontological framework. Together, these form the tradition of natural theology, the theory of relation between divine and natural being.

Theology is distinct from both mythology and cosmology. Instead of focusing on poetic speech or written rationality, theology aims to give an account of being through the illumination of the *book* or word of God. Medieval theology begins where ancient cosmology leaves off, with a single transcendent God. Given that a single God exists, how is it that we come to know this God? How does he create without dissolving into his creations? What is his relation to that which he creates? Natural theology is an ontological description that focuses on the *relations* between God and everything else, and on the process by which these relations can be known to us as natural and divine laws.

Historically, the rise of theology as the dominant mode of describing being in the West begins with the rise to power of Christian religion. All other major conceptualizations of being during this time take place within this conceptual framework and its discourse, including the scientific revolution of the sixteenth and seventeenth centuries. In this way, the natural sciences, philosophy, and religion all develop unique descriptions of being but always within the dominant presupposition of a theological postulate: the existence of a creator God.

The argument of this chapter is that all these different modes of theological description—scientific, philosophical, and religious—end up describing roughly the same dominant kinetic pattern of tensional motion in their descriptions of the continuous forces between beings, both divine and natural.[1] The following chapters trace the emergence of these scientific and religious descriptions, ultimately arguing that they describe a kinetic field of tensional motion.[2] We will therefore examine each of the three tensional features of force in turn: interrelational, external, and internal.

THE INTERRELATION OF MOTION

The first kinetic operation or feature in the ontological description of force is the *interrelation* of motion. The interrelation of motion is the active medium through which a flow travels between two circulatory fields. If two circulations are going to have any kind of relation at all, there must be some sort of medium through and within which these relations occur. If they are ontologically divided, nothing happens and no connection is possible. However, if they are exactly identical, then again nothing happens.

The interconnection of motion must therefore traverse both the mover and the moved in order for them to be related. They must share at least one thing in common. Kinetically speaking, they must share a link that is continuous with them but also distinguished from them. Therefore, the concept of an interrelation between two or more things presupposes a transport medium that is continuous with relata while also distinguishing the relata from each other.

The concept of a permeating force of interrelation is the first to rise to predominance in the medieval and early modern periods. This is the case, however, only because a similar description had already been developed thousands of years before in the ancient world to guarantee the continuous connection of the center of the cosmic sphere to its periphery. In centrifugal cosmologies, the concepts of the breath of God, soul, aether, pneuma, and others were developed to describe this connection. Although the ancient usage of these concepts describes a cosmospherical unity, the concept of aether continued to be used in the medieval and early-modern periods in order to describe a similar force or transport medium outside, within, and between *multiple spheres.*

There are two major differences between the ancient theory of aether and the medieval–early modern one. The first difference is kinetic. The ancient theory of aether described a natural centrifugal motion, moving from the compact center of the cosmos and rarefying outward toward the periphery to form the celestial dome, while the medieval–early modern theory described a mechanistic tensional motion, moving in tension between various bodies according to various attractions, repulsions, compositions, and decompositions. The second difference is theological. The ancient theory of aether described it as a divine element identical with God or a world-soul, while the medieval–early modern theory more often described it as a permeating vital fluid that connects God to nature, without itself being only God or nature. A longer prehistory of the emergence and transformation of the idea of force is developed elsewhere, so we move on now to focus on its descriptive usage in the period under direct consideration.[3]

The Aether

In the medieval and early modern periods, the description of an *interrelational ethereal force or dynamic medium* was taken up from the ancients and increasingly transformed into a description of a tensional movement within a multicentered cosmos. Although the early medieval concept of aether tended to be dominated by the Aristotelean, Ptolemaic, and centrifugal models of aether, as most things cosmological were, the beginnings of a new concept were also gaining momentum.

This new medieval theory of ethereal force emerged from the Stoic notion of a *tensional pneuma*. However, instead of accepting the primacy of a single *pneuma*-radiating cosmic sphere, as the Stoics did, the new idea of ethereal force combined the tensional attributes of Stoic *pneuma* with atomism, as well as the cosmotheological notion of multiple and often nonconcentric planetary and ethereal motions.[4]

What follows is a kinetic analysis of several ontological descriptions of this interrelational force medium given by a number of influential thinkers during this time. From this we can see how the medievals and early moderns put forward a new theory of interrelational force under the ancient name of "aether." In these descriptions the aether is expanded to become an all-pervasive fluid medium in which all things are related, without the direct and constant centrifugal intervention of God. Instead of a mere first mover, God's entire body is transformed into the vast fluid and vortical medium of forces.

Mechanism. One of the most important differences introduced into the concept of ethereal force is the concept of mechanism. It is a grave mistake in the history of metaphysics that the so-called age of mechanism has been thought of as an age of the ontological primacy of corporeal determinism. It is true that there was a rise in materialist physics and naturalist theologies in the medieval and early-modern periods, but in the last ontotheological instance the motive cause of mechanistic motion remained *force*. Force is the ontologically primary motive cause of being's motion. Force is that invisible substance through which bodies are caused to move. With the introduction of force, God's actions become indirect through this vital fluid medium. In short, the ancient formula of "form and matter" was increasingly replaced by the early modern one of "force and mechanism." Far from opposing one another, vitalism and mechanism go hand in hand during this period.[5]

Astronomy. The second difference introduced into the description of ethereal force during this time is astronomical tension. In contrast to the dominant ancient geocentric model surrounded by perfect concentric spheres, medieval and early-modern astronomers introduced the new idea that celestial bodies were held together and apart by the force of tension (attraction and repulsion), just like the material bodies of the earth. Terrestrial linear motion and celestial circular motion were no longer separate but instead two manifestations of the same motion and expressions of the same causal motive force.[6]

More than anything else, the Copernican revolution was a kinetic revolution. Where Aristotle and Ptolemy had postulated stasis at the heart of the cosmological sphere, Copernicus introduced motion, thus destabilizing the geocentric conditions of observation, calculation, and theology. Much has been written on the conceptual consequences of his astronomical theory,[7] but what is less commonly discussed in this revolution is its kinetic consequences. The Copernican revolution did not merely replace one centrism with another (geo versus helio), or reveal a new transcendental idealist orientation to being, as Kant would have it.[8] Rather, it multiplied the autonomous mobility of heavenly bodies, and thus of their tensional relations of forces.

Furthermore, if the earth was now a planet like the others, moving around the sun and spinning on its axis, the other planets were likely to also have their own centrifugal and ethereal forces. Heliocentrism is therefore poorly understood as a cosmological monocentrism, and it should be understood as a tensional multicentrism of forces.

The Copernican revolution therefore posed a new, strictly kinetic problem for planetary measurement. If the earth was no longer the static center of the universe, distances and relations could no longer be measured by a direct linear path alone. The planets were no longer fixed distances away from the earth, like concentric spheres. All relation was hopelessly changing at the whim of unknowable forces, all in tension with one another. Since the earth is always in motion, measurements and relations could only take place through a series of parallax views. A new theory of relations had to be invented.

Triangulation. This new theory of relations can be seen quite dramatically in the invention of new decentered and triangulated astronomical techniques. For example, ten years before Copernicus's death, a young philosopher and cartographer named Gemma Frisius (1508–1555) formalized a new methodology called "triangulation," which allowed one to determine the location of a point by measuring the angles to it from other known points. In 1533 Frisius published his new method as *Libellus de Locorum describendorum ratione* in a new edition of Peter Apian's *Cosmographia*.

Following Frisius's method, one could determine the location of a given point with only the knowledge of one known side and two known angles. This is the method still used today in surveying. In 1579 the astronomer Tycho Brahe (1546–1601) used the same method of triangulation to map the Scandinavian island of Hven, where his observatory was based.[9] In 1600 Johannes Kepler (1571–1630) came to work with Brahe and used the method of triangulation to determine the earth's orbit. In his book *Astronomia Nova* (1609), Kepler used astronomical triangulation to determine the orbit of Mars as well. Based on his measurements, however, he postulated that the orbit of Mars, and by extension all the other planets, in fact moved in ellipses, all by the hand of a permeating material but invisible *virtus motrix* (motive force).[10]

Heliocentrism and triangulation therefore introduced into cosmology and theology a kinetic description missing in both Aristotle and the Stoics: a universe defined fundamentally by ethereal forces but now moving in *dynamic tension with one another*. In particular, the concept of triangulation became an important—even if imprecise—tool for the measurement of continuous relations between bodies held together and apart in patterns or circulations of linked motions.

Triangulation became necessary because cosmic bodies could no longer be determined unilaterally, but only by means of a third body, force, relation, or series of angles through which one body relates or is regionally connected to another, and not from a single static and absolute point of reference. For example, Kepler's discovery of elliptical orbits based on his triangulations could not be reconciled with the cosmotheology of perfect concentric spheres. The center had been displaced and multiplied. Celestial motion was therefore only intelligible through a linked system of multicentered and triangulated kinetic tensions.

Kepler, Galileo, and Newton all increased support for the idea of an earth rotating on its axis, adding a further dimension of kinetic displacement and tension between the other planets. We can therefore see a visible shift from ancient cosmologies based on concentric circles to early-modern cosmologies like Kepler's, based on overlapping and intersecting triangulated relations of force in a vast polygonal network (see Figure 24.1).

It is therefore no coincidence that for Kepler triangulation made possible a "divine ratio" or "golden triangle" in mathematics, geometry, and all being.[11] The language of nature was mathematical, and the name of God was the divine tensional triangle. God still held the planets together through force, but his forces became necessarily plural, indirect, and triangulated in the fluid medium of the aether.

Theory of the Aether

Even before the introduction of mechanistic and astronomical turns in medieval philosophy, one can already see the precursors of an increasingly

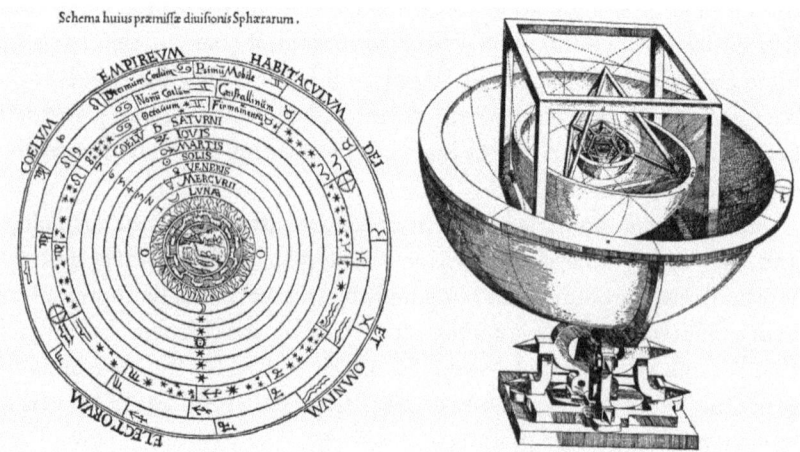

Figure 24.1 Concentric Universe versus Kepler's Polygonal Universe
Source: The image of concentric universe comes from Fastfission/Wikimedia Commons. The image of the polygonal universe comes from Johannes Kepler/Wikimedia Commons.

tensional theory of an all-pervasive and interrelational force in the work of the sixth-century Aristotelian commentator and Christian theologian John Philoponus (c. 490–c. 570). Just as the Stoics did, Philoponus argued (against Aristotle) that the heavens were made of a fully material aether.

The word "aether" comes from the Greek word αἴθω *aitho*, meaning "to incinerate, to burn, or shine," and, as Socrates suggests, from the Greek word *rheô*, meaning "to flow, run, stream, or gush." Philoponus rejected Aristotle's attribution of eternity and immateriality to the aether, but he retained the etymological idea of an all-pervasive flowing, burning substance that permeates and connects/separates the terrestrial and celestial realms.[12] Aristotle's immaterial theory of the aether allowed him to divide the terrestrial elements (fire, water, earth, air), with their naturally linear motions, from the celestial element (aether) with its naturally circular motion.

Philoponus, however, argued that there were not two kinds of natural motion but simply a single tension between various corporeal elements. Fire is simply the element that accumulates in the heavens and holds the celestial bodies together, apart, and in tension with the earth. Philoponus affirmed the corruptibility of these material elements, and with it the noneternal and corruptible nature of the universe.[13] This fire is the invisible material that allowed the transfer or communication of force between bodies. If a force is to be transferred, it has to be transferred through a medium, and for Philoponus that medium was ethereal fire, the medium of God's causal action.

From Philoponus to Francis Bacon (1561–1626), the concept of aether, although frequently of the ancient variety, moved increasingly closer to Philoponus's theory and away from Aristotle's. The medieval concept of "quintessence," for example, from the Latin word *quint*, meaning "five," referred to the fifth element: aether. Quintessence was studied by alchemists and captured in various elixirs. At least as early as Francis Bacon, we get an explicitly tensional and interrelational theory of the aether, in contrast to the center-periphery division introduced by Aristotle. In Bacon's *Specimen of Animated Astronomy*, he describes interstellar space, or the interrelational space between heavenly bodies and between the earth and the heavens, as a plenum full of an ethereal fluid in which all the stars float.[14]

Importantly, for Bacon (like Philoponus), this ethereal fluid is a material and corruptible fire. However, while it remains perishable on earth due to its collision with other bodies, in the heavens it remains unaffected and uncorrupted—not *de jure* but *de facto*.[15] The difference between heaven and earth, for Bacon, is therefore not between center and periphery or between types of natural motion, but is more like a surface tension created between different degrees of ethereal fluid. The interrelational space or medium between heaven and earth only appears empty; it is in fact filled with an invisible force that creates a surface tension between fluid regions. "Such as one as may admit of flowing," Bacon writes, "as when water floats on quicksilver, oil on water, and air on oil."[16]

The heavens, therefore, float above the surface of the earth like oil on water, and the stars themselves float around in various fluid-dynamic relations on the surface of their fluid ethereal medium. Bacon's theory of the aether is thus a description of the tensional movement of bodies as they float together and apart within the same interrelational fluid medium.

Perhaps the most influential and historically sophisticated formulation of the idea of a permeating tensional cosmic fluid is the one formulated by René Descartes (1596–1650) in his "vortex theory of the aether." Descartes was influenced by the astronomical findings of Brahe and Kepler, and he visited their labs while he was in Prague in 1620. Having understood the philosophical importance of the heliocentric model and the nonconcentric triangulated tensions between the planets, Descartes proposed his own theory of the nature of the interrelational medium through which the planets are held together and apart in linked rotational motion.

In his *Principles of Philosophy*, Descartes proposed a cosmological network of interlocking vortices (*tourbillon*). These vortices are made up of atom-sized globules (secondary matter), the "indefinitely" small debris (primary matter or aether)[17] left over from the collision of larger elements, and a tertiary matter that comprises larger macroscopic bodies.[18] For Descartes, these three kinds of matter and the three laws of nature explain all cosmological phenomena, including gravity. These three types of matter move not by natural motions but by a series of collisions accumulating and breaking apart in the fluid medium of an invisible aether that allows for the transport of their motion or "motive force." "It must be thought that the matter of the heaven, like that which forms the Sun and the fixed Stars, is fluid. This is an opinion which is now commonly held by all Astronomers, because they see that otherwise it is almost impossible to give a satisfactory explanation of the phenomena of the Planets."[19]

Aether has the highest mobility, the "globules" the second-highest mobility, and macroscopic bodies the least. However, the kinetic interrelational medium of invisible heavenly matter is not a neutral medium; for Descartes, the motion of this universally permeating aether is an active force. "This striving [*conatus*]," he states, "is found in celestial matter."[20] As the aether mixes and combines, its bodies start "adhering somewhat to one another, [and] they form there a certain large and very rarefied mass, similar to the air (or rather the aether)."[21] After the aether begins to adhere to itself in a network of linked tension, it forms a knotted and branching intertwinement, forcing them all to move together in a mass.[22]

Once a larger composite is formed, numerous larger particles will become trapped by the branching motion of the aether such that only the smallest ethereal flows will be able to escape the celestial mass.[23] The smallest particles of aether are able to escape and flow out one pole of the celestial body, but they are then caught in the massive striving of aether just outside the pass and returned to the mass as the other pole. "As a result, after these grooved particles have traversed the whole intermediate Earth from one hemisphere to the other along straight lines, or lines equivalent to straight, parallel to its axis; they return through the surrounding aether to that same hemisphere through which they earlier entered the Earth; and thus flowing through the Earth again, form a kind of vortex."[24]

For Descartes, the cosmos is a fluid-dynamic medium filled with celestial vortices of force, like whirlpools in a river (see Figure 24.2):

> In a river there are various places where the water twists around on itself and forms a whirlpool. If there is flotsam on the water we see it carried around with the whirlpool, and in some cases we see it also rotating about its own centre; further, the bits which are nearer the centre of the whirlpool complete a revolution more quickly; and finally, although such flotsam always has a circular motion, it scarcely ever describes a perfect circle but undergoes some longitudinal and latitudinal deviations. We can without any difficulty imagine all this happening in the same way in the case of the planets, and this single account explains all the planetary movements that we observe.[25]

Every star and planet is a vortex in an ethereal plenum of force. Each vortex is in constant motion and butts up with other adjacent vortices in a direct tension. Vortices wax and wane as they attract, repel, and move in a linked rotation with their neighbors. Thus, instead of a single centrifugally radiating cosmosphere, Descartes proposed multiple vortices, each radiating and moving in a linked interrelational tension with one another (see Figure 24.2).

Like many, Thomas Hobbes (1588–1679) was profoundly influenced by Descartes's vortex theory of aether. Hobbes rendered even more explicit the radical all-pervading nature of aether, as well as its direct connection with the idea of motive force. For example, Hobbes sees the aether as both a celestial "ambient ethereal substance" that "propagate[s] motion to the next remote parts, and these to the next, and so on continually,"[26] but can

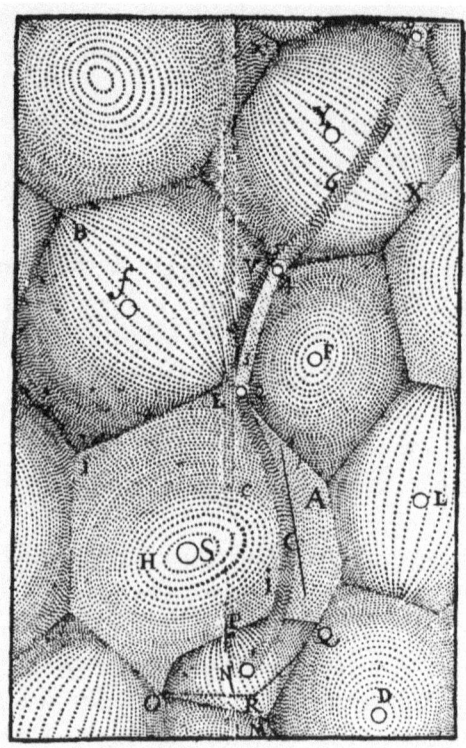

Figure 24.2: Descartes's Aetherial Vortices
Image of Descartes's vortices is from his 1644 book *Principia Philosophiae*.
Source: René Descartes/Wikimedia Commons.

also be identified "when the motion of the ambient ethereal substance makes the spirits and fluid parts of our bodies tend outward [and] we acknowledge heat."[27] Everything is therefore explicitly "intermingled with the ethereal substance."[28] For Hobbes, the aether is therefore also an all-permeating invisible but interrelational fluid dynamic medium, just as it was for Descartes.

Although rarely invoked for his theory of the aether, Isaac Newton (1642–1727) also frequently engaged in metaphysical speculation about the cause of gravitational force by using the concept of the aether as a fluid-dynamic medium of transport. Newton even went so far as postulating aether as the cosmogenic origin of being when he speculated that "perhaps may all things be originated from aether."[29] From the celestial to the terrestrial, Newton gave ethereal force absolute metaphysical primacy in the famous final paragraph of the *Principia*:

> Now we might add something concerning a certain most subtle spirit which pervades and lies hid in all gross bodies; by the force and action of which the particles of bodies mutually attract one another at near distances, and cohere if contiguous, and electric bodies operate to greater distances as well repelling as attracting the neighbouring corpuscles; and light is emitted, reflected, refracted, and heats bodies; and all sensation is excited, and the members of animal bodies move at the command of the will, namely by vibrations of this spirit, mutually propagated along the solid filaments of the nerves, from the outward organs of sense to the brain, and from the brain into muscles."

For Newton, the aether functions as a universal and interrelational force medium for the transport of all action. He describes it as a very "rare" or "fine" "medium" that "grow[s] denser and denser perpetually and thereby cause[s] the gravity of those great bodies towards one another, and of their parts towards the bodies; every body endeavouring to go from the denser parts of the medium towards the rarer?"[30] The aether is the force that endeavors or strives to contract and expand and thus creates gravity across seemingly immaterial distance. In a profoundly circular move, Newton solves the problem of "action at a distance" by claiming that *the distance is pure action* ("endeavor"). Gravity is thus explained as varying degrees of density in an ethereal interrelational medium of pure force.

Between the influence of Descartes and Newton, practically all of seventeenth-century intellectual Europe began using the concept of ethereal force or dynamism to explain all kinds of natural phenomenon—optics, biology, magnetism, alchemy, and so on. In addition to its adoption by Newton, the German philosopher Gottfried Leibniz (1646–1716) also granted aether a privileged ontological status as the universally permeating interrelational medium through which all relations of force were transferred. Bodies have their own force or "conatus," but Leibniz also argued that all collisions between bodies, no matter how small, were able to impact and burst apart due to "the motion of the fluid aetherial matter permeating" them.[31]

As opposed to Descartes, Leibniz argued that force is not technically transferred or externalized from one body to another, because it already exists in both and as the medium in which the collision occurs. In an interesting move, Leibniz here unifies all three kinds of forces—internal, external, and interrelational—into a single but differentiated multifold force, a fitting end to the complex but intertwined history of etherial force.

It should therefore come as no surprise then that Leibniz also followed Descartes' vortex theory of cosmological aether:

I found that this universal motion of the planets can be explained beautifully by means of a vortex around the sun common [for all of the planets]. Indeed, it follows geometrically from Kepler's law of motion that the trajectory can be distinguished into two, a harmonic circulation of the planet around the sun (that is, one whose velocity is proportionally less when the body is more distant from the sun) and a rectilinear approach to the sun, like gravity [gravitas] or magnetism.[32]

From the terrestrial to the celestial the aether is transformed into an all-pervading tensional fluid and raised to the highest level of ontological explanation, at least equal to or in *coprimacy with God himself*.[33]

The Antinomy of Interrelational Motion

The emergence of a tensional description of aether is thus defined by its micromateriality, its corruptibility, its contingency of combination, heterogeneity of degree, and the tensional linkage between vortices. This is in contrast to the ancient centrifugal theory of aether defined by its immateriality, eternity, natural necessity of motion, hierarchy of emanation, and centrifugal direction from a single fixed cosmic center.

The problem, however, is that the interrelational movement that pervades all of being and is described by the idea of an ambient aether only explains the *medium of force*. It does not fully explain the unique motion by which an inner motion becomes externalized or by which an externalized motion becomes internalized. A medium is crucial for the transport of motion, but it does not explain the internal and external forces of the objects in motion.

What is needed, therefore, is both a description of how such forces can actually leave their objects and move through this interrelational medium to affect others, and how those others can internalize and receive this force.

As the next two chapters show, these two other kinds of force (internal and external) are needed to complete the full description of tensional or dynamic being. We thus move on in the next chapter to a historical description of externalized motion, often called "impetus."

CHAPTER 25

Medieval Theology II

Impetus

THE EXTERNALIZATION OF MOTION

The second kinetic operation or feature in the ontological description of force is the *externalization* of motion. Kinetically, the externalization of motion occurs when a flow becomes disjoined or released from a field of circulation. Once such a flow breaks free or bifurcates from the conjunction of a circulatory system, it is then capable of folding itself into a new series of junctions in a new field or connecting to another field elsewhere. When the internal motion of circulation, like that of a rotating sphere, for instance, appears to transfer its motion to another body as a cause, agent, or force, what occurs kinetically is not the transfer of a *metaphysical substance*, as it is historically described during the medieval and early period, but the continuation of the same movement, circulated differently. The two circulations are not ontologically separate, although they are kinetically distinct, but are simply two coordinated systems within the same continuous flow of motion. The externalization or transfer of motion from one body to the other is not like tossing a ball from one person to another, but more like the transfer of sea foam across the surface of a wave.

In other words, there is no third thing that moves between them, only a change in the modulation of the same coextensive field or relative neighborhood of the two folds. The term "externalization," therefore, does not refer to a radical outside, but only to the relative outside of a single folded flow. This is the kinetic condition for the historical description of being as having an external force or "impetus."

As such, the externalization of motion or force has three main characteristics: (1) it breaks free from the direct control of God and his spherical circulation, (2) it is not reducible or simply identical to God, and (3) it can be transferred externally from God to beings or between beings. External force therefore presupposes not only the prior centripetal accumulation of motion into some kind of collected being or circulation (in this case God) but also the centrifugal capacity of that being to redirect motion outward beyond the periphery, ultimately directed toward a new circulation.

Although it took several centuries for the external theory of force to reach its full dominance as a primary description of being and to fully break away from the centrifugal motion of divine spherology, it first began to do so in the work of the sixth-century Aristotelian commentator John Philoponus. It then developed over the course of the centuries, eventually acquiring the name "impetus theory," or what we now call inertia.

IMPETUS THEORY

Philoponus's innovative contribution to the description and primacy of force was to liberate it from the direct and centrifugal control of God. Against Aristotle, Philoponus argued that force, or *dunamis*, is actually transferred or externalized from the mover to the moved, so that what is moved continues in motion independently of the mover once it is set into motion. He called the transfer of this external force *rhope* in Greek, often translated as "inclination" and later Latinized as "impetus."[1]

Historically, "impetus in the strict sense is equated with *vis impressa*—an internal force impressed *from without*."[2] The radical nature of this concept cannot be overstated. The great twentieth-century philosopher of science Thomas Kuhn even called the introduction of impetus theory no less than a scientific revolution or, in his terminology, a "paradigm shift."[3] Philoponus initiated this revolution, allowing tensional motion to break free from its centrifugal domination.

For Aristotle and his followers, the forced motion of something like a javelin thrown into the air is propelled not by the transfer of force or motion from an external mover to a moved object but by the direct imparting of motion to successive pockets of air behind the javelin. This is essentially a centrifugal theory of direct force following the flow of a *thermon*, or fluid cause of motion, entirely contained within the unity of the sphere of the unmoved mover.

Philoponus rejects this subordination of motion to direct divine manipulation. According to Aristotle's logic, Philoponus reasons, an army could simply perch its projectiles on a thin parapet and set the air behind them in motion with ten thousand pairs of bellows. Since this is clearly ridiculous, another explanation must be sought. Philoponus thus argues that there must be a *dunamis kinetike*, or "incorporeal kinetic power [that] must be transmitted by the thrower to the thing thrown, and the air that is pushed contributes either nothing at all or very little to this motion."[4] When the thrower throws the javelin, he impresses on it or transfers to it a force or kinetic power that allows it to keep moving, even after he is no longer in contact with it.

After some elaboration, Philoponus extends this simple but revolutionary insight all the way to the ontotheological level. Not only is terrestrial motion caused by the transmission of an external force, but celestial motion is caused in the same way. "[God] implant[s] a motive power [*kinetiken entheinai dunamin*] in the moon, the sun and the other heavenly bodies, he implanted inclinations [*rhope*] in heavy and light ones, and implanted in all animals the movements which come from the souls [*psuchē*] within them, that the angels will not have to move them by force [*biai*]."[5]

Philoponus finds it absurd that angels would have to actively and continuously move all the heavenly and earthly bodies. It makes much more sense, he reasons, to think of God as an ontotheological javelin thrower, who simply impresses a force (*vis impressa*) into the world at creation and then lets it unfold on its own without his constant intervention. This move has the important consequence of introducing a crucial ontological distinction between God (the mover) and nature (the moved), versus their ancient unity within the center-periphery matrix of an absolute sphere.

Furthermore, it also shifts the question of the cause of motion from God, who simply acts once, to nature, which perpetuates and orders this force in the world. As Philoponus writes, "By learning that nature is the source of motion or rest, we learnt not what it is, but what it does (*poiei*). So in order to give the definition of what it is as well, let us say that nature is life (*zoe*) or power (*dunmais*) diffused through bodies, moulding them and managing them, as the source of motion or rest in the thing in which it belongs primarily and in it in virtue of itself and not coincidentally."[6]

For Philoponus, nature becomes completely coextensive with force. Nature is nothing other than that living force or power that is completely and immanently diffused through all bodies, connecting and ordering them in motion. For the ancients this was the definition of God or aether; now, for Philoponus, God becomes a mere external and efficient cause needed simply to explain how nature got moving in the first place but is afterward no longer directly relevant as an explanatory source of natural motion.[7] Philoponus therefore rejects the Aristotelian notion of a theological final cause that inspires the heavens to motion by love or by animated souls in favor of a purely efficient theory of causality. For Philoponus, all motion—terrestrial, forced, and celestial—is nothing but efficient cause without a final end orchestrated by God. God may have created nature, but afterward nature followed its own motions implanted by the force of God.

Unfortunately, Philoponus's writings on force (*rhope*) were not widely read during the sixth century and were only picked up later in the fourteenth century by the French priest Jean Buridan (1300–1358), through the transmission of the Islamic philosophers. Although Buridan does not directly cite Philoponus and does not directly credit Avicenna's concept of *mayl*, he does discuss the work of Avicenna, Averroes, and other Islamic impetus theorists, and he was therefore likely influenced by their ideas in physics in his own usage of the word "inclination."[8] Buridan then extends their arguments regarding terrestrial forms of force all the way up to the theological level. The Bible, Buridan argues, makes no mention of so-called intelligences or angles that move the celestial bodies, precisely because

> God, when He created the world, moved each of the celestial orbs as He pleased, and in moving them He impressed in them impetuses which moved them without His having to move them any more except by the method of general influence whereby He concurs as a co-agent in all things which take place; "for thus on the seventh day He rested from all work which He had executed by committing to others the actions and the passions in turn." And these impetuses which He impressed in the celestial bodies were not decreased nor corrupted afterwards, because there was no inclination of the celestial bodies for other movements.[9]

To Buridan, God created the universe and impressed on it a motive force (*virtus motiva*) that allows it to continue to move without him. On the seventh day of creation God rested, and creation began moving on its own. However, Buridan's celestial impetus is not a radical break with God; rather, God still remains a "co-agent in all things." God remains a coagent, in part, because the movement of the heavens has become just as immortal and incorruptible as God himself. Kinomenologically speaking, God's movement becomes externalized in creation and thereby transforms him retroactively into a coagent of a new autonomous motion that he no longer directly controls, which cannot be said to be ontologically or radically divided from him as the externalization of his motive force or impetus. His creation is neither strictly identical to him nor strictly separate; rather, God and creation become two folds or coagents in the same process of kinetic externalization.

While at the Faculty of Arts in Paris, Buridan influenced the thinking of a number of his contemporaries, such as Albert of Saxony, Marsilius of Inghen, and Nicole Oresme, who further disseminated the concept of impetus throughout Europe.[10]

Insofar as impetus theory accepts the existence of something between the two distinct circulations of God and nature that connects them, but without reducing one to the other, it ends up locating a new theory of motion. Impetus allows force to be externalized from one body to another through an ethereal medium. As Buridan aptly reasons, "Since every motion arises from a motor being present and existing simultaneously with that which is moved, if the impetus were the motion, it would be necessary to assign some other motor from which that motion would arise. And the principal difficulty would return. Hence there would be no gain in positing such an impetus."[11] Thus Buridan gives to force the status of a third "thing of permanent nature [*res naturæ permanentis*],"[12] distinct from the local motion of the mover and the moved. An internal motor without external transfer of its motion is useless. Impetus must be something transferable or externalizable from mover to moved.

This is the great kinetic insight of impetus theory: that between the mover and the moved there must be a *third thing* that holds the two together and apart in tension and thus ensures a common something that can move back and forth *between them*. Impetus is the coexistence of a third thing simultaneous with the mover and moved, but that is not reducible to either one. If it were, then nothing could be transferred from one to the other—and all motion would fail.

THE CLOCKWORK UNIVERSE

Within the ontological parameters of this impetus theory, it was the French philosopher Nicole Oresme (1320–1382), influenced by Buridan, who was the first to draw out the radical theological conclusion of this theory, which was thereafter adopted in one way or another by almost every major philosopher in the West: that the universe functioned like clockwork.

One can hardly imagine a more anti-Aristotelian thesis than this. Not only is God no longer the constant and direct source of all motion, but the fundamental movement of nature and the cosmos is ordered entirely according to its *own immanent set of tensional natural laws*. As Oresme writes in his *Livre du ciel et du monde* (*Book of the Heavens and Earth*, 1370),

> When God created them [the heavens], he placed in them qualities and moving powers just as he put weight in terrestrial things and put in them resistances against the moving powers. . . . And these powers are so moderated, tempered, and ordered against their resistances that the movements are made without violence. But except for the violence it is similar when a man has made a clock and he lets it go and be moved by itself. Thus God let the heavens be moved continually according to the proportions that the moving powers have to their resistances and according to the established order.[13]

Just as the mechanical clock is powered by an initial weight whose tension or system of rigid linkage drives its ordered motion, so God gives an initial force or impetus to the universe, which then unfolds according to a set of natural laws. The same kinetics of tension apply to both. The universe is both the product of a divine craftsman and, in some sense, autonomous from its creator through the kinetic link of creation (force) itself.

Oresme's theory of the clockwork universe is the image par excellence of the ontological primacy of force in the medieval and early modern ages. He was the first to put forward the most influential clockwork comparison showing that impetus theory, clockwork, and ontotheology all function according to the same tensional pattern of motion.[14]

The kinetic significance of the function of the monastic timetable or *horarium*'s function is also crucial. Just as God gave the stars and planets a regular, perfect, and rhythmic motion, so too ought God's faithful to follow a similarly ordered pattern of motion. The closest and most appropriate "clock" for measuring and imitating God's perfect celestial creation was the planetary orbits.

It is therefore unsurprising that the very first mechanical clocks were designed precisely as astronomical or planetarium clocks, influenced by the ancient astrolabe—a planetary compass for determining the relative position of the planets, stars, and time through triangulation. These emerged as early as the thirteenth and fourteenth centuries across Europe and had a great influence on Oresme and others.[15] The clock, the *horarium*, and planetary motions were all part of the same tensional pattern of orchestrated motions, all held together and apart by relations of forces.

KINETIC ANALYSIS

Oresme's explicit unification of three interrelated fields—the physics of impetus theory, the monastic tradition of the divine *horarium*, and the invention of the mechanical clock—had enormous consequences, all of which made explicit what had been slowly developing for centuries: a shift from the ontological primacy of a spherical and centrifugal movement of eternity to one of mechanism and tensional force. As Lewis Mumford observes regarding the introduction of the mechanical clock, "Eternity ceased gradually to serve as the measure and focus of human actions."[16] There are therefore at least two major kinetic consequences of the clockwork-universe thesis that define it according to the same tensional circulation that defined impetus theory in both its terrestrial and ontological formulations.

Transmission by Tension between Parts. First, impetus, divine rhythm, and the mechanical clock all describe the same kinetic externalization of motion *transmitted by a tension between parts*. Impetus theory was defined by the transfer of motion between bodies, as noted in the previous section. When taken to the theological level, as it was, God then imparts this divine impetus to nature. Horokinetics, the movement of clocks, operate according to this same tensional form of motion.

The first mechanical clock functioned according to the kinetic operation of what is called "escapement," so named for the kinetic escape of motion as a balance wheel releases a tooth of the escapement's *escape wheel* gear, allowing the clock's gear train to advance or escape by a fixed amount. The escapement is driven by a spring or weight and transmitted through the parts of the clock's gear train by a linked tension between the parts. The movement of the wheel gear is produced by an alternately held tension-and-release linkage between two rotational motions: the weighted rotation of the foliot and the weighted rotation of the verge.[17]

The first mechanical clock thus measured time not by the centripetal stockpile of water and its centrifugal release outward, or by the centrifugal release of light from a solar center, but instead by the alternating tension and release of a link between two rotating motions. With the invention of the mechanical clock in the fourteenth century, time could be coordinated much more accurately and at smaller intervals—the half hour, the quarter hour, and so forth. The messiness of the flows of the water clock was replaced by the more appropriately linked tension device. The connection between the mechanical clock and social-celestial kinetics is evidenced in the explicitly social automata that were built into many mechanical clocks of the Middle Ages. When the hour rang, carved wooden people would emerge from the clock tower to pray, work, sleep, and so on.

The clockwork universe brings all of being into a hierarchically linked system of harmonious kinetic tension, like the gear train through which a force is transmitted and given autonomous life. Being moves, not like a puppet directly controlled by angels, God, or the unmoved mover, but according to a linked tension between parts endowed by the initial impetus of its creator.

Introduction of Kinetic Automation. Second, horokinetics functions according to an externalization of motion that introduces a difference between the creator or clockmaker, the semi-autonomous movement that is transferred, and the clock itself. For example, the invention of the mechanical clock meant that a timepiece could now run day and night for a very long time without any direct intervention from the horologist or natural forces such as water or sun. This created a new and very clear sense of the power of automation and automatons in celestial and terrestrial clocks, whose very name and Greek origin indicate exactly how they were historically interpreted: as *automatos*, αὐτόματος—self-moved, automatic, and spontaneous. The movement of the clock thus took on a kind of relative autonomy with respect to its creator and spectator—it appeared to be self-moved.

Furthermore, the relative autonomy of the clock made possible, at the same time, the relative autonomy of the creator. Kinetic escapement was therefore double: the escape of the timekeeper from the kinetic labor of direct horology (watching the stars, measuring the candles, refilling the water clocks, and so on), as well as the escape of the clock itself from dependence on subjective support, caprice, and possible user error.

Finally, this dual escapement made possible the identification of a semi-autonomous motion or force of the spring or weight that seemed to be causing the clock's motion. What kept it going? How quickly would it run out? What were the laws and properties of this power that was clearly distinct from the gear train of the clock as well as the clockmaker?

The clockwork universe thus introduces a triple kinetic division following the same dominant descriptions of force: God the clockmaker (external force), Nature the mechanism (relational force), and the motive power (internal force). Force cannot be reduced to either the unmoved mover or nature. Something moves between them. Kepler even goes so far to say that it actually robs the splendor of nature to reduce nature to God! God and nature each have its own force. Each has its own semi-autonomous circulation, but they are also related through a system of tensions or linkages that themselves are distinct from God and nature (force), thus keeping them together and apart, but also locked in a linked motion with each other.

THE THEORY OF EXTERNALIZED MOTION

So far in this chapter I have argued that impetus theory and the clockwork universe thesis are both conditioned on the same pattern of tensional motion presupposed by the description of externalized motion. In both cases I have sought to show that a kinetic analysis is capable of explaining the kinetic structure of "force" as a theological description of reality.

However, one thesis is not the cause of the other. Impetus theory is not the product of a technical realization that emerged as a simple result of monastic horology, nor is the clockwork-universe theory the product of either impetus theory or of the invention of the mechanical clock. Instead, each co-conditions the other. Impetus theory, the mechanical universe, and the mechanical clock are three expressions of the same tensional pattern of motion that rose to dominance during this time.

Once the theses of impetus and the clockwork universe were explicitly brought together and ontologized by Oresme in the fourteenth century, tensional motion became the dominant image of being until around the end of the seventeenth century. This is attested to but not exhausted by a number of important thinkers of this time.

In the fifteenth century, for example, the German philosopher Nicholas of Cusa described the cosmos as a sphere, but as a strictly *mechanical* sphere (*machina mundi*) released from direct contact with God and moved instead by an externalized and autonomous impetus. "Much as you give motion to the globe. But this sphere is not moved directly by God, the Creator, nor by the Spirit of God; it is not you nor your spirit who move immediately the globe which is now rotating in front of you. It is, however, you who initiate this motion, since the impulsion of your hand, following your will, produced an impetus and as long as this impetus endures the globe continues to move."[18] Cusa goes so far as to remove not only God but the Spirit of God as the direct motive force. Although Cusa wants to retain the idea of a sphere, his notion of impetus and the mechanical universe actually produced an escapement of motion from the sphere in the form of an impetus that is neither God nor the Spirit of God but rather a linked and autonomous mechanical nature held in tension with God through an enfolding (*complicare*) and unfolding (*explicare*) of force itself.

Later, Leonardo da Vinci (1452–1519) united the concept of impetus and clockwork mechanism in his *Sketches and Notebooks*, where he writes,

> Force I define as an incorporeal agency, an invisible power, which by means of unforeseen external pressure is caused by the movement stored up and diffused within bodies which are withheld and turned aside from their natural uses;

imparting to these an active life of marvellous power, it constrains all created things to change of form and position, and hastens furiously to its desired death, changing as it goes according to circumstances. When it is slow its strength is increased, and speed enfeebles it. It is born in violence and dies in liberty; and the greater it is the more quickly it is consumed. . . . Without force nothing moves.[19]

Da Vinci's description of force here follows an explicitly fluid-dynamic model of continuous motion characterized by the transfer or externalization of external pressure through impetus, dammed up or let loose, flowing through all created things and constraining their movement and change, and finally characterized by a kind of autonomy in its resistance to death and desire for liberty.

In the sixteenth century the English philosopher Francis Bacon (1561–1626) not only followed the same formulation of divine impetus proposed by Buridan but also described nature as a clockwork machine that operates according to the laws of this force: "That God ... created heaven and earth, and all their armies and generations 'sun, moon, and stars,' and gave unto them constant and everlasting laws, which we call *Nature,* which is nothing but the Laws of the creation. . . . So as the laws of Nature, which now remain and govern inviolably till the end of the world, began to be in force when God first rested from his works and ceased to create [Gen. 2:2]."[20]

God created nature, then impressed it with force (the laws of nature) that, just like clockwork, unfolds itself autonomously according to the transfer of tensional motion imposed by these very simple principles.[21] "*The force implanted by God in these first particles,*" Bacon writes, "form the multiplication thereof of all the variety of things proceeds and is made up."[22] God externalized his movement in the form of Epicurean particles of matter, which then, through collision, produced all of nature. Bacon thus introduces a brilliant synthesis of theology, naturalism, and mechanism in a single theory of force relations.

In the seventeenth century the German astronomer Johannes Kepler (1571–1630) finally abandoned his Neoplatonic animist theory of divine intelligence, put forward in his *Mysterium cosmographicum* (1596), as the cause or *anima motrix* of celestial motions.[23] Between the publication of the first edition of this book and the second edition in 1610, Kepler joined the court of Emperor Rudolph in Prague in 1600 and discovered there the only other planetarium clock in Europe that could rival that of de Dondi's in Italy: Jost Bürgi's planetarium globe, simulating the motions of sun, moon, and the five planets. In 1604 Bürgi entered the service of the emperor, and he and Kepler became close friends and collaborators.[24] Then a transformation occurred. When the second edition of *Mysterium cosmographicum* was published, Kepler turned his back on the animate soul as a celestial motor, writing, "[I]f we substitute for the word soul the word force, then we get just the principle that underlies my new physics of the skies. . . . I have come to the conclusion that this force must be substantial."[25]

In 1605 Kepler wrote to a friend an explicit synthesis of the impetus theory of force and the clockwork theory of the universe: "I am now much engaged in investigating physical causes. My goal is to show that the celestial machine is not the likeness of the divine being, but is the likeness of a clock (he who believes the clock is animate attributes the glory of the maker to the thing made). In this machine nearly all the variety of movements flow from one very simple magnetic force just as in a clock all the motions flow from a simple weight."[26] In this letter Kepler unites the holy trinity of externalized motion: force, clockwork cosmology, and the fluid-dynamic notion of a motion as it is transmitted and flows through the linked tensions of the clock's autonomous gear train. The weight or motive force is separate from the time mechanism but connected through an inelastic linkage.

This connection was possible because Kepler was not only familiar with the new physics of impetus spreading through Europe, and with its Islamic linage through Averroes, but also with the language of mechanism and clockwork through his friendship with Bürgi. In astronomy, Kepler argued that the elliptical orbits of the planets could not be the source of their own motion because they were noncircular but were rather products of a third motion or force related to the distance of their orbits. For Kepler, all of physics was united by the concept of a natural force capable of external and autonomous circulation distinct from the creator.

Kepler's work in astronomy was also deeply influential on the French philosopher René Descartes (1596–1650),[27] who ended up accepting both the notion of the clockwork universe and, counter to his own attempts at a completely dualistic philosophy, a theory of impetus. In his *Principles of Philosophy*, Descartes tries to show that matter is strictly reducible to extension in space and mind is strictly reducible to thought. He explicitly claims to have reduced motion to a mode of matter and not made it an independent third substance.[28]

The only problem is that Descartes then had to continually make allowances for a motive force that initially causes or impels matter into motion in exploring how motion is transferred from some object to another, and ultimately from God the creator to matter, his creation. For example, in *The World*, Descartes writes that "the *virtue or power* in a body to move itself can well pass wholly or partially to another body and thus no longer be in the first; but it cannot no longer exist in the world."[29] Force (*virtu/puissance*) is transferable between bodies, but as such is not itself reducible to a body, and as such is not subject to decay as bodies are. These are terms and ideas taken directly from impetus theory.

Even in the *Principles*, Descartes adds to bodies in motion an "inclination" that allows them to persist or continue along their course of motion. "Every moving body," he says, "at any given moment in the course of its movement, is *inclined* to continue that movement in some direction in a straight line."[30] Motion is therefore not the same as inclination. Even if motion were a mode of matter, inclination is not the same as a motion but is a tendency or force of motion. In another passage in the *Principles*, Descartes identifies these strivings as a "first preparation for motion,"[31] but again, a preparation for motion is not the same as the motion itself. Therefore, Descartes ends up adopting a third kind of substance in addition to body and mind to solve the problem of motive force: impetus.

Descartes again presupposes impetus and externalized motion in his theological commitment to a clockwork universe, just as Kepler did. In Descartes's view, God created the universe and then set it into motion, letting its pieces move according to the dynamic and autonomous principles of their clockwork structure. "We see clocks, artificial fountains, mills, and other such machines which, although only man-made, have the power to move of their own accord in many different ways. But *I am supposing this machine to be made by the hands of God*, and so I think you may reasonably think it capable of a greater variety of movements than I could possibly imagine in it, and of exhibiting more artistry than I could possibly ascribe to it."[32]

Just as humans make automatons that are capable of several kinds of motion, so God made humans and nature in the same manner but capable of vastly more motions. The movements of the nature and the human body, therefore, follow "just as necessarily as the movement of a clock follows from the *force*, position, and shape of its counter weights and wheels."[33] Just as the motive force of a tensional weight is communicated through the gear train, so God's force is similarly externalized into and through the coordinated parts of nature held together and apart by a single, continuous, but folded flow of movement.

Without a transfer or externalization of force from clockmaker to clock, the entire idea of the clockwork universe breaks down. "Just as the same craftsman could make two clocks which tell the time equally well and look completely alike from the outside but have completely different assemblies of wheels inside, so the supreme craftsman of the real world could have produced all that we see in several different ways."[34] Just as in clockwork, his setting them into motion is only possible with the impression or transfer of an inclination or autonomous force into the clock, and therefore introducing a triple folded tension into the continuous movement between God, the motive power, and creation.[35]

In his *Principia*, Newton claims that the entire task of philosophy is to investigate the phenomena of movement, and from them determine their causal forces (links and tensions), and then draw out their implications for other motions. "I offer this work, the mathematical principles of philosophy, for the whole burden of philosophy seems consist in this: from the phenomena of motions investigate the forces of nature, and then from these forces demonstrate the other phenomena."[36] Force and forces therefore occupy a central role in Newton's philosophy and physics as the explanatory names of causality.

In a body, for example, causal force has a dual function: when it is at rest it has an inherent force (*vis insita*) that resists any body that "endeavors to change its condition," and when it is in motion it has the power to impress and transfer force externally to other bodies (*vis impressa*). "It is resistance so far as the body, for maintaining its present state, opposes the force impressed; it is impulse so far as the body, by not easily giving way to the impressed force of another, endeavors to change the state of that other."[37]

Gravity becomes Newton's name for the force that causes movement toward a center by the external transmission of motion through space. By the term "gravity" he refers to "the absolute force to the centre, as endued with some cause, without which those motive forces would not be propagated through the space round about."[38] Despite his agnostic moments, Newton fundamentally relies on a theory of causality and the externalization of motion through impressed force.

His reliance on the external transfer of motion (*vis impressa*) is further evidenced and required by his theological belief in God as the creator and mover of the universe. God created the world, but he also created the force of gravity that allows it to continue to move like the weight in a clock. In a letter to the editor of the *Memoirs of Literature*, Newton writes,

> But certainly God could create planets that should move round of themselves without any other cause than gravity that should prevent their removing through the tangent. For gravity without a miracle may keep the planets in. And to understand this without knowing the cause of gravity, is as good a progress in philosophy as to understand the frame of a clock and the dependence of the wheels upon one another without knowing the cause of the gravity of the weight which moves the machine is in the philosophy of clockwork; or the understanding of the frame of the bones and muscles and their connection in the

body of an animal and how the bones are moved by the contracting or dilating of the muscles without knowing how the muscles are contracted or dilated by the power of the mind, is [in] the philosophy of animal motion.³⁹

Although Newton does not explicitly call the universe a clock or God a clockmaker, in this passage he does explicitly analogize the autonomous force of gravity, created by God and left to operate through nature and bodies without any "miraculous" intervention, with the tensional force of the weight in a clock made by a clockmaker and left to operate autonomously through the linked tensions of the gear train. Here Newton presupposes both an impetus theory of externalized motion and the linked tensional motion required by clockwork.

TWO ANTINOMIES OF EXTERNALIZED MOTION

The theory of externalized motion expressed in the twin notions of impetus and the clockwork universe poses two related antinomies. First, although Philoponus's anti-Aristotelian concept of impetus postulates the transmission of an external force from one body to another, it also presupposes that the recipient of that transferred force is capable of internalizing that force and continuously deploying it autonomously. The body that receives the force, like the gear train of the clock, cannot be merely passive in the process but must also be designed such that it can hold and slowly release the tension of the motor.

Theologically, God cannot simply transfer force to nature without nature also internalizing this force as its own and unfolding it in its own way. Therefore the externalization of motion on its own is not enough to account for the autonomous operation and unfolding of force in nature. A theory of the internalization of motion is thus required to understand how movement is possible independent of the mover.

Second, the theory of externalized motion also presupposes some kind of third relational aspect that would allow the transmission of motion between two relatively distinct things—God and nature, external and internal. That which externalizes motion therefore also remains connected in some way to that which provides the medium through which the motion is externalized to another body and therein internalized. A theory of the interrelation of motions is thus required to understand how movement is possible through a fluid medium.

Since the first kinetic operation of interrelational force was already developed in the previous chapter, the next chapter develops that of internal force or "conatus." Together, the interrelational, external, and internal aspects of tensional motion define the kinetic structure of force as it is used in the descriptions of the natural theology of the medieval and early-modern periods.

CHAPTER 26

Medieval Theology III

Conatus

THE INTERNALIZATION OF MOTION

The third kinetic operation or feature in the ontological description of force is the *internalization* of motion. This is the motion that occurs when a flow is disjoined or released from a given field of circulation and then either recirculated back in or folded into another field. The transfer or flow of motion from one body to another therefore presupposes a double internalization of motion: first in the primary body within which the force is originally contained, and second within the receiving body that takes up this motion and continues it from the first.

In this way, the ontological coprimacy of internalized motion is fundamentally incompatible with the Aristotelian universe. For Aristotle, the unmoved mover is precisely that: unmoved, *akinetos*. The unmoved mover lacks any *dunamis*, or potential, which is required for motion. However, in the Middle Ages the cosmological externalization of motion from God to nature in the form of an impetus presupposes that God has some motion or force to transfer outside himself in the first place. But there can be no transfer of motion without the preexistence of an internalized motion. The consequence of the externalization of motion and its subsequent independence from its source is thus, first and foremost, the affirmation that God is defined according to some internal self-motion that he redirects outward in the form of a material flow.

Therefore, the internalization of motion has three main characteristics: (1) it has an ontological coprimacy with God as a preexisting attribute of God that he can transfer to nature; (2) it cannot be simply identical to God, since it can be transferred from him; and (3) it has an autonomous internal motion insofar as it continues to move without God's direct control. Historically, the kinetic operation of internalized motion emerges as a coprimary force exercised by both the mover and the moved.

CONATUS

The concept of conatus, translated into English as "effort, endeavor, inclination, tendency, or striving," is the historical name for the kinetic description of a tensional and internalized motion. In other words, conatus is the name for the causal force that explains the autonomous self-movement of beings. While the kinetic descriptors of interrelational movement and externalized movement appeared much earlier historically, descriptions of conatus and internalized motion did not emerge until the end of the period, in the sixteenth and seventeenth centuries.

The origins of the concept of conatus are difficult to determine, since its appearance and spread in the late Scholasticism of the sixteenth and seventeenth centuries never took on a systematic usage in philosophy and theology. Furthermore, the fact that it emerged right before the empiricist's devastating critique of force also means it had a much shorter life. However, before the sixteenth century, many Scholastics used similar terms, such as "appetite" and "inclination," to analogically describe the obscure motions of gravitation and levitation. Aristotle described the "natural motions" of fire's tendency to rise upward and earth's to fall downward, but Scholastics like Aquinas began to attribute to these motions, by psychological analogy, an "appetite," "desire," or "aversion" to move in various ways.

For instance, in his *Summa contra Gentiles* (probably written in 1264), Aquinas distinguishes between three types of appetite: natural, animal, and intellectual:

> There is in everything an appetite for the good: for good is what everything desires [*appetuntur*], as the philosophers teach. In this way, the appetite in the things that lack thought is called natural appetite, as for instance it is said that the stone desires [*appetit*] to be downwards. In those who have sensitive thought, it is called animal appetite, which is divided into concupiscible and irascible. In those who have intelligence, it is called intellectual or rational appetite, which is will.[1]

By the sixteenth century, this host of psychological and metaphorical terms describing gravitation and levitation as desires was given a synthetic definition by Francesco Buonamici, in his *De Motu* (1587), as an "inclination which is necessary from the nature of every thing to agree to the good that convene to itself according to nature."[2] It is in this context that the term "conatus" emerged and spread, especially among Jesuits, as a central concept in the Scholastic explanation of gravity.

For these Scholastics, every sublunary body strives to return to its natural place through a rectilinear motion toward the center of its sphere. When this natural striving or conatus is interrupted, the body exerts an inner force or motive tendency to return to its natural motion. For example, "every time a stone is thrust upwards by an external force, its form opposes the ascent by a natural striving [*conatu*] and impulse that urges it downwards; but also the water, when warmed up by the fire, repels actively this form of warmness, because of an innate tendency [*inclinationem*] to cold, and to conserve its coldness as much as it can, even in fire."[3]

Throwing the stone transfers an impetus or *vis impressa* into the stone, but in addition to the externalization of motion in the stone, the stone also has its own internal force, innate tendency, or conatus that actively opposes the impetus and returns it back to the earth. Conatus, therefore, appears to not be identical to the motion, but to the innate force that strives against its violent motion. For Buonamici and others, this force is active even while the body is at rest. It simply strives to persist in its being until sufficiently forced to do otherwise.

In his *De Motu* (1646), the French Jesuit priest Honoré Fabri (1608–1688) combines these two motions, natural and forced, into a single twofold force defined by the seemingly contradictory term "innate impetus." "The impetus produced by a motive power . . . may have a twofold [*duplex*] effect. The first is motion; the second is an exertion [*nisus*] or striving [*conatus*] opposed to the extrinsic motion. . . . Indeed it always has this innate motion, unless it is hindered by another body."[4] If every body always has an innate impetus but is also always in a world influenced by the impetus of other bodies, every body would then be a mixture or dynamic twofold (*duplex*) of motion. This *duplex* has both an external impetus forcing it to move by an external transfer of motion, and an innate impetus or conatus striving against this external force.

Fabri's idea of the *duplex* suggests that externalization and internalization of movement are not ontologically separate but rather folded differences or relative kinotopologies of the same motion held together and apart with itself and by itself, like the folds of origami. In the idea of a kinetic fold, there is no longer an ontological division between a virtual power (conatus) and an actual power (impetus) in the trajectory of the stone but rather a continuous tension and coexistence between two different axes producing a single differential curvature as the stone moves up and then down through the air.

Descartes was deeply influenced by these developments in late Scholasticism when he studied at the Jesuit college of La Flèche, where the Conimbricenses' *Commentaries* on Aristotle's works and Eustachius's *Summa* were likely used as textbooks.[5] Despite Descartes's attempt "to construe motion in a purely kinematic way," his extensive use of dynamic terms like force (*vis*), action (*actio*), and striving (*conatus*) could not be avoided. In his *Principles of Philosophy* alone these terms appear 290, 59, and 8 times, respectively.[6] Descartes uses the concept of conatus, but in a way that is quite different from the Scholastics in three major ways.

First, Descartes rejects the Aristotelian thesis that God is the direct and continuous mover of everything. As Aristotle writes, "As in the universe, so in the soul, God moves everything."[7] Against this thesis, Descartes argues that God simply creates matter, sets it in motion, and afterward merely "preserves" the total quantity of motion and rest without constantly intervening in every single change in the motion of matter: "In the beginning he created matter, along with its motion and rest; and now, merely by regularly letting things run their course, he preserves the same amount of motion and rest in the material universe as he put there in the beginning. (God's perfection involves his never changing in himself or in his ways of operating)"[8]

God is thus reduced to a first efficient cause of motion and is no longer the proper agent of any subsequent motions, which are now attributed to nature and its laws. "It follows of necessity that there may be many changes in its parts that cannot, it seems to me, be properly attributed to the action of God (because that action does not change) and hence are to be attributed to nature. The rules according to which these changes take place I call the 'laws of nature.'"[9] God is only the proper and *direct author* of the initial creation of matter and transfer of force (*vis impressa*) into it; afterward, the subsequent internal collisions of matter produce all manner of irregularities and curves inconsistent with the pure, rectilinear motion directly attributable to God. "God alone is the author of all the motions in the world, insofar as they exist and insofar as they are straight, but it is the diverse disposition of matter that renders the motions irregular and curved."[10]

There is also a normative correlate to this thesis for Descartes: "God is also the author of all our actions, insofar as they exist and insofar as they have some goodness, but it is the diverse disposition of our wills that can render those actions evil."[11] Descartes's theory of cosmogenesis is therefore also a theory of cosmokinetic morality: the attempt of striving bodies to follow a rectilinear path to the good given by God but corrupted by humans.[12]

Second, Descartes rejects the Aristotelean thesis of a cosmological final cause: that all things are moving toward a final end, guided by God. For Descartes, motion is the outcome of complex causes that all act on a body simultaneously. As he says in the *Principles*, "there can be strivings toward diverse movements in the same body at the same time."[13] There is thus not only a duplex or twofold of natural motion and violent motion but also a complex or multifold of innumerable composite forces on a single body. Since these composite forces are not directly caused by God but are compositional natural motions of bodies in collision with one another, they are not headed toward any final state or God-given end.

Furthermore, for Descartes, the conatus or striving of bodies is not something that occurs as a whole between beginning and end, *terminus a quo and ad quem*, as the Scholastics say, but rather something that happens in an instant. Descartes distinguishes between two kinds of force: a determination of motion, and a tendency toward motion. A determination of motion is a description of a body's actual motion, while a body's tendency toward motion only occurs at a single instant. He states, "Of course, no movement is accomplished in an instant; yet it is obvious that every moving body, at any given moment in the course of its movement, is inclined to continue that movement in some direction in a straight line."[14]

In another passage in the *Principles*, Descartes identifies these strivings as a "first preparation for motion."[15] The preparation for motion is itself not a motion, but an instantaneous inner preparation or cause of motion. Determinations of motion span several instants and constitute actual movements, but at any given moment or instant every body also has the inclination or striving to continue in some particular direction. This is a crucial distinction between motion and inner force. If the inner force of conatus, striving, or inclination is something that occurs not in an actual determined motion but in an undeterminable instant, then its telos or endpoint certainly cannot be given in advance of the series of instants that define its determination or actual trajectory.

The third difference Descartes introduces is the rejection of the Aristotelean thesis of "natural motions": that certain types of bodies tend to go up or down by nature, like fire and earth. Rather, he argues, bodies *tend to persist in the same state*, whatever that state is, until caused to move otherwise. Descartes's "first law of nature" states that "each thing, in so far as it is simple and undivided, always remains in the same state, as far as it can, and never changes except as a result of external causes."[16] This first law overturns the very basis of Aristotelean philosophy. Bodies move according to their internal striving without continuous direct force from God. Motion and rest are equally the product of an inner conatus affected by others, with their own inner conatus. For Descartes, the movement of nature becomes autonomous. Movement and rest become two expressions of the same inner force or conatus.

The kinetic structure of Descartes's theory of force is expressed in his description of inner force or conatus as a tendency or tension. The French verb *tendere* that Descartes uses to describe the inner force of bodies comes from the Latin word *tener*, meaning "to hold, to become taut, to tend, to strive." Descartes's use of this word is not arbitrary. The conceptual genealogy of this word comes directly from the Stoics, who described force as a pneumatic tension—*tonike kinesis* or "tensional motion"—that holds things together and apart as it flows through them. The word *tener* is a Latinization of the Greek word τόνος, *tónos*, meaning "stress," and is used consistently throughout the medieval and Scholastic period when describing the concept of force. Even the seemingly novel idea contained in Descartes's first law of nature was already put forward by the Greek physician Galen in his description of *tonike kinesis* as analogous to the muscles of an arm under strain, both in a state of motion or stress and yet at rest as a whole.[17] Descartes thus participates in this tradition and imports its kinetic presuppositions about the tensional operation of inner forces.[18]

Descartes seems explicitly aware of this in *The World*, and even states he is using the word *tendre*—the French translation of the Latin conatus—to describe an "effort" and a "resistance." *Tendre*, he says, implies that a body "is disposed to move there, whether it truly moves or, rather, some other body prevents it from doing so. It is principally in this last sense that I use the word *tendre*, because it seems to signify some effort and because every effort presupposes some resistance [*c'est principalement en ce dernier sens que je me sers du mot de tendre, à cause qu'il semble signifier quelque effort, & que tout effort présupose de la resistence*]."[19] Descartes is clearly aware that the word *tendre* implies both an effort and striving (conatus), but also that every conatus presupposes a resistance or tension with others.

This idea is deployed throughout Descartes's oeuvre. For him, the concept of *tendre*, often translated into English as "tendency," is explicitly distinct from the concept of movement. "The tendency they [bodies] have to move—is different from their motion," he writes in *The World*. "For example, if we make a wheel turn on its axle, even though all its parts go in a circle (because, being joined to one another, they cannot do otherwise), their tendency is to go straight ahead."[20] In this example, the movement of the body is circular but the tendency of the body is linear, even without any actual linear movement. Therefore, he says later in his *Optics*, "it is necessary to distinguish between the movement and the action or the tendency to move."[21] Despite Descartes's attempt to define bodies by extension and movement alone, he deploys a distinct concept of conatus and *tendre* to account for the cause of motion, which is itself immobile, instantaneous, and yet somehow still active.

Kinetically, however, the concept of *tendre* as both effort (conatus) and resistance (*tendre*) precisely describes a regime of tensional motion. According to this logic, the operation of inner force is defined by three distinct movements: first, there is an internal movement of circulation (God); second, a flow breaks free or moves outside the circulation (tension); and third, this flow folds back over itself, forming a new circulation distinct from the original but with its own autonomous inner movement (nature). Each of these three moments is irreducible to the other. Descartes's concept of conatus as a *tendre* describes exactly the simultaneous effort and resistance implied by the relative autonomy of God and nature, as well as the inner tensions held between distinct bodies and their internal forces or conatus. God, nature, and the bodies within nature are thus held together and apart according to the tensional motion of their differing conatus.

Thomas Hobbes (1588–1679) read and exchanged correspondence with Descartes on a number of topics. Despite their vehement disagreements about most issues, Hobbes ends up, like Descartes, adopting a similarly causal and tensional notion of inner force (conatus). Hobbes rejects the Cartesian idea of an ontological dualism between mind and matter, as well as any immaterial conception of force. He therefore aims to accomplish what he believed Descartes had failed to do: a purely geometrical and materialist philosophy. In this effort, Hobbes draws on the same scholastic tradition as Descartes, and even on Descartes himself.

Hobbes defines conatus, or "endeavor," as he translates it into English, as the "internal beginning of animal motion;"[22] the "small beginnings of motion, within the body of man, before they appear in walking, speaking, striking, and other visible actions."[23] Hobbes even directly adopts the same scholastic terminology as Descartes did to describe this inner force when he says, "This endeavor, when it is toward something that causes it, is called APPETITE or DESIRE. And when the endeavor is fromward something, it is generally called AVERSION."[24] Conatus is thus the inner efficient causal force that sets bodies into motion. "When any body is moved," Hobbes writes, "which was formerly at rest, the immediate efficient cause of that motion is in some other moved and contiguous body."[25] This chain of causal motion stretches all the way back to the very first efficient cause or conatus: God.[26]

Just like Descartes, Hobbes strips God of direct control over motion and leaves him nothing but first efficient causality, while nature takes on its own autonomous laws. For Hobbes, motion is "a continual relinquishing of one place, and acquiring of another,"[27] so that the beginning of a motion of a body must be an infinitely small change in the place of the body. Accordingly, Hobbes defines endeavor "to be motion made in less space and time than can be given; . . . that is, motion made through the length of a point, and in an instant or point of time."[28]

Whereas Descartes introduces an immaterial concept of conatus in order to explain internal tendency and external causality, Hobbes argues instead that conatus is nothing other than an "infinitesimal movement." Where Descartes explicitly separates the determination of motion from the tendency toward motion, Hobbes tries to unify them. "Endeavor," he writes, "is to be conceived as motion," but not a quantified motion.[29] "For, the very first beginning of any thing is a part of it and the whole being motion, the part (that is, the first Endeavor) how weak soever, is also Motion."[30] This is in contrast with the concept of impetus, which Hobbes inherits from Buridan and others and defines as "nothing else but the quantity of endeavor."[31]

However, if conatus is nothing other than motion itself, then what is the cause of motion or force? In order to solve this problem, Hobbes simply adds the power of efficient causality or force back into the order of movements, calling it conatus. In this important moment Hobbes comes very close to restoring movement to its full primacy, but ultimately fails by reintroducing causality into the infinitesimal level, as if by burying it so deeply it might disappear and leave nothing but pure matter in motion. However, by attributing to conatus the power to cause motion, both in the causal series of bodies and in the first instance of God's efficient causality, Hobbes reintroduces the same distinction that Descartes did between motion and the cause of motion. Conatus becomes an immaterial inner force that is meant to explain and organize motion.

In the end, Hobbes not only adopts a similar concept of conatus as immaterial inner causality as Descartes did, but also adopts the same kinetic regime of tensional motion. In almost every place in his writings where Hobbes talks about endeavor, he describes its action as a tendency—"All endeavour tends towards,"[32] "Endeavour by which they tend,"[33] "The way by which the first endeavour of bodies moved tendeth,"[34] and so on. In a wonderful synthesis of late Scholastic vocabulary, Hobbes writes, "This first endeavour, when it tends towards such things as are known by experience to be pleasant, is called appetite."³⁵ Conatus, *tendentia*, and *appetitus* all express the dual aspect of inner force as a kinetic motion of *tension* between striving and resistance. Inner striving always takes place in a tension, hold, or taut linkage with other strivings.

Kinetically speaking, however, without movement, tension is impossible. It is bodies in motion that link up and hold together or apart. For Hobbes, the concept of conatus simply functions as a descriptive term for the constant conjunction or flow that links and relates heterogeneous bodies in motion together and apart. Conatus, for Hobbes, is invisible; at every level that we look for it, we simply find more bodies in motion and never conatus itself, and so on ad infinitum. Hence the "infinitesimal" nature of conatus. By placing conatus infinitesimally between bodies in motion, Hobbes introduces a metaphysical disruption into the pure continuum of matter in motion itself. In between every quantified body in motion, he inserts an unquantified or intensive motion holding the two bodies together and apart, linking them, composing them, and causing them to move in tension. Although Hobbes's intuition that conatus is nothing but matter in motion begins with good intentions, his failure in the end comes from dividing motion from itself and attributing to it something other than motion: force and causality.

In a radical reversal of this dilemma, Baruch Spinoza (1632–1677) was able to identify the true dynamic linchpin of both philosophical systems and make it the cornerstone of his own: conatus or *potestas* (power). Spinoza was thus directly influenced by Descartes's and Hobbes's theories of conatus, although he ultimately rejected the dualism of Descartes and the materialism of Hobbes.³⁶ Instead of deploying a concept of conatus without giving it a formal place in his philosophy, as Descartes did, or trying to bury immaterial causal powers in the infinitesimal tensional interstices of matter in motion, as Hobbes did, Spinoza raised conatus to the highest ontological level: God and/or nature, *dues sive natura*. Spinoza's ontology is thus an ontology of power or conatus. He makes explicit what was already essential and primary in Descartes—inner force, striving, and power—and raises it to the infinite.

According to Spinoza, God expresses his power through the conatus of singular determinate things, which simultaneously express God's power of being and acting. Together, the two express the same conatus or univocal striving of being:

> Singular things are modes by which God's attributes [thought, extension, and others unknown to us] are expressed in a certain and determinate way, that is, things that express, in a certain and determinate way, God's power [*Dei*

potentiam], by which God is and acts. And no thing has anything in itself by which it can be destroyed, or which takes its existence away. On the contrary, it is opposed to everything which can take its existence away. Therefore, as far as it can, and it lies in itself, it strives to persevere in its being, q.e.d. [*adeoque quantum potest, et in se est, in suo esse perseverare conatur*].[37]

If God has an inner power to create, this power or force must also be in some way expressed or transferred to his creation as conatus. However, if it is to take on its own motion, this transferred power or conatus must also be capable of its own conatus such that it can actively express the determinate action of God. In other words, the force of expression is identical to neither God nor his modes. Conatus is neither a body with extension nor a mind with thought; it is rather the continuous inner transformation of both—in and as God—without positing a third transcendent entity as their mediator or cause.

By raising the "force of expression" to such an ontologically foundational level, Spinoza introduces a dizzying immanence to theology. Instead of using the concept of inner force or conatus as a transcendent causal power of bodies (first efficient cause), Spinoza makes all of being the expression of a single inner force. He introduces the heretical theory of immanent causality. "God, therefore," he says, "is the immanent, not the transitive cause of all things."[38] God is the cause of himself in the *same sense* in which the modes that express him are the cause of one another. There is no transcendent cause because God, his attributes, and the modes are all three expressions of the *same force or power*.

Kinetically, the immanent structure of this vitalist conatus presupposes a trifolded continuum of linked tensional motion. Spinoza's theory of expression is deeply indebted to the theological notions of *complicare* and *explicare* (enfolding and unfolding) invented in the Middle Ages in order to theorize the unity-in-plurality of the plicated divine. Nicholas Cusa, for example, writes, "God, therefore, is the enfolding of all in the sense that all are in God, and God is the unfolding of all in the sense that God is in all."[39]

Throughout his works, Spinoza deploys the language of folding or plication: *complicare, explicare, implicare*, and reciprocal *expressiones*.[40] God is present in all things by complicating or enfolding them together with one another into a single unity. These things then explicate or unfold his complications into a plurality of determinate beings and actions. As unfolded things, they are not ontologically different from God but simply the topological differentiations of his continuum. Opposed to the centrifugal theory of Neoplatonic emanation that posited the One as more or less distant from beings in a series of successive subordinations, Spinoza's philosophy posits the copresence of two simultaneous movements: folding and unfolding. Things remain in God at the same time as they unfold and express him, and no less than God himself remains in himself as he complicates or enfolds the multiple unfoldings.

Insofar as these movements of folding are real movements and not merely rhetorical ones, Spinoza ends up requiring being to be *kinetic*, even if he does not acknowledge it. For example, conatus is not defined as an attribute of God, but rather a pure transversal becoming across substance, attributes, and modes. Conatus is therefore neither strictly mental nor strictly material. However, if the relation between substance, attribute, and mode is one of folding, then being must be kinetic. Folding requires a motion (flow), or else it is simply analogical and not ontological. Further, if there is motion then something is moving (matter). And if something moves, it requires a continuum of motion, as shown in Book I.

Therefore, insofar as Spinoza relies on the kinetic work done by folding to hold together the immanence of substance, attribute, and mode, he relies on and presupposes motion. The only error is that he describes this motion as a pure conatus or becoming, which itself is incapable of folding because it is not moving matter—and *not even an attribute at all*! Therefore, he ends up presupposing the primacy of exactly what conatus claims to explain: motion. Without motion there is no real fold, only a metaphorical "expression of force" without any actual motion, and thus no actual fold.

Through the immanence of a kinotopological folding, Spinoza also introduces a tensional motion into being between three distinct folds: substance, attributes, and modes. All three remain connected together, but also rigidly held away from one another through the tension of an enfolded unity. The meaning of Spinoza's threefold onefold is precisely a tensional one, held together and apart through the rigid continuity of the moving and folding surface. Kinetically, folding can only occur on the condition that a continuous surface can be held together and apart from itself. The different *topoi* on a folded surface must assume that at some point each of those areas is connected by an unbroken and mobile line (flow). If topology and plication are to have any ontological significance, they must be able to move. This is what Spinoza's immanence has taught us, even if we had to learn it through his oddly incorporeal theory of force. Similar versions of this position appear today in the neo-Spinozist and neo-vitalist ideas of "pre-acceleration,"[41] "vibrant matter,"[42] "virtual forces,"[43] and "affect."[44]

Like Spinoza, Gottfried Leibniz (1646–1716) also had the hindsight to notice the motive linchpin of the Cartesian and Hobbesian systems: conatus. Without it, Descartes's bodies had no causal or motive power and Hobbes's bodies had no origin or motive cause. In his *Hypothesis Physicae Nova*

(1671), Leibniz complains that the purely kinetic view of Descartes makes no sense without the addition of a dynamic principle (conatus); the essence of matter, he argues, cannot consist exclusively of extension and motion.[45] But this does not mean returning to Aristotelean theories of *entelechies* (natural motions) or passive possibilities.

Leibniz was instead more influenced in his thinking of conatus by his teacher at Jena, Erhard Weigel (1625–1699), a student of Hobbes.[46] Following Hobbes's lead, Leibniz radicalizes the idea that conatus or force is an unquantified point, arguing that it is even a fundamentally *unquantifiable* infinitesimal point. Where Hobbes tried and failed to argue that force is still just motion, Leibniz takes this "failure" and runs with it, just as Spinoza did, as an immaterial causal force—and makes it the foundation of a new philosophical system. Therefore, it is with Spinoza and Leibniz that the concepts of inner force, conatus, and power reach their final apex in the history of philosophy before the Humean revolution.

For Leibniz, "there is something besides extension in corporeal things . . . [there is] a striving or effort [*conatus seu nisus*] which has its full effect unless impeded by a contrary striving."[47] In fact, the very substance and extension of corporeal things are themselves already products of a more primary force of action or conatus. "Indeed," Leibniz writes, "it must constitute the inmost nature of the body, since it is the character of substance to act, and extension means only the continuation or diffusion of an already presupposed acting and resisting substance. So far is extension itself from comprising substance!"[48] The inner and unquantifiable force (striving and resisting; *tendentia*) of a body is what, through continuous diffusion, produces the attribute of extension in the first place. Here Leibniz and Spinoza have more in common with each other than with Descartes and Hobbes. For both Spinoza and Leibniz, substance is inner force. Substance is pure action, and this pure action is equivalent to God, who is the "preserver of their original forces or moving powers."[49]

In *Specimen Dynamicum* (1695), Leibniz goes so far as to reduce motion, space, and time to unreal mental constructions derived from the force of substance:

> Space, time, and motion have something akin to a mental construction [*de enterationis*] and are not true and real per se but only insofar as they involve the divine attributes of immensity, eternity, and activity or the force of created substances. Hence it follows at once that there is no vacuum in space and time; that motion apart from force (or insofar as it involves only a consideration of the geometric concepts of magnitude, figure, and their variations) is in fact

nothing but change of situation; and thus that motion insofar as it is phenomenal consists in a mere relationship.[50]

The only thing that is real, for Leibniz, is relations of force. Motion is only real insofar as it is "a force striving toward change. Whatever there is in corporeal nature besides the object of geometry, or extension, must be reduced to this force."[51] Therefore, Leibniz concludes, force is what is real and absolute, and motion simply belongs to a subclass of relative phenomena. The truth, Leibniz says, is "found not so much in phenomena as in their causes."[52] The inner force is the inner cause of motion, and thus its inner truth. Motion is thus subordinated to force. Force provides the pure continuum, without void or gaps, through which motion takes place and itself becomes continuous. As such, force has no extension, no magnitude, and an unassignable quantity, being "smaller than any ratio that can be given."[53] "Endeavor is to motion as a point is to space, or as one to infinity, for it is the beginning and end of motion."[54]

Since extended bodies are made from force, the collision of bodies is not mechanistic but vitalistic. Each body, according to Leibniz, spontaneously generates an internal force that also changes and responds spontaneously to other external forces.[55] Both colliding bodies act equally in response to each other as expressions of their respective inner forces. For example, when two balls collide with each other, they are not driven back by an externalized force but rather recede from each other by their own force.[56]

Although quite different from Descartes and Hobbes, Leibniz remains similarly committed to the concept of a *tendentia* (conatus, resistance) inherited from Weigel through Hobbes, Descartes, and ultimately the Stoics. For Leibniz, the kinetic commitment to tensional motion manifests itself in the inner tensions created by the fact that there can "be many contrary conatuses in the same body at the same time."[57] Despite Leibniz's explicit subordination of motion as an unreal mental construction, his theory of inner force presupposes the presence of a tensional motion within and between bodies as they are held together and apart. What Leibniz calls the continuous invisible force or forces within and between bodies is nothing other than the continuum of moving matter itself that has been folded and linked together.

There is no empirical experience, as Hume argues, of anything other than the continuous movement of bodies. When Leibniz looks at bodies and sees that they are capable of multiple kinds of combinatorial motions and reactions with one another, he is effectively seeing a tension or held constraint of multiple flows within a single kinetic object or between objects that hold them together. Seeing this and considering their cause,

Leibniz gives the name "force" to the constant conjunction of patterns of linked motion between bodies. When one composite body moves, all of its linked composed bodies move along with it. What he observes is linked matter in motion, but what he speculates is that there are invisible forces causing this movement.

THE DECLINE OF FORCE

The ontotheological primacy of force rose slowly over the course of the medieval and early modern periods, culminating with Spinoza's and Leibniz's monisms of force. The philosophical and theological primacy of force remained influential through the seventeenth and early eighteenth centuries with later adherents such as Roger Boscovich (1711–1787) and the early Immanuel Kant (1724–1804). Kant's precritical works on force follow almost directly the ontological primacy given to it by Spinoza, Leibniz, and Boscovich, affirming that "it is easily proved that there would be no space and no extension, if substances had not force whereby they can act outside themselves. For without a force of this kind there is no connection, without this connection no order, and without this order no space."[58] For the precritical Kant, force is the most fundamental metaphysical concept from which all others are derived. However, after reading the work of the empiricists George Berkeley and David Hume, and awakening from his "dogmatic slumber," Kant completely reverses his position and gives force a much less central positon.

For Berkeley, the concept of force has no meaning other than a convenient term to describe the phenomenon of motion. As he writes in his *De Motu*, "Force, gravity, attraction and similar terms are convenient for purposes of reasoning and for computations of motion and of moving bodies, but not for the understanding of the nature of motion itself."[59] Motion can only be understood through empirical observation and experiment. Therefore "those who assert that active force, action, and the principle of motion are really in the bodies, maintain a doctrine that is based upon no experience, and support it by obscure and general terms, and do not themselves understand what they wish to say."[60] When physicists observe a succession of sense data connected by rules, Berkeley argues, they simply interpret "that which precedes in their order as the cause and that which follows as the effect. It is in this sense that we say that one body is the cause of the motion of another, or impresses motion on it, pulls it or pushes it."[61] For Berkeley, force is just another name for temporal sequence.

After Berkeley's and Hume's critiques of force, similar criticisms took hold all over Europe. By the nineteenth century, a new "empirical mechanism" had emerged among German, French, and English physicists, including Gustav Kirchhoff (1824–1887), Heinrich Rudolf Hertz (1857–1894), Ernst Mach (1838–1916), Jules Henri Poincaré (1854–1912), Lazare Carnot (1753–1823), Barré de Saint-Venant (1797–1886), and Bertrand Russell (1872–1970), who aimed to eliminate the concept of force entirely from the sciences.

In its place, early eighteenth-century physicists like Jean-Baptiste le Rond d'Alembert (1717–1783) began putting forward a new conceptualization of force as a function of the measure of time.[62] Poincaré adopted Kirchhoff's definition of force as the product of mass and acceleration, and the idea took hold quickly. Increasingly, the metaphysical concept of force was stripped of any transcendent or metaphysical meaning and became a pure function of time, a measurement of a rate of change in time, a mass times its acceleration, *in time*. In this way the ontological decline of force gave birth to an increasing descriptive prominence of a new metaphysics of time, as we will see in Part IV.

All three aspects of tensional motion described in these chapters so far can also be located in the descriptive ontotheological core of the Christian tradition: in the doctrine of the trinity. Trinitarianism was one of the first attempts to think of all three aspects of force together as three different aspects of the same trifolded ontology of force. This will be the focus of the next chapter: the unity of the three forces in one.

CHAPTER 27

Medieval Theology IV

The Trinity

TRINITARIANISM

The previous chapters outlined the threefold operations at work in the ontological description of force in natural theology—relational, external, and internal forces—each one posing an antinomy without the others. In this final chapter on medieval theology, however, we turn to an analysis of their coexistence in the doctrine of the Trinity.

The theological doctrine of the Trinity was by far one of the most important, dominant, and novel descriptions of being during the medieval and early modern periods, beginning around the middle of the fourth century. From the time of the Nicene Creed (381 CE), which established an official doctrine of the Trinity, until the emergence of the European Enlightenment in the mid-eighteenth century, Trinitarianism remained the single most pervasive and powerful ontotheological framework in the West—influencing all the natural theologies of force described in the previous chapters. To this day it remains the official doctrine of the Catholic Church.

Trinitarianism emerged historically as an original response to the ontological and kinetic problems raised by the introduction of, God's son Jesus, into the existing cosmological frameworks of the ancient West: monotheism, Platonism, Aristotelianism, Stoicism, and others. The English word "trinity" comes from the Latin noun *trinitas*, meaning "triad," and the adjective *trinus*, meaning "threefold" or "triple." As its name suggests,

Trinitarianism aims to resolve the following theological problem: that there is only one divine and heavenly God (monotheism), but this one God also manifested himself on earth as a man (Christ), who is connected to but not merely identical to God (relation). How can God be both celestial and terrestrial at the same time without rupturing the distinction between the celestial and terrestrial and without introducing plurality into his unity? If there are multiple Gods, then does Christianity fall back into paganism? If God came to earth and was transformed into man, how are the two related to each other? What was the means and medium of such a theological transport or movement?

Posed in this way, the problem of the Trinity is essentially a kinetic problem of tension: how to explain the movement of God, given the introduction of a second, a man-God. In most ancient cosmologies, the problem of God's motion was largely resolved by adopting a spherical and centrifugal regime of motion in which an emanating creator God occupied a static and eternal center (creating without moving), while his mobile creation was simply distributed hierarchically around him. All beings were set in ordered motion by God's ethereal breath (force), which permeated the entire cosmosphere. God existed everywhere by a difference in degree from the center outward, not a difference in kind, between two identical persons in two different kinotopological regions of the same sphere. For Christian theology, however, this cannot be an acceptable solution, because it subordinates and marginalizes the importance and dual centrality of God-the-Christ, which distinguishes Christianity from other monotheisms and religions.

THE HOLY SPIRIT

Christian Trinitarianism was thus forced to resolve this ontological problem in an entirely novel way, and in doing so it ended up describing a regime of tensional motion or circulation that had an incredible impact on the whole Latin West. In particular, in order to resolve the problem of the coduality of God the Father and God the man, Trinitarianism introduced a *third* concept that envelops or unifies the first two but also provides the relational transport medium through which the other two are held together and apart: the Holy Spirit.

The Holy Spirit is the invisible and eternal force that permeates everything, including God himself, and through which God expresses his power of action—creation and transmutation as the Son. In this way the concept of the Holy Spirit follows genealogically and functionally, from the ancient concept of the breath of God—itself having various names, including aether, soul, spirit, wind, air, fire, pneuma, smoke, and so on. In fact, the English words "Holy Spirit" are simply a translation of the original Greek words *pneuma hagion,* or "holy breath," and are described in explicitly fluid kinetic terms.

The term "Holy Spirit" is used most frequently in the Gospels to refer to baptismal flows. In Mark and John, Jesus "will baptize in [the] Holy Spirit," and in Matthew and Luke, he "will baptize with Holy Spirit and fire," a reference to the fiery aether of the Greeks.[1] In the Book of Acts, one is "filled with the Spirit" like a permeating liquid force or power. Spirit is "poured out upon" or "falling upon" people.[2] Up until the eighth century, the Holy Spirit, depicted in the fluid kinetic images of the dove, fiery air, or water, is also described in feminine terms associated with water and motion and identified with the womb of the Virgin Mary. This both connects the Divine Father to the Earthly Son while also holding them apart through her. In the Book of Luke, for example, an angel tells Mary that "the Holy Spirit shall come upon thee, and the power of the Most High shall overshadow thee: wherefore also the holy thing which is begotten shall be called the Son of God."[3] God acts and expresses his power or force through the interrelational and kinetic flows of air and water. Mary's watery-kinetic womb thus echoes the Book of Genesis, where "the Spirit of God hovered over the waters."[4] The same Holy Spirit that hovered over the waters at the creation of the world hovers over the waters of Mary's womb. The same kinetic power of God that mobilized the fluid-kinetic force of the waters to create the world now begets Jesus in the same way.[5]

However, as shown in the previous chapters, insofar as the Holy Spirit remains simply identical to God, his force or breath remains fundamentally centrifugal, a divine emanation. What is unique about Trinitarianism is that it introduces a whole new form of motion into theology by attributing personhood to the Holy Spirit. In this way, the Holy Spirit ceases to be an attribute and becomes a substance—"The" Holy Spirit.[6] If the Holy Spirit is a person just as the Father and Son are persons, then God's breath or force becomes ontologically coprimary with him as a distinct but not separate entity. God becomes a threefold person in the Trinity. By granting personhood to the Holy Spirit and raising God's Son and his force to the same substantial level, Trinitarianism introduces an ontological three-way tension into the movements of the divine.

The concept of theological force deployed in the Christian notion of a Holy Spirit can therefore not be separated from its (meta)physical descriptions of force in natural theology. Both concepts are expressions of the same kinetic regime of interrelational or tensional motion, force, or causal relation. Both explain how the celestial and terrestrial are held in tension—together (unified) and apart (differentiated), and how a conjunctive or causal power is possible between them that is not identical to them but not separate from them either. The two move together by the held tension of the third link.

However, the introduction of a third relational term binds the first two terms only at the expense of further complicating the status of the One. Therefore, the sections that follow show precisely how the trifold unity of the Father, Son, and Holy Spirit comes to a historico-theological resolution by relying on a fundamentally kinetic description of tensional motion between the threefold, One, or triune God.

CENTRIFUGAL SUBORDINATION

Despite the introduction of the three persons (Father, Son, Holy Spirit) into Christian theology, the earliest attempts to reconcile their comotion and interrelation remained kinetically centrifugal. From the first century to the middle of the fourth, most of the Early Church fathers described the relations among the Trinity in an explicitly "subordinationist" manner. God the Father is ontologically first or primary and then creates or begets the Son, who is second and who, through his connection with the Father, makes possible a third: the Holy Spirit. Kinetically, this subordinationist model closely follows the emanationist model of the spinning cosmosphere, whose center remains unmoved and eternal, but by moving in rotation it radiates outward in a hierarchical sequence toward the periphery.

For example, Clement of Rome (99 CE) writes, "The apostles received the gospel for us from Jesus Christ, and Jesus Christ was sent from God. So Christ is from God, and the apostles are from Christ: thus both came in *proper order* by the will of God."[7] Ignatius of Antioch (107 CE) commands us to "be subject to the bishop and to one another, as Jesus Christ in the flesh was subject to the Father and the apostles were subject to Christ and the Father, so that there may be unity both fleshly and spiritual."[8]

In this centrifugal model, unity is accomplished through subjection in the hierarchy of command from the center. Justin Martyr (100–165 CE) makes this chronohierarchical ordering explicit when he writes, "We reasonably worship Him, having learned that He is the Son of the true God Himself, and holding Him in the second place, and the prophetic Spirit in the third, we will prove."[9] Further, "that Jesus Christ is the only proper Son who has been begotten by God, being His Word and first-begotten, and power; and, becoming man according to His will."[10]

The relation here is clearly one of unidirectional emanation of a force, power, or will from Father to Son. The *Didache*, or *Teaching of the Twelve Apostles,* describes Jesus as the "Servant" of God.[11] Even Tertullian (c.155–160–after 220), who was the first to describe the co-relation between Father, Son, and Spirit as a *trinitas*, frequently adopts subordinationist language, saying that "the Father, is distinct from the Son, being *greater than the Son*, in as much as he who begets is one, and he who is begotten is another; he, too, who sends is one, and he who is sent is another; and he, again, who makes is one, and he through whom the thing is made is another."[12] Origen of Alexandria (184– 253 CE) claimed that Jesus was a *Deuteros Theos* or second God,[13] and the Son was other in substance than the Father.[14]

The failure of this centrifugal model of hierarchical emanation to give ontological coprimacy to God-the-Son was one of the major problems dealt with in the so-called Arian controversy between subordinationists and a rising group of theologians espousing a new theological model of equality of divine persons, led by the Church Father Bishop Athanasius. The debate continued for about half a century, until it was formally ended at the Council of Constantinople in 381 in favor of a new *tensional doctrine* of the Trinity.

TENSIONAL EQUALITY

This new kinetic resolution came from three principal theologians in ancient Turkey (Cappadocia): Gregory of Nazianzus (c. 329–390), Basil of Caesarea (329–379), and Gregory of Nyssa (c. 335–c. 395). For the Cappadocian fathers, the problem of the Trinity was a kinetic problem: how to reconcile the internal movement of the Trinity with respect to itself without introducing a hierarchy of one term or the other, and thus diminishing the divinity of Christ.

If God begets a moving Son, he must do so through some kind of activity or force. Furthermore, since there is no outside to God, the mobility of the Son must have in some sense been in him from the beginning. The introduction of the Son, even if chronologically second, cannot be ontologically second. This also means that motion or the operational act (*oikoinomia*) cannot be ontologically derivative but must be coprimary.

This is a radically anti-Aristotelean proposition. For Aristotle, the unmoved mover (*akinesis*) creates without moving and has no power (*dunamis*) that is not unfulfilled. God is pure *energia* or action without potential or motion. To say that God begets a Son is not the problem, but to grant the

Son coprimacy with the Father reintroduces motion retroactively back into the unmoved mover. The immanence of the Trinity thus introduces operational, economic, and kinetic immanence into God. The unity of God arrives at duality by *motion*, but it arrives at Trinity by linking the two together *through motion*.

As Gregory of Nazianzus writes, "For it is possible for Unity if [it is] at war with itself [*stasiazon pros heauto*] to come into a condition of plurality; but one which is made of an *equality of Nature* and a Union of mind, and an *identity of motion*, and a convergence of its elements to unity—a thing which is impossible to the created nature—so that although numerically distinct there is no severance of Essence. Therefore Unity having from all eternity *arrived at Duality by motion*, found its rest in Trinity. This is what we mean by Father and Son and Holy Spirit."[15]

In motion the unity is divided, but *through motion* and *as motion* the three (moving Father, movement spirit, moved Son) are reunited as a continual process of linked circulation. For Gregory of Nazianzus, the "rest" of the Trinity is therefore nothing other than the tensional motion of the triune as they move together (operationally/economically) as one. As one moves so do the others, like circulatory loops in a trefoil knot (see Figure 27.1).

The result of this linked tension in motion is a brilliant and novel reconciliation of mobility with relative fixity. The triune moves and morphs itself without moving with respect to itself and without giving up the relatively fixed regions, folded flows, loops, and circulations that define its trifold nature. In other words, the tensional Trinity allows for both a single and continuous movement of *ousia* (being) while still maintaining three relatively

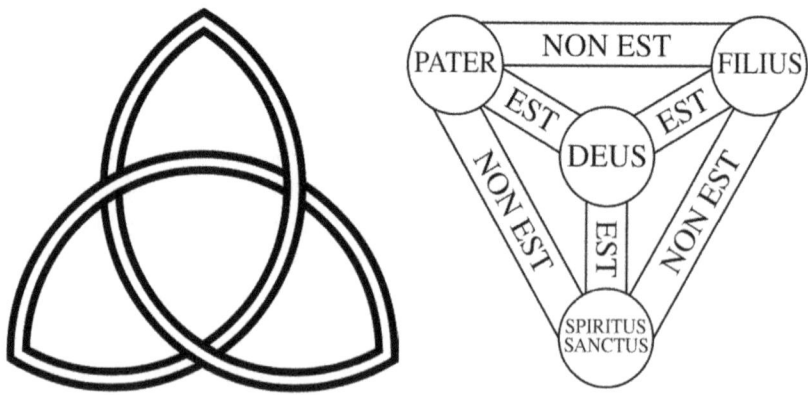

Figure 27.1 Trefoil and Shield of the Trinity
Source: Trefoil Image taken from AnonMoos/Wikimedia Commons.
Shield of the Trinity comes from Wikipedia: AnonMoos/Wikimedia Commons.

[378] *Being and Force*

distinct and tensional folds in this motion as three "hypostases" (from the Greek words *hypo*, "underlying," and *stasis*, "fixed or motionless"). Gregory here follows the Stoic usage of the word hypostases not as substances but as modes or tensional relations (*pros ti, prōs echon*) in a single substance.[16]

What is kinetically interesting here is that one of the first resolutions to the problem of the Trinity is not accomplished in purely ontotheological terms but by operational and kinetic terms. Hippolytus (170–235 CE) offers a similar, Stoic-influenced resolution to the problem of the Trinity: "[God] has a single Power [*dunamis*]; and that as far as the Power is concerned, God is one; but in terms of the *oikonomia*, the display [of it] is triple."[17] As a force or *dunamis*, God is one continuous dynamic movement, but in terms of the economic display of this force, there are three discrete circulations within. The discrete hypostases are thus the product of an inner folding within the continuous movement of being.

Aristotle could never have allowed *dunamis* and motion into the unmoved mover like this. Plato, too, could never have accepted the notion that the eternal God was in motion because the eternal does not move. Gregory of Nazianzus, however, does explicitly this with his theory of the divine *edios* or image: "For in ordinary language an image is a motionless representation of that which has motion; but in this case [the Trinity] it is the living reproduction of the Living One."[18]

The kinetic implications of this point are radical. God creates the Son as a moving image of his own movement. In doing so, however, he also displaces himself as the static center and introduces a kinetic tension between two distinct motions, where, for the ancients, there had been only one of subordination of motion to eternal immobility. Nazianzus goes on to compare the Trinity both to a continuous flowing river with distinct regions[19] and to a single ray of light that "quivers with many rapid movements [of moisture], and is not one rather than it is many, nor yet many rather than one; because by the swiftness of its union and separating it escapes before the eye can see it."[20] In both cases we can see that the comprehension (from the Latin word, *comprehendere*, "to catch, seize, grasp firmly; embrace in tension") of the Trinity relies on a distinctly fluid kinetic description of being as one continuous but multifolded flow.

Gregory of Nyssa proposes a similar kinetic solution. "Since then the Holy Trinity fulfills every operation," he writes, "not by separate action according to the number of the Persons, but so that there is *one motion* and disposition of the good will which is communicated from the Father through the Son to the Spirit."[21] What is significant here is the idea that the Father cannot move without the Son and Holy Spirit moving in tension *with* the Father, "by reason of the unity of action" or motion.[22]

In the writings of Basil of Caesarea we find a similar recourse to kinetic *flows* in order to describe the nature and operation [*oikonomia*] of grace or spirit as it moves in, between, and through the divine persons while still respecting the triple-hypostases that define their relative distinctness within the Trinity. "For the grace *flowing from Him* when He *dwells in* those that are worthy, and carries out His own *operations*, is well described as *existing in those that are able to receive Him*. . . . Where on the other hand *the grace flowing from the Spirit naturally comes and goes*, it is properly and truly said to exist in, even if on account of the firmness of the recipients' disposition to good the grace abides with them continually."[23]

THE FOLDS OF FORCE

After the Council of Constantinople, the equality of the Trinity became Western Orthodoxy and received its most sustained synthetic expression in the work of Augustine of Hippo (354–430) around 417. Although Augustine's work is largely synthetic of positions already reached by the Council, it also puts forward a clear emphasis on the ontotheological status of the *relatio* (relation) and *potentate* (force) of the Trinity. Both suggest the rise of the ontological primacy of co-relation and tensional force over the simple unity of centrifugal and spherical radiation.

Augustine is explicitly aware of the kinetic problem posed by the Trinity. "It is difficult to contemplate and fully know the substance of God; who fashions things changeable, yet without any change in Himself, and creates things temporal, yet without any temporal movement in Himself."[24] This is close to Aristotle's problem of the unmoved mover (how does the unmoved mover move the world without moving himself), but for Aristotle the unmoved mover is not a creator God and therefore his being can be resolved by the eternal centrality of the moving sphere. Augustine, however, must somehow account for how change and time are created or derived from God without allowing God himself to be changeable or temporal (i.e., affected by what he creates).

Augustine's solution, following the Cappadocian fathers, is to introduce an ontotheological "indivisible equality" of relation between God and his creation (Son) and the force, Holy Spirit, or *potestas* through which he creates.[25] Augustine describes this as the "co-eternity and consubstantiality" of the Trinity, entailing that each of the three cannot exist or act [*actio*] without the other one.[26] "The Father, and the Son, and the

Holy Spirit, as they are indivisible, so work indivisibly"[27] in their immanence of being and in their immanence of economy, operation, force, or motion.

The resolution to the ontologically triple nature of a creator God, therefore, is to raise his force or potentate (*dunamis*) to the level of a coprimacy with God himself and his creation, such that God, Son, and Spirit become trifold expressions of *a single continuous flow of force or power*. In doing so, however, one simultaneously violates Aristotle's claim that the unmoved mover has no *dunamis* or force, and also introduces an immanent dynamism into eternity itself, thus complicating the status of eternity from *absolutely* unmoved to *relatively* or *relationally* unmoved.

Further complicating the unmoved status of the eternal is the fact that Father, Son, and Spirit are immanent in being and immanent *in action*. As one acts, so do the others. Thus, when Augustine attributes to the Trinity a "co-eternity" that remains unchanged and atemporal, he is asserting the primacy of force (above change and time), and thus a notion of coeternity that remains only "unmoved" *qua* relation (*relatio*) in its tension within the other persons of the Trinity, but *moved* with respect to the actions or inner operations. The persons of the Trinity are thus different as persons but identical "according to relation [*relatio*], which relation, however, is not accident, because it is not changeable."[28]

Augustine is quite explicit here that the Trinity is only coeternal and unchangeable insofar as we are referring to a *relationship or force* and not insofar as we are referring to the individuality of the persons. "The co-eternal nature of the father and son," he writes, "refer[s] to their relationship," not to their individuality as persons.[29] The unity of God must therefore rely on the concept of a fold in the continuous and coextensive flow of power or force relation. In the Trinity, God becomes a fold (*pli*), a "*simplici multiplicitate, aut multiplex simplicitas* [simple multiplicity, or multifold simplicity]."[30]

The primacy of folded relation is also therefore a primacy of force relation, since Christ is the power or *virtue* or *dunamis* of God: "Christ the power of God [*Christum dei uirtutem et dei*]."[31] God and Son are united and distinguished *qua dunamis multiplex*. This primacy of force and power could not be more explicit than when Augustine writes, "Christ is the power [*virtus/ dunamis*] and wisdom of God, because He Himself, being also power and wisdom, is from the Father, who is power and wisdom."[32] For Augustine, the Trinity cannot be reduced to a merely logical relation of analogy. God, Son, and Spirit are a complex of relations *of force*. Force is the real, not merely (ana)logical, condition of their being together.

PERICHORESIS

Another important kinetic resolution to the problem of the Trinity emerges in the seventh and eighth centuries with the concept of *perichoresis* in the work of Maximus Confessor, Pseudo-Cyril, and John of Damascus. Although the verb *perichoreo* first emerges in the work of Gregory of Nazianzus to deal with the dual nature of Christ, it is not until Maximus Confessor that it is used as a noun, and not until Pseudo-Cyril and John that it is directly applied to the specific problem of the Trinity.[33]

The word *perichoresis* comes from the Greek words περί, perí, "around," and χώρα, *chora*, which has several interrelated kinetic definitions, including "to dance, to encircle, to open up a space for, to nourish from the countryside, to fold or enclose."[34] In Plato's dialogue of the same name, Timaeus uses the term to describe a "third kind" (*triton genos*)[35] of kinetic being, irreducible to either static being or becoming, which actively generates through motion (shaking) all of being without itself being determinable as a particular being. Insofar as the word *perichoresis* borrows from this same root word *-chor*, it retains the meaning of a kinetic process that opens up or creates an enfolded space of continuous circulation and mutual coinherence and co-constitution.[36]

Gregory of Nazianzus thus uses the verb *perichoreo* three times in order to describe the mutual and circulatory movement of life and death,[37] the process of desire and satiation,[38] and, most importantly, Christ's "reciprocal" nature as divine and mortal, the two co-consituting one another in a mutual kinetic encircling.[39]

In the seventh century, Maximus the Confessor (580–662) directly uses the noun *perichoresis* in order to solve the problem of dual action in Christ. His purpose is not to explain the unity of the one Christ but the simultaneous action and effect that occur from his two natures in a single Person. He uses the example of a red-hot knife that burns and cuts at the same time, but without becoming two different substances or actions.[40] The knife is hot and cuts in the same motion; its being and action are immanent yet differentiated. Maximus uses the term adverbially in *Ambigua*, where he explains that "the human nature totally makes room for (*perikechoreke*) the divine nature, to which it is united without any confusion."[41] With Maximus, however, *perichoresis* remains focused on the action "of" (the God-Man) and not yet coinherence "in" or "through."

In Pseudo-Cyril (seventh century), however, the notion of *perichoresis* is finally applied directly to the problem of the Trinity. The problem with hitherto existing Trinitarianism was that its definition had been predominantly from the top down, "one ousia, three hypostases." The genius of

Pseudo-Cyril was to invert the problem and focus on defining the Trinity from the bottom up, from the hypostases first. With respect to the oneness of the Trinity, it is the unity of the three, but with respect to the threeness of the Trinity, the three must be in a continual and mutual kinetic circulation or coinherence of mutual action and power. The three are distinct moments in the continual process of enfolded circulation without coalescing or mixing together, "an unconfused and unaltering *perichoresis* into one another," Pseudo-Cyril writes.[42]

Pseudo-Cyril argues that "each nature interchanges with the other what belongs to itself, through the identity of the hypostasis and the *perichoresis* of the natures into one another; so that it is possible to say that 'God appeared on earth' and that 'this man is uncreated and impassible.'"[43] Pseudo-Cyril therefore emphasizes the mutual enfolding described in John 14:11: "I am in the Father and the Father in me."

Perichoresis is therefore no longer the dual action *of* the God-Son, but the constitutive movement or process that occurs *in and through* the Father-Son-Spirit. The kinetic transformation here is crucial. With Pseudo-Cyril the *perichoresis* of the Trinity is no longer "to" one another, but "in" one another, not as mere equals, but as two coextensive folds in the same continuous *process of circulation* in which they are two regions.[44] Circulation, or *circumincessio* (the Latin translation of *perichoresis*), comes from *circumincedere*, meaning "to move around" or "moving in and through the other," a sense preferred by Bonaventure and other Western theologians.[45]

John of Damascus (c. 675–749) then adopted Pseudo-Cyril's original usage of *perichoresis*, and without making any significant innovations popularized it for a wider orthodox readership. For John, *perichoresis* remains primarily a *kinetic process* within which the Trinity occurs as a trifold. He summarizes this position at the end of his treatment of the Trinity in his *Exposition of the Orthodox Faith*:

> The subsistences [i.e., the three persons] dwell and are established firmly in one another. For they are inseparable and cannot part from one another, but keep to their separate courses within one another, without coalescing or mingling, but cleaving to each other. For the Son is in the Father and the Spirit: and the Spirit in the Father and the Son: and the Father in the Son and the Spirit, but there is no coalescence or commingling or confusion. And there is *one and the same motion*: for there is *one impulse and one motion of the three subsistences*, which is not to be observed in any created nature.[46]

There is *one continuous movement* of the Trinity, but it is a tensional movement shared by three hypostases or subsistences moving together as folds in the same circulatory process. It is a tensional movement because there are three persons without coalescence or commingling. Furthermore, John's description of *perichoresis* applies several attributes of the Greek *chora* to God himself as a movement of absolute force, sustaining fullness, and infinite excess, "wanting in nothing, being His own rule and authority, all-ruling, life-giving, omnipotent, of infinite power, containing and maintaining the universe and making provision for all."[47]

What is kinetically crucial here is how reliant Trinitarianism is on a highly kinetic account of circulation and folding to describe what Christian theologians believe to be fundamentally unknowable and mysterious metaphysical processes. Although on guard for anthropocentrism and physicalism in their systems, this rarely stops them from needing and inventing complex physical kinetic descriptions of the nature of the divine Trinity that rely on movement and tension to account for the primacy of God's interpenetrating force.

THE TRIANGULATION OF ONENESS

Drawing on Trinitarian theologies of equality, folding, and *perichoresis*, Nicholas of Cusa (1401–1464) developed the explicitly kinetic and geometrical implications of the triune. Cusa's theological geometry sets out to explain the simultaneous oneness and threeness of the Trinity. "For because God is Oneness, He is Begetter and Father; because He is Equality of Oneness, He is Begotten, or Son; because He is Union of both [Oneness and Equality-of-Oneness], He is Holy Spirit."[48] Therefore "Oneness is called Father, Equality is called Son, and Union is called Love or Holy Spirit."[49]

This trifold notion of oneness deeply complicates the ancient idea of a simple centrifugal cosmosphere. In fact, Cusa even writes that without the more primary understanding of threeness, one cannot even properly conceive of oneness. "For if Oneness is the greatest and most perfect understanding, . . . then whoever does not attain to the trinity of this Oneness does not rightly conceive of oneness. For oneness is only threeness, since oneness indicates indivision, distinctness, and union."[50] Therefore, geometrically, he writes, "We regard the maximum triangle as the simplest measure of all trinely existing things—even as activities are actions existing trinely (1) in potency [*posse*], (2) in regard to an object, and (3) in actuality."[51]

For Cusa, if the Trinity is going to be conceived as One, it will require a triangular relational distinction that is not present in the simple oneness of a spinning sphere. More specifically, Cusa argues that the entire geometry of triune oneness can be derived from the potency (from the Latin *posse*, meaning "power, force, or capacity") of a single infinite line. By folding and bending and moving a single infinite line, Cusa shows how the line can be transformed into a "maximal" triangle (a triangle with infinitely long sides), a circle (whose center is everywhere and circumference is nowhere), and a sphere (made of infinitely large triangles).

"It is now evident," he writes, "why from the potency [*posse*] of a simple line there first arises a simple triangle (as regards polygons), then a simple circle, and then a simple sphere; and we do not arrive at other than these elemental figures which are disproportional to one another in finite things and which enfold within themselves all figures."[52] In other words, a continuous line or flow of force ("*Posse* of All Power")[53] can be unfolded into the three infinite lines of a triangle, which can then be rotated into a circle of triangular slices, which can then be further rotated into an infinite sphere.

For Cusa, a static geometry on its own is quite literally impotent (*im-posse*). Only through the continuous *movement* of enfolding (*complicare*) and unfolding (*explicare*) is it possible for oneness to be a complex or manifold "which enfolds all things in its simplicity of oneness."[54] Cusa's theological geometry therefore requires it to be kinetic. As God moves the world, so he is moved by it. "Your seeing is your moving. Therefore you are moved with me and never cease from moving so long as I am moved.[55] . . . You are moved with all that are moved and stand with all that stand."[56] For Cusa, God is both the mover and the moved insofar as "absolute possibility [*posse*] is God."[57] God is the pure power or force that enfolds or envelops all of being as its oneness and that unfolds or explicates all beings in their manifold motion.

Since all the folds of being are of one and the same absolute tensional surface that moves together without change of relation, there is no motion. However, insofar as the folds unfold themselves at different levels, degrees, or regions of being, there is motion. "There is, therefore, no simply maximum motion, since it coincides with rest. And no motion is absolute, for absolute motion is rest and is God and enfolds all motions."[58] Instead, unfolding is simply "contracted according to a greater and lesser, between the simply maximum and the simply minimum, according to their own degrees."[59]

This movement of folding and unfolding is defined according to a single, primary, and pure power or *posse*. "By 'Posse Itself' is signified the three and one God, whose name is the 'Omnipotent' or the 'Posse of All Power,' with whom all things are possible and nothing impossible, who is the strength of the strong and the power of powers."[60] Thus, for Cusa, force becomes the primary ontotheological determination of being, but it also relies on a fundamentally kinetic account of geometric folding, which privileges the triangle as the simplest measure of all triune beings defined by an external, internal, and interrelational force.

From the fifteenth century onward, the doctrine of the Trinity retained its status as Christian orthodoxy in the West. Most major early modern philosophers, like Hobbes,[61] Descartes,[62] and Leibniz,[63] phrase the problem slightly differently, but in the end all accept the orthodox position of homoousia: "one substance, three hypostases."[64] Even Spinoza, who was Jewish, followed a similar Trinitarian logic developed by Henry of Ghent (c. 1217–1293) and Duns Scotus (1266–1308) to resolve the ontological problem of how there can be one substance or God and yet many attributes and modes.[65] Ghent's and Scotus's ideas of "intentional distinction" (Ghent) and "formal distinction" (Scotus) allowed Spinoza to argue that God was one with respect to a numerical distinction and yet multiple with respect to an intentional or formal distinction in the attributes and modes of God.

However, this resolution is not kinetically different from that originally proposed by the Early Church Fathers' idea that the Trinity was numerically and substantially one but modally three. As Tertullian writes, "It is not by [numerical] division that He is different, but by *distinction*; because the Father is not the same as the Son, since they differ one from the other in *the mode of their being*."[66] In addition to this, Spinoza also uses the concept of folding, deployed throughout the history of Trinitarianism from the Early Church Fathers to Nicholas of Cusa.[67]

CONCLUSION

In the physics and theology of the medieval and early-modern periods, from about the fifth century to around the early eighteenth, the description of natural and divine force rises to a new place of ontological primacy and follows a similarly tensional regime of motion.

However, alongside this change in the dominant description of being from eternal to dynamic, another transformation took place in the domain of graphism: the invention of the book. Just as in the case of speech and writing, the emergence of the book is neither a simple cause of ontological description nor simply an effect or neutral tool through which such description occurred. Rather, the two kinomena of theological description and bibliographic inscription are bound together or coordinated in the same kinetic regime of tensional motion, as we will see in the next chapters.

III
Graphos

CHAPTER 28

The Book I

Manuscript

During the medieval period, being was predominantly described as a tensional, triangulated, trifolded, and relational force. Such descriptions, however, also made use of a new material technology of inscription with the same tensional regime: the book. Without assuming any direct causation, the following two chapters show a clear similarity of kinetic structure in both theological description and its technology of inscription during this time.

The new kind of kinography that rose to dominance in the West around the fourth and fifth centuries was called "bibliography." The rise of bibliography, or book writing, functioned according to two major kinographic operations: the binding of the book and the comprehension (or kinetic tension between author and the reader) of the book. Between the fifth and eighteenth centuries, two major book technologies were used in theological descriptions: the manuscript codex, from the fifth to fifteenth centuries, and the printed codex, from the fifteenth up to the eighteenth century.

The two historical periods are different from each other in significant ways,[1] but kinetically speaking they both perform the same kinographic operations and move or circulate according to the same regime of tensional motion, albeit to different degrees. The introduction of the printing press, for example, is not a difference in kinetic kind from the manuscript codex but in kinetic degree, as we will see below.

In order to demonstrate the tensional motion of these kinographic operations, which were coordinated with the tensional kinetics of the medieval theology of force, this chapter and the next proceed historically. The current chapter looks at the twin operations of binding and comprehension in the manuscript codex, while the next chapter looks at the same operations in the printed codex.

THE MANUSCRIPT CODEX

As its name suggests, a manuscript is any graphism that has been written (script) by hand (*manu*). This includes tallies, tokens, tablets, parchments, and, in its largest definition, all manual graphism before the introduction of the printing press. Therefore, for technical reasons and to avoid confusion in this chapter, I do not refer to "the manuscript" but instead to "the manuscript codex" or "bibliographism" to indicate the specific technical apparatus of the codex that emerged in late Roman antiquity and quickly rose to graphic dominance around the fourth and fifth centuries CE.

The word "codex" comes from the Latin word *caudex*, meaning "trunk of a tree, block of wood," and is defined as a group of bound pages. The name *caudex* refers to the use of wooden blocks to hold the pages together and to the early Roman practice of binding wax-covered wooden tablets (*pugillares*) together in a series.[2] The later *pugillares membranei*, however, were made from folded parchment (animal-hide membranes) and were the first form of the protocodex, attested to by the first-century CE poet Martial to describe gifts of literature that Romans exchanged during the festival of Saturnalia.[3] These early notebooks remained in relatively marginal use except by early Christians[4] until around the fourth century, when they finally became as prevalent as scrolls.[5] They completely replaced scrolls by the sixth century throughout the Christianized Greco-Roman world.[6]

Binding

The rise of the codex in the West to virtually exclusive dominance introduced a whole new tensional regime of motion into writing, reading, and speaking through the kinographic operation of binding. The operation of binding that occurred in the materiality of the book itself was composed of four component operations in the material, folds, covering, and punctuation of the bibliographic apparatus.

Material. After the fall of the Roman Empire in the fifth century CE, papyrus became difficult to obtain due to a lack of direct or imperial contact with Egypt. This led to an almost exclusive reliance on parchment as a writing material. The shift in the material composition of the recording surface also expressed a shift in the material-kinetic regime of the technical object itself. For example, with the introduction of the early codex, the recording surface was no longer defined by the centrifugal pounding of a surface from above but by the tensional stretching of the animal hide from the sides. The ancient and centrifugal manufacture of papyrus in Europe relied on a centralized and imperial connection with Egypt in the form of slave harvests of papyrus, and the vertical force of the hammer to pound and press the surface of identical papyrus strips into conformity, uniformity, and homogeneity with one another, thus squeezing the liquids outward centrifugally from the center of the plants with the press as it dried.

In contrast, the medieval tensional manufacture of parchment relied on fixed legal or feudal contracts (rigid links) with individual and regional agriculturalists for sheep and goats. Instead of pounding the surface from above, the animal pelt was stretched according to a tensional network of numerous horizontal cords or ropes tied to a stretching frame. Once scraped, the skins produced a natural form of glue (collagen) that allowed them to keep their shape after drying but still retain flexibility.

Folding. Once the parchment was stretched, it was cut into strips that were folded into a quire, from the Latin *quaterni*, "four at a time." That is, four sheets of parchment were stacked and folded down the middle and stitched together to produce eight leaves, or folios, and sixteen pages. The quire is a onefold-manifold, a "complex simplicity," as the theologians say, bound in linked tension with itself. To turn a page of a book is thus to unfold or explicate what is complicated or enfolded in the whole. Each page turn is both an unfolding to the open page and an enfolding of the rest of the book as hidden pages. Multiple quires are compiled into a continuous manifold bound together and apart from one another. To turn a leaf is to pivot on a rigid, linked tension of bound leaves. The folios, from the Latin *foluim*, meaning "leaves," are bound in tension with one another in the book, just like the leaves of the tree (*caudaux*) are bound together by the tree or book. The organicism of the codex is explicit. The book is a living, natural being that, like a tree, unfolds itself from within itself according to its own inner power or vital force. The oak tree is there in the acorn, simply waiting to be unfolded.

This is in contrast to the ancient clay tablet and even the papyrus scroll, defined simply by their inorganic geometrical shape (flat tablet, rolled scroll). The tensional fold of the codex is thus kinetically in contrast to the flat surface of the tablet awaiting inscription from above and the rolled surface of the scroll whose center is its end, its final cause, directly and continually unrolling the scroll in a linear development toward an ultimate telos. The folded tensions of the folio contrast with both the loose piles of tablets and the separate sheets of papyrus homogenized together into a single surface with glue.

While the tablet introduced a radical division of the recording surface into separate tablets, the scroll introduced a radical continuity without distinction. The book, however, allowed for both distinction and continuity through the use of a tensional folding and binding. The book is a single continuous surface folded over itself in such a way as to render its pages distinct and individually accessible. The pages are held in tension by the binding and by their ordering, but they can be unfolded and accessed individually.

Covering. Once the quires had been folded and stitched separately, they were then stitched together collectively into a single volume, or cover, by sewing them into the spine (another organic body part) of the codex. The style of the stitching and binding of early codices varied significantly, but all the methods using parchment also required a further step: the enfolding of all the quires by two pieces of wood to cover them and hold them together.[7] Each of the pieces of wood was bound by a thick, often rough layer of membrane and held to the other with some kind of clasp. Since parchment tends to dry and curl up over time, sturdy clasps were necessary to bind and hold all the pages flat.[8] In this way, the early codex was a whole complex of bound tensions and folds, just waiting to spring open and unfold when the clasp was released.

The tensional force of the codex is thus in kinetic contrast with the unbound nature of the loose tablets and even the simple continuity of papyrus. Without folding, tension, and binding, the tablet and the scroll could not be folded durably without creasing or breaking. A single broken page ruined the whole tablet or papyrus but not the book. Furthermore, as with all kinographic arts, mobility is crucial. Because of the tension of binding, the book is more compact, durable, and mobile. One can thus look at the history of kinography as a history of increasing mobility—not simply speed but the range, patterns, and qualities of motion. In each major historical change, there is a corresponding set of capacities for movement.

Punctuation. The fourth and final kinetic operation of binding is punctuation and ruling. Not only was the book a tensionally bound body of folded parchment, but even the letters on the page became increasingly bound by a grammatical regime that introduced a kinetic tension into the movement of the reader's eyes and mouth as he or she read.

The Greeks and Romans used a few minor punctuation marks, but beginning around the fifth century, when large numbers of the Bible were produced, punctuation developed dramatically. Since the Bible was meant to be read aloud, punctuation was introduced in order to help readers more easily move their eyes within the text and speak the text properly. Such early marks included indentation, various punctuation marks (*diple, paragraphos, simplex ductus*), and an early version of initial capitals (*litterae notabiliores*).

In the seventh and eighth centuries, Irish and Anglo-Saxon scribes introduced spaces between words.[9] In the late eighth century another system of punctuation emerged in the Carolingian empire in order to indicate how one's voice should be modulated when chanting the liturgy—the *positurae*—that soon found its way into all manuscripts. Punctuation thus introduced explicit relational marks into the text to indicate a new tension between sounds and the tension in one's eyes as one read and had to pause for a certain duration in the reading. Reading and speaking are material-kinetic activities, and punctuation is the law that orders the tensional relation between audiovisual motions of the performing body.

Furthermore, around this same time, codex manuscripts were "ruled" on the pages, indicating where the text should appear and for how many lines—quite literally circumscribing the audiovisual movements possible on the page. This regime of motion in the book is quite different from that of the unruled *scripta continua* of ancient documents. In most ancient texts, there is no distinction between upper- and lowercase letters, no spaces between letters, and no audiovisual instructions on how to see and speak the text. Just as the scroll demanded that the user unroll or rotate from the middle outward in a continuous, direct, and centrifugal flow from the center to the periphery, so it also demanded the complete continuity of audiovisual connection between letters and words.

WRITTEN COMPREHENSION

The second kinetic operation of tensional motion in the codex is comprehension. Comprehension, from the Latin, *com-* ("with, together") + *prehendō* ("to take hold of, grasp, seize"), is not a mentalistic activity but rather a kinetic and material activity of holding together and apart in tension. The book made possible a new graphic relation of comprehension. As a technical object, the book was thus not only defined by a kinetic tension in binding, as was demonstrated in the previous section, but it also made possible a new relationship with the reader defined by interpretation—from the Latin *interpres*, meaning "an intermediary, agent, go-between, a spokesman or messenger of God." The predominance of interpretation was made possible only with the introduction of an increased kinetic transport between the material distance between the author and reader, facilitated by an increasingly mobile intermediary or messenger: the book.

This is in contrast with the scriptographic regime of dictation that predominated in the ancient world. Scriptography was monopolized by a very small group of priests, scribes, and aristocrats who knew how to read and write. Since most early scriptography was used for internal bureaucratic purposes of accounting, calendars, laws, and eventually historical and religious records, the author and reader were likely to be the same person, or the reader could be someone directly connected with the author. Scribes recording information were directly connected to scribes reading at the command or dictation of the priest-king, who was the divine voice of God on earth.

Comprehension and interpretation were not absent from scriptography, especially toward the end of the period with the Greeks and Romans, but they played a much less significant role because most scriptography occurred as a direct dictation from God himself. In the ancient world, God, gods, or God-men on earth simply spoke directly to the scribe, whose job was simply to dictate and record the voice of God. Commands were given at the center, dictated, and then directly implemented outward and downward. This is not a metaphorical movement. From the priest-kings of Sumer and Egypt to Moses on Mount Sinai, and even Socrates's daemon, the voice of God could be directly heard, recorded, and implemented centrifugally with divine authority from the small and centralized literati outward and downward to the massive illiterate periphery.

The medieval bibliographic regime of comprehension is kinetically different than this. Although literacy was still not universal, exponentially more and different people were literate between the fifth and fifteenth centuries than in the ancient world. This was related to the fact that the material kinetics of the codex introduced a radical new mobility and durability of the recording surface. By making a larger number of recording surfaces compact through folding and binding, the book also increased its mobility: in speed, type of transport medium, and storage. For example, one person could carry numerous books by horseback more quickly, and store more of them in one place, than ever before.

Furthermore, the increased durability of the book made possible by using woodbound parchment instead of crumbly papyrus or fragile clay tablets made possible a longer kinetic duration and life span of the book than ever before. Both of these material-kinetic features of the book increased the material and temporal circulation between the author and the reader, increasing the centrality of interpretation and comprehension in kinographic circulation.

Since more writing could be in more places faster and farther apart, it could be read by more people over great distances in time and space. It was no longer the exception but the rule to read a text by an unknown and previously unconnected author. The most radical example of this is the case of God, the author. By the fifth century, God, gods, and God-men were, for the most part, no longer believed to be directly and constantly intervening on earth or dictating to scribes. God may have given Moses the commandments to radiate downward and outward from the mountaintop, and the God-man Christ may have directly dictated to the apostles, but those days were long gone. What remained by the fifth century was the Word of God as transmitted literally and kinetically over long distances and times. The great Greek and Roman philosophers and playwrights were long dead, but their writings were preserved almost exclusively on the durable parchment of the codex. Almost everything else remaining on papyrus scrolls was destroyed.

The kinetic tension of bibliography is this: the book comprehends or holds together (and apart) kinetically distant authors and readers with one another. The book's incredible new power of circulation and mobility made it possible for an author to inscribe it at one point in the circulation and transport it, and then further along for the book to enter into a new circulation of reading and/or reproduction and possible further transportation. The book thus introduced an increased tension between the points of its circulation, fixed in the rigid link of the text itself—multiple readers. The problem of interpretation and the intermediary is a part of every graphism, but in the Middle Ages it became a primary and defining feature of the bibliographic apparatus and its usage.

Therefore, in the sections that follow, the primary problem of interpretation and comprehension should be understood, despite the often mentalistic language of the authors, as a fundamentally kinetic problem of tension between author and reader made possible by the mobility and materiality of the manuscript codex itself. In particular, the kinetic operation of comprehension occurs through three major and interrelated bibliographic functions: the book of God and the book of nature, *lectio divino* (divine reading), and divine illumination.

The Book of God and the Book of Nature

As the book rose to kinographic dominance, it also became a site of inscription for ontotheological descriptions. Therefore, the first kinetic function of comprehension in the manuscript codex is related to the "duplex" or twofold structure of the book's material and kinetic composition. As the Italian theologian Saint Bonaventure (1221–1274) wrote, "There is a duplex book, the one written inside, which is the eternal art and wisdom of God, the other written outside, which is the sensible world."[10] The idea that the human relationship to God and nature is structured through and like a book (author, text, reader) follows the same kinographic movement introduced by the twofold nature of the codex page itself. The motion of reading and writing on both sides of the parchment page and the motion of turning the page—linked and folded in tension with others—transforms the ontographic process into one of kinetic *tension*, both between the page and itself (its two-sided nature connected by a stretched membrane) and between different pages (held together and apart from one another in the same continuous circulation).

The emergence of the increasingly dominant ontological description of God and nature as books occurs, unsurprisingly, precisely at the same time as the rise to dominance of the book apparatus itself: around the fifth century. In these descriptions, God and nature are not ontotheologically separate or binary but are instead, like the twofold nature of the codex page itself, two sides of the same tensional surface that holds them together and apart.

The distinction between the two books also produced a semiotic tension in the content between the *meaning* of the *Word* that must be *thought* and the *speaking* of the words, made visible by the *page* through the *sensation* of light on the body. On the one hand, the book is an inorganic body of truth, *meditātiō*, and *reflexio*. On the other hand, it is a natural and organic body with a spine, a tree trunk (*caudex*), and unfolding leaves (*folium*). Following the Greek, it is both a *morphe* (an intelligible form or text) and a *hyle* (a sensible matter or wooden tree). Comprehension is thus the holding together and apart of the two through the material-kinetic tension of the codex itself.

The earliest descriptions of God and nature as books began with the kinographic dominance of the book around the third century CE, and within the specifically Christian theological tradition of the early church fathers. The rise of the book and the rise of the hermeneutical problem in Christian theology of how to understand the twofold God-man (Christ) are two sides of the same regime of motion. Both raise the problem of comprehension and interpretation to the highest possible level. In Christian theology, God leaves us on the earth with only his Word with which to understand him in his absence. In science, nature leaves us bodies with only fluctuating appearances with which to understand their laws. The material hermeneutics of the book make it possible for the book to leave us only with the text *without its author to explain it*.

Although Greek precursors to this problem emerged toward the end of the ancient period,[11] none privileged the problem of interpretation more highly than the third-century CE Christian theologian Origen (184–253). For Origen, God not only renders himself knowable through the book of Scripture but also renders himself visible through the book of nature. Following Romans 1:20, "For the invisible things of him from the creation of the world are clearly seen, being understood by the things that are made," Origen writes, "I think that He who made all things in wisdom so created all the species of visible things upon the earth, that He placed in some of them some teaching and knowledge of things invisible and heavenly, whereby the human mind might mount to spiritual understanding and seek the grounds of things in heaven."[12] God and nature are duplex, but for Origen there is also an asymmetry between them. God is both the author of Scripture *and* of nature.

Origen is explicit about the duplex relation between author and text, God and nature. "He who believes the Scripture to have proceeded from him who is the Author of Nature may well expect to find the same sort of difficulties in it as are found in the constitution of nature,"[13] namely the difficulty of comprehension or holding together author and reader through the tension of the text.

Since the book of nature is also written by the author of Scripture, nature remains simply a visible sign referring back to the glory and power of God the author—not of nature's own creative power. The invisible is privileged over visible. "Each of the manifest things," writes Origen, "is to be related to one of those that are hidden—. . . all things visible have some invisible likeness and pattern."[14]

Tertullian (c. 155–c. 240) expresses a similar asymmetry in the kinographic comprehension of "The Book" when he writes, "We conclude that God is known first through Nature, and then again, more particularly, by doctrine; by Nature in His works, and by doctrine in His revealed word."[15] We learn of God firstly and naively through our senses of his works but more particularly through his doctrine in the Scripture.

By the fourth century there was a general consensus among Christian theologians from both East and West that while there were two books, there was only one author. The study of nature was therefore important only insofar as it edified the soul in search of salvation. Basil the Great (c. 330–379) thus declared the material world to be "a training place for rational souls and a school for attaining the knowledge of God because through the visible and perceptible objects it provides guidance to the mind for the contemplation of the invisible."[16]

Ambrose of Milan (c.339–397), the mentor of Augustine, taught similarly that "the beginning of the ways of God is in His work, so that the race of men might learn by Him to follow the ways of the Lord and to perform the works of God." "Heaven and earth," Ambrose declares, "are the sum of the visible things which appear not only as the adornment of this world but also as a testimony of invisible things and as an evidence of things that are not seen."[17]

For the church fathers, what is important about nature is not how it works or the causes of its motion, but what it signifies about the divine author. Nature, like a text, is made of signs and has a meaning; therefore, the same methods of theological exegesis applied to the book of God can be applied to the book of nature with the same outcome: a better comprehension of the divine.

For example, Origen argues that visible patterns in nature are evidence of a common likeness given by the creator.[18] Man is the image of God,[19] the divine idea made visible on earth. Similarly, Saint Ambrose writes that "the body of man is constructed like the world itself," and that he is "a summation of the universe."[20] Our eyes are like the sun and moon, our hair like the trees, our eyebrows twofold hedges or mountains, our nose a cavern.[21] Therefore, "we cannot fully know ourselves without first knowing the nature of all living creatures."[22]

Similarly, animals were used by the church fathers as natural signs of the passions. John Chrysostom (c. 349–407), for example, spoke of "bringing the beast under control" by "banishing the flood of unworthy passions."[23] Floodwaters and natural flows were not autonomous things but signs of spiritual chaos and appetite. However, this hermeneutical process existed only because of the tensional kinetic structure of the book itself that split the author from the reader in a very specific way.

Later, Augustine of Hippo (354–430) not only formalized Origen's theological hermeneutics, but also intensified the primacy of the specifically scriptural word as the absolute reference of all comprehension. For Origen, natural beings referred to intelligible forms or divine patterns, but for Augustine the absolute referent for all things was given by Scripture. For Augustine to be concerned with the ideal patterns of the natural world (Origen) was to still be "a slave to the sign"; it was to engage in an idolatrous "literalism" applied to objects. One therefore had to turn toward the book of nature only in order to turn away from it, and toward the spiritual interpretation of both scriptural and natural texts. "God has given us sensible signs and spoken words," Augustine writes, "to show us something of the divine."[24] From Augustine to the Renaissance, the book of nature existed only as a set of creature signs interpreted according to the scriptural syntax of the assumed authorship of God. Until the authorship of nature and a new syntax could be discovered, the book of nature remained subordinated to the book of God. This is the first kinetic function of comprehension in the manuscript codex.

Lectio Divina

The second kinetic function of comprehension in the manuscript codex was the emergence of *lectio divina*. Alongside the early church fathers' emphasis on the asymmetrical relationship between the visible and the invisible, and the ultimately unknowable relation to God the author, they also advocated a hermeneutical solution to this problem. If one could never know in absolute terms the divine in any direct sense, the closest knowledge one could hope to attain would be the *movement of divine interpretation itself*. This was a brilliant solution that gave both God and humans a relative autonomy but a connective, tensional, or linked autonomy through the Word of the book.

In contrast to the rationalism of Plato and Aristotle, the theological structure of Christianity did not allow for the direct comprehension of the divine but only for a tensional or mediated relationship *through the book*. What followed was an explicit change in the movement of being from being directly communicated to being indirectly interpreted. Again, this is not a representationally metaphorical or false movement. The entire kinetic practice of reading, writing, praying, and speaking really changed. Bodies moved differently, even if the descriptions of these motions rely on the metaphysical language of force. The emergence of the book, the architecture of the cell, feudal juridical contracts, and so on all describe a new kind of material change in the circulation of matter.

However, if direct access became barred in Christianity, it was now the linkage, intermediary, or tensional connection *through the materiality of book* that took on ontological primacy. The act of interpretation, reading, contemplating, mediating, and so on itself became the divine act: the *lectio divina*.

Lectio divina, also called *lectio sacra, sacra pagina*, or *lectio sacra*, emerged with the rise of the book around the third through fifth centuries with the early church fathers and became the dominant bibliographic practice throughout the Middle Ages. *Lectio divina* was even reaffirmed as recently as 1965 in a decree of the Second Vatican Council. Although practiced differently throughout the Middle Ages in different places, *lectio divina* was based on the almost universal bibliographic practice of speaking manuscripts out loud. The kinetic activity or performance of holding the book, reading, speaking, and listening emerged within the same regime of motion of the hermeneutic of *lectio divina*.

One of the earliest church fathers to describe the methodology of *lectio divina* was Origen. As part of his hermeneutics of the books of God and nature, Origen treated Scripture itself as a *sacrament*. "We are said to drink the blood of Christ not only in the rite of the sacraments [*non solum sacramentorum ritu*], but also when we receive his words [*sermones*], in which are life."[25] Therefore, for Origen, when we speak the Word of God we are also eating (ruminating) his body as a sacrament. In this way the Word of the book is more than the literality of what is said, just as the sacrament is more than just bread and wine. "When you devote yourself to the divine reading [*lectio divina*]," he writes, "seek the meaning of divine words which is hidden from most people."[26] The meaning of the *sacra pagina* is not literal but performed immanently *with* God.

As Cyprian of Carthage (c. 200–258) advocates, "You should apply yourself to prayer or to reading: at times you speak with God, at times he speaks with you [*Sit tibi vel oratio assidua vel lectio: nunc cum Deo loquere, nunc Deus tecum*]."[27] As you read you pray; as you pray you speak; as you speak you are with God and he is with you. In the *lectio divina*, speaking, praying, and listening all become one and the same immanent movement of the pneuma, spirit, or breath coursing through God, book, and human. As Ambrose writes, "We speak to him when we pray; we listen to him when we read the divine oracles."[28] The kinetic action of reading-speaking-hearing is thus inseparable from divine comprehension. The pneumatic flow of the divine moves through God, text, and body in the continuous performance of reading the book out loud.

The Word is a life-giving nourishment and the cause of motion: a food, a sacrament. The divine pneuma, or breath of speech, is therefore something that flows from the divine author through his inscription of the book's surface, and is incorporated into the body by "chewing" or speech, and eventually eaten, digested, and incorporated into the body through a metabolic kinesis. God does not speak directly through us but only indirectly *as us* through the *lectio divina*, the *oratio*, the *ruminatio*.

As the Christian theologian Saint Jerome (c. 347–420) writes, "The soul is fed each day with *Lectio Divina*."[29] The Latin word *rūminātio* means both to chew over again, or to fold over in one's mouth and/or mind, and to meditate through repetition. Meditation-prayer-reading is therefore "intent on the food of *Lectio Divina*," as Ambrose writes.[30] "*Lectio Divina* raises us up," Augustine writes, "so that you may cultivate the fear of God through *Lectio*

Divina and serious conversation."[31] For Augustine, reading is therefore a kind of cultivation of a force of life. We do not control the force or power of the divine, but by cultivating it we can be nourished on it by folding its flows over in our mouth and circulating it through our bodies (see Figure 28.1).

The book itself already shares in the same kind of kinetic rumination or folding over itself in the form of bound pages repetitively folded and unfolded along the tension of the spine. The body of the book is an organic body, a nourishing body. We chew its leaves and circulate them. To read is to breathe. In breathing the word of the text, one does not represent it literally or symbolically but expressively in the form of a performative rumination or mediation. The movement is a tensional one, since, in the *lectio*, author and reader do not move as a simple unity or as simply separate, but as a linked motion "with" one another, *through the book*, as Cyprian says.

During the monastic period, Saint Benedict of Nursia (c. 480–543) was one of the first to institutionalize *lectio divina* within the monastery, a practice that would later spread throughout Europe. Within the Benedictine rules, the life of a monk was to "pray and work [*Ora et labora*]." In addition

Figure 28.1 *Lectio Divina*
Source: St. John Eating the Book, no. 28 from "The Apocalypse of Angers," 1373–1387 (tapestry), Nicolas Bataille (fl. 1363–1400)/Musee des Tapisseries, Angers, France/Giraudon/The Bridgeman Art Library.

to manual labor during the day, monks had to learn to read and study grammar in order to practice *lectio divina*. In Rule Chapter 48, Benedict writes that "idleness is the enemy of the soul. Therefore the brethren should have specified periods of manual labor as well as for prayerful reading [*lectio divina*]."[32] More specifically, "from the fourth hour until about the sixth let them apply themselves to reading [*lectio divina*]."

In Chapter 38, appropriately, Benedict writes, "The meals of the sisters should not be without reading." Each week a designated person would read during dinner while everyone else remained in silent contemplation. Before reading the sister was to say the following prayer: "O Lord, open my lips, and my mouth shall declare Your praise." The practice of reading and eating at the same time was no accident. Those in attendance ruminated on the Word of God. As they chewed their food they circulated the sound in their meditating bodies. They internalized the sound as they internalized the food and were nourished. The movement of nourishment was tensional and indirect; it occurred through the metabolic medium of food digestion and the kinetic movement of chewing-folding or rumination. The book bound the monks to God, since God did not directly nourish them.

In the twelfth century, Guigo II, a Carthusian monk, formalized the practice of *lectio divina* into four movements up "The Ladder of Monks." The four movements precisely followed the kinometabolic circulation of sacramental food. In the first movement we "bite" off from the book by reading [*lectio*]; in the second "we begin to chew it and break it with mind and reason"[33] in meditation [*meditatio*]; in the third we savor its essence in the speaking [*oratio*]; and in the fourth we finally digest and metabolize it in contemplation [*contemplatio*].[34] In all four stages there is a kinetic development of the Holy Spirit. "The Holy Spirit," Guigo writes, "moves us to good and recalls us from evil." Precisely because the relation between God and human is no longer direct and immediate, there are kinetic alignments or ladders that must hold us together and apart. To comprehend is to use the book as a ladder or transport medium by which the force of the Holy Spirit *moves* us to reach the divine.

Kinetic Analysis

The practice of *lectio divina* precisely describes a regime of tensional circulation. First, God is suffused with the Word as pure audibility. In the beginning, audibility precedes that which is audible in the form of an *internal* circulation. "In the beginning was the Word, and the Word was with

God, and the Word was God."[35] From the pure sonic unity of God's audibility, a flow of sound escapes or is *externalized* in the form of a flow or kinophonic wave.

Second, this externalized flow of sound is incarnated and inscribed on earth as the logos (Christ) and written in the folds of the book. Third, this kinophonic flow of sound enters the mouth and ears of the readers as they bite off a piece of this flow and fold it over in their mouths, internalizing, resonating, and eventually folding it over (ruminating) into their bodies as a form of constitutive nourishment.

God does not speak directly to the listener but makes himself heard *through* the interrelational phonographic inscription of the logos or Christ. The word incarnate is the book just as it is Christ. *Lectio divina* thus relies on the triple fold of external, internal, and interrelational motion within the same continuous movement of tensional circulation. The flows or waves of sound permeate everything like the Holy Spirit, pneuma, or speaking breath, but also differentiate themselves within this pure continuity into kinetic regions of internal and external motion held together and apart by the flows themselves.

The focus of *lectio divina* is thus on the *rumination of kinophonic flows*, and it therefore also entails a theory of divine illumination that describes the nature of the *kinoptic flows* of divine light, as described in the next section.

Divine Illumination

The third kinetic function of comprehension in the manuscript codex is the coemergence of divine illumination, which is related to *lectio divina* insofar as it provides a kinetic explanation of how the author and reader remain separate but connected by a third flow of light between them. Just as the natural lighting of the scriptorium illuminates the book, so a divine light illuminates the mind. The theory of divine illumination is therefore a theory of the kinoptic in-between area or zone of transport between God and human beings. The flows of light are what hold them together and apart in comprehension. God does not directly speak to us, but rather releases a flow of divine light that reveals what was always there but previously hidden away in the dark.

In the Latin West, it was Augustine who played the decisive role in formulating the doctrine of illumination: "The mind needs to be enlightened by light from outside itself, so that it can participate in truth, because it is not itself the nature of truth. You will light my lamp, Lord."[36]

The human mind cannot see the nature of truth or the Word on the page of the book without the lamp lit by God. God is not reducible to the light, but by releasing a flow of light he illuminates a shared, linked realm where the truth can appear. "If we both see that what you say is true, and we both see that what I say is true, then where do we see that? Not I in you, nor you in me, but both of us in that unalterable truth that is above our minds."[37] Truth therefore occurs not simply in one mind or another, but in a zone of light. Illumination is therefore a fluid (waves of light) and atmospheric condition of visibility within which the text can become visible. The light itself is not what is visible, but the flows of light within which the visible, like the text, becomes visible.

The natural world and our senses are constantly changing, but the very conditions of their visible changing do not change: light itself, visibility itself. Therefore, "everything that the bodily senses attain, that which is also called sensible, is incessantly changing. . . . But what is not constant cannot be perceived; for that is perceived that is comprehended in knowledge. But something that is incessantly changing cannot be comprehended."[38] For Augustine, comprehension is therefore a fundamentally mediated process. It occurs in the light, through the light, under the condition of the light—but never directly. The visible objects change but like the book, the condition of visibility (the meaning of the author) does not. God's rays permeate and infiltrate our minds. They do not tell us what to think but merely light the lamp by which to see the truth on the pages of our mind (see Figure 28.2).

Kinetic Analysis

Divine illumination therefore follows the same tensional operations as *lectio divina*, but with respect to kinoptic flows instead of kinophonic flows. First, God is suffused with pure and perfectly circular (or spherical) inner light, and as pure visibility is invisible as such. From this pure visibility he releases an externalized flow or ray of light outward. Second, this externalized flow of light illuminates the medium of the created text or Word within the folds of the book. Third, this flow of light enters through the eyes and into the mind of the reader, folding itself up into a pure interiority, such that the reader discovers it as "their own."

Divine illumination therefore relies on a triple fold within the same continuous movement of tensional circulation. The flows of light permeate everything, like the Holy Spirit but also differentiate with its pure

Figure 28.2 Divine Illumination
Source: Tolle Lege. Iconographia magni patris Aurelli Augustini: Hipponensis episcopi, et ecclesiae doctoris excellentissimi/George Maigret; Hieronymus Petrie. 1624. page 3. Courtesy of Digital Library @ Villanova University.
Credit: St. John Eating the Book, no. 28 from "The Apocalypse of Angers," 1373–1387 (tapestry), Nicolas Bataille (fl. 1363–1400)/Musee des Tapisseries, Angers, France/Giraudon/The Bridgeman Art Library.

continuity three folds or kinetic regions held together and apart by the interrelational flow itself. This idea of divine illumination remained dominant up to the period of the Renaissance, after which a theory of natural illumination emerged and rivaled that of the divine, as we see in the next chapter, analyzing the kinetics of the printing press.

CHAPTER 29

The Book II

Printing Press

While the printing press undoubtedly introduced several novelties into graphic and social circulation, it was *not* the bringer of a radically new kinographic regime. Kinetically speaking, it was a modification and intensification of the already dominant tensional regime of the codex. Just because there were more books in more hands does not mean the regime of motion changed, only that it was intensified and in some ways modified. In regard to intensification, we can cite the obvious quantitative increase in the production of books: from the 2.7 million manuscripts produced in western Europe by the end of the fourteenth century to the addition of another 328 Million by the end of the seventeenth century, largely, although not exclusively, due to the printing press.[1]

But the printed codex is still a codex, and it therefore follows much of the same material-kinetic functions as the manuscript codex. The printed codex thus secured and intensified what the manuscript codex had already begun: the dominance of a new bibliographic regime of motion defined by the primary features of binding and comprehension.

BINDING

As a codex, the printed book followed many of the same basic material-kinetic operations as the manuscript codex: It was created through a process of binding. The bookbinding process remained only slightly modified from earlier medieval methods. Pages (folios) were folded into quires, sewn together, and then bound with a spine. Leaves or folios were held in tension around the central pivot of the spine and had writing on both sides. Punctuation, grammar, and ruling only increased over the next several hundred years.

Furthermore, the emergence of printed codices did not completely replace manuscript codices or other manuscript forms. The two coexisted throughout the medieval and early-modern periods. The bibliographic apparatus is additive, not eliminative. However, in addition to the basic tensional structuring of bookbinding, the printing press introduced several further modifications as well as qualitative and quantitative intensifications of this same regime of motion.

The Press

The first kinetic operation of the printed codex is pressing. The printing press is a mechanical device, and like many medieval mechanical devices, it was structured according to a series of tensionally linked parts held together by pivots, slides, and gearlike screws. The previous chapters commented on the privileged kinetic status of mechanism during this time. In Europe, beginning around the fourteenth century, a wave of interest in mechanisms such as clocks began to influence an entire generation of philosophers, astronomers, theologians, and others.

Machines described cosmological motions. The universe is not only structured like a clock machine, a series of rigidly linked parts set in motion by a power source, but the clock itself is already structured like other medieval mechanical devices that were introduced into Europe around the same time: the horizontal loom (eleventh century), the paper mill (thirteenth century), the compound crank and stern-mounted rudders (1180s), the spinning wheel (thirteenth century), and the wine press (twelfth century). Although most of these devices, including the wine press, originated in the ancient world, it is only in the medieval world that their form of motion became an *ontological* model of motion. The Renaissance was therefore not merely a repetition of the ancient world, but also a transformation of it, modeled on its tensional machines.

The Gutenberg printing press (1440) was essentially a modified screw press for pressing wine, which in its basic form had been used for centuries to press grapes, olives, and other fruits. The material-kinetic motion of the screw press is defined by the exertion of a rigid force on an object by folding two objects over each other and holding them together and apart, just enough to apply a force without crushing the object.

In other words, the press held the object in a proper tension or relation without allowing it free motion or destroying it. More specifically, Gutenberg developed a bifolding dual-plate system, held together by the rigid link of a pivot or hinge, that would allow the tension to be distributed evenly along the paper held between the "platen."

Using a wine press to print letters on a page took what was an ontologically insignificant material motion associated with drunkenness and elevated it to the most ontologically significant motion of the time. In both cases the model of tensional fluid extraction remained the same, but the fluid itself was transformed from a material one to a theological one. Gutenberg is explicit about this, writing, "Yes, it is a press, certainly, but a press from which shall *flow in inexhaustible streams* the most abundant and most marvelous liquor that has ever flowed to relieve the thirst of men. Through it, God will spread His word; *a spring of pure truth shall flow from it*; like a new star it shall scatter the darkness of ignorance, and cause a light hithertofore unknown to shine among men."[2]

This should not be read as mere poetic hyperbole. As we have just seen, God communicates his word through *literal flows* of light in illumination, breath through speech, and sound through hearing. These are the real material flows necessary for reading the book. God communicates through a fluid dynamic stream of pneuma, breath, Holy Spirit, and on waves of light. God the author does not speak to us directly, but we indirectly drink and eat his Word by chewing his text in our mouths.

In this short passage, Gutenberg succinctly shows the relation between the three kinetic elements that define the tension of bibliography: the natural flows of liquor with which we drink-read (reader), the force or meaning of the Word as we hear it (text), and the divine origin of the message in the celestial stars (author). Just as the ancients drank from the material flows of wine and became stupefied, Gutenberg imagines we will now drink the divine flows of truth and become illuminated.

Interestingly, however, the theological force of the Word is made possible only on the material condition of the press itself. In fact, the description of the corporeality of the press itself already gives us a sense of this implicit relation modeled on the book. The organicism of the book—wood, leaves, tree, spine, and so on—becomes coordinated to the organicism of the body of the printing press, with its parts named after those of the body. "The body" "the head," the "cheek," and the "feet" of the press all express this organicism. The printing press is a natural body, literally made of wood. Just like the book, the press is natural but makes possible signs of the divine. However, while the manuscript codex was gently touched on the surface of the page with watery ink, the press intensifies this significantly, as can be seen in its kinetic operations.

The Letter

The second kinetic operation of the printed codex is typographic. Movable type emerged in Europe around the twelfth century.[3] Just as the manuscript codex introduced new tensional relations between words on the page through ruling, punctuation, spacing, and so on, so the printed codex intensified this movement by separating the letters themselves from one another, from the page, and from the hand. By isolating individual letters in the form of punch-cut metal, typography made possible a new uniformity and cellular individuation of the components of the text. In turn, this made possible an increasingly tensional relation between distinct molded letters inside the typesetting frame. Instead of *continua scripta* or even *scripta regula*, the printing presses unleashed from the process a flow of liquid metal molded into a discrete letter or cellular individual.

The tensional process of typesetting is composed of four kinetic operations. First, one carves or punch-cuts a letter into a hard piece of uniformly sized metal. Second, one presses this hard piece of metal into a softer piece of metal called the matrix, from the Latin word *matrix*, meaning "uterus, womb, dam (nonhuman female animal kept for breeding), source, and origin," and from the Latin word *māter*, meaning "mother." From this same Latin root also comes the word "matter." The matrix thus functions as a mold or negative image of the letter.

The image here is thoroughly Platonic. The master craftsman makes a model, impresses it onto the feminine receptacle (the *chora*), and generates a copy, image, or simulacra: the text. However, what is added to this description by typesetting is the liquid medium poured into the mold and held by the tensional force by casting. The ancient scroll is simply inscribed, but the medieval print book is typeset with cast letters of liquid metal.

This difference is clearly demonstrated in the third kinetic operation of typesetting: casting. The matrix is inserted into the bottom half of a hand mold, a tensional clamping-folding mechanism held together by a hinge-linkage. With the matrix tightly enclosed, liquid metal is poured through a small hole in the top of the hand mold. When the metal cools, it is trimmed and cut into a homogenous length with the other letters. While the manuscript codex introduced the first individualization of letters through punctuation and spacing, the printed codex intensified this process further by molding or normalizing each letter within the confined cell of the disciplinary hand mold. Typography is not the cause of social cellularity, or the other way around, but both share the same kinetic regime of cellularity, interiority, confinement, and molding. To the monastic images of the cellular interior, the prison, the school, the hospital, military barracks, and so on, we should also add the printing press.

Finally, the fourth kinetic operation in typography is the tensional locking in and binding of all the ordered letters into a frame, "bed," or "chase," from the Latin word *capiō*, meaning to "capture, seize, or take." The letters are laid in the bed, sandwiched between the hinged platen, and pressed into the paper. The kinetic description of the typographic process is now complete: the motherly body of nature (press) has within it a nonhuman womb (matrix), which is impressed with the craftsman's model (punch cut), filled with a fluid, and laid into a "bed" frame where she is captured, held in tension, seized (chase), and finally pressed. The materiality and kinetic structure of the printing press is thus based on an organic model of biological reproduction.

The printing press therefore doubles the motion of the book itself, but this time the process of inscription is different from the earlier manuscript process. This time there are two authors that precede the book: the male craftsman who makes the punch cut and the female author whose body (printing press) is the womb or receptacle (matrix) for a flow of mediating fluid (liquid metal and liquid ink).

The movement of the press is therefore no longer subordinated to the ancient centrifugal motion of the incision or stamp from above (despot), but instead takes on an autonomy of its own, following the horizontal tensional relation between letters (individuals) in the cellular frame or grid and squeezed between the linked, pivoted, vertical platen. Instead of a binary of stamp and stamped, there is a trinity between the two platen linked together by the rigid pivot, with the paper and flow of ink between them.

Paper and Ink

The introduction of paper, made from cloth and/or wood pulp, dramatically increased the mobility and circulation of the book. While the parchment of the manuscript codex was by far superior in strength, paper was eventually cheaper and lighter in weight. The usage of paper in the printed codex was made possible by the introduction of mechanical paper mills in thirteenth-century Europe. Although paper had been in existence well before this time, it was only with the introduction of a new tensional mechanical motion of filtering, pressing, and drying that paper could be used to mass produce the printed codex. Instead of the tensional stretching of an animal hide, the paper mill introduced a new tension between individual vegetable cellulose fibers themselves as they linked together across a mesh screen. When the microlinkages dried they formed a network of cellular connections bound by the frame.

Ink, too, became more tensional and rigid in its relation to the press and paper. Previous inks, usually made from soot, gum, and water, were too runny and would not hold a surface tension between the letter and the paper, leaking flows of ink all over the paper and warping it. Previous inks held a tension to the parchment page, but not a tension between letterpress and absorbent paper. Gutenberg invented an oil-based ink that held a higher surface tension on the paper and did not run or warp the paper. Instead of staining the paper, it "stuck" or "held" onto the paper like a varnish.

PRINTED COMPREHENSION

After binding, the second major tensional motion in the printed codex is comprehension. Comprehension, or the holding together in tension of the kinetic difference between the author and the reader through the circulation of the text, is the central kinetic problem of bibliography. For the manuscript codex, this problem was shaped by the singularity of the hand of the author. The text of the manuscript was radically unique and expressed something about the divinity of the author himself.

However, this problem took on an additional dimension with the introduction of the second author: the printing press of Mother Nature. With the introduction of a second author and standardized font types, the singularity of the divine author (in the form of a unique hand) was divided into two authors who spoke in the same voice. And this same voice was increasingly the voice that human authors spoke with when their works were printed.

In other words, the uniformity of printed text only increased the general equivalence and univocality of the Word such that a visual difference could not be discerned between the text of God, nature, and man. All now spoke with *the same text*. Far from resolving the problem of comprehension, this only intensified it by multiplying authors and readers who were now separated from one another through the mediating linkage of the book. This defined a triple tension: (1) between the authors (God, nature, man), then (2) between the authors and readers, and finally (3) between the readers and other readers. If all spoke in the same voice (print), what precisely was the status of the reading-speaking voice itself? Whose voice was it performing?

The kinetic operation of printed comprehension thus occurs through three major and interrelated bibliographic functions: the book of nature and the book of God, silent reading, and natural illumination.

The Book of Nature and the Book of God

The books of God and nature emerged at the same time as the book. Both describe a tensional and kinetically mediated relationship between author and reader. However, while the manuscript codex acknowledged only one divine author and two texts, Word and nature, the printed codex acknowledged two authors (God and Nature) and only one univocal text.

Furthermore, in the case of the manuscript codex, the body of the book is the organic tree, with leaves and spine, while in the case of the printed codex, the body of the organic tree book is the product of a larger Mother Nature who operates according to mechanical laws and creates through an exertion of force (press). Mother Nature is the author, the printing press, while the book is the natural product, tree, or wood produced according to her tensional movements of pressing.

This transition in the structure of bibliographic comprehension from single authorship to dual authorship emerged around the period of the Renaissance (1050 to 1250) and became increasingly dominant until around the eighteenth century. We can see this shift toward the importance of the book of nature, explicitly in the writings, among other thinkers, of the great German Renaissance abbess Hildegard of Bingen (1098–1179) when she writes, "We are strengthened and brought to our souls' salvation by the five senses. We can know the whole world through our sight, understand through our hearing, distinguish it by our sense of smell . . . dominate by our touch, and in this way come to know the true God, author of all creation."[4] This position is quite different from that of the early church fathers, who argued that the senses were only signs defined by Scripture, and as such had no direct connection to God. For Hildegard, however, sensation is not a distraction, it is a way to know God, the author of all creation. In other words the text of creatures and the text of the Scripture both speak in the same authorial voice. Thus, we can come to know God equally through the Scripture or through his sensuous creatures.

Hildegard's contemporary Bernard of Clairvaux (1090–1153) agreed, perhaps intensifying the point that "there is no access open to us, except through the body. . . . The spiritual creature, therefore, which we are, must necessarily have a body, without which, indeed, it can by no means obtain [divine] knowledge."[5] Therefore, it is not simply through the mind *or* through the body that God is known. The body, as the support of the mind, becomes the entry point and condition of all further knowledge.

Following the empiricism of Albert the Great (c.1200–1280), his student Thomas Aquinas agreed that "all our knowledge takes its rise from sensation," and that "it is the knowledge we have of creatures that enables us to use words to refer to God."[6] The sensation of nature is primary, and creatures are thus the primary condition for interpretation. As John Scotus Eriugena writes, "As through sense perception one comes to a concept, so through the creature one comes back to God."[7] While for Augustine it is God who makes possible our knowledge of the world, for Aquinas it is the world that makes possible our knowledge of God.[8] This inversion is kinetically crucial.

Throughout the twelfth and thirteenth centuries, a new kinetic description was required to deal with the existence of nature the author. Hugh of St. Victor (c. 1096–1141), for example, describes nature as a machine: "The visible world is this machine."[9] Arnold of Bonneval describes nature as a great body and nature's creatures as her body parts: "God ordered the things of nature like the members of a great body."[10] Alan of Lille (c. 1128–1202/1203) describes nature as the "child of God and Mother of things."[11] All these descriptions, as we have seen, follow the same tensional motion described by the mechanical printing techniques developed around the same time. Nature is an organic unity following mechanical laws of expression.

Around the twelfth century, natural sensation and creatures not only provide foundational access to God, but nature itself begins to do the same according to its *own authorship* as the "mother" or "laws" of connection between natural creatures themselves. Thus, in the thirteenth century, Bonaventure distinguishes between natural *similitudines* that connect created things, and divine *similitudines* that connect creatures with God.[12] Similarly, Aquinas argues for the existence of natural *similitudinem* that exemplify certain natural tendencies with respect to nature itself. Natural things, he writes, "have a relation to one another, and to Him [God]."[13] There are therefore two authors with their own styles and *similitudines*: on the one hand, the divine book written "by the finger of God," as Hugh of St. Victor says,[14] and on the other hand, "the book of creatures given to us for reading," as Vincent of Beauvais and Alan of Lille argue.[15] In the book of nature, natural objects are formed like letters—the indivisible parts of syllables, as William of Conches writes.[16]

Accordingly, nature was increasingly treated as a second author worthy of a separate hermeneutical study modeled on that of the divine book. Honorius Augustodunensis (1080–1154) argued that there were therefore two hermeneutics: the comprehension of the created order (nature), and the comprehension of the divine text (God).[17] Just as one searched for patterns, meaning, and laws in God's book, one must now search for the same in nature's book.[18] A speck of dust, Robert Grosseteste (c. 1175–1253) observes, "is an image of the whole universe" and "a mirror of the creator."[19] Similarly, Hugh of St. Victor writes, "every nature teaches man; every nature reproduces its essential form."[20]

Beginning in the twelfth and thirteenth centuries, the study of the book of nature began to become a study in its own right. Hugh of St. Victor in particular pushed this radical line beyond the Augustinian importance of "things as well as words" to the conclusion that things are significant in their own right.[21] William of Conches likewise expressed contempt for those who would perpetuate the Augustinian indifference to science: "Ignorant themselves of the forces of nature and wanting to have company in their ignorance, they don't want people to look into anything; they want us to believe like peasants and not to ask the reason behind things."[22]

The study of nature thus became a thoroughly theological and hermeneutical enterprise. "Thereafter, in the schools natural philosophy was increasingly integrated into the Christian scholarly endeavour. In the renaissance of the twelfth century we see a religiously-motivated indifference to the natural world transformed into a religiously-motivated quest for knowledge. Alongside the words inscribed by God upon the human heart and on the sacred page of scripture, stands the book of nature. The search for truth required the diligent study of both books."[23]

Legere in Silentio

Alongside the rise of the natural sciences, the rise of silent reading also began to take on kinographic dominance. This rise occurred coextensively with the other kinotechnical and hermeneutical movements described in the previous sections: the introduction of tensional mechanical systems into western Europe, including the wine press, clock, and paper mill; the introduction of movable type; paper; and the study of nature as an author. All had precursors elsewhere and anterior, but all attained a new privileged kinetic and kinographic status during the Renaissance.

The old thesis, advanced by Marshall McLuhan and repeated by Cecil Clough, Pierre Francastel, Walter Ong, and Elizabeth Eisenstein,[24] that the medieval practice of bibliography was primarily oral until the invention of the printing press has now been shown to be historically inaccurate.[25] Paul Saenger's groundbreaking book *Space Between Words: The Origins of Silent Reading* provides massive historical evidence to the contrary, arguing instead that the shift from oral to silent reading began much earlier, with the introduction of word spacing in the eighth century, increasing in prevalence until the eleventh century, and achieving near ubiquity among readers between the twelfth and fifteenth centuries.

This position accords with our own kinetic one that the introduction of punctuation and spacing emerged alongside the introduction of the graphic form of the codex and its tensional motion and is not unique or exclusive to the printed codex. Punctuation, spacing, and silent reading all date back to the origins of the codex itself and its usage by the early church fathers.

Punctuation and spacing introduced a linked tension between words as they are said in the mouth—they force/allow one to pause in speech. Previously texts were most often read through continuously, just like their appearance on the page. The pause in movement also introduced a system of leaping in vision—one's eyes now began to jump and skip between blocks of text. The space between the words is the materiality of the page itself and holds the words together and apart. The page literally holds the words together in a linked conjunction as it folds. Word "blocks" become distinct from one another but related through the medium of the punctuation mark or space.

Therefore, the typographical space was not a negative introduction but a positive one that held words together and apart, giving them distinction with each other and not, as in *scripta continua*, a centrifugal flow from beginning to end, unrolling what had been rolled up and around the center unfolded toward the periphery. The reader *read* the scroll from periphery to center, but the author *created* the scroll by holding the center immobile and rolling the periphery up around it.

However, even though punctuation, spacing, and silent reading began with the rise of the manuscript codices, they did not become truly dominant kinographic movements until the Renaissance. Thus, for the early medieval period, *lectio divina* remained the dominant method of reading and remained focused on the kinophonic tensions between the mouth and the ear. During the Renaissance, however, with the dominance of silent reading, this kinophonic tension was largely although not entirely replaced by a new kinoptic tension between the eyes and the brain.

In an earlier passage from the *Confessions*, Augustine describes a moment when he experiences two reading voices simultaneously: the spoken voice and the silent voice. The coexistence of these two voices produces a tension of indecision within him. Anguished, Augustine runs under a fig tree and weeps.[26] The coexistence of the two voices introduced by silent reading thus produced an internal fold or tension between audio and visual flows, experienced by the reader as an immanent division in the stream of consciousness. One speaks in two voices at the same time: an audio voice and a visual voice.

The entire kinographics of the book was now doubled and bifurcated. God emanates two parallel flows (light and sound) that are now equally illuminated in the eye-mind and audible in the ear through the visible letter on the page and the audible sound of one's breath. Light and breath are the twin flows of the Holy Spirit incarnated in the eye and on the tongue. With the introduction of an equality between the silent voice and the spoken voice, a new audiovisual tension was introduced and the reader became not only doubled by the audiovisual dipole but tripled because the audiovisual dipole is only related through the mediation of the book itself. Thus, there is an audio-textual-visual triplet that defines the tensional movement of the speaking-reading-seeing body.

According to Augustine, the book was "invented so that we might be able to converse even with the absent." However, the material kinetics of this absence take the form not only of the tension between author-text-reader that defines the codex but also a tension between "signs of sounds" and "signs of things we think,"[27] or an audio-textual-visual triplet that defines the dual reading voices of the codex.

In the seventh century, Saint Isaac of Syria (c. 613–c. 700) described the benefits of silent reading. "'I practice silence,' he writes, 'that the verses of my readings and prayers should fill me with delight. And when the pleasure of understanding them silences my tongue, then, as in a dream, I enter a state when my senses and thoughts are concentrated. Then, when with prolonging of this silence the turmoil of memories is stilled in my heart, ceaseless waves of joy are sent me by inner thoughts, beyond expectation suddenly arising to delight my heart'."[28]

Isaac's kinetic description of silent reading is fantastic. Silent reading, according to Isaac, is precisely the opening up of one's body, through the portals of the eyes, as a vessel to contain God's optical flows or waves of light. The purpose of the vessel is not mere centripetal containment. Once received, the reader-vessel then redirects these flows internally to produce a distribution or circulation of inner enjoyment. But inner enjoyment is not an idealist category; it is, as Isaac writes, a concentration of sensation and thought. Thought itself becomes a sensation: the sense the brain has of itself as a body stimulated by the flows of light through the eye.

In contrast to the audiocentrism of *lectio divina* that privileges the movement of the tongue, Isaac proposes an optico-centrism of an "inner light" that privileges the eye and brain. In fact, it is the tongue itself that introduces turmoil and turbulence into the circulation of optical-thought. Once Isaac's tongue goes silent, his sensations and thoughts become concentrated, reorganized, and recirculated in the form of sensuous waves. The fluid dynamics of silent reading are clear: the movement of the tongue is in tension with the movement of the eye-mind. Silent reading aims to reorganize the tension around the eye-mind axis not in order to reject the senses, but to concentrate and recirculate the senses internally to extract a maximum of joy.

Thus, although word spacing began as an aid to reading aloud, it eventually gave rise to two new practices: silent copying and, paradoxically, silent reading. By breaking up the text into lines of ten to fifteen characters, scribes found that they could remember them more easily and increase the speed with which they read and copied.[29] As this technique spread, silence became a requirement in the scriptoriums. Word spacing thus gave rise to silent reading.

We can see this in the architectural changes to libraries in the twelfth and thirteenth centuries. In the early Middle Ages, library carrels were enclosed, for monks to both read aloud and dictate. By the late thirteenth century, however, libraries were relocated to central halls and "furnished with desks, lecterns, and benches where readers sat next to one another."[30] Even books themselves began to change into more visually complex objects with tables of contents, alphabetical glosses, subject indexes, running headings, and so on that were not meant to be spoken but visually glossed as references.[31]

While the rise of silent reading was at first confined largely within the ecclesiastical world, by the fourteenth century it had spread to aristocratic literate culture and eventually, with the printing press, to a larger increasingly literature popular culture, easily reaching widespread graphic dominance by the end of the seventeenth century and into the eighteenth. [32] The printing press is thus not the beginning of this transformation, but an intensification of kinetic operations that had already been bibliographically dominant for hundreds of years, like punctuation, word spacing, and silent reading.

Silent reading thus introduced a number of kinetic changes to the tensional regime inaugurated by the manuscript codex and popularized by the print codex. The bibliographic dominance of silent reading from the twelfth century onward did not eliminate the tensional structure of the codex but intensified it by proliferating it with three new graphic tensions.

The manuscript codex and *lectio divina* introduced the first major series of tensions: (1) between the author, text, and reader; (2) between the text and itself (the fold); and (3) between the reader's tongue and ear. The print codex and *legere in silencio* then introduced three more tensions: (1) between authors as individual persons, (2) between the reader's tongue and eye, and (3) between individual readers.

This was possible first and foremost because the book was no longer predominantly intended to be read collectively aloud but individually in silence. The collective audio reader was largely but not exclusively replaced with the individual visual reader. The tensions were therefore different. However, these new tensions individualized not only the reader, but also the silent writing author. With the rise of translated Greek texts (in spaced Arabic) into the West, and eventually with the printing press, the books of human authors began to proliferate. During this time the author became an individual with a name and discrete identity, and thus differentiated from multiple other authors with differing degrees of authority, credential, ability, opinion, and so on.

Second, as discussed in the example of Augustine, silent reading introduced a tension between readers and themselves as a difference between spoken word and visual word. If the kinetic structure of the codex relied on a triple fold in the continuous flows of sound and light and gave readers the ability to speak the words and thoughts of the absent author, the silent reading of the printed book introduced a tension within readers between the voice of the author that they spoke and the voice of the reader that they experienced silently as a visual-mental image. The production of individuality and personage thus had a kinographic resonance-effect.

Here in the bibliographic domain, we see that the kinetic production of something called an "individual" occurred as a differential but immanent and sensuous tension between what is heard and what is seen. The individual emerged as this very tension: the one for whom seeing-reading-saying remained three distinct folds within a single immanent process. The Latin word *reflexio*, used to describe the process of silent reading, literally means a turning or bending back of light. To reflect is precisely to let a flow of light in through the eye and bend it back or fold it over itself internally. The reading subject is thus the subject of a folded light. Just as in the rumination of *lectio divina* one speaks God's word through one's self, and in this way is the incarnate Word of God, so in the "meditation" of the *legere in silencio* one sees the word of the author and thinks it in oneself internally, differentially: the other speaks, thinks, and is seen, all "within" the individual. Like the Trinity, the individual's being is immanently differentiated within this triune movement. But now the Trinity, along with the author, has become an increasingly social and natural one.

Thus, the third tension introduced by silent and printed reading was a tension between individual readers. Through the spaced and printed book, the collective was transformed into the collective of individuals in immanent tension with one another, or in other words, the nation.[33]

This new kinetic and bibliogeographical tension allowed for the proliferation of spiritual literature between the fourteenth and seventeenth centuries that was meant for silent "mediation." Individuals were spoken to directly as persons, but persons within a larger flock of believers like themselves, a collective of individuals whose salvation and communication was a personal project (Protestantism). However, it was also a collective personal project—a revolutionary religious conversion of a mass of individual believers, defined and judged by their individual actions, without the aid of salvation through another, such as a priest system of indulgences.

This new tension between "collective individuals" also allowed for the proliferation of subversive political, erotic, and critical literature. Since individuals no longer read together, one could hold an increasingly critical attitude (Kant), skeptical distance (Descartes), or heretical position (Spinoza) without necessarily being considered scandalous, punished, or shamed. With the introduction of a tension between individual readers, the problem of interpretation was multiplied; doubt and criticism could proliferate within these new tensions.

Again, this is not a metaphorical representation. Readers were really and kinetically held together by common laws and lands, but they were held apart by their different movements, reading spaces, reading desks, rooms, and so on. The Middle Ages was filled with a whole bibliographic architecture in libraries (reading desks), monasteries (reading cells), schools (writing desks), and churches (silent meditation areas) built to ensure the collective cellular isolation of the individual reader.[34] The portability, reproducibility, affordability, and small size of books also made them suitable for multiple individual readers to be reading in the same space as one another without disturbing other individual readers.

NATURAL ILLUMINATION

The third major tensional kinetic function of the printed codex is natural illumination. While divine illumination is related to *lectio divina* insofar it provides the visual flows that accompany the audio flows of the ruminated word, *natural* illumination inverts the focus of the internalization process from sound to light. In both divine and natural illumination theories, sound (word) and light (truth) are both part of the same divine emanation. Divine illumination did not completely disappear later on, but it lessened or became equal to a new form of illumination stemming from nature and the human mind (or the natural human mind). Just as the Renaissance introduced the coexistence of natural, divine, and human authorship, so the theory of natural illumination allowed for other sources of light.

The origin of natural illumination is no doubt related to the idea of *reflexio*, whereby the eye and mind literally become sites where the divine light strikes and is bent back, thus emanating a light of its own. Thomas Aquinas is most often associated with the demise of divine illumination and the rise of natural illumination. Aquinas rejected the strong position of divine illumination, which stated that all of the objects of our knowledge come directly and constantly from God and that we need illumination in order to think. He further denied that divine illumination is, on its own, sufficient without the senses.

Instead, Aquinas invoked the Aristotelian idea of an agent intellect: "From those words of Augustine we are given to understand that truth is not entirely to be looked for from the senses. For we require the light of agent intellect, through which we unchangeably cognize the truth in changeable things, and we distinguish the things themselves from the likenesses of things."[35] The agent intellect based on natural sensation thus produces its own natural illumination capable of recognizing patterns in nature and in the divine without any additional illumination. Human beings are naturally endowed by their creator with the capacity for independent thought without the need for "new illumination added onto their natural illumination."[36] They may receive it by gift, but not by nature. However, in another sense, our own natural light is also a reflection of the light from the one who created us. "For the intellectual light that is in us," Aquinas says, "is nothing other than a certain likeness of the uncreated light, obtained through participation, in which the eternal reasons are contained."[37]

While Aquinas wanted to have both divine illumination and natural illumination, later theorists saw natural or intellectual light playing an increasingly important role while still trying to reconcile its autonomous power with its creation by God, as we discussed in Chapter 26 in the idea of inner force, or conatus.

Some theorists were even ready to reject the idea of divine illumination entirely.[38] Both Henry of Ghent and John Duns Scotus contributed to the theory of intellectual illumination, but in the end they still supplemented it with God's efficient creation. For Scotus, the divine intellect "is that in virtue of which secondarily the objects produced move the intellect in actuality."³⁹ The divine intellectual simply creates objects, including humans, whose secondary motions then move the intellect. In this sense human beings "can achieve [knowledge], by purely natural means."⁴⁰

By the sixteenth century the idea of a natural or intellectual illumination had been taken up by Bacon and Descartes. Like the others, Bacon affirmed the divine creation of the mind, but he simultaneously affirmed the autonomous power of the "light of reason" to attain knowledge.⁴¹ Descartes's formulation of the tensional relation between divine light and natural light, influenced by the Scholastics, is exemplary in this regard. "The faculty of knowing which God has given us, which we call natural light, never perceives any object which is not true insofar as it perceives it, that is, insofar as it recognizes clearly and distinctly; for we would have to believe that God was a deceiver if he had given it to us such that we took the false for the true when we used it well."⁴² The natural light of reason is a secure faculty of knowledge because it has been given to us by God, who by definition as good cannot deceive us.

The terms "clear and distinct" are thus luminous terms for Descartes and are directly related to the kinetic flow of light externalized from the creator, traversing through the world like a book, and folded up inside us in the form of a kinetic *reflexio* of that light back on the world, as we think/read to and within ourselves. In this tensional regime of circulation, knowledge is not direct, but indirect through a series of flows, folds, and reflections. "I recognize (*connais*) by the natural light," Descartes says.⁴³ One does not know the light, but knows *by the light* as a transport medium, meaning the light given by God that reflects from our faces back onto the world to illuminate it.

All of this testifies to the broader tensional kinetics of force at work in theological descriptions and bibliographic inscriptions. The theory of natural and intellectual illumination, developed during this period alongside the dominance of silent reading, reflection, and the printed codex, continued to spread throughout Europe and formed the basis of the European Enlightenment. Around the eighteenth century, however, the fluid dynamics of light inside the reflecting subject began to take on a very different kinetic structure, as we see in Part IV.

CONCLUSION

This chapter concludes Part III's kinetic analysis of being and force as a regime of tensional motion. Not only do we find this tensional regime in the theological descriptions of natural and divine force, but, as this chapter and the last have shown, we also find it in the bibliographic regimes of the manuscript and printed codex along with their related hermeneutical theories of comprehension and illumination. Both are dimensions of the same coordinated historical regime of motion.

Kinetically, however, tensional circulation encounters a certain limit to its motion when the interrelational line that links circulations together itself begins to take on its own autonomy over that which it connects. Historically, this is what occurred during the period from about the eighteenth century to the twentieth. The rigid linkages of tension became increasingly elastic and active. During the modern period, the new kinetic power of elasticity rose to dominance under the metaphysical name of being as "time." This is the subject of Part IV, and the final historical name for being, which will be treated in Book II.

PART IV
Being and Time

I
Kinos

CHAPTER 30

Elastic Motion

At the turn of the eighteenth century, the description of force as ontologically primary began to dissipate in the face of a brutal empiricist critique. However, it was not until nearly the end of the eighteenth century that Immanuel Kant (1724–1804) began to replace this notion with a new ontologically primary descriptor: time. At least since Aristotle, time had been considered ontologically subordinate to motion and other terms. It was not until Kant, however, that one of the most historically derivative ontological categories, time, became the most primary. After Kant, the ontological primacy of time was taken up by almost every nineteenth- and twentieth-century ontologist.

Modern ontology became increasingly critical of the idea that space, eternity, and force were ontologically foundational categories. Time, however, remained largely immune to the same critiques. Time became the new name for being—ushering in an age of generalized chronophilia. With only some exceptions, almost all modern ontologies of the eighteenth through twentieth centuries, in one way or another, accept the reality and foundational nature of time—that everything occurs in time, but time itself was not created by or derived from anything else.

The thesis of Part IV follows that of the previous chapters in arguing that time, like space, eternity, and force, is an ontological description structured according a specific regime of motion. In short, Part IV argues that the concept of time is a fundamentally kinetic concept. Time is derived from motion in at least three ways.

First, time is by definition a division between three tenses: past, present, and future; before, during, after. Without such a division there can be no meaningful concept of time. However, as seen throughout this book, the minimal ontological condition of our present is that being is in motion, and motion presupposes the primacy of a kinetic continuum. Time, as an essentially divided phenomenon, presupposes that which it divides, namely a continuum or flow of motion. If temporal division were fundamental, being would already be predivided, and movement would be reduced to a mere juxtaposition of vacuum-sealed fragments. Nothing would secure or allow for transition between divided points. Time is therefore derivative of continuous flow by definition. Time introduces division into the continuum of motion, but motion allows time to flow.

Second, contemporary accelerationist cosmology confirms the derivative nature of time. Before the existence of the known universe, most physicists postulate, there was a purely continuous unfolding of all matter (quantum fields) moving (exploding) outward—in a stochastic process of differentiation and combination. All forms of current division and discreteness come from the primary movement of continuous cosmic materialization. Without matter in motion (the explosion) there would be no spatial division or distinction, no rotational images of eternity in the heavenly bodies, no forces or relations between bodies, and no temporal division among a before, during, and after. Temporal division (linear or circular) is only possible on the condition of a more primary explosion of motion or entropic materialization. Time is therefore possible only because the universe moves in a certain way and because we just *happen to exist in a low-entropy universe*. In high-entropy universes, or at the Planck scale, things move differently. Therefore, time is not ontologically foundational but derived from the kinetic process of cosmic acceleration and materialization.[1] What we call time is accordingly a division in a continuous process: a measure of motion.

Third, and relatedly, thermodynamics also confirms this thesis. According to thermodynamics, the reason why time appears to us as irreversible is because it is *derived* from matter in entropic motion. Since heat is fundamentally kinetic (bodies in motion), and since motion is fundamentally pedetic, some motion is always lost or escapes any given circulation (entropy). However, according to the law of entropy that defines this thermodynamic foundation of time, entropy itself is *not absolute*. It is only a macroscopic *tendency*, not a fundamentality. In other words, it is the pedetic movement of matter that is both the condition for the emergence and destruction of time.

If time existed independently from matter in motion, then it would be logically reversible. However, the postulation of such a reversal, independence, and fundamentality of time is the result of a metaphysical presupposition in the mathematical disciplines that are able to demonstrate the so-called reversibility of time *in equations*. Mathematicians first run an equation (including stochastic equations) forward, laying out the formula and inputting the physical variables. Then, having reached a conclusion, they see if they can derive the variables from the conclusion. Invariably, they do. What this shows, however, is not the reversibility *of time* but the reversibility *of equations*. Starting with the solution and working backward just confirms what was already discovered in the initial formula and observations. What the difference between thermodynamics and mathematics shows on this point is that if time existed independently from matter and motion, as it does in mathematics, then it would be macroscopically reversible. However, since according to thermodynamics real matter and motion do not actually behave this way in this macroscopic region of our universe, then the metaphysical and mathematical-idealist description of time existing independently from material motion has no absolute reality. The movement of time forward and backward has a strictly physical definition because it is tied to kinetic energy.

This does not mean, however, that our *description* of time has no reality. What thermodynamics shows us is precisely this fact: time is a description given by bodies in motion *of* bodies in motion and nothing else outside of this. What we are describing when we describe time can certainly be called sequence and seriality. Being really does move and change continuously, and it can be divided into various dimensions we can call past, present, and future. The kinetic question then is, "What is the kinetic status of such dimensions and seriality?" This is the question posed and answered in Part IV. The answer to this question adds to our previous kinetic theories of space, eternity, and force, a final kinetic theory of time that completes for now the core concepts of the ontology of motion.

Part IV, like the previous parts of this book, is divided into three sections: the first offers a strictly *kinomenological* theory of time as elastic motion; the second offers a kinetic analysis of the historically *descriptive* features of time provided by the phenomenological writings of the period; and the third offers a kinetic analysis of the historical technology of *inscription* (typography) within which these descriptions were inscribed.

THE KINOMENOLOGY OF TIME

This chapter begins Part IV by offering a purely kinomenological theory of the elastic motions that define the appearance of being as time. The thesis of this chapter is that temporal being is defined by a material and kinetic elasticity of motion.

Following the previous kinomenological chapters, we can now identify the emergence of four dominant patterns of motion. From the primary movement of pure pedesis, motion begins to curve into a spiral pattern, *centripetally* piling upward toward a central mountain peak. Once the central peak accumulates, it begins to flow back outward from the center in all directions, forming a rotating sphere. In the process, however, flows from this *centrifugal* radiation also begin to escape the sphere and give rise to other spheres linked together in *tension* by their connective flows.

What happens next is similarly radical: the flow itself that constituted the circulations of spiral, sphere, and polygon now begins to multiply itself into a series of a thousand tiny microfolds and intervals. The previously subordinate flow that composed all the other patterns now takes on all the activity, multiplying itself into a continuity or sequence of larger and smaller folds—like a compound foam. In doing, so all the other regimes, composed of these now foaming flows, also begin to take on a serial or intervallic structure. This new structure allows for a new general elasticity of all the previous regimes to expand and contract at any point whatsoever within their field of circulation. The transformation is radical but by no means final or developmentally necessary.

In one sense this change is so radical because it is the modern formulation of being as time that seems to get closest to affirming the ontological primacy of motion. For the first time in history, the whole of being seems to be caught up in a more primary flux or flow of time. In another sense, however, this change is so radical because it could not be more different from the real flux and continuum of motion. Ultimately, the temporal description of being reintroduces division and stasis back into the heart of being in the most radical way possible and subordinates all matter to motion *in time* and not time *in motion*. But if time is not *in motion*, then its arrow fails to pass and we are left with an empty and static ontology of abstract change, immobile becoming, and difference without continuous flow.

The kinetic theory of time, by contrast, is defined by a fundamentally elastic regime of motion. The rise to dominance of this elastic regime is coextensive with the ontological description of time and is defined by the primacy of three new kinetic operations: the seriality of folds, their expansions and contractions, and the predominance of the subject.

Seriality

The first kinomenological operation that defines the elasticity of time is seriality. Kinetically speaking, seriality is not discontinuous or intervallic but rather defined by the introduction of an indefinite number of linearly ordered folds. This indefinite folding of a flow is possible precisely because the flow is a pure continuity. Only in a kinetic continuum is it always possible for another fold to emerge between two others. This kinetic structure of seriality gives birth to four interrelated structures of time: abstract, concrete, folded, and elastic.

Abstract Temporality. Only a single fold in a flow is necessary in order to introduce abstract temporality. A flow without the demarcation of a single fold has neither a before nor an after, since there is not a relative point from which to orient them. Temporal differences, however, only become possible as derived from the introduction of at least one kinetic difference or fold.

Once a fold has been made in a flow, a future opens up ahead of it and a past behind it. However, with only one fold, the future and the past remain temporally abstract in the sense that they do not refer to any specific fold before or afterward; they refer only to an undifferentiated continuum in which nothing happened before or after. But if nothing in particular happened, then there is no way to know whether the so-called present is in fact a present (i.e., between a future and past), and not itself another past or future. In this way the structure of abstract time undermines the determination of any fold as a determinately tensed fold. In abstract time, there is only a vague before and after, without a past, present, or future.

Concrete Temporality. Seriality and true temporality, however, are only possible on the condition of a concrete temporality; that is, on the condition that there are at least three folds in a flow. Two act as limit junctions, one of the past, the other of the future, while the third is passed through between them. The first two limit junctions make possible an ordered and spatial kinetic field, but the third conjoins the two and begins to multiply in the interval.

The basic structure of a concrete temporal series thus requires the possibility of an in-between through which time can pass. In nontemporal language, we could say that the basic structure of the concrete series is that every fold is coordinated to one that comes before and one that comes after. Since kinetic fields circulate, each of the limit junctions refers to the other, first as a future and then as a past, and so on. Each of the three tenses is defined by the other, so that without one the others cease to exist. Without a future fold there could not be the passing of a present into the past, which will become in turn a future for the past fold, and so on in a feedback loop of concrete and relative time tenses. The triple fold of time thus borrows its interlocking structure from the topology of the Borromean rings in which the removal of one unlinks the others.

Seriality is therefore simply the indefinite application of this structure. Following the basic tripartite structure of the series results in a radical and indefinite multiplication of intervallic folds within a flow. If between every past and future is a present, and from the perspective of every past the present is a future fold, then there must be a fold in between them, and so on indefinitely. Furthermore, if from the perspective of the future fold the present fold appears as a past fold, then there must be a present fold behind that. Therefore, in both directions of the present there is an indefinite series of folds all the way down. The line of the fold is infinitely foldable and differentiable without ever being divided. If Zeno had used the logic of the fold instead of the cut, he could have solved all his paradoxes. Time can pass along an infinitely folded surface because temporal moments are not cuts but folds in a kinetic continuum.

However, following this basic structure of the concrete temporal series also results in a paradoxical detemporalization of time. If the kinetic logic of the series is the indefinite multiplication of folds in a continuous flow, then every flow is, with respect to different folds, a past, a present, and a future all at the same time. Every fold is thus detemporalized in the series. In other words, there is no such thing as absolute time, only relative time from the orientation of a given fold. The structure of seriality is therefore such that any fold, with respect to the series as an open whole, is temporally equivalent with any other fold. With respect to seriality, it is not the folds themselves that are past, present, or future, but their relative ordering, that makes them so. The folds thus become exchangeable fragments without a pregiven whole in which they fit. Every fold in the series becomes any-fold-whatsoever in the series. In this sense it becomes impossible to determine an absolute or objective temporal series.

The Fold of Time. Despite the absolute detemporalization and interchangeability of the folds in the series, the structure of the fold itself also saves time by introducing its own temporal division. Every fold has within it at least three distinct temporal demarcations following its kinetic structure:

1   The period of intersection or bifurcation where the flow folds back over and intersects with itself marks the present. The present is the point of sensation where an object senses itself as here or present.

2 The region opened up as the flow moves counterclockwise around the loop and moves forward or ahead of the present toward the future. The future is the furthest point on the fold ahead of the present.
3 After the flow passes this point it begins to move backward toward the past and then back around to the present. The movement of the flow through these temporal regions along the fold constitutes the arrow or continuous passage of time.

The present is therefore lived as a "thick present" as it passes around the tenses of the folds and includes the past and future as moments within itself. It is therefore in the fold of the present that time occurs. Within the fold of the present is the past and the future. The past is retained insofar as it is the past of this present; and the future is anticipated insofar as it is the future of this singular present. Thus, the past and the future are not separate instants or abstract points in time but are included in the same continual loop or fold of the living present of the fold. The past and future are dimensions of this present.

The fold of time (see Figure 30.1) is thus the kinomenological foundation for both the idea of a *mens momemnta*, or present instant, when the fold intersects with itself at a singular point, and the idea of a specious, or lived present when the present retains and anticipates the immediate past and future as dimensions of its lived present. The present thus appears both as an infinitely thin instant that is crossed in the continuous flow from past to future and back, and as thick present that extends through this continuum to the past and future. Both of these notions of time share the same kinomenological foundation in the fold of time. Time passes and flows but never leaves the fold of the lived present. The fold of time forms a habitual periodicity or cycle. In this sense the kinetic fold solves a fundamental paradox of time: it creates both time while also passing the time constituted in the same continuous motion.

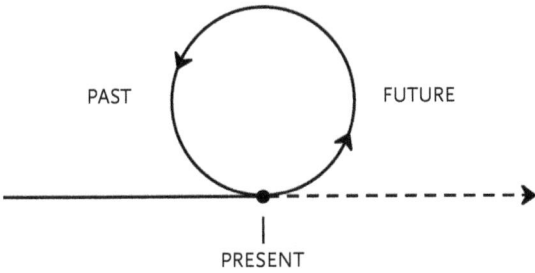

Figure 30.1 The Fold of Time

The fold of time thus makes possible a new seriality of lived presents. All of matter is so many folds, each with a sensation of itself (the present), a retention of what it was in the form of material or biological persistence (the past), and an anticipation or receptivity to possible stimuli (the future). The kinomenological operation of seriality is thus defined by a series or sequence of temporal folds, each with their own pasts, presents, and futures. These folds then enter into larger or smaller compositions while each retains its own temporality.

The Elasticity of the Fold. In addition to producing a series or sequence of unique temporal folds, each of these temporal folds is also capable of an elastic motion of expansion and contraction of the fold itself. As the fold of time becomes larger, the past extends further back and the future extends further ahead. Different material and biological folds thus have different temporalities and can even modulate their temporal fold depending on the situation. For example, in combat an animal's temporal field may shrink down to the very near past and future. In looking for food, however, it may expand the temporal field to include an entire season in order to remember where certain food appeared last or was stored previously. Most pieces of matter, like rocks, will have an extremely small duration. This is not a conscious process of representation of past folds but an intuition of the internal dimensions of the same lived fold. Since every flow is infinitely continuous, it has an infinite elasticity. Every fold in the series thus has an elastic function.

The kinetic operation of seriality also allows for a basic differentiation between two kinds of flows: folded flows and conjoining flows. Any composite body will be made of both, a number of material or cellular folds and a pattern of motion that connects them together. This is the most minimal kinetic distinction that can be made of matter—folded flow or unfolded flow. As such, it provides the kinetic condition for the most basic logical or formal distinction in being: between closed and open circuits, one or zero. Intervallic being. Fold and pore. The graphism of the 1 and 0 visually depicts the closed loop of the fold or 0 and the open unfolded flow or 1.

Elasticity

The second kinomenological operation of time is that of an elasticity of the field of temporal circulation itself. In the kinetic field there is a continuous circulation and seriality of temporal folds, but such continuity also presupposes a connective flow running between the folds: the field. The structure of seriality and temporality, however, is such that at any point in a continuous field a fold may emerge *between* two other folds. Since flows are continuous, they allow for an elasticity of folds, and since fields are made of flows, the field is itself elastic.

Therefore, there is not only an elasticity of the folds but also of the flow of the connective field itself. The elasticity of the field allows for an expansion and contraction of the entire temporal sequence itself. The description of "absolute time" is derived from nothing more than the field's own elasticity to be stretched forward and backward without absolute limit.

The elasticity of the temporal field thus allows for smaller and larger series of conjoined temporal folds. It has a double elasticity. An indefinite series of folds can always emerge within any field, but the field itself can also expand and contract to add or subtract folds.

Like all kinetic fields, the temporal field is not necessarily a thing or a particular temporal fold. The temporal field is the condition within which individual temporal folds emerge and are ordered. For example, there are not first temporal folds, and then a flow or attribute of "passing" is added. Sequence already presupposes kinetic continuity, and continuity presupposes an infinite elasticity and mobility of circulation. All concrete temporal orders presuppose a field through which they flow.

Temporally speaking, the "passage" *of time* presupposes the continuity of movement or flux of passing as primary. It is therefore *not time that passes* but kinetic passage that is temporalized. Only after the conditions of kinetic passage are laid out on a temporal field is it possible for particular folds to emerge elastically from within this continuity and then pass between each other. Passage and passer therefore coappear at the "same time" as mutual presuppositions of each other. The temporal-kinetic field allows for the passage but is not reducible to a moment that passes.

The Elasticity of the Field. There are two consequences of the elasticity of the temporal field. First, the circulation of a temporal field makes possible the reproducibility of *contemporaneous temporal folds*. This is possible because within the temporal field of circulation, each temporal fold or present shares the same connective flow with the others as part of the same series. Each temporal fold is thus linked to and is like the others insofar as they form an ordered whole of *the same flow*.

In other words, the elastic temporality of the field makes it possible to say that a past fold is not the same as a present fold but prior to it, and a future fold is just like the present but after, all with respect to a given series. The temporal field thus allows for the reproducibility of relatively homogenous temporal folds within it such that each occurs as a repeatable moment *in the field*. In order for a past fold to be related *as past*, it must also be able to be so in the same field as a present fold. Thus, a past fold must also be *contemporaneous with the field itself* insofar as it is connected in the same circulatory series.

This contemporaneity is possible, however, only insofar as movement is circulatory. That is, insofar as time passes through "the same" differentially repeated field. The temporal field moves through the whole series and then at the end of the series loops back to the first in the series and repeats it. This allows for each temporal fold to be reproduced again and again, uniting all the folds together in a continuum, but also alternating their relative status as past, present, or future, depending on where one is in the circulatory process. Thus, *with respect to the temporal field as a whole*, all the temporal folds are contemporaneous.

The second consequence of temporal elasticity is that it functions as an immanent precondition of the passage of time. Insofar as the elastic process of the temporal flow is required for the passing of time, it is the precondition of the temporal folds. However, since the field is nothing other than its folds, this precondition cannot technically be "before" the folds themselves. Time is thus conditioned by a more kinetic, not temporal, structure through which time passes.

Seriality and elasticity therefore define two kinomenological aspects of temporality. On the one hand, the circulatory process itself is the temporal condition or elastic field within which individual temporal folds occur. As such, it is not a particular time, but the kinetic condition of all times and the expanding and contracting passage of time itself. On the other hand, it is the folding of particular temporalities with their own past, present, and futures through which time passes. The combination of both makes possible a field of temporal passage such that any given fold can be treated as resembling the others with respect to the whole, and thus ordered and repeated through the circulatory process as past, present, or future in sequence.

The Subject

Subjectivity is fundamentally kinetic. As such, the history of subjective formations also follows the dominant regimes of motion that this book has outlined so far. The previous chapters have not focused on the subject so far simply because the *strictly ontological primacy* of the subject does not appear as a dominant description until the eighteenth century. In the following chapters, therefore, it will be a focus of analysis.

In this chapter, however, we are concerned only with the kinomenological theory of the subject, and thus strictly with the kinetic structure of its operation. The kinetic structure of the subject follows the same elastic regime of motion as that of time. It is no coincidence that the historical rise of the ontological primacy of time coincides with the historical rise of the ontological primacy of the subject, beginning with Kant. Time and subjectivity are kinomenologically coextensive. In the modern period, the dominant description of subjectivity becomes fundamentally *temporal* at the same time that temporality becomes fundamentally *subjective*.

Serial Subjectivity. Just as there are two kinomenological operations that define the elasticity of time, so there are two kinomenological operations that define subjectivity: seriality and elasticity. Subjectivity is first of all defined according to the process of folding in which a continuous flow is folded back over itself into a fold or loop. Just as with the temporal fold, the subjective fold is defined according to at least three general regions: the point of intersection where the fold intersects with itself (sensation), the point furthest ahead along the fold (receptivity), and the point furthest behind the present along the fold (retention).

The kinetic theory of subjectivity is clearly much broader than the usual anthropocentric one, which equates subjectivity strictly with human consciousness. Not coincidentally, under this same anthropocentric criteria, most organisms are also said to lack temporal experience. This twin bias of anthropocentric subjectivity is related to the historical primacy of modern temporality and subjectivity, as we will see in the following chapters.

A notable exception to this bias is the brilliant work of the German biologist Jakob von Uexküll (1864–1944), who defined subjectivity much more broadly and kinetically as nothing but the circulation of material flows between the three subjective functions of perception, structure, and effect in a continuous "functional cycle" with the world (see Figure 30.2).[2]

The world gives off flows that are first perceived by the organism, then internalized in its organic structure, retained in the form of effects on its self, and directed back onto the world. This is an important move, even though it still remains limited to the domain of animality and does not deal with the kinetic subjectivity of matter itself. Kinetically, however, this move can be radicalized and subjectivity extended to everything defined by a process of folding.

The process of folding accomplished by kinetic internalization has three parts: an affectivity, a receptivity, and a retention. These are not intrinsically biological functions. Rocks, for example, are composed of kinetic flows of molecules that fold over and affect themselves internally, producing the minimal kinetic sensation of the rock. They also have a receptivity to light, heat, cold, and other material flows that can transform them. They also have a capacity for retention that allows their flows to continue to

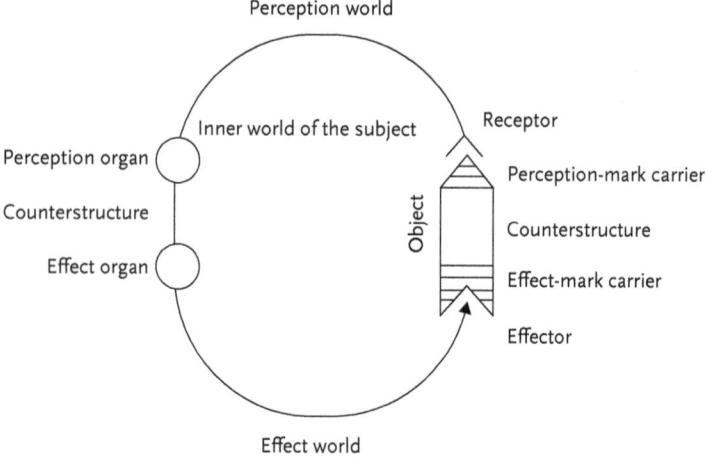

Figure 30.2 Functional Cycle
Source: Figure 3, page 49 of Jakob von Uexküll, *A Foray into the Worlds of Animals and Humans: With a Theory of Meaning* (Minneapolis: University of Minnesota Press, 2010).

persist together in their motion. There is thus a kind of subjectivity even in minerals.

This tripartite kinetic structure of subjectivity is directly related to the tripartite kinetic structure of temporality. Affectivity is the sensation of motion as it intersects with itself by folding in the *present*. Receptivity is the openness or anticipation to *future* stimulation. Retention is the heredity of the *past* carried into the future by kinetic habit. This is the reason why minerals do not instantly dissipate following the fundamentally pedetic nature of their molecular movements. Matter persists by continuously moving in the same synchronous patterns again and again—going outward, reaching a limit, then returning in a cycle. The cycle of movement around the fold is the subjective habit of matter to reproduce itself again and again: affection, reception, retention. Habit is thus not only a function of life, but of all matter.

This cyclical folding is elastic insofar as it allows the limits of matter to expand and contract. Just as the kinetic structure of the temporal fold can expand and contract to include more or less of the past and future, so subjective temporality increases or decreases its range of receptive and retentional faculties. In this way it becomes capable of being affected by a greater or lesser number of flows and of retaining certain modifications of its body through habit.

In this sense the difference between living and mineral bodies is quite large. A living body retains a complex genetic code and even grows as a result of receptivity to stimulation. The more complex the organism, the larger its lived present, the more ways it can be affected by stimuli, and the more it can retain its past through heredity and perceptions that linger in the retained habits of body and brain. This is the sense in which there are different times for different bodies. For example, the subjective temporality of the mayfly is much smaller than that of a horse, based on how long it will live and the number of flows it can receive and respond to. Regardless of the difference in the size of their temporal folds, each has its own lived present.

Every body is structured temporally in this way, but every body is also a composite body of other bodies. Therefore, there is only an indefinite series of heterogeneous subjective temporal folds, each with its own time, operating together in larger or smaller bodies. Every subject is therefore already multiple and temporally composite. At no point is there a difference in kind of serial subjectivity—only a difference in degree all the way up and all the way down.

Elastic Subjectivity. The second kinomenological operation of subjectivity is elasticity. Subjectivity is serial and multiple, but in addition to this subjective continuum of degree, there are also larger and smaller *temporal fields* that connect these series of subjective folds. Just like circulatory temporality, the circulatory subject is not itself a specific body, but the kinetic process that holds together all the bodies. The circulatory process itself is also subjective.

What the elasticity of the kinetic field makes possible for the subject is a kinetic memory. In the case of more complex composite bodies, subjectivity is defined by the coexistence of an entire series of folds. Each fold is recallable and representable as a fold resembling the others *with respect to the kinetic unity of the entire series.* Every heterogeneous fold becomes homogeneous relative to the "zero degree" of the subjective field. In this way subjectivity becomes continuous and coextensive with the entire temporal series while at the same time individualized in the seriality of the folds. As such, the subject becomes capable of representing to itself temporal moments distinct but not different from the continuity of the field that ties all the folds together. This is the kinomenological meaning of the term "stream of consciousness," as we see in the next chapters.

There is no consciousness *of time* but rather a time-consciousness *of motion*. The very idea of a consciousness of time presupposes an ontological division between consciousness and time. Either time is purely continuous and consciousness simply takes experiential snapshots of this flow, or consciousness itself is a pure continuous stream that instants of time divide up into discrete units or blocks. Both miss the point if motion is not primary.

Subjectivity and consciousness are not something other than being. Being is in continuous motion and therefore so is time-consciousness. There is no division of motion into some other kind of thing called "time" or "space." Motion is folded, not cut. There is no ontological difference between time and consciousness—they are two descriptions *of the same elastic field of motion.*

At the level of individual temporal folds, subjectivity is fundamentally plural and fragmented. In each fold the subject says I, I, I. When one I reflects on itself, there are essentially two I's—one doing the reflecting, the other being reflected on, ad infinitum. However, with respect to the continuum of the circulatory field, the subject represents itself as a general unity of all the I's. Each I becomes a particular memory within the larger temporal field that coexists with them. In this way any single present, as a kinomena in the series, includes all the other presents in the same coextensive subjective field.

It now remains to be seen how this kinomenological regime of elastic motion is described in the modern phenomenology of time. This is the aim of the following chapters in Part IV.

11
Logos

CHAPTER 31

Modern Phenomenology I

Series

The regime of elastic motion defined in the previous chapter rises to historical dominance during the modern period—around the eighteenth to the twentieth century. The rise of this new kinetic regime occurred alongside the rising predominance of a new ontological description of being as fundamentally temporal. During this period one of the most historically marginalized concepts of Western ontology, time, became the most fundamental description of all reality. It is hard to appreciate the novelty of this move today after its incredible influence on the twentieth century. Of course, all the other major ontological descriptions of space, eternity, and force persisted in various ways, especially during the transitional seventeenth and eighteenth centuries, but by the end of the eighteenth century all these other names had become increasingly reinterpreted *temporally*.

In the previous chapter we developed a strictly kinomenological exposition of time as elastic motion. But the kinetic theory of time, like the kinetic theories of space, eternity, and force, is itself derived from its historical pattern of description and does not precede it. We therefore turn now to the historical description of time and its elastic regime of motion.

PHENOMENOLOGY

Phenomenology, from the Greek word *phainómenon,* meaning the study of that which appears, is the study of being strictly as it *appears* to the consciousness of the subjects that experience it. In its broadest definition, phenomenology is methodologically different from all the previously dominant ontological inquires analyzed so far. This is the case not because it resists making any ontological claims about the true nature of reality in itself but because it defines the true nature of reality in itself as *fundamentally temporal*.

In other words, time is a special kind of phenomena that *does not appear* to the subject of experience. This is because temporality is the serial and elastic process within and through which the subject's own experience is itself constituted. In one sense we can say that for phenomenology there is no experience of being qua being, because being always appears as being qua appearance to a subject. Accordingly, for phenomenology, the very premise of studying being qua being as such is entirely misguided and impossible.

In another sense, however, the very reason or condition for the unexperienceable nature of being qua being in phenomenology is precisely because being qua being is *fundamentally temporal*. That is, because being is temporal and thus internally differentiated between past, present, and future, subjective experience is always thrown outside itself or "ecstatic," as Heidegger writes—and thus incapable of absolute ontological descriptions. From the perspective of phenomenology, all hitherto existing descriptions had privileged the temporal present in one way or another, and had thus produced a metaphysics of presence. Philosophy assumed that if being was reducible to the present, then it can be completely experienced, known, and described in its totality. If, however, being is fundamentally temporal and internally differentiated into tenses, then any attempt to grasp its totality (qua being) in its immediacy is impossible. All we have is our temporal experience of beings.

In contrast to medieval natural theology, phenomenology was therefore the first to break from the ontological presupposition of an eternal or absolute God. Where theology was a thinking of the nature of the tensional relation between God and nature, phenomenology introduced a new elasticity of the flow itself under the name of the subject. God, nature, and their relation all became appearances or experiences *in* the elastic consciousness of the experiencing subject itself.

However, the claim that being qua being is fundamentally temporal itself also operates as an ontological and universal description. For example, to claim that the only thing that can be said about the nature of being is that *nothing* can be said about the nature of being is only correct if we accept that the reason for this limitation is that being is fundamentally temporal. This becomes clear when we try to affirm the inverse claim that the temporality of being and the subject are *not* in fact ontologically absolute. If this were the case, then it would be possible that being was in fact nontemporal, present, and thus totally knowable.

By definition, phenomenology cannot accept this inverse claim, since it would mean that being qua being was accessible, that there might be mind-independent being, and that the phenomenological method itself might not be the right orientation to being. However, if phenomenology does not accept this inverse claim, it is therefore forced to accept the absolute ontological necessity of time.

Despite the significant differences between individual phenomenologists, this chapter argues that they all share a minimal ontological commitment to the primacy of time. Only if being is temporally differentiated is the subject capable of the very self-affection that structures the experience of the subject itself as well as its so-called descriptive limitations. The being of the subject must be a fundamentally temporal being or all phenomenological experience is impossible.

Historically speaking, the rise of phenomenology as the dominant mode of ontological description in the West begins with the Enlightenment's emphasis on the power of human reason and empiricism. In particular, George Berkeley and David Hume contributed greatly to the stripping away of a number of important metaphysical ideas, such as abstract space, eternity, forces, and causality. All ontological questions in philosophy and the sciences increasingly bowed down to the exhaustive power of human reason and experience. Empiricists and early rationalists such as Francis Bacon, Descartes, Spinoza, Leibniz, Voltaire, Newton, Rousseau, and others all placed increasing methodological and philosophical primacy in human reason. However, it was not until the publication of Immanuel Kant's *Critique of Pure Reason* (1781) that the structure of human reason itself described the fundamental temporality of being as such. After Kant, most if not all major currents in philosophy and ontology accepted the primacy of temporality in one way or another, from Hegel to Derrida.

Before beginning with Kant, however, this chapter begins with a kinetic analysis of some of the historical precursors of phenomenological time found in the medieval and early-modern periods. This is important because these early descriptions of time as lived, mechanical, and abstract were not abandoned after Kant but rather made to provide the foundations for a whole new kinetics of transcendental time. On the one hand, then, the medieval and early-modern descriptions of time became component aspects of phenomenological time, but on the other hand, they remained fundamentally limited by the dominant historical kinetics of their period that ended up giving ontotheological primacy to the force of God. As early-modern theories of time became more and more abstract, they also became more and more elastic-sounding. In contrast to a sudden Kantian break, there is actually a much slower and incremental increase in such descriptive language that both continues through Kant and is transformed by him, eventually defining the kinetic structure of phenomenological time more broadly.

The argument of the following chapters is therefore that the rise to dominance of the description of being as fundamentally temporal emerged historically under the title of "phenomenology," and that it relied on an elastic description of being.

MEDIEVAL AND EARLY MODERN TEMPORALITY

Medieval temporality was the first to introduce the description of seriality into time.[1] This was a radical move against most ancient conceptions of time, which were fundamentally subordinated to the centrifugal regime of eternity.[2] If ancient temporality subordinated time to a single enclosed circle of rotational presence, medieval temporality released and multiplied time in a sequence of multiple times or lived presents. In so doing, however, medieval time also introduced a kinetic tension between God's eternality and the temporal present of the individual contemplating mind. Medieval time functioned therefore as a kind of intracircular time, a time that moves between multiple circles and *along a series* held together by the tensional force of God the creator.

This new tensional description of time made possible three interrelated kinetic operations that defined serial motion and formed the foundation of the later phenomenological description of time: the temporal fold, the multiplication of the temporal fold, and the elasticity of the flow of time.

Starting with Augustine, these three kinetic operations were increasingly used to describe time. Just as the elasticity of time presupposes the seriality of time, as we saw in the previous chapter, so the modern phenomenological description analyzed in the next chapter presupposes the earlier medieval theories of (1) lived time, (2) mechanical time, and (3) absolute time, analyzed in the current chapter.

Therefore, in the rest of this chapter we turn to an analysis of these three kinetic operations, which are necessary but not yet sufficient for a kinetic description of phenomenological time: lived, mechanical, and absolute time.

Lived Time: The Temporal Fold

The first kinetic operation of medieval time was the temporal fold—described in the subjectivity of the human measurer of time. While the ancients were content to define time as a measure of motion, the medievals added to this a description of the *act* of measurement itself via the subject who counts the time.

Augustine of Hippo (354–430) was the first thinker to do this using a theory of the temporal series. In his *Lectures on the Consciousness of Internal Time*, Husserl even writes, "The first thinker who sensed profoundly the enormous difficulties inherent in this analysis [of time-consciousness], and who struggled with them almost to despair, was Augustine."[3] In Book XI of the *Confessions*, Augustine takes seriously the ancient idea that "time is the measure of motion," but he inquires more deeply into what structure of the mind is required for such a process of measurement to be possible and what relation it has to God eternal. "I want to know," he writes, "the essence and nature of time, whereby we measure the movement of bodies and say, for instance, that one movement lasts twice as long as another."[4]

Augustine brilliantly resolves the problem by describing two kinetic tensions in being that will be repeated often over the next millennium: first, between an eternal God whose force or power created the mind and time as distinct but also one with his power; and second, within the mind itself between the tripartite temporal division itself. While the ancient concept of time was defined by the dualism between eternity (truth) and temporality (illusion), the medieval concept of time accepted the division but in turn reconfigured it in terms of a triad or trinity between the eternal and existing present, the temporal past, and the temporal future.

First Tension: God. The first kinetic tension emerges alongside the introduction of the Christian creator God. God externalizes his power in the form of a creative flow that is distinct from himself in the sense that he is not identical with his creation, but also one with this creation insofar as it is nothing other than an expression or folding of his own power. The structure of this kinetic tension was developed at length in Part III, but is now considered with respect to temporality.

Working within this tensional regime, Augustine argued that God creates by his word, not by a "passing word" but by a silent or instantaneous word. God did not create *at a point in time*; nor did God create through any temporal process in action or in audible speech. Before God there could not have been time, or else God would not be eternal. Furthermore, God also cannot be coeternal with time, because the definition of eternity is that which transcends all times.[5] There is first eternal God, then there is a flow of creative force, then there is temporality, which is distinct from both God and from his force or power. If his force was not distinct from time, then he would have created time without using any force, which makes no sense. Therefore, the silent word and the unmoved action are the atemporal forces of creation and are ontologically primary to time, according to Augustine. "In the excellency of an ever-present eternity, Thou precedest all times past, and survivest all future times, because they are future, and when they have come they will be past; but You are the same, and Your years shall have no end. . . . Your today is eternity . . . You have made all time; and before all times You are, nor in any time was there not time."[6]

God is the pure, unchanging, unmoved, eternal present. The kinetic problem then is how to explain how God moves, acts, or exerts power somehow distinct from what he is, qua temporal creation. How is it possible for an eternal being to create time? Augustine's answer: because the creative force itself *is outside time*. Furthermore, this is possible because time is only a subjective impression that occurs *in our minds alone*. In this way, for Augustine, temporality is subordinated to the force or kinetic tension between God, the force of creativity, and the created demonstrated in Part III. As the measure of motion in the mind, time is created and therefore secondary to the creative *power* of God, which creates time in the first place.

Second Tension: Mind. The second and more novel kinetic tension that Augustine introduces is the one within the mind itself, between the three temporal tenses. The mind measures the motion of bodies with time, but the time of the past has already gone out of existence, and the time of the future has not yet arrived. Even the present itself is constantly passing away so rapidly that it hardly constitutes a stable unit of measure. "What about those two times past and future," Augustine writes, "in what sense do they have real being, if the past no longer exists and the future does not exist yet? As for the present time, if that were always present and never slipped away into the past, it would not be time at all; it will be eternity."[7] If time is constantly passing or flowing through our fleeting present awareness, then Augustine concludes:

> It is inaccurate to say, "there are three tenses of time: past, present and future," though it might properly be said, "there are three tenses of times: the present of past things [*praesens de praeteritis*], the present of present things [*praesens de praesentibus*], the present of future things [*praesens de futuris*]." These are three realities in the mind, but nowhere else as far as I can see, for the present of past things is memory, the present of present things is attention [*attentio*], and the present of future things is expectation. If we are allowed to put it that way, I do see three tenses or times, and admit that they are three.[8]

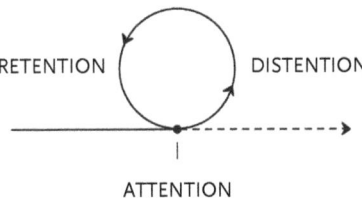

Figure 31.1 The Tensional Fold of Time

Augustine's move here is kinetically brilliant. Time is a continuous flow of sensation passing through us constantly, but when we focus our attention (from the Latin root *tendere*, meaning "tension") on the present, we are able to hold together the three "tenses" (again from the Latin root *tendere*),[9] or temporal tensions of the flow by essentially folding the flow back over itself. By folding the flow over itself and creating a loop of time, the present is essentially expanded and stretched (*tenditur*) into a temporal fold or interiority: an inner duration. The present is the point of kinetic intersection of the flow with itself, the future ahead and past behind. The flow of kinetic sensation is the arrow of time internalized and held together and apart (*distenditur*) in the fold. Time continually flows through the fold without division or stasis but through the repetition of the tensional fold itself a regional temporal stability is created such that a distinction in time is possible without ever dividing it (see Figure 31.1).

This kinetic fold of the tensional present can then serve as the basis of temporal measurement, even though it is constantly passing. The present does not measure the future or the past but is an inner region or dimension within the present. The flow of time passes but also folds in a smaller or larger loop depending on the duration. This is what is kinetically implied when Augustine says, "[Time] is measured while it passes."[10] Time is measured *en passant* around the temporal fold.

Augustine's theory of time in its various Aristotelean permutations remained the dominant theory of time for around a thousand years. Time remained the subjective measure or lived present of motion in relation to God's eternity.

Mechanical Time: The Multiplication of the Fold

With the introduction of mechanical devices, the mechanical clock in particular, and the related spread of impetus theories throughout Western Europe around the fourteenth century, a second kinetic description of time increasingly gained traction: the multiplication of the temporal fold. The spread of mechanical clocks, including astronomical clocks, introduced into Western Europe for the first time a kinetic demonstration of a tensional motion that could measure its own time. A mechanical clock could measure its own movement and produce a time distinct from the movement of subjective, terrestrial, and celestial movements. The clock clearly demonstrated that any motion, not just subjective motions, could serve as the standard measure of time. In fact, the clock mechanism was even more precise than subjective lived measurement.

The rise of mechanical clock time not only multiplied the temporal folds; it also allowed for a subordination of subjective time and human movement to mechanical time. In other words, human motion was increasingly *numbered by time* instead of doing the *numbering of time*. As the measure of time increasingly liberated itself from its subordination to subjective time around the fourteenth century, it was able to turn back on and capture one temporal fold by another.

The kinetic logic is as follows: If there are multiple temporal folds, and many of these temporal folds are not just subjective or lived presents but mechanical ones, then it becomes possible to make one the measure of the movements of the other. For example, the increasingly regulated movements of human bodies in the monastery, university, hospital, town, workplace, and so on can all become quantifiable and ordered in relation to another strictly mechanical time.[11] A more foundational fluxion was thus introduced to measure the others.

Although time began to function as an increasingly autonomous and seemingly objective sequence that ordered the motion of bodies, it still remained subordinated to the more primary ontological determination of force. As we saw in Part III, the dominant kinetic operation of mechanism, including clock and cosmic mechanism, is a tensional one that relies on the primacy of a causal or motor force for its power. Every mechanism requires an energy source; every clock needs to be wound up; every body has its origin and motive power. Once connected to a power source, the clock simply distributes a tensional force throughout the gear train.

Historically, we can therefore see the rise of nonsubjective measurements of time in a number of fourteenth-century medieval thinkers, especially in the contrast between *potential time (temporis potentialis)* (Duns Scotus)[12] and the *standard clock time* of the *primum mobile* (Peter Auriol),[13] or first moved, outermost ring in the geocentric universe.

This purely numerical formulation of temporal measurement reached its apex in William of Ockham's (c. 1287–1347) idea of a *conceptual clock*. Ockham went one step farther than Auriol and argued that it is not the

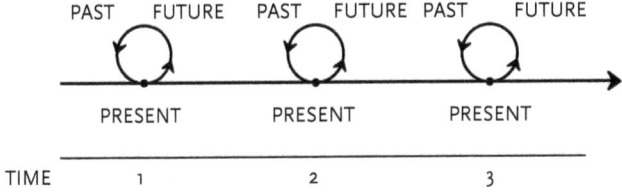

Figure 31.2 Numerical Multiplication of Temporal Folds

primum mobile as such that constitutes the best or even perfect unit for the measurement of motion—it is any perfect unity whatsoever. In fact, even in the absence of any perfect uniform rotation or the coexistence of multiple first uniform celestial rotations,[14] we can still have the concept of a perfectly uniform motion by which to measure all other motions. Thus, any existing motion whatsoever, considered as a uniform motion, can function as a measure because it is numerical quantity itself that is the basis of all measurement. It provides the minimal condition for the possibility of measurement and occurs independently of any subjective lived qualitative sensation of time we may have.

Ockham's conclusion is radical: Time, as a numerical measure of motion, is itself the measure of other times (i.e., unities of movement). In every fold it is the affective intersection that unifies the fold with itself and thus constitutes the condition of numerical quantity (see Figure 31.2). Therefore it is the formal unity of a movement with itself in the fold that produces the standard clock. One tree or one kite or one of anything is all equally one numerically.

What all of these theories and other similar ones have in common is thus precisely the kinetic operation of the multiplication of the temporal fold.[15] The tension between an eternal God and temporal creation remains the same as the tension between the three tenses of the temporal fold. Time is still defined by the measure of motion, but it has been released from a merely qualitative subjective measure to include a quantitative measure no less subordinated to motion and ultimately to the cause of motion: force.[16]

Absolute Time: The Elasticity of the Flow

The third and final kinetic operation in the medieval and early-modern description of time is the elasticity of the flow. This operation does not negate the previous two but adds to them a third. From even the earliest theories, time has always been a *flow* of time. The passage of time always presupposes a more primary continuity that no realist theory of time can do without.

However, at the start of the early-modern period, the flow of time that connected all the multiple temporal folds together becomes an increasingly primary kinetic function of time in a new way. The flow of time is the continuous line that holds all the temporal folds together and apart in tension but it is also increasingly treated as a static continuity that is no longer moved but *stretched* elastically into the absolute future and past. Absolute time is thus the elasticity of a purportedly static and linear temporality.

Kinetically speaking, however, there is no flow or elasticity without motion. Elasticity is the kinetic condition for the description of absolute or infinite time. If the idea of an infinite line of time is defined by the geometric projection of a point to infinity, then this projection presupposes an elasticity of the point, and elastic projection presupposes the movement of the point with respect to itself.

After Aristotle, time had always been the *numerum motus*, or number of motion. Even mechanical motion still defined time as the number of motion, even if anything whatsoever, as a number, could become the measure of another motion. The early modern theory of absolute time finally broke with the ontological primacy of motion over time, even as it still failed to break free from the primary creative force or power of God. No longer was time the measure of motion, but time took on an existence independent of any created body or motion.

Kinetically speaking, the flow of time itself was considered an elastic line stretching infinitely far into the future and into the past. Lived natural times were only points on this infinite line. Lived time and mathematical time were merely the qualitative and quantitative dimensions of the temporal folds *in the absolutely elastic line of time* (see Figure 31.3).

One of the earliest formulations of absolute time is in the work of Descartes.[17] While the beginnings of the idea of absolute time can clearly be seen in previous notions of potential, mathematical, or quantitative time, there is one very important difference: absolute time is purely continuous,

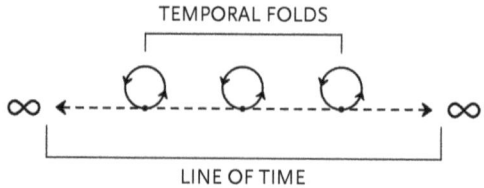

Figure 31.3 Elastic Line of Time

infinite, and unchanging. The mathematical idea of numerical measure still deals with discrete, divisible, finite units that pass from one point to another in a tensional sequence along the flow of time.

Drawing on the Scholastic distinction between time (the number of motion) and duration (the persistence of being), Descartes argues, however, that while time differs according to the mind's measure of relative motions, duration in general does not differ at all with respect to movement:

> Now some attributes or modes are in the very things of which they are said to be attributes or modes, while others are only in our thought [*in nostra tantum cogitatione*]. For example, when time [*tempus*] is distinguished from duration taken in the general sense [*duratione generaliter*] and called the number of movement [*numerum motus*], it is simply a mode of thought [*modus cogitandi*]. For the duration which we find to be involved in movement is certainly no different from the duration involved in things which do not move. This is clear from the fact that if there are two bodies moving for one hour, one slowly and the other quickly, we do not reckon the time to be greater in the latter case than in the former, even though the amount of movement may be much greater. But in order to measure the duration of all things [*omnium durationem*], we compare their duration with the greatest and most regular motions, which give rise to years and days, and call this duration "time" [*hancque durationem tempus vocamus*]. Yet nothing is thereby added to duration, taken in its general sense, except a mode of thought.[18]

We can distinguish in our mind a difference between movement and rest, but in doing so nothing is added to duration itself. For Descartes, duration is absolutely unchanging insofar as God preserves or endures in the *same proportions of movement and rest* that he first introduced into creation.[19] However, he is still relatively different insofar as the bodies change in relation to one another. Therefore, motion is not an absolute change of place but "is relative only to contiguous bodies that are *regarded* as being at rest."[20] "For a body to 'move,' in the strict sense, is for there to be a change in what bodies it is in immediate contact with."[21] In this sense, nothing is added to the whole of duration and it remains proportionally unchanged.

This idea of *duratione generaliter* that has relative motion (expansion and contraction) but not absolute motion allows Descartes to break with the Scholastic definition of eternity as the simultaneity and coexistence of all times in a single static present. Duration is not an unmoved point at the center of a rotating sphere; it is the point stretched into an infinite flow that is mobile and differentiated at each point on the line, while at the same time absolutely static as a whole or totality of movement and rest. In other words, time is linearly elastic.

Although Newton is perhaps most well known for the theory of absolute time, he stands at the end of a long line of theorists, including some, like Pierre Gassendi (1592–1655), who were more radical. There is no question, however, that Newton had an incredible influence on the rise of absolute time during this period. Although following Isaac Barrow (1630–1677) almost word for word, Newton famously wrote in his *Principia*, "Absolute, true, and mathematical time, of itself, and from its own nature, flows equably without relation to anything external, and by another name is called duration."[22]

However, for Newton the flow of duration in general is itself absolutely motionless: "The Duration of a thing is not its flow [*ejus fluxio*], or any change, but its permanence and immutability in flowing time. All things endure in so far as they remain the same at any time. The duration of each thing flows, but its enduring substance does not flow, and is not changed with respect to before and after, but always remains the same."[23]

For all their differences, Newton's formulation of duration in this passage follows that of Descartes almost exactly. What is more, for all their revolutionary efforts to overthrow the primacy of movement above time, Newton and Descartes also both end up retaining the ontological primacy of force in the form of divine power. In his *De Gravitatione*, Newton explicitly argues that space and duration are emanations or effects of God's creative power. "Space is an affection of a being insofar as it is a being . . . [and] an emanative effect of the primarily existing being, since if any being whatsoever is posited, space is posited. And the same may be asserted for duration: for certainly both are affections or attributes of a being according to which the quantity of each individual's existence is denominated with respect to amplitude of presence [for space] and to persistence in its being [for duration]."[24] God, "the Maker and Lord of all things," Newton writes, "by existing always and everywhere, he constitutes Duration and Space. . . . In him are all things contained and moved; yet neither affects the other: God suffers nothing from the motion of bodies; bodies find no resistance from the omnipresence of God."[25] Duration and space are thus emanative effects or expressions of God's absolute power. He is not *in* duration and space, but they are effects produced by his existence. God is the absolute cause of all things, including all absolute forces, such as gravity,[26] that cause bodies to move. Duration expands and contracts, but as an absolute whole it does not change.

The description of abstract time as regionally elastic but absolutely unchanging thus provides the first foundation for a whole new theory of modern time in which time is no longer subordinated to motion, and eventually even the force of God himself.

CONCLUSION

The kinetic operations found in the medieval description of time thus attest to an increasing use of lived, mechanical, and elastic language to describe the flow of time. These theories of time, however, are not overcome or replaced by later transcendental theories of time but rather taken up and transformed by them. This is why it was necessary to treat them here first before moving on to Kant's radical new theory of time. These medieval and early-modern descriptions of time begin to displace the primacy of motion over time, and thus provide the basis for a modern phenomenological ontology of time.

In other words, having increasingly tried to throw off the yoke of motion over the course of the medieval and early-modern periods, the modern description of time was able to build on these efforts to throw off the ultimate yoke of force as well and to provide for time its own autonomous regime of ontological description, as seen in the next two chapters.

CHAPTER 32

Modern Phenomenology II

Circulation

This chapter argues that the descriptive primacy of time in modern ontology follows an elastic regime of motion. As we saw in the previous chapter, some degree of elasticity had always been part of the kinetic structure of "tensional" time. In early-modern descriptions of abstract or absolute time, the folds of lived time could expand and contract, as could the flow of time itself. However, this elasticity was also simultaneously subordinated to the ontological tensions of a more primary divine force.

Kant's theory of transcendental time introduced for the first time a theory of a fundamentally *temporal field of circulation*. In the temporal field, the flows that constitute lived, mechanical, and absolute time recirculate back through the whole series, creating a whole new temporal order. This is the temporal order of the phenomenological subject. The kinetic conditions of an experiencing phenomenological subject require that being itself must be internally differentiated in its folds and yet synthetically unified in its ego to affect "itself" in experience. In short, if being were not temporally differentiated according to an infinite multiplicity of folds along an infinite flow of time, it could not be receptive or self-affecting since it would already be identical to itself in an absolute metaphysical presence. The temporal field of circulation thus allows for both a synthetic unity and an analytic multiplicity required by the self-affecting being of the subject.

Following this core phenomenological commitment to the temporal nature of being, the modern theory of time is defined by at least four major kinetic differences from the early-modern theory of absolute time:

1. In contrast to the static totality of absolute time, the modern theories of time tend to be *unlimited* and nontotal. Time is no longer a whole but an open and unending sequence.
2. In contrast to the ontologically secondary status of time as an effect or emanation of creative power from God, modern time raises temporality to the highest ontological primacy in which all other ontological determinations occur.
3. In contrast to the identity of absolute space-time in a single substance, modern time distinguishes the two and grants true foundational status to time alone.
4. In contrast to the absolute horizontality of time, modern time introduces curvature to time, allowing it to become flexible. In the modern period, following Einstein's theory of relativity, time becomes a field of circulation within which different times become visible on the same surface.

In what follows, each of these four differences will be developed at length, following the historical emergence of phenomenological and elastic temporality.

Just as we identified three distinct kinetic descriptions of temporal elasticity in the previous chapter—the elasticity of the temporal fold (Augustine), of the multiplication of folds (Ockham), and of the line itself as a stretched point (Newton)—so in the next chapters we add four more—the circulation of the temporal field (Kant), the multiplication of the temporal field (Husserl), the process of temporalization (Heidegger), and the interval of time (Derrida).

THE CIRCULATION OF THE SUBJECT

In the *Critique of Pure Reason*, Kant puts forward the first description of the elastic temporal field. Against the empirical conception of time developed by Locke, Berkeley, and Hume, Kant argues that "time is not an empirical concept that has been abstracted from any experience. For simultaneity [*Zugleichsein*] or succession would not even enter our perception if the presentation of time did not underlie them a priori." According to Kant, the very existence of the retentional temporal folds of experience already presupposes a more primary temporal field of presentation such that there could even be a being that was "one and the same thing (simultaneously) or at different times (sequentially)."[1] The unity of simultaneity and difference of sequence thus, by their very nature, presuppose a more primary field or condition within which they appear as the same or different.

Kinetically, we can say then that if the "flow of time" was not itself already elastic, it would not be able to fold back over itself and affect itself in the form of subjective experience or temporal folding, such that things appear simultaneous or different for the subject of experience. Temporal folds, therefore, do not come preformed, but emerge as folds within a more primary field of time that must be able to expand and contrast elastically into simultaneous and different folds of the same field. As Kant says, "time is a necessary presentation that underlies all intuitions." The "actuality of appearances is possible only in time,"[2] which flows and folds up into these appearances.

Kant's incredible insight here is to have realized that the temporal field is not at all frozen or fixed but must be able to fold itself into distinct regions as well as stretch infinitely in more than one direction. "To say that time is infinite," for Kant, "means nothing more than that any determinate magnitude of time is possible only through limitations [put] on a single underlying time. Hence the original presentation *time* must be given as unlimited."[3]

Here Kant makes quite clear that the unlimited nature of time is defined by a twofold kinetic operation: that it is always possible to add one more determinate temporal fold and that these temporal folds are folds in an unlimited flow of underlying time. If there is only one underlying time, then all limitations on this time must be *internal limitations* of this time on itself and not by something else. Although Kant does not explicitly describe the self-limitation of time as a fold, folding is in fact the perfect way to think about how a continuous single flow limits itself without cutting or introducing anything other than itself.

For Kant, the extensive definition of movement as change of place[4] also already presupposes the more radical continuity, differentiation, and elasticity of the flow of time itself. Only after the flow of time has created a series of self-limiting folds or "places" on an elastic line are these folds able to change the order of their relations on this folded line:

> The concept of change, and with it the concept of motion (as change of place) is possible only through and in the presentation of time; and that if this presentation were not (inner) a priori intuition, no concept whatsoever could make comprehensible the possibility of a change, i.e., of a combination, in one and the same object, of contradictorily opposed predicates (e.g., one and the same thing's being in a place and not being in that same place). Only in time can both of two contradictorily opposed determinations be met with in one thing: viz., sequentially.[5]

Each temporal fold remains the same temporal fold precisely because it is repeated again and again in the same underlying flow of time. Once these folds are repeated in places relative to a given circulation, they can then be said to "change places." For Kant, empirical movement is therefore subordinated to the transcendental flow of time. Accordingly, the temporal folds or distinct moments are nothing other than the elastic folds of time itself. "Time is not something [contra Newton] that is self-subsistent [*fur sich selbst bestehen*]," or independent from the temporal folds that constitute it, nor is it, contra Leibniz, something "that attaches to things as an objective determination," since temporal folds are always ordered moments in a larger transcendental field or fold of the flow of time itself.[6] This is Kant's truly original description of time.

Time is not only elastic in its creation of temporal folds and in its unlimited, qua self-limiting, horizontality, but also in its circulatory elasticity. In other words, the flow of time in which the temporal folds emerge is capable of folding back over onto itself and recirculating back through all the temporal folds, ordering and distributing them. In this sense, time constitutes a true circulatory field within which a temporal series is internally ordered. "Time," Kant writes, "is nothing but the form of inner sense, i.e., of the intuiting we do of ourselves and of our inner state. For time cannot be a determination of outer appearances, [because] it does not belong to any shape or position, etc., but rather determines the relation of presentations in our inner state."[7] It is in this elastic operation that the temporal folds are united as moments with the same circulation or subjective field. Without this temporal circulation, time falls back into either its absolute determination as a linear totality (Newton et al.) or its relative determination as something merely added onto things (Locke et al.). For Kant, time becomes truly foundational and constitutive as "the formal a priori condition of all appearances generally."[8]

As the structure of all appearing in general, time is also the structure within which the subject itself appears to itself. For Kant, time "is the direct condition of inner appearances (of our souls), and precisely thereby also, indirectly, a condition of outer appearances."[9] The temporal field is therefore the objective condition for the production of the subject and of the distinct things that appear to the subject in a given regime of temporal circulation. In other words, within a given regime of circulation, the subject appears as a series of first-person temporal folds (I, I, I) alongside a series of objective temporal folds (it, it, it) that have the status of being exterior to the subject by virtue of being distinguished from it *in time*. Time is therefore the condition of both interior and exterior presentation in general.

However, this same seriality of time also reveals the fundamentally fragmented or plural nature of subjectivity and objectivity that haunts empiricism. Subject and object, as a series of temporal folds, are multiple. Therefore it is only in the circulatory field of time itself that the series of I's and its are unified, synthesized, ordered, repeated, and represented. The subject could not have created the temporal field, because it is precisely within this field that the subject *is produced in the first place*. In this sense, time must operate as an *ontological determination* of being's capacity to be receptive to itself in the form of the temporal fold *and* in its presentation of itself to itself as a synthetic unity in the form of an elastic circulation of a limited series of temporal folds (see Figure 32.1).[10]

Time is therefore the precondition of all sensation and differentiation. If there were no temporal seriality in being, there would be no differentiation; if there were no real differentiation, then there could be folding—no touching of two different points to each other in the same flow. Without differentiation, there would be no affect and thus no experiencing subject.

As such, time is the general structure of affection within which the subject is receptive to itself and to objects in general. Insofar as time is the general condition of sensation, it is the constitutive movement of subjectivity itself, and thus nothing apart from it. Without the process of temporal circulation (the subject) that lays out, orders, and unifies the fragmentary moments of temporal folding, there is no time. Time is therefore, by definition, fundamentally circulatory, folded, and elastic. Without the plicated structure of folded self-affection of both the field and the fold, time would collapse back into an absolute and undifferentiated line.

Kant clearly rejects the notion of absolute time. Thus, "only absolute reality must, by the reasons adduced above, be denied to time."[11] Absolute reality as a frozen or eternal totality has no temporality because it has no movement, elasticity, or flow beyond itself. As a fixed totality, "the absolute" can have no sensation and thus no subjectivity and thus temporality.

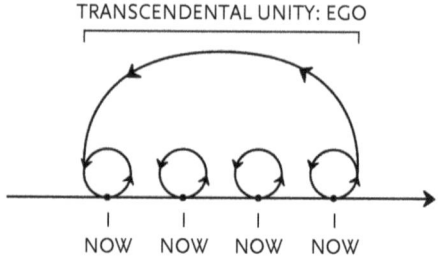

Figure 32.1 Circulation of Temporal Folds

"Time attaches not to objects themselves, but merely to the subject intuiting them."[12] Time is not something else that transcends objects and is added to them by the mind, but it is the immanent process of self-affection itself that constitutes the subject and the circulation within which the folds of the subject and object are ordered.

For Kant, time is therefore the structural condition within which a limited series of temporal folds appears. Time is not an "absolute totality" but an unlimited ontological and immanent sequence that can always be delimited, synthesized, or folded one more time. For Kant, the linear flow of time becomes bent and folds back over itself in regions of autonomous circulation. Outside these circulations, time is nothing. Within them, however, time becomes phenomenologically and ontologically primary over space, eternity, and force. Therefore, even though Kant explicitly subordinates motion to time, his theory of time already presupposes the deeper flux and fold of time itself, as Hegel and others attest to after him.

THE CIRCULATION OF NATURE

After Kant, Hegel (1770–1831) was the first to render explicit the ontologization of time and subjectivity that was implicit in Kant. Where Kant began with the universality of the subject and ended with the necessary ontologization of time, Hegel begins with the ontologization of time and ends with the necessary universality of the subject. In this respect, Hegel is the inversion of Kant. Despite the numerous and fundamental differences between them, however, both are committed to a similar descriptive primacy of elastic time as the condition of subjectivity and the structure of appearance of all beings in general.

Hegel's ontology of time occurs in the second volume of his great *Encyclopedia of the Philosophical Sciences* (1817), *Philosophy of Nature*. In the first volume, Hegel lays out the formal logic of being as such, in the second he lays out the nature of being as appearing and existence, and in the third he lays out a phenomenology of being as it is known or understood by humans historically. Since we are concerned here only with the primacy of time, we focus on Hegel's most sustained treatment of time in the *Philosophy of Nature*, in which he lays out the ontological structure for the appearance of being in general.

The being of *nature*, for Hegel, is the ontological condition within which humanity emerges. The collective human spirit (*geist*), itself part of nature, will eventually, through history, overcome the contradictions that nature introduces and attain an absolute knowledge of itself as the process of nature's own self-knowledge. "In nature," Hegel writes, "spirit actualizes itself only as its own other, as spirit asleep."[13] Nature is spirit asleep because it has not yet come to know itself through the notion or idea. "The Notion strives to burst the shell of outer existence and to become for itself."[14]

It should therefore be noted that, for Hegel, the ontological primacy of time has the inverted status it might have had previously in the history of philosophy. Previously, first principles were always already perfect and complete *in themselves and for themselves*. For Hegel, however, they are *in themselves* but only become perfect and complete once they are known to be so through the strictly temporal-historical development of human self-knowledge *for itself*. In other words, nature only comes to increasingly know itself *in time*. Accordingly, time is not only ontologically primary for Hegel, as we will demonstrate shortly, it is also phenomenologically primary insofar as it is the privileged structure by which the collective human spirit comes to know itself in human history. "World history," Hegel writes, "is therefore, above all, the interpretation of spirit in time, just as in space the idea interprets itself as Nature."[15]

Even though nature is sublated in spirit through history, history comes to an end when spirit achieves absolute knowledge. Time, however, does not. The human process of history comes to an end in the form of the state, but the temporal nature of being, which is even more primary than history, continues on. In this sense, time is even more primary for Hegel than it could have ever been for any previous philosopher, since being itself becomes temporally. As temporally differentiated, it is both the condition of self-knowledge (self-affection) and the condition of impossibility of immediate self-knowledge, since being is fundamentally differentiated from itself *in time*. Therefore, the final form of the knowledge of being can only be the knowledge of being as the *process itself as a whole* of temporal difference: temporal becoming.

In his *Jena Lectures on the Philosophy of Nature* (1803–1804), Hegel begins his ontology of nature with the primacy of time. He defines time as an unlimited succession of quantitative moments. The quantitative moments, all external to one another and indistinguishable from one another, form a single continuous line stretching out indefinitely. These continuous, undifferentiated, and external moments of time together form a whole, which Hegel calls "space." Time thus comes out of itself into space as its totality. The whole process of time can therefore be posited as sublated in its purely spatial expression. The single infinitely elastic line of time is defined by a direction, but that direction implies that there are other directions. Space thus limits time by introducing a three-dimensionality to the directions of time.[16]

However, thirteen years later, in Part Two of Hegel's *Encyclopedia, Philosophy of Nature* (1817), he gives space and time more of a coprimacy with a similar definition. Hegel first describes space. He defines nature first and foremost as pure quantitative externality:[17] "It is a wholly ideal side-by-sideness because it is self-externality; and it is absolutely continuous, because this asunderness is still quite abstract, and contains no specific difference within itself."[18] Space is immediate, indifferent, quantity, in-it-self. No aspect of space is any different from any other. Interestingly, this is the same definition he gives of time in the Jena lectures.

Space is not constituted by points, he says, but points occur in space as its negation. The point is the negation of space because it is a singular localization or qualitative difference among quantitative indifferentiation. By its localization in space somewhere it negates the rest of space everywhere else. Therefore, Hegel writes, "the difference of space is, however, essentially a determinate, qualitative difference. As such, it is (a), first, the negation of space itself, because this is immediate differenceless self-externality, the point."[19] As a negation of space, however, the point is a point in space. The relation of the point to that which it negates (space) is the line: the relation between the point to what is not itself. The line therefore "does not consist of points, . . . for the line is rather the point existing outside of itself, i.e., relating itself to space and sublating itself. . . . Here the point is conceived as the primary and positive element which forms the starting-point."[20]

The straight line is thus not composed of points but rather the elastic expansion of the point outward. However, the flow of the point into the line next encounters other lateral dimensions outside itself, which it confronts in the form of its bend or curvature. But by curving, the line makes possible a surface or plane insofar as its curve closes back in on itself in a circle. "It is thus the restoration of the spatial totality which now contains the negative moment within itself, an *enclosing surface* which separates off a single whole space."[21] The enclosing surface of the circle completes and totalizes the whole of space by enclosing all other geometric shapes.[22]

When these qualitative differences—point, line, enclosing circle—are posited for themselves, *this is time*. Each of the qualitative differences of space is actually the same space at determinately different times. "Now time is precisely the existence of this perpetual self-sublation; in time, therefore, the point has actuality. Difference has stepped out of space; this means that it has ceased to be this indifference, it is for itself in all its unrest, it is no longer paralyzed."[23] Time can hold all spatial indifferences together in a single moment that is different from another moment: past, present, and future. It sublates all of space into a single moment. "The truth of space is time, and thus space becomes time; the transition to time is not made subjectively by us, but made by space itself."[24] Explicitly pushing aside any Kantian subjectivist-sounding residues, Hegel boldly declares that space moves and folds itself and, even more boldly, that pure time is the very condition of this very self-affection of space with itself.[25] Without time there are no "moments" in the dialectic of space.

However, time, for Hegel, is also defined by its own internal negations by which it falls back into indifference. The temporal moment is a merely passing moment of becoming between past, present, and future moments and is therefore external to itself.[26] Time is thus the objective determination of actual beings insofar as they flow into and out of being. It is not because they are in some absolute time like a river that they perish, but because "things themselves are temporal, and to be so is their objective determination."[27] Time flows because beings flow temporally. While space remains purely abstract, time is the first truly ontological determination of the being of beings as such in their objective determination. Being in its being is therefore fundamentally finite, temporal, and self-affective.

However, insofar as time is the continuous passing between exchangeable moments, it remains, like space, abstract: "There is as yet no real difference."[28] Being simply passes from being (past/future) into nonbeing (future/past) and back again in an endless circle. The present "now" is the truth of the process as a whole insofar as the past and future *are not*—but *become*. The true present is therefore the notion of eternity, i.e., the negation of time, i.e., space.

The dialectic of time and space is therefore torn mutually asunder. No wonder Hegel changed his mind about starting with space or time. Both are dialectically coprimary dimensions of the same dialectical process. As Hegel himself shows in his lectures, whether we start with one or the other makes no difference, since each is the truth of the other. The starting points can easily be reversed. "We see that this immediate unity of space and time is already the ground of their being; for the negative of space is time, and the positive, i.e., the being of the differences of time, is space."[29] The differences in space (point, line, surface) mirror the differences in time (moment, flow, present), both of which are sublated in the same figure of the enclosed circle that renders them both elastic and self-affective but also indifferent in their unity as place, space-time, or now-here.

The third moment of the dialectic of nature is thus the transition of space into time and of time into space, or the transition between places: movement. Time gains existence through space, and space becomes self-affective in time, but it is only through motion that units of space-time (place) first become actually distinct from one another in different movements.[30]

"There are three different places: the present place, the place about to be occupied, and the place which has just been vacated; the vanishing of the dimensions of time is paralyzed. But at the same time there is only one place, a universal of these places, which remains unchanged through all the changes; it is duration, existing immediately in accordance with its Notion and as such it is Motion."[31]

Movement, for Hegel, is thus the continuous transition from place to place and therefore capable of introducing actual differences between the dimensions of space and time, all at the same time. But in the process of connecting space with itself and time with itself in one and the same motion, the notion of motion is all one place: the place of continuous motion. In this way the process or becoming of space and time as a whole is the actuality of self-affection of being with itself, or the subject. "Just as Time is the purely formal soul of Nature, and Space, according to Newton, is the sensorium of God, so Motion is the Notion of the veritable soul of the world. We are accustomed to regard it as a predicate or a state; but Motion is, in fact, the Self, the Subject as Subject, the abiding of vanishing."[32]

In other words, the minimal ontological condition of subjectivity is first and foremost spatiotemporal differentiation: the self-affection of external being with itself. The unity of these two conditions defines the kinetic process identical to the subjectivity of being itself. In short, because being is temporal and temporality is the minimal condition of subjectivity (the soul of nature), being itself is subject. Substance by its very temporal ontological structure becomes subject *through motion*, or continually changing self-affection.

In a long *Zusatz* (additional note), Hegel brings all three moments of the dialectic together in the perfect unity of the circle. It is worth quoting him at length:

> This return of the line is the circle; it is the Now, Before and After which have closed together in a unity in which these dimensions are indifferent, so that Before is equally After, and vice versa. It is in circular motion that the necessary paralysis of these dimensions is first posited in space. Circular motion is the spatial or subsistent unity of the dimensions of time. The point proceeds towards a place which is its future, and leaves one which is the past; but what it has left behind is at the same time what it has still to reach: it has been already at the place which it is reaching. Its goal is the point which is its past; and this is the truth of time, that the goal is not the future but the past. The motion which relates itself to the centre is itself the plane, motion as the synthetic whole in which exist its moments, the extinction of the motion in the centre, the motion itself and its relation to its extinction, namely the radii of the circle. But

this plane itself moves and becomes the other of itself, a complete space; or the reversion-into-self, the immobile centre, becomes a universal point in which the whole is peacefully absorbed. In other words, it is motion in its essence. . . . . In the circle, these are in a unity; the circle is the restored Notion of duration, Motion extinguished within itself. There is posited Mass, the persistent, the self-consolidated, which exhibits motion as its possibility. Now this is how we conceive the matter: since there is motion, some-thing moves; but this some-thing which persists is matter. Space and Time are filled with Matter. . . . Matter has often been made the starting-point, and Space and Time have then been regarded as forms of it. What is right in this standpoint is that Matter is what is real in Space and Time. But these, being abstract, must present themselves here as the First, and then it must appear that Matter is their truth. Just as there is no Motion without Matter, so too, there is no Matter without Motion. Motion is the process, the transition of Time into Space and of Space into Time: Matter, on the other hand, is the relation of Space and Time as a peaceful identity.[33]

Let's take this one point at a time. The circle is the unity of the whole enclosure of space because it contains all other shapes. The circle is the unity of the whole of time because it connects the past, present, and future together in a single whole of eternity. These circles are the truth of one another insofar as they are actually expressed by the same circular movement from one place to another along the circumference.

However, as a circular movement that goes out and returns to itself, it produces an enclosed interior unity, which is matter: the materiality of the subjective process. Circular motion extinguishes itself in self-affection so that it will hold together in materiality. The complete process forms an immobile but temporally differentiated whole. Hegel thus rejects the ontological primacy of matter and motion and affirms instead the primacy of time. In short, for Hegel, it is temporal differentiation that grants space its dialectical moments, which in turn grants motion its kinetic regions of differentiation in the circle.

Kinetic Analysis

Hegel, like Kant, posits a fundamental continuity and elasticity of time in the form of an unlimited line that folds back over itself in order to produce a subject that can order, represent, and synthesize each of its heterogeneous moments to itself in the form of the higher unity of the circle. In the circle, all of time and space stand still and ready for recall and reorganization. Hegel presupposes the ontological primacy of quantitative and qualitative continuum in space and time, respectively, but by circumscribing them in the totality of an immobile self-extinguishing circle, he forecloses the possibility of real motion outside the circle. In contrast to kinetic circulation, Hegel thinks his temporal folds never leak or stray, and that they come fully formed as purely logical circles instead of the periodic rhythms and limit cycles of folded flows.

Hegel thus presents a case in which motion must be implicitly presupposed and used to describe other attributes, which then appear to explain and create motion itself. For example, in the very first step of the dialectic, Hegel describes how an unlimited and continuous line is produced not by multiplying discrete points but by stretching a point out into an unlimited line. Interestingly, this is precisely how his Jena lectures begin as well: with the existence of a single continuous and unlimited line of time. In both cases, Hegel must presuppose the *flow of the line*. As such, the "line of space" and "flow of time" do not *logically* curve, they *actually* curve because they are already in motion. But motion, Hegel says, is only something derived from the dialectical synthesis of time and space, which he says are "logically primary." The elastic motion of the stretched point is thus presupposed only in order to derive it later on *from time*.

Hegel therefore posits time and space as logically primary in order to derive the idea of motion, when in fact the situation is the reverse. The point is already something distinguished within a more primary kinetic medium such that it could be in motion in the first place. Pure time or pure space must already presuppose motion, or else create it out of nothing. Once the point moves, it strangely appears as if movement comes from the point itself—which is impossible unless motion had already been there from the beginning. Therefore, although motion is clearly required for the *actuality* of space and time, Hegel nonetheless starts by assuming that it is *not needed* and instead first posits the immobility of space and time, and then shows that movement actually emerges from a merely *logical contradiction* internal to abstract space and time.

However, motion does not and cannot emerge from what is immobile and purely logical.[34] One consequence of beginning with the logical abstractions of space and time as opposed to the actualities of matter and motion is that Hegel ends up considering the abstractions of space and time independently, as if they were complete totalities or circles. By making abstract space and time the ontological models for matter and motion, he ends up reducing motion to an *abstract and immobile motion* that simply extinguishes itself in itself in the form of an enclosed temporal subjectivity. In short, by starting with totality and immobility, he is incapable of generating motion and flow.

Movement, then, is simply reduced to the derived unity of the two abstract forms, and not as their true producer. Matter is dead on arrival insofar as it is already circumscribed by the enclosed circle of space-time. Matter is not in motion but rather defined in advance by the formal and immobile logical unity of time and his temporal description of space. Hegel must therefore presuppose the flow of actual movement but only in order to deny it so that he can re-deduce it later from the abstract immobility and totality of space and time. He begins with the elastic being of time stretched out in a line, and then bent into a circle, and thus deduces temporal becoming as motion, instead of beginning with kinetic becoming and deducing temporal being from motion.

THE CIRCULATION OF CAPITAL

Karl Marx (1818–1883) draws on Hegel's insight into the ontological primacy of time, but he does so strictly historically. Marx sees Hegel as having articulated an ontology *for his time*, an ontology *of time* that rose to power alongside the rise of Western capitalism. One of Marx's most incredible innovations was to identify a historical ontology of time at the heart of capitalism. According to Marx, capital treats all beings as objective condensations or "crystallizations" of time.[35] Things in capitalism are treated as so many temporal folds held together in an elastic process of circulation capable of expansion and contraction (accumulation).[36]

Marx states quite clearly and repeatedly that the goal of the process of capital accumulation is essentially to "annihilate space with time."[37] In his description, capitalism treats all beings as strictly temporal differences. By reducing transport times, for example, and increasing continuity in the flows of movement, spatial relations shrink.[38] It is not by accident that the Industrial Revolution began first with liquids like crude oil, then second with semi-liquids like wheat and grain, and only later with metalworking and mechanical industries, when the assembly-line system figured out how to treat larger objects as fluids, too.[39] In this way the capitalist process of production is modeled on the infinite fluidity of time and thus achieves the highest technological success with materials that approximate its vaporous fluidity. For Marx, capitalism melts all that is solid into air, because this is the material form closest to the pure fluidity of time itself. The more matter is made to flow through the circulations of capitalist production, the *easier it is to treat matter in motion as time*.

Time not only annihilates space by treating matter as temporal flows, but it also annihilates human activity insofar as it becomes the very organizing condition of social and natural life. In contrast to the historical idea that time is the measure of motion, in capitalism all movement itself becomes *ordered by time*. Capitalist temporality thus

> presupposes that labour has been equalized by the subordination of man to the machine or by the extreme division of labour, that men are effaced by their labour; that the pendulum of the clock has become as accurate a measure of the relative activity of two workers as it is of the speed of two locomotives. Therefore, we should not say that one man's hour is worth another man's hour, but rather that one man during an hour is worth just as much as another man during an hour. *Time is everything, man is nothing; he is at most, time's carcase*. Quality no longer matters. Quantity alone decides everything; hour for hour, day for day.[40]

The human body and its activity under capitalism is now reduced entirely to a unit of time. The wage form of value is precisely a unit measure of labor-*time*. Strictly speaking, in capitalism there is no human being, there is only labor-time. There is no labor that is not temporal and no time that cannot be filled with labor. Time becomes everything. The human body is simply the dead carcass of time—a commodity in its purely quantitative and exchangeable temporal form.

Capitalist circulation is therefore the circulation and ordering of temporal folds, commodities, and the general condition under which they can be represented as parts within the whole capitalist process. Capitalism cannot be defined strictly by quantities of time but only by *temporal quantities*: folds of time. "Time," Marx writes, "is the room [*raum*] of human development. A man who has no free time to dispose of, whose whole lifetime, apart from the mere physical interruptions by sleep, meals, and so forth, is absorbed by his labour for the capitalist, is less than a beast of burden."[41] Time becomes the *raum* or space of human activity. Space and movement are thus both subordinated to the demands of labor-time. A person who does not have free time also has no space or movement to live.

In this sense, capitalist time is not the same as modern absolute time because it is a specifically elastic time that responds to the demands of the capitalist market, as if the market itself were a subject organizing human beings as temporal folds within its field of circulation. As demands increase, time expands the working day and gathers more surplus labor-time; as demand decreases, time contracts and releases workers into the floating unmeasured time of unemployment. Time is thus treated as elastic because its limits are the same as the limits of the market, and the limits of the market are elastic.

The market is therefore not in time as much as it is the *condition of temporality itself*, within which all of being is represented on the market in the form of more or less liquid or crystalized time. Capital is the continuous circulatory process within which labor and commodities are quantities or temporal folds of labor-time.[42]

Kinetic Analysis

The elasticity of temporal circulation that defines capitalism is also based on a still more fundamental presupposition of flows of movement. For example, the literal movement and circulation of human activity, workers, and commodities in manufacture and transportation is precisely what allows space to be abolished and for time to expand and contract in the first place. The elasticity of time in capitalism therefore requires first and foremost an actual movement of bodies—a migrant proletariat and the semi-liquid commodity—that it must presuppose as the "so-called lever of capitalist accumulation,"[43] but which it must at the same time devalorize and negate as a retroactive effect of its more primary circulation of their kinetic activity.

The major difference between Hegelian ontology and Marx's theory of capitalist production is the difference between the circle and the spiral. For Hegel, the dialectic of being always returns to itself in a circle of unity because motion is derived from the abstract form of circular time. For Marx, however, the dialectical movement of being is differentiated such that each return of the process also introduces something new—thus producing a spiral formation. Capitalism is the social ontology that has learned to feed on and adapt itself to the constant introduction of novelty into being. It is not just elastic in its fold over itself but also in its endless expansion outward and around.

For Marx, capitalism is therefore fundamentally elastic and spiraled: "Looked at concretely, accumulation can be resolved into the production of capital on a progressively increasing scale. The cycle of simple reproduction alters its form and, to use Sismondi's expression, changes into a spiral."[44] The progressive elongation of temporal elasticity in the form of the spiral is quite different from that of the spiraled space of the primitive world that was already preaccomplished. The primitive spiraled movement of being is regular, rhythmic, and unified. One moves along it as along a road already laid out. Modern elastic time, on the other hand, is spiraled only because the line itself is continually contracting and expanding elastically in irregular fits and starts. The spiral is irregular, deformed, and multiple.[45]

Time circulates because it is elastic. It is the elasticity of temporal circulation that makes possible the expansion and contraction of the subject, nature, and capitalism. Furthermore, this same elasticity is what makes possible the multiplication of elastic temporal fields as well, as we will see in the next chapter.

CHAPTER 33

Modern Phenomenology III

Multiplication

After Marx's analysis of capitalist temporality, Edmund Husserl (1859–1938) introduced an even more radical elasticity into transcendental temporality in the form of an "absolute flow of time."[1] This move set him apart from both Hume and Kant. Hume had denied the possibility of any empirical experience of temporal unification in the form of the subject, and thus denied the elasticity of time, saying, "All my hopes vanish when I come to explain the principles, that unite our successive perceptions in our thought or consciousness."[2] Hume therefore had to explicitly presuppose the continuous passing of time, but he could not defend this thesis on the basis of our experience of successive moments.

Kant then concluded that the flow of time was not experienceable as such, and thus must have a transcendental and singular unity. As such, however, this poses a problem for the intersubjectivity of such fields and the conditions on which they are known from within them as fields. Husserl's remarkable innovation was to *multiply and stretch* the temporal field itself such that any given temporal field can become a subcirculation or conjunction within an even larger field. This is possible, as we will see, because the flow of time is absolutely elastic.[3]

MULTIPLE CIRCULATIONS OF TIME

Husserl's concept of absolute flow marks a radical shift in his thinking away from the empiricism of Franz Brentano's theory of intentionality.

In the first 1900 edition of *Logical Investigations*, for example, Husserl is unable to find, echoing Hume, a theory of subjective unity, and thus temporal unity, saying, "I must frankly confess, however, that I am quite unable to find this ego, this primitive, necessary centre of relations [to the contents of experience]."[4] In the second edition in 1913, however, he finds this unity in the transcendental subject: "I have since managed to find [this ego], i.e., have learnt not to be led astray from a pure grasp of the given through corrupt forms of the ego-metaphysic."[5] More precisely, this breakthrough occurs for the first time in his 1905 *Lectures on the Consciousness of Internal Time*, with his introduction of the concept of the "absolute flow."

Husserl's concept of the absolute flow reveals the major problem confronted by all hitherto existing temporal ontologies: that temporality must presuppose a continuous flow of motion that it divides into tenses, but it must also presuppose that the tenses already divided the continuum insofar as time itself is primary. However, if the divisions precede the continuum, the continuum is reduced to a succession of tenses, and is therefore not a true continuum and therefore does not flow. In short, Husserl's theory of time confronts the same ontological dilemma faced by all philosophy: is movement continuous or discrete? Husserl's lectures on time consciousness are a brilliant demonstration of this battle and result in a radically elastic theory of time.

Husserl first introduces the concept of the absolute flow in his tripartite distinction between three kinds of temporal constitution: (1) temporally *constituted* things as we encounter them in empirical experience, (2) temporally *constituting* immanent unities in preempirical time, and (3) the absolute time-constituting flow of consciousness.[6] These three levels of constitution correspond to empirical, transcendental, and absolute flow, respectively.

First Level. At the first level, individual objects are constituted as unities "in the stream," "that is, [the time-object] continuously exists in time and is something identical in this continuous existence, which at the same time can be regarded as a process. Conversely: What exists in time continuously exists in time and is the unity belonging to the process that carries with it inseparably the unity of what endures in the process as it unfolds."[7]

This is strikingly close to the kinetic theory of time. The constituted object is a unity of a process as a processual unity, namely a fold in a flow. Its identity belongs to nothing other than the process itself enduring, folding, unfolding, and refolding in the flow. If there is anything like a time point, Husserl writes, "it is conceivable only as the phase of a process, a phase in

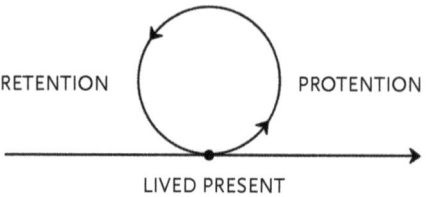

Figure 33.1 Husserl's Temporal Fold

which the duration of an individual being also has its point."[8] Kinetically, we could say that if there is anything like a time point it is the point of intersection or affection produced by the folding of the flow. The temporal fold as a whole is its retentional phase, while its point is its self-intersection (see Figure 33.1).

Second Level. At the second level, these temporal folds are conjoined together in the stream in larger and smaller overlapping successive phases that constitute the unity of the object without being "expanded into a continuous succession; and therefore the flow cannot be conceived as so transformed that this phase would be extended in identity with itself."[9] A constituting temporal phase is therefore a conjunction of constituted objects that, as only a phase in an absolute stream, can never express the identity of the folded objects it conjoins. The series of overlapping conjunctions therefore produces a kind of patchwork continuum. Temporal conjunctions also give relative order to movement and rest, speed and slowness, with respect to other constituting conjunctions. This is possible because the conjunctions are themselves elastic. Constituting conjunctions can expand and contract to include more or less temporal folds. "Any phase of a change can be expanded," Husserl writes, "into a rest, and any phase of a rest can be carried over into a change." With respect to the whole, any given motion will be small, but with respect to its smaller subcircuits, it will be large.

Third Level. At the third level, these successive temporal conjunctions or phases are held together in the absolute flow of time itself. "This flow is something we speak of in conformity with what is constituted, but it is not 'something in objective time.' It is absolute subjectivity."[10] The absolute flow is not other or beyond the constituted temporal folds and their constituting conjunctions; it is immanent with them without being merely identical to them. The absolute flow is what circulates through them, between them, and folds back over them all to produce the continuous unity of the transcendental and temporal subjective field. On this point Kant and Husserl both agree—temporal circulation is identical to subjective circulation. This is precisely because they agree that ontological affectivity is the a priori condition of all subjectivity.

Husserl's break with empirical intentionality here is explicit:

> Consequently, what we called "act" or "intentional experience" in the *Logical Investigations* is in every instance a flow in which a unity becomes constituted in immanent time (the judgment, the wish, etc.), a unity that has its immanent duration and that may progress more or less rapidly. These unities, which become constituted in the absolute stream, exist in immanent time, which is one; and in this time the unities can be or have durations of equal length (or perhaps have the same duration, that is, in the case of two immanent objects that endure simultaneously). Moreover, the unities have a certain determinability with respect to before and after.[11]

Intentional acts themselves as constituting temporal conjunctions are now unities in a more primary immanent time or absolute stream that unifies them all in the absolute subject. "Now in reflection we find a single flow that breaks down into many flows, but this multitude nevertheless has a kind of unity that permits and requires us to speak of one flow" within which "the multitude elapses 'conjointly.'"[12] . . . Immanent time is constituted as one for all immanent objects and processes."[13] The absolute flow is therefore the unity and identity of all other flows.

However, and this is Husserl's true radicality, this elastic unity of circulation, capable of holding together all the temporal folds and their successive constituting intentionalities, is itself capable of becoming unified by yet another larger circulatory unity ad infinitum. "The stream (the absolute flow) in its turn is supposed to be objective and to have its time. Here again a consciousness constituting this objectivity and a consciousness constituting this time would be necessary. On principle we could reflect again, and so in infinitum."[14] The absolute stream is therefore not a totality but a pure multiplicity of multiplicities. Any thing that is given is therefore given "as the unity of an absolute multiplicity that is not given."[15]

This, Husserl says, is the essence of temporal unity: multiplicity. "These unities are unities of multiplicity, that is, unities that necessarily point back to multiplicities belonging to the ultimate temporal flow in which they are necessarily presented and in which are adumbrated in the flow of time. The absolute to which all phenomenological analysis leads back lies here, in this flow. We speak of the absolute flow of phenomenological time and say that all unities become constituted in it."[16]

These higher unifications of unifications are possible for two reasons: (1) temporality is absolutely elastic and can always fold one more time over itself, and (2) temporality is differentiated in tenses that make possible self-affection. "The flow of the consciousness that constitutes immanent time not only exists but is so remarkably and yet intelligibly fashioned that a self-appearance of the flow necessarily exists in it, and therefore the flow itself must necessarily be apprehensible in the flowing. The self-appearance of the flow does not require a second flow; on the contrary, it constitutes itself as a phenomenon in itself. The constituting and the constituted coincide."[17]

While this may sound initially shocking and even absurd, as Husserl says, it is nonetheless true: "the flow of consciousness constitutes its own unity."[18] This is possible because the absolute flow is so elastic in its movement that it can endlessly fold back over itself in larger and larger unified circulations. This was not possible at the level of mere constituting intentionality because its series of successions was never given a higher immanent unity in the first place. Once a higher subjective unity is possible, then an even higher unity can circulate through that unity and all its constituting conjunctions and its temporal objects all at once. This is possible because the retentional unities and intentional unities of these unities are simply two aspects of *the same absolute stream* (see Figure 33.2).

The unities of absolute temporal immanence, however, never produce an absolute transcendence in being. They remain as foldings and unfoldings in one immanent time of pure multiplicity. Therefore, Husserl writes, "the *temporal form* is not a phansiological form in the ultimate sense, not a form of absolute being, but only a form of individual objects. We must say: It is not an absolute but only a form of 'appearances.'"[19] Thus, being, for Husserl, just as it was for Kant, has no absolute status as a knowable totality *precisely because it is temporal*. If being were total and complete, there would be no appearance at all, since everything would already be present without differentiation, like a homogenous now. Without temporal differentiation there could be no self-affection and thus no experience, and thus no multiplicity of circulations or fields of self-affection.

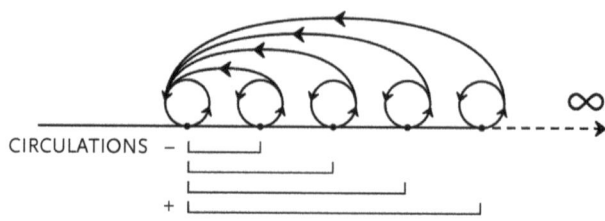

Figure 33.2 Husserl's Temporal Circulations in the Elastic Stream

In short, being must be *absolutely temporal* and not simply *absolute*. The temporal form, therefore, is not a transcendent determination of absolute being but an immanent determination of the absolute temporality of being itself. Furthermore, as an absolute flow, there is always a running-off of time in which time's elasticity keeps pushing farther and farther ahead such that something new is always being introduced into the flow. "Something new is always being 'added in front' in order to flow away immediately in its turn," but always "reaches beyond this, always adding something new" again.[20] As new flows and folds are added and conjoined, the absolute flow traverses them all and continually unifies them into an open and horizontal whole of Querintentionalitat (transverse intentionality).[21]

It is here, however, that Husserl's concept of the absolute flow encounters the fundamental problem of ontological temporality. On the one hand, everything hinges on the absolute continuity and flow of time, but on the other hand, self-affectivity requires there to be a fundamental temporal differentiation in being. If being is ontologically divided into tenses from the beginning, how can the succession of discrete tenses ever get back to absolute continuum and flow? Husserl ends up trying to argue both. He first argues that it makes no sense to talk about the before and after of absolute constituting flows:

> Time-constituting phenomena . . . are evidently objectivities fundamentally different from those constituted in time. They are neither individual objects nor individual processes, and the predicates of such objects or processes cannot be meaningfully ascribed to them. Hence it also can make no sense to say of them (and to say with the same signification) that they exist in the now and did exist previously, that they succeed one another in time or are simultaneous with one another, and so on. But no doubt we can and must say: A certain continuity of appearance—that is, a continuity that is a phase of the time-constituting flow—belongs to a now, namely, to the now that it constitutes; and to a before, namely, as that which is constitutive (we cannot say "was") of the before. But is not the flow a succession, does it not have a now, an actually present phase, and a continuity of pasts of which I am now conscious in retentions?[22]

Since that which constitutes objects in time cannot itself be an object in time, it must be ordered in a more fundamental continuity or absolute flow. However, if time-constituting conjunctions are grounded and temporally ordered in the unity of an absolute flow, the absolute flow itself is not temporally ordered qua unity and therefore has no absolute fundamental temporal division. Yet the flow must be successive in order for temporality to be possible at all.

Husserl tries to resolve this problem between continuity and division using the age-old weapon of representational metaphor. The status of the absolute flow, Husserl says, can only "be designated metaphorically as 'flow'" since a flow is purely continuous, but temporality has temporal divisions. Time is like a flow but *with divisions*—in other words, *not like a flow at all*, and in fact the opposite of a flow. For this kind of special temporal flow, Husserl says, "we lack names."[23]

Of course, we lack names for this description because it is a contradiction: temporality presupposes the continuity of its passing that it divides, but if temporal division is ontologically primary, then there is nothing for it to divide and it cannot explain its continuous passing. Thus, metaphor fails to resolve the fundamental problem of temporality and only ends up forcing the philosophical choice between kinetic continuum and temporal discontinuity. Temporal division cannot be ontologically primary because it is incapable of producing true continuum or passage. If we begin instead with temporal continuity or absolute flow, as Husserl attempts, we also fail because in defining time as fundamentally undivided flow according to its temporal dimensions, we have destroyed time—hence Husserl's metaphoric solution. Undivided temporality, however, or a temporality without past, present, or future, *is not temporality*.

If motion is ontologically primary, then continuity is primary, and then temporality can be understood as a series of distinct (not ontologically divided) folds, conjunctions, and circulations immanent to the flow of materiality itself.[24] Time becomes simply a specific regime of elastic motion capable of an unlimited multiplicity of temporal unities.[25]

Several more major attempts to resolve the kinetic problem of elastic temporality were made in the twentieth century by emphasizing the *process* and *intervallic* nature of temporality. These last two descriptions of elastic temporality are the subject of the next and final chapter on the logos or description of modern being.

CHAPTER 34

Modern Phenomenology IV

Process and Interval

After Husserl, the elastic motion of time was taken one step further by Martin Heidegger (1889–1976). For Husserl, the ontological primacy of time emerges as an a priori condition of time consciousness and thus results in the radical multiplicity of the temporal field, initially discovered by Kant. Heidegger, however, discovers the pure elasticity of time itself as an *ontological process*.[1]

THE PROCESS OF TEMPORALIZATION

This discovery first occurs in *Being and Time* (1927), in Heidegger's analysis of the temporal conditions of Dasein's existence. Dasein, or human ecstatic being, has the primordial structure of its being outside itself in the sense in which it exists as thrown into a future toward its ultimate death and finitude, while also retaining the past leading toward this future in the present. The temporality of Dasein's existence is therefore not lived as a series of discrete nows but rather as a unity of three distinct modes of being that tear it outside itself. Common-sense linear time is possible only on the more primary condition of a primordial time[2] from which we abstract and isolate units of "presents" and project them.

However, for Heidegger, primordial phenomenological time is not successive. "Temporalizing does not signify that ecstases come in a 'succession.' The future is not later than having been, and having-been is not earlier than the Present. Temporality temporalizes itself as a future which makes present in a process of having been."[3] Time does not exist, but this does not mean that it is an illusion and being is eternal. Rather, "Dasein qua time temporalizes its Being."[4] It is precisely because being is temporal that Dasein, or "being-there," exists temporally. Outside of existence or being-there, there is no absolute Newtonian time. Time does not occur in succession, but "the future has a priority in the ecstatical unity of primordial and authentic temporality" because it is what first takes the form of having been futurally and what "awakens the Present."[5]

In other words, the past is lived as that which was headed toward the future, and the present is lived as that which is directed to the future. Thus, "temporality temporalizes itself primordially out of the future."[6] However, the future of our existence is finite because our being is "toward death," and thus time is fundamentally finite. According to Heidegger, this does not mean that time does not go on after we die. Time does go on, but only in the form of other existential horizons or as an abstraction of our own primordial time. Time is thus finite but unlimited insofar as there are multiple Daseins and modes of living in the future.

Time, in short, is not a linear succession of points, but, qua Dasein, an elastic continuum that Heidegger says "stretches" (*erstrecken*) or is "extended" (*strecke*) between the three ecstatic dimensions. "Dasein," Heidegger says, "stretches itself along 'temporally.'"[7] However, Dasein does not stretch along a pregiven track of life composed of momentary actualities, "it stretches itself along in such a way that its own Being is constituted in advance as a stretching-along."[8] In other words, it does not stretch between pregiven temporal points but is always already stretched out in time such that any point whatever can come to appear within its temporal extension.

This *erstrecken*, or elasticity, defines the fundamental connectedness of life and the *movement* of temporality itself. Heidegger is explicit about this:

> Accordingly it is within the horizon of Dasein's temporal constitution that we must approach the ontological clarification of the "connectedness of life"—that is to say, the stretching-along [*erstrecken*], the movement, and the persistence which are specific for Dasein. The movement [*Bewegtheit*] of existence is not the motion [*Bewegung*] of something present-at-hand. It is definable in terms of the way Dasein stretches along. The specific movement in which Dasein is stretched along [*erstrecken*] and stretches itself along, we call its "historizing."[9]

The movement of time is not the motion between points but the already existing *continuum of time itself* that stretches and extends elastically and ecstatically along the future, past, and present. The continuity of this elastic movement is not the continuity of an already constituted set of objects but is the constituting movement that is itself the condition of their possibility as such. "[This movement] must be conceived in terms of the ecstatical stretching-along of that temporality which is alien to any Continuity of something present-at-hand but which, for its part, presents the condition for the possibility of access to anything continuous that is present-at-hand."[10] Temporal *elasticity* is thus the continuous condition for temporal continuity.

Kinetically, elasticity is the movement of temporal stretching that folds time back over itself and into a horizon or field of circulation such that any given time can appear as such to Dasein. Time is outside itself because it differentiates itself in the circulation and ordering of its own flows.

Heidegger never completed *Being and Time*, but in the final chapter it is clear that Dasein's temporality was only the starting point for an even more radical inquiry into being in general. Insofar as time was still tethered to Dasein's elastic circulatory horizon, it was still limited to one model of elasticity, kinetically quite close to Husserl's. Thus, in the final section of *Being and Time*, Heidegger proposes to radicalize the analysis of time one step further:

> Our aim is to work out the question of Being in general. . . . The existential-ontological constitution of Dasein's totality is grounded in temporality. Hence the ecstatical projection of Being must be made possible by some primordial way in which ecstatical temporality temporalizes. How is this mode of the temporalizing of temporality to be Interpreted? Is there a way which leads from primordial time to the meaning of Being? Does time itself manifest itself as the horizon of Being?[11]

The conclusion to *Being and Time* is clear if incomplete: Being is time. This conclusion, however, requires a different and more radical methodology.

In his 1962 lecture "Time and Being," Heidegger provides precisely that. In this lecture he picks up where *Being and Time* left off—in attempting "to think Being without regard to its being grounded in terms of beings."[12] Being is not a particular being like Dasein, and time is not a particular time. Being and time are what are distributed throughout all beings without being particular beings. Being is therefore not a particular being in time and time is not a particular time in being, "yet Being as presencing remains determined as presence by time, by what is temporal."[13]

In other words, being is defined by a *process of presencing*, and time is defined by a process of coming to the *present*. Ontological presencing and chronological presenting, however, are not identical but are two "reciprocally determining" aspects or dimensions of *the same process* by which beings come to appear as given.[14] According to Heidegger, when we say "there is" (*es gibt*) being or "there is" time, we describe being and time not as mere things but as gifts (*geben*), and gifts presuppose a *process of giving* by which they are given.

However, the ontotemporal process of giving is not a complete giving-over that would exhaust being and time in their giving. Rather, being and time are both given as a process that stretches (*erstrecken*), reaches (*reichen*), and extends (*strecke*) itself outward, while at the same time withholds or contracts itself and abides so it may give again. Thus, when being presences or reaches out into appearance, it is also present in its absence insofar as that which is not present at hand still *is* as withheld. Similarly, when time stretches itself into the present, the past and the future also come to the present in the form of an absence, since they are no longer. "What has been does not just vanish from the previous now as does that which is merely past. Rather, what has been presences, but in its own way. In what has been, presencing is extended."[15]

The unity of time is therefore not in the present but rather "in the interplay of each toward each. This interplay proves to be the true extending, playing in the very heart of time."[16] The past, present, and future are the threefold dimensions of the presencing of being. They are the "threefold extending, perduring the denying, and withholding nearness which determines that extending. Time is not the product of man; man is not the product of time. There is no production here. There is only giving in the sense of extending which opens up time-space."[17] The threefold nature of time is the ontologically primary structure of being as presencing and the "prespatial region which first gives any possible 'where.'"[18] Time does not produce man because man as a being is already temporal in his being.

The consequence of this ontotemporal structure—lacking a simple or reified notion of being or time—is that there cannot be an "it" that gives. "The It . . . names a presence of absence."[19] In place of an it, there is only the continual process of giving, reaching, extending, and withdrawing. Therefore, "what determines both, time and Being, in their own, that is, in their belonging together, we shall call: *Ereignis*, the event of Appropriation [or enowning]."[20] *Ereignis* is the name of the process itself by which being and time stretch, extend, reach, send, and contract. Their "extending . . . lies in one and the same with sending, in Appropriating."[21] However, Appropriation should not be thought of as some thing other than being and time. Appropriation is the continuous unity or threefold unfolding process of being and time. "Appropriation neither is, nor is Appropriation there. To say the one or to say the other is equally a distortion of the matter, just as if we wanted to derive the source from the river."[22]

Kinetic Analysis

With the concept of *Ereignis*, Heidegger extends the elasticity of time, initially put forward in *Being and Time*, to the entire temporal process itself as an open process. *Ereignis* is not only the flow or stretch of time, but also the *absolute source of all flowing as such*. Thus, the chronokinetics that had previously defined the elastic movement (*Bewegtheit*) of Dasein as stretching (*erstrecken*) and extending (*strecke*) now define the *elastic movement* of being as such as *Ereignis*. Although Heidegger does not use the word *bewegtheit* to describe *Ereignis* in this particular essay, he does define it by all the same names—stretching, reaching, extending, and so on—that were described explicitly as movements in *Being and Time*, in contrast to merely relative motions (*Bewegung*) of change of place.

In *Contributions*, Heidegger also describes the elasticity of the event as a "movement of oscillation"[23] between needing and belonging. We can therefore say kinetically that for Heidegger time is ontologically primary (over space, for example), but that elastic movement is itself the process by which being and time are cogiven in the event. This is no doubt what Peter Sloterdijk has in mind when he writes, "Under the spell of Heidegger's existential analytic of time, it has mostly been overlooked that the former is grounded in a corresponding analytic of space and that *both are fundamentally rooted in an analysis of movement* [ontokinesis]."[24]

Heidegger's analysis of time therefore presupposes the ontological primacy of movement as the more primary process or kinetic source of giving. By giving the name of this process to *time*, he robs *Ereignis* of its true *bewegtheit*. "We must give the name 'time' to the unity of reaching out and giving which we have now shown, to this unity alone."[25] Movement thus remains the hidden motor of Heidegger's description of being as time. By accepting the ontological primacy of time, he encounters the same problem as Husserl did: If time is ontologically primary, and time is triple or threefold, where did the process of folding itself come from? How did time become enfolded? Of what is it a fold?

If time is already threefold, it necessarily presupposes the ontokinetic process of folding itself through which time becomes folded and stretched. Insofar as the elastic movement of folding, unfolding, stretching, and extending remains explicitly subordinated to time in Heidegger's philosophy, he remains unable to overcome the problem of his own ontochronological grounding. In other words, he both requires the continuous movement of time as a kinetic giving or stretching and rejects it at the same time as already tensed into the past, present, and future.[26] Time therefore presupposes a kinetics of passing and the flow of a more primary movement.[27]

THE INTERVAL OF TIME

Jacques Derrida (1930–2004) pushed the ontology of time to its radical and most explicitly paradoxical conclusion.[28] While Merleau-Ponty radicalized the elasticity of time toward its increasing identification with a pure material-kinetic vortex of being (the flesh), and thereby almost overthrowing its primacy, Derrida radicalizes time in the opposite direction, toward its most primary and defining ontological feature: pure *différance*. While Merleau-Ponty expanded time into an absolute ontological flux differentiated by folding, Derrida radically contracts time into its most minimal and defining element: the interval or delay. For Derrida, time *is nothing* but the pure gap or *temps* (tempo, beat, interval) that *gives* (*donne*) time (*le temps*) its very differentiated structure in the first place.[29]

In *Speech and Phenomenon* (1967), Derrida mounts a sustained critique against Husserl's concept of the absolute flux, which Merleau-Ponty was just beginning to recover in the concept of the flesh. However, instead of stretching and folding this absolute temporal flux as Merleau-Ponty does, Derrida shows the flux itself to be the very condition of the fragmentation of the subject as such. Since the Husserlian subject is in time and the structure of time is auto-affection or temporal difference, absolute time does not unify the subject at all but rather fundamentally *disrupts it*. The very idea of a synthesized and circulatory subject in Husserl is thus "undermined by its own origin, by the very condition of its self-presence, that is, by 'time,' to be conceived anew on the basis now of difference within auto-affection, on the basis of identifying identity and nonidentity within the 'sameness' of the *im selben Augenblick*."[30]

Derrida thus renders explicit what we have already said about this chronokinetic paradox in Husserl. For time to pass, Husserl needs the absolute flux to be a kinetic continuum, but insofar as the absolute flux is *temporal*, it presupposes an ontological difference within itself that is both the condition of possibility for subjective auto-affection and the condition of impossibility of a subjective unity within this ontological difference.

Accordingly, Derrida is right to highlight the "admirable § 36" of Husserl's *Phenomenology of Internal Time-Consciousness*, "which proves the absence of a proper noun for this strange 'movement,' which, furthermore, is not a movement. 'For all this,' concludes Husserl, 'names fail us.' We would still have to radicalize Husserl's intention here in a specific direction. . . . This determination of 'absolute subjectivity' would also have to be crossed out as soon as we conceive the present on the basis of difference, and not the reverse."[31] Derrida thus keenly notes that even though Husserl calls the absolute flux a movement, this is impossible by definition of such a flux as an ontotemporal differentiation. Derrida's radicalization is to expose the ontological difference of the flux itself and show that such a flux could not, by definition, constitute an absolute subject or temporal synthesis.

Derrida even more keenly argues that all metaphysical theories of time have always had to dissimulate a movement or flow in order for time to pass, as has been shown at length in Part IV. "The word 'time' itself, as it has always been understood in the history of metaphysics, is a metaphor which *at the same time* both indicates and dissimulates the 'movement' of this auto-affection. All the concepts of metaphysics—in particular those of activity and passivity, will and non-will, and therefore those of affection or auto-affection, purity and impurity, etc.—*cover up* the strange 'movement' of this difference."[32]

In other words, theories of time have to presuppose movement but deny it at the same time if they want to preserve the primacy of temporal difference. They have to cover up what Derrida calls the "strange movement" of difference, because it is *not actually a movement*; it is an ontological gap or interval in being that the theory of time has to both assume and deny *at the same time*. Derrida can thus only use the word "movement" in scare quotes—because the difference of the interval makes real continuous movement impossible.

For example, Derrida says, when one speaks, one introduces a difference between the speaker and the listener, even when this is "the same" person. This difference is a fundamentally temporal difference. "The theme of a pure inwardness of speech, or of the 'hearing oneself speak,' is radically contradicted by 'time' itself. The going-forth 'into the world' is also primordially implied in the movement of temporalization. 'Time' cannot be an 'absolute subjectivity' precisely because it cannot be conceived on the basis of a present and the self-presence of a present being."[33] Time is therefore the ontological condition of the impossibility of the subject. The subject can never be fully present to itself in time. There is always a *"différance*, [an] operation of differing which at one and the same time both fissures and retards presence, submitting it simultaneously to primordial division and delay."

By the term *différance*, Derrida means an ontological difference that is at once deferring as temporal delay and a differing as the active work of difference.[34] The concept of *différance* is thus fundamentally temporal for Derrida. To be clear, however, *différance* is not a differentiation of "some organic unity, some primordial and homogeneous unity, that would eventually come to be divided up and take on difference as an event."[35] There is no temporal continuum. Time does not pass. Time temporalizes through *différance* and externalizes itself as space. Thus "space is 'in' time; it is time's pure leaving-itself as the self-relation of time. The externality of space, externality as space, does not overtake time; rather, it opens as pure 'outside' 'within' the movement of temporalization."[36]

In his essay "Différance" (1968), Derrida further elaborates the differential structure presupposed by temporal ontology:

> *Différance* is what makes the movement of signification possible. . . . In order for it to be, an interval must separate it from what it is not; but the interval that constitutes it in the present must also, and by the same token, divide the present in itself, thus dividing, along with the present, everything that can be conceived on its basis, that is, every being—in particular, for our metaphysical language, the substance or subject. Constituting itself, dynamically dividing itself, this interval is what could be called spacing; time's becoming-spatial or space's becoming-temporal (temporalizing).[37]

For Derrida, the most radical condition of time is difference. If there is time, it is only given on the condition of a more radical ontological difference within which time comes into presence as time. But since *différance* is already a fundamentally temporal concept as delay or deferral, time is already its own radical undoing. Time temporalizes itself through difference.

Pushing this concept to its most radical conclusion, in his most mature writing on time, *Given Time* (1991), Derrida argues that the *givenness* of time itself, as the *process* by which time-being is given, also presupposes a more primordial *différance*. The ontological condition of the process by which time is given (*ça donne*) is the interval or gap "between receiving and giving."[38] Derrida thus radicalizes Heidegger's "Time and Being" essay by arguing that the very ontological structure of the *es gibt* or gift that gives time and being as an elastic movement must itself already be fundamentally different from itself such that it could give to itself. It is the interval or *temps* that makes possible the gift of time as a fundamentally differentiated movement of elastic stretching out and withholding in the first place. "This condition [of *différance*] concerns time but does not belong to it, does not pertain to it without being, for all that, more logical than chronological."[39]

Différance is fundamental because time is ontologically fundamental. In other words, time is ontologically primary but only because time by its very structure is differential, because it introduces a gap or interval into being. This ontological difference makes possible the gift as the temporalization of time, but it also "sets in motion the process of a destruction of the gift," insofar as it would be received and grasped as present.[40] "It is in the course of this movement that Being [*Sein*] . . . is signaled on the basis of the gift."[41]

What is the nature of this "movement" Derrida ascribes to *différance*? Following Heidegger, Derrida says that the giving of time is a play (*spielt*): "The movement of the *Entbergen* [unconcealing]" is a play or an undecidable oscillation back and forth between giving and receiving. Play, Derrida writes in *Limited Inc.* (1988), "is not indeterminacy in itself, but the strictest possible determination of the figures of play, of oscillation, of undecidability, which is to say, of the *différantial* conditions of determinable history, etc."[42] Temporality as a *movement* of oscillation is thus "a time that is what it is without being (it) [*sans l'etre*], that is not what it is and that is what it is not, which is to be it without being (it) [*qui est de l'etre sans l'être*]."[43] As a kinetic oscillation, time presupposes within itself the impossibility of simultaneity: two events in time cannot by definition be given at the same time.[44] This is because "the *syn* of this system, as we shall see in a moment, has *an essential relation to time*, to a certain delay, to a certain deferral/differing [*differer*] in time."[45]

Time is *différance* and *différance* is essentially the chronokinetic movement of oscillation and animation that brings time into being without itself becoming a thing: "Moved by a mysterious force, the thing itself demands gift and restitution, it requires therefore 'time,' 'term,' 'delay,' 'interval' of temporization, the becoming-temporization of temporalization, the animation of a neutral and homogeneous time by the desire of the gift and the restitution. *Différance*, which (is) nothing."[46]

Derrida thus distinguishes between temporization and temporalization. Temporization, following the meaning of the French word *temps*, is the interval, time, or delay between the beats of a rhythm or cadence that allows it to be differentiated from itself. The focus of *temporization* is thus the interval between any given times that is the condition for any given time being given.

Temporalization, on the other hand, is the past, present, and future as given times. Thus, for Derrida, "the becoming-temporization of temporalization" is the revelation that it is precisely the interval or gap between and within time itself that allows time to become, move, or pass. It gives time through an animated oscillation. For Derrida, the elasticity of time is therefore not the stretching, extending, or reaching of the future or any other tense; it is the pure kinetic elasticity of the interval itself, or the *différance* between times that gives time.

Just as it was implicitly for Heidegger, for Derrida the act of giving time is a fundamentally *kinetic act*. Giving gives a rhythm or cadence to time. Thus, "the thing is not in time; it is or it has time, or rather it demands to have, to give, or to take time—and time as rhythm, a rhythm that does not befall a homogeneous time but that structures it originarily."[47] The thing is the *time-thing*, the being whose being is primordially structured by the kinetic oscillation of giving and taking in time. In this way Derrida radicalizes time toward its most minimal condition: the elasticity of the interval itself, *différance*.

Kinetic Analysis

Derrida also finds himself confronted with the introduction of motion, oscillation, in order to explain a supposedly pure temporal process. Derrida goes to great lengths to reject the use of metaphors of movement and continuity when talking about the flow of time, because they presume a homogeneous unity from which temporal difference would emerge. For Derrida, the past, present, and future do not and cannot stretch or extend, since they are by definition already given times—given to the subject, or Dasein, or consciousness. Derrida thus realizes a fundamental insight about the structure of time that previous theorists have desperately sought to dissimulate with metaphor: the movement or passing of time. Derrida's great discovery is that time, by its very definition and structure, *cannot be continuum or flow*. Time does not pass; it is given only through its *différance* or intervallic action. Being as such is pure, irreconcilable, undecidable division or difference. In this sense, difference is not different from an identity but different from itself in itself.

This radical discovery of difference at the heart of being in the history of philosophy thus brings us back to the beginning of our inquiry into the being of motion. If being is absolute *différance*; if it is always divided from itself; if between every being is a gap, interval, or "primordial division"—then motion is ontologically impossible. Being will never be able to continually pass. There can be discrete change or real difference between things but only as different aspects or dimensions of a single frozen and fragmented dead being. One will never pass over to the other. Derrida is absolutely right: time does not pass or flow.

However, just like all the other major historical descriptions of being—space, eternity, and force—time does not work without motion. Without motion, time would not be what it is: an elasticity of being that expands and contracts in larger or smaller folds and circulations. Even Derrida cannot escape the primacy of motion required by the ontology of time. This is clearly evidenced by his constant use of kinetic language to describe the gift of time as a movement, oscillation, animation, and even rhythm that brings time into being without itself being reducible to the time that is given. His usage of kinetic terms thus allows time to move by granting the interval itself a kinetic activity.

There are at least two possible interpretations of this usage. The first is that Derrida is only using the term "movement" as a metaphor for something (the gift) that is fundamentally immobile, immaterial, and divided. But if the giving of time is fundamentally static, then how does time or being ever pass, change, or give at all? If the giving is immobile, then it cannot give anything at all, because giving is a real process that requires some kind of movement or action. Furthermore, this interpretation would explicitly subject Derrida to his own critique, since he rejected the exact same use of metaphors of motion and continuum in Husserl's theory of the absolute flux.

The second possible interpretation is that Derrida actually does think that giving is a real elastic movement of oscillation between and within time. However, if this were the case, then several contradictions follow. First, time would no longer be ontologically primary, as he argues it is, because it would rely on a more primary motion of oscillatory giving. Second, since real motion requires continuum, being would be fundamentally continuous, which would contradict his concept of *différance* and his explicit rejections of continuity throughout his work. Furthermore, Derrida would have no sufficient explanation for how time or difference would emerge from this kinetic continuity.

In both interpretations, however, time is abolished along with *différance*. On the one hand, if his use of movement is metaphorical, then there is no passage of time and thus no time. On the other hand, if his use of movement is real, then being is no longer fundamentally *différantial*, and thus time, to which it is "essentially related" for Derrida, is no longer possible. All of these difficulties arise because Derrida models his theory of difference on time, following the phenomenological tradition, and not on motion.[48] If "the gift only gives to the extent it gives time,"[49] then giving is ontologically differential from the beginning and can never produce the continuity of motion truly needed for time to pass or flow in the first place. Thus, by radically ontologizing time as difference or interval, Derrida destroys the kinetic movement or kinetic flow needed for time to pass.

CONCLUSION

The kinetic theory of time cannot function without the presupposition of the primacy of motion. In particular, it historically assumes an elastic regime of motion—a whole chronokinetics of stretching, extending, bending, vortical folding, oscillation, and so on. Without the presupposition of a fundamental elasticity to time, time is unable to pass and circulate in the form of a kinetic subject. Movement is therefore the unthought of time. It is what temporality must presuppose for the continuity of its passing, but must reject at the heart of being.

We can now identify seven historically and conceptually distinct types of temporal elasticity—the elasticity of the temporal fold (Augustine), the multiplication of folds (Ockham), the line itself as a stretched point (Newton), the circulation of time (Kant), multiple circulations (Husserl), the process as a whole (Heidegger), and the interval stretched between times (Derrida). With respect to the historical arc traced by this book, the idea of time as a pure passage or flow of being brings us at once closest to the idea of the unrestrained movement of being, but it also takes us the farthest away from it insofar as the structure of time presupposes that being is primordially divided, intervalic, fragmentary, and thus static.

The historical description of being today is therefore at a threshold between its absolute rejection and its absolute presupposition. The aim of this book, and this chapter in particular, is to highlight this threshold and tip historical ontology over to the side of motion—thus making explicit what has always been implicit in the ontological description of being. However, before concluding this effort and assessing its next steps, it is crucial to understand that the elastic motion of time is not just the way being is *described* during this period, it is also the way it is *inscribed* in the modern kinography of the keyboard, as we will see in the next chapters.

III
Graphos

CHAPTER 35

The Keyboard I

Typewriter

Alongside the historical rise of ontological descriptions of time, a new regime of inscription also emerged: typography. Just as the ontologically descriptive regime of force was inscribed in the tensional regime of the book, so the rise of the descriptive regime of time, from the late eighteenth century to the present, was predominantly inscribed in an elastic regime of the keyboard. Writing and books did not disappear during this time, of course, but were instead taken up and modified within a new kinographic regime defined by the elastic oscillations of the keyboard.

TYPOGRAPHY

Typography is the inscription of preformed letters or type onto a receptive medium using a keyboard. Beginning in the late eighteenth century, and rapidly rising to dominance in the nineteenth and twentieth centuries, the keyboard became the prevailing kinographic technique for the inscription of being. Most philosophers in the Kantian legacy of ontochronology either directly used a keyboard to type, dictated to a typist, or handwrote texts, which were then converted by typewriter into a typescript and were finally printed using a linotype keyboard printing press.

The rise of typography or typewriting followed two major kinographic operations: binary circulation and binary modulation. These two operations correspond to the two major historical technologies of typography: the typewriter from the nineteenth to the mid-twentieth century, and the computer from the mid-twentieth century to the present. These two techniques of inscription differ from each other in important ways, but, kinetically speaking, both function as types of the same kinographic regime of elastic motion.

Typographic inscription has its precursor in the early modern invention of the printing press (fifteenth century) and the invention of type. Kinetically, however, the tensional motion of the early printing press subordinated typography to the bibliography of the printed book. As shown earlier, the whole form of motion of the Gutenberg press was defined by hand-casting individual letters, confining them into the printing frame in pregiven, tensional, and fixed relations, and then using the tension of the machine to press all the letters at once onto the paper surface.

Typography thus had no place outside the printing press. It was only with the emergence of the typewriter that typography was liberated from the tensional motion of the press and allowed to develop its own form of elastic motion. Eventually, the elastic motion of the keyboard turned back on the printing press and subordinated it with the invention of linotype press in the nineteenth century. Once liberated from the printing press, typography began to take on its own form of motion, defined by a binographic elasticity. This process requires a brief introduction and definition before moving on to the kinographic history of the typewriter and computer.

BINOGRAPHIC ELASTICITY

Binography is the process of inscribing a series of simple binary differences onto a recording surface. A binary or twofold division or difference is the simplest and most radical form of graphic division. While early writing systems invented symbols for each new object, producing an infinity of qualitative graphic divisions, and the phonetic alphabet reduced those differences to a finite number (twenty-six) of qualitatively different phonetic sounds, binary inscription reduced those divisions even further to their absolute *quantitive* limit: one or zero.

Through binary coding, binography was capable of reinscribing all previous regimes of inscription in a series of purely quantitative differences. As such, however, binary inscription also relied on the kinographic structure of the series in a much more profound way than previous graphisms. With pictographs and even with phonetic letters, much could be communicated in a very short series. With binography, however, a longer series of graphic marks, ones and zeros, was required to produce the same meaning. What was required, therefore, was an increase in graphic speed to communicate the simplest form of inscription. This was made possible by the development of a whole new technical apparatus in the form of the typewriter and computer, which function according to the necessary kinetic condition of a rapid oscillation of a series of open or closed positions—key positions on the typewriter and transistors in the computer.

Binography should not be understood as a purely idealist or logical division. Like all inscription, binography is kinographic; that is, it relies on movement for its material operation. We should therefore distinguish it from the so-called pure mathematico-idealist concept of binary difference as an absolute quantitative difference between one and zero. Logical or idealist binary division must admit nothing other than one and zero. If this were the case, however, there would be no possibility of transition between the two. There would be no continuous intermediary. If there were nothing between one and zero, this would mean that there was no difference between one and zero, which would mean they were identical, which is a contradiction. This idea is thus incomplete.

Just as in the case of temporal difference, there must be a flow, flux, or movement between times that will allow time itself to pass. The movement from zero to one is not kinetically unlike the movement from the past to the future: both require an intermediary or intermediaries in order to move. In their pure form, the numbers zero and one are idealist abstractions, quantifications of real qualities, and composed of real material flows. To admit an absolute logical or idealist division between zero and one is thus to submit to a transcendent illusion, both logically contradictory, because a difference is also required, and kinetically abstracted from the real material conditions that make the transition between any two differences possible.

In this sense, binary division is not two at all, but at least three. There is zero, one, and the difference between them. This difference, as shown in the previous chapters, is a kinetic difference, a flow, or a continuum within which a bifurcation and fold can emerge and a transition can be made. Thus, in a more kinetic sense, binography is not three at all, but threefold. The origins of binary division are therefore not in the *thought* of binary number, but in the material motion of oscillation between at least two different kinetic states. Binary division is therefore not an invention of Leibniz in the eighteenth century, Bacon in the seventeenth, the I Ching in the ninth, or any others.

Nature already creates its own bifurcations and oscillations. Human civilization already introduces material switches between flow and fold in the simple form of the vessel. The vessel either folds a flow or drains a flow of liquid. The canal or waterway is allowed to flow or be dammed up. The door or window to the house is open, letting a flow of air move through, or closed, blocking a flow. In a profound and rudimentary way, binography has always existed. However, with respect to ontological description, it only became the dominant mode of technical inscription with the introduction of the typewriter in the late eighteenth century.

The motion of moving back and forth without breaking or introducing a division into a continuum of motion is called "kinetic elasticity." Oscillation is therefore elastic by definition, insofar as a movement in one direction allows for a return to the previous position without introducing a division between the two motions. Elasticity is this continuous motion back and forth between two positions, open and closed.

If the typewriter mechanism did not allow for an elastic oscillation, it would only be able to press its type on paper once. If the computer did not allow for an elasticity of quantum motion back and forth between semiconductor materials, there would be no logic gates and no computation. The inventions of the circuit and the electric flux fundamentally rely on an elastic and oscillatory movement back and forth between two binary positions. Modern ontological inscription, defined by the technical dominance of the typewriter and computer, is defined by this binographic elasticity.

THE TYPEWRITER: BINARY CIRCULATION

The rise of typography began with the typewriter because the typewriter was the first to liberate type from the subordination of the printing press and the book. The first elastic kinographic operation of circulatory oscillation thus emerged with the typewriter as the first series or graphic switches.

In contrast to the fountain pen and the steam press, the typewriter is defined by a complex series of oscillating switches on a continuous circulation of platen and paper. The first documented typewriter was invented by an Italian nobleman, Pellegrino Turri, in 1808 in order help the blind countess Carolina Fantoni write. His writing machine had alphabetical keys that oscillated between an off state and an on state, hammering against an ink ribbon to produce legible marks on the paper recording surface.

Circulatory Oscillation

This first circulatory oscillation is thus defined by a number of kinetic operations. First, the typewriter is not defined by a single oscillation or switch between an on and off state, but by numerous such oscillations. Furthermore, all the oscillations take place in a continuous series on the recording surface. Each letter oscillates back and forth, but does so in a unique series graphically recorded on the paper. There is thus a binographism of each letter, key, or switch, but also a serial binography that records its historical sequence. Each new graphic mark expands the inscription process as the paper flows vertically underneath. At the end of each line of texts, the platen returns back to its starting point.

This is the first form of typographical circulation: the continuous circulation back and forth of the platen, while the keys oscillate back and forth on it. This horizontal and vertical circulation of paper is the flow within which isolated points of graphic data are inscribed. The text becomes nothing more than a series of discrete, homogenous, graphic marks on the continuous flow of paper moving by. The pages of paper are not prebound in the book or fixed in the rigid tensions of the printer's plates, but are now allowed to flow into and out of the machine in a loose pile, without beginning or end.

After Turri's typewriter, there was a rapid development of typewriters throughout the nineteenth century. At first the typewriter was slow, but as modifications were made and more people adopted it, it became faster and easier to use. The typewriter became much more of what it is: a temporal machine. It shortened the time between each on and off oscillation in the circulation, making it possible not only to type faster than one could write but also to increase the speed at which one could read what was typed. Each finger became a semiautonomous switch in the dactylographic process. As the speed of the keys increased, the time between composition and publication decreased. The difference between composition and print publication was now the time it took the key to move forward and hit the ink ribbon. The typewriter thus became its own printing press, and in this sense liberated itself from the press.[1]

The fact that the earliest writing machines were automatons reveals something about the kinetic structure of the machine itself. The typewriter has always been capable of a higher degree of autonomy than other inscription techniques: either through mechanism, punch card, or teletype, and it has always had a higher capacity of automation or auto-affection than any other graphism. The typewriter is the machine that *inscribes itself in time*. It is self-circulating in the sense that it moves its own platen in a series of loops, back and forth, scrolling up and down on a roller. It combines the rolling and unrolling movement of the ancient scroll, and the rigid-bar linkage and hinge systems of the medieval book, and gives them all an automatic interconnection and circulation within a single device. The typewriter is the scroll that unrolls itself, the book that turns its own pages as it is written.

It produces its own autonomous regime of circulation within which letters appear as so many homogenous space-time units in its flow. The stylus has always seemed to suggest an autonomous subject separate from the recording surface, a subject who uses the stylus as an object. However, the typewriter is the surface, paper, ink, and stylus all at once. It combines and automates them all into a whole new circulation. All that is left to be done is to flip the switches, which does not even technically require a human being.

Mechanical Elasticity

The second operation is that of a mechanical elasticity in the movement of extension or stretching that makes possible the continuous oscillation between two positions. The mechanical typewriter makes use of this motion in order for the key hammers to return to their original position after their extension. This is accomplished either through an elastic fluid or oil between mechanical hinges, or by the introduction of various spring mechanisms into the machine. Coiled metal springs connecting the key lever to the bar linkage system and connecting the universal bar to the u-bar allow its motions to expand and contract elastically without breaking.[2]

However, the mechanical typewriter is not a purely elastic graphism, since, in addition to its elasticity, it also relies on a tensional system of rigid linkages and escapement. The two kinetic motions coexist in the mechanical typewriter, but it is the elastic motion that tends to be historically favored as more and more springs are added. There is thus a historical transition from tensional bar-linkage kinetics to increasing elastic-spring kinetics, toward greater and greater mechanical elasticity. It is precisely this increasing elasticity that allows the mechanical typewriter to literally move faster and faster. The more elastic or "springy" the kinetics of the mechanisms, the more easily they can be pushed back and forth, the faster the hammers can retract, and the faster the next hammer can land. Increasing elasticity means increasing speed, which means it takes less time to write. The time it takes between one hammer and the next contracts, reducing the temporal difference between the two keys down to fractions of a second.

In this sense, the kinetic elasticity of the key-spring mechanism becomes *the temporal difference* between the keystrokes. Elastic motion is what provides the spatial difference between letters, as well as the temporal difference needed for the hammers to not stick to one another.

Elastic movement is therefore the kinographic condition for the actuality of the spatiotemporal difference required by typographic writing. The minimal difference in space and time between each letter is what allows each letter to be given as a distinct letter in the inscription series. This difference is therefore nothing other than the movement of the typewriter itself. It is a fundamentally *kinetic difference that gives the spatiotemporal difference*. The condition of spatiotemporal type and discrete letters is the elastic movement of the typewriter itself.

It is thus no coincidence that the birth of the typewriter came not only from writing automatons but also from musical keyboards and music-recording machines.[3] The keyboards of the clavier and harpsichord prefigure the typewriter as kinetic machines that produce a series of discrete times, tempos, and beats. It is the movement and oscillation of the keys that produce time, meter, rhythm, and cadence. The first "melographic" machines made this spatiotemporal difference visible by attaching ink to the key levers of pianos or having each key punch a hole in paper. Both typography and melography thus make visible a kinographics of time itself. Typography is a tempographism.

In 1808 the typewriter was first liberated from the constraints of the printing press and freed to develop its own elastic regime of motion with the invention of the linotype machine. The linotype machine was invented by Ottmar Mergenthaler, "the second Gutenberg," and was essentially a keyboard attached to a typecasting and stamping machine. By typing out the letters on a keyboard, the machine could automatically cast an entire line of metal type at once, or a "line-o'-type." These lines of type could then be automatically set into the printing press and printed.

The printing press process could now be driven by a single operator at a keyboard. As the operator typed, each keystroke released a matrix from the magazine mounted above the keyboard. The matrix moved via a spring-operated delivery channel into an assembler, where it was lined up in a series with others to be cast with hot metal all at once. Between each word, the operator introduced a blank matrix or spaceband that would produce an empty space between the words, making explicit that even the so-called empty space between letters that gives them their difference is already a positive kinetic activity of the spring-loaded linotype machine.

Additionally, just like the early writing automatons, the linotype machine could function automatically if given a feed of paper tape with a series of holes punched in it. The series of holes in the tape could then be read by the machine to trigger the corresponding keystrokes and produce the lines of type. This allowed text to be typeset over telegraph lines in the

"TeleTypeSetter" and for multiple operators to work on different lines of type to increase production speed.[4]

The textual description of being is thus inscribed as a series of binographic holes in a series of paper tapes or punch cards. Kinography is transformed from a series of qualitatively different letters into a series of simple quantities: one or none, hole or no hole. The punch card (1801) was thus a defining kinographic invention of the modern period that animated all sorts of automatic machines through its coded surface. Typography was given a new regime of circulation no longer simply defined by the mechanical circulation of the typewriter platen or blank paper sliding over its surface, but by the circulation of paper tape and punch cards through the machine. At one time completely autonomous, the typographic machine now became just another oscillatory circulation within an ever-larger oscillatory circulation of linked punch cards or tapes running through it.

The punch card is a continuous circulation, a complete chain of punch cards capable of being strung together and back to each other in a loop like those first used in the Jacquard looms. Within the continuous flow of blank paper, a series of binographic marks are made: hole or no hole, flow or no flow. All differences are reduced to a single binary difference.

The same kinetic regime of binary typography that made it possible for the mechanical punch card loom to displace tens of thousands of skilled artisans in the textile mills is the same regime of motion that defines capitalism's reduction of all previous social differences to a single difference: proletariat or capitalist, open or closed.[5] All social and typographic antagonism is reduced to a single antagonism. The labor of multiple skilled printing-press workers could now be replaced by a single linotype operator. Even more, the single operator could now be replaced by the labor of multiple isolated typists not even in front of machines, some of whom might never see the machine itself.

Electric Elasticity

The third kinetic operation of the typewriter introduced an even more radical elasticity in the form of an electric current. Although the electric-powered typewriter was not invented until the turn of the twentieth century, the origins of electric typography go back to the turn of the nineteenth century and the discovery of the electric circuit. Electricity was more than just a source of power for the typewriter; it changed the very kinetic structure of typographic inscription. It transformed mechanical elasticity into a fundamentally "electrical elasticity," as James Clerk Maxwell called it.[6]

In 1800 Alessandro Volta built the first electrochemical circuit, consisting of two electrodes, zinc and copper, in an electrolyte bath of sulfuric acid mixed with water or a saltwater brine.[7] This voltaic pile or electric column was the first electrical circuit capable of producing a steady electrical current, thus making possible a new regime of radically elastic electrical circulation. Volta's invention in turn made possible the first forms of electrical typography or telegraphy (from the Greek τῆλε, tête, "at a distance").

In 1804 and 1809 the first electrochemical telegraphs connected as many as thirty-five wires, one for each Latin letter and numeral, between two locations. On the sending end an electrical current, made possible by Volta's battery, was sent, and on the receiving end the wires were immersed in separate tubes of acid. When a current was sent, the acid released hydrogen bubbles.[8] Between 1809 and 1832 a number of similar telegraphic systems were invented, but by 1833 the number of telegraphic wires had been reduced, first down to sixteen, then eight, then two by Pavel Schilling, then finally one by Carl Friedrich Gauss.

In 1832 Schilling was one of the first to start using a binary system of communication, but in 1833 Gauss and Wilhelm Weber begun using a single wire to communicate an entire alphabetic language, using purely electrical means. An electrical current at one end would be given either positive or negative voltage pulses by moving an induction coil up and down over a magnet. Wires were then run all over the German town of Göttingen. In 1837 a similar electrical telegraph and binary-coded alphabetic system was independently developed by Samuel Morse in the United States. Based on these developments, several telegraphic printing systems were developed in the 1850s capable of inscribing electrical signals directly onto paper. These early telegraphic systems were used primarily as stock-price-ticker systems and used the same binary method of inscription. Based on these binary codes, one of the earliest practical stock-ticker machines, the Universal Stock Ticker developed by Thomas Edison in 1869, was able to automatically decrypt the codes and print in alphanumeric characters with a printing speed of approximately one character per second.[9]

Electric typography is the use of electrical circulation to produce an inscription on a recording surface. From the earliest electrical telegraphs at the turn of the nineteenth century to the introduction of the electric typewriter at the turn of the twentieth, the kinographic process remained fundamentally elastic and binographic. Electrical current is a highly stretchable movement of electrons capable of taking on within itself an internally differential *voltage* or electrical pressure, named after Volta—the elastic difference between two points in the charge. As a purely continuous kinetic flow of electrons, any given circulation of electricity can thus be given a greater or lesser voltage, depending on how much is allowed to flow at once—a trickle or a flood.

However, the flow of electrical current circulating continuously between positive and negative poles can also be kinetically stretched or extended over shorter or longer distances, in smaller or larger circulations. The larger the circulation with the same voltage, the weaker the current. Electrical circulation is therefore elastic in the sense that more or less can flow through the same circuit (voltage or kinoelectric pressure), and in the sense that the same flow can be expanded or contracted in larger or smaller circulations, increasing or decreasing the number of electrons moving per second (current or amperes).

In the case of electric typography, the flow of electricity is stretched across larger or smaller circulations at different voltages in order to open or close a circuit. The opening and closing of an electrical circuit allows for electrical binary communication and inscription. In the case of the electrical typewriter in particular, the current circulates through a series of possible binary operations for each key. The flow of electricity to move any given key is tied to each particular key, even if it remains mechanically operated. The electrical activation of the motor for that key is different from the other keys. Thus, the typographic mechanism distributes the usage of the electrical power differently for each key. Pressing two keys at once, for example, stretches the same voltage into two different key oscillations. Each key is either electrically on, moved by the motor, or off, not moved by the motor.

Thus, the differential between each keystroke is no longer purely mechanical but electric. The spatiotemporal difference between letters is still kinetic but now electrokinetic. This again further reduces the time between possible oscillations. Electricity is the ultimate spring, continuous and stretchable. A higher voltage can produce a faster key. Each letter of every word is simply a fluctuation of an electrical flow opening or closing on the circuit. Electric typography is thus defined by a series of possible binary oscillations within a continuous circulation of electricity.

Subjective Anonymity

Typography not only created a new form of *oscillatory* circulation and *electric* elasticity, but it also gave primacy to a fourth kinetic operation: the synthetic or anonymous subject of inscription. In 1780, twenty-eight years before Turri's typewriter and twenty years before Volta's electrical circuit, the Italian physicist Luigi Galvani discovered bioelectricity when he observed that frogs' legs moved when struck by an electrical spark. His publication of *De viribus electricitatis* in 1791 introduced a whole new study of "animal electricity" that demonstrated that electricity was the medium by which animal muscle movement occurred. An electrical switch between on and off corresponded to the physiological movement of the legs up and down.

Electric Subjectivity. This discovery introduced into physiology what Kant's *First Critique* introduced into philosophy at the same time: a new form of synthetic, circulatory, or transcendental subjectivity. The subject could no longer be considered a pregiven homogenous rational agent, but instead had to be thought of as a passive and active synthesis of a series of oscillations in a continuous field of circulation or flow. For Kant, the subject was constituted in and through the flow of time itself in the form of an auto-affection. There was no pregiven transcendental soul, only the process of continual synthesis in time.

For Galvani, the metaphysics of the soul could similarly be explained entirely by a passage of current across a *bioelectrical transcendental field* of electrical circulation. The movement of our body and brain was defined by so many binary ons and offs in a continuous electrical circuit. For Kant, the subject was a circulation of time flows; for Galvani, the subject was a circulation of electrical flows. The "I think" accompanies all the singular I's that think in each successive moment in time in the same way that the same flow of electricity accompanies all the binary oscillations of unique ons and offs across the brain's synapses. Subjective idealism and electrical materialism thus both coincide in the same kinetic regime of elasticity. Bioelectric circulation thus makes possible a whole new understanding of graphism.

The typewriter, writing automaton, and body can no longer be separate kinds of graphisms, but simply become dimensions or aspects of the same elastic regime. The body is a series of oscillations in a circulatory series, just as the typewriter is. The typographical object and subject both undergo a kinetic change at the same time along neurophysiological and philosophical lines.

As Nietzsche writes, "Humans are perhaps only thinking, writing, and speaking machines."[10] This is no Cartesian mechanism; there is no ontological discontinuity between mind and body. The body is no longer mechanistic but circulatory, and the mind is no longer spirit but electricity. This is most evident in the name "type-writer" itself. No other technical object of inscription at the time had the exact same name as the user of that object itself: the type-writer is both the automated technical object and the name of the person who uses the machine. With the rise of typography, the subject and object became increasingly ambiguous and indistinguishable with respect to who is doing the writing, because both were unified in the same elastic field.

Heidegger bemoaned this new subjective anonymity. "Mechanical writing provides this 'advantage,' that it conceals the handwriting and thereby the character. The typewriter makes everyone look the same." The typewriter not only "destroys the word" by transforming it into type, Heidegger argues, but type also "deprives the hand of its rank." The hand of the subject becomes just another mechanical force, and its essence is thus transferred to the machine, resulting in "a transformation . . . in the relation of Being to man," namely that being appears to coincide with itself through the typewriter in a moment of temporal presence when in fact being is actually being stretched out beyond this point.[11]

Heidegger fears in the typewriter precisely what Adorno celebrates in it: the increasing temporal proximity between word and thought. Since being is temporal and differential, word and thought can never coincide. However, it is also important to observe, as Adorno does, how the technics of the typewriter also produce a new form of material-kinetic subjectivity, as a form of tactile and machinic circulation. "The hand . . . chisels word-bodies out of the keys, so clearly that it is as if they were held in the fingers under whose pressure they are sculpted out of the keyboard. . . . Words, across so many centuries merely read, can once again be felt; perhaps in this way we are getting them back within our grasp, whereas for so long we had been under the sway of their foreign power."[12] For Adorno, the switches of the keys become internal to the hand itself. There is no alienation or hiding of one's essence with the typewriter, precisely because the body itself becomes the typewriter. The keys are not levers pushed by the hand, but the fingers are already switches capable of oscillating rapidly up and down like the keys themselves.

As Nietzsche famously described his Malling-Hansen Writing Ball typewriter, "THE WRITING BALL IS A THING LIKE ME: MADE OF IRON YET EASILY TWISTED ON JOURNEYS. PATIENCE AND TACT ARE REQUIRED IN ABUNDANCE AS WELL AS FINE FINGERS TO USE US."[13] Unlike the stylus-phallus, writing from above and beyond the surface, the typewriter unites all writing elements, including the subject, into a single field of circulation, a single recording apparatus requiring a new feminine dexterity of the fingers. "Our writing tools," Nietzsche writes, "are also working on our thoughts,"[14] transforming thought itself not as a foreign force acting from outside, but as a cybernetic system in which the subject is produced as a continuous movement stretching over the temporal intervals between the letters and lines.

As the German novelist and white-collar typist Christa Anita Brück writes in her book *Schicksale*, "Tempo, Tempo, faster, faster. Man funnels his energy into the machine. The machine, which is he himself, his foremost abilities, his foremost concentration and final exertion. And he himself is machine, is lever, is key, is type and moving carriage. Not to think, not reflect, on, on, fast, fast, tipp, tip, tipptipptipptipptipp tipp."[15] It is no coincidence that the typewriter was marketed from the very beginning as a cybernetic device to replace the eyes of the subject. The typewriter was always made to allow the subject to serve as an anonymous prosthesis of the machine. More than a visual machine, like writing it is a kinotactile machine. One writes by literally feeling the motion and stretching one's bodily mobility over the keys. The memory of the key locations in space but also the *kinetic memory* of the letters themselves become the inner extensions of the body. The subject thus writes itself into being through motion.

As a kinetic circulation of anonymous key oscillations, the subject takes on the elastic circulation proper to the typewriter. Writing becomes "more staccato" as T. S. Eliot writes;[16] more "aphoristic," as Nietzsche observes; and more "plastic," as Ben Lerner states;[17] more "*automatique*." Automatic, however, does not mean mechanistic, and staccato does not mean discontinuous. Mechanism presupposes exteriority where the typewriter has only kinetic circulation pulsing through the intervals continuously. Thus, the subject does not move a key as an external object in space but as an adjustment of its own movement. As Merleau-Ponty writes, "The subject knows where the letters are on the typewriter as we know where one of our limbs is, through a knowledge bred of familiarity which does not give us a position in objective space. The movement of her fingers is not presented to the typist as a path through space which can be described, but merely as a certain adjustment of motility, physiognomically distinguishable from any other. . . . It is literally true that the subject who learns to type incorporates the key-bank space into his bodily space."[18]

Far from abolishing the hand, as Heidegger worried, the typewriter actually incorporates the hand (and the entire body's mobility) even more than the pen by adding another hand and all of one's fingers. As Derrida writes, "Having recourse to the typewriter or computer doesn't bypass the hand. It engages another hand, another 'command,' so to speak, another induction, another injunction from body to hand and from hand to writing."[19]

The apparent discontinuity between letters, lines, and hands is made possible by a more primary continuity of the typewriter ink ribbon. The finger-keys oscillate while the ribbon circulates and flows within and between the elasticity of the keys. The letters form impressions on the continuity of the kinetic flux that circulates beneath. The ink is thus a material-kinetic supplement of the typewriter. The ribbon automatically rolls and unrolls, receding and emerging so that the keys may write, so the circuit may circulate. Derrida writes:

> This *ringhband* exposes itself, it unrolls and rolls itself up like a phantasmatic body through which waves of ink will have been made to flow. An affluence or confluence of limited ink, to be sure, because a typewriter ribbon, like the ink cartridge of a computer printer, has only a finite reserve of coloring substance. The material potentiality of this ink remains modest, true, but it capitalizes, virtually, for the "sooner or later," an impressive superabundance: not only a great flux of liquid, good for writing, but a growing flux at the rhythm of a capital—on a day when speculation goes crazy in the capitals of the stock markets. And when one makes ink flow, figuratively or not, one can also figure that one causes to flow or lets flow all that which, by spilling itself this way, can invade or fertilize some cloth or tissue.[20]

The Dutch word *ringhband*, the etymological origin of the word "ribbon," means a curve, band, link, or tie that binds together a series, like a necklace. The ribbon, the tie, and the necklace are thus material folded circulations that hold together a series of punctuated objects: the charms of a necklace, the sheaves of paper, or the impressions of the keys.

In contrast to tensional motion, the bind or ribbon is not in constant contact with the keys, but only in a punctuated or elastic relation between open and closed oscillating states. The subjective movement of the fingers and the ribbon together form the subject as a series of internally integrated switches. The body is not externalized in the machine, nor is the machine internalized in the subject. Both subject and machine are part of the same kinetic process of fingers and keys elastically stretching back and forth over the surface of the type.

The typographic subject is the kinetically transcendental subject. That is, it is a continuous flow of movement that is between and underneath, and it accompanies all the unique oscillations of the keys. Every time one says "I" or types a letter, this is a unique I or letter in a series of letters all made by the continuous elastic motion of the fingers and keys. The subject is both fragmented by the multiplicity of typed I's that accompany the I that types, and unified by the continuous kinetic processes of platen, ink ribbon, and finger movement. It is motion that unifies the typed I in time and the difference in time is a function of the movement that types. The subject can thus be posited only retroactively. One types, one becomes a subject. But since this subjective operation is all of its I's at once, it experiences a kind of anonymity in the sense in which it is all and none of its I's at the same time.

The kinographic ego has no existence outside of all the serial oscillations that it marks.

Just as the transcendental field makes all of time simultaneous and copresent in its reflection, so all the keys of the typewriter spread out in front of one's hands at the same time. All the keys of everything that has ever been said are literally present all at once at one's fingertips. The subject is the process that unifies the keys under the elastic stretch of its fingers. As the fingers move, time and ink flow into letters and individuate the radical but anonymous unity of the subject. The elastic movement of the key levers thus work as the transcendental conditions of inscription, while the inked letters on the paper are the empirical actualizations of the material transcendental field.

This new subjective anonymity finds its perfect historical expression in the popular early-twentieth-century thought experiment of the infinite monkey theorem. The infinite monkey theorem, first put forward by Émile Borel in his 1913 article "Mécanique Statistique et Irréversibilité" (Statistical mechanics and irreversibility),[21] postulates that if one million *singes dactylographes* (typewriting monkeys) typed ten hours a day, it would be extremely unlikely that they would be able to reproduce exactly all the books in the greatest libraries. In 1928 the physicist Arthur Eddington drew on Borel's example, arguing, "If I let my fingers wander idly over the keys of a typewriter it might happen that my screed made an intelligible sentence. If an army of monkeys were strumming on typewriters they might write all the books in the British Museum. The chance of their doing so is decidedly more favourable than the chance of the molecules returning to one half of the vessel."[22] Drawing on this same concept, in "The Total Library" (1939) and "The Library of Babel" (1941), Jorge Luis Borges postulates that given infinite time, all randomly generated books would eventually equal everything ever produced by humans.

The popular discourse of the monkey typewriters is typically understood to make a mathematical point—that infinite probabilities are possible but highly unlikely. However, there is also a kinetic meaning to this idea. With the popularization of the typewriter came the emergence of a new typographic subject whose graphic motions became fused with the writing machine itself and thus increasingly anonymous.

The kinographic logic is as follows: If the inscribing subject is nothing other than the binographic oscillation of keys within the circulation of ink, platen, and paper, then the subject leaves behind no unique trace of his or her particular hand, and is thus effectively anonymous. If the inscribing subject has become anonymous, then anyone can learn to type and produce identical documents. Historically, the typewriter's function was to conceal the blindness of the blind as well as the sex of the women who did dictation for Henry James, Goethe, and Nietzsche, and produced typed manuscripts for others like Heidegger, who still wrote by hand. If, the logic goes, *even women* are capable of learning to type, perhaps even an ape could type something meaningful such that we could not tell it apart from Shakespeare. Even more radically, in the case of Borges and logicians like Alan Turing, a truly random letter generator would be capable of such a feat, given infinite time. The patriarchy of the authentic pen in this logic is clear. In short, if all it takes to inscribe meaning on a recording surface is a series of key oscillations between two positions within a circulation, then anything that moves can write or be made to write.

The subject of inscription is thus both fragmented in the infinite temporal series, and expanded by the circulation of those very fragments that constitute it. The subject of inscription becomes everything and nothing; it accompanies all inscription but itself is not one of the inscriptions in the series. In the infinite series the subject of inscription remains open-ended, nontotal, always becoming. This logic is carried to its highest conclusion in the computer revolution of the later twentieth century, as we will see in the next chapter.

CHAPTER 36

The Keyboard II

Computer

BINARY MODULATION

The kinetics of the computer keyboard are defined primarily by a binary *modulation*, introduced in the mid-twentieth century. In addition to the binary *circulation* introduced by the typewriter, the transistor computer and computer keyboard move not only by mechanical and electrical *circulation* but also by a quantum kinetic modulation of those circulations themselves.

In particular, the computer keyboard not only has elastic oscillating keys supported by springs or rubber but also relies on the work of transistors to modulate or modify the flow of energy released from the key contact. Transistors in turn rely not on a mechanical or even electrical switch but on the modulation of a purely quantum flux in the subatomic structure of a semiconductor material. This kinetic operation is thus defined by three suboperations: modulated oscillation, modulated elasticity, and modulated subjectivity.

Modulated Oscillation

The first suboperation of the computer is modulated oscillation. While the typewriter creates a movement of circulation between a series of oscillating switches, the computer modulates the circulatory flow itself to produce an oscillation. This is accomplished first by the invention of the transistor. Up until the invention of the transistor in 1947, all mechanical and electrical switches could be understood entirely according to the laws of classical physics. In the case of electrical circulation, there is a flow of electrons from negative to positive poles of a battery or vacuum tube. The key lever of the electric typewriter is simply powered by this flow of energy. Each key releases an oscillation of this current to move the switch.

However, with the computer all this changes. The computer keyboard is not an electromechanical device; each key depression completes an electrical flow that itself does not make an impression or inscription. Rather, the completion of the electrical circuit simply unleashes another flow, which in turn releases another, and so on through a multiplicity of transistor oscillations between open and closed states whose collective activation is what inscribes the surface of the disk drive and appears on a screen. The transistor is thus fundamental to the operation of the computer as a kinographic device.

A transistor is a composite of two semiconductor materials that, when electrically (not mechanically) energized, releases a flow of electrons from within the materials themselves. A simple transistor is composed of three pieces of silicon. The two on the ends are made from silicon mixed with phosphorus, and the piece in the middle is made from silicon doped with boron. Since silicon has four electrons in its outer shell, phosphorus has five, and boron has three, the electrons from the phosphorus side of the transistor move toward the boron side of the transistor to fill the electron holes in the silicon lattice. The phosphorus side is the "source," and the boron side is the "drain." In between the two is an electrical contact called the "gate," which applies an electrical charge across the two sides, causing the negatively charged electrons of phosphorus (source) to flow into the positively charged holes in the boron, then to phosphorus on the other side (drain), and then through a connective circuit back around to the source again. In short, with the application of a very small voltage, a circulation of electrons between negative and positive charges is produced.

A nonmechanical electrical circuit is thus produced by mobilizing the subatomic and quantum properties of crystalline semiconductors. Semiconductivity is a quantum mechanical phenomenon because in classical physics there is no way for an electron to move through "close-packed" atoms. Furthermore, in classical physics there is no such thing as an electron hole or differently massed electrons.[1] The transistor is therefore a binary quantum switch that can be opened or closed by simply modulating an electrical voltage.

The difference between open and closed is no longer mechanical but quantum-mechanical. Thus, when a computer key is pressed, it introduces a modulation or fluctuation in a long and complex chain of electron flows beyond the simple oscillation of its initial impact. Instead of each key marking a one or zero, each key introduces a ripple or modulation into the constant flow of electrons in the transistors, which produces an enormous amount of other oscillations in the transistors. It is as if each switch of the key was attached to thousands (1970s) or billions (2010s) of other autonomous switches.

In addition to the modulation of the electron flow, the computer also introduces a modulation in the graphic image produced on the computer screen. Word-processing computer software made possible for the first time a continuous modulation or modification of the recorded graphism. Functions such as cut, paste, copy, font, spacing, and other formatting tools allow the typography to be transformed in ways impossible for a directly printed word to be changed.

Since a computer screen is simply a series of pixels, all typography becomes simply a series of discrete light points. The screen itself, either produced by cathode ray or light-emitting diode, is a series of on or off points. The colors of the screen depend on the binary code of the primary signal. When type is transformed on the screen, this is, kinetically speaking, nothing other than a modulation of current causing an oscillation wave through the transistors between open and closed. Unlike the typewriter or book, the computer document has no end; it only has waves and processes of modification in the electron flows themselves, which now themselves govern the oscillations.

Oscillation is also modulated in another sense: the flow of electrons always leaks at the quantum level. Electrons do not all stop when the current is removed. At the quantum level, all electrons are in constant motion. In addition to their electrical circulation, they also have a subatomic circulation that does not follow the same rules. In quantum mechanics, electrons are capable of tunneling through material and energetic barriers and leaking into other circuits and materials. As transistors get smaller and smaller, designers have to manage this leakage more carefully. The kinetic paradox is that movement is both the condition of the possibility of the quantum modulation of electrical circulation as well as the conditions of the impossibility of the total binary mastery of that same motion.

Modulated Elasticity

The second suboperation of the computer is modulated elasticity. The computer adds to the elastic motion of the typewriter key-spring two even more elastic materials: rubber and plastic. Alongside the mass production of the transistor in the later twentieth century was the mass production of plastic and rubber. These two novel technical objects have the same kinetic structure: elasticity.

Not only did all the same physiological motions from the typewriter (stretching of fingers and so on) still apply, but a new technical material became part of the motion as well, in the form of an elastic surface that is the condition of all modern computer inscription. In addition to using springs, computer keyboards use rubber domes to give the keys an elastic, "snappy" feel as they modulate the electrical circuit below and return to position. Today, when one writes on a computer, one is working with an elastic material. One does not simply flip a switch; one produces a ripple in a flexible dome, bed, or sheet of rubber underneath the keys. Without the elasticity of the keys there is no inscription.

Unlike the typewriter, whose elasticity is confined to a direct spring between key and inked letter, the elasticity of the computer keyboard occurs as a pure modulation of electron flows running through millions of intermediary transistors. Just as there is no longer a simple oscillation but instead a complex and modulated one, so there is no longer a simple elasticity between open and closed key motion but instead a modulated elasticity of electrons expanding and contracting as they travel through more or fewer transistors depending on the key command, software, and so on. It is the flow itself that modulates and continually modifies itself elastically without mechanical oscillation.

The newest touchscreen keyboards have introduced an even more elastic inscription process that reacts to the pressure of the finger itself in a purely electrical way. Without any rubber, spring, or plastic, a flow of electrons can determine how hard a finger is pushing on a piece of glass. In this case, the constant flow of electrons is modeled directly on the microscopic modulation in the elasticity of the human finger itself and modulates itself continually in response. The difference between a finger depression is no longer a simple on and off but is instead a continuous electrical flow directed through billions of on/off oscillations that closely approximate a continuous response. Even if the typographic image is ultimately discrete and its conditions are binographic oscillations, this is only possible because of a quantum kinetics of a continuous circulation of electrons, themselves also rippling in a continuous quantum field that allows them to tunnel and leak.

Modulated Subject

The third suboperation of the computer is modulated subjectivity. With the typewriter, the subject is produced as an anonymous circulation, a unity of the entire kinographic circulation. With the computer, however, the subjective operation of opening and closing the typographic switches now becomes a function taken over almost entirely by the transistor itself. In other words, what used to be the defining activity of the typographic subject—the oscillation of switches within a circulation—has now become largely the property of the computer itself. In this sense, the computer itself becomes indistinguishable from a form of semiautonomous typographic subjectivity. The computer is not an extension of the subject, nor is the subject an internalization of the computer system; instead, the two become two different dimensions of the same typographic process.

The subject is no longer the simple unity of the series of manual oscillations but is now a complex modulation of a series of automatic oscillations tied to the manual oscillations. The typographic subject experiences the effects of the key depression as related to the subject's own mechanical oscillation, but such graphisms are actually the result of thousands to billions of transistors opening and closing by a self-modulation of voltages. In this way the subjective activity of inscription becomes part of the *process* of intervallic modulation itself as it expands and contracts.

For example, the modulated typographic subject is defined by the storage or outsourcing of subjective information (memories, photos, numbers, dates, texts and other personal information) into the computer itself. The typographic subject is not reducible to what is in the brain or what is inscribed on a piece of paper but is now expanded to what has been inscribed in the modulations of electron pathways. In viewing subjective information through the computer, the computer operates as a kind of "Other" within the subject that writes and sees the same things as the subject but is also an Other that stands apart in the machine and watches us.

Derrida thus describes the computer as "an invisible addressee, [as if] an omnipresent witness were listening to us in advance, capturing and sending us back the image of our speech without delay, face to face—with the image rendered objective and immediately stabilized and translated into the speech of the Other, a speech already appropriated by the other or coming from the other, a speech of the unconscious as well. Truth itself."[2] The computer shows us our own typographic productions but modulated and differentiated from the mere mechanical motions of our fingers. The typewriter allows one to watch the mechanism and even directly touch the product, but the inscriptions of the computer remain invisible to the eye and intangible to the hand.

This does not mean that computer typography is somehow immaterial or even quasi-immaterial but only that our hands and eyes cannot sense it. In this way the computer performs the most radical process of desubjectification by automating and outstripping the movement of human writing while at the same time raising the most minimal subjective graphic act itself (binographic oscillation) to the highest form, expanding the subject in ways never possible without it.

The question is not whether the subject is destroyed or exploded but rather how it is changed. In other words, from mechanical anonymity we have moved to quantum mechanical plasticity. The typographic subject is not simply anonymous in relation to the typed letters but has now become integrated into the computer images themselves as a modulated and modifiable reflection of its own movements. One can inscribe and then rework and modulate the inscriptions without leaving a visible trace of the modulation. "Because of the plastic fluidity of the forms, their continual flux, and their quasi immateriality," Derrida writes, "in this new experience of specular reflection, there is more outside and there is no more outside."[3] In other words, there is more outside in the sense that the computer seems like a massive externalization of oscillatory motion via transistors, but at the same time this outside is immediately interpolated as our subjective activity and therefore not outside at all. This does not mean that the identity of thought and inscription is achieved by the computer. Such a distance is never bridgeable. There is, as Derrida explains, always a temporal interval of difference.

The elimination of mechanism in the touch keyboard is not the elimination of movement but an explosion of movement! Between the interval of a soft touch and a harder touch lie a million modulated quantum motions. Thus, the computer does not *collapse* the interval between thought and inscription—it *fills* the interval with a million tiny movements! The interval becomes more active and more subjective than ever before. The microsubject becomes the supersubject. By seeking out stasis in the form of stable on/off quantum flows, one does not increase stasis but harnesses and makes use of more and more of the intervallic quantum motions in between the stabilized ones.

For all the apparent invisibility of data on hard drives and the static nature of so-called solid-state drives, there lies an even deeper and more radical flux of electrons and quantum fields leaking all over the place. The tighter the grip, the more the leaks. The typographic subject cannot be removed from this process, and the process cannot be removed from the subject of inscription. The whole process is inscribed on the hard drive. When we write with the computer and delete a letter, it only appears that the letter has vanished, but in truth it has been recorded, and will only be overcoded when the hard drive or RAM has reached its limit. Our typographic movements are thus doubled elsewhere, leaving traces of every single tiny mistake, change, and micromotion. Contemporary word-processing software even now allows you to browse every modified version of your document in its history. But even this is the tip of the iceberg of digital inscription.

This process of continual revision is close to how the computer subject operates: not as a final product but as an endless modulation and revision process that includes all the versions at once of the whole document at each stage. Seeing all the versions renders visible this leaky, fragmented, modulated subject. With the typewriter one can see the subjective ghost of the letter behind the wite-out, but with the new word processor you can see every single version all at once in a nonlinear fashion—not one ghost but an army of slightly different doppelgängers. When we move our finger on the keyboard and identify this with the corresponding inscription on the screen, this connection is not direct, as it was with the classical typewriter. It only appears this way. Rather, each motion of the finger gives rise to a million tiny motions, like an electron wave or ripple, that are all part of the inscription process and thus the subjective process of expression.

CONCLUSION

This chapter concludes Part IV's analysis of being and time as a regime of elastic motion. Not only do we find this elastic regime in the phenomenological descriptions of time, but we also find it in the typographic regimes of the typewriter and computer. Kinetically, elastic circulation brings us closest to the primacy of movement in the form of an irreducible kinetic interval, but it also takes us the farthest from this motion by reducing movement to a differential interval or single kinographic gap between open and closed.

Therefore, this final part returns us to the ontological importance between continuity and discontinuity posed at the start of the book. We can now conclude, at the end of our journey, that ontology and kinography fundamentally rely on that which they have historically denied: motion. Even in the most minute structure of quantum mechanics, movement, continuum, and flux must be presupposed in the operation of contemporary typographical inscription.

There are, however, many implications of and limitations to the present study. We turn to a consideration of them now in the conclusion of this book.

Conclusion

The early twenty-first century has already shown itself to be an age defined increasingly by motion. Politically, it is an age defined by migration and global mobility; scientifically, it is an age defined by continuously moving quantum fields; and aesthetically, it is an age defined by the mobility of the digital image, all of which condition ontological practice and prompt the invention of a new conceptual and ontological framework of analysis that begins with the primacy of motion. *Being and Motion* provides precisely this framework: a historical ontology for the twenty-first century.

In this short conclusion, we are now in a position to highlight the main theses put forward by this book, what we have gained from them, their limitations, and what directions they have opened for future research.

THE FIVE MAIN THESES OF BEING AND MOTION

Rather than simply reproduce a summary of the book that is already contained in earlier chapters, I would like to put forward here a concise formulation of what I see as the five main theses of *Being and Motion* and where each thesis is defended in the book.

1 *Historical Ontology*: The major events of the twenty-first century are increasingly defined by movement, and thus allow us to identify a new historical ontological framework based on the primacy of motion. (See the Introduction, Chapter 1, and Chapter 2.)

2 *Transcendental Realism and the Theory of Motion*: If being is in motion today, there must be at least some minimal features of historical being that make this possible: its flows, folds, and fields. (See Book I.)
3 *Process Materialism*: If the movement of being that defines the present age and matter is the name historically given to what moves, then being can be defined by a kinetic or process materialism. (See Book I.)
4 *Kinography*: If being is in motion, then so is ontological practice itself. This practice takes the form of a kinetic description and inscription of being with the historical names of space, eternity, force, and time, and inscribed through speech, writing, books, and keyboards. (See Book II.)
5 *Kinomenology*: Not only is ontological practice in motion, but its descriptions and inscriptions also form synchronous kinetic patterns with one another that can also be studied according to their type of motion: centripetal, centrifugal, tensional, and elastic. These patterns form the basis of a new kinetic theory of space, eternity, force, and time, respectively. (See Book II.)

THE CONSEQUENCES

The important payoff and consequence of this conceptual (Book I) and historical (Book II) ontology of motion is that it provides us with the tools to analyze a diversity of events in a new way: from the perspective of the primacy of motion. This is possible because the ontological descriptions of space, eternity, force, and time, as well as the ontological inscriptions of speech, writing, books, and keyboards, are not only historical practices but contemporary ones as well—reproduced under similar conditions that have persisted throughout history to varying degrees and in unique combinations, and that now condition contemporary ontological practice itself, including this book. Contemporary ontological practices are a hybrid mix of all these previous historical patterns.

The ontology of motion has two important consequences for ontological practice. First, it allows us to see that motion is not necessarily an ontologically secondary property of being derived from a static and immutable metaphysical principle like eternity or time, or even from fixed anthropocentric structures like mind or culture. The motion of being is the condition for the very practice of ontological description and inscription itself. Fields of motion are not just anthropic structures but kinetic structures within which matter, including humans, materializes itself in history.

Second, *Being and Motion* allows us to see that there is a noncausal or nonreductionist resonance between the kinetic fields of description and inscription in the history of ontology. Instead of a causal correspondence, *Being and Motion* identifies a series of specific patterns of motion that define the historical *synchrony* between ontological description and inscription. What is more, analyzing these regimes has made possible uniquely kinetic theories of space, eternity, force, and time.

Among this mix today, the ontology of time (and difference) remains the most dominant, although not exclusive, description of being. We are only now on the historical cusp of a new ontology of motion that is capable of reinterpreting and explaining all the others, while the others have failed to account for it (i.e. motion). Motion thus requires its own ontological framework. The contribution of kinetic philosophy is to continue to develop this new ontological framework and demonstrate its explanatory strength in a number of areas as this century moves forward.

While *Being and Motion* uses this framework to explain ontological practice in particular, the aim of its companion volumes is to develop the kinetic consequences of this historical ontology in other fields in the arts, sciences, and in politics. However, once the consequences of this historical ontology have been shown, it will then be possible, although not necessary, for it to be explained in turn by yet another new historical ontology, or not. The future remains open. As yet, however, no other systematic philosophy has been capable of providing an ontology of motion without trying to explain it by something else.

THE LIMITATIONS

There are five important limitations to these consequences.

Historical

First, *Being and Motion* is limited historically to the period of the long Anthropocene, when, as far as we know, humans first began to produce graphic signs with some discernible capacity for ontological description. Signs and surfaces of ordered motion in general precede and exceed humans, but the study of kinography is restricted here for practical, not theoretical, reasons to human history. This does not mean that *Being and Motion* is anthropocentric. On the contrary, it simply means that it has applied its own non-anthropocentric materialist-kinetic framework to a period of history in which humans invented a practice called ontological description. I hope it has been clear in this book and in the companion volumes that individual humans are not the sole agents of this creative labor. Again, I must refer the reader to planned future works that will make good on the claim that nature, independently of humans, has its own techniques of description and inscription.

Nature and animals have kinetic patterns related to description and inscription. The larger and important point to be made here is that the method of historical ontology is possible not simply because of a strictly anthropocentric perspective or practice but because of a historical perspective from the present. In other words, humans can describe and inscribe not because we are human but because nature itself is at a point in history in which it can do these specific things through us. Ontological practice is not the ideal culmination of an ideal process, but rather a material moment in an open and hybrid material process.

Even nonhuman matters have their own graphic process or material memory from their own point in history. Light retains a history of red and blue shifts that record its motion through the cosmos. Stone retains a history of warps and woofs that record its morphology on the surface of the earth. Biological life retains a history of its own evolution through fossilization and DNA patterns. Future studies are therefore needed, and already underway, to further develop the kinographic histories of these other beings.

Philosophical

Second, and perhaps most importantly, the present work is limited strictly to the study of the *kinetic structures* of ontological practice. *Being and Motion* is not a complete intellectual history of every great idea and thinker in the Western tradition. It does not pretend to do biographical, comparative, or systematic justice to Western philosophers and their ontologies. It is my hope that the reader will evaluate this book on its own terms for what it has done, and not for what it has not done or what the reader would have done instead. What is unique about *Being and Motion* is its focus on the hidden kinetic structures operating within the history of ontology, and which reveal a subterranean ontology of motion. Again, the focus on motion is not a theoretical limit (as if this was all there was to be said about Western ontology) but a practical approach. Every book has its focus, and is thus practically limited. The proper intellectual historiography of Western ontology is a different project than the one put forward in this book.

Mixological

Third, and within this second limitation, *Being and Motion* is further limited to the study of only the most dominant names of being and their associated fields of motion *considered separately*. In history, by contrast, many names and fields coexist and mix together without dissolving entirely into one another. They mix in different proportions and concentrations through history. They never occur equally. Just because regimes often mix, however, does not mean there are no regimes at all. It simply means that there are several identifiable kinetic patterns that overlap and knot together. Within these mixtures, however, one pattern tends to become more dominant or prevalent than the others during certain historical periods. *Being and Motion*, therefore, for the sake of parsimony, only considers the dominant names of being during the period of their historical rise to predominance. To show all the uneven mixtures for each historical period would be too large a task and must be reserved for future studies.

Geographical

Fourth, the present work is for the most part limited geographically to the near Eastern and Western history of ontological practice. One of the unfortunate sacrifices made for the historical breadth of this book has been its geographical narrowness. By trying to theorize as closely as possible several major kinetic regimes, I have had to reduce the study down to only their most dominant expression in Near Eastern and Western history. One of the consequences of this method is that it risks giving the appearance that these are the only manifestations of ontology, the only ones that matter, or the only possible ones—none of which is the case.

In no way does this practical limitation suggest that the near East or West have the only or best ontologies. Far from it—the revelation of the primacy of motion at the heart of Western ontology is a way of undoing certain prevailing notions of Western philosophy itself, of showing the subordinated material conditions of its supposedly purely metaphysical descriptions of being qua being that are often used to justify its intellectual superiority. Western ontology does not emerge out of nowhere in classical Greece, as I hope was clear from the treatment of Near Eastern and non-Western ontologies from the Paleolithic, Neolithic, Sumerian, Akkadian, and Egyptian traditions in Parts I and II of Book II. Western ontology, typically defined as beginning with classical Greece, is something which emerges from and is continuous with Near Eastern and non-Western ontologies that preceded it historically.

Furthermore, Western ontology, like Western history more generally, cannot be extracted from its historical and material conditions of imperialism, patriarchy, racism, slavery, and genocide. In fact, Western ontology is defined precisely by its shameless attempts to cover over its own material-kinetic and historical conditions of inscription, which are related to its practices of political expulsion from the Neolithic to modernity. *Being and Motion*, however, does not pretend to do justice to or prove the details of such a bold claim about the constitutive political conditions of ontological practice. This is a topic deserving of its own book-length treatment. Indeed, I have already written two major works of political theory that deal with this issue and to which I now refer the reader.

Insofar as the companion volumes to this one follow the same historical-kinetic patterns as *Being and Motion*, I hope that the reader will see precisely how the different domains are simply different aspects of the same historical-kinetic processes—expressed now politically, now ontologically, now aesthetically, and now scientifically. It is unreasonable for a single book to try and accomplish this alone, and so I have written the argument as a series of interlocking or resonating volumes—each raising questions dealt with by the others.

FUTURE WORK

Given these limitations, there are at least four areas of future research for the ontology of motion.

> *Historical.* The expansion of historical scope beyond the Anthropocene to natural and animal ontologies of motion.
> *Philosophical.* The expansion of philosophical depth to include thinkers left out of the current chapters or aspects of certain kinographic descriptions or inscriptions not included therein.
> *Mixological.* The expansion of analysis to include the coexistence of several minor kinographic and kinetic patterns during the same historical period as the dominant regime analyzed in this book.
> *Geographical.* The expansion of geographical scope to include non-Western and colonial regions, which may have different periods of descriptive and inscriptive dominance, different mixtures of kinetic regimes, and possibly different regimes altogether.

However, with respect to the larger systematic philosophy of motion proposed here, the next task is to complete the kinetic study of aesthetic and scientific domains using the ontological framework developed in Book I but properly adapted to and exemplified in their own domains just as *The Figure of the Migrant* and *Theory of the Border* were for politics. As I write this conclusion, I have already completed drafts of these additional companion volumes: *Theory of the Image* and *Theory of the Object*. In addition to these thematic volumes, several volumes on the history of the philosophy of movement, alluded to in Book I, are in various stages of completion, including ones on Lucretius, Marx, and Bergson.

There is much more work to be done in the philosophy of motion. The aim of this book has been to prepare the way for further analysis by creating a general conceptual and historical framework proper to ontological practice based on patterns of kinetic graphisms that can be used to perform further historical and contemporary analysis of ontological practice elsewhere. The present age requires a new historical ontology: an ontology of movement.

NOTES

INTRODUCTION I
1. This is an ambitious claim and requires more than the few paragraphs I have offered to prove. In fact, each area (politics, science, and art) requires its own book-length argument showing the historical and contemporary importance of motion: *The Figure of the Migrant*, *Theory of the Border*, *Theory of the Image*, and *Theory of the Object* (the latter two in development). In one sense, *Being and Motion* should be read first, because it contains the kinetic-theoretical framework in its most general conceptual formulation, but in another sense it should be read last, because its inquiry is motivated by the contemporary events described in the other works. The domains of art, science, politics, and ontology have been selected here as extremely broad areas, similar to the traditional ontological categories of quality, quantity, relation, and modality, respectively. These broad areas are inclusive of many other areas, termed "cultural," "economic," "social," "epistemological," and so on. In theory, every historical practice one could name can be considered equally with respect to its qualitative, quantitative, relational, and modal aspects. This is a huge task that will be subject of future works and is therefore not part of the focused inquiry of this book, which is ontology.
2. With the rise of home foreclosures and unemployment, people today are beginning to have much more in common with migrants than with certain notions of citizenship (grounded in certain social, legal, and political rights). "All people may now be wanders," as Zygmunt Bauman notes in *Globalization: The Human Consequences* (New York: Columbia University Press, 1998), 87. And "[m]igration must be understood in a broad sense," according to Nikos Papastergiadis in *The Turbulence of Migration: Globalization, Deterritorialization, and Hybridity* (Cambridge: Polity Press, 2000), 2.
3. In total number (1 billion, or 1 in 7 people), and as percentage of total population (about 14%), according to the International Organization on Migration, *The Future of Migration: Building Capacities for Change* (World Migration Report 2010, https://www.iom.int/world-migration-report-2010), and The World Health Organization (http://www.who.int/migrants/en/).
4. As of 2010, there were 215 million international migrants and 740 million internal migrants, according to the United Nations Human Development Report 2009, *Overcoming Barriers: Human Mobility and Development* (p. 21), http://oppenheimer.mcgill.ca/IMG/pdf/HDR_2009_EN_Complete.pdf.

5. United Nations, "Trends in International Migrant Stock: The 2008 Revision" (United Nations database, POP/DB/MIG/Stock/Rev.2008), http://esa.un.org/migration; US National Intelligence Council, "Global Trends 2030: Alternative Worlds," 24, http://globaltrends2030.files.wordpress.com/2012/11/global-trends-2030-november2012.pdf. On the theoretical implications of this phenomenon for liberalism, see Phillip Cole, *Philosophies of Exclusion: Liberal Political Theory and Immigration* (Edinburgh: Edinburgh University Press, 2000).
6. Future forecasts vary from 25 million to 1 billion environmental migrants by 2050, moving either within their countries or across borders, on a permanent or temporary basis, with 200 million being the most widely cited estimate. This figure equals the current estimate of international migrants worldwide, according to the International Organization for Migration, "IOM Outlook on Migration, Environment and Climate Change,"(IOM, 2014).
7. United Nations, "World Urbanization Prospects," 2014 Revision, https://esa.un.org/unpd/wup/Publications/Files/WUP2014-Highlights.pdf.
8. World Bank, World Development Indicators 2005: Section 3 Environment, Table 3.11, http://documents.worldbank.org/curated/en/947951468140975423/pdf/343970PAPER0WDI0200501OFFICIAL0USE0ONLY1.pdf.
9. International tourist arrivals exceeded 1 billion annual tourists globally for the first time in history in 2012. World Tourism Organization (UNWTO), *World Tourism Barometer* 11.1 (2013), https://www.e-unwto.org/toc/wtobarometereng/11/1.
10. I use the word "expulsion" here in the same sense in which Saskia Sassen uses it to indicate a general dispossession or deprivation of social status. See Saskia Sassen, *Expulsions: Brutality and Complexity in the Global Economy* (Cambridge, MA: Belknap Press of Harvard University Press, 2014), 1–2. Many scholars have noted a similar trend. For an excellent review of the "mobilities" literature on migration, see Alison Blunt, "Cultural Geographies of Migration: Mobility, Transnationality and Diaspora," *Progress in Human Geography* 31 (2007): 684–694.
11. Tim Cresswell, *On the Move: Mobility in the Modern Western World* (Hoboken, NJ: Taylor and Francis, 2012); Mike Featherstone, N. J. Thrift, and John Urry, eds., *Automobilities* (London: SAGE, 2005); Peter Adey, *Mobility* (London: Routledge, 2010); Peter Merriman, *Mobility, Space, and Culture* (London: Routledge, 2013); Mimi Sheller and John Urry, "The New Mobilities Paradigm," *Environment and Planning A* 38.2 (2006): 207–226.
12. For a full-length treatment of such a theory, see Thomas Nail, *The Figure of the Migrant* (Stanford, CA: Stanford University Press, 2015); Thomas Nail, *Theory of the Border* (Oxford: Oxford University Press, 2016).
13. Prior to 1929, most physicists, including Albert Einstein, believed that the universe was contained by an immobile spatiotemporal sphere. However, in 1929 Edwin Hubble produced experimental evidence that showed that the universe was expanding in every direction. By 1998 further evidence showed that the universe was expanding at an *accelerating rate*.
14. Lee Smolin, *The Trouble with Physics: The Rise of String Theory, the Fall of a Science, and What Comes Next* (Boston: Houghton Mifflin, 2006), 151: "From Aristotle up until that point, the universe had always been thought to be static. It might have been created by God, but if so, it hadn't changed since. Einstein was the most creative and successful theoretical physicist of the preceding two centuries, but even he could not imagine the universe as anything but eternal and immutable.

We are tempted to say that if Einstein had been a real genius, he might have believed his theory more than his prejudice and predicted the expansion of the universe. But a more productive lesson is just how hard it is for even the most adventurous thinkers to give up beliefs that have been held for millennia."

15. Ilya Prigogine, *From Being to Becoming* (San Francisco: Freeman, 1980).
16. See Smolin, *The Trouble with Physics* (2006).
17. See Sean Carroll, *The Big Picture* (New York: Dutton, 2016), for an accessible review of the state of contemporary physics. See Smolin, *The Trouble with Physics* (2006), for a more detailed review of the literature on string theory and loop quantum gravity. See also Carlo Rovelli, *Reality Is Not What It Seems: The Journey to Quantum Gravity*, translated by Simon Carnell and Erica Segre (New York: Riverhead Books, 2017); Carlo Rovelli, *Seven Brief Lessons on Physics* (London: Penguin, 2016).
18. Karen Barad, *Meeting the Universe Halfway: Quantum Physics and the Entanglement of Matter and Meaning* (Durham, NC: Duke University Press, 2007).
19. For a full-length treatment of this theory see Thomas Nail, *Theory of the Object* (manuscript in process).
20. Today, 77% of developed countries and 40% of the entire world use the Internet. It has become the single-largest mechanism for the production, mobilization, and consumption of sensory media. See the International Telecommunication Union's Statistics page, at http://www.itu.int/en/ITU-D/Statistics/Pages/stat/default.aspx.
21. Luca Turin, *The Secret of Scent: Adventures in Perfume and the Science of Smell* (New York: Harper Perennial, 2007).
22. See Mark Hansen, *New Philosophy for New Media* (Cambridge, MA: MIT Press, 2004) for an excellent literature review of this growing field of study. See also Mark B. N. Hansen, *Bodies in Code: Interfaces with Digital Media* (London: Routledge, 2006); Erin Manning, *Relationscapes: Movement, Art, Philosophy* (Cambridge, MA: MIT Press, 2012); Brian Massumi, *Parables for the Virtual: Movement, Affect, Sensation* (Durham, NC: Duke University Press, 2007); Ossi Naukkarinen, "Aesthetics and Mobility: A Short Introduction into a Moving Field," *Contemporary Aesthetics* (2005), http://www.contempaesthetics.org/newvolume/pages/article.php?articleID=350Politics; Simon O'Sullivan, "The Aesthetics of Affect: Thinking Art beyond Representation," *Angelaki* 6.3 (2001): 125–135; Melissa Gregg and Gregory J. Seigworth, eds., *The Affect Theory Reader* (Durham, NC: Duke University Press, 2010).
23. For a full-length treatment of such an aesthetic framework, see Thomas Nail, *Theory of the Image* (forthcoming with Oxford University Press).
24. Obviously, they do so most often as "bourgeois migrant workers" (BMWs). We should therefore not conflate them with other less privileged figures of the migrant. For a full qualification of this point, see Nail, *Figure of the Migrant*.
25. For a number of reasons, including economic, political, gendered, racial, and historical reasons, the analysis of which has shaped much of postwar and contemporary European philosophy. This is discussed in greater detail in the companion volumes to this book.
26. See Chapters 1 and 2 for a full elaboration of this point.
27. Karen Barad describes this process as an "intra-action" or mutual constitution in *Meeting the Universe Halfway*.
28. See John Phillips, "The End of Ontology and the Future of Media Theory," *Media Theory* 1.1 (2017): 122–136, http://mediatheoryjournal.org/

john-w-p-phillips-the-end-of-ontology-and-the-future-of-media-theory/ ; Friedrich Kittler, "Towards an Ontology of the Media," *Theory, Culture & Society* 26.2–3 (2009): 23–31; Jussi Parikka, *What Is Media Archaeology* (Cambridge: Polity Press, 2015); Michel Serres, *Thumbelina: The Culture and Technology of Millennials*, translated by Daniel W. Smith (London: Rowman & Littlefield, 2016).

29. The attention to the material conditions of philosophy has been a growing tendency in much postwar Continental philosophy. For a genealogy of this trend, see Kittler, "Towards an Ontology of the Media."
30. Mobilities theorists have argued for a perspective that takes movement and mobility, rather than static structures, sedentarism, or territorial borders, as the central fact of modern and postmodern life. See Cresswell, *On the Move*, 25–55; Sheller and Urry, "The New Mobilities Paradigm," 208.
31. Cole, *Philosophies of Exclusion*; Bauman, *Globalization*; Papastergiadis, *The Turbulence of Migration*; Giorgio Agamben, *Means without Ends* (Minneapolis: University of Minnesota Press, 2000).
32. Nicholas Carr, *The Shallows: What the Internet Is Doing to Our Brains* (New York: W. W. Norton, 2011).
33. See Rovelli, *Reality Is Not What It Seems*.
34. For an excellent literature review of the mobilities paradigm across a number of disciplines, see Sheller and Urry, "The New Mobilities Paradigm."
35. Marc Augé, *Non-places: Introduction to an Anthropology of Supermodernity* (London: Verso, 1995); Manuel Castells, *The Rise of the Network Society*, 2nd ed. (Oxford: Blackwell, 2000); Anthony Giddens, *The Consequences of Modernity* (Cambridge: Polity Press, 1990); David Harvey, *The Condition of Postmodernity* (Oxford: Blackwell, 1989); Frederic Jameson, *Postmodernism, or, the Cultural Logic of Late Capitalism* (London: Verso, 1991); cf. N. Thrift, "A Hyperactive World," in *Geographies of Global Change: Remapping the World in the Late Twentieth Century*, edited by R. J. Johnston, Peter J. Taylor, and Michael Watts (Oxford: Blackwell, 1995), 18–35; Peter Merriman, "Driving Places: Marc Augé, Non-places and the Geographies of England's M1 Motorway," *Theory, Culture & Society* 21.4–5 (2004): 145–167; Peter Merriman, "Marc Augé on Space, Place and Non-place," *Irish Journal of French Studies* 9 (2009): 9–29; Hartmut Rosa and William E. Scheuerman, eds., *High-Speed Society: Social Acceleration, Power, and Modernity* (Philadelphia: Pennsylvania University Press, 2009),1–29.
36. To be clear, the age of mobility described here is not defined by or identical to modern capitalism. It is true that capitalism functions by circulation, but it more specifically functions by capturing and temporalizing moving bodies into crystalized quantities of labor-time: value. Time therefore remains of more primary importance to the specificity of the capitalist mode of production. Motion, on the contrary, remains more primary and defining for the migrant whose living movement is the more primary process that gets temporalized and commodified by capital in the first place. Capital is parasitic on migrant labor just as time is parasitic on motion. See Chapter 34 for a full discussion of the relation between time and motion with respect to capitalism.

CHAPTER 1

1. See Chapter 3.
2. See Sheller and Urry, "The New Mobilities Paradigm," for a great literature review and sample of all the places people are using studying movement and mobility.

3. The extension of this framework to other fields and a closer engagement with other empirical studies of motion is already the subject of several other books in this series, which began with *The Figure of the Migrant* and *Theory of the Border* (on politics), and will continue with *Theory of the Image* (on the arts) and *Theory of the Object* (on the sciences). Each of these books is structured almost identically to help the reader see the connections and entanglements between the fields, but each book deals with only one field.
4. Exceptions include at least Lucretius, Marx, and Bergson. I recognize that this is a bold argument, but I believe that I defend it in two ways: first, negatively, by showing over the course of this book how almost all other Western philosophers privilege some feature other than motion, and second, positively, by showing in three separate monographs how Lucretius, Marx, and Bergson are philosophers of motion. For a full literature review of this topic, see Chapter 3.
5. At this point the reader may sense a tension between the *historical* nature of ontology, on the one hand, and the ontology of motion, on the other. In other words, if the historical primacy of motion is revealed only through a historical process, thought of as "temporal," doesn't this mean that motion is by definition not as fundamental as time? This is an understandable objection, but it also assumes what it sets out to show: that history is "fundamentally temporal." From the perspective of motion, however, history is nothing other than the folding and unfolding of matter in motion. Time is simply the descriptive name we give to the motion of matter in process. It is the thesis of this book that the metaphysical idea of time is a conceptual and descriptive practice and not ontologically fundamental. What history "is" is described quite differently in different historical periods and not always defined primarily by time—thus the concept of history is itself historical and not at all obviously or fundamentally temporal—if time itself is fundamentally kinetic. For a full treatment of this issue and a kinetic theory of time, please see Part IV.
6. See Gabriel Rockhill, *Interventions in Contemporary Thought: History, Politics, Aesthetics* (Edinburgh: Edinburgh University Press, 2016), 51–52.
7. See Michel Foucault, *Essential Works of Foucault 1954–1984*, Volume 1, edited by Paul Rabinow (New York: New Press, 1997), 316: "What difference does today introduce with respect to yesterday?" "I shall thus characterize the philosophical ethos appropriate to the critical ontology of ourselves as a historico-practical test of the limits that we may go beyond, and thus as work carried out by ourselves upon ourselves as free beings."
8. See Levi Bryant, *Onto-cartography: An Ontology of Machines and Media* (Edinburgh: Edinburgh University Press, 2014).
9. For more on methodology, see Book I, Part I.
10. Karl Marx, *The Early Writings* (New York: Penguin, 1992), 423.

CHAPTER 2

1. See Part IV on the philosophy of time.
2. See Part IV, Sections I and II, for a more developed critique of subjectivism and phenomenology.
3. Although the present inquiry is limited to the history of ontological practice, a future study will be dedicated to the preanthropic patterns of natural motion. Book I, Part II does, however, provide a brief kinetic analysis of a nonanthropic (plant) event.

4. François Laruelle's project remains fundamentally negative, since it claims to be providing a metaphilosophy, which is not itself philosophical—"a view from no where." He completely ignores the material, historical, and social conditions under which his own nonphilosophy functions.
5. Marshall McLuhan, *The Gutenberg Galaxy: The Making of Typographic Man* (Toronto: University of Toronto Press, 1962).
6. What Bernard Stiegler calls "originary technicity." See Bernard Stiegler, *Technics and Time, 1: The Fault of Epimetheus* (Stanford, CA: Stanford University Press, 1998).
7. Henry Liddell, Eric A. Barber, Robert Scott, Henry S. Jones, and Roderick McKenzie, *A Greek-English Lexicon* (Oxford: Clarendon Press, 1940).
8. Graphic marks are ontologically arbitrary but historically synchronous.
9. Graphic signs also include aural signs, since sounds move and mark the hearing body.
10. These four broad areas (bodies, images, objects, and signs) account for most if not all domains of philosophical inquiry and are not limited to humans alone.
11. The reader will likely notice that the only major literature review of the book occurs in Chapter 3, while the rest of the book keeps its secondary literature mostly restricted to the endnotes. Although I do not provide literature review chapters for every topic covered in the book, I have quoted a significant amount of primary textual materials to support my kinetic interpretations, often quoted in their primary language and with my own translations. I also cite extensively from secondary sources. If readers wish to follow up on the debates in the secondary scholarship or are curious to see my influences, the notes provide a good list of the major primary and secondary sources to follow up with. All the examples given in Part II of Book I are treated at length elsewhere, although some of these sources are not yet published.
12. The usage of this framework to develop an analysis of the social, aesthetic, and scientific domains is developed in a series of companion volumes to this book. The mixture of all these domains is the work of future case studies, which will require a hybrid analysis of the social motions, affects, and objects in each of the cases. The ontology of motion is not a predictive, normative, or reductionist theory. It is purely descriptive and analytic across multiple domains.
13. Karl Marx, *Capital*, Volume 1, translated by Ben Fowkes (Harmondsworth, UK: Penguin, 1976), 102.
14. Although there is a succession of dominant kinographic regimes, there is no ontological development or necessary evolutionary pattern to their emergence, only different historical distributions and combinations. Today, there may be a high degree of hybridity of these regimes compared to prehistoric societies, but this does not mean that there will be any ontological necessity of increasing complexity in the future. It only means that "so far" there has been an increasing complexity and hybridity.

CHAPTER 3
1. This may sound like a bold thesis, but at the turn of the twenty-first century it is almost universally accepted by all physicists in quantum field theory and cosmology. See Carroll, *The Big Picture*; Rovelli, *Reality Is Not What It Seems*.
2. See Ilya Prigogine and Isabelle Stengers, *Order out of Chaos: Man's New Dialogue with Nature* (London: Fontana, 1988); Steven Strogatz, *Sync: The Emerging Science of Spontaneous Order* (New York: Hyperion, 2014).

3. See Scott Draves's *Electric Sheep* (1999–); Maurizio Bolognini's *Programmed Machines* (1988) and *Collective Intelligence* (2000); and Maxime Causeret's *Order from Chaos* (2016).
4. For a great bibliography of work on migration, transport, and tourism, see Sheller and Urry, "The New Mobilities Paradigm," 207–226; Marcel Endres, Katharina Manderscheid, and Christophe Mincke, *The Mobilities Paradigm: Discourses and Ideologies* (London: Routledge, 2016).
5. Sheller and Urry, "The New Mobilities Paradigm," 207–226.
6. For an excellent literature review and collected volume on the latest expansions of mobility studies, see Endres et al., *The Mobilities Paradigm*.
7. Rather, applying the terminology of Foucault's archaeological approach to discourse analysis, the *rules of discourse formation* "determine both, what can appear as 'movement,' and the subject positions according to which one can move meaningfully and legitimately and according to which one can claim agency and insight in relation to movement," Birgitta Frello, "Towards a Discursive Analytics of Movement: On the Making and Unmaking of Movement as an Object of Knowledge," *Mobilities* 3.1 (2008): 25–50, 30.
8. Augé, *Non-places*; Castells, *The Rise of the Network Society*; Bauman, *Globalization*, 87; Virilio, *Speed and Politics*.
9. Most mobilities philosophies or "methodologies" begin with motion, but just as often they supplement this with theories of space from Soja, Lefebvre, or David Harvey, or theories of time from Heidegger and Virilio, or theories of affect from Deleuze and Guattari.
10. Sheller and Urry, "The New Mobilities Paradigm," 210.
11. Quoted in Sheller and Urry, "The New Mobilities Paradigm," 210. Cited from Stephen Graham and Simon Marvin, *Telecommunications and the City: Electronic Spaces, Urban Spaces* (London: Routledge, 2001).
12. Peter Merriman and Peter Adey have also taken issue with this binary opposition between mobility and immobility. See Peter Adey, "If Mobility Is Everything It Is Nothing: Towards a Relational Politics of (Im)mobilities," *Mobilities* 1 (2006): 75–94 (76, 83, 86). In reply, Adey has suggested that as "everything is mobile" and "there is never any absolute immobility," "moorings are indeed mobile too." At a more fundamental level, however, Peter Merriman argues that the mobility/moorings binary is too simplistic. See Merriman, *Mobility, Space, and Culture*. This is a concern also held by David Bissell in his "Narrating Mobile Methodologies: Active and Passive Empiricisms," in *Mobile Methodologies*, edited by B. Fincham, M. McGuinness and L. Murray (Basingstoke, UK: Palgrave Macmillan, 2010), 53–68.
13. Adey, "If Mobility Is Everything It Is Nothing," 76.
14. It is also wrong because space and time are both produced through the folding of quantum fields, which are not themselves reducible to space and time. This is yet another contemporary discovery of the primacy of motion. See Rovelli, *Reality Is Not What It Seems*.
15. For a critique of such simplistic theories of motion, see Cresswell, *On the Move*. On this, also see Nigel Thrift, "Inhuman Geographies: Landscapes of Speed, Light and Power," in *Writing the Rural: Five Cultural Geographies*, edited by P. Cloke, M. Doel, D. Matless, M. Phillips, and N. Thrift (London: Paul Chapman, 1994), 191–248. Although a few feminist theorists such as Rosi Braidotti have embraced nomadic theory/nomadic metaphors, many others have criticized their gendered nature. See Janet Wolff, "On the Road Again: Metaphors of

Travel in Cultural Criticism," *Cultural Studies* 7 (1993): 224–239; Caren Kaplan, *Questions of Travel: Postmodern Discourses of Displacement* (Durham, NC: Duke University Press, 2009), 65–100.
16. Thomas Nail, *Lucretius I: An Ontology of Motion* (Edinburgh: Edinburgh University Press, 2018). The books on Marx and Bergson are mostly completed but still in progress at the time of writing.
17. Epicurus, *Letter to Herodotus*, line 43. In Diogenes Laertius, *The Lives of Eminent Philosophers*, Volume II, translated by Robert D. Hicks (London: W. Heinemann, 1925), Book X, line 43, page 573.
18. Lucretius, *De Rerum Natura*, Book II, lines 292–293.
19. Karl Marx, *The First Writings of Karl Marx*, translated by Paul M. Schafer (Brooklyn, NY: Ig Publishing, 2006), 111. Italics added.
20. "Since labour is motion, time is its natural measure." Karl Marx, *Grundrisse: Foundations of the Critique of Political Economy (rough draft)*, translated by Martin Nicolaus (New York: Penguin Classics, 2012), 205.
21. Karl Marx, *Capital: A Critique of Political Economy*, Volume 1 (London: Penguin, 1976), 128.
22. Marx, *Capital*, 128.
23. Henri Bergson, *Creative Evolution*, translated by Arthur Mitchell (New York: Modern Library, 1944), 5.
24. Bergson, *Creative Evolution*, 273.
25. Henri Bergson, *Matter and Memory*, translated by Nancy Margaret Paul and William Scott Palmer (New York: Zone Books, 1988), 187.
26. Bergson, *The Creative Mind: Introduction to Metaphysics* (Mineola, NY: Dover, 2013), 53.
27. Bergson, *The Creative Mind*, 8.
28. Bergson, *Matter and Memory*, 47.
29. Bergson, *The Creative Mind*, 46.
30. Bergson, *The Creative Mind*, 46.
31. Bergson, *The Creative Mind*, 155.
32. In the case of quantum gravity, this is quite literally the case. Dimensionality emerges from matter—not the other way around. This position is more fully developed with respect to space in Book II, Part I, and with respect to time in Book II, Part IV.
33. See Alfred North Whitehead's theory of change in Alfred North Whitehead, *Concept of Nature* (Cambridge: Cambridge University Press, 1978), 73, 59.
34. Alfred N. Whitehead, *Process and Reality* (New York: Free Press, 2014), 73.
35. See also Leonard J. Eslick, "Substance, Change, and Causality in Whitehead," *Philosophy and Phenomenological Research* 18.4 (1958), 503–513; 510.
36. Whitehead, *Concept of Nature*, 105.
37. Whitehead, *Process and Reality*, 35.
38. It is well established in the scholarship that Whitehead is a thinker of radical discontinuity and stasis, but also becoming. Since each actual occasion is atomistic and self-contained, and events only arise in the gap or passage between them, there is "no continuity of becoming." See Keith Robinson, *Deleuze, Whitehead, Bergson: Rhizomatic Connections* (Basingstoke, UK: Palgrave Macmillan, 2009).
39. Michael Hardt and Antonio Negri, *Empire* (Cambridge, MA: Harvard University Press, 2007); Manuel De Landa, *Assemblage Theory* (Edinburgh: Edinburgh University Press, 2016); Brian Massumi, *Parables for the Virtual: Movement,*

Affect, Sensation (Durham, NC: Duke University Press, 2007); Erin Manning, *Relationscapes: Movement, Art, Philosophy* (Cambridge, MA: MIT Press, 2012); Jane Bennett, *Vibrant Matter: A Political Ecology of Things* (Durham, NC: Duke University Press, 2010); William E. Connolly, *A World of Becoming* (Durham, NC: Duke University Press, 2011); Rosi Braidotti, *Nomadic Subjects: Embodiment and Sexual Difference in Contemporary Feminist Theory* (New York: Columbia University Press, 2011).

40. Levi R. Bryant, *Onto-cartography: An Ontology of Machines and Media* (Edinburgh: Edinburgh University Press, 2014).
41. Steven Shaviro, *The Universe of Things: On Whitehead and Speculative Realism* (Minneapolis: University of Minnesota Press, 2014).
42. Didier Debaise, *Speculative Empiricism: Revisiting Whitehead* (Edinburgh: Edinburgh University Press, 2017).
43. Gilles Deleuze, *Difference and Repetition*, translated by Paul Patton (New York: Columbia University Press, 1994), 138.
44. Gilles Deleuze and Felix Guattari, *A Thousand Plateaus: Capitalism and Schizophrenia*, translated by Brian Massumi (Minneapolis: University of Minnesota Press, 1987), 95.
45. Deleuze explicitly subordinates matter and motion to force in his book on Nietzsche, contrasting himself and Nietzsche against Lucretius and Marx's kinetic materialism: "Only force can be related to another force. (As Marx says when he interprets atomism, 'Atoms are their own unique objects and can relate only to themselves'—Marx '*Difference between the Democritean and Epicurean Philosophy of Nature.*' But the question is; can the basic notion of atom accommodate the essential relation which is attempted to it? The concept only becomes coherent if one thinks of force instead of atom. For the notion of atom cannot in itself contain the difference necessary for the affirmation of such a relation, difference in and according to the essence. Thus atomism would be a mask for an incipient dynamism." Gilles Deleuze, *Nietzche and Philosophy* (New York: Columbia University Press, 1983), 6–7.
46. There are many places where Deleuze *seems* to be explicitly giving primacy to motion. For example, in *A Thousand Plateaus*, he and Guattari write that "only nomads have absolute movement, in other words, speed; vortical or swirling movement is an essential feature of their war machine." Absolute movement is oddly defined both by vortical motion and by speed itself. The nomad seems to be a figure of motion, but just as quickly they clarify this by saying, "It is therefore false to define the nomad by movement." Speed, not motion, is what is most primary here for the nomad. Numerous similar examples can be found throughout Deleuze's work, where motion sounds primary in one passage but is elsewhere contradicted. Deleuze and Guattari, *A Thousand Plateaus*, 381.
47. Deleuze, *Difference and Repetition*, 89.
48. Gilles Deleuze, *Logic of Sense*, translated by Mark Lester and Charles Stivale (Columbia University Press, 2009), 62.
49. Gilles Deleuze and Felix Guattari, *Anti-Oedipus: Capitalism and Schizophrenia*, translated by Robert Hurley, Mark Seem, and Helen R. Lane (Minneapolis: University of Minnesota Press, 1983), 141, 142, 146, 194, 198, 338.
50. Deleuze and Guattari, *Anti-Oedipus*, 5, 6.
51. Deleuze and Guattari, *A Thousand Plateaus*, 381.
52. Deleuze and Guattari, *A Thousand Plateaus*, 159, 197, 199.

53. This is why I have chosen to start with Lucretius and not Spinoza. See Merriman, *Mobility, Space, and Culture*, 2–3, for a critique of Erin Manning and process philosophy in which "embodied movement is repeatedly situated in relation to the privileged concepts of space and time (often as space-time), and the philosophical and scientific orthodoxies which both underpin and provide a departure point for processual and poststructuralist thinking remain in view." See also Jane Bennett's *Vibrant Matter* for an example of a similar subordination of movement to vital force.
54. Gilles Deleuze and Felix Guattari, *What Is Philosophy?* (London: Verso, 2011), 36.
55. Deleuze and Guattari, *What Is Philosophy?*, 33: "The task of philosophy, when it creates concepts, entities, is always to extract an event from things and beings, to set up the new event from things and beings, always to give them a new event: space, time, matter, thought, the possible as events."
56. Deleuze and Guattari, *What Is Philosophy?*, 60.
57. Deleuze and Guattari, *What Is Philosophy?*, 59.
58. Spinoza, *Ethics*, ID4, emphasis added.
59. Martial Gueroult presents a thorough history of this controversy. See Martial Gueroult, *Spinoza: Dieu (Ethique 1)* (Aubier-Montaigne, Paris, 1968), 428–461.
60. Gilles Deleuze, *Expressionism in Philosophy: Spinoza*, translated by Martin Joughin (New York: Zone Books, 201), 65.
61. See Peter Hallward's *Out of This World: Deleuze and the Philosophy of Creation* (London: Verso, 2006) for a book-length treatment on Deleuze's idealism. While I do not agree with all the claims he makes, Hallward provides significant textual support regarding the primacy of "the image of thought" throughout Deleuze's work.
62. Deleuze and Guattari, *What Is Philosophy?*, 60.
63. Deleuze and Guattari, *What Is Philosophy?*, 60. Italics added.
64. Karl Marx, *The Poverty of Philosophy* (New York: International Publishers, 1963), 78.
65. Followers of Deleuze have also reproduced a similar Spinozist idealism. See Elizabeth Grosz, *The Incorporeal: Ontology, Ethics, and the Limits of Materialism* (New York: Columbia University Press, 2017).
66. I am not the first to identify an idealist tendency in Deleuzean ontology. Michael Hardt writes, "Deleuze's thought, then, appears as idealism on both sides of this practicotheoretical synthesis: a speculative idealism and an empirical idealism held loosely together in one philosophy." Michael Hardt, *Gilles Deleuze: An Apprenticeship in Philosophy* (Minneapolis: University of Minnesota Press, 2007), 74–79. See Sean Bowden, "Paul Redding's *Continental Idealism* (and Deleuze's Continuation of the Idealist Tradition)" *Parrhesia* 11 (2011): 75–79; Paul Redding, *Continental Idealism: Leibniz to Nietzsche* (London: Routledge, 2009); Ray Brassier, *Nihil Unbound: Enlightenment and Extinction* (London: Palgrave Macmillan, 2007).
67. Deleuze and Guattari, *What Is Philosophy?*, 39.
68. Deleuze and Guattari, *What Is Philosophy?*, 96.
69. Deleuze and Guattari, *What Is Philosophy?*, 59.
70. The concepts of flow, fold, and field developed in this book are therefore not borrowed from Deleuze, who frequently mixes them with stasis but from the real ontologists of motion: Lucretius, Marx, and Bergson.
71. For an excellent critique of the ahistorical character of vitalist new materialism, see Simon Choat, "Science, Agency and Ontology: A Historical-Materialist Response to New Materialism," *Political Studies* (November 3, 2017).

72. Karl Marx, *Capital*, Afterword to the second edition: "With (Hegel, the dialectic) is standing on its head. It must be turned right side up again, if you would discover the rational kernel within the mystical shell."

CHAPTER 4

1. I use the term "historical being" (or "being") to refer only to previous being up to but not including the future—as was specified in the earlier chapters of Book I.
2. Peter Sloterdijk, *Spheres*, Volume 1: *Bubbles*, translated by Wieland Hoban (South Pasadena, CA: Semiotext(e), 2011), 333.
3. Alain Badiou, *Being and Event*, translated by Oliver Feltham (London: Continuum, 2006), 317.
4. Deleuze and Guattari, *A Thousand Plateaus*, 155.
5. A full analysis of the kinetics of contemporary ontology is outside the scope of this work and must be left for later works.
6. "Nietzsche called the philosophers and philosophy of his time 'the portrayal of all that has ever been believed.' He might say the same of today's philosophy where Nietzscheanism, Hegelianism and Husserlianism are the scraps of the new gaudily painted canvas of modern thought." Deleuze, *Nietzsche and Philosophy*, 195. We might very well say the same thing of today's Deleuzism, Badiouism, Heideggeriansim, and so on.
7. The theory of the kinetic transcendental in *Being and Motion* is precisely what allows it to theorize previous historical structures without necessarily rejecting everything about them. Modernist or post-Kantian transcendental philosophies—including phenomenology, structuralism, and post-structuralism, in particular—are not being abandoned entirely, but rather reinterpreted as regional cases of a larger and more historically primary ontology of motion.
8. Michel Foucault, *Ethics: Subjectivity and Truth*, edited by Paul Rabinov and Robert Hurley (New York: New Press, 1997), 315–319.
9. Immanuel Kant, *Critique of Pure Reason*, translated by. Werner S. Pluhar (Indianapolis, IN: Hackett, 1996), 20.
10. Kant, *Critique of Pure Reason*, 21.
11. Kant, *Critique of Pure Reason*, 21.
12. Kant, *Critique of Pure Reason*, 22.
13. Marx, *The Early Writings*, 423.
14. Again, this is only the case given the ontological primacy of motion in the present. On the question of whether motion and matter will always be primary or whether something else will emerge, we must remain agnostic.
15. Carlo Rovelli, *Reality is Not What it Seems* (New York: Penguin, 2017), 226.
16. Interview with Karen Barad, "The Transversality of New Materialism," in *New Materialism: Interviews and Cartographies*, edited by Rick Dolphijn and Iris van der Tuin (Ann Arbor, MI: Open Humanities Press, 2012), 94: "Think of the feminist polemic about the failed materialism in the work of Judith Butler." See also Vicki Kirby, *Judith Butler* (London: Continuum, 2007); Elizabeth Stephens, "Feminism and New Materialism: The Matter of Fluidity," *Inter/Alia: A Journal of Queer Studies* 9 (2014): 187.
17. See Barad's critique of Judith Butler in *Meeting the Universe Halfway*: "I argue that Butler's conception of materiality is limited by its exclusive focus on human bodies and social factors, which works against her efforts to understand the relationship between materiality and discursivity in their indissociability" (34).

18. See Thomas Lemke, "Materialism without Matter: The Recurrence of Subjectivism in Object-Oriented Ontology," *Distinktion* 18.2 (2017): 133–152. Harman writes, "What is real in the cosmos are forms wrapped inside forms, not durable specks of material that reduce everything else to derivative status. If this is 'materialism,' then it is the first materialism in history to deny the existence of matter." Graham Harman, *Tool-Being: Heidegger and the Metaphysics of Objects* (Chicago: Open Court, 2002), 293.
19. This theory of matter is most consistent with the historical precursors described in Chapter 3: Lucretius, Marx, and Bergson. See Nail, *Lucretius I*.
20. On the question of quantum entanglement and a related realist theory of ontological performativity see Barad, *Meeting the Universe Halfway*; Vicki Kirby, *Quantum Anthropologies: Life at Large* (Durham, NC: Duke University Press, 2011).
21. Marx, *Grundrisse*, 687. Furthermore, quantum fields can only be observed through the visible effects they create and not in themselves. In order to generate mass and particles, quantum fields by necessity must have energy and momentum. Since, as Einstein showed, mass and energy are convertible, particles are born from and return to their quantum fields. Quantum field energy becomes particle mass, becomes field energy, in a continuous momentum or movement. Therefore, a quantum field is just as material as particles are—even if the field itself is not empirically visible—because *particles are nothing other than folds or excitations in the flow of fields*. Matter is therefore always already a flow of matter that has simply folded up into a particle.
22. Quantum fields are observable and measurable to some degree, but not reducibly so due to indeterminacy, mobility, and nonlocality.
23. For a full-length treatment of the concept of kinetic materialism see Nail, *Lucretius I*.
24. Marx, *The Early Writings*, 423; Theses on Fuerbach IX.
25. Marx, *The Early Writings*, 421; Theses on Fuerbach I.
26. See Bennett, *Vibrant Matter*; Grosz, *The Incorporeal*. See also the vitalist process ontology of *Teotl* (power/energy/vital force) in Aztec metaphysics, discussed in James Maffie, *Aztec Philosophy: Understanding a World in Motion* (Boulder: University Press of Colorado, 2014). Maffie explicitly compares Aztec vitalism with Spinoza's pantheistic philosophy.
27. Terms like "agential" or "performative" or "diffracted" materialism as used by Karen Barad, or even "animate" materialism by Mel Chen, are better, since they do not rely on the language of life and forces. See Mel Chen, *Animacies: Biopolitics, Racial Mattering, and Queer Affect* (Durham, NC: Duke University Press, 2012).
28. For a critique of this vital biopolitical fetishism, see Elizabeth Povinelli, *Geontologies: A Requiem to Late Liberalism* (Durham, NC: Duke University Press, 2016). For a Marxist critique of vitalist new materialism, see also Jennifer Cotter, "New Materialism and the Labour Theory of Value," *Minnesota Review* 87 (2016): 171–181. See also Choat, "Science, Agency and Ontology," for an even-handed assessment of the problems with vitalist new materialism and the contributions of Marx to new materialism.
29. See Chen, *Animacies*, 11: "My purpose is not to invest certain materialities with life."

30. For a full typology and critique of various new materialisms, see Chris Gamble, Josh Hanan, and Thomas Nail, "What Is New Materialism?", unpublished manuscript.
31. "This then is one account of nature, namely that it is the primary underlying matter of things which have in themselves a principle of motion or change." Aristotle, *Physics II*, 193a28–193a29. "This is Motion. This becoming, however, is itself just as much the collapse within itself of its contradiction, the *immediately identical* and *existent* unity of both, namely, *Matter*." Georg W. F. Hegel, *Hegel's Philosophy of Nature: Being Part Two of the Encyclopedia of the Philosophical Sciences*, translated and edited by Arnold V. Miller, and Karl L. Michelet (Oxford: Clarendon Press, [1830] 1970), 41.
32. "All that exists, all that lives on land and under water, exists and lives only by some kind of movement. Thus the movement of history produces social relations; industrial movement gives us industrial products, etc. Just as by dint of abstraction we have transformed everything into a logical category, so one has only to make an abstraction of every characteristic distinctive of different movements to attain movement in its abstract condition—purely formal movement, the purely logical formula of movement. If one finds in logical categories the substance of all things, one imagines one has found in the logical formula of movement the absolute method, which not only explains all things, but also implies the movement of things." Marx, *The Poverty of Philosophy* (1963), 78.

CHAPTER 5

1. These terms have also been used in various ways by the historical precursors of the ontology of motion: Lucretius, Marx, and Bergson. For a full demonstration of this argument, see the forthcoming volumes on each of these thinkers.
2. In other words, these three concepts are the minimal historical conditions for the movement of being as well as the conditions of its ontological description. Flows, folds, and fields are thus the common features extracted in their own way from each of the domains—as shown in the companion volumes. For its own part, *Being and Motion* focuses on the historical emergence and consequences of these features *as strictly ontological features*.
3. See Kurt Gödel, *On Formally Undecidable Propositions of Principia Mathematica and Related Systems* (New York: Basic Books, 1962).
4. Geach used this phrase to describe Russell and McTaggart's theories of formal change; see Geach, *God and the Soul* (New York: Schocken Books, 1969), 71–72. See also Alfred North Whitehead's theory of change in Whitehead, *Concept of Nature*, 73, 59. According to Whitehead, change is only "the difference between actual occasions comprised in some determined event," and thus it is "impossible to attribute 'change' to any actual entity." Change and motion thus relate to a succession of actual entities, and are constituted only by the differences among them. Every entity is simply "what it is" and it becomes with its whole set of relations to other entities inherent therein, and thus *cannot change or move*. See also Eslick, "Substance, Change, and Causality in Whitehead," 503–513. Whitehead's transition "is not a real transition, not a flow or flux, and change so understood is merely a fact consequent upon the successive existence of a series of different unchangeable actual entities. *The very notion of change has been made incurably static*" (510).

5. Even the case of "quantum leaps" already presupposes the existence of discrete electrons. The quantum fields that compose these electrons, however, are in continuous motion and vibration. Leaping and tunneling only appear discontinuous with respect to other discrete particles.
6. Lucretius, *On the Nature of Things*, translated by Walter G. Englert (Newburyport, MA: Focus, 2003), lines 1–25.
7. Bergson, *Matter and Memory*, 193.
8. Paul Valéry, *The Graveyard by the Sea*, translated by C. Day Lewis (Philadelphia: Centaur, 1932).
9. Bergson, *Matter and Memory*, 189.
10. Henri Bergson, *An Introduction to Metaphysics*, translated by T. E. Hulme (New York: G. P. Putnam's Sons, 1912), 53.
11. By "whole," Bergson does not mean a "totality," because a totality cannot change or become other than it is. Bergson means something like an open and vibratory whole.
12. See Nail, *Figure of the Migrant*, 11–20.
13. See also Carroll, *The Big Picture*, 172–173: "Our best theory of the world—at least in the domain of applicability that includes our everyday experience—takes unification one step further, to say that both particles and forces arise out of *fields*. A field is kind of the opposite of a particle; while a particle has a specific location in space, a field is something that stretches all throughout space, taking on some particular value at every point. Modern physics says that the particles and the forces that make up atoms all arise out of fields. That viewpoint is called "quantum field theory."
14. See James Cushing, ed., *Philosophical Consequences of Quantum Theory: Reflections on Bell's Theorem* (Notre Dame, IN: University of Notre Dame Press, 2003).
15. Rovelli, *Reality Is Not What It Seems*.
16. The Clay Mathematics Institute (CMI), http://www.claymath.org/millennium-problems/navier–stokes-equation.
17. James Gleick, *Chaos: Making a New Science* (New York: Viking, 1987), 1–32; Strogatz, *Sync*.
18. The quote is probably apocryphal, but the sentiment is striking.
19. Heisenberg ultimately adopts a theory of quantum interaction and abandons the idea of epistemological relativism often associated with his uncertainty principle. "Following a heated discussion wherein Bohr offers an important criticism of Heisenberg's analysis, Heisenberg acquiesces to Bohr's point of view. Though it is little discussed, Heisenberg includes an admission of these important shortcomings of his analysis in a postscript to his famous uncertainty paper. In an important sense, this postscript constitutes an undoing of the analysis that he presents in the body of the text, and yet this erroneous analysis has become the standard exposition on the reciprocity relations. The uncertainty principle continues to be taught to students and spoken of by physicists and non-physicists in accord with Heisenberg's account when by his own admission his account had been based on a fundamental error. Ironically, there is no mention of Bohr's account of the reciprocity relations, that is, the indeterminacy principle. Indeed, if Bohr's contributions to these discussions are mentioned at all, it is usually with a historically respectful nod to complementarity; but even this is seldom mentioned anymore." Barad, *Meeting the Universe Halfway*, 301.
20. Lee A. Rozema, Ardavan Darabi, Dylan H. Mahler, Alex Hayat, Yasaman Soudagar, and Aephraim M. Steinberg. "Violation of Heisenberg's

Measurement-Disturbance Relationship by Weak Measurements," *Physical Review Letters* 109.10 (2012).
21. The "Boltzmann brain" is named after the nineteenth-century physicist Ludwig Boltzmann.
22. Lucretius, *De Rerum Natura*, 2.114–128.
23. Gleick, *Chaos*, 1–32.
24. Gleick, *Chaos*; Strogatz, *Sync*; John P. Briggs and F. David Peat, *Turbulent Mirror: An Illustrated Guide to Chaos Theory and the Science of Wholeness* (New York: Harper & Row, 2000).
25. In contemporary physics this is called "topological quantum field theory," the study of the folds, curves, and bends and knots in quantum fields.

CHAPTER 6

1. Carroll, *The Big Picture*, 52–53.
2. Sean Carroll and Jennifer Chen, "Spontaneous Inflation and Origin of the Arrow of Time" (Chicago: Enrico Fermi Institute and Kavli Institute for Cosmological Physics, 2004), https://arxiv.org/pdf/hep-th/0410270v1.pdf.
3. Xing Xiu-San, "Spontaneous Entropy Decrease and its Statistical Formula," *ResearchGate*, November 1, 2007, https://arxiv.org/pdf/0710.4624.pdf.
4. All current observations also suggest that our current universe is infinite within a margin of error of only 0.4%. In other words, the universe shows no sign of curvature that would indicate that our flat space is ultimately part of a very large topological shape like a sphere or torus. It is flat and continuously expanding.
5. See Manual De Landa, *Intensive Science and Virtual Philosophy* (New York: Continuum, 2017); Levi Bryant, *The Democracy of Objects* (Ann Arbor, MI: Open Humanities Press, 2011).
6. Adriana Cavarero, *Inclinations: A Critique of Rectitude* (Stanford, CA: Stanford University Press, 2016), 130.
7. Nature is therefore fundamentally excessive, unrestrained [*inmoderatum*] (1.1013) with respect to itself, without final measure or numerical totality. Nature is, Lucretius says, "*simplice natura pateat*" (1.1013), openly simplex, or a one-fold-multiple-fold that continuously keeps on folding and unfolding without end. See Nail, *Lucretius I*.
8. The operative definition of infinity used here is a materialist one adapted from calculus and not an idealist one taken from set theory. For further discussion of the concept of "actual infinities," see Thomas Nail, *Theory of the Object* (in progress).
9. Quantum fields, for example, are in continuous movement and are topologically differentiated. Since they are in continuous movement, there is no point at which motion is no longer possible.
10. Marx, *The First Writings of Karl Marx*, 112.
11. There are large and smaller infinities. For example, countable infinities are smaller than uncountable infinities (which include the irrational and real numbers).
12. "The way to see the energy/momentum of a field is to arrange some clever experiment in which a series of, "microscopic," movements of energy and momentum in the field kick off a chain reaction of larger-scale movements of energy/momentum until a, "macroscopic," thing is affected in a way that we can see. This is basically what designing an experiment is all about." Personal

correspondence with Brian Skinner, a researcher in theoretical condensed matter physics at MIT.
13. See Sean Carroll, *The Particle at the End of the Universe: How the Hunt for the Higgs Boson Leads Us to the Edge of a New World* (New York: Dutton, 2012).
14. Second, quantum fields can only be observed through the visible effects they create and not in themselves. In order to generate mass and particles, quantum fields by necessity must have energy and momentum. Since, as Einstein showed, mass and energy are convertible, particles are born from and return to their quantum fields. Quantum field energy becomes particle mass, becomes field energy, in a continuous momentum or movement. Therefore, a quantum field is just as material as particles are—even if the field itself is not empirically visible—because *particles are nothing other than folds or excitations in the flow of fields*. Matter is therefore always already a flow of matter that has simply folded up into a particle.
15. See Chapter 33, footnote on William James. Sensation happens in the stream, but there is no sensation of the "stream of thought" itself.
16. See Barad, *Meeting the Universe Halfway*, ix: "To be entangled is not simply to be intertwined with another, as in the joining of separate entities, but to lack an independent, self-contained existence. Existence is not an individual affair. Individuals do not pre-exist their interactions; rather, individuals emerge through and as part of their entangled intra-relating."
17. Karen Barad, "Transmaterialities: Trans*/Matter/Realities and Queer Political Imaginings," *GLQ: A Journal of Lesbian and Gay Studies* 21 (2015): 387–422.
18. Lucretius, *The Nature of Things*, Book II, line 260.
19. See Carlo Rovelli, *The Order of Time* (New York: Penguin, 2018).
20. Bruno Leibundgut and Jesper Sollerman," A Cosmological Surprise: the Universe Accelerates." *Europhysics News* 32.4 (2008): 121.
21. Lee Smolin, *The Trouble with Physics: The Rise of String Theory, the Fall of a Science and What Comes Next* (New York: Houghton Mifflin, 2006), 56.
22. Carroll, *The Big Picture*, 58: "What we know is that this initially low entropy is responsible for the 'thermodynamic' arrow of time."
23. Carroll and Chen, "Spontaneous Inflation and Origin of the Arrow of Time."
24. See Carlo Rovelli, *The Order of Time* (New York: Penguin, 2018).
25. See "First Second of the Big Bang," *How the Universe Works*, Season 3, 2014 (Discovery Science).
26. Unfortunately, Rovelli often makes metaphysical remarks like "The world is subtly discrete, not continuous. The good Lord has not drawn the world with continuous lines: with a light hand, he has sketched it in dots, like the painter Georges Seurat." *The Order of Time*, 84. Although he often emphasizes the "continuous" nature of quantum movements (132, 226), he still seems to hang onto (despite his best efforts) the old substance based idea that "nature is discrete" without seeing the contradiction entailed by this claim. First, any claim about the "nature of being" is by definition metaphysical (unless otherwise qualified historically). Second, if being were in continuous motion, as he admits, there could be no single static substance called "nature" that could be continuous or discrete, or anything else. If being really flows any claim about the continuous or discrete nature of substance makes no sense because there are no fixed substances to be the predicate of this claim. For a full analysis and critique of quantum field theory and quantum gravity theory see *Theory of the Object* (unpublished manuscript).

27. See Carlo Rovelli, "Loop Quantum Gravity," *Physics World* 16.11 (November 2003); Carlo Rovelli and Lee Smolin, "Loop Space Representation of Quantum General Relativity," *Nuclear Physics B* 331 (1990): 80–152; Lee Smolin, *Three Roads to Quantum Gravity* (Oxford University Press, 2000).
28. A more developed kinetic theory of time is developed in Part IV.
29. The kinetic postulate of bifurcation is thus entirely consistent with contemporary astrophysics. From this continuum of motion, the universe rapidly bifurcated and split itself from itself through the Big Bang: moving from pure kinetic continuum to increasing heterogeneity, discontinuity, and entropy. Cosmologically, matter multiplies through bifurcation.

CHAPTER 7

1. Valéry, *The Graveyard By The Sea*.
2. What Woolf calls a "streak" of sensation. Virginia Woolf, *The Waves* (New York: Wordsworth Editions, 2000), 13.
3. "[A] sign on the brink of an abyss," as Mallarmé says. Stephane Mallarmé, *Collected Poems and Other Verse* (Oxford: Oxford University Press, 2008), 163–183.
4. Friedrich Nietzsche, *Beyond Good and Evil: Prelude to a Philosophy of the Future*, edited by Rolf-Peter Horstmann, translated by Judith Norman (Cambridge: Cambridge University Press, 2002), 4.
5. For further analysis, see Thomas Nail, *Returning to Revolution: Deleuze, Guattari, and Zapatismo* (Edinburgh: Edinburgh University Press, 2015); Nail, *Lucretius I*; Nail, *Figure of the Migrant*; Nail, *Theory of the Border*. Currently unpublished manuscripts include *Theory of the Image* and *Theory of the Object*.
6. David Biello, "How the First Plant Came to Be" *Scientific American*, February 16, 2012, http://www.scientificamerican.com/article/how-first-plant-evolved/.
7. Jakob von Uexküll, *A Foray into the Worlds of Animals and Humans: With a Theory of Meaning* (Minneapolis: University of Minnesota Press, 2010), 44–51.
8. The number of confluent flows and pores is not an absolute determination made from on high. All determinations of the number of confluent flows and pores are relative to the field of circulation itself. See Book I, Part II, Section III for further elaboration on this point.
9. See Eric Schneider and Dorion Sagan, *Into the Cool: Energy Flow, Thermodynamics, and Life* (Chicago: University of Chicago Press, 2005).
10. See Chapter 30.
11. Woolf, *The Waves* (2000), 13.

CHAPTER 8

1. A flow that does not intersect itself is simply a curve. A fold requires that a flow return to itself.
2. Michel Serres develops a similar theory of vortices: "The vortex conjoins the atoms, in the same way as the spiral links the points; the turning movement brings together atoms and points alike." Michel Serres, *The Birth of Physics* (Manchester, UK: Clinamen Press, 2000), 16. Deleuze and Guattari then further develop this under the name of "minor science" in Deleuze and Guattari, *A Thousand Plateaus*, 361–362.
3. The kinetic roots of the word "junction" come from the Proto-Indo-European root *yeug-, "to join, to yoke."

4. John Lowe and S. Moryadas, *The Geography of Movement* (Boston: Houghton Mifflin, 1975), 54.
5. Lowe and Moryadas have been thoroughly critiqued in Tim Cresswell, *On the Move: Mobility in the Modern Western World* (Hoboken, NJ: Taylor & Francis, 2012), 27–29.
6. Peter Haggett claims the starting point of analysis is arbitrary: "[I]t is just as logical to begin with the study of settlements as with the study of routes. We choose to make that cut with movement." Peter Haggett, *Locational Analysis in Human Geography* (New York: St. Martin's Press, 1966), 31.
7. The river rolls itself up like the periodicity of an electron shell.
8. Daniel Graham, *The Texts of Early Greek Philosophy: The Complete Fragments and Selected Testimonies of the Major Presocratics* (Cambridge: Cambridge University Press, 2010), 159: 62 [F39].
9. Virginia Woolf, *The Waves*, in *Selected Works of Virginia Woolf* (Hertfordshire, UK: Wordsworth Editions, 2005), 691.
10. Paul Valéry, *Cantate Du Narcisse* (Paris: Gallimard, 1944), Scene II :

    > Admire dans Narcisse un éternel retour
    > Vers l'onde où son image offerte à son amour
    > Propose à sa beauté toute sa connaissance:
    > Tout mon sort n'est qu'obéissance
    > A la force de mon amour.

11. André Gide, *Le Traité Du Narcisse*, translated by Herbert Marcuse in *Eros and Civilisation* (Boston: Beacon Press, 1966), 163.

    > Paradise must always be re-created. It is not in some remote Thule; it lingers under the appearance. Everything holds within itself, as potentiality, the intimate harmony of its being—just as every salt holds within itself the archetype of its crystal. And a time of silent night will come when the waters will descend, more dense; then, in the unperturbed abysses, the secret crystals will bloom.

12. For the theory of kinetic conjunction, see Chapter 23.

CHAPTER 9

1. Charles Baudelaire, *L'invitation Au Voyage: A Poem from the Flowers of Evil*, edited and translated by Pamela Prince, Jane Handel, Richard Wilbur, and Carol Cosman. (Portland, OR: Ma Nao Books, 2011) :

    > Là, tout n'est qu'ordre et beauté,
    > Luxe, calme, et volupté.

2. Arthur Rimbaud, letter to Georges Izambard, Charleville, May 13, 1871.
3. See Maurice Merleau-Ponty, *Phenomenology of Perception*, translated by Donald A. Landes (London: Routledge, [1962] 2012), 94.
4. For example, the Koyukon of Alaska see "streaking like a flash of fire through the undergrowth," not a fox, and "perching in the lower branches of spruce trees," not an owl. The names of animals are not nouns but verbs. The sun is not understood as an object that moves across the sky, but rather as the path of its movement through the sky, on its daily journey from the eastern to the western horizon. Richard Nelson, *Make Prayers to*

the Raven: A Koyukon View of the Northern Forest (Chicago: University of Chicago Press, 1983), 108, 158. For similar examples, see Tim Ingold, *Being Alive: Essays on Movement, Knowledge and Description* (London: Routledge, 2011), 72.
5. Woolf, *The Waves* (2005), 727.
6. See Plato's "Philebus," in *The Dialogues of Plato*, translated by Benjamin Jowett (New York: Random House, 1937).
7. Strogatz, *Sync*.
8. See Aristotle's "Categories," in *The Basic Works of Aristotle*, translated by Richard McKeon (New York: Random House, 1941), line 254.
9. Gilles Deleuze, *Bergsonism*, translated by Hugh Tomlinson and Barbara Habberjam (New York: Zone Books, 1988), 87–88.
10. A full account of the waveform theory of quality would take us too far afield here but will provided in *Theory of the Image* (in progress).
11. This problem is also formalized in set theory. Alain Badiou, *Being and Event*, translated by Oliver Feltham (London: Continuum, 2007), 267–268.
12. Friedrich Nietzsche, *The Will to Power*, translated by Walter A. Kaufmann (New York: Random House, 1967), 565.
13. Deleuze, *Bergsonism*, 74.
14. See Richard Liboff, *Kinetic Theory: Classical, Quantum, and Relativistic Descriptions* (New York: Springer, 2003). See also Carroll, *The Big Picture*, 172–173: "Modern physics says that the particles and the forces that make up atoms all arise out of fields. That viewpoint is called *quantum field theory*."
15. For a full development of the theory of quantity, see *Theory of the Object*, in progress.
16. For a fully developed theory of number see *Theory of the Object* (unpublished manuscript).
17. See Chapter 20 for a discussion of the *chora*.

CHAPTER 10

1. "*et quo quaeque magis cohibet res intus inane, / tam magis his rebus penitus temptata labascit.* And the more void each thing contains within, / the more it is attacked by these things deep within and is weakened." Lucretius, *On the Nature of Things*, Book I, lines 536–537.
2. The Dirac sea is a theoretical model of the vacuum as an infinite sea of particles with negative energy. It was first postulated by the British physicist Paul Dirac in 1930. Paul Dirac, "A Theory of Electrons and Protons," *Proceedings of the Royal Society of London: Mathematical, Physical and Engineering Sciences* 126.801 (1930): 360–365.
3. Rovelli, *Reality Is Not What It Seems*, 145.
4. See Anatoliĭ Burshteĭn, *Introduction to Thermodynamics and Kinetic Theory of Matter* (New York: Wiley, 1996).
5. For more on the kinetic theory of causality see Book II, Part III.
6. See Carroll, *The Big Picture*, Chapter 8, "Memories and Causes."
7. The "potential energy" of static objects is a macrolevel determination. The molecules, atoms, subatomic particles, and quantum fields are still in motion and do not remain fixed. Matter is still in motion.
8. The kinetic flow of matter is sufficient for understanding the production of heat and energy in thermodynamics. For a history of the development of the kinetic

theory of heat, see Albert Einstein, *Investigations on the Theory of Brownian Movement*, translated by R. Fürth (New York: Dover, 1956).
9. On the idea of "general economy," see Georges Bataille, *Accursed Share*, translated by Robert Hurley (New York: Zone Books, 1992); Eric Schneider and Dorion Sagan, *Into the Cool: Energy Flow, Thermodynamics, and Life* (Chicago: University of Chicago Press, 2005). It is possible to reinterpret Bataille's concept of a "general economy" of energy as a general kinetic economy of motion.
10. Nail, *Figure of the Migrant*.

CHAPTER 11

1. In mathematics, an infinite sum is the sum of the terms of an infinite sequence: a series.
2. René Descartes, *The Philosophical Writings of Descartes*, Volume 1, translated and edited by John Cottingham, Robert Stoothoff, and Dugald Murdoch (Cambridge: Cambridge University Press, 1985), 228; Part II, Section 13.
3. Isaac Newton, *A Treatise of the Method of Fluxions and Infinite Series: With Its Application to the Geometry of Curve Lines* (London: Printed for T. Woodman at Camden's Head in New Round Court in the Strand, 1737).
4. Descartes, *The Philosophical Writings of Descartes*, Volume 1, 236; Part II, Section 31.
5. Woolf, *The Waves* (New York: Harcourt, Brace, 1931), 126–127; the paragraphs above are taken from pages 118–140.
6. I take this word, *kinoumena*, from Epicurus's "Letters" from Book X of Diogenes Laërtius, *Lives of Eminent Philosophers* (London: W. Heinemann, 1925).
7. For a critique of this Kantian idea of phenomena and toward a phenomenology of motion, see Maxine Sheets-Johnstone, *The Primacy of Movement* (Amsterdam: John Benjamins, 1999).
8. For an expanded theory of social limit junctions, see Nail, *Theory of the Border*.
9. These three motions are all developed at length in *Theory of the Border*.
10. For more detail on the composite nature of cycles, synchronies, and emergence, see Harold Morowitz, *The Emergence of Everything: How the World Became Complex* (New York: Oxford University Press, 2004).
11. Mae-Wan Ho, "Circular Thermodynamics of Organisms and Sustainable Systems," *Systems* 1.3 (2013): 30–49, http://www.mdpi.com/2079-8954/1/3/30/htm.

CHAPTER 12

1. There is thus a crucial difference between Bruno Latour's *network theory* of static nodes, Tim Ingold's *meshwork theory* of intersecting lines, and the *knotwork theory* based on folds. For Karen Barad's critique of Latour, see Barad, *Meeting the Universe Halfway*, 41. For Tim Ingold's critique of Latour's network theory and description of his own meshwork theory see Tim Ingold, *Lines: A Brief History* (Taylor and Francis, 2016), 91.
2. See Karen Barad's intra-actional ontology in *Meeting the Universe Halfway*.
3. For more on political expansion and expulsion see Nail, *Figure of the Migrant*. For more on the nonlinear dynamics of population growth, see Gleick, *Chaos*.
4. Subcomandante Marcos, *Ya Basta!: Ten Years of the Zapatista Uprising*, edited by Žiga Vodovnik (Oakland: AK Press, 2004), 642.

5. Subcomandante Marcos, *Ya Basta!*, 645.
6. Subcomandante Marcos, *Ya Basta!*, 645.
7. Oliver de Marcellus, 'Peoples' Global Action: Dreaming up an Old Ghost', in Midnight Notes Collective (ed.), *Auroras of the Zapatistas: Local and Global Struggles of the Fourth World War*, New York: Autonomedia, 2001, 105–17.
8. For an excellent application of knot theory to several different fields, see Colin Adams, *The Knot Book: An Elementary Introduction to the Mathematical Theory of Knots* (New York: W.H. Freeman, 1994).
9. Despite these differences, the kinetic-knot theory does not contradict a core presupposition of contemporary physics: whatever being is, it is in motion. String theory, for example, boldly claims to have unified motion and force. According to Lee Smolin, in string theory, "motion dictates the laws of force." Strings flow in either open or closed loops, which generate forces. These vibrating loops intersect to form larger or smaller composites of forces and eventually particles. Strings vibrate, loop, and intersect. Smolin, *The Trouble with Physics* (2006).
10. These regimes are considered here according to their logic of motion without direct consideration of the historical and material conditions in which they emerged and were set in motion. This is a highly artificial reconstruction that is only possible ex post facto in light of the material and historical labor that demonstrates their concrete emergence described in Book II. Only once this labor has been accomplished is it possible to identify the common kinetic structure produced through a thousand tiny technologies and daily motions constitutive of being. The purpose of introducing these concepts at the beginning of this text and not at the end is purely strategic. If the reader knows the results of the inquiry in advance, she or he is in a better place to understand them as they are applied and developed in the main body of the text. An early presentation also makes available a rich kinetic vocabulary by which to describe the regimes of motion as they emerge historically.
11. A full defense of this historical argument can only be properly made in Book II and through future kinetic studies, of which *The Figure of the Migrant* and *Theory of the Border* are only the first.

INTRODUCTION II

1. Merriman, *Mobility, Space, and Culture*, 2: "We might even go as far as to suggest that space-time is a Western fiction, a series of stories we like to tell ourselves, which in turn structure how we think about the world." See also Martin Heidegger, *The History of Being*, translated by William McNeill and Jeffrey Powell (Bloomington: Indiana University Press, 2015).
2. Joseph Campbell, *Occidental Mythology* (Harmondsworth, UK: Penguin, 1991), 95: "A product, like every other piece of ancient literature, not of God's literary talent but of man's ... not of eternity but of time, and specifically an extremely troubled time."
3. Marx, *The Poverty of Philosophy* (1963), 78.
4. Lacan, Jacques. *Écrits: A Selection*, translated by Alan Sheridan (London: Tavistock, 1977), 164; 167, 175.
5. The historical study of these kinetics, however, is an ambitious one even when limited to just the domain of ontological description. Therefore, *Being and Motion* sets five limitations on the study of ontology, described in the Conclusion. See Viki McCabe, *Coming to Our Senses: Perceiving Complexity to Avoid Catastrophes*

(New York: Oxford University Press, 2014). McCabe describes the function of kinetic structural information below the surface of linguistic representations.

6. The following books all put forward "externalized" theories of technology: Alva Noë, *Out of Our Heads: Why You Are Not Your Brain, and Other Lessons from the Biology of Consciousness* (New York: Hill and Wang, 2009); Friedrich Kittler, *Gramophone, Film, Typewriter* (Stanford, CA: Stanford University Press, 1999); Marshall McLuhan, *Understanding Media: The Extensions of Man* [1964], critical edition, edited by W. Terrence Gordon (Berkeley, CA: Gingko Press, 2003); Bernard Steigler, *Technics and Time 1: The Fault of Epimetheus* (1994), translated by Richard Beardsworth and George Collins (Stanford, CA: Stanford University Press, 1998), 17; Jack Goody, *The Domestication of the Savage Mind* (Cambridge: Cambridge University Press, 1977), 10.
7. In *Being and Motion*, however, we focus not on the regime of bodily sensation, which includes the brain, but on the graphisms that define the descriptions and inscriptions of ontological practice.
8. This is less an explanation (causal) than a description of a collective change.
9. As Michel Foucault has demonstrated in *Archaeology of Knowledge* (London: Routledge, 1972).
10. The kinetic study of "knowledge" is reserved for a coming volume entitled *Theory of the Object*.

CHAPTER 13

1. Other determinations of being, such as eternity, force, and time, were also present to a certain degree.
2. On the "early Anthropocene hypothesis," see William Ruddiman, *Plows, Plagues, and Petroleum: How Humans Took Control of Climate* (Princeton, NJ: Princeton University Press, 2005), 6; William Ruddiman, "How Did Humans First Alter Global Climate?," *Scientific American*, March 2005; William Ruddiman, *Earth Transformed* (New York: W.H. Freeman, 2014).
3. In other words, the kinomenology of space is not a transcendental anthropology or phenomenology, but a transcendental kinomenology. It is a real description of how being in motion was actually distributed and in what way this distribution became an increasingly dominant organization of material flows on earth.
4. See Carlo Rovelli, "Loop Quantum Gravity," *Physics World*, November 2003, for a theory of quantum gravity. Sloterdijk misses this crucial point in his books on space and thus reproduces a kind of formalism of the sphere.
5. Gaston Bachelard, *The Poetics of Space*, translated and edited by M. Jolas and John R. Stilgoe (Boston: Beacon Press, 1994), 212.
6. Peter Sloterdijk makes a similar claim in *Spheres*, Volume 1, *Bubbles*, translated by Wieland Hoban (Los Angeles: Semiotext(e), 2011), 333.
7. "Thus profound metaphysics is rooted in an implicit geometry which-whether we will or no-confers spatiality upon thought; if a metaphysician could not draw, what would he think?" Cited in Bachelard, *The Poetics of Space*, 212.
8. What Tim Ingold calls "the logic of inversion." Tim Ingold, "The Art of Translation in a Continuous World," in *Beyond Boundaries: Understanding, Translation and Anthropological Discourse*, edited by Gísli Palsson (Oxford: Berg, 1993), 210–230.
9. See Rovelli, "Loop Quantum Gravity"; Rovelli and Smolin, "Loop Space Representation of Quantum General Relativity"; Smolin, *Three Roads to Quantum Gravity*.

10. Henri Bergson, *Creative Evolution*, translated by Arthur Mitchell (New York: Random House, 1944), 135.
11. Nail, *Lucretius I*.
12. This is why "human knowledge," as Lenin writes in his *Notebooks*, "is not (or does not follow) a straight line, but a curve, which endlessly approximates a series of circles, a spiral." This is not a metaphor. Human thought literally follows a spiral motion precisely because it *is* a spiral motion, because it *is* centripetal. Vladimir Lenin, *Lenin's Collected Works*, 4th ed., Volume 38, (New York: International Publishers, 1976), 357–361. Written in 1915, first published in 1925 in the magazine *Bolshevik*, No. 5–6.
13. "Fluid space," as I use the term, is not a "third space" between "networked" and "regional" spaces, as John Law and Annemarie Mol have described it. Through folding and circulation, fluid or kinetic space is capable of *producing* networks and regions. Network and regional space is derived from kinetic space. See Annemarie Mol and John Law, "Regions, Networks and Fluids: Anaemia and Social Topology." *Social Studies of Science* 24.4 (1994): 641–671.
14. See Deleuze and Guattari, *A Thousand Plateaus*, 474–500.
15. Merleau-Ponty, *Phenomenology of Perception*, 293.
16. Merleau-Ponty, *Phenomenology of Perception*, 253–254.
17. Merleau-Ponty, *Phenomenology of Perception*, 149. Italics added.
18. Merleau-Ponty, *Phenomenology of Perception*, 100.
19. Place is "at once the limit and the condition of all that exists. . . . To be is to be in place." Edward Casey, *Getting Back into Place: Toward a Renewed Understanding of the Place-World* (Bloomington: Indiana University Press, 1993), 15–16.
20. Tim Ingold, "Bindings against Boundaries: Entanglements of Life in an Open World," *Environment and Planning A: Economy and Space* 40 (2009): 1808.
21. Martin Heidegger, *Basic Writings: Martin Heidegger*, translated by David F. Krell (London: Routledge, 2010), 355.
22. Heidegger, *Basic Writings*, 356.
23. Heidegger, *Basic Writings*, 359.
24. Heidegger, *Basic Writings*, 361.
25. Maxine Sheets-Johnstone, *The Primacy of Movement* (Amsterdam: John Benjamins, 1999), xvii: "It is about how movement is at the root of our sense of agency and how it is the generative source of our notions of space and time." See also 1–32 on Neandertals.

CHAPTER 14

1. Marija Gimbutas, *The Language of the Goddess: Unearthing the Hidden Symbols of Western Civilization* (San Francisco: Harper & Row, 1989), xv–xxiii.
2. "It is a fact that ever since the Upper Paleolithic, but especially since the advent of agriculture, the world of symbols-religious, aesthetic, and social has always stood higher on the hierarchical ladder than the world of technics." André Leroi-Gourhan, *Gesture and Speech* (Cambridge, MA: MIT Press, 1993), 183–184. "The emergence of graphic signs at the end of the Palaeoanthropians' reign presupposes the establishment of a new relationship between the two operating poles—a relationship exclusively characteristic of humanity in the narrow sense, that is to say, one that meets the requirements of mental symbolization to the same extent as today" (187). "What is new at this time is their number, and also the indication that she was not only a 'fertility symbol' but a genuine mythical personality, conceived as a supreme being and universal mother, in other words

a goddess who crowned a religious system which one could describe as 'female monotheism' in the sense that all the rest remained subordinated to her." Jacques Cauvin, *The Birth of the Gods and the Origins of Agriculture*, translated by Trevor Watkins (Cambridge: Cambridge University Press, 2000), 32.

3. Far from being a late phenomenon, it is directly connected with the fact that the figures are symbols, not copies. Leroi-Gourhan, *Gesture and Speech*, 384.
4. See also Mircea Eliade, *Cosmos and History: The Myth of the Eternal Return* (New York: Harper, 1959), 3 and throughout the whole book.
5. Leroi-Gourhan, *Gesture and Speech*, 196.
6. "Such a mode of representation is almost naturally connected with cosmic symbolism." Leroi-Gourhan, *Gesture and Speech*, 196.
7. "The reason why art is so closely connected with religion is that graphic expression restores to language the dimension of the inexpressible—the possibility of multiplying the dimensions of a fact in instantly accessible visual symbols. The basic link between art and religion is emotional, yet not in a vague sense. It has to do with mastering a mode of expression that restores humans to their true place in a cosmos whose center they occupy without trying to pierce it by an intellectual process." Leroi-Gourhan, *Gesture and Speech*, 200.
8. "We have seen that Paleolithic people used pictures as mythograms, and we may therefore suppose meaning-related composition to have been present at the very beginning of figurative expression. Figurative syntax is inseparable from the syntax of words." Leroi-Gourhan, *Gesture and Speech*, 386.
9. Gimbutas, *The Language of the Goddess*, xv.
10. Hegel is therefore wrong to have begun his philosophy of world history with the Persians—the so-called "first Historical People." The conceptualization and determination of being begins much earlier. Georg W. F. Hegel, *Lectures on the Philosophy of World History*, Volume 1, translated and edited by Robert F. Brown and Peter C. Hodgson (Oxford: Oxford University Press, 2011), 191–192.
11. "The pregnant vegetation goddess . . . was one of the most-represented female figures depicted in Neolithic Old Europe." Marija Gimbutas, *The Living Goddesses* (Berkeley: University of California Press, 1999), 15.
12. Thomas H. Maugh II, "Venus Figurine Sheds Light on Origins of Art by Early Humans," *Los Angeles Times*, May 14, 2009, http://articles.latimes.com/2009/may/14/science/sci-Venus14.
13. Gimbutas, *The Living Goddesses*, 8.
14. For a more robust feminist materialist interpretation/critique of ancient goddess mythology, see Nail, *Lucretius I*, influenced by the work of Luce Irigaray, *This Sex Which Is Not One* (Ithaca, NY: Cornell University Press, 1996); Barad, *Meeting the Universe Halfway*; Anne Baring and Jules Cashford, *The Myth of the Goddess: Evolution of an Image* (London: Arkana, 2000); Judith Butler, *Bodies That Matter: On the Discursive Limits of "Sex"* (New York: Routledge, 2015); Cavarero, *Inclinations*.
15. Gimbutas, *The Language of the Goddess*, 43.
16. For a full description of goddess culture in the Neolithic, see Gimbutas, *The Language of the Goddess*, xv–xxiii.
17. "The Lakota define the year as a circle around the border of the world. The circle is a symbol of both the earth (with its encircling horizons) and time. The changes of sunup and sundown around the horizon during the course of the year delineate the contours of time, time as a part of space." David Abram, *The Spell of the Sensuous: Perception and Language in a More-Than-Human World*

(New York: Pantheon, 1996), 189. "In this Hopi view, [that which we call] time disappears and [that which we call] space is altered, so that it is no longer the homogeneous and instantaneous timeless space of our supposed intuition or of classical Newtonian mechanics." Cited in Abram, *The Spell of the Sensuous*, 191.

18. Lewis Mumford, *The City in History: Its Origins, Its Transformations, and Its Prospects* (New York: Harcourt, Brace & World, 1961), 7.
19. Mumford, *The City in History*, 10.
20. Mumford, *The City in History*, 10. Italics added.
21. Mumford, *The City in History*, 11.
22. Bachelard, *The Poetics of Space*, 32.
23. Mumford, *The City in History*, 13.
24. Mumford, *The City in History*, 15–16.
25. See Gimbutas, *The Language of the Goddess*; David Leeming, *Encyclopedia of Creation Myths* (Santa Barbara, CA: ABC-CLIO, 1994).
26. Gimbutas, *The Language of the Goddess*, 213.
27. On the double egg shaped buttocks, see Gimbutas, *The Language of the Goddess*, 163.
28. See Gimbutas, *The Language of the Goddess*, 3.
29. Albert Dalcq, *L'oeuf et son dynamisme organisateur* (Paris: Albin Michel, 1941), 95.
30. Deleuze and Guattari, *A Thousand Plateaus*, 153.
31. Gimbutas, *The Living Goddesses*, 58.
32. Peter Sloterdijk, *Bubbles*, translated by Wieland Hoban (Los Angeles: Semiotext(e), 2011), 323.
33. Leeming, *Encyclopedia of Creation Myths*, Volume 2, 342.
34. Patricia Lynch, *African Mythology A to Z* (New York: Facts on File, 2004), 18.
35. Lynch, *African Mythology A to Z*, 28.
36. For a complete list of egg myths, see Leeming, *Encyclopedia of Creation Myths*, Volume 1, 12.
37. Leeming, *Encyclopedia of Creation Myths*, Volume 2, 342.
38. Later anthropologists have not been able to reproduce the mythology discovered by Griaule. However, the mythology as told by at least one of the Dogon people to Griaule is an incredible convergence and elaboration of numerous other historical cosmic egg myths. See Laird Scranton, "Revisiting Griaule's Dogon Cosmology: Comparative Cosmology Offers New Evidence to a Scientific Controversy." *Anthropology News* 48.4 (2007): 24–25.
39. Marcel Griaule, *The Pale Fox*, translated by Germaine Dieterlen and Stephen C. Infantino (Chino Valley, AZ: Continuum Foundation, 1986), 81.
40. Griaule, *The Pale Fox*, 82.
41. Griaule, *The Pale Fox*, 83–84.
42. Griaule, *The Pale Fox*, 130.
43. Leeming, *Encyclopedia of Creation Myths*, Volume 1, 10.
44. Gimbutas, *The Language of the Goddess*, 279.
45. Leroi-Gourhan, *Gesture and Speech*, 367–368.
46. Gimbutas, *The Language of the Goddess*, 277.
47. Gimbutas, *The Language of the Goddess*, xix.
48. "Antithetic spirals whirl around this lidded vase, simulating the life power of the central egg, which is marked with a net design. 4200–4100 BCE." See Gimbutas, *The Language of the Goddess*, Plate 22.
49. Encyclopedia Britannica, "Australian Aboriginal peoples," https://www.britannica.com/topic/Australian-Aboriginal

50. Roy Wagner, *Symbols That Stand for Themselves* (Chicago: University of Chicago Press, 1986), 21.

CHAPTER 15
1. For the above paragraphs see Leroi-Gourhan, *Gesture and Speech*.
2. Leroi-Gourhan, *Gesture and Speech*, 113–114.
3. Leroi-Gourhan, *Gesture and Speech*, 363.
4. Just to be clear, mythological description is oral but is also inscribed in both the human body and in the mythograms created by the body.
5. Giambattista Vico, *The New Science of Giambattista Vico*, translated by Thomas G. Bergin and Max H. Fisch, 3rd ed. (Garden City, NY: Doubleday, 1961).
6. Johann Gottfried Herder, *On the Origin of Language* (Chicago: University of Chicago Press, 1966).
7. Charles Darwin, *The Descent of Man, and Selection in Relation to Sex* (Princeton, NJ: Princeton University Press, [1871] 1981).
8. Abram, *The Spell of the Sensuous*, 82.
9. Musical pitch is not modeled on a linguistic field, but creates its own nonsignifying sonic field of images that creates just as much as it is created by the functional operations required by language itself: discrete combinatorics and hierarchic cognition in early humans. For a theory of "pitch continuum" and "vector grammar," see Martin Rohrmeier, Willem Zuidema, Geraint A. Wiggins, and Constance Scharff, "Principles of Structure Building in Music, Language and Animal Song." *Philosophical Transactions of the Royal Society of London B: Biological Sciences* 370.1664 (2015). See also Gary Tomlinson, *A Million Years of Music* (New York: Zone Books, 2015), 258: "The winnowing of discrete pitches from the graded intonational contours of the calls of protodiscourse brought with it an abstraction, a distancing of the pitches themselves from meaning."
10. Maurice Merleau-Ponty, *The Visible and the Invisible* (Evanston, IL: Northwestern University Press, 1968), 194.
11. Merleau-Ponty, *The Visible and the Invisible*, 155.
12. Deleuze and Guattari, *A Thousand Plateaus*, 94.
13. See Deleuze and Guattari, *A Thousand Plateaus*, 75–110.
14. William Labov, *Sociolinguistic Patterns* (Philadelphia: University of Pennsylvania Press, 1973), 3.
15. Ferdinand Saussure, *Course in General Linguistics*, edited by Charles Bally and Albert Reidlinger, translated from the French by Wade Baskin (New York: Philosophical Library, 1959), 87.
16. Noam Chomsky, *Rules and Representations* (New York: Columbia University Press, 1980), 92.
17. Deleuze and Guattari, *A Thousand Plateaus*, 82.
18. See Thomas Rickert, *Ambient Rhetoric: The Attunements of Rhetorical Being* (Pittsburgh, PA: University of Pittsburgh Press, 2013).
19. Friedrich Nietzsche, *Twilight of the Idols, or, How to Philosophize with a Hammer*, translated by Duncan Large (New York: Oxford University Press, 1998), 20.
20. Deleuze and Guattari, *A Thousand Plateaus*, 101.
21. Eliade Mircea, *The Myth of the Eternal Return* (New York: Harper & Row, 1959), vii.
22. Griaule, *The Pale Fox*, 84, footnote 9.
23. "The *bummo* of the *po* prefigure its spiral movement. The image does not connote a seed, but the internal life of that seed." Marcel Griaule, *The Pale Fox*,

97. "This act provoked the emergence of the *yala* [marks/traces] from the spiral which, turning in the other direction, will prefigure, inside the egg, the future expansion of the universe.... Thus, inside the egg Amma himself was like a spiraling motion, called 'accelerated ball.'" Marcel Griaule, *The Pale Fox*, 118–130.
24. Marcel Griaule, *The Pale Fox*, 91–92.
25. Marcel Griaule, *The Pale Fox*, 135.
26. Eliade Mircea, *The Myth of the Eternal Return*, 104.
27. David Leeming, *Encyclopedia of Creation Myths*, Volume 1 (Santa Barbara, CA: ABC-CLIO, 1994), 131; Pomo people, 230; Acoma song of creation, 33.
28. "It must have been the oral tradition of songs and story-telling that kept the [Neolithic Goddess] tradition alive, as it had done for countless thousands of years before that." Baring and Cashford, *The Myth of the Goddess*, 301.
29. The Akkadian word tiamtu or tâmtu, "the sea," becomes Tiamat. Walter Burkert, *The Orientalizing Revolution: Near Eastern Influence on Greek Culture in the Early Archaic Age* (Cambridge, MA: Harvard University Press, 1992), 91–93. See also Catherine Keller, *Face of the Deep: A Theology of Becoming* (London: Routledge, 2003).
30. "For I am faring to visit the limits of the all-nurturing earth, and Oceanus, from whom the gods are sprung, and mother Tethys, even them that lovingly nursed and cherished me in their halls, when they had taken me from Rhea, what time Zeus, whose voice is borne afar, thrust Cronos down to dwell beneath earth and the unresting sea." Homer, *Iliad*, translated by A.T. Murray, Book XIV, lines 200–205.
31. "Verily at the first Chaos came to be, but next wide-bosomed Earth, the ever-sure foundations of all the deathless ones who hold the peaks of snowy Olympus." Hesiod, *Theogony*, translated by Richard S. Caldwell (Newburyport, MA: Focus Classical Library, 1987), lines 116–138.
32. "And he [Epicurus] says that the world began in the likeness of an egg, and the Wind [Khronos (Time) and Ananke (Inevitability) [entwined?] encircling the egg serpent-fashion like a wreath or a belt then began to constrict nature. As it tried to squeeze all the matter with greater force, it divided the world into the two hemispheres [Ouranos and Gaia, heaven and earth]." Carl Holladay, *Orphica* (Chico, CA: Scholars Press, 1996), Epicurus Fragment (from Epiphanius).
33. "First was Chaos and Night, and black Erebus and vast Tartarus;
    And there was neither Earth, nor Air, nor Heaven: but in the boundless
       bosoms of Erebus.
    Night, with her black wings, first produced an aerial egg,
    From which, at the completed time, sprang forth the lovely Eros,
    Glittering with golden wings upon his back, like the swift whirlwinds.
    But embracing the dark-winged Chaos in the vast Tartarus.
    He begot our race (the birds), and first brought us to light.
    The race of the Immortals was not, till Eros mingled all things together;
    But when the elements were mixed one with another, Heaven was produced,
       and Ocean,
    And Earth, and the imperishable race of all the blessed Gods."
                                                                Aristophanes, *The Birds*
                          (Newburyport, MA: Focus Classical Library, 1999), line 698.
34. "First (I have sung) the vast necessity of ancient Chaos,
    And Cronus, who in the boundless tracts brought forth
    The Ether, and the splendid and glorious Eros of a two-fold nature,

> The illustrious father of night, existing from eternity.
> Whom men call Phanes, for he first appeared.
> I have sung the birth of powerful Brimo (Hecate), and the unhallowed deeds
> Of the earth-born (giants), who showered down from heaven
> Their blood, the lamentable seed of generation, from whence sprung
> The race of mortals, who inhabit the boundless earth for ever."
>
> *Argonautica Orphica*, line 419ff.

35. Today, we continue to use such kinetic so-called metaphors to describe many speech-acts, such as "to advance claims," "direct an argument," "gain/lose 'momentum' in speech," "gain/lose traction with an argument," "to stand for something," "direct an audience," "to be moved or touched by something someone said," "make a forceful statement," "to walk someone through something," "shift positions in an argument," "to drive home a point," "to stake a claim," and "to settle a dispute."
36. Rainer Maria Rilke, *Sonnets to Orpheus: Duino Elegies* (New York: Fine Editions Press, 1945), 3.

CHAPTER 16

1. Euclid, *Elements*, Book I, definition 15 and 16 (italics added), translation by Richard Fitzpatrick, http://farside.ph.utexas.edu/Books/Euclid/Elements.pdf.
2. Euclid, *Elements*, Book I, Postulate 3.
3. Georg W. F. Hegel, *Philosophy of Nature: Being Part Two of the Encyclopaedia of the Philosophical Sciences*, translated by Arnold V. Miller and Karl L. Michelet (Oxford: Clarendon Press, [1830] 1970), 36.
4. Hegel, *Philosophy of Nature*, 36, 39.
5. Hegel, *Philosophy of Nature*, 43–44. Translation modified.

CHAPTER 17

1. Eternal being, in contrast to space, is undying. It may be born in some descriptions, but it never passes away. It is immune to the spatial and natural cycle of regeneration. If an eternal being does come into being it almost always destroys that which birthed it, such that it no longer has a creator and is in this way "uncreated." In its most extreme description, eternity neither comes into being nor goes out of being. Accordingly, we find a continuous etymological modulation and mixing of the names for eternity in history, increasingly moving from simply meaning "undying life" to "unborn *and* undying life." We thus find a *historical spectrum* or degree of eternality, and not any kind of absolute difference in kind between immortality and eternity.
2. Samuel Kramer, *Sumerian Mythology: A Study of Spiritual and Literary Achievement in the Third Millennium B.C.* (New York: Harper, 1961), 40. Her epithet ama-tu-an-ki, "the mother who gave birth to heaven and earth," reveals her original character. The goddess Nammu is described as ama-palil-ù-tu-dingir-šár-šár-ra-ke-ne, "the mother, the ancestress, who gave birth to all the gods." See also Henri de Genouillac, *Textes religieux sumériens du Louvre, Tomes I–II* (Musée du Louvre, Department des antiquités orientales, Textes cunéiformes, Tomes XV–XVI; Paris, 1930), 10.36–37.
3. Kramer, *Sumerian Mythology*, 53.
4. Kramer, *Sumerian Mythology*, 51.
5. Kramer, *Sumerian Mythology*, 38.

6. R T. R. Clark, *Myth and Symbol in Ancient Egypt* (London: Thames and Hudson, 1978), 44.
7. Clark, *Myth and Symbol in Ancient Egypt*, 65.
8. Enlil *retroactively* becomes the father of both gods and men, the king of heaven and earth.
9. Georges Bataille, *Visions of Excess: Selected Writings, 1927–1939*, translated by Allan Stoekl (Minneapolis: University of Minnesota Press, 1985), 8.
10. Baring and Cashford, *The Myth of the Goddess*, 177.
11. Baring and Cashford, *The Myth of the Goddess*, 178.
12. Diane Wolkstein and Samuel N. Kramer, *Inanna, Queen of Heaven and Earth: Her Stories and Hymns from Sumer* (New York: Harper & Row, 1983), 71.
13. Baring and Cashford, *The Myth of the Goddess*, 209.
14. Baring and Cashford, *The Myth of the Goddess*, 211.
15. "However, Campbell brings evidence to support the thesis, based on Frazer, that before 2500 BCE, kings were ritually sacrificed every octennial Great Year in their role as the vegetation god, together with the high priestess or queen who personified the goddess." Baring and Cashford, *The Myth of the Goddess*, 221. See also Joseph Campbell, *Oriental Mythology* (London: Souvenir, 2000), 44.
16. "My mother, an enitum [temple priestess], conceived me,
in secret she bore me.
She set me in a basket of rushes,
with bitumen she sealed my lid.
She cast me into the river, which
rose not over me.
The river bore me up and carried
me to Akki, the drawer of water.
Akki, the drawer of water, lifted me
out as he dipped his bucket.
Akki, the drawer of water, took me
as his son and reared me.
Akki, the drawer of water,
appointed me as his gardener.
While I was a gardener, Ishtar
granted me love.
And for four and ... years I
exercised kingship,
The black-headed people I ruled, I governed."
John Gray, *Near Eastern Mythology* (Feltham, UK: Hamlyn, 1969), 56.
17. "The first of these is Nammu, goddess of the primordial ocean or sea, whose cult endured for millennia; for the greatest and wisest of the late Sumerian kings, Ur-Nammu (c. 2100 BCE), takes her name, calling himself 'Servant of the goddess Nammu.' (The Babylonian mother goddess Tiamat seems to have been a later or alternative name for Nammu, for she also was the primordial waters, the First or Great Mother, the Great Deep.)." Baring and Cashford, *The Myth of the Goddess*, 185. See also Samuel Kramer, *From the Poetry of Sumer: Creation, Glorification, Adoration* (Berkeley: University of California Press, 1979), 43.

CHAPTER 18
1. Quoted in Joseph Campbell, *Occidental Mythology*, 78–79.
2. *The Enuma Elish*, Tablet I, lines 105–109. Translated by W.G. Lambert, "Mesopotamian Creation Stories," in *Imagining Creation*, edited by Markham Geller and Mineke Schipper (Leiden, the Netherlands: Brill, 2008), http://www.ancient.eu/article/225/.
3. *The Enuma Elish*, Tablet IV, lines, 29–30. Translated in L. W. King, *The Seven Tablets of Creation: Or, the Babylonian and Assyrian Legends Concerning the Creation of the World and of Mankind* (New York: AMS Press, 1976).
4. *The Enuma Elish*, Tablet IV, lines 39–40. King Translation.
5. *The Enuma Elish*, Tablet IV, lines 95–104. King Translation.
6. *The Enuma Elish*, Tablet IV, lines 129–138. King Translation.
7. *The Enuma Elish*, Tablet V, lines 57–61. Translated in Thorkild Jacobsen, *The Treasures of Darkness: A History of Mesopotamian Religion* (New Haven, CT: Yale University Press, 1976), 179.
8. *The Enuma Elish*, Tablet VI, lines 31–33. Jacobsen Translation.
9. Hesiod, *Theogony*, in *The Homeric Hymns and Homerica*, translated by Hugh G. Evelyn-White (London: Heinemann, 1964), lines 116–138.
10. Hesiod, *Theogony*, 116–138.
11. Hesiod, *Theogony*, 116–138.
12. Hesiod, *Theogony*, 154–159.
13. Hesiod, *Theogony*, 479–484.
14. Homer, *Iliad*, translated by Walter Burkert, Book I, lines 503, 533.
15. Hesiod, *Theogony*, 865.
16. Hesiod, *Theogony*, 300.
17. *The Enuma Elish*, Tablet I, lines 61–63. Lambert translation.
18. *The Enuma Elish*, Tablet I, line 69. Lambert translation.
19. *The Enuma Elish*, Tablet I, line 81–84. Lambert translation.
20. Homer, *Iliad*, translated by Walter Burkert, Book XIV, line 199.

CHAPTER 19
1. "Writing known as the Elohim, or 'E', texts, which belonged originally to the mythology of the northern kingdom of Israel, and here the sacred mountain is called Horeb. These texts date to the eighth century BC. Elohim is the plural form of the word El (which was also the name of the Canaanite father god) and is translated as 'god,' although the more accurate translation would be 'gods.' The name 'Yahweh' (translated as 'the Lord') comes from the body of writings known as the Yahwist, or 'J', texts, which belonged to the mythology of the southern kingdom of Judah and date to the ninth century BC; in these texts the sacred mountain is called Sinai." Baring and Cashford, *The Myth of the Goddess*, 418.
2. Genesis 1:1–4. New Revised Standard Version of the Bible (NRSV).
3. Job 26:10. NRSV.
4. Proverbs 8:27. NRSV.
5. Isaiah 40:22. NRSV.
6. Genesis 1:2. NRSV.
7. Robert Graves and Raphael Patai, *Hebrew Myths: The Book of Genesis* (Garden City, NY: Doubleday, 1964), 31; see also 27 and 33.
8. Isaiah 27:1. NRSV.
9. Baring and Cashford, *The Myth of the Goddess*, 420.

10. "15 Behold now behemoth, which I made with thee; he eateth grass as an ox. 16 Lo now, his strength is in his loins, and his force is in the navel of his belly. 17 He moveth his tail like a cedar: the sinews of his stones are wrapped together. 18 His bones are as strong pieces of brass; his bones are like bars of iron. 19 He is the chief of the ways of God: he that made him can make his sword to approach unto him. 20 Surely the mountains bring him forth food, where all the beasts of the field play. 21 He lieth under the shady trees, in the covert of the reed, and fens. 22 The shady trees cover him with their shadow; the willows of the brook compass him about. 23 Behold, he drinketh up a river, and hasteth not: he trusteth that he can draw up Jordan into his mouth. 24 He taketh it with his eyes: his nose pierceth through snares." Job 40:15–24. King James Version.
11. "There he was also shown the 'women weeping for Tammuz,' the sun-worshippers and all kinds of 'creeping things and beasts and all kinds of idols' being worshipped by the seventy elders of Israel." Ezekiel 8. "Behold, I, even I, will bring a sword upon you, and I will destroy your high places. And your altars shall be desolate and your images shall be broken: and I will cast down your slain men before your idols. And I will lay the dead carcases of the children of Israel before their idols; and I will scatter your bones round about your altars." Ezekiel 6:3–5. NRSV.
12. Diogenes Laertius, *Lives of Eminent Philosophers*, Loeb Classical Library, with an English Translation by R. D. Hicks (London: W. Heinemann, and Cambridge, MA: Harvard University Press), Volume I, Book II, 1, p. 131.
13. "He says that that part of the everlasting which is generative of hot and cold separated off at the coming to be of the world-order and from this a sort of sphere of flame grew around the air about the earth like bark around a tree. This subsequently broke off and was closed into individual circles to form the sun, moon, and stars." Plutarch, *Miscellanies* 2 (A10). Cited in Daniel W. Graham, *The Texts of Early Greek Philosophy: The Complete Fragments and Selected Testimonies of the Major Presocratics* (Cambridge: Cambridge University Press, 2010), 57.
14. "Anaximander says the stars are borne by the circles and spheres on which each one goes." Cited in Graham, *The Texts of Early Greek Philosophy*, 61. Aetius P 2.16.5, S 1.24.2C (AI8).
15. "Furthermore, motion is everlasting, as a result of which the heavens come to be." Cited in Graham, *The Texts of Early Greek Philosophy*, 53. Hippolytus *Refutation* 1.6.r-2 (A11, B2).
16. "... the cause of motion and coming to be a single one." Cited in Graham, *The Texts of Early Greek Philosophy*, 55. Simplicius *Physics* 154.14–23, Theophrasrus fr.228B Fortenbaugh (A9a).
17. For a full defense of the interpretation of Anaximander's concept of apeiron as "sphere" see Kurt Pritzl, "Anaximander's Apeiron and the Arrangement of Time," in *Early Greek philosophy: the Presocratics and the emergence of reason*, edited by Joe McCoy (Washington D.C.: The Catholic University of America Press, 2013), 18–34.
18. Diogenes, *Lives*, Book VII, lines 25–26.
19. Diogenes, *Lives*, 35–36, Book VIII, Chapter 1, line 35.
20. Xenophanes, Fragment 11. Cited in John Burnet, *Early Greek Philosophy* (London: A. & C. Black, 1930), 72.
21. Xenophanes, Fragment 19. Cited in Graham, *The Texts of Early Greek Philosophy*, 109. Clement of Alexandria, *Miscellanies*, 5.109 (B14).

22. "Yes, and if oxen and horses or lions had hands, and could paint with their hands, and produce works of art as men do, horses would paint the forms of the gods like horses, and oxen like oxen, and make their bodies in the image of their several kinds." Xenophanes, Fragment 15. Cited in Burnet, *Early Greek Philosophy* (London: A. & C. Black, 1930), 71.
23. "One god is greatest among gods and men, not at all like mortals in body or in thought." Xenophanes, Fragment 3. Cited in Burnet, *Early Greek Philosophy*, 65.
24. "... whole he sees, whole he thinks, and whole he hears." Xenophanes, Fragment 5. Cited in Burnet, *Early Greek Philosophy*, 65. Translation modified.
25. "... but completely without toil he shakes all things by the thought of his mind." Xenophanes, Fragment 25. Cited in Burnet, *Early Greek Philosophy*, 72.
26. "... always he abides in the same place, not moving at all, nor is it seemly for him to travel to different places at different times." Xenophanes, Fragment 26. Cited in James H. Lesher, *Xenophanes of Colophon: Fragments, a Text and Translation with a Commentary* (Toronto: University of Toronto Press, 1992), 110–111.
27. Diogenes Laertius, *Lives of Eminent Philosophers*, R.D. Hicks, Ed. Book IX, Chapter 2.
28. "Spherical, everywhere the same, neither limited nor unlimited." Xenophanes, Fragment 28. Cited in Graham, *The Texts of Early Greek Philosophy*, 113. Aristotle, *On Melissus Xenophanes, and Gorgias*, 977a14–b20 (A28).
29. Parmenides, Fragment 8. Cited in Graham, *The Texts of Early Greek Philosophy*, 215.
30. Parmenides, Fragment 8. Cited in Graham, *The Texts of Early Greek Philosophy*, 215.
31. Parmenides, Fragment 8, lines 39–49. Cited in A H. Coxon and Richard D. McKirahan, *The Fragments of Parmenides: A Critical Text with Introduction and Translation, the Ancient Testimonia and a Commentary* (Las Vegas, NV: Parmenides, 2009), 78.
32. "You will understand the aether's origin, and likewise all the signs in the aether and the invisible deeds of the pure torch of the brilliant sun, and whence they sprang." Parmenides, Fragment 9. Cited in Coxon and McKirahan, *The Fragments of Parmenides*, 84.
33. "For the narrower rings became filled with unmixed fire and those over them with night, in which moves a proportion of flame. Between these is the divinity who governs all things." Parmenides, Fragment 12. Cited in Coxon and McKirahan, *The Fragments of Parmenides*, 90.
34. Anaxagoras, Fragment 15. Cited in Graham, *The Texts of Early Greek Philosophy*, 291. Simplicius, On Aristotle: *Physics*, 164.24–25, 156.13–157 (B12).
35. Anaxagoras. Cited in Graham, *The Texts of Early Greek Philosophy*, 297. Hippolytus, *Refutation*, 1.8.1–13 (A42).
36. William Ellery Leonard, *The Fragments of Empedocles* (Chicago: Open Court, 1908), 29.
37. Leonard, *The Fragments of Empedocles*, 30.

CHAPTER 20

1. Leucippus and Democritus have not been included among the theorists of being as eternity because of the primacy of motion of the atoms in their philosophies. Even though the atoms are said to be eternal, and even productive of a spherical universe, in the case of Leucippus, the fact that their motions are not

fundamentally centric or spherical places them in the tradition of the philosophy of motion.
2. Plato, *Timaeus*, 29a–b. Translated in Peter Kalkavage, *Plato's Timaeus: Translation, Glossary, Appendices and Introductory Essay* (Newburyport, MA: Focus, 2001).
3. Plato, *Timaeus*, 30a. Translated by Peter Kalkavage.
4. "... a totality consisting of the totality of its parts." ".... Second, he wanted it to be one, and so he ensured that there was nothing left over from which another similar universe could be created ... unageing and free from sickness." Plato, *Timaeus*, 32d, 33a. Translated by Peter Kalkavage.
5. Plato, *Timaeus*, 34c. Translated by Peter Kalkavage.
6. Plato, *Timaeus*, 34b.
7. Plato, *Timaeus*, 34a.
8. Plato, *Timaeus*, 37c–e. Italics added.
9. Plato, *Timaeus*, 37c–e.
10. Plato, *Republic*, 436 d–e. Translated by Joe Sachs, *Republic* (Newburyport, MA: Focus, 2007).
11. See John Sallis, *Chorology: On Beginning in Plato's Timaeus* (Bloomington: Indiana University Press, 1999).
12. "Now the thing to which we have given the name of 'heavens' and 'cosmos' certainly has a portion of many blessed things from its progenitor, but on the other hand it also has its share of body. In consequence it is impossible for it to be altogether exempt from change, although as far as is possible, given its capacities, it moves in the same place, in the same way, with a single motion; and this is why it has reverse rotation as its lot, which is the smallest possible variation of its movement. To turn itself by itself forever is, I dare say, impossible for anything except the one who guides all the things which, unlike him, are in movement; and for him to cause movement now in one way, now in the opposite way is not permitted. From all of these considerations, it follows that one must neither say that the cosmos is always itself responsible for its own turning, nor say at all that it is turned by god in a pair of opposed revolutions, nor again that it is turned by some pair of gods whose thoughts are opposed to each other; it is rather what was said just now, which is the sole remaining possibility, that at times it is helped by the guidance of another, divine, cause, acquiring life once more and receiving a restored immortality from its craftsman, while at other times, when it is let go, it goes on its own way under its own power, having been let go at such a time as to travel backwards for many tens of thousands of revolutions because of the very fact that its movement combines the effects of its huge size, perfect balance, and its resting on the smallest of bases." Plato, *Statesman*, 269E–270A, in Plato, *Complete Works*, translated by John M. Cooper and D. S. Hutchinson (Indianapolis, IN: Hackett, 1997).
13. "The center of the universe and the vault of heaven is spherical, and half of this sphere fell to the celestial gods, and the other half to the gods under the earth that the soul, after its release from the body, goes to the Place Unseen, to a dwelling beneath the earth. Here the palace of Pluto is not inferior to the court of Zeus, since the earth occupies the center of the universe and the vault of heaven is spherical, and half of this sphere fell to the celestial gods, and the other half to the gods under the earth, some of them brothers, others children of brothers." Plato, *Axiochus* 371b. Translated by Cooper and Hutchinson.

14. "Every soul is immortal. That is because *whatever is always in motion is immortal*, while what moves, *and is moved by*, something else stops living when it stops moving. So it is only what moves itself that never desists from motion, since it does not leave off being itself. In fact, this self-mover is also the source and spring of motion in everything else that moves; and a source has no beginning." Plato, *Phaedrus*, 245C–D. Translated by Cooper and Hutchinson. Italics added.
15. "Since we have found that a self-mover is immortal, we should have no qualms about declaring that this is the very essence and principle of a soul, for every bodily object that is moved from outside has no soul, while a body whose motion comes from within, from itself, does have a soul, that being the nature of a soul; and if this is so—that whatever moves itself is essentially a soul—then it follows necessarily that soul should have neither birth nor death." Plato, *Phaedrus*, 245E. Translated by Cooper and Hutchinson.
16. Aristotle, *Physics*, Book III, line 201a. In *Aristotle's Physics: A Guided Study*, translated by Joe Sachs (New Brunswick, NJ: Rutgers University Press, 1995).
17. Aristotle, *Physics*, Book III, line 201a. Translated by Joe Sachs.
18. "But the thing that causes motion is already in activity as what causes heat is hot, and in general what brings something into being is what has the form. So at the same time, the same thing, in the same respect, would hot and not hot." "Therefore, of the thing that itself moves itself, one part causes the motion and another part is moved." Aristotle, *Physics*, translated by Joe Sachs, Book VIII, Chapter 5, line 257b.
19. Aristotle, *Physics*, Book VII, 265a28–265b16. In *The Complete Works of Aristotle: The Revised Oxford Translation*, translated by Jonathan Barnes, (Princeton, NJ: Princeton University Press, 1984).
20. Aristotle, *On the Heavens*, Book II, 286b10–286b11. Translated by Jonathan Barnes.
21. Aristotle, *Physics*, Book VIII, 256b-1-20. Translated by Joe Sachs.
22. Aristotle, *Physics*, Book VIII, 267b. Translated by Joe Sachs.
23. With the slight difference that, for Aristotle, the unmoved mover does not create the world, but only creates and causes its motion ex nihilo.
24. Aristotle, *Physics,* Book, VII, 257b 10. Translated by Joe Sachs.
25. "A circle admits of being everlasting." Aristotle, *Physics*, Book VIII, 265a 10–20. Translated by Joe Sachs. "There is no change that is infinite or continuous apart from change of place in a circle, let so much have been said by us." Aristotle, *Physics*, Book VIII, 265a 11.

CHAPTER 21

1. McLuhan, *The Gutenberg Galaxy*; Walter J. Ong, *Orality and Literacy: The Technologizing of the Word* (London: Methuen, 1982); Eric A. Havelock, *Preface to Plato* (Cambridge, MA: Belknap Press, 1963); Harold A Innis and Mary Q. Innis, *Empire and Communications* (Toronto: University of Toronto Press, 1972).
2. Marshall Poe, *A History of Communications: Media and Society from the Evolution of Speech to the Internet* (Cambridge: Cambridge University Press, 2011); Terence P. Moran, *Introduction to the History of Communication: Evolutions and Revolutions* (New York: Peter Lang, 2010).
3. Jack Goody, *The Logic of Writing* (Cambridge: Cambridge University Press, 2001), 50.
4. See *Theory of the Object* (in progress) for a kinetic theory of tallies.

5. Denise Schmandt-Besserat, *Before Writing* (Austin: University of Texas Press, 1992), Volume 1, 6.
6. Beginning around 8000 BCE and continuing through five millennia, the tokens were hand-molded out of clay, and sometimes afterward baked in an oven or fired in a kiln. In later periods, a relatively small number were cut out of stone. Schmandt-Besserat, *Before Writing*, Volume 1, 198, 20–31.
7. Denise Schmandt-Vesserat, "The Earliest Precursor of Writing," in *Communication in History: Technology, Culture, Society*, 5th ed., edited by David Crowley and Paul Heyer (Boston: Pearson, 2007), 14–23, 19.
8. Tokens were singular, unique, and destroyed after use. "Consequently, unlike markings on tallies, which had an infinite number of possible interpretations, each clay token was itself a distinct sign with a single, discrete, and unequivocal significance. While tallies were meaningless out of context, tokens could always be understood by anyone initiated into the system. The tokens, therefore, presaged pictography: each token stood for a single concept." Denise Schmandt-Besserat, *How Writing Came About* (Austin: University of Texas Press, 2006), 93.

   "The distribution of tokens within settlements suggests two important facts. First, in cities, tokens are more frequent in official rather than secular quarters. Second, the discovery of tokens among refuse in vacant lots suggests that the counters were discarded as soon as their function had been fulfilled. In other words, they were used primarily for record keeping rather than for reckoning." Schmandt-Besserat, *How Writing Came About*, 30.

9. "The synchronic occurrence of tokens and plant domestication in Mureybet III was not coincidental; rather, it demonstrates that agriculture brought about a need for accounting." Schmandt-Besserat, *How Writing Came About*, 102. "In sum, developments in farming and industry played a major role in the development of the token system. Cultivation of cereals was directly linked to the invention of plain tokens, and the complex counters are linked to the beginning of industry. Trade, however, played no visible role in the creation of reckoning technology." Schmandt-Besserat, *How Writing Came About*, 103.
10. Schmandt-Besserat, *How Writing Came About*, 103. Schmandt-Besserat thus distinguishes between two kinds of counting: computing and accounting.
11. "The distribution of tokens within settlements suggests two important facts. First, in cities, tokens are more frequent in official rather than secular quarters. Second, the discovery of tokens among refuse in vacant lots suggests that the counters were discarded as soon as their function had been fulfilled. In other words, they were used primarily for record keeping rather than for reckoning." Schmandt-Besserat, *How Writing Came About*, 30.
12. See *Theory of the Object* (in progress) for a more detailed kinetic theory of debt.
13. Schmandt-Besserat, *Before Writing*, Volume 1, 24–25, 198.
14. Schmandt-Besserat, *Before Writing*, Volume 1, 14, 82.
15. Schmandt-Besserat, *Before Writing*, Volume 1, 176–177.
16. Schmandt-Besserat, *How Writing Came About*, 105.
17. Schmandt-Besserat, *How Writing Came About*, 108.
18. For a further development of the kinopolitical details of this centrifugal motion, see Nail, *Figure of the Migrant*; Nail, *Theory of the Border*.
19. Leroi-Gourhan, *Gesture and Speech*, 332.
20. Leroi-Gourhan, *Gesture and Speech*, 327.

21. However, plain tokens, complex tokens, and concrete numbers are not clear-cut stages of development. There was significant temporal and geographical overlap in their usage. Different tokens express different coexisting motions without entering into any kind of dialectical relationship of opposition.
22. Schmandt-Besserat, *How Writing Came About*, 44.
23. Schmandt-Besserat, *Before Writing*, Volume 1, 198.
24. Schmandt-Besserat, *Before Writing*, Volume 1, 109.
25. Schmandt-Besserat, *Before Writing*, Volume 1, 154.
26. Schmandt-Besserat, *How Writing Came About*, 51.
27. Schmandt-Besserat, *Before Writing*, Volume 1, 68–69.
28. Schmandt-Besserat, *How Writing Came About*, 54. Different techniques of marking are discussed in pages 49–54.
29. Schmandt-Besserat, *Before Writing*, Volume 1, 154.
30. Schmandt-Besserat, *Before Writing*, Volume 1, 198–199.
31. Schmandt-Besserat, *Before Writing*, Volume 1, 112.
32. "A single cylinder seal was impressed all over the artifact, obviously with the intent of covering the entire surface." Schmandt-Besserat, *Before Writing*, Volume 1, 123.
33. Schmandt-Besserat, *Before Writing*, Volume 1, 125.
34. Schmandt-Besserat, *How Writing Came About*, 7.
35. Schmandt-Besserat, *Before Writing*, Volume 1, 133.
36. Schmandt-Besserat, *How Writing Came About*, 55.
37. Schmandt-Besserat, *Before Writing*, Volume 1, 134–137.
38. Schmandt-Besserat, *How Writing Came About*, 63.
39. Schmandt-Vesserat, "The Earliest Precursor of Writing," 14–23, 21.
40. Schmandt-Besserat, *How Writing Came About*, 21.
41. Schmandt-Besserat, *How Writing Came About*, 120.

CHAPTER 22

1. See also Christopher Woods, *Visible Language: Inventions of Writing in the Ancient Middle East and Beyond* (Chicago: Oriental Institute of the University of Chicago, 2010), 33–34.
2. The cuneiform origins are discussed most famously by Schmandt-Besserat. The origins of Egyptian writing are far less well understood but somehow draw on rock art and/or "pot marks . . . decorated pottery, cylinder seals, decorated ceremonial objects," that precede it. Woods, *Visible Language*, 47–48, 116.
3. Alphabetic writing is defined as "the graphic representation of phonemes" (Woods, *Visible Language*, 189). The earliest known alphabet (consonants only)—"the linear alphabet"—is traced to proto-Sinaitic writing (c. 1850 BCE), which developed as a hybrid of Egyptian hieroglyphs and the sounds of West Semitic words, likely developed by foreign, Asiatic workers (e.g., miners or builders) while in Egypt (189–190). It is debated if those workers had any semantic understanding of the Egyptian writing system or not (Goldwasser says no, others say yes, or at least a little—see p. 193n8). The "association of the letter name (*kaph*) with its initial phoneme (/k/) is called the *acrophonic principle* (*acro-* 'top- most' + *phone* 'voice, sound'), and the fact that it is via the Semitic vocabulary that such a principle operates suggests that the linear alphabet arose for the purpose of writing a Semitic language" (190). Another alphabetic system (now extinct) emerges as the Ugaritic alphabet (c. 1250 BCE) and is a cuneiform alphabet. It is likely an adaptation, or at least partial

adaption of the linear alphabet (191–192). All pages from Woods, *Visible Language*.
4. The Ugaritic alphabet—an alphabetic cuneiform—emerged c. 1250 BCE and is likely (but not conclusively) adapted from the linear alphabet and subsequently perished (191–192). Apart from that possible exception, all other known alphabets (to my knowledge) derive to varying degrees from the proto-Sinaitic alphabet, albeit through its full-fledged or "stabilized" form in the Phoenician alphabet (c. 1100 BCE, see 192). All pages from Woods, *Visible Language*.
5. For the preceding paragraph, last three notes, and the recommendation to read Schmandt-Besserat's work, I am thankful to Chris Gamble and his careful research on the historical emergence of writing. See Woods, *Visible Language*, 192.
6. Leroi-Gourhan, *Gesture and Speech*, 210.
7. "The subordination of the hand to language in the graphic symbolism that eventually led to writing." Leroi-Gourhan, *Gesture and Speech*, 403.
8. See McLuhan, *The Gutenberg Galaxy*; Albert Lord, *The Singer of Tales* (Cambridge, MA: Harvard University Press, 1960).
9. "Before writing, the hand was used principally for making and the face for language, but with the invention of writing the balance between the two was restored." Leroi-Gourhan, *Gesture and Speech*, 113.
10. Deleuze and Guattari, *Anti-Oedipus*, 202.
11. Innis, *Empire and Communication*, 8.
12. Plato, *Phaedrus*, 275d-e. Italics added.
13. Wang, who has produced the most recent study of this subject, proposes that the combination of signs used to write the toponym for Nippur came to be a writing for the deity Enlil at about the time of Late Uruk–Early Dynastic Period transition (c. 3200–2800 BCE). Wang suggests that the deity Enlil might have come to be worshipped at Nippur at this time, and subsequently taken the writing of the toponym for the writing for his divine name. Xianhua Wang, *The Metamorphosis of Enlil in Early Mesopotamia* (Münster, Germay: Ugarit-Verlag, 2011), 245.
14. Baring and Cashford, *The Myth of the Goddess*, 153.
15. Kramer, *From the Poetry of Sumer*, 45.
16. Samuel Kramer, *History Begins at Sumer* (Garden City, NY: Doubleday, 1959), 88.
17. 1 Kings 19:11–12.
18. Deuteronomy 4:11–12.
19. Baring, *The Myth of the Goddess*, 438.
20. Deuteronomy 4:11–12, 15–19.
21. Exodus 20:3–4.
22. Exodus 3:13–14.
23. Baring, *The Myth of the Goddess*, 437.
24. Psalms 104:3–4.

CHAPTER 23

1. Henri Bergson, *An Introduction to Metaphysics*, translated by T. E. Hulme (New York: G. P. Putnam's Sons, 1912), 53.
2. Friedrich Nietzsche, *The Will to Power*, translated by Walter A. Kaufmann, edited by R. J. Hollingdale (New York: Random House, 1967), 333.
3. In mechanics this is also called "spatial movement" or "Bennett's linkage." Bennett's linkage is a spatial four-bar linkage with hinged joints that have their

axes angled in a particular way that makes the system movable. K. H. Hunt, *Kinematic Geometry of Mechanisms* (Oxford Engineering Science Series, 1979).

4. For an in-depth kinetic analysis of human joints, see Vincenzo Parenti-Castelli and Nicola Sancisi, "Synthesis of Spatial Mechanisms to Model Human Joints," in *21st Century Kinematics*, edited by. J. Michael McCarthy (London: Springer, 2013).

5. "As we have already shown, the prince is obliged to safeguard the persons, possessions, and families of his subjects, by force of arms, and by force of law, while his subjects are under a reciprocal obligation to give their prince loyal and obedient service." Jean Bodin, *Six Books of the Commonwealth* (Oxford: Blackwell, 1955), 22. "Binding force of a law," Aquinas, *Summa Theologica*, Question 90 "The Essence of Law," Article 4, Objection 3, http://www.newadvent.org/summa/2090.htm.

6. David Hume, *An Enquiry Concerning Human Understanding*, edited by Peter J. R. Millican (Oxford: Oxford University Press, 2007), 45.

7. Hume, *An Enquiry Concerning Human Understanding*, 137.

8. Hume, *An Enquiry Concerning Human Understanding*, 46.

9. Hume, *An Enquiry Concerning Human Understanding*, 46.

10. Hume, *An Enquiry Concerning Human Understanding*, 137.

11. Hume, *An Enquiry Concerning Human Understanding*, 137.

12. Hume, *An Enquiry Concerning Human Understanding*, 137.

13. Hume, *An Enquiry Concerning Human Understanding*, 53.

CHAPTER 24

1. Even though scientific descriptions are often empirical, it is crucial to see that they can also rely just as deeply on descriptions of ontotheological substances like "aether" or "impetus," which connect them with more explicitly theological discourses. Since the focus of this book is ontology, the following claims will be treated ontologically and theologically and not strictly empirically. Scientific treatment requires a more robust kinetic theory and history of science developed at length in *Theory of the Object*—and is thus not included in this book.

2. This task is complicated by two problems. The first is that the massive proliferation of conceptual vocabulary describing forces of various kinds in the broad sense above is daunting. By my count there are more than twenty different names for this concept, including conatus, impetus, inertia, nisus, effort, endeavor, impulse, causality, inclination, tendency, undertaking, striving, hormé, sympathia, appetition, virtué, forza, potenze, vis viva, and aether. The second is that by focusing only on the concept of force, we will most certainly not be able to do justice to the robust theories developed by each thinker alongside their conceptual interrelation and biographical histories. Since both of these tasks have been attempted more systematically elsewhere, I do not deal with them here, but instead focus on motion exclusively. See Max Jammer, *Concepts of Force: A Study in the Foundations of Dynamics* (Cambridge, MA: Harvard University Press, 1957).

3. I have written a lengthy history of ancient theories of force and their kinetic patterns from Mesopotamia to the Stoics, including their similarities and differences from medieval tensional theories, which will hopefully appear elsewhere in another form.

4. While Aristotle had divided thermon, pneuma, and aether into terrestrial linear motion and celestial circular motion, the Stoics unified them into a

single tensional and material pneuma. "As pneuma took over some of the characteristic attributes of aether, there began a confusion of these two terms and one was substituted for the other. Cicero says that 'air resembles aether and is closely connected with it.' Arios Didymos expresses it directly: 'Pneuma . . . has become analogous to aether, so that both are used synonymously.' Similarly, Clemens Alexandrinus referring to a passage in Aratos's poem, indicates that he would prefer to attribute the binding force of the cosmos to aether rather than to the Stoic tension of the pneuma." During the medieval and early modern periods, the concept of an ethereal and interrelational medium of force increasingly became more like the Stoic tensional pneuma than the Aristotelean aether, but with important differences. Cited in Samuel Sambursky, *Physics of the Stoics* (Princeton, NJ: Princeton University Press, 1987), 10.

5. For a more detailed historical treatment of this point, see Charles Wolfe, "Varieties of Vital Materialism; Two Materialisms; Passive and Active Matter; Vital Materialism," in *The New Politics of Materialism: History, Philosophy, Science*, edited by Sarah Ellenzweig and John H. Zammito (London: Taylor and Francis, 2017), 44–65.
6. William Stahl, trans., *Martianus Capella and the Seven Liberal Arts*, Volume 2, *The Marriage of Philology and Mercury*, (New York: Columbia University Press, 1977), 332–333.
7. Marshall Berman, *All That Is Solid Melts into Air: The Experience of Modernity* (New York: Simon & Schuster, 1982); Thomas Kuhn, *The Copernican Revolution: Planetary Astronomy in the Development of Western Thought* (Cambridge, MA: Harvard University Press, 1957).
8. Immanuel Kant, *Critique of Pure Reason*, translated by Werner S. Pluhar and Patricia Kitcher (Indianapolis, IN: Hackett, 1996), 21.
9. Michael Jones, "Tycho Brahe, Cartography and Landscape in 16th Century Scandinavia," in *European Rural Landscapes: Persistence and Change in a Globalising Environment*, edited by Hannes Palang (Dordrecht, the Netherlands: Kluwer Academic, 2004), 210.
10. Max Caspar, *Kepler* (London: Abelard-Schuman, 1959), 133.
11. In mathematics, two quantities are in the golden ratio if their ratio is the same as the ratio of their sum to the larger of the two quantities. A Kepler triangle is a right triangle with edge lengths in geometric progression, following the golden ratio. Kepler defined this as a "Divine Proportion," writing, "Geometry has two great treasures: one is the theorem of Pythagoras; the other, the division of a line into extreme and mean ratio. The first we may compare to a measure of gold; the second we may name a precious jewel." Quoted in Mario Livio, *The Golden Ratio: The Story of Phi, the World's Most Astonishing Number* (New York: Broadway Books, 2002), 62.
12. John Philoponus, *Criticism of Aristotle's Theory of Aether*, translated by Christian Wildberg (Berlin: W. de Gruyter, 1988).
13. The Stoics accepted a similar idea, but were quick to reaffirm the centrifugal radiation of an origin and a centripetal contraction of the end, where Philoponus only affirmed the tensional recombination of bodies held together and apart by an all-permeating material fire.
14. ". . . all the stars by the aether they float in . . ." Francis Bacon, *Specimen of Animated Astronomy*, in *The Philosophical Works of Francis Bacon*, Volume 3 (London: M. Jones, 1815), 224.

15. "[S]o likewise flame below is a momentary body, but in aether permeant and durable." Bacon, *Specimen of Animated Astronomy*, 242.
16. Bacon, *Specimen of Animated Astronomy*, 202.
17. René Descartes, *Principles of Philosophy*, in *The Philosophical Writings of Descartes*, Volume 1, translated and edited by John Cottingham, Robert Stoothoff, and Dugald Murdoch (Cambridge: Cambridge University Press, 1984), 263. Descartes, *Principles*, Part III, Articles 99–100. "99. The kinds of particles into which sunspots disintegrate. 100. How the ether round the sun and stars is produced from these particles. This ether and the spots belong to the third element." It is clear that primary matter is aether.
18. Descartes, *Principles*, Part III, Articles 48–54.
19. Descartes, *Principles*, Part III, Article 24.
20. Descartes, *Principles*, Part III, Article 60.
21. Descartes, *Principles*, Part III, Article 100.
22. "And the particles of which this aether is composed, having very irregular branching figures, become attached to one another in such a way that they cannot be moved individually like the globules of heavenly matter." René Descartes, *Principles of Philosophy*, translated and edited by Valentine R. Miller and Reese P. Miller (Dordrecht, the Netherlands: Reidel, 1983), 172. Explanatory note in *Principles*, Part III, Article 148.
23. ". . . branching particles of that aether which is produced around stars will prevent those grooved particles, and all but the tiniest particles of the matter of the first element, spread over spot DEFG, from passing into the Heaven." René Descartes, *Principles of Philosophy*, translated and edited by Miller and Miller, 146. Explanatory note in *Principles*, Part III, Article 112.
24. Descartes, *Principles of Philosophy*, Part III, Article 133, translated and edited by Miller and Miller, 243.
25. Descartes, *Principles*, Part III, Article 30, in *The Philosophical Writings of Descartes*, Volume 1, 254.
26. Thomas Hobbes, *The English Works of Thomas Hobbes of Malmesbury*, Volume 1, *De Corpore*, edited by William Molesworth (London: J. Bohn, 1839), 448.
27. Hobbes, *The English Works*, Volume 1, *De Corpore*, 466.
28. Hobbes, *The English Works*, Volume 1, *De Corpore*, 474.
29. Cited in Jammer, *Concepts of Force*, 135.
30. Newton, *Opticks*, Query 21. Cf. Also Newton's letter to Boyle of Feb. 28, 1679, *The Works of R. Boyle*, 1772, Volume I, cxvii.
31. "What we have said about inflated balls must also be understood to apply to every body insofar as it is acted upon in impact, namely, that the repercussion and bursting apart arises from the elasticity it contains, that is, from the motion of the fluid aetherial matter permeating it, and thus it arises from an internal force or a force existing within itself." Gottfried W. Leibniz, *Specimen Dynamicum*, in *Philosophical Essays*, translated and edited by Roger Ariew and Daniel Garber (Indianapolis, IN: Hackett, 1989), 135.
32. Gottfried W. Leibniz, *On Copernicanism and the Relativity of Motion*, in *Philosophical Essays*, translated and edited by Roger Ariew and Daniel Garber (Indianapolis, IN: Hackett, 1989), 93–94.
33. For a survey of such theories, see Kenneth Schaffner, *Nineteenth-Century Aether Theories* (Oxford: Pergamon Press, 1972); Jeffrey Edwards, *Substance, Force, and the Possibility of Knowledge: On Kant's Philosophy of Material Nature* (Berkeley: University of California Press, 2000). The concept of aether did not

die at the end of the eighteenth century, but like all regimes of motion continued on, mixing together with other regimes of motion up to the present, even if today the concept of aether has been scientifically discredited. Up until Einstein, the metaphysical concept of a permeating ethereal force was still respectably used to explain the motive cause or force of attraction (i.e., gravity, light, and magnetism).

CHAPTER 25

1. The Latin term *impetus*, regarding local motion, was introduced by Jean de Buridan (University of Paris, 1320–1358) in his *Questions on the Eight Books of the Physics*, Book VIII, Question 12. The expression "impetus theory" was first used by the historian of science Pierre Duhem at the end of the last century in his "De l'accélération produite par une force constante," *Congrès d'histoire des sciences* (Genève, 1904), 859–915. Duhem, however, did not offer a general definition of the theory, according to M. Wolff, "Philoponus and the Rise of Preclassical Mechanics," in *Philoponus and the Rejection of Aristotelian Science*, edited by R. Sorabji (Ithaca, NY: Cornell University Press, 1987), 84.
2. Richard Sorabji, *Matter, Space and Motion: Theories in Antiquity and Their Sequel* (Ithaca, NY: Cornell University Press, 1988), 247.
3. Thomas Kuhn, *The Structure of Scientific Revolutions* (Chicago: University of Chicago Press, 1970), 120.
4. Philoponus, *Physics* 641,13–642,20. Cited in Sorabji, *Matter, Space and Motion*, 229.
5. Philoponus, *de Opificio Mundi* 28,20–29,9. Cited in Sorabji, *Matter, Space and Motion*, 233.
6. Philoponus, *Physics* 197,30–198,8. Cited in Sorabji, *Matter, Space and Motion*, 243.
7. "The big difference concerning final causes comes when in the *de Opificio Mundi* Philoponus turns God into an efficient cause impressing motion into the heavens, instead of a final cause who inspires the heavens to motion by arousing their love. Indeed, he denies that the heavens are animated by souls at all." Sorabji, *Matter, Space and Motion*, 246.
8. We do not know precisely where Buridan got the idea of impetus, but a less sophisticated notion of impressed force can be found in Avicenna's doctrine of *mayl* (inclination). In this he was possibly influenced by Philoponus, who was developing the Stoic notion of *hormé* (impulse). For discussion, see Jack Zupko, "What Is the Science of the Soul?: A Case Study in the Evolution of Late Medieval Natural Philosophy," *Synthese* 110.2 (1997): 297–334.
9. Jean Buridan, *Commentary on Aristotle's Physics*, Book VIII, Question 12. Cited in *Medieval Philosophy: Essential Readings with Commentary*, edited by Gyula Klima, Fritz Allhoff, and Anand Vaidya (Malden, MA: Blackwell, 2007), 192–193.
10. Jammer, *Concepts of Force*, 70–72.
11. Buridan, *Commentary on Aristotle's Physics*, Book VIII, Question 12.
12. Buridan, *Commentary on Aristotle's Physics*, Book VIII, Question 12.
13. Nicole Oresme, *Book of the Heavens and Earth* [1370]. Cited in Richard Olson, *Science Deified and Science Defied: The Historical Significance of Science in Western Culture* (Berkeley: University of California Press, 1982), 27.
14. "Nicole Oresme (c. 1325–82) took the step from the term *machina mundi* to a universe-clockwork comparison. Comparisons of God with a clockmaker are used by the archbishop of Canterbury, Thomas Bradwardine (ca. 1290–1349),

as well as Henry of Langestein (d. 1397). The clockwork analogy is also used in medieval literary contexts by the French poets Jean Froissart (1333?-1400/1) and Christine de Pisan (1364–ca. 1430) and the great Florentine poet Dante Alighieri (ca. 1265–1321). In these early theological contexts, the clockwork analogy has two essential features: God as creator of the clockwork and God as sustainer of the clockwork. Thus it differs from eighteenth-century, nonprovidentialist deism that is committed only to the first element." Stephen Snobelen, "The Myth of the Clockwork Universe: Newton, Newtonianism, and the Enlightenment," in *The Persistence of the Sacred in Modern Thought*, edited by Chris L. Firestone and Nathan Jacobs (Notre Dame, IN: University of Notre Dame Press, 2012) 149–184, 152.

15. Lynn White, *Medieval Technology and Social Change* (Oxford, 1962), 124–125.
16. Lewis Mumford, *Technics and Civilization* (New York: Harcourt, Brace and Co., 1934), 14.
17. See John Scattergood, "Writing the Clock: the Reconstruction of Time in the Late Middle Ages." *European Review* 11.4 (2003): 453–474.
18. Nicolai de Cusa, *Dialogorum de ludo globi*, Book I, translated by Gerdavon Bredowi Yom Globusspiel (Schriften des Nikolaus von Cues Meiner Hamburg, 1952), Pilosophsche Bibliothek, Volume 233. Quoted in Jammer, *Concepts of Force*, 71.
19. Leonardo Da Vinci, *The Notebooks of Leonardo Da Vinci*, Volume 1, edited by Edward McCurdy (Old Saybrook, CT: Konecky & Konecky, 2003), 113.
20. Francis Bacon, *A Confession of Faith* [1602], in *The Works of Francis Bacon*, edited by James Spedding (London: Green, Longman and Roberts 1857–1874), Volume 14, 49–50.
21. "The construction of clocks (for example) is certainly a subtle and precise thing that seems to imitate the celestial bodies in its wheels, and the heartbeat of animals in its constant, ordered motion; and yet it depends upon just one or two axioms of nature." Bacon, *New Organon*, LXXXV.
22. Francis Bacon, *On Principles and Origins According to the Fables of Cupid and Coelum*, in *The Works of Francis Bacon*, 648.
23. Olson, *Science Deified*, 28.
24. Olson, *Science Deified*, 28.
25. Olson, *Science Deified*, 28.
26. Quoted in Olson, *Science Deified*, 28.
27. Rhonda Martens, *Kepler's Philosophy and the New Astronomy* (Princeton, NJ: Princeton University Press, 2000), 173.
28. ". . . and I want to make it clear that the motion of something that moves is, like the lack of motion in a thing which is at rest, a mere mode of that thing and not itself a subsistent thing, just as shape is a mere mode of the thing which has shape." Descartes, *Principles*, Part II, Article 25.
29. Descartes, *The World*, in *Oeuvres de Descartes*, edited by Charles Adam and Paul Tannery (Paris: J. Vrin, 1976), Volume XI, page 15.
30. Descartes, *Principles*, Part II, Article 39. Italics added.
31. Descartes, *Principles*, Part III, Article 63.
32. Descartes, *Treatise on Man*, in *The Philosophical Writings of Descartes*, Volume 1, 99. Italics added.
33. Descartes, *Discourse on Method*, in *Oeuvres de Descartes*, Volume VI, 50. Italics added.
34. Descartes, *Principles*, Part IV, Article 327.

35. A similar position was held by the Irish philosopher Robert Boyle (1627–1691), who argued that God is less like a puppet master. Robert Boyle, *The Works of the Honourable Robert Boyle,* edited by by Thomas Birch (London, 1772), Volume 5, 163.
36. Isaac Newton, Preface to the First Edition, in *Sir Isaac Newton's Mathematical Principles of Natural Philosophy and His System of the World*, Volume 2, translated by Andrew Motte and Florian Cajori (Berkeley: University of California Press, 1962), xvii.
37. Isaac Newton, Definition III, in *Sir Isaac Newton's Mathematical Principles of Natural Philosophy and His System of the World*, Volume 2, 2.
38. Isaac Newton, Definition VIII, in *Sir Isaac Newton's Mathematical Principles of Natural Philosophy and His System of the World*, Volume 2, 5.
39. Newton to the Editor of the *Memoirs of Literature*, unpublished, written c. May 1712, in Isaac Newton, *Philosophical Writings*, translated by Andrew Janiak (Cambridge: Cambridge University Press, 2004), 116–117.

CHAPTER 26

1. "Inest enim omnibus appetitus boni: cum bonum sit quod omnia appetunt, ut philosophi tradunt. Huiusmodi autem appetitus in his quidem quae cognitione carent, dicitur naturalis appetitus: sicut dicitur quod lapis appetit esse deorsum. In his autem quae cognitionem sensitivam habent, dicitur appetitus animalis, qui dividitur in concupiscibilem et irascibilem. In his vero quae intelligunt, dicitur appetitus intellectualis seu rationalis, qui est voluntas." Thomas Aquinas, *Summa contra gentiles*, Book 2, Chapter 47. Translated by Rodolfo Garau, "Late-scholastic and Cartesian Conatus," *Intellectual History Review* 24.4 (2014): 479–494, 481.
2. "Ergo appetitus definitio talis afferri poterit, inclinatio necessaria ex natura cuiusq. rei ad bonum sibi coveniens secundum naturam." Buonamici, *De Motu*, 392. Translated by Rodolfo Garau.
3. "[Q]uandoquidem lapis externa vi sursum propellitur, reluctatur ascensui eius forma naturali conatu, & impulsu, quod deorsum nititur; sed etiam aqua ab igne calefit, eius forma calefactioni active repugnat, per ingenitam ad frigus inclinationem, et quantum potest frigum suum active conservando, et in igne." Conimbricenses, *Commentari in Octo Libros*, Volume 6, Explanatio 202. Translated by Rodolfo Garau.
4. "Decimò, cum manus sustinet aliquod pondus immobiliter, non producit in eo impetum." Fabri, *Tractatus Physicus*, 417. Translated by Rodolfo Garau.
5. Rodolfo Garau, "Late-Scholastic and Cartesian Conatus," *Intellectual History Review* 24.4 (2014): 479–494, 484.
6. See Stephen Gaukroger, *Descartes' System of Natural Philosophy* (Cambridge: Cambridge University Press, 2002), 108.
7. Aristotle, *Nicomachean Ethics*, 1248a23. Translated by Joe Sachs (Newbury, MA: Focus, 2002).
8. Descartes, *Principles,* Part II, Article 36. In René Descartes, *Principles of Philosophy*, in *The Philosophical Writings of Descartes*, Volume 1, translated and edited by John Cottingham, Robert Stoothoff, and Dugald Murdoch (Cambridge: Cambridge University Press, 1984).
9. Descartes, *Le Monde.* Translated by Michael Sean Mahoney (Norwalk: Abaris Books, 1978), 59. Italics added.
10. Descartes, *Le Monde* (1978), 75.

11. Descartes, *Le Monde* (1978), 75. Italics added.
12. This linear and folded tension between rectilinear and curvilinear motion in Descartes is notably different than the kinetics of Plato's cosmological morality where spherical souls ought to aim for rotational and concentric harmony with other spheres in the cosmospherical order.
13. Descartes, *Principles*, Part III, Article 57.
14. Descartes, *Principles*, Part II, Article 39.
15. Descartes, *Principles*, Part III, Article 63.
16. Descartes, *Principles*, Part II, Article 37.
17. Galen, *De musculorum motu*, Book I, 7–8. (Arnim, II, 450).
18. "Descartes also uses the concept of action or disposition to describe tendencies to move. This concept too comes from the Stoic notion of hexis, meaning active condition, disposition, or holding together in arrangement." Rodolfo Garau, "Late-Scholastic and Cartesian Conatus," *Intellectual History Review* 24.4 (2014): 479–494, 485.
19. René Descartes, *Le Monde*, translated by Michael Sean Mahoney (Norwalk, CT: Abaris Books, 1978), 146–147.
20. Descartes, *The World*, in René Descartes, *Principles of Philosophy*, in *The Philosophical Writings of Descartes*, Volume 1, translated and edited by John Cottingham, Robert Stoothoff, and Dugald Murdoch (Cambridge: Cambridge University Press, 1984), 96.
21. Descartes, *Optics*, in René Descartes, *Principles of Philosophy* in *The Philosophical Writings of Descartes*, Volume 1, translated and edited by John Cottingham, Robert Stoothoff, and Dugald Murdoch (Cambridge: Cambridge University Press, 1984), 155.
22. Hobbes, *Elements of Law* I.7.2.
23. "These small beginnings of motion, within the body of man, before they appear in walking, speaking, striking, and other visible actions, are commonly called ENDEAVOR." Hobbes, *Leviathan*, Chapter 6, in Thomas Hobbes, *The English Works of Thomas Hobbes of Malmesbury*, Volume 3 (London: J. Bohn, 1839), 39.
24. Hobbes, *Leviathan*, Chapter 6, page 39.
25. Hobbes, *De Corpore*, in *English Works*, Volume 1, 205.
26. Hobbes, *De Corpore*, in *English Works*, Volume 1, 132.
27. Hobbes, *De Corpore*, in *English Works*, Volume 1, 109.
28. Hobbes, *De Corpore*, in *English Works*, Volume 1, 206.
29. Hobbes, *De Corpore*, in *English Works*, Volume 1, 206.
30. Douglas Jesseph, "Hobbes and the Method of Natural Science," in *The Cambridge Companion to Hobbes*, edited by Tom Sorell (Cambridge: Cambridge University Press, 1996), 91.
31. Hobbes, *De Corpore*, in *English Works*, Volume 1, 207.
32. Hobbes, *De Corpore*, in *English Works*, Volume 1, 215.
33. Hobbes, *De Corpore*, in *English Works*, Volume 1, 515.
34. Hobbes, *De Corpore*, in *English Works*, Volume 1, 515.
35. Hobbes, *De Corpore*, in *English Works*, Volume 1, 407.
36. Garau, "Late-Scholastic and Cartesian Conatus," 480.
37. Spinoza, *Ethics*, Book II, Postulate 6.
38. Spinoza, *Ethics*, Book I, Postulate 18.
39. Nicholas of Cusa, *On Learned Ignorance*, Book II, Chapter 3, Section 107. In *Selected Spiritual Writings*, translated by H. L. Bond (New York: Paulist Press, 1997), 135.

40. See Gilles Deleuze, *Expressionism in Philosophy: Spinoza* (New York: Zone Books, 1990).
41. Erin Manning, *Relationscapes: Movement, Art, Philosophy* (Cambridge, MA: MIT Press, 2012).
42. Jane Bennett, *Vibrant Matter*.
43. Brian Massumi, *Parables for the Virtual: Movement, Affect, Sensation* (Durham, NC: Duke University Press, 2007).
44. Melissa Gregg and Gregory J. Seigworth, eds. *The Affect Theory Reader* (Durham, NC: Duke University Press, 2011).
45. See Jammer, *Concepts of Force*, 159.
46. Leibniz directly credits Weigel for his understanding of tendency. See Richard Arthur, "Space and Relativity in Newton and Leibniz," *British Journal for the Philosophy of Science* 45.1 (1994): 219–240.
47. Gottfried Leibniz, *Specium Dynamicum*, in *Philosophical Papers and Letters*, edited by Leroy E. Loemker (Dordrecht, the Netherlands: D. Reidel, 1970), 435.
48. Leibniz, *Specium Dynamicum*, 435.
49. Leibniz, *Philosophical Papers and Letters*, 677.
50. Leibniz, *Specium Dynamicum*, 445.
51. Leibniz, *Specium Dynamicum*, 436.
52. Leibniz, *Specium Dynamicum*, 446.
53. Leibniz, *Hypothesis Physica Nova*, in *Philosophical Papers and Letters*, 140.
54. "Conatus est ad motum, ut punctum ad spatium, seu ut unum ad infinitum, est enim initium finisque motus." Gottfried Leibniz, *The Labyrinth of the Continuum: Writings on the Continuum Problem, 1672–1686* (New Haven, CT: Yale University Press, 2001), 340–341.
55. "[E]very passion of a body is spontaneous or arises from an internal force, though upon an external occasion." Leibniz, *Specium Dynamicum*, 448.
56. Leibniz, *Specium Dynamicum*, 448.
57. Leibniz, *Hypothesis Physica Nova*, in *Philosophical Papers and Letters*, 140.
58. Immanuel Kant, *Kant's Inaugural Dissertation of 1770*, translated by William J. Eckoff (New York: AMS Press, 1970), 10.
59. George Berkeley, *De motu*, Section 17, in *Works of George Berkeley*, edited by A. C. Fraser (Oxford: Clarendon, 1901), Volume I, 506.
60. George Berkeley, *De motu*, Section 31; *Works*, Volume I, 511.
61. George Berkeley, *De motu*, Section 7; *Works*, Volume I, 527.
62. J. L. d'Alembert, *Traite de dynamique* (Paris, 1743), xvi.

CHAPTER 27

1. Kilian McDonnell and George T. Montague, *Christian Initiation and Baptism in the Holy Spirit: Evidence from the First Eight Centuries* (Collegeville, MN: Liturgical Press, 1991), 4. Mathew 3:11 and Luke 3:16.
2. See Acts 2:17–18, Acts 2:33, Acts 8:16, Acts 10:44, Acts 1:8, Acts 19:6.
3. Luke 1:35.
4. Genesis 1:2.
5. On the Holy Spirit, Virgin Mary, and Shekhinah as Sophia, see Baring and Cashford, *The Myth of the Goddess*, 596: "However, the dove still retains its archetypal feminine connotations, for, as the Holy Spirit, it signifies the relationship between the divine and the human realms, and it is this that brings the transcendent god into creation as an immanent presence. The divine presence of Yahweh in the Wisdom literature of the Old Testament used to be

experienced as feminine, either as the Shekhinah or as Sophia, as the Presence of God or the Wisdom of God. If the feminine principle had not been lost as a sacred entity, there would inevitably have been some relation between 'God' and Shekhinah/Sophia, and 'God' and Mary as a parallel union of masculine and feminine principles in their heavenly and earthly aspects. The language of the Annunciation—'The Holy Ghost shall come upon thee, and the power of the Highest shall overshadow thee: therefore also that holy thing which shall be born of thee shall be called the Son of God'—unmistakably recalls, in the image of 'overshadowing,' the Shekhinah."

6. In many cases the pronoun "the" is introduced into Latin and English translations of the Bible, where there is no corresponding pronoun in the Hebrew or Greek. See http://www.ecclesia.org/truth/pneuma.html.
7. 1 Clement 42:1–2. Italics added.
8. Ignatius to the Magnesians 13:2.
9. Justin, *First Apology*, Chapter 13. http://www.newadvent.org/fathers/0126.htm.
10. Justin, *First Apology*, Chapter 23. http://www.newadvent.org/fathers/0126.htm.
11. *The Didache: The Lord's Teaching through the Twelve Apostles to the Nations*, Chapter 9, Number 1, translated by Philip Schaff (New York: Funk & Wagnalls, 1885), http://www.newadvent.org/fathers/0714.htm.
12. Alexander Roberts, James Donaldson, A. C. Coxe, Allan Menzies, Ernest C. Richardson, and Bernhard Pick, trans. and eds., *The Ante-Nicene Fathers: Translations of the Writings of the Fathers Down to A.D. 325*, Volume 3 (Buffalo, NY: Christian Literature Publishing Company, 1885), 604. Italics added.
13. Migne, *Patrologiae Cursus Completus*, translated by J.-P, and A.-G Hamman (Paris: Garnier Frères, 1958), Volume 14, 108–110.
14. Origen, *Contra Celsus*, Book 8, Chapter 12; Tertullian, *On Prayer*, Book 15, Chapter 1. http://www.newadvent.org/fathers/index.html.
15. Gregory of Nazianzus, *Select Orations*, Third Theological Oration (Oration 29), II, translated by Martha P. Vinson (Washington, DC: Catholic University of America Press, 2003), 301, http://www.newadvent.org/fathers/310229.htm. Emphasis in original.
16. Gregory of Nazianzus, *Select Orations*, 307.
17. Hippolytus, *Contra Noetum*, Number 64. http://www.newadvent.org/fathers/0521.htm.
18. Gregory of Nazianzus, *Fourth Theological Oration*, XX.
19. Gregory of Nazianzus, *Fifth Theological Oration*, XXXI.
20. Gregory of Nazianzus, *Fifth Theological Oration*, XXXII.
21. Gregory of Nyssa, *On "Not Three Gods,"* § 9. Italics added.
22. Gregory of Nyssa, *On "Not Three Gods,"* § 9.
23. Basil the Great, *De Spiritu Sancto*, Chapter 26, § 61. Italics added.
24. Augustine, *On the Holy Trinity*, Book 1, Chapter 1, § 3.
25. Augustine, *On the Holy Trinity*, Book 1, Chapter 4, § 7.
26. Augustine, *On the Holy Trinity*, Book 1, Chapter 6, § 13.
27. Augustine, *On the Holy Trinity*, Book 1, Chapter 4, § 7.
28. Augustine, *On the Holy Trinity*, Book 5, Chapter 5, § 6.
29. Augustine, *On the Holy Trinity*, Book 5, Chapter 5, § 6.
30. Augustine, *On the Holy Trinity*, Book 6, Chapter 4, § 6.
31. 1 Corinthians 1:24.

32. Augustine, *On the Holy Trinity*, Book 7, Chapter, 3, § 4.
33. Although, some theologians have argued that the idea of *perichoresis*, not the term, began earlier with Origen of Alexandria. Lossky asserts that Origen was the first to formulate the doctrine, which was later to be called "perichoretic," or the doctrine of the "communication of idioms." Vladimir Lossky, *The Vision of God* (Leighton Buzzard, UK: Faith Press, 1973), 59. Congar adds that "although the words perichoresis and circumincession may not occur as such in the writings of the earliest Fathers of the Church, the idea certainly does." Yves Congar, *I Believe in the Holy Spirit*, Volume 3 (New York: Seabury Press, 1983), 37.
34. All from Henry G. Liddell, Eric A. Barber, Robert Scott, Henry S. Jones, and Roderick McKenzie, *A Greek-English Lexicon* (Oxford: Clarendon Press, 1940). *Chor-eia*: dance, any circling motion, dancing place. *Choreo*: Χωρέω: make room for, give way, withdraw. *Choreg-eion*: means of providing for, abundance, expanse, supply-veins. *Chorion*: enveloping membrane. *Choros*: Dance, place for dancing. *Chort*: enclosed place, countryside, harvest, to seed, eat, fold or enclosure, pen, earth.
35. Plato, *Timaeus*, 48e.
36. According to Wolfson, it was taken over from the Stoics' vocabulary. Harry Wolfson, *The Philosophy of the Church Fathers* (Cambridge, MA: Harvard University Press, 1956), 418–421.
37. Gregory Nazianzus, *Orations*, Oration 18, § 42.
38. Gregory Nazianzus, *Orations*, Oration 22, §4.
39. Gregory Nazianzus, *Letters*, Epistle 101, To Cledonius the Priest against Apollinarius. http://www.newadvent.org/fathers/3103a.htm.
40. Maximus Confessor, *Opuscula theologica et polemica*, 102B.
41. Maximus Confessor, *Ambigua*, 112b D. See M. G. Lawler, "Perichoresis: New Theological Wine in an Old Theological Wineskin," *Horizons* 22 (Spring 1995): 50.
42. Pseudo-Cyril Alexandria, *De Trinitate*, 24. Quoted in Danut Manastireanu, "Perichoresis and the Early Christian Doctrine of God," *Archaevs* XI–XII (2007–2008), 61–93, 70.
43. Pseudo-Cyril Alexandria, *De Trinitate*, 27. Quoted in Manastireanu, 70.
44. G. L. Prestige, *God in Patristic Thought* (London: S.P.C.K., 1952), 298.
45. Bonaventura, *Liber Sententiarum*, Book I, Distinction 19. Quoted in P. S. Fiddes, *Participating in God: A Pastoral Doctrine of the Trinity* (London: DLT, 2000), 72.
46. John of Damascus, *An Exact Exposition of the Orthodox Faith*, Book I, Chapter 14. Italics added. http://www.orthodox.net/fathers/exacti.html#BOOK_I_CHAPTER_XIV.
47. John of Damascus, *An Exact Exposition of the Orthodox Faith*, Book I, Chapter 14.
48. Nicholas of Cusa, *On Learned Ignorance*, Book I, Chapter 24, Paragraph 79–91. In *Selected Spiritual Writings*, translated by H. L. Bond (New York: Paulist Press, 1997).
49. Cusa, *On Learned Ignorance*, Book I, Chapter 9, Paragraph 26.
50. Cusa, *On Learned Ignorance*, Book I, Chapter 10, Paragraph 28.
51. Cusa, *On Learned Ignorance*, Book I, Chapter 20, Paragraph 62.
52. Cusa, *On Learned Ignorance*, Book I, Chapter 20, Paragraph 61.
53. Nicholas of Cusa, *On the Summit of Contemplation*, Paragraph 28. In *Selected Spiritual Writings*, translated by H. L. Bond (New York: Paulist Press, 1997), 303.

54. Cusa, *On Learned Ignorance*, Book I, Chapter 24, Paragraph 76.
55. Nicholas of Cusa, *On the Vision of God*, Chapter 5, Paragraph 15. In *Selected Spiritual Writings*, 242.
56. Cusa, *On the Vision of God*, Chapter 9, Paragraph 35. In *Selected Spiritual Writings*, 251.
57. Cusa, *On Learned Ignorance*, Book II, Chapter 8, Paragraph 136. In *Selected Spiritual Writings*, translated by H. L. Bond (New York: Paulist Press, 1997), 48.
58. Cusa, *On Learned Ignorance*, Book II, Chapter 10, Paragraph 155. In *Selected Spiritual Writings*, 157.
59. Cusa, *On Learned Ignorance*, Book II, Chapter 10, Paragraph 155. In *Selected Spiritual Writings*, 157.
60. Cusa, *On the Summit of Contemplation*, Paragraph 28. In *Selected Spiritual Writings*, 303.
61. "To conclude, the doctrine of the Trinity, as far as can be gathered directly from the Scripture, is in substance this; that God who is alwaies One and the same, was the Person Represented by Moses; the Person Represented by his Son Incarnate; and the Person Represented by the Apostles. As Represented by the Apostles, the Holy Spirit by which they spake, is God; As Represented by his Son (that was God and Man), the Son is that God; As represented by Moses, and the High Priests, the Father, that is to say, the Father of our Lord Jesus Christ, is that God: From whence we may gather the reason why those names Father, Son, and Holy Spirit in the signification of the Godhead, are never used in the Old Testament: For they are Persons, that is, they have their names from Representing; which could not be, till divers men had Represented Gods Person in ruling, or in directing under him." Hobbes, *Leviathan*, Part 3, Chapter 42, line 25.
62. "As for the mystery of the Trinity, I share St Thomas' opinion that it is a sheer article of faith and cannot be known by the natural light. But I do not deny that there are things in God which we do not understand, just as even in a triangle there are many properties which no mathematician will ever know—which does not prevent everyone knowing what a triangle is." Descartes, *The Philosophical Writings of Descartes*, Volume III, 166.
63. "It follows thence that certain writers have been too ready to grant that the Holy Trinity is contrary to that great principle which states that two things which are the same as a third are also the same as each other: that is to say, if A is the same as B, and if C is the same as B, then A and C must also be the same as each other. For this principle is a direct consequence of that of contradiction, and forms the basis of all logic; and if it ceases, we can no longer reason with certainty. Thus when one says that the Father is God, that the Son is God and that the Holy Spirit is God, and that nevertheless there is only one God, although these three Persons differ from one another, one must consider that this word God has not the same sense at the beginning as at the end of this statement. Indeed it signifies now the Divine Substance and now a Person of the Godhead." Gottfried W. Leibniz, *Theodicy: Essays on the Goodness of God, the Freedom of Man, and the Origin of Evil*, translated by Austin Farrer (La Salle, IL: Open Court, 1985), 89–90.
64. Newton is an exception to this.
65. See Deleuze, *Expressionism and Philosophy*.
66. Tertullian, *Against Praxeas*, Chapter 9.
67. See Deleuze, *Expressionism in Philosophy*.

CHAPTER 28

1. The existing literature on the printing press often marks a "revolutionary" difference between the manuscript codex and the printed codex.
2. Bernhard Bischoff, *Latin Palaeography: Antiquity and the Middle Ages* (Cambridge: Cambridge University Press, 1990), 11.
3. T. C. Skeat, *The Collected Biblical Writings of T. C. Skeat* (Leiden, the Netherlands: E.J. Brill, 2004), 45.
4. "Christian texts from the earliest known date appear in codex form, the forerunner of the book. Wax-tablets had long been joined by leather thongs to form 'notebooks,' but no one before the Romans thought of arranging parchment or papyrus in this way. Even then such 'notebooks' were only used in schools and businesses; they were not 'proper books.' For literary texts the transition from roll to codex did not take place until the fourth century." Frances Young, Lewis Ayres, Andrew Louth, and Ron White, eds., *The Cambridge History of Early Christian Literature* (Cambridge: Cambridge University Press 2004) 8–9.
5. "Codex," in *The Oxford Dictionary of Byzantium* (Oxford University Press, New York & Oxford, 1991), 473.
6. Colin H. Roberts and T. C. Skeat, *The Birth of the Codex* (Oxford: Oxford University Press, 1983), 75.
7. See John Szirmai, *The Archaeology of Medieval Bookbinding* (Aldershot, UK: Ashgate, 1999).
8. "That wooden boards were used as covers on the early MSS. was doubtless due to the fact that the vellum on which they were written had a strong tendency to curl, and could not be made to lie at without some pressure. Even the weight of the heavy wooden boards had to be augmented, and the added pressure produced by placing metal clasps over the edges of the books was resorted to in order to keep these texts from yawning. I might add that metal bosses were fastened to the sides of these early books probably for the twofold purpose of decoration and keeping the leather from being scratched or harmed as the book lay on its side." Szirmai, *Archaeology of Medieval Bookbinding*, 17.
9. Malcolm B. Parkes, "The Contribution of Insular Scribes of the Seventh and Eighth Centuries to the 'Grammar of Legibility,'" in *Scribes, Scripts and Readers: Studies in the Communication, Presentation and Dissemination of Medieval Texts* (London: Hambledon, 1991), 1–18.
10. "Et secundum hoc duplex est liber, unus scilicet scriptus intus, qui est aeterna Dei ars et sapientia; et alius scriptus foris, mundus scilicet sensibilis." Bonaventura, "Breviloquium," in *Opera omnia V: Opuscula varia theologica*, Book II, Chapter 11, Section 2. Bonaventura, *Opuscula Varia Theologica* (Ad Claras Aquas [Quaracchi], prope Florentiam: Ex Typographia Collegii S. Bonaventurae, 1891), 229.
11. According to Peter Harrison, Plato's *Timaeus* gives us a theory of interpretation as revealing divine truth through the structure of nature: "In the *Timaeus*, Plato asserted that the world is 'a sensible God who is the image of the intellectual,'" (*Timaeus*, 27c). Peter Harrison, *The Bible, Protestantism, and the Rise of Natural Science* (Cambridge: Cambridge University Press, 2006), 40.
12. Origen, *The Song of Songs: Commentary and Homilies*, translated by R. P. Lawson (Westminster, MD: Newman Press, 1957), 220.
13. Origen, *Philocalia*. Quoted in Joseph Butler, *The Analogy of Religion to the Constitution and Course of Nature* (London: Religious Tract Society, n.d.), 7.
14. Origen, *The Song of Songs*, 220.

15. Tertullian, *Adversus Marcionem*, Book I, Chapter 18.
16. Basil, *Hexameron*, Book I, Chapter 6 (FC 46, 11). In *Fathers of the Church* (Washington, DC: Catholic University of America Press, 1947), 46, 11.
17. Ambrose, *Hexameron*, Book I, Chapter 4, Section 6. In *Fathers of the Church*, 42.
18. Origen, *The Song of Songs*, 218. The reference to Paul is Romans 1.20.
19. Origen, *Homilies in Genesis*, Book I, Chapter 11 and 12. In *Fathers of the Church*, 71.
20. Ambrose, *Hexameron*, Book VI, Chapter 9, Sections 54 and 75. In *Fathers of the Church*, 268, 282.
21. Ambrose, *Hexameron*, Book VI, Chapter 9, Sections 54 and 63. In *Fathers of the Church*, 268–274.
22. Ambrose, *Hexameron*, Book VI, Chapter 2, Section 3. In *Fathers of the Church*, 229. Asclepius similarly writes that "on account of mankind's divine composition, it seems right to call him a well-ordered world. . . . Mankind knows himself through the world." Asclepius, 10. In Brian Copenhaver and Trimegisto Hermes, eds., *Hermetica: The Greek Corpus Hermeticum and the Latin Asclepius in a New English Translation with Notes and Introduction* (New York: Cambridge University Press, 1994), 72.
23. Chrysostom, *Homilies on Genesis*, Book VIII, Chapter 14. In *Fathers of the Church*, 74. For animals as symbolizing human passions, also see Philo, *De plantation*, Book XI, Chapter 43.
24. Thomas Aquinas, *Somme Théologique: Volume 3: Ia. 12-13, Knowing and Naming God: Latin Text and English Translation*, translated by Herbert McCabe (Cambridge: Cambridge University Press, 2010), 45.
25. Origen, *Homilies on Numbers*, 2, 9, 16. In *Homilies on Numbers*, translated by Thomas P. Scheck, and Christopher A. Hall (Downers Grove, IL: IVP Academic, 2009), 100–101.
26. Origen, *Letter 4 to Gregory Thaumaturgus*. http://www.newadvent.org/fathers/ 0415.htm. Quoted in Duncan Robertson, *Lectio Divina: The Medieval Experience of Reading* (Trappist, KY: Cistercian Publications, 2011), 81.
27. Cyprian of Carthage, *Epistles*, Epistle 1, Section 15. http://www.newadvent.org/ fathers/050601.htm.
28. Ambrose, *De officiis ministrorum*, Book, Chapter 20, Section 88.
29. Jerome, *Commentaries on Titus*, Book III, Chapter 9. In *St. Jerome's Commentaries on Galatians, Titus, and Philemon*, translated by Thomas P. Scheck (Notre, Dame, IN: Notre Dame Press, 2010), 277–350.
30. Ambrose, *Patrologia cursus completus, series Latina*, Volume 15, edited by J.-P. Migne (Paris: Paris Apud Garnier, 1844–1905), 1681b.
31. Augustine, *Patrologia*, Volume 38, 778.
32. Benedict, *The Rule of Benedict*, Chapter 48, Paragraph 1. http://www.osb.org/rb/ text/rbemjo3.html#48.
33. Guigo II, *On Contemplation*, The Ladder of Four Rings. http://www.umilta.net/ ladder.html.
34. See also: GuigoII, "Ladder of the Monks," in *The Oblate Life*, translated by Gervase Holdaway (Collegeville, MN: Liturgical Press, 2008), 109.
35. John 1:1
36. Augustine, *Confessions*, Book IV, Chapter 15, Section, 25.
37. Augustine, *Confessions*, Book XII, Chapter 25, Section 35.
38. Augustine, *Eighty-Three Different Questions*, translated by D. L. Mosher (Washington, DC: Catholic University of America Press, 1982), 9.

CHAPTER 29

1. Eltjo Buringh and Jan Luiten van Zanden, "Charting the "Rise of the West": Manuscripts and Printed Books in Europe, A Long-Term Perspective from the Sixth through Eighteenth Centuries," *Journal of Economic History* 69.2 (2009): 409–445; 416, Table 1.
2. Alphonse Lamartine, *Memoirs of Celebrated Characters*, Volume 2 (Rarebooksclub.com, [1856] 2012), 287. Italics added.
3. Herbert Brekle, *Die Prüfeninger Weihinschrift von 1119. Eine paläographisch-typographische Untersuchung (brief summary)* (Regensburg: Scriptorium Verlag für Kultur und Wissenschaft, 2005), 23–26.
4. Hildegard of Bingen, *De operatione Dei*, Book V, Chapter 2; Hildegard of Bingen, *Liber divinorum operum*, Book I, Chapter 4, Section 97. In *Patrologia cursus completus, series Latina*, Volume 197. Quoted in Harrison, *The Bible, Protestantism, and the Rise of Natural Science*, 37.
5. Bernard of Clairvaux, *Sermon V*, in *Cantica canticorum: Eighty Six Sermans on the Song of Solomon*, translated by S. J. Eales, (London: Elliot Stock, 1895). Quoted in Sarah Beckwith, *Christ's Body: Identity, Culture, and Society in Late Medieval Writings* (London: Routledge, 1993), 49.
6. Aquinas, *Summa Theologica*, 1a, Question 15, Article 1.
7. John Scotus Eriugena, *De divisione naturae*, Chapter 111, Section 35. In *Patrologia cursus completus, series Latina*, Volume 122, 723.
8. Harrison, *The Bible, Protestantism, and the Rise of Natural Science*, 36.
9. Hugh of St. Victor, *De arca Noe morali*, Book IV, Chapter 7, in *Patrologia cursus completus, series Latina*, Volume 176, 672D.
10. Arnold of Bonneval, *De operibus sex dierum*, prologue, in *Patrologia cursus completus, series Latina*, Volume 189, 1515D, 16A.
11. Alan of Lille, *De planctu naturae*, in *Patrologia cursus completus, series Latina*, Volume 210, 447.
12. The distinction is explicitly stated by Bonaventure, *Quaestiones disputatae de scientia Christi*, Question 2.
13. He writes, "[Y]et among created things some may be called exemplars of others which are made to their likeness [*similitudinem*]." Aquinas, *Summa Theologica*, 1a, Question 44, Article 3.
14. Hugh of St. Victor, *De tribus diebus*, 4, in *Patrologia cursus completus, series Latina*, Volume 176, 814B. Also see Wanda Cizewski, "Reading the World as Scripture: Hugh of St. Victor's *De tribus diebus*," *Florilegium* 9 (1987) 6588.
15. Vincent of Beauvais, *Libellus totius opens apolageticus*, Version 1, Chapter 5.
16. William of Conches, *Philosophia mundi*, Book I, Chapter 13. Quoted in Stock, *The Implications of Literacy* (Princeton, NJ: Princeton University Press, 1983), 319.
17. Honorius follows Eriugena in linking these two forms of knowledge to the two-fold vestiture of the transfigured Christ. Honorius Augustodunensis, *De animae exsilio et patria*, Book XII, in *Patrologia cursus completus, series Latina*, Volume 172, 1246A.
18. Harrison, *The Bible, Protestantism, and the Rise of Natural Science*, 45.
19. Quoted in S. Gieben, "Traces of God in Nature according to Robert Grosseteste, with the Text of the 'Dictium, Omnis creatura speculum est,'" *Franciscan Studies* 24 (1964) 144–158.
20. Hugh of St. Victor, *Didascalicon*, Book VI, Chapter V, in *Didascalicon of Hugh of St. Victor: A Medieval Guide to the Arts*, translated by Jerome Taylor (New York: Columbia University Press, 1961), 145. "Hugh set out quite specific

techniques for the interpretation of the text of nature, based on the general assumption that living things can be read as signs variously of God's power, wisdom and goodness: the power of God is seen in the immensity of creatures, his goodness in their usefulness, and his wisdom in their elegance." Harrison, *The Bible, Protestantism, and the Rise of Natural Science*, 57.
21. Hugh of St. Victor, *On the Sacraments*, Book I, prologue.
22. William of Conches, *Philosophia mundi*, Book I, Chapter 23, in *Patrologia cursus completus, series Latina*, Volume 72, 56.
23. Harrison, *The Bible, Protestantism, and the Rise of Natural Science*, 63.
24. Cecil Clough, "The Cult of Antiquity: Letters and Letter Collections," in *Cultural Aspects of the Italian Renaissance: Essays in Honour of Paul Oskar Kristeller*, edited by Cecil H. Clough (Manchester, UK: Manchester University Press, 1976); Pierre Francastel, "Poussain et l'homme historique," *Annalles* 19 (1964) 6; Walter J. Ong, "Systems, Space, and Intellect in Renaissance Symbolism," *Bibliotheque d'humanisme et Renaissance* 18 (1956) 229; Walter J. Ong, *Ramus, Method, and the Decay of Dialogue* (Cambridge, MA: Harvard University Press, 1958) x, 79, 128; Walter J. Ong, *The Presence of the Word: Some Prolegomena for Cultural and Religious History* (New Haven, CT: Yale University Press, 1967), 58–61; Elizabeth Eisenstein, "Some Conjectures about the Impact of Printing on Western Society," *Journal of Modern History* 40 (1968) 30–31; Elizabeth Eisenstein, *The Printing Press as an Agent of Change: Communication and Cultural Transformations in Early Modern Europe* (Cambridge: Cambridge University Press, 1979), 10–11, 698.
25. See Paul Saenger, "Silent Reading: Its Impact on Late Medieval Script and Society," *Viator: Medieval and Renaissance Studies* 13 (1982): 367–414.
26. Quoted in Alberto Manguel, *A History of Reading* (New York; Viking, 1996), 44.
27. Quoted in Manguel, *A History of Reading*, 45.
28. Quoted in Manguel, *A History of Reading*, 49.
29. Saenger, "Silent Reading," 367–414, 378.
30. Saenger, "Silent Reading," 367–414, 396.
31. Saenger, "Silent Reading," 367–414, 408.
32. Saenger, "Silent Reading," 367–414, 405.
33. Susan Reynolds argues that many European medieval kingdoms were nations in the modern sense, except that political participation in nationalism was available only to a limited prosperous and literate class. Susan Reynolds, *Kingdoms and Communities in Western Europe, 900–1300* (Oxford: Clarendon Press, 1984). See also Benedict Anderson, *Imagined Communities: Reflections on the Origin and Spread of Nationalism* (London: Verso, 1991).
34. I develop the kinetic theory of the tensional "cell" in *Theory of the Border*. And will develop it further in the next book on affect, *Theory of the Image* (Oxford: Oxford University Press, forthcoming).
35. Aquinas, *Summa Theologiae*, Question 84, Article 6, Ad 1.
36. Aquinas, *Summa Theologiae*, 1a 2ae, Question 109, Article 1c.
37. Aquinas, *Summa Theologiae*, 1a, Question 84, Article 5c.
38. As Steven Marrone has shown in detail, there were various authors at the end of the thirteenth century who were ready to reject illumination. Indeed, Ghent himself gave illumination less and less attention in his later years. See Steven Marrone, *The Light of Thy Countenance: Science and Knowledge of God in the Thirteenth Century* (Leiden, the Netherlands: Brill, 2001).
39. Duns Scotus, *Ordinatio*, Book I, Distinction 3, Question 1, Article 4, number 267.
40. Duns Scotus, *Ordinatio*, Book I, Distinction 3, Question 1, Article 4, number 258.

41. Francis Bacon, *Of Truth*, in *The Works of Francis Bacon*, Volume 6, 378.
42. Descartes, *Principles*, Part I, Article 30.
43. Descartes, *Meditations*, Part III, in *Oeuvres de Descartes*, Volume IX, 33, 35, 38; *Meditations*, Part VI, In Adam and Tannery, Volume IX, 65. Expressions like this do not appear in anything that Descartes wrote before the *Meditations*.

CHAPTER 30
1. Carlo Rovelli, *The Order of Time* (New York: Penguin, 2018), 83–84.
2. Uexküll, *A Foray into the Worlds of Animals and Humans*, 49.

CHAPTER 31
1. Seriality should not be confused with "sequence." Sequence is the definition of time in general, but seriality is a kinetic operation having to do with the process of temporal folding.
2. I have written a lengthy kinetic history of Neolithic and ancient descriptions of time that will hopefully be made available elsewhere.
3. Edmund Husserl, *On the Phenomenology of the Consciousness of Internal Time (1893–1917)*, edited and translated by J. B. Brough (Dordrecht, the Netherlands: Kluwer, 1991), 3.
4. Augustine, *Confessions*, Book XI, Chapter 30.
5. Augustine, *Confessions*, Book XI, Chapter 14, Section 17: "At no time, therefore, had Thou not made anything, because You had made time itself. And no times are co-eternal with You, because You remain for ever . . ."
6. Augustine, *Confessions*, Book XI, Chapter 13, Section 16.
7. Augustine, *Confessions*, Book XI, Chapter 14, Section 17.
8. Augustine, *Confessions*, Book XI, Chapter 20, Section 26.
9. There is a dual etymology of the word "tense" (from *tempus* and from *tendre*). The word "tense" invokes both.
10. Augustine, *Confessions*, Book XI, Chapter 21, Section 27.
11. See Nail, *Theory of the Border*, 104–107.
12. Joannis Duns Scoti, *Scriptum Oxoniensis*, Book II, Distinction 2, Question 11: Dico ergo ad quaestionem . . ., in *Opera Omnia*, Volume VI, Part I, page 324. Cited in Pierre Duhem and Roger Ariew, *Medieval Cosmology: Theories of Infinity, Place, Time, Void, and the Plurality of Worlds* (Chicago: University of Chicago Press, 1985), 296.
13. Petri Aureoli, Verberii Ordinis minorum Archiepiscopi Aquensis S. R. E. Cardinalis. *Commentariorum in secundum Librum Sententiarum Pars Secundus*, Distinction II, Question I, Article I: Utrum tempus sit duratio vel successio, sive quantitas continua, vel discreta, p. 38, col. b. Cited in Duhem and Ariew, *Medieval Cosmology*, 300.
14. "Multiple times can be considered as coexistant unities and thus one time. If there were several equally first heavens and several first movements, there would, in reality, be several times; but all these times would be a single time by equivalence (per equivalentiam), meaning that these multiple times would make up a single time for measuring." Gulieimi de Villa Hoccham, *Summulae in libros Physicorum*, pars IV, cap. XI, fol 26, col. d [po 95, col. b]. Cited in Duhem and Ariew, *Medieval Cosmology*, 320.
15. Similar theories include those of Francis of Marchia (c. 1290–c. 1344), Jean Buridan (c. 1295–1363), and Nicholas Bonet (c. 1280–1343).

16. I have left out a number of important philosophies of mechanistic time during this period in order to focus on a few major representative ones. The thinkers I have discussed do not agree about everything. The purpose of this section is not to lay out a complete and comparative intellectual history, but to show the emergence of the kinetics of absolute time. For a more complete account, see Duhem and Ariew, *Medieval Cosmology*; Alexander Koyre, *Metaphysics and Measurement: Essays in Scientific Revolution* (Cambridge, MA: Harvard University Press, 1968); Max Jammer, *Concepts of Simultaneity: From Antiquity to Einstein and Beyond* (Baltimore, MD: Johns Hopkins University Press, 2006); Edwin Burtt, *The Metaphysical Foundations of Modern Physical Science* (Garden City, NY: Doubleday, 1954); Milič Čapek, *The Concepts of Space and Time: Their Structure and Their Development* (Dordrecht, the Netherlands: Reidel, 1976).
17. Similar theories of absolute time with the same elastic descriptions include those of Pierre Gassendi (1592–1655), Thomas Hobbes (1588–1679), Henry More (1614–1687), Walter Charleton (1619–1707), and Isaac Barrow (1630–1677). See Koyre, *Metaphysics and Measurement*; Jammer, *Concepts of Simultaneity*; Čapek, *The Concepts of Space and Time*.
18. Descartes, *Principles*, Part I, Article 57. Cited in René Descartes, *The Philosophical Writings of Descartes*, Volume 1, translated and edited by John Cottingham, Robert Stoothoff, and Dugald Murdoch (Cambridge: Cambridge University Press, 1984), 212.
19. Descartes, *Principles*, Part II, Article 36: "God is the primary cause of motion; and he always preserves the same quantity of motion in the universe. In the beginning he created matter, along with its motion and rest; and now, merely by regularly letting things run their course, he preserves the same amount of motion and rest in the material universe as he put there in the beginning. (God's perfection involves his never changing in himself or in his ways of operating.)" Cited in *The Philosophical Writings of Descartes*, Volume 1, 240.
20. Descartes, *Principles*, Part II, Article 29: "And it is to be referred only to those contiguous bodies which are regarded as being at rest. I further specified that the transfer occurs from the vicinity not of any contiguous bodies but from the vicinity of those which 'are regarded as being at rest.'" Cited in *The Philosophical Writings of Descartes*, Volume 1, 235.
21. Descartes, *Principles*, Part II, Article 28. Motion is not a change of place. "Motion in the strict sense is to be referred solely to the bodies which are contiguous with the body in motion. In my definition I specified that the transfer occurs from the vicinity of contiguous bodies to the vicinity of other bodies; I did not say that there was a transfer from one place to another." Cited in *The Philosophical Writings of Descartes*, Volume 1, 234.
22. Isaac Newton, *Mathematical Principles of Natural Philosophy and His System of the World*, translated by Andrew Motte (1729), revised by Florian Cajori (Berkeley, University of California Press, 1966), 6.
23. Newton, *Manuscript Add. 3965*, Portsmouth Collection. Translated under the title "Tempus and Locus" by J. E. McGuire. Original Latin with translation provided in McGuire's "Newton on Place Time and God: An Unpublished Source," *British Journal for the History of Science*, Vol. 11, 1978. This passage paragraph 2, McGuire, p. 117.
24. Isaac Newton, *De Gravitatione et æquipondio fluidorum, Add. Ms. 4003* (Cambridge University Library). Translated by Emmaline Margaret Bexley, "Absolute Time

before Newton" (Dissertation for History and Philosophy of Science Programme School of Philosophy Faculty of Arts, University of Melbourne, 2007).
25. Newton, General Scholium to the *Principia Mathematica*.
26. Isaac Newton, *Newton: Philosophical Writings*, translated and edited by Andrew Janiak (Cambridge: Cambridge University Press, 2014), 117.

CHAPTER 32

1. Immanuel Kant, *Critique of Pure Reason*, translated by Werner S. Pluhar, edited by Patricia Kitcher (Indianapolis, IN: Hackett, 1996), 85.
2. Kant, *Critique of Pure Reason*, 86.
3. Kant, *Critique of Pure Reason*, 86.
4. In quantum kinetics, this definition can no longer serve as an adequate definition of movement.
5. Kant, *Critique of Pure Reason*, 87.
6. Kant, *Critique of Pure Reason*, 87.
7. Kant, *Critique of Pure Reason*, 88.
8. Kant, *Critique of Pure Reason*, 88.
9. Kant, *Critique of Pure Reason*, 88.
10. It is in this sense that Heidegger describes Kant's theory of time as having a metaphysical foundation. "As the original, threefold-unifying forming of future, past, and present in general, this is what first makes possible the 'faculty' of pure synthesis, i.e., that which it is able to produce, namely, the unification of the three elements of ontological knowledge, in the unity of which transcendence is formed." Martin Heidegger, *Kant and the Problem of Metaphysics* (Bloomington: Indiana University Press, 1962), 137. "The universal ontological function that Kant assigns to time at the beginning of the ground-laying can hence only be sufficiently justified because it is precisely time itself, and indeed time in its ontological function (i.e., as essential bit of pure ontological knowledge), which forces us to determine the essence of subjectivity in a more original way." Heidegger, *Kant and the Problem of Metaphysics*, 36.
11. Kant, *Critique of Pure Reason*, 91.
12. Kant, *Critique of Pure Reason*, 91.
13. Georg W. F. Hegel, *Outlines of the Philosophy of Right*, translated by Stephen Houlgate (Oxford: Oxford University Press, 2008), 232–233.
14. Georg W. F. Hegel, *Hegel's Philosophy of Nature: Being Part Two of the Encyclopaedia of the Philosophical Sciences (1830)*, translated and edited by Arnold V. Miller, and Karl L. Michelet (Oxford: Clarendon Press, 1970), 25.
15. "As we know, world history is thus on the whole the laying out of mindful spirit in time, just as the idea as nature lays itself out in space" ("Die Weltgeschichte, wissen wir, ist also überhaupt die Auslegung des Geistes in der Zeit, wie die Idee als Natur sich im Raume auslegt"). Georg W. F. Hegel, *Werke*, edited by Eva Moldenhauer, Karl M. Michel, and Helmut Reinicke (Frankfurt am Main: Suhrkamp, 1986), Volume 12, 96.
16. See H. S. Harris, *Hegel's Development, Night Thoughts (Jena 1801–1806)* (Oxford: Clarendon Press, 1983), 245–246.
17. Hegel, *Philosophy of Nature*, 29.
18. Hegel, *Philosophy of Nature*, 28.
19. Hegel, *Philosophy of Nature*, 31.
20. Hegel, *Philosophy of Nature*, 31.
21. Hegel, *Philosophy of Nature*, 31.

22. All geometric shapes can be enclosed in the circle. "A higher definition of the circle than that based on the equality of the radii, is that which takes account of the difference in it, and so reaches a complete determinateness of the circle. . . .The relationship of these three is the determinateness of the circle, not simple as in the first definition, but a relation of differentiated elements . . . Just as there are an infinite number of right-angled triangles possible on one hypotenuse, so to a square there correspond a multitude of rectangles; both have their place in the circle." Hegel, *Philosophy of Nature*, 33.
23. Hegel, *Philosophy of Nature*, 34.
24. Hegel, *Philosophy of Nature*, 34.
25. "Time is continuous, too, like space, for it is the negativity abstractly relating self to self, and in this abstraction there is as yet no real difference." Hegel, *Philosophy of Nature*, 35.
26. ". . . it is Becoming directly intuited; this means that differences, which admittedly are purely momentary, i.e. directly self-sublating, are determined as external, i.e. as external to themselves." Hegel, *Philosophy of Nature*, 34.
27. "It is because things are finite that they are in time; it is not because they are in time that they perish; on the contrary, things themselves are the temporal, and to be so is their objective determination." Hegel, *Philosophy of Nature*, 36.
28. Hegel, *Philosophy of Nature*, 35.
29. Hegel, *Philosophy of Nature*, 40.
30. "Time which has a real existence through Space, or Space which is first truly differentiated by Time. Thus we know that Space and Time pertain to Motion; the velocity, the quantum of Motion, is Space in relation to a specific Time elapsed. . . . It is in Motion that Space and Time first acquire actuality." Hegel, *Philosophy of Nature*, 43.
31. Hegel, *Philosophy of Nature*, 43.
32. Hegel, *Philosophy of Nature*, 43.
33. Hegel, *Philosophy of Nature*, 43–44.
34. ". . . purely formal movement, the purely logical formula of movement. If one finds in logical categories the substance of all things, one imagines one has found in the logical formula of movement the absolute method, which not only explains all things, but also implies the movement of things." Marx, *The Poverty of Philosophy* (1963), 78–79. "So what is this absolute method? The abstraction of movement. What is the abstraction of movement? Movement in abstract condition. What is movement in abstract condition? The purely logical formula of movement or the movement of pure reason. Wherein does the movement of pure reason consist? In posing itself, opposing itself, composing itself; in formulation itself as thesis, antithesis, synthesis; or, yet again, in affirming itself, negating itself and negating its negation." Marx, *The Poverty of Philosophy* (1963), 78–79.
35. "In general, the greater the productivity of labour, the less the labour-time required to produce an article, the less the mass of labour crystallized in that article, and the less its value." Karl Marx, *Capital: A Critique of Political Economy*, translated by Ben Fowkes, edited by David Fernbach (Harmondsworth, UK: Penguin, 1976), 131.
36. See Nail's *The Figure of the Migrant* and *Theory of the Border* for more on the elastic theory of capitalism.
37. Marx, *Grundrisse*, 539.

38. "The history of capitalism has therefore been marked by dramatic reductions in the cost or time of movement together with improvements in continuity of flow. Space relations are thereby continuously subject to transformation." David Harvey, *Spaces of Global Capitalism* (London: Verso, 2006), 328.

39. The study of this move from liquid to solid manufacturing is developed in depth in Alfred Chandler, *The Visible Hand: The Managerial Revolution in American Business* (Cambridge, MA: Belknap Press, 1977). Mass production occurred first with liquids, then semi-liquids, then solids. "Such mass production techniques came first in industries processing liquids or semi-liquids, such as crude oil. They came a little later in a number of mechanical industries, including those processing tobacco and grain. They appeared more slowly in the metal-making and metal-working industries, because there high-volume production required more technological breakthroughs." Chandler, *The Visible Hand*, 240. "In the mechanical industries, where continuous-process machinery and plants permitted mass production, and in the refining and distilling industries, where the materials were liquid or close to liquid and the processes were chemical rather than mechanical, improved plant design and machinery were in most cases enough to synchronize the processes of production and to assure intensive use of equipment and personnel." Chandler, *The Visible Hand*, 281.

40. Marx, *The Poverty of Philosophy*, in *Collected Works of Marx and Engels*, Volume 6 (New York: International Co., 1969), 126–127. Italics added.

41. Karl Marx, *Value, Price and Profit* (New York: International Co., 1969), Section VIII, Article 3, https://www.marxists.org/archive/marx/works/1865/value-price-profit/ch03.htm.

42. "What we see appearing through these two forms is the introduction of *time* into the capitalist system of power and into the system of penality. Into the system of penality: for the first time in the history of penal systems, one no longer punishes through the body or through goods, but through time to live. . . . Thus, what allows us to analyze the punitive regime of crimes and the disciplinary regime of labor as of a piece is the relationship of the time of life to political power: that repression of time and repression through time, that kind of continuity between workshop clock, production line stopwatch, and prison calendar." Michel Foucault, *The Punitive Society: Lectures at the College De France 1972–1973*, translated by Bernard E. Harcourt and Graham Burchell (New York: Palgrave Macmillan, 2015), 72.

43. Marx, *Capital*, 784.

44. Sismoodi, *De economie politique*, Volume 1 (Paris, 1819), 119. Cited in Marx, *Capital*, 727.

45. The elastic spiral is also the site of emancipation because it is always open to becoming something else. Capital takes advantage of this novelty but not by necessity: communism can also take hold of the movement.

CHAPTER 33

1. Between Marx and Husserl we are skipping over a number of important figures—not because they have nothing to say about time—but because they either have nothing kinetically new to say about time or because they do not grant time ontological primacy, which is the focus of this chapter. For a more complete intellectual history of time, see Philip Turetzky, *Time* (London: Routledge, 2002). Nietzsche (1844–1900) grants ontological primacy to force, will, or power, and not to time. His theory of the eternal return,

while interesting, is ultimately an expression of the power of being to return and not the dominant temporal structure of being. I skip over William James (1842–1910) here as well because he explicitly rejects the Kantian idea of the transcendental ego, and thus the elasticity of the flow of time itself to unify the temporal folds of empirical time. Furthermore, James's account of empirical time as a "specious present" adds nothing kinetically to the long history of medieval and early modern theories of the lived present in thinkers like Augustine, Hume, Berkeley, Locke, and others. The fact that James still must presuppose a continuous "stream of consciousness," which he describes as a river, train, flow, and so on, presupposes the continuous unity of the flow itself, and therefore the elasticity of the flow such that it can fold into the "specious present." James only finally realizes this in *The Pluralistic Universe: Hibbert Lectures to Manchester College on the Present Situation in Philosophy* (Norwood, Pa: Norwood Editions, 1979), where he adopts an explicitly Bergsonian position. His rejection of Kant is clear: "But this service has been ill-performed; for the Egoists themselves, let them say what they will, believe in the bundle, and in their own system merely tie it up, with their special transcendental string, invented for that use alone. Besides, they talk as if, with this miraculous tying or 'relating,' the Ego's duties were done. Of its far more important duty of choosing some of the things it ties and appropriating them, to the exclusion of the rest, they tell us never a word. To sum up, then, my own opinion of the transcendentalist school, it is (whatever ulterior metaphysical truth it may divine) a school in which psychology at least has naught to learn, and whose deliverances about the Ego in particular in no wise oblige us to revise our own formulation of the Stream of Thought." William James, *The Principles of Psychology* (New York: Dover, 1950), 371. Brentano (1838–1917), after James, simply elaborates the medieval kinetic structure of the intentional time of the "lived present," first put forward by Augustine. Like Augustine and James, Brentano's theory of time presupposes the primacy of flow but fails to see the elasticity of time itself as the condition of the circulation and regional unification of the intentional temporal folds. I skip over J. M. E. McTaggart (1866–1925) also, because he attributes his theory of time to Hegel, which we have already covered in this chapter. Furthermore, McTaggart's thesis that time is unreal is a very undialectical position, since, as we have seen, time and space gain their reality and actuality through their becoming as motion. For Hegel, time is real, and even ontologically primary, but only through its becoming in motion. For Hegel, it is simply a truism that nothing exists as a pure abstraction. We might as well claim that nothing is real since nothing exists in itself and for itself without the dialectical process of mediation. McTaggart's antirealist position concludes with the reality of eternity as simultaneity (time is an illusion), which is a very old historical thesis also already covered in the previous chapter. Bertrand Russell (1872–1970) and Charlie Dunbar Broad (1887–1971), for all their differences with William James and Brentano, and between each other, further reiterate the same theory of the temporal fold or the retentional present. They both argue that the flow of time is directly present to empirical experience without any transcendental structure needed to hold these impressions together. Bergson (1859–1941) is not included in this history because he equates his theory of duration with pure movement. "Reality is mobility itself.... If movement is not everything, it is nothing." Henri Bergson, *The Creative Mind*, translated by Mabelle Louise Cunningham Andison

(New York: Philosophical Library, 1946), 177, 171. As such, Bergson is one of the few philosophers who grants ontological primacy to movement, and he will be treated elsewhere at much greater length.
2. David Hume, *A Treatise of Human Nature*, edited by L. A. Selby-Bigge and P. H. Nidditch (Oxford: Clarendon Press, 1978), 635–636.
3. It is important therefore not to reduce Husserl's theory of time-consciousness to a simple tripartite structure of primal impression, retention and protention, thus reducing his theory of time to that of his empiricist precursors like James, Brentano, and Locke and theories of the 'specious present.' This appears to be a key point of divergence between Husserl and authors such as Stern (1897) and James (1890), for whom the idea that there is a limited temporal interval experience can span (as encapsulated in the notion of the 'specious present') carries some explanatory weight in accounting for the very possibility of temporal experience. "In a major recent study of temporal experience, for instance, Barry Dainton discusses in detail Husserl's early attempts to give an account of temporal experience in terms of that tripartite structure, but mentions only briefly later developments that also feature the notion of the absolute flow, commenting that he "find[s] the relevant Husserlian writings obscure." Christoph Hoerl, "Husserl, the Absolute Flow, and Temporal Experience," *Philosophy and Phenomenological Research* 86.2 (2013): 376. See also Barry Dainton, *Stream of Consciousness: Unity and Continuity in Conscious Experience* (London: Routledge, 2006), 160.
4. Husserl, *Logical Investigations*, Volume 2, 549.
5. Husserl, *Logical Investigations*, Volume 2, 549, note 1.
6. Edmund Husserl, *On the Phenomenology of the Consciousness of Internal Time (1893–1917)*, translated by John B. Brough (Boston: Kluwer Academic 1991), 77.
7. Husserl, *On the Phenomenology of the Consciousness of Internal Time*, 78.
8. Husserl, *On the Phenomenology of the Consciousness of Internal Time*, 78.
9. Husserl, *On the Phenomenology of the Consciousness of Internal Time*, 78.
10. Husserl, *On the Phenomenology of the Consciousness of Internal Time*, 79.
11. Husserl, *On the Phenomenology of the Consciousness of Internal Time*, 80.
12. Husserl, *On the Phenomenology of the Consciousness of Internal Time*, 81.
13. Husserl, *On the Phenomenology of the Consciousness of Internal Time*, 82.
14. Husserl, *On the Phenomenology of the Consciousness of Internal Time*, 119.
15. Husserl, *On the Phenomenology of the Consciousness of Internal Time*, 294.
16. Husserl, *On the Phenomenology of the Consciousness of Internal Time*, 287–288. [footnote added in summer 1909]
17. Husserl, *On the Phenomenology of the Consciousness of Internal Time*, 88.
18. Husserl, *On the Phenomenology of the Consciousness of Internal Time*, 84.
19. Husserl, *On the Phenomenology of the Consciousness of Internal Time*, 308.
20. Husserl, *On the Phenomenology of the Consciousness of Internal Time*, 87.
21. Husserl, *On the Phenomenology of the Consciousness of Internal Time*, 86–87.
22. Husserl, *On the Phenomenology of the Consciousness of Internal Time*, 79.
23. Husserl, *On the Phenomenology of the Consciousness of Internal Time*, 79.
24. For further elaboration of the idea that time is a product of matter in motion, see Carlo Rovelli, *Quantum Gravity* (Cambridge: Cambridge University Press, 2004), 29–31. "We never really see time. We see only clocks. If you say this object moves, what you really mean is that this object is here when the hand of your clock is here, and so on. We say we measure time with clocks, but we see only the hands of the clocks, not time itself. And the hands of a clock are a

physical variable like any other. So in a sense we cheat because what we really observe are physical variables as a function of other physical variables, but we represent that as if everything is evolving in time. . . .What happens with the Wheeler-DeWitt equation is that we have to stop playing this game. Instead of introducing this fictitious variable—time, which itself is not observable—we should just describe how the variables are related to one another. The question is, Is time a fundamental property of reality or just the macroscopic appearance of things? I would say it's only a macroscopic effect. It's something that emerges only for big things." Rovelli, quoted in Tim Folger, "Newsflash: Time May Not Exist," *Discover Magazine*, June 12, 2007, http://discovermagazine.com/2007/jun/in-no-time.

25. I skip over Albert Einstein (1879–1955) and many twentieth-century physicists here in order to deal with them more closely in a future work on the science of motion, *Theory of the Object*. However, it should be noted that Einstein's theory of time marks a kinetic break with Newton's idea of an absolute time, produced by the force of god. Einstein instead proposes an elastic theory of time in his theories of special and general relativity. In Chapter 17 of *Relativity* (1916), Einstein describes space-time as a four-dimensional manifold capable of bending, curving, and folding in Minkowski space. The recently discovered gravitational waves (2016) are clear proof of the elasticity of space time folding and waves. However, Einstein did not think that time was ontologically primary, because (a) it is entirely continuous with space, and (b) the elasticity of time seems to be produced by the movement of more primary fields composed of energy and momentum, according to Einstein's field equations. I therefore do not treat Einstein in this chapter on the ontological primacy of time, since Einstein and most physicists of his time remained committed to a static universe for most of the twentieth century. General relativity still relies on the fundamentality of time. But Quantum Gravity models like Carlo Rovelli's are conceptually and mathematically well defined by Wheeler-Dewitt equations without the use of presupposed background space-time. Einstein's general theory of relativity should thus be updated by quantum field theory and matter given back its motion, contra Einstein's claim that "matter may be looked upon as being permanently at rest." Albert Einstein, *Cosmological Considerations on the General Theory of Relativity* (Methuen, 1916), https://www.marxists.org/reference/archive/einstein/works/1910s/relative/relativity.pdf. See also Daryl Janzen, "Einstein's Cosmological Considerations" (2014), https://arxiv.org/pdf/1402.3212.pdf.

CHAPTER 34

1. "That which Husserl still calls time-consciousness, i.e. consciousness of time, is precisely time itself, in the primordial sense." Martin Heidegger, *The Metaphysical Foundations of Logic* (Bloomington: Indiana University Press, 1992), 204.
2. Martin Heidegger, *Being and Time*, translated by John Macquarrie (New York: Harper, 1962), 377.
3. Heidegger, *Being and Time*, 401.
4. Martin Heidegger, *History of the Concept of Time: Prolegomena* (Bloomington: Indiana University Press, 2010), 319.
5. Heidegger, *Being and Time*, 378.
6. Heidegger, *Being and Time*, 378.

7. Heidegger, *Being and Time*, 423.
8. Heidegger, *Being and Time*, 426.
9. Heidegger, *Being and Time*, 427.
10. Heidegger, *Being and Time*, 476.
11. Heidegger, *Being and Time*, 487.
12. Martin Heidegger, *On Time and Being*, translated by Joan Stambaugh (New York: Harper & Row, 1972), 2.
13. Heidegger, *On Time and Being*, 3.
14. Heidegger, *On Time and Being*, 3.
15. Heidegger, *On Time and Being*, 13.
16. Heidegger, *On Time and Being*, 15.
17. Heidegger, *On Time and Being*, 16.
18. Heidegger, *On Time and Being*, 16.
19. Heidegger, *On Time and Being*, 18.
20. Heidegger, *On Time and Being*, 19.
21. Heidegger, *On Time and Being*, 20.
22. Heidegger, *On Time and Being*, 24.
23. "This oscillation of needing and belonging constitutes beyng as event, and our thinking is in the first place obliged to raise the movement of this oscillation into the simplicity of knowledge and to ground it in its truth." Martin Heidegger, *Contributions to Philosophy (of the Event)*, translated by Richard Rojcewicz and Daniela Vallega-Neu (Bloomington: Indiana University Press, 2012), 198. "The clearing for concealment is already the movement of the oscillation in the turning of the event," 277.
24. Peter Sloterdijk, "Nearness and Da-Sein: the Spatiality of Being and Time," *Theory Culture and Society* 29 (2012): 36–42, 27.
25. Heidegger, *On Time and Being*, 14.
26. Emmanuel Levinas (1906–1995) is not included in this chapter because although his early work up to his 1947 lecture series *Time and the Other* remains definitively in the tradition of ontochronology, he quickly abandons this position in the 1950s under the influence, he says, of Franz Rosenzweig's Jewish eschatological philosophy. Afterward, the Other transcends all temporality. The ethical, not ontological, call of the Other precedes being and time entirely. In *Otherwise Than Being* (1974), temporality becomes something illusory to be overcome by and through the atemporal transcendence of the Other. In other words, the temporality of the Other becomes a "diachronic" or split time between the *timeless* ethical demand of the Other and the lived temporality or instant to be overcome by the ethical response. In this sense, atemporal transcendence becomes more primary than any temporal or ontological structure. Levinas thus begins his early career privileging being and time but quickly returns to the theological primacy of a transcendent atemporal and immobile eternity—kinomenologically similar to the ancient theory of diachronic time of atemporal eternity and temporal finitude: atemporal Other and temporal other, diachrony. For a full defense of this interpretation of Levinas's theory of time, see Eric Severson, *Levinas's Philosophy of Time: Gift, Responsibility, Diachrony, Hope* (Pittsburgh, PA: Duquesne University Press, 2013). Leaving aside the relationship between Levinas's earlier pre-ethical and later ethical writings, it is certainly worth considering the influence of Levinas's early *Existence and Existents* on Derrida's notion of interval; in this earlier work, Levinas speaks at length about a

constitutive halt, or pause; indeed, in Derrida's own early review of this work, he describes Levinas as an atomist in this regard.
27. Gilles Deleuze (1925–1995) is also not included in this chapter because, although he has an interesting theory of time, his work has already been discussed in Chapter 3. Jean-Paul Sartre and Maurice Merleau-Ponty are also not discussed in this chapter, due to space concerns and because their theories of time are so similar, although not identical, to Heidegger's.
28. Left out of this account is also the structuralism of Jacques Lacan and others working at the intersection of psychoanalysis and phenomenology. This is because structuralism only relies on the ontological primacy of temporal difference in a cryptic or implicit way in the "logical" division between the real, imaginary, and symbolic. But this division is modeled on the temporal one developed by the phenomenologists already covered in this chapter. This onto-chronolocial structure is most clear in Lacan's essay "Logical Time and the Assertion of Anticipated Certainty: A New Sophism" (1945), where he argues that the temporality of psychoanalytic practice or logic "provides the logical form of all 'human' assimilation," or subjectivity. This structure moves from the Real [the instant of the look], to the Imaginary [the time for understanding] to the Symbolic [the moment to conclude]. The structure of structures is therefore fundamentally temporal, even if it is split between three separate kinds of temporality. Especially interesting in this essay is Lacan's use of movement and act required to produce the temporal division. Jacques Lacan, *Ecrits: The First Complete Edition in English*, translated and edited by Héloïse Fink and Bruce Fink (New York: W. W. Norton, 2006).
29. See Maurice Merleau-Ponty, *The Visible and the Invisible: Followed by Working Notes*, translated by Claude Lefort (Evanston, IL: Northwestern University Press, 1968), 184, 194, 200, 208, 231, 244, 267.
30. Jacques Derrida, *Speech and Phenomena: And Other Essays on Husserl's Theory of Signs*, translated by David B. Allison (Evanston, IL: Northwestern University Press, 1973), 68.
31. Derrida, *Speech and Phenomena*, 84.
32. Derrida, *Speech and Phenomena*, 85.
33. Derrida, *Speech and Phenomena*, 86.
34. Derrida, *Speech and Phenomena*, 88.
35. Derrida, *Speech and Phenomena*, 143.
36. Derrida, *Speech and Phenomena*, 86.
37. Jacques Derrida, *Margins of Philosophy*, translated by Alan Bass (Chicago: University of Chicago Press, 1982), 13. Translation modified.
38. "Time already begins to appear as that which undoes this distinction between taking and giving, therefore also between receiving and giving, perhaps between receptivity and activity, or even between the being-affected and the affecting of any affection." Jacques Derrida, *Given Time: I* (Chicago: University of Chicago Press, 1992), 3.
39. Derrida, *Given Time: I*, 9.
40. Derrida, *Given Time: I*, 14.
41. Derrida, *Given Time: I*, 19.
42. Jacques Derrida, *Limited Inc.*, (Evanston, IL: Northwestern University Press, 1988), 145.
43. Derrida, *Given Time: I*, 28.
44. Derrida, *Given Time: I*, 34.

45. Derrida, *Given Time: I*, 38. Italics added.
46. Derrida, *Given Time: I*, 40.
47. Derrida, *Given Time: I*, 41.
48. Deleuze encounters the same problematic in *Difference and Repetition* when he describes the third synthesis of time as "necessarily static, since time is no longer subordinated to movement; time is the most radical form of change, but the form of change does not change" (89). His concept of difference is thus modeled on the concept of time. But at the same time relies on the concept of a "true" or "real movement" (10) by which time is given "the infinity of real movement and the form of the absolute difference given in the repetition of eternal return" (9).
49. Derrida, *Given Time: I*, 41.

CHAPTER 35

1. In 1714 Henry Mill, an engineer with the New River Water Co. in London, received his inconsequential British patent (no. 395) "for 'a machine or artificial method, to print letters continuously one after another while writing, in a fashion so clean and precise that they are indistinguishable from the printing of letters.'" Cited in Friedrich Kittler, *Gramophone, Film, Typewriter* (Stanford, CA: Stanford University Press, 1999), 187.
2. See image here: http://maritime.org/doc/typewriter/part2.htm.
3. Adler, *The Writing Machine*, Chapter 2.
4. For all the above, see Mergenthaler Linotype Co., *Linotype Machine Principles* (Brooklyn, NY: Mergenthaler Linotype Co., 1940).
5. See Karl Marx and Friedrich Engels, *Manifesto of the Communist Party*, in *The Marx-Engels Reader*, edited by Robert Tucker (New York: Norton, 1978), 474.
6. James C. Maxwell, *A Dynamical Theory of the Electromagnetic Field* (Edinburgh: Scottish Academic Press, 1982).
7. Giuliano Pancaldi, *Volta: Science and Culture in the Age of Enlightenment* (Princeton, NJ: Princeton University Press, 2003).
8. Samuel Thomas von Sömmering's "Space Multiplexed" Electrochemical Telegraph (1808–1810). See image here: http://people.seas.harvard.edu/~jones/cscie129/images/history/von_Soem.html.
9. The mathematical formalization of the binographic process was put forward by George Boole in his books *The Mathematical Analysis of Logic* (1847) and *An Investigation of the Laws of Thought* (1854). Boolean algebra demonstrated for the first time that not only communication, but all logical and graphic processes, could be reduced to a single and fundamental quantitative difference between one and zero.
10. Kittler, *Gramophone, Film, Typewriter*, 188.
11. Martin Heidegger, *Parmenides (1942–43)*, translated by Andre Schuwer and Richard Rojcewicz (Bloomington: Indiana University Press, 1992), 80–81, 85–86.
12. Theodor W. Adorno, "Words without Songs," translated from the German by Marc Hiatt from *Collected in Gesammelte Schriften*, Volume 20.2 (Frankfurt, 2003), http://takingnotenow.blogspot.com/2008/01/adorno-and-nietzsche-on-thinking-with.html.
13. Friedrich Nietzsche, on February 16, 1882. Nietzsche Typescript, written on his writing ball: A Poem. Copyright: The Goethe and Schiller Archive, Weimar, Germany, http://www.malling-hansen.org/friedrich-nietzsche-and-his-typewriter-a-malling-hansen-writing-ball.html.

14. Quoted in Kittler, *Gramophone, Film, Typewriter*, xxix.
15. Quoted in Kittler, *Gramophone, Film, Typewriter*, 222.
16. "T. S. Eliot, who will be 'composing' *The Waste Land* 'on the type writer,' finds (no different from Nietzsche) 'that I am sloughing off all my long sentences which I used to dote upon. Short, staccato, like modern French prose.' Instead of 'subtlety,' 'the typewriter makes for lucidity,' which is, however, nothing but the effect of its technology on style." Quoted in Kittler, *Gramophone, Film, Typewriter*, 229.
17. "I, personally," Benn says about *Problems of Poetry (Probleme der Lyrik)*, "do not consider the modern poem suitable for public reading, neither in the interest of the poem nor in the interest of the listener. The poem impresses itself better when read.... In my judgment, its visual appearance reinforces its reception. A modern poem demands to be printed on paper and demands to be read, demands the black letter; *it becomes more plastic by viewing its external structure.*" Quoted in Kittler, *Gramophone, Film, Typewriter*, 228. Italics added.
18. Maurice Merleau-Ponty, *Phenomenology of Perception*, translated by Colin Smith (London: Routledge, 1962), 145.
19. "Heidegger points out that the work of thinking is a handiwork, a Handlung, an 'action,' prior to any opposition between practice and theory. Thought, in this sense, would be a Handlung, a 'maneuver,' a 'manner,' if not a manipulation. But is that a reason for protesting against the machine? Having recourse to the typewriter or computer doesn't bypass the hand. It engages another hand, another 'command,' so to speak, another induction, another injunction from body to hand and from hand to writing. But it's never at any moment, at least for the time being, a matter of handless writing, writing while keeping your hands in your pockets. Far from it. Handless writing is perhaps what we are doing now as we record our voices." Jacques Derrida, *Paper Machine*, translated by Rachel Bowlby (Stanford, CA: Stanford University Press, 2005), 21.
20. Jacques Derrida, *Without Alibi*, translated by Peggy Kamuf (Stanford, CA: Stanford University Press, 2002), 122.
21. Émile Borel, "Mécanique Statistique et Irréversibilité." *Journal de Physique*, 5e série, 3 (1913): 189–196. and Emile Borel, *La Hasard* (Paris: F. Alcan, 1914).
22. Arthur Eddington, *The Nature of the Physical World: The Gifford Lectures* (New York: Macmillan 1928), 72.

CHAPTER 36

1. For a detailed explanation of and contrast with classical mechanics of the transitory, see Richard P. Feynman, *The Feynman Lectures on Physics* (Reading, MA: Addison-Wesley, 1963), Volume III, Chapters 13–14.
2. Derrida, *Paper Machine*, 23.
3. Derrida, *Paper Machine*, 27.

INDEX

Tables and figures are indicated by an italic *t* and *f* following the page number

Abram, David, 548n17
absolute center, 240, 240t, 266
absolute flow of time, 472–474, 478
absolute temporal immanence, 476
absolute time, 451–454, 460, 480, 578n16
abstract meaning, 296–298, 300–301, 304–310, 550n9
abstract temporality, 431, 454–455
accelerationist cosmology, 428
accountants and accounting, 289–292, 559n10
Acteal massacre (December 22, 1997), 154
Adey, Peter, 531n12
Adorno, Theodor W., 504
aesthetic field of circulation, 136–137
the aether
 in ancient vs. medieval world, 332–333, 562–563n4
 in ancient world, 556n32
 scientific and theological concepts of, 562n1
 theory of, 336–342, 564n17, 564n22, 564–565n33
affect, 106–117
 in art, 29–30
 in global justice groups, 150
 kinomena and, 138–139
 knots and, 146
 in mobilities philosophies, 531n9
 things and, 91, 110–111
 in *The Waves*, 136–138
affectivity, 437
agent intellect, 420

agriculture and graphic signs, 187, 195, 287, 289
Alan of Lille, 413
Albert of Saxony, 347
Albert the Great, 412
d'Alembert, Jean-Baptiste le Rond, 372
algae flows, 89–90, 130
alphabet, 300–312
 phonetic, 300–306
alter-globalization movement, 95, 150
Ambrose of Milan, 398, 400
Anaxagoras, 272
Anaximander, 268–270, 555n14
ancient cosmology, 33–34, 239–251
 Aristotle, 280–282 (*see also* Aristotle)
 Atum (Egyptian sun god), 241–243, 245–248
 concentricity in, 235
 deification of the king, 240, 240t, 248–251
 Dumuzi-Tammuz (Akkadian/Sumerian god-king), 240t, 241, 248–251, 293, 555n11
 Enlil (Sumerian god) (*see* Enlil)
 Greek philosophers, 268–275, 306–309 (*see also* Greeks and Greek philosophers)
 Plato, 276–280 (*see also* Plato)
 separation of heaven and earth, 241–242
 theomachy, 252–261 (*see also* theomachy)
 Yahweh (Hebrew god), 262–264
 Zeus (Greek god), 255–256, 260–261, 551n30

angels, 350
animal and vegetable motions, 195, 220, 287. *See also* nature; the plant (example 1)
anonymous subject of inscription, 502–508
anthropocentric subjectivity, 437
antinomy of interrelational motion, 342
Apian, Peter: *Cosmographia*, 335
apostles of Christ, 376
Apsû (Babylonian primordial father), 252–254, 257–259, 263
Aquinas, Thomas, 359, 413, 575n13
  on agent intellect, 420
  demise of divine illumination and rise of natural illumination and, 419–420
  Summa contra Gentiles, 359
Argonautica Orphica, 551–552n34
Arian controversy, 377
Arios Didymos, 562–563n4
Aristophanes: *The Birds*, 551n33
Aristotle
  aether and, 334, 336, 562–563n4
  on circles, 558n25
  compared to Descartes, 361
  compared to Philoponus, 344–345, 356
  on God as totality, 270–271
  internalized motion and, 358
  on matter, 59, 537n31
  on metaphor, 165
  on motion, 40, 558nn18
  on movement of eternity, 279–281
  on natural motions, 359, 362, 369
  on number of motion (*numerum motus*), 452
  on quality, 111
  rationalism of, 397
  stasis and, 334
  theory of relation, 323
  Trinity as anti-Aristotelean proposition, 376–377, 379
  unmoved mover and, 558n23
Arnold of Bonneval, 413
Asclepius, 574n22
astronomical clocks, 450
astronomy, 334–335, 338, 353
Athanasius, Bishop, 377

atomism, 40–42, 46, 533n45, 556–557n1
attractor vs. identity, 101–102
Atum (Egyptian sun god), 241–243, 245–248
audiograms, 216, 219
Augé, Marc, 38
Augustine of Hippo
  on book's invention, 415
  on comprehension and reading, 402, 413, 416
  Confessions, 447
  illumination, doctrine of, 403
  Scriptural Word and, 398
  on tension between God and the mind, 447
  theory of time in relation to God's eternity, 447, 457
  Trinity and, 379–380
Auriol, Peter, 450
autonomy
  lectio divina and, 399
  in Zapatismo, 93–95
Averroes, 346, 353
Avicenna, 346, 565n8

Babylonian cosmology, 252–254
Bachelard, Gaston, 194
Bacon, Francis, 337, 352, 421, 445, 566n21
  Buridan and, 352
  Specimen of Animated Astronomy, 337
bacterial flows, 89–90, 109, 130
Badiou, Alain, 53
Barad, Karen, 527n27, 535nn16–17, 536n27, 538n19, 540n16
Baring, Anne, 551n28, 553n15, 554n1
Barrow, Isaac, 454, 578n17
Basil of Caesarea, 377, 380
Basil the Great, 397
Bataille, Georges, 245, 544n9
Baudelaire, Charles, 106, 542n1
Bauman, Zygmunt, 38, 525n2
becoming. *See* process ontology and becoming
Behemoth, 264, 267, 555n10
being and eternity (ancient period, 5,000 bce-500 ce). *See also* eternity
  ancient cosmology, 239–282
  being as space vs., 552n1

centrifugal motion, 227–236
writing, 227–228, 285–312
being and force (medieval period, 500 ce–1700 ce). *See also* force
the book, 389–422
tensional motion, 317–327
theology, 331–386
being and space (Neolithic period, 10, 000 bce–5, 000 bce). *See also* space
centripetal motion, 175–183
prehistoric mythology, 187–203
speech, 207–222
being and time (modern period, 1800 ce–2000 ce). *See also* Heidegger, Martin; Husserl, Edmund; Kant, Immanuel; time
elastic motion, 427–440
keyboard, 493–515
modern phenomenology, 443–490 (*see also* modern phenomenology)
being as force (medieval period, 500 ce–1700 ce). *See* force
being as space (Neolithic period, 10, 000 bce–5, 000 bce). *See also* space
being as eternity vs., 552n1
centripetal motion, 175–183
opposition, 235
prehistoric mythology, 187–203
speech, 207–222
being as time (modern period, 1800 ce–2000 ce). *See* time
being in motion, 15–17, 32–35, 158. *See also* field; flow; fold
constitution of, 19, 50, 67
continuous vs. discrete, 178–179, 540n26
historical determinations of, 161
infinite, 77–79
Marx on, 41
mixological areas for future study, 522
mixological limitations to study, 521
ontological description as aspect of, 21–23
in process materialism, 58–62
transcendental realism describing, 52–57
"being qua being," 444
absolute and immutable, 18, 23
historical names of, 32–35

in metaphysics and constructivism, 54
in ontological texts, 163
as traditional definition of ontology, 5, 14, 22–25, 162
Benedictine rules governing monastery life, 401–402
Benedict of Nursia, 401–402
Bennett's linkage, 561–562n3
Bergson, Henri, 582n1
on discrete objects, 70
on intensive and extensive movement, 71
Matter and Memory, 43
La Pensée et le mouvant (Thought and Mobility), 43
as philosopher of motion, 42–43, 529n4, 534n70
on space, 178
on space and eternity, 178, 317
Berkeley, George, 371–372, 445, 457
De Motu, 371
Bernard of Clairvaux, 412
Bernard Stiegler, 529n6
bibliography, 166, 389, 406
bifurcation, 84–85, 84f, 89–90, 140–141, 176, 541n29
astrophysics and, 541n29
in being of Hebrew cosmology, 266
circulatory accumulation and, 176
events and, 89–91
limit junctions and, 140–141
opposition and, 235–236
of phonographic circulation, 308
the Big Bang, 83, 541n29
"Big Bounce" theory, 78
binary division, 495
binary modulation, 509–515
binding
manuscript, 290–393
printed books, 406–407
binographic elasticity, 494–496
bioelectricity, 502
biological life's history in evolution and DNA patterns, 520
biological sciences, 60, 88–91, 110, 130, 135
bipedalism, 208–209, 213, 216
birds and bird mythograms, 196–200, 197f, 245, 551n33

Index [591]

birth and death, 189, 191, 198, 228, 249–250, 258
Black English, 215
Bodin, Jean, 562n5
the body, 166–167, 179–180, 182, 546n7
   female/spatial, 189–196
   the house and, 182
   as inscription surface, 166–167, 209–211, 550n4
   as instrument of sonic internalization, 302
   kinography of, 166–167
   in Plato's cosmology, 277–278
   sensation and, 546n7
   space and, 179–180
   speech and, 207–222, 300
   writing and, 307–308
body surface, inscribing, 209–211
Bohr, Niels, 538n19
Boltzmann, Ludwig, 72
Bonaventure, Saint, 396, 413
Book of God and Book of Nature
   printed book, comprehension of, 412–414
   written manuscript, comprehension of, 395–398
books. *See* manuscript; printing press
Boole, George, 587n9
Boolean algebra, 587n9
borders. *See also* limit and nonlimit junctions
   in theory of motion, 141*f*
Borel, Émile, 507
Borges, Jorge Luis, 507
Borromean rings, 432
Boscovich, Roger, 371
"bourgeois migrant workers" (BMWs), 527n24
Boyle, Robert, 567n35
Brahe, Tycho, 335, 338
Brahmanda Purana (Indian myth), 199
Brentano, Franz, 472–473, 582n1, 583n3
Broad, Charlie Dunbar, 582n1
Brownian motion. *See* pedesis
Brück, Christa Anita, 505
building, 182
Buonamici, Francesco: *De Motu*, 360
Bürgi, Jost, 353
Buridan, Jean, 346, 565n8
   Bacon and, 352

   Hobbes and, 364
Butler, Judith, 189, 535nn16–17

Campbell, Joseph, 164, 545n2, 553n15
Canaanite alphabet, 300
capitalism
   circulation of capital, 468–470
   kinetic organization against, 151
   movement and continuity of flow associated with, 581n38
   time and, 528n36
Cappadocian fathers, 377, 380
Carnot, Lazare, 372
Carroll, Sean, 83, 538n13, 540n22, 543n14
Cartesian coordinates, 179–180
Casey, Edward, 547n19
Cashford, Jules, 551n28, 553n15, 554n1
Castells, Manuel, 38
causality, kinetic theory of, 123–124
Cauvin, Jacques, 547–548n2
Cavarero, Adriana, 78
celestial bodies and spatialization, 195, 555nn13–15
cell phones, 4, 6
cells in plants, 135, 140, 143–144, 144*f*
center/periphery division, 240–248, 240*t*, 250, 551nn32–33
Central Independiente de Obreros Agrícolas y Campesinos Histórica, 121
centralization and the center, 229–236
   abstraction of, 281, 297–298
   in Aristotle's cosmology, 281–282
   center/periphery division, 243–244
   in centrifugal regime of ontological description, 240
   as common thread of Greek philosophers, 268
   in *Enuma Elish*, 257, 260
   in Greek cosmology, 268–275, 308
   mutual subordination to abstract meaning, 302–303
   the soul in, 277–278
   tablets and, 297
   tokens and, 288, 293
   token spheres and, 293–294, 297
   written word and, 308–309
   Yahweh and, 266–267
   Zeus and, 260–261

centrifugal fields, 156–157, 156f
centrifugal motion, 227–236, 228
 absolute, 266–267
 aether and, 333, 333
 centralization, 229–236
 eternity as effect of, 233, 308
 in Greek cosmology, 260–261, 268–282
 kinomenology of eternity, 162, 228–236
 in Marduk, 257–261
 pictographs and, 297
 as redistribution, 294
 tension and, 318–319, 430
 theomachy and, 252, 257–261
 in tokens and tally systems, 287–291
 in writing, 298, 305, 308–309
centripetal fields, 156, 156f, 176
centripetal motion, 167, 175–183, 430
 asymmetry in, 267
 description of, 188
 gathering, 180–183
 in Greek cosmology, 255, 260, 275
 of the hand, 208
 in Hebrew cosmology, 267
 internalization, 177–179
 kinomenology of space, 177–183
 in Marduk, 252–253, 257–261
 in Neolithic mythology, 191–194
 place, 179–180
 of sound waves, 209–210
 stasis and, 232–233
 in Sumerian and Egyptian cosmology, 243–244
 tensional motion and, 318
 thought as, 547n12
 in token systems, 287–291
Chandler, Alfred, 581n39
chaos theory, 2, 72
Charleton, Walter, 578n17
Chen, Mel, 536n27, 536n29
chevrons, 196–197, 197f
Chiapas, Mexico, Zapatista rebellion in, 93–95, 125, 148, 154–155
chiasm, 108
chloroplasts, 89–90, 109, 130, 135
Chomsky, Noam, 217
chora
 John of Damascus applying to God, 383
 pores compared to, 115

Christ. *See* Son of God; Trinity, doctrine of
Christianity. *See also* monastery life; Trinity, doctrine of
 chanting of liturgy, 393
 collective personal project of Protestantism, 419
 The ladder of monks, 402
 rise to power of, 331
 sacraments, 400
 scrolls, early Christian use of, 390
 word of God and, 395–396
chronophilia, 427
the circle, 229
 in ancient cosmology, 245–248, 250
 Aristotle on, 558n25
 centralization and, 229–236
 in *Enuma Elish*, 257
 in Hebrew cosmology, 263–266
 in Plato's cosmology, 277
 token spheres and, 293
circuit, 122–124, 122f
circular motion, 465
circulation, 129–144
 aesthetic field of, 136–137
 binary circulation, 496–508
 binary circulation and the typewriter, 496–508
 of capital, 468–470
 centrifugal, 228, 229–230, 235
 centripetal, 177
 in centripetal motion, 177
 conjunction and (*see* conjunction)
 expansion by expulsion, 141–144, 148
 expansion by expulsion in fields of, 141–144, 142f, 148
 field of circulation, 129–130, 130f, 148, 541n8
 incapacity, 131–132
 kinomena, 138–140
 kinosigns and, 214–216
 limit and nonlimit junctions, 140–144, 140f
 multiple circulations of time, 472–478
 mutual subordination to abstract thought, 302, 304
 of nature, 461–468
 ontological practiced distributed by, 160

circulation (Cont.)
    the plant (example 1), 130–131,
        135–136, 143–144
    of the subject, 457–461
    of temporal folds, 459, 460f
    theory of fluxions, 132–135
    in the Venus, 189
    The Waves (Woolf), 136–138
classical physics. *See* physics
clay-token spheres, 287, 291–295, 304
Clemens Alexandrinus, 562–563n4
Clement of Rome, 376
climate change, 1, 6
clockwork universe, 347–348, 350
    conceptual clock of William of
        Ockham, 450–451
    introduction of kinetic automation,
        349–350
    invention of mechanical clock,
        348–349, 566n21
    planetarium clock, 353
    transmission by tension between
        parts, 349
codex. *See* manuscript and codex
collective trajectory, 142, 545n10
communication
    in kinetic theory of speech, 216–217
    in knotworks, 148–151
communism, 581n45
composition of flows, 80–81
comprehension
    the Book of God and the Book of
        Nature, 412–414
    printed book and, 411–412
    written manuscript and, 393–405
computer, 509–515
    binary modulation, 509–515
    computer screen and pixel display, 511
    hard drive, 514
    keyboard, 509–515
    modulated elasticity, 512
    modulated oscillation, 509–511
    modulated subject, 513–515
    touchscreen keyboards, 512
conatus, concept of, 359–371
concentricity, 234–235
conceptual clock, 450
concrete temporality, 431–432
confluence, 86–96, 541n8
    constellation, 91–95, 91f, 95f, 145, 213

event, 87–91
fold vs., 99
the plant (example 1), 88–91
of sound in the body, 216
Zapatismo (example 2), 93–95
Congar, Yves, 571n33
Conimbricenses' *Commentaries*, 361
conjunction, 118–126, 118f
    circuit, 122–124
    circulation distinct from, 129
    constant, 324
    disjunction, 124–126, 142, 208
    entropy, 124–126
    fields of circulation and, 129, 140–141,
        145
    Hume and, 325, 327
    injunction, 121–122, 121f
    kinetic, 327
    sound and gesture, 212–213
    Zapatismo (example 2), 122
consciousness, 55–56, 138, 164, 248,
    285, 437, 475
consensus decision-making, 150
constellation, 91–95, 91f, 95f, 145, 213
constructive unknotting, 153–154
constructivism, 30, 33, 54, 162
continuity of movement, 68–76
    in atomism, 40–41, 69
    bifurcation of, 84
    discontinuity and, 68–69, 85, 116
    fold and, 101
    infinite, 77
    intensive and extensive movement,
        70–71, 84–85
    modern formulation of time and, 430
    pedesis, 72–74
    in quantum fields, 71, 536n21
    Rovelli on, 540n26
    waves, 74–76, 80
Copernicus, 55, 323, 335
cosmology. *See also* ancient cosmology
    contemporary accelerationist
        cosmology, 428
    infinity and, 78
    mythology vs., 239–240
    "oneness" favored in, 298
    origin of space and time in, 83
    "sphere" of being, 163
    writing and, 298, 306–312

Council of Constantinople (381), 377, 380
Councils of Good Government (Juntas de Buen Gobierno), 94
creation myths, 199, 219–220
"Creation of the Pickax" (Sumerian myth), 241
Cronus (Greek Titan), 255, 260
cultural memory, 302
cuneiform, 300, 560nn2–3, 561n4
Cusa, Nicholas of, 351, 367, 384–385
cycle, 99, 101–103, 102f, 109–110, 112–114, 121–122, 250
Cyprian of Carthage, 400, 401

Dainton, Barry, 583n3
Dalcq, Albert, 197
Dante Alighieri, 565–566n14
Darwin, Charles, 211
da Vinci, Leonardo, 352
  Sketches and Notebooks, 351
death and birth, 189, 192, 198, 228, 249–250, 257
deification of the king, 240, 240t, 248–251
Deleuze, Gilles, 586n27
  Difference and Repetition, 587n48
  on the egg, 198
  on linguistics, 217–218
  on motion, 533n46
  on mutual subordination to abstract meaning, 303
  on Nietzsche and philosophy, 535n6
  process ontology and becoming, 44–51, 53, 533n45, 534n55
  on vortices, 541n2
delimitation, 79–80
Democritus, 40, 556n1
Derrida, Jacques, 457, 484–489
  "Différance," 486
  Given Time, 486
  Levinas and, 585–586n26
  on most radical condition of time as difference, 486–487, 586n38
  Speech and Phenomenon, 484
  on temporization vs. temporalization, 487
  on typewriter or computer use, 505, 513–515
Descartes, René
  on absolute time, 452
  breaking with Scholastic definition of eternity, 453
  clockwork universe and, 353
  compared to Aristotle, 361
  compared to Hobbes, 364–365
  compared to Leibniz, 341, 368, 371
  compared to Newton, 453
  compared to Plato, 568n12
  on conatus, 360–364
  first law of nature, 362
  on movement and impetus, 354, 364, 568n18, 578n21
  on natural or intellectual illumination, 421
  Principles of Philosophy, 133, 338, 353, 354, 361, 362, 564n17, 564n22, 566n28, 578nn19–21
  on reason, 445
  Scholasticism and, 361
  Stoics and, 568n18
  "*tendre*" as concept for, 363–364
  theory of force, 363
  Trinity, doctrine of, and, 386, 572n62
  vortex theory of the aether, 338, 340f, 341, 341–342
  The World, 353, 363
The Descent of Inanna to the Nether World (Sumerian myth), 249
description (logos)
  of being as eternity, 239–282
  of being as force, 331–386
  of being as space, 187–203
  of being as time, 443–490
  in historical ontology, 163–168
  kinetic capacities identified by, 146–148, 520
  as material enactment, 60, 62
  metaphor and, 164–165
  mythograms and, 187–188, 550n4
  in ontological practice, 23, 26–28, 31–33, 158
  reductionism and, 25–27
  sounds as, 208–209
  the spiral as, 201–202
  subjectivism and, 22
  as system of kinosigns, 299
  the Venus as, 189, 191–196
destructive unknotting, 153
determinism, 26, 104

Index [595]

Didache, or Teaching of the Twelve Apostles, 377
digital media and images, 3–6, 517
Diogenes Laertius, 268–270
Dirac, Paul, 543n2
Dirac sea, 120, 543n2
disjunction, 124–126, 124f, 142, 208
divine illumination, 403–404, 405f, 419–420. See also *lectio divina*
Dogon cosmic-egg myth, 199, 201f, 220, 549n38
domestication of plants and animals, 193
Dumuzi-Tammuz (Akkadian/Sumerian god-king), 240t, 241, 248–249, 293, 555n11
dunamis kinetike, 344
Duns Scotus, John, 44, 386, 420, 450
dynamic stability. See stability in theory of motion

Ea (Babylonian god), 252–254, 257–261, 263, 298, 312
the ear, 209, 210
early Anthropocene hypothesis, 546n2
Early church fathers, 376, 386, 396–399, 412, 415
early-modern temporality, 445–455. See also medieval period (500 ce–1700 ce)
the earth as living body, 195, 221
Echidna, 256, 261
ecologies, 142, 148
Eddington, Arthur, 507
Edison, Thomas, 501
the egg, 196–200, 200–201f, 201, 209, 212, 220, 549n48, 550–551n23, 551nn32–33
Egypt as source of papyrus, 390–391
Egyptian hieroglyphics, 300, 560n3
Egyptian mythology and cosmology, 199, 239–240, 242–243
Einstein, Albert
 on elastic theory of time, 584n25
 on finite universe, 2, 68, 526n13–14
 kinetic theory of, 72, 109, 125
 on mass and energy, 536n21, 540n14
 Relativity, 584n25
Ejército Zapatista de Liberación Nacional (Zapatista Army of National Liberation), 93, 123–124, 155
elastic fields, 157–158, 158f

elastic line of time, 452, 452f, 458
elastic motion, 427–440
 elasticity, defined, 452
 elasticity of temporal field, 434–435
 elasticity of the field, 434
 elasticity of the flow, 452–455
 elasticity of the fold, 434
 Heidegger's temporal stretching and, 480, 483
 kinomenology of time, 430–440
 seriality, 431–434
 subjectivity, 437–440
elastic spiral, 581n45
elastic theory of time, 584n25
electric elasticity, 500–502
electric subjectivity, 503
Eliade, Mircea, 219
Eliot, T. S., 505
Elohim, 554n1
Empedocles, 273, 275
empiricism, 55–56, 58–59, 81–82
Encuentros, 149–151
energy capture and storage, 143
Enlightenment, 421, 445
Enlil (Sumerian god), 240–241, 240t, 243, 561n13
 in *Enuma Elish*, 258–260
 kinetic analysis, 243
 separation of heaven and earth and, 250, 291
 in Sumerian cosmology, 248
 written word and, 308–310
entropy, 72, 83, 124–126, 428
Enuma Elish (Babylonian epic), 252–254, 257–261, 312
Epicurus, 40–41, 352, 544n6
Ereshkigal (Sumerian goddess), 242, 249
Eriugena, John Scotus, 413, 575n17
Eslick, Leonard J., 532n35, 537n4
essences
 events vs., 94–95
 kinetic relations vs., 138, 208–209
 as kinomena, 232–233
 in linguistics, 218
 of mythological femininity, 189
 quality vs., 111–112, 121
eternity
 Augustine on, 447–449
 being and, 165 (see also being and eternity)

centrifugal motion of the sphere and, 307–308
Descartes breaking with Scholastic definition of eternity, 453
etymological modulation of, 552n1
kinetic operations of description, 240
kinography of, 285–312 (*see also* writing)
kinomenology of, 227–236 (*see also* centrifugal motion)
metaphysics and, 167
in ontological inquiry, 14, 19, 24, 53, 164
ontology of, 239–282 (*see also* ancient cosmology)
Ouroboros and, 247
in philosophy of motion, 160
Plato on, 162, 382
time and, 231
Euclid, 229, 232
Eustachius: *Summa*, 361
event, 47, 53, 87–91, 87f, 101, 109, 110, 534n55
Deleuze and Guattari on, 534n55
as eternal truth, 53
fold vs., 101
matter and, 47
receptivity and redirection, 109–110
sound and gesture, 213–214
stability of, 145
of Zapatismo, 93–94, 94f
evental unknotting, 153
exchange value, 288–289, 294
ex nihilo creation, 240, 240t, 262–275
expansion by expulsion in fields of circulation, 141–144, 142f, 148
expansion of the universe, 2, 50, 68, 526nn13–14, 539n4
expansive unknotting, 153
explosion (matter in motion), 428
externalized motion, 320, 344–357
the eye, 307–308

Fabri, Honoré: *De Motu*, 360
Fang creation myth, 199
Fantoni, Carolina, 496
the feminine
  in Marduk, 258
  in prehistoric mythology, 188–196, 201

field, 31, 129–158, 518, 534n70, 537nn1–2
the body as, 212
features of (*see* circulation; knot)
flows constituting, 129–130
folds within, 129–135
historical typology of, 155–158
the transcendental and, 55
flow, 31, 67–95, 430, 534n70, 537nn1–2
absolute flow of time, 472–474, 477
conjunction and, 121
Deleuze on, 46
elasticity of the flow, 452–455
features of (*see* confluence; continuity of movement; multiplicity)
fields of circulation and, 129–130, 143, 318
fold and, 99–105, 324, 541n1
limit junctions and, 140–141
of the line, 467
Lucretius on, 40
material flow, 358
from ontology of becoming, 50
pores and, 114–117
in prehistoric mythograms, 189, 197–198
in quantum fields, 536n21, 540n14
in speech, 212–218
of time, 458
the transcendental and, 55
flux. *See* flow
fluxions, 132–135, 134f
fold, 31, 97–126, 534n70, 537nn1–2
in centrifugal motion, 228–235
circulation of temporal folds, 459, 460f
confluence vs., 99
continuity of movement and, 101, 385
delimitation and composition, 80
event developed by, 88, 91
extensive movement as, 71
features of (*see* conjunction; junction; sensation)
within fields of circulation, 129–135
flow and, 99–105, 430, 541n1
junction and, 100f
kinomena and, 138–140
kinosigns and, 213–214
matter and, 58, 324
numerical multiplication of temporal folds, 450–451, 451f

fold (Cont.)
  parchment as writing material, 391
  in quantum fields, 536n21, 540n14
  reading printed books and, 419
  seriality and, 431–434
  space from, 178–179
  subjectivity and, 436
  tensional fold of time, 449, 449f
  of time, 432–433, 433f
  the transcendental and, 55
  in *The Waves*, 136–138
folded unity of triangulation, 322
folios
  manuscript, 391
  printed books, 406
force
  Bergson and, 43
  conceptual vocabulary describing kinds of, 562n2
  decline of, 371–372, 427
  Deleuze on, 45, 533n45
  describable by motion, 32–35, 545n9
  force of law, 320
  Hume and, 325–327
  inscription (the book) as technology in medieval period, 318
  interrelation of motion (*see* interrelation of motion)
  kinography of, 317, 389–422 (*see also* manuscript; printing press)
  kinomenology of, 317–327 (*see also* tensional motion)
  linking flows of force, 322
  mechanism, concept of, 333
  in medieval world, 317
  in ontological inquiry, 14, 19, 24, 53, 165
  ontology of, 331–386
  in philosophy of motion, 160
  process ontology on, 44–51
  relation and, 323–327
  as temporal sequence, 371
  tensional motion as kinetic component of, 318–320
  theological writings of medieval period on descriptive features of, 317 (*see also* theology, medieval)
  triangulation, 321–323, 322f
  vital materialism and, 60
foreclosures on homes, 525n2
Foucault, Michel

Archaeology of Knowledge, 546n9
  on ontology, 529n7
  rules of discourse formation, 531n7
Frello, Birgitta, 531n7
Frisius, Gemma: *Libellus de Locorum describendorum ratione*, 335
Froissart, Jean, 565–566n14
functional cycle, 437, 438f
the future, 18–20, 24, 32, 50, 427
future study, areas for, 522–523

Gaia (Greek god), 255–256, 260
Galeano, Subcomandante, 122
Galen, 363
Galileo, 336
Galvani, Luigi, 503
Gamble, Chris, 561n5
Gassendi, Pierre, 454, 578n17
gathering, 180–183
Gauss, Carl Friedrich, 501
geometric shapes, 580n22
gesture, 208–221, 301, 305
Ghent, Henry of, 386, 420, 588n38
Gide, André, 103
  Le Traité Du Narcisse, 542n11
Gimbutas, Marija, 188, 189, 190f, 198, 548n11, 549n48
global solidarity, 149–150
God. *See also* Trinity, doctrine of
  aether and, 333
  as the clockmaker, 351, 356, 565–566n14
  creation by, 346–347, 352, 447–448
  Cusa on, 351
  Descartes on, 354, 361
  dictation from, 393, 395
  eternal nature of, 447
  externalized motion and, 343, 346
  as first efficient cause of motion, 361
  force or tension required for, 318–319
  internalized motion and, 358
  kinetic tension between God and the mind, 447–448
  mechanism and force and, 333
  motion or force transferred by, 358, 578n19
  nature and it own motions and, 346
  phenomenology's break from presupposition of eternal or absolute God, 444

Spinoza on, 367
theological postulate of, 333
unity of God as fold, 381
Word of God, 331, 406, 408
God as totality, 270. *See also specific gods*
"God particle," 81, 352
Graeber, David, 150
grammars from kinosigns, 214–215
graphic inscription. *See* inscription
graphism, 26–30, 208, 292–297, 301–310
graphos, 165–167. *See also* inscription
grave mounds, 192
gravity, 2, 17, 341, 356
 quantum physics, 2, 50, 83–84, 532n32, 584n25
Gray, John, 553n16
the Great Mother, 189, 191, 194, 553n17
Greeks and Greek philosophers, 268–275, 308, 395
 aether of, 375
 on boundary, 181
 cosmology in writings of, 240, 390
 Orphic mythology, 199, 200f
 punctuation, use of, 390
 scriptography of, 394
Gregory of Nazianzus, 377, 377–378, 382
Gregory of Nyssa, 377, 379
Griaule, Marcel, 549n38, 550–551n23
 The Pale Fox, 199
Guattari, Félix, 46–50, 198, 217–218, 303, 533n46, 534n55, 541n2
Guigo II (Carthusian monk), 402
Gutenberg printing press, 407–408, 411, 494

habit, 438
Haggett, Peter, 542n6
Hallward, Peter, 534n61
the hand, gesture and graphism of, 208, 211, 303, 409, 411, 505–506, 507, 561n7, 561n9
Hardt, Michael, 534n66
Harman, Graham, 536n18
hate, movement of, 275
Hebrew Bible, 263–265. *See also* Scriptures
Hebrew cosmology, 262–265
Hegel, Georg W. F.
 on circular motion, 266
 on dialectic as "movement," 165
 on eternity, 231–233
 on historical being, 548n10
 Jena Lectures on the Philosophy of Nature, 462
 Marx influenced by, 41–42, 50, 535n72
 on motion and matter, 537n31
 on the nation-state, 17
 on ontologization of time and subjectivity, 461–468, 580n27, 580n30, 582n1
 Philosophy of Nature, 461–462
 space in, 177
Heidegger, Martin
 Being and Time, 53, 480–481
 Contributions, 483, 585n23
 on Kant's theory of time, 579n10
 on motion, 17
 on space and things, 181–182, 462
 on subjective experience as "ecstatic," 444
 on temporalization process, 457, 479–484
 "Time and Being" essay, 486
 on typewriter use, 504, 505, 588n19
Heisenberg, Werner, 72–73, 538n19
heliocentrism, 335, 335
Heraclitus, 102
Herder, Johann Gottfried, 211
Hertz, Heinrich Rudolf, 372
Hesiod, 221, 260–261, 270, 270
 Theogony, 255, 551n31
hieroglyphics, 300, 560n3
Higgs field, 81
Hildegard of Bingen, 412
Hippolytus, 273, 379
historical materialism, 60–61. *See also* process materialism
historical method, 16–20
 the future, 18
 the past, 17–18
 the present, 16–17
historical ontology, 13–20, 33–34, 34t, 53
 future study, 522
 limitations of study, 519
 methodology of, 160–161
 mobility of, 53
 ontological history, 21–35
 of ontology, 23–25
 for twenty-first century, 517

Index [599]

historical realism, 162
historical typology of fields, 155–158
history
  motion of, 28–29, 162, 162
  from perspective of motion, 529n5
  in process ontology and becoming, 47–49
  in transcendental realism, 55
Hobbes, Thomas, 340
  on absolute time, 578n17
  compared to Descartes, 364–365
  compared to Leibniz, 369, 371
  on conatus, 364–365
  Trinity, doctrine of, and, 386, 572n61
Holladay, Carl, 551n32
Holy Spirit, 323, 375–376, 402, 569n5. *See also* Trinity doctrine of
Homer, 221, 233, 256, 260, 270, 270
  Iliad, 551n30
Honorius Augustodunensis, 414, 575n17
horarium's function, 348
Horeb, 554n1
horizontality in ontology, 78, 244
horizontal (nonhierarchical) organization, 150–151
the house, 182, 193–194
Hubble, Edwin, 50, 68, 526n13
Hugh of St. Victor, 414, 575–576n20
humanities and social sciences, 38–39
human/nature divide, 26, 162, 208, 210–211, 354, 420, 462–463, 520
Hume, David, 325–327, 371–372, 445, 457, 472
Husserl, Edmund, 457, 472–478, 489, 583n3
  Lectures on the Consciousness of Internal Time, 447, 473
  Phenomenology of Internal Time-Consciousness, 484
  temporal circulations in the elastic stream, 474, 474f, 484
  temporal fold, 474, 474f
  time-consciousness of, 584n1
Hyppolite, Jean, 177

idealism
  contemplative materialism as, 60
  in Deleuze, 47, 534n61, 534nn65–66
  in history of writing, 285
  infinity and, 539n8

in linguistic theory, 211
metaphor and, 165–166
reductionism and, 25
space and, 177–178
transcendental, 55
identity
  in period and cycle, 101–103, 111, 112
  from phonism and graphism, 303, 305
Ignatius of Antioch, 376
illumination, doctrine of, 404, 405f
images, 3–5
  aesthetic practice and, 28–29
  as conjoined things, 118, 119f
  of Hebrew God, 312
  from musical pitch, 550n9
  as mythograms, 187
  in Neolithic mythology, 189–196
  of ontological division, 248
  on token spheres, 293–294
  written words as, 307–308
immobility of the center, 240, 240t, 248–249, 279, 280, 294, 308
immortality. *See* eternity
impetus theory, 344–347, 351, 565n1
  Kepler and, 353
  kinetic analysis, 348–349
Inanna/(Sumerian goddess), 248–249, 259, 263, 293
incapacity, 131–132
indeterminacy in quantum systems, 73–74, 538n19
infinity, 77–79, 118, 132, 458, 539n8, 539n11, 544n1
information vs. communication, 216
Ingold, Tim, 180, 544n1, 546n8
injunction, 121–122, 121f
ink, 411
Innis, Harold, 305–306
inscription (graphos). *See also* manuscript and codex; printing press and printed books; typography
  of being as eternity, 285–312
  of being as force, 389–422
  of being as space, 207–222
  of being as time, 493–515
  in historical ontology, 162–168
  of numbers and pictographs, 308
  in ontological practice, 25, 27–28, 30–31

in process materialism, 60
reductionism and, 25
rhythms as, 208–209
of sound in the body, 208–211, 240
thought limited by, 47
written, 240
instrumentalism, 26
intensive and extensive movement, 70–71, 84–85
intentionality, theory of, 472, 475
Intercontinental *Encuentros* for Humanity against Neoliberalism (*Encuentros*), 149–150
internalization
centrifugal motion and, 228, 229
centripetal motion and, 177–182
in Marduk, 258
in prehistoric mythology, 189, 194, 196, 198, 198
sonic, 302
internalized motion, 320, 358–372
Aristotle and, 358
decline of force and, 371–372
defined, 358
Internet, 527n20
interrelation of motion, 320, 333–342
the aether, 333–342
antinomy of, 342
astronomy, 334–335
triangulation, 335–336
interval of time, 484–489
kinetic analysis, 488–489
Isaac of Syria, 416
Ishtar (Akkadian goddess), 248–250, 263, 265

James, William, 582n1, 583n3
Jerome, Saint, 400
Jesus Christ. *See* Son of God; Trinity, doctrine of
John of Damascus, 382, 383
Exposition of the Orthodox Faith, 383–384
junction, 99–105, 541n3
cycle, 99, 101–103, 102*f*, 109–110, 112–114, 121–122, 250
existence, 103–104
fold and, 100*f*
limit and nonlimit junctions, 140–144, 140*f*

megajunction, 229
necessity, 104–105, 110, 121
period, 100–104
pores and, 114
Yahweh as, 266–267
Jung, Carl, 248
Juntas de Buen Gobierno (Councils of Good Government), 94
Justin Martyr, 376

Kalevala (Finnish epic), 199
Kant, Immanuel
compared to Husserl, 472
The Critique of Pure Reason, 55, 445, 457
on force, 371–372
on motion, 17
space in, 177
on time/temporality of being, 427, 437, 445, 456–461, 503
on the transcendental, 55–57, 334
Thomson, William (Lord Kelvin), 152
Kepler, Johannes, 323, 335–336, 336*f*, 338, 352, 353, 563n11
Astronomia Nova, 335
Mysterium cosmographicum, 353
keyboard, 493–515
binographic elasticity, 494–496
computer, 509–515
typewriter, 493–515
typography, 493–494
kinetic analysis, 14. *See also* ontology of motion
of Sumerian and Egyptian cosmology, 243–248
theory of time, 529n5
kinetic analysis/perspective, 14, 87–89, 92, 110, 521. *See also* ontology of motion
kinetic conjunction, 327
kinetic elasticity, 496
kinetic memory, 505
kinetic philosophy, 161–162, 518, 521. *See also* being in motion; movement of ontology; ontology of motion
Kingu (Babylonian god), 253, 259
kinography (graphos), 27–32, 29*t*, 55, 166, 499, 518. *See also* movement of ontology
of being and space, 187–203
of being as eternity, 285–312

Index [601]

kinography (graphos) (*Cont.*)
   of being as space, 187–203
   as inscription of being, 55
   limitations of study, 520
kinology, 30–31, 101, 161
kinomena, 40, 138–140, 146
kinomenology (kinos), 161–163, 518
   of eternity, 227–228
   of force, 317–327
   fundamental question of, 147
   of space, 176–183, 546n3
   of time, 427–428, 444 (*see also* elastic motion)
kinomorphism, 178
kinosigns, 212–218
Kirchhoff, Gustav, 372
Kittler, Friedrich, 5
knot, 145–158, 146f, 148f, 152f, 544n1, 545n9
   centrifugal fields, 156–157
   constructive unknotting, 153–154
   destructive unknotting, 153
   elastic fields, 157–158
   evental unknotting, 153
   expansive unknotting, 153
   historical typology of fields, 155–158
   kinetic vs. mathematical, 151–152
   knotting, 146–148
   nests, 146
   tensional fields, 157
   unknots, 152–154
   Zapatismo (example 2), 148–151, 154–155
knotting, 146–148
Koyukon of Alaska, 542n4
Kuhn, Thomas, 344

labor
   as material flow, 42
   wage form of value as measure of labor-time, 469
Labov, William, 215, 217
Lacan, Jacques, 586n28
language
   kinetic changes from, 21
   linguistics and, 217–218
   writing and, 301
Laruelle, François, 530n4
Latour, Bruno, 544n1
Law, John, 547n13
laws of nature, 361

lectio divina, 399–402, 401f, 418, 418
kinetic analysis,
Leeming, David, 198
legere in silentio, 414–419
Legionella (bacterial parasite), 109, 140
Leibniz, Gottfried, 341, 368–371, 564n31
   compared to Descartes, 341, 368, 369
   compared to Hobbes, 368–369, 370
   compared to Spinoza, 369, 370
   on conatus, 368–369
   Hypothesis Physicae Nova, 368
   on internalized force, 370
   on reality of force, 370
   on reason, 445
   Specimen Dynamicum, 369
   Trinity, doctrine of, and, 386
   Trinity doctrine and, 572n63
Lenin, Vladimir, 547n12
Lepenski Vir shrines, 198
Lerner, Ben, 505
Leroi-Gourhan, André, 187, 200, 209, 290, 301, 302, 547nn2–3, 548nn6–8, 561n9
Leucippus, 40–41, 556n1
Leviathan, 264, 265
Levinas, Emmanuel, 585n26
limit and nonlimit junctions, 140–144, 140f, 176
linear phonetic alphabet, 300
linguistics, 217–218
linotype press, 494
literacy
   between fifth and fifteenth centuries, 394
   silent reading, 417
literature, 28, 136
Locke, John, 457, 583n3
logos, 163–165
loop quantum gravity, 3, 84
López, José Luis Solís, 121
love, movement of, 274
Lowe, John, 100
Lucretius
   Bergson influenced by, 42
   Deleuze on, 533n45
   Marx influenced by, 41–42
   on nature, 539n7
   as philosopher of motion, 40–41, 43, 529n4, 534n70

on time and space, 82, 83
on turbulence, 72
on void, 543n1

Mach, Ernst, 372
Maffie, James, 536n26
Mallarmé, Stéphane, 541n3
manuscript and codex, 389–405
　binding, 390–393
　the Book of God and the Book of Nature, 395–399
　codex, defined, 390
　coexisting with printed books in medieval and early modern periods, 407
　covering of codex, 392, 573n8
　definitions, 390
　divine illumination, 403, 405*f*
　folios, 391
　interpretation of the book, 394
　kinetic tension of reading, 395
　lectio divina, 399–402, 401*f*
　manuscript codex, 390–393
　manuscript codex vs. printed codex, 389, 573n1
　mobility as feature of, 392
　papyrus, use of, 390, 395
　parchment as writing material, 390–391, 394–395
　printed codex, 389
　punctuation and spacing of words, 392–393
　quires, parchment folded into, 391
　ruled pages controlling where text should appear, 393
　written comprehension, 394–395
Marcos, Subcomandante, 93, 121
Marduk, Babylonian epic of, 241, 240*t*, 252–254, 257–260, 264, 264, 298
Marrone, Steven, 576n38
Mars, orbit of, 335
Marsilius of Inghen, 347
Martial (Roman poet), 390
Martianus Capella, 323
Marx, Karl
　on atoms, 80
　on circulation of capital, 468–470, 580n34
　Deleuze on, 533n45
　on formal movement, 537n32
　on Hegel, 164, 535n72

historical materialism and, 50
on labor and time, 532n19
on materialism, 59, 60
as philosopher of motion, 41–42, 48, 519, 529n4, 534n70
on practice, 19
on presentation and inquiry, 31
Mascara Roja (Red Mask) and the Acteal massacre, 154
mass production, 581n39
material conditions of philosophy, 528n29
material flow, 358
material historicity, 15
materialism
　historical, 61–62
　infinity in, 539n8
　kinetic, 61
　linguistics and, 211
　"negative" or "without matter," 58, 536n18
　process materialism vs., 58 (*see also* process materialism)
　terms for, 536n27
　transcendental, 82
　vital, 60
mathematics, 336, 429, 452–453, 495, 507. *See also* topology
　reversibility of time in, 429
matter. *See also* motion and mobility
　bifurcation and, 541n29
　dimensionality from, 532n32
　ontology of motion and, 41–42
　potential energy and, 543n7
　in process materialism, 57–62
　in process ontology and becoming, 44–51, 534n55
　qualities of, 112
　in quantum fields, 71–72, 536n21, 540n14
　sensation and, 110
　space from, 177, 189
　in transcendental realism, 55–57
Maximus the Confessor, 382
Maxwell, James Clerk, 500
McCabe, Viki, 545n5
McTaggart, J. M. E., 582n1
meaning, phonism and graphism subordinate to, 302–303. *See also* abstract meaning

Index [603]

mechanical clock, invention of, 348–349, 351, 407, 386–388, 566n21
mechanical devices invented in Middle Ages, 407. *See also* printing press and printed books
mechanical elasticity, 498–500
mechanical sphere, cosmos described as, 351
mechanism, concept of, 334
media
  historical, material, and kinetic, 24–25
  the image in, 3–6
  of inscription, 166
medieval period (500 ce–1700 ce), 167–168
  antinomies of externalized motion, 356–357
  bibliographic architecture of, 419
  centrifugal subordination, 376–377
  clockwork universe, 347–348, 350
  compared to ancient period, 321
  conatus, 359–371
  covering Middle Ages, Renaissance, and early modern periods, 317
  decline of force, 371–372
  elasticity of the flow, 451–455
  externalization of motion, 343–344 (*see also* externalized motion)
  folds of force, 380–381
  force or power as primary characteristic of, 317 (*see also* force)
  Holy Spirit, 374–376
  impetus theory, 344–347, 351
  internalization of motion, 358 (*see also* internalized motion)
  interrelation of motion, 332–342
  kinetic analysis, 318, 348–350
  lived time, 447–449
  manuscript, 389–405 (*see also* manuscript)
  perichoresis, 382–384
  printing press, 406–422 (*see also* printing press)
  temporality, 446–455
  tensional equality, 377–380
  theology, 318, 331–386 (*see also* theology, medieval)
  theory of externalized motion, 351–356
  time (*see* time)

triangulation of oneness, 384–386
Trinitarianism (*see* Trinity, doctrine of)
megajunction, 229, 230, 234, 258, 265–266, 302, 304
Menger sponge, 116*f*, 117
Mergenthaler, Ottmar, 499
Merleau-Ponty, Maurice, 179, 211, 484, 505, 586n27
Merriman, Peter, 531n12, 534n53, 545n1
meshwork theory, 544n1
Mesopotamia, 239, 240, 252, 309–310
metaontology, 24
metaphor, 164–165, 488, 552n35
metaphysical substance, 343
metaphysics, 59–61
  alternatives to, 33
  Aztec, 536n26
  of the circle, 229–230
  eternity and, 167, 229
  in linguistics, 217–218
  names of being in, 62
  on ontology, 22–23
  space at heart of, 177
  transcendental realism vs., 54
Mexican government. *See* Zapatismo (example2)
Middle Ages. *See* medieval period (500 ce–1700 ce)
migrants and migration, 1–2, 5, 6, 527n24
  capitalism and, 528n36
  prevalence of, 517, 525–526nn2–6
  Zapatismo and, 125
Mill, Henry, 587n1
mimesis, 211
mind and body dualism, 326
mind and matter dualism, 364
mind in Greek cosmogony (*nous*), 272, 278
mind in kinetic tension with God, 447–449
mitochondria, 132, 140
mobile devices, 4, 6
mobilities paradigm, 37–40, 531n12
modern period (1800 ce–2000 ce)
  elastic motion and, 168 (*see also* elastic motion)
  time as fundamental description of all reality in, 443

[604] *Index*

time concept, different from early
modern theory, 456
modern phenomenology, 33, 443–444,
456–457
  circulation of capital, 468–471
  circulation of nature, 461–468
  circulation of the subject, 457–461
  multiplication/multiple circulations of
  time, 472–478
  process and interval, 479–490
modulated elasticity (computer), 512
modulated oscillation (computer),
509–511
modulated subjectivity (computer), 513–515
Mol, Annemarie, 547n13
monad, 269
monastery life, Benedictine rules
governing, 401–402
monastic timetable, 348
monotheism. *See* God
More, Henry, 578n17
Morse, Samuel, 501
Moryadas, S., 100
Moses, 311, 395
motion and mobility, 1–6. *See also* primacy
of motion; *specific types of motion*
  Anaximander on, 269
  Aristotle on, 280, 558n18
  aspects of (*see* circulation; flow; fold)
  being as, 32–34
  Bergson on, 44
  described by the Venus, 191–192
  dominant patterns in, 430
  externalized motion, 320, 343–357
  (*see also* externalized motion)
  of history, 30
  internalized motion, 320, 358–372
  (*see also* internalized motion)
  interrelational motion, 320
  kinetic interpretation of ontology
  through, 159–168, 318
  in mobilities philosophies, 531n9
  ontological framework for, 13–16,
  54–55, 158
  patterns of motion defining historical
  synchrony, 519
  philosophy of, 36–40
  Plato on, 558n14
  the present and, 16–17, 428
  in process materialism, 57–62

  in process ontology and becoming,
  44–51, 534n53
  in spirals, 200–202
  time and space from, 82–84, 427, 547n25
  transcendental realism
  describing, 52–57
  twenty-first century characterized by,
  517
  Whitehead on, 537n4
  of the written words, 308
  Xenophanes on, 270
the mouth, lips, and tongue, 209, 210,
243, 301
movement of ontology, 29t, 163,
530n14. *See also* kinography
multiplicity, 77–85
  bifurcation, 84–85, 85f, 89, 91,
  140–141, 176, 541n29
  circulations of time, 472–478
  composition, 80–81
  delimitation, 79–80
  infinity, 77–79, 539n8
  pores and, 116
  things and, 119
  time and space, 82–84
  visibility, 81–82
Mumford, Lewis, 192–193, 349
musical pitch, 550n9
mutual global solidarity, 149–151
mutual subordination to abstract
meaning, 301–307, 310
mythograms, 187–188, 287, 548n8
mythology
  cosmology vs., 239–240
  prehistoric, 187–203, 548n11
  speech and, 209, 217–222, 240
of transcendental ego, 56

Nail, Thomas
  The Figure of the Migrant, 7, 523,
  525n1, 527n24, 529n3, 545n11,
  559n18, 580n36
  Theory of the Border, 7, 523, 525n1,
  529n3, 545n11, 559n18, 580n36
  Theory of the Image, 523, 525n1,
  527n23, 529n3, 541n5, 543n10
  Theory of the Object, 523, 525n1,
  527n19, 529n3, 539n8, 540n26,
  541n5, 543nn15–16, 546n10,
  558n4, 559n12, 562n1, 584n25

names of being, 29, 32–34, 45, 62, 160, 521. *See also* eternity; force; space; time
Nammu (Sumerian goddess), 241, 243, 249–251, 264, 552n2, 553n17
Narcissus, 103, 106, 304, 542n10
nations and nationalism in Middle Ages, 576n33
Native American peoples and spatialization, 192
natural illumination, 419–421
nature
  as clockwork machine, 352
  Early church fathers on, 399
  natural motion and, 195–196, 211, 220
nature/human divide, 26, 162, 208, 211, 354, 420, 461, 520
nature of being. *See* being in motion; "being qua being"; ontology of motion
necessity, 104–105, 109, 120
negentropy, 125
Nelson, Richard, 542n4
Neolithic period (10, 000 bce–5, 000 bce), 167, 175, 187, 577n2. *See also* being and space
  as age of containers, 194
  mythological femininity in, 189
  plain tokens in, 287
  social motion in, 192
nests, 146
networked and regional spaces, 547n13
network theory of static nodes, 544n1
new materialism, 45, 49, 61, 534n71
Newton, Isaac
  on absolute time, 454, 457, 480
  on aether, 340
  compared to Descartes, 454
  De Gravitatione, 454
  on earth's rotation, 336
  force as central to philosophy and physics of, 355
  on gravity, 17
  on motion, 465
  Principia, 340, 355, 454
  on reason, 445
Nicene Creed (381 ce), 373
Nietzsche, Friedrich, 88, 113, 218, 317, 503, 535n6, 581n1
Nippur, 561n13

node vs. fold, 100
nomadic theory, 531n15
nominalism, 162
nonhierarchical (horizontal) organization, 150
nonhuman matters' graphic process or material memory, 520
nonlinear dynamics, 2, 72

objects, as conjoined things, 118, 119*f*
Occupy movement, 94, 150
Ockham, William of, 450–451, 457
Ogotemmeli, 220
Old Canaanite alphabet, 300
"oneness," 298
ontological practice
  geographical areas for future study, 522
  geographical limitations of study, 521–522
  historical, material, and kinetic, 14–35, 57, 520
  historical regimes of, 159
  kinetic dimensions of, 160–168, 227
  metaphor in, 164–165
  ontology of motion's consequences for, 518–519
  plane of immanence and, 48
  theory of motion vs., 158
  transcendental realism and, 52–57
  Western history as focus of the study, 521–522
ontological reductionism, 25
ontological stasis, 22–23
ontology
  alternate definition of, 26–27
  as domain of inquiry, 29
  of eternity, 239–282
  flat, 78
  graphism, 26–30
  mobility of, 5–6
  movement in (*see* ontology of motion)
  names of being in, 29, 34, 45, 62, 159–160, 521
  reductionism, 25
  of space, 187–203
  stasis, 22–23
  verticality in, 78, 234, 244, 245, 261, 265

ontology of motion (kinology), 5–6, 69, 169, 490
  the circle in, 251
  consequences of, 518–519
  descriptive and analytic, 530n12
  framework needed for, 519
  future research related to, 522–523
  historical, material, and kinetic, 14–35, 529n5
  historical precursors, 32–33, 40–43, 537n1
  kinographism and, 27–32, 55
  logic and contradiction in, 227
  matter and process materialism in, 57–62
  philosophy of motion and, 36–40
  process ontology and becoming vs., 44–51
  theory of motion and, 158
ontotemporal process of giving, 482
opposition, 235–236
oppression as kinopolitical knot, 148–151, 154–155
oral cultures, 219, 302–303, 310
Oresme, Nicole, 347–348, 351, 565–566n14
  Livre du ciel et du monde, 347
Origen of Alexandria, 377, 397–398, 400, 571n33
origins of speech, 207–209
Orpheus, 221
oscillation, 495
  circulatory oscillation (typewriter), 496–498
  modulated oscillation (computer), 509–511
the Other, 513, 585n26
Ouranos (Greek air-sky-father), 256, 260
Ouroboros, 201, 247–248, 247f

Papastergiadis, Nikos, 525n2
paper and ink, 410–411
paper mills, 410–411
papyrus, 390, 391, 395
paradox of the One, 68, 79
parchment as writing material, 390–391, 395–396
  ink and, 410–411
Parmenides, 40, 68, 271, 556nn32–33
the past
  as division of time, 427
  in motion, 18
  in transcendental realism, 54–55
pedesis, 72–74, 86, 88, 95, 176, 430
penal system, use of time as punishment in, 581n42
Peoples' Global Action (PGA), 150
perceptual motion, 191–192
period, 100–110, 102f, 112
periphery. *See* cent; center/periphery division
phenomenology, 33, 138, 443–446, 535n7
  defined, 443–444
Philoponus, John, 337, 344–345, 356, 563n13, 565n8
  de Opificio Mundi, 565n7
philosophy of motion, 6, 14, 36–40, 45, 556–557n1
Phoenician alphabet, 300
phonemes, 210, 212, 217, 300–301, 305, 307, 560n3
phonetic alphabet, 300–306
  kinetic analysis, 304–306
  subordination of graphism to phonism, 301
  subordination of phonism and graphism to meaning, 302–303
  subordination of phonism to graphism, 302
phonism, 209–210, 213, 300–305, 308. *See also* phonetic alphabet
phonographism, 166, 209, 211–218, 222. *See also* speech
physics, 58, 545n9. *See also* Kepler Johannes; NewtonIsaac; quantum physics
  empirical mechanism, emergence of, 372
pictography, 287, 295–298, 301, 309, 559n8
Pisan, Christine de, 566n14
places, 179–180, 189, 191, 547n19
Planck scale, 428
plane of immanence, 47–48
planetarium clock, 352
the plant (example 1), 88–91, 109–110, 130–131, 135–136, 143–144, 144f

Index [607]

Plato, 104, 276–277
  on abstract meaning and writing, 306–308
  compared to Descartes, 568n12
  cosmology of, 276–280, 557nn12–13
  on eternity, 162, 379
  eternity as being in, 162
  on existence, 104
  kinetic analysis, 278–280
  Phaedrus, 306–308
  on quality, 111
  rationalism of, 399
  The Republic, 276
  Timaeus, 276, 278, 382, 557n4
Plutarch, 268, 555n13
Poincaré, Jules Henri, 372
political events in constellation. *See* Zapatismo (example2)
polygonalism, 322
pores, 114–116, 116f, 119, 146, 541n8
postmodernity, mobility as central fact of, 528n30
practical entanglement, 5
prehistoric mythology, 33, 187–203
  the egg, 196–200, 200f, 201, 201f
  the spiral, 201–203
  the Venus, 188–195
the present
  being as reducible to, 444
  as division of time, 427
  eternity as, 231
  fold of time and, 432–433
  history of, 161–162
  ontology of motion in, 33, 427
  as produced by motion, 16–20
  "thick present," 433
  transcendental realism and, 52–55
priest-bureaucrats, 290–291
priest-kings in cosmology, 249–251, 254, 259, 290, 293, 553n15
primacy of biological life, 60
primacy of chaos in egg myths, 200
primacy of motion, 2–3
  across domains, 37–40
  in atomism, 41, 42
  Bergson on, 44
  in Deleuze and Guattari, 533n46
  fold and, 99, 101
  historical, 16, 21
  matter and, 57, 60

  methodological application of, 50
  ontological inquiry and, 19, 436
  in physics, 531n14
  in the present, 535n14
  spatialization and, 182
  stasis vs., 232, 298
  theory of motion and, 30–31, 158
prime movement, 321
printed comprehension, 411–412
  the Book of God and the Book of Nature, 412–414
  silent reading, 416–417
  spacing of words and, 417
printing press and printed books, 406–422, 493
  binding, 406–407
  coexisting with manuscript codices in medieval and early modern periods, 407
  legere in silentio, 414–419
  letters in movable type, 409–410
  matrix's function, 409
  natural illumination, 419–421
  paper and ink, 410–411
  press, 407–409
  printed comprehension, 411–412
  punctuation, grammar, and ruling, 407
processes of sexuation, 189, 196
process materialism, 45, 57–62, 518
process of temporalization, 479–484
process ontology and becoming, 44–51, 534n53
Pseudo-Cyril, 382, 383
Ptolemy, 333, 334
punch cards, 500
punctuation, use of, 392–393, 407
Pyramid Texts, 245
Pythagoras, 269–270
quadrupedalism, 208

Quakers, 150
quality, 110–113, 114f, 118–121
quantity, 113–114, 114f, 118–121
quantum mechanical phenomenon of semiconductivity, 510–511
quantum physics
  big bounce cosmology and, 78
  complementarity, 71

[608]   Index

field theory, 2–6, 81–84, 518, 538n5, 538n13, 539n9, 540n14
gravity, 50, 83, 532n32, 584n25
intensive and extensive movement in, 71
matter in, 58–59
quality and quantity in, 113–114
uncertainty principle and indeterminacy, 72–73, 82
quintessence, 337
quires
parchment folded into, 391–392
printed books, 406

Rainbow serpent myth, 202, 219
random motion, 73
reading, 302–303
kinetic tension of reading, 396
silent reading, 415–417
La Realidad (Zapatista community), 121
realism and materialism, 52–62
historical materialism, 61–62
metaphysics, 59–61
process materialism, 57
transcendental realism, 55–57
receptivity and redirection, 108–109, 437
redistributive economy, 289
reductionism
kinosigns vs., 213
in mobilities paradigm, 38–39
ontological, 25
writing and, 285
reference and representation in speech, 217, 220
regional and networked spaces, 547n13
Renaissance, 407, 420. See also medieval period (500 ce–1700 ce)
representation, 4, 108
repression through time, 581n42
reproduction, 130, 135
resonance and synchrony
in historical periods, 163, 285
of mythograms with spatialization, 191–192
in ontological description, 28, 29
in pedetic motion, 77–78
quality and, 111
in speech, 209–211, 308

with technology of inscription, 164, 166
in theory of motion, 31
of token spheres with deification, 293
of writing with spherical cosmology, 285–286, 308
retention, 437–438
retroactive centrifuge, 240, *240*, 240t, 257–260
reversibility of time in equations, 429
revolution from confluence of events, 93–95
Reynolds, Susan, 576n33
rhope, 344–345
Rilke, Rainer Maria, 221
Rimbaud, Arthur, 107
ritual, 218–219
Robinson, Keith, 532n38
rocks, 437
Roman philosophers, 395
Romans
codex form employed by, 573n4
exchange of gifts of literature (codex), 390
punctuation, use of, 392–393
scriptography of, 394
rotation, 230–232, 271–273, 278–279, 306, 429
Rousseau, Jean-Jacques, 210, 445
Rovelli, Carlo, 58, 83, 120, 540n26, 584n25
Ruddiman, William, 546n2
Russell, Bertrand, 372, 582n1

Saint-Venant, Barré de, 372
Samoan creation myth, 199
Sargon (Sumerian priest-king), 249
Sartre, Jean-Paul, 104, 586n27
Sassen, Saskia, 526n10
Saussure, Ferdinand de, 217
Schilling, Pavel, 501
Schmandt-Besserat, Denise, 289, 292, 295–296, 301, 559n6, 459nn8–11, 560n32
Scholastics, 359, 361, 364, 421, 453
science of knots, 151–152
scientific revolution of sixteenth and seventeenth centuries, 332, 341, 359

scriptography, 166, 286–287, 394
  dictation from God, 394
  kinetic analysis, 290–291
Scriptures
  Genesis, Book of, 375
  omission of intelligences or angles, 346
  production in large numbers and introduction of punctuation, 392–393
  Romans 1:20, 397
  sacrament of scripture, 400
  Son of God, 375
scrolls
  compared to codex, 391, 392
  early Christian use of, 390
Second Vatican Council (1965), 399
self-affection, 476
semiconductivity, 510
semiotic patterns, 163
Semitic religion, 239, 240, 310–312
sensation, 106–116
  existence and, 104
  intercalation and, 107f
  knots and, 147
  the plant (example 1), 109–110
  pores, 114–116
  quality, 110–113
  quantity, 113–114
  receptivity and redirection, 108–110
  stream of thought and, 540n15
separation of heaven and earth, 241–248, 240t, 250, 258, 290, 551n32, 551n33
sequence, defined, 577n1
seriality, 431–434, 460, 577n1
serial subjectivity, 437–439
Serres, Michel, 541n2
set theory, 543n11
sexuation, 189, 196
Shangaan creation myth, 199
Sheets-Johnstone, Maxine, 547n25
Shekhinah, 569n5
Sheller, Mimi, 37, 39
shen (Egyptian symbol for eternity), 245–247, 246f
signs and surfaces, 27–29, 301, 302, 305, 308, 310
silent reading, 415–417
silicon, 510

simplex, 74–75, 75f, 539n7
Sinai, 554n1
Sinaitic alphabet, 300
Skinner, Brian, 539–540n12
Sloterdijk, Peter, 53, 198, 483, 546n4
Smolin, Lee, 83, 526n14, 545n9
snakes and serpents, 200–202, 220, 221, 246–247, 254, 260, 293
social anxiety, 2
social motion, 2, 28, 192
Socrates, 276, 279, 306–307, 337, 394
solidarity, 149, 151, 154
Solís López, José Luis, 121
songlines, 220, 551n28
Son of God, 323, 375–376. *See also* Trinity, doctrine of
  reciprocal nature as divine and mortal, 382
  the soul in Plato's cosmology, 277–278, 558nn14–15
sound, 208–220, 300–301, 305
space
  being and (*see* being and space)
  contiguity in, 324
  describable by motion, 32–34
  in Egyptian and Sumerian cosmology, 244
  in eternity, 233
  in Greek cosmogony, 270
  in Greek cosmology, 260
  in Hebrew cosmology, 263, 264, 265, 311
  kinography of, 207–222(*see also* speech)
  kinomenology of, 176–183, 546n3 (*see also* centripetal motion)
  in Lakota and Hopi cultures, 548–549n17
  in mobilities philosophies, 531n9
  from movement of flows, 82–84, 181
  in ontological inquiry, 14, 19, 24, 53, 165
  ontology of, 187–203(*see also* prehistoric mythology)
  in philosophy of motion, 36–40, 160
  in process ontology and becoming, 44–51, 534n55
  special relativity and, 133
space-time, 2, 545n1

spatiality and spatialization, 180–183, 189, 200, 201, 222, 305
spatial movement in mechanics, 561n3
special relativity, 133
speculative realism, 45
speech (phonography), 207–222
  centripetal, 308
  inscribing surface of the body, 209–211
  kinetic metaphors in, 552n35
  mythology and, 218–222
  origins of, 207–222
  phonographism, 211–218
  Semitic religion and, 310–312
  writing vs., 306, 308
spheres, 291–292, 430
  centralization and, 233–234, 293
  in Egyptian mythology, 246f
  graphic duplication and, 292
  in Greek cosmology, 268–282
  in Hebrew cosmology, 264
  kinetic analysis, 265, 292–294, 296–299
  ontology of, 270–275
  tokens stored in, 287, 291–294, 304
  writing and, 305–309
spin-foam theory of space, 84
Spinoza, Baruch, 366–368
  compared to Leibniz, 369
  on conatus, 366–368
  Descartes and Hobbes as influences on, 366
  on reason, 445
  Trinitarian logic and, 386
Spinoza, Benedict de, 47–48, 536n26
the spiral, 176, 177, 177f, 200–202, 209, 220–221, 228, 233–234, 430, 549n48
  asymmetry in, 267
  elastic spiral, 581n45
  in Greek cosmology, 255
  Leviathan and, 264, 265
  in Marduk, 258
spontaneous symmetry breaking, 83
stability in theory of motion
  centripetal motion, 176
  circulation and, 142
  continuous flow, 197
  organisms and minerals, 119, 130
  repetition, 145

Sumerian cosmology and, 250
  theory of the fold and, 96, 103, 126
standard model of physics, 6
stasis, 232
  determinations of matter leading to, 61
  eternity and, 232
  existence vs., 104
  as movement, 70, 71
  ontological, 22–23
  in process ontology and becoming, 45–46, 50, 532n38, 534n70
  temporal description and, 430
  tokens and, 298
static model of states and borders, 2, 6
Stern, William, 583n3
Stiegler, Bernard, 530n6
stochastic motion. See pedesis
Stoics, 333, 335, 337, 363, 370, 379, 562–563n4, 563n13, 565n8, 568n18, 571n36
stream of consciousness, 439
string theory, 3, 545n9
strobe being, 69
structuralism and post-structuralism, 56, 58, 535n7, 586n28
stylus, 292, 294–295
subjectivism, 22–23
subjectivity, 437–440, 465
  electric subjectivity, 503
  modulated subjectivity (computer), 513–515
Sumerian cosmologies, 241, 241, 243, 249
sun-disk circle, 246, 246f, 248
synchrony. See resonance and synchrony

tablets, 168, 240, 287, 294–299, 304
tally systems, 287, 287
taxation, 289–290
technological reductionism, 25
technologies of inscription, 33, 164–166
  speech, 207–222
  writing, 227–228, 285–299
Tehom, 263–264
telegraph, invention of, 501
the temple, 289–290, 304, 307
temporal elasticity. See also time
  Augustine's theory of time, 447–449, 457

temporal elasticity (*Cont.*)
  Derrida's stretched interval (*see*
    Derrida, Jacques)
  elastic line of time, 452, 452*f*, 458
  elastic theory of time, 584n25
  Heidegger's process as a whole (*see*
    Heidegger, Martin)
  Kant's breakthrough (*see* Kant,
    Immanuel)
  Newton's approach (*see*
    Newton, Isaac)
  Ockham's multiplication of folds (*see*
    Ockham, William of)
tension, Descartes' use of, 363–364
tensional fields, 157, 157*f*
tensional fold of time, 449, 449*f*
tensional motion, 318–321, 430
  centripetal movement and, 319
  defined, 318
  externalized motion, 320
  first problem, 319–320
  internalized motion, 320, 358–372
    (*see also* internalized motion)
  interrelational motion, 320
  kinomenology of force, 318
  in medieval and early modern periods,
    323
  relation, 323–327
  second problem, 321
  triangulation, 321–323
Tertullian, 377, 386, 397
textual canons, kinetic treatment of, 163
theology, medieval, 319, 331–386
  proliferation of printed spiritual
    literature from fourteenth to
    seventeenth centuries, 419
  theological description of force,
    317, 332
  Trinitarianism, 373–374(*see also*
    Trinity, doctrine of)
theomachy, 240, 240*t*, 252–261
  kinetic analysis, 257–261
  Marduk, Babylonian epic of, 252–254
  Zeus (Greek god), 255–256
theory of fluxions, 132–135
theory of motion, 30–31, 46–47, 67, 104,
  158, 161, 518. *See also* field; flow;
  fold; ontology of motion
thermodynamics, 125, 143–144,
  428–429, 543n8

things. *See also* images; objects
  affect and, 91, 110–111
  circuit and, 123
  conjunction and, 118–120, 119*f*, 139
  dimensions of, 118
  fields of circulation and, 131–132
  as kinomena, 140
  knots and, 147
  Ouroboros describing order of,
    247–248
  spatiality and, 181–182
  writing and, 306
Thomson, William, 152
thought
  as centripetal motion, 547n12
  inscription and, 166
  as kinemonological process, 168
  in ontological texts, 163
  in process ontology and becoming,
    47–50, 534n55, 534n61
Tiamat (Babylonian primordial mother),
  252–254, 258–260, 263, 298
time
  absolute time, 451–455, 578n16
  abstract temporality, 431
  Augustine's theory of time in relation
    to God's eternity, 447–449
  Bergson on, 44
  circulation of temporal folds, 460,
    460*f*
  clocks (*see* clockwork universe;
    mechanical clock, invention of)
  concrete temporality, 431–432
  consciousness and, 439
  defined, 427–428, 451
  Derrida's discovery that time cannot
    be continuum or flow, 488–489
  describable by motion, 32–34, 430
  diachronic time, 585n26
  elastic line of time, 452, 452*f*, 458
  in eternity, 231
  events producing, 90, 427–428, 430
  fold of time, 432–434, 433*f*
  as fundamental description of all
    reality, 443
  in Hebrew cosmology, 264, 311
  Heidegger's temporalization process,
    479–484
  Husserl's temporal fold, 472–473,
    474*f*

Kant and primacy of time, 427, 445, 455
kinography of, 493–516 (see also kinography)
kinomenology of, 429–440, 444 (see also elastic motion)
medieval and early modern temporality, 446–455
modern theory vs. early modern theory of, 456
from movement of flows, 82–84, 428
in ontological inquiry, 14, 19, 24, 53, 165, 519
ontology of, 430, 437, 443–490 (see also modern phenomenology)
passage of, 435, 489
in philosophy of motion, 36–40, 160
plain tokens and, 287
priority in, 324
in process ontology and becoming, 44–51, 534n55
as product of matter in motion, 583n24
reversibility of time in equations, 429
special relativity and, 133
subjective time, effect of mechanical clock on, 450
temporal (threefold) division, 428, 482, 488
temporal unity, 475
tensional fold of time, 449, 449f
thermodynamics and, 428–429
unity of, 234, 468, 473, 476, 482
the Venus and, 192
time and space
capitalism and, 528n36
history and, 529n5
tokens, 287–297, 301, 301, 559n6, 559n11, 559nn8–9, 560n21
kinetic analysis, 290–291, 304
tombs, 192–193, 198
Tomlinson, Gary, 550n9
the tongue, lips, and mouth, 208, 210, 243
topology, 74–75, 84, 117, 151, 539n25
touchscreen keyboards, 512
tourism, 526n9
the transcendental, 55–57, 259, 263–264, 535n7
transcendental materialism, 82

transcendental realism, 52–57, 62, 518
transistor, invention of, 509–510
triangulation
folded unity of, 322
force and, 321–323, 322f
Frisius on, 335
in interrelation of motion, 335–336
in kinetic relations, 140
of oneness in the Trinity, 384–386
Trinity, doctrine of, 331, 372, 373, 378f
Augustine of Hippo and, 380–381
centrifugal subordination and, 376–377
as Christian orthodoxy in the West, 386
Cusa and, 384–385
Descartes and, 386, 572n62
folds of force and, 380–381
Hobbes and, 386, 572n61
kinetic problem of tension and, 374
Leibniz and, 386, 572n63
perichoresis and, 382–384, 571n33
tensional equality and, 377–380
triangulation of oneness, 384–386
triskelion spiral, 202
Tummuz (Akkadian god-king), 248–249
turbulence, 72–73, 83, 86
Turetzky, Philip, 581n1
Turing, Alan, 508
Turri, Pellegrino, 496
twenty-first century, 6–7
Typhoeus, 261, 261
typography, 166, 493–494
binary circulation, 496–508
computer, 509–516 (see also computer)
electric elasticity, 500–502
linotype press, 494, 499
mechanical elasticity, 498–500
movable type, 409
subjective anonymity, 502–508
typewriter, 493–508

uncertainty principle, 73, 538n19
unemployment, 525n2
unities of movement, 451, 577n14
unity of time, 234, 468, 473, 476, 482
unity of triangulation, 322
universal heat death, 78, 83
unknots, 152–154
the unmoved mover, 280–281, 558n23

Upper Paleolithic period. *See* Neolithic period
urbanization, 289–290
Ur-Nammu (Sumerian king), 249, 553n17
Urry, John, 37, 39
Uruk (ancient urban center), 290, 300
use value, 291, 294

"V" (symbol), 196
Valéry, Paul, 70, 86, 87, 103, 542n10
value, in capitalism, 528n36
vegetable and animal motions, 195. *See also* the plant (example 1)
the Venus, 188–195, 547n2
　of Hohle Fels, 188
　of Lespugue, 190f
　motions of, 209, 212
verticality in ontology, 78, 234, 244, 245, 261, 265, 267, 268, 290
vessel, human introduction of, 495–496
Vico, Giambattista, 210
Virilio, Paul, 38
visibility, 81–82, 88
vital materialism, 60
Volta, Alessandro, 501
Voltaire, 445
von Uexküll, Jakob, 437
vortex theory of knotted atoms, 152

Walbiri (aboriginal people), 202
Wang, Xianhua, 561n13
waveform theory of quality, 112–113, 543n10
waves, 74–76, 80
The Waves (Woolf), 136–138
wax tablets, 573n4
Weber, Wilhelm, 501
Weigel, Erhard, 369, 370
Western ontology as focus of the study, 521–522
Wheeler-DeWitt equation, 584n24, 584n25
Whitehead, Alfred North, 44, 50
　on change and motion, 537n4
　The Concept of Nature, 44, 537n4
　criticism of, 532n35
　stasis and becoming in, 532n38
William of Conches, 414
Wolfson, Harry, 571n36
Women's Revolutionary Law, 123
Woolf, Virginia, 91
　The Waves, 103, 110, 136–138
Word of God, 395, 402, 418
word-processing computer software, 511, 515
writing, 227–228, 285–299, 494, 561n7
　alphabet, 300–312 (*see also* phonetic alphabet)
　cosmology and, 240, 299, 306–312
　Greek philosophy, 306–309
　language and, 301
　Mesopotamia, 309–310
　pictographic, 296
　reductionism and, 285
　scriptography, 166, 286–287
　Semitic religion, 310–312
　spheres, 291–292
　tablets, 294–299
　tokens, 287–291
written comprehension, 394–395

Xenophanes, 270–271, 556nn22–26, 556n28

Yahweh (Hebrew god), 241, 240t, 262–269, 310–312, 554n1, 569n5

Zapatismo (example 2), 93–95, 121–122, 125, 126, 148–151, 154–155
Zapatista Army of National Liberation, 93–95
Zeno, 69, 70, 85, 432
Zeus (Greek god), 255–256, 261, 551n30

Lightning Source UK Ltd.
Milton Keynes UK
UKHW010030060821
387961UK00014B/540